EDITORS' PREFACE

The fourth edition of *Legislation on International Private Law* is notably longer than earlier editions, evidencing the increasingly legislative nature of the subject.

The materials are arranged in the same manner as in previous editions. As before, changes to the wording of an original enactment are indicated by the use of square brackets round the affected text. The use of '[...]' indicates a repealed provision. The use of '...' indicates provisions which, in our discretion, have been omitted for reasons of relevance or brevity.

Parts I and II have been enlarged, principally through inclusion of material pertaining to family law, but also concerning succession. Significant changes in Scots and UK domestic law to authorise same sex marriage have necessitated the inclusion of primary and secondary legislation pertaining to the conflict of laws dimension of that topic. Separately, there is included a suite of legislative provisions on forced marriage. New material concerning overseas adoptions has been added, as has legislative provision governing parental order applications in surrogacy cases.

In the commercial sphere, the materials have been updated to take account of the accession in 2014 by the EU on behalf of Member States to the 2005 Hague Convention on Choice of Court Agreements. We have excised from this edition the EU Insolvency Regulation (Regulation (EC) 1346/2000), in view of its being replaced, with effect from June 2017, by the recast version (Regulation (EU) 2015/848). Annex D of the Recast Regulation, containing the Correlation Table, is included in this volume, as is the jurisdiction provision of the Bankruptcy (Scotland) Act 2016.

To accommodate new legislation, we have taken the decision to omit from Part IV Regulation (EC) 1896/2006 creating a European Order for Payment Procedure, Regulation (EC) 861/2007 establishing a European Small Claims Procedure, and Directive 2008/52/EC on mediation. Conversely, we have included Regulation (EU) 655/2014 establishing the European Account Preservation Order; although the UK did not adopt the Regulation, UK creditors and debtors yet may be affected by it.

Part IV, devoted to EU materials, reflects the Europeanised character, to date, of international private law rules operative in the UK. On 23 June 2016, the UK voted to leave the EU. In principle, the process of exiting the EU, once triggered by invocation of Article 50 of the Treaty on European Union, ought to be accomplished within two years. The post-Brexit character and content of Scots and UK international private law rules cannot be known at the date of this Preface. Similarly it cannot be predicted what will be the post-Brexit content of the international private law of EU Member States vis-à-vis the UK. The EU materials in Part IV – extant; about to take effect; or even, as in the case, for example, of Brussels II *bis*, subject to change while the UK remains an EU Member State – are presented in the expectation that they will continue to apply until such point as Brexit is effected, and subject to the detail of that negotiation.

EBC
JMC

University of Glasgow
31 July 2016

EDITORS' PREFACE TO FIRST EDITION

This is an entirely new publication in an area of Scots law which, increasingly, has become legislation based and subject to European and global regulation. The legislative profile of the subject today is in striking contrast with its largely common law character as late as 1970. It is essential for lawyers to have ready access to relevant materials, the more so in view of the varied sources from which the legislative materials derive: the Scottish Parliament, the UK Parliament, the EU Institutions, and the Hague Conference on Private International Law. This collection of materials is wide-ranging in subject matter, as dictated by the nature of Scots international private law, which is co-extensive with the entirety of Scots private law.

This book is intended to be a resource for students and for practitioners, and to stand as a companion to Crawford and Carruthers, *International Private Law in Scotland* (2nd edn, 2006, W Green & Sons).

The materials are arranged in six Parts, namely: Part I (Statutes – UK and ASP); Part II (Statutory Instruments); Part III (Scottish Statutory Instruments); Part IV (EC Materials); Part V (International Conventions); and Part VI (Draft Material).

The unremitting nature of the European harmonisation programme means that legislative revision and refinement exercises must be logged, and projected changes, where near completion, must be intimated. We are pleased that it has been possible to include the final version of Rome II (choice of law rules for non-contractual obligations). We have included the most up-to-date version of the draft Lugano Convention. We have taken the decision not to include the proposed Rome I Regulation (choice of law rules for contractual obligations), negotiations at a European level being ongoing, and the attitude of the UK towards the instrument being unsettled.

In general, where a UK statute has been amended by a later instrument (examples being the Prescription and Limitation (Scotland) Act 1973, and the Divorce (Scotland) Act 1976), our practice is to present the Act in its amended form, incorporating later changes. An important exception to this practice concerns section 2 of the Family Law (Scotland) Act 2006, which inserts a new provision (section 20A) into the Marriage (Scotland) Act 1977; in this instance, the new provision is narrated in both places.

Changes to the wording of an original enactment are indicated by the use of square brackets round the affected text. The use of '[...]' indicates a repealed provision. The use of '...' indicates provisions which, in our discretion, have been omitted for reasons of relevance or brevity.

EBC
JMC

University of Glasgow
August 2007

CONTENTS

Preface . . . . *iii*
Preface to First Edition . . . . *iv*

Part I: Statutes (UK and ASP)
Foreign Marriage Act 1892, ss 1, 4(3), 7, 8, 13, 18, 19, 22, 23   1
Administration of Justice Act 1920, ss 9, 12, 14   4
Foreign Judgments (Reciprocal Enforcement) Act 1933   6
Maintenance Orders Act 1950, ss 16–18, 21, 22, 27   11
Wills Act 1963   15
Succession (Scotland) Act 1964, ss 8, 9   16
Administration of Estates Act 1971, ss 1–6.   19
Maintenance Orders (Reciprocal Enforcement) Act 1972, ss 1, 2, 5–9, 21, 25,
   26, 31.   22
Matrimonial Proceedings (Polygamous Marriages) Act 1972, s 2.   31
Domicile and Matrimonial Proceedings Act 1973, ss 1, 4, 7, 8, 8A, 10, 11,
   Schs 1B, 3, paras 8,9.   31
Prescription and Limitation (Scotland) Act 1973, s 23A   40
Evidence (Proceedings in Other Jurisdictions) Act 1975, s 1.   41
Divorce (Scotland) Act 1976, s 3A.   41
Marriage (Scotland) Act 1977, ss 1, 3–3B, 5, 7, 20, 20A, 22.   42
Unfair Contract Terms Act 1977, s 27   47
Adoption (Scotland) Act 1978, ss 38, 39, 41–44.   47
State Immunity Act 1978, ss 1–6, 9, 14   49
Civil Jurisdiction and Judgments Act 1982, ss 1–23, 27, 28, 30–35, 41–45, 49,
   50, Schs 2, 4, 6–8.   52
Matrimonial and Family Proceedings Act 1984, ss 28, 29, 29A   89
Child Abduction and Custody Act 1985, ss 1–9, 24A, 25, Sch 1   91
Family Law Act 1986, ss 8–15, 17–18, 25–42, 44–52, 54   98
Recognition of Trusts Act 1987, s 1, Schedule. 113
Contracts (Applicable Law) Act 1990, Schs 1, 3 116
Foreign Corporations Act 1991, s 1. 120
Children (Scotland) Act 1995, s 14 120
Private International Law (Miscellaneous Provisions) Act 1995, ss 7, 9–15B . 121
Scotland Act 1998, ss 29, 30, 57, 126, Sch 5, para 7. 124
Adoption (Intercountry Aspects) Act 1999, ss 1, 2, 17, 18, Sch 1. 126
Immigration and Asylum Act 1999, ss 24, 24A. 135
Adoption and Children Act 2002, ss 83–89, 91, 105. 137
Civil Partnership Act 2004, ss 1, 85, 86, 125, 210–219, 225–227, 233–238. . . . 142
Family Law (Scotland) Act 2006, ss 4, 22, 25–29A, 38–41. 153
Adoption and Children (Scotland) Act 2007, ss 39, 40, 58–70, 119. 159
Human Fertilisation and Embryology Act 2008, s 54. 167
Forced Marriage etc (Protection and Jurisdiction) (Scotland) Act 2011 168
Defamation Act 2013, s 9. 174
Marriage (Same Sex Couples) Act 2013, ss 1, 9–11, 13, 15, 20. 175
Anti-Social Behaviour, Crime and Policing Act 2014, ss 121, 122 178
Marriage and Civil Partnership (Scotland) Act 2014, ss 4, 9–11, 28(3) 180
Succession (Scotland) Act 2016, ss 1, 2, 9. 183
Bankruptcy (Scotland) Act 2016, s 15. 184

Part II: Statutory Instruments
Civil Jurisdiction and Judgments Act 1982 (Provisional and Protective
   Measures) (Scotland) Order 1997, arts 2, 3 186

Civil Jurisdiction and Judgments Order 2001, regs 2–3A, Sch 1   186
Cross–Border Insolvency Regulations 2006.   190
Adoption (Recognition of Overseas Adoptions) Order 2013   209

Part III: Scottish Statutory Instruments
Registration of Foreign Adoptions (Scotland) Regulations 2003, regs 1, 2, 7.   211
European Communities (Matrimonial and Parental Responsibility
    Jurisdiction and Judgments) (Scotland) Regulations 2005, regs 1, 6, 7. . . .   212
Divorce (Religious Bodies)(Scotland) Regulations 2006, regs 1, 2.   212
Adoptions with a Foreign Element (Special Restrictions on Adoptions from
    Abroad) (Scotland) Regulations 2008   212
Adoptions with a Foreign Element (Scotland) Regulations 2009   214
Parental Responsibility and Measures for the Protection of Children
    (International Obligations) (Scotland) Regulations 2010.   240
International Recovery of Maintenance (Hague Convention 2007) (Scotland)
    Regulations 2012   243
Adoption (Recognition of Overseas Adoptions) (Scotland) Regulations
    2013   246
Marriage (Same Sex Couples) (Jurisdiction and Recognition of Judgments)
    (Scotland) Regulations 2014.   248

Part IV: European Materials
Treaty on the functioning of the European Union (Consolidated version),
    art 81   250
Treaty establishing the European Community (Amsterdam consolidated
    version) ('Treaty of Amsterdam'), Arts 61, 65   251
Protocol (No 21) to the Treaty of European Union and the Treaty on the
    functioning of the European Union in respect of freedom, security and
    justice.   251
Council Regulation (EC) No 44/2001 on jurisdiction and the recognition
    and enforcement of judgments in civil and commercial matters
    ('Brussels I')   254
Council Regulation (EC) No 1206/2001 on cooperation between the courts
    of the Member States in the taking of evidence in civil or commercial
    matters   270
Council Regulation (EC) No 2201/2003 concerning jurisdiction and the
    recognition and enforcement of judgments in matrimonial matters and
    matters of parental responsibility ('Brussels II bis').   278
Regulation (EC) No 805/2004 creating a European Enforcement Order for
    uncontested claims.   297
EC/Denmark agreement of 19 October 2005 on jurisdiction and the
    recognition and enforcement of judgments in civil and commercial
    matters   307
Regulation (EC) No 864/2007 on the law applicable to non-contractual
    obligations ('Rome II')   313
Regulation (EC) 1393/2007 on the service in the Member States of judicial
    and extrajudicial documents in civil and commercial matters   324
Regulation (EC) 593/2008 on the law applicable to contractual obligations
    ('Rome I').   334
Council Regulation (EC) 4/2009 in matters relating to maintenance
    obligations   348
Council Regulation (EU) No 1259/2010 implementing enhanced cooperation
    in the area of the law applicable to divorce and legal separation ('Rome III')   374
Regulation (EU) No 650/2012 in matters of succession and on the creation
    of a European certificate of succession   382

Regulation (EU) No 1215/2012 on jurisdiction and the recognition and
  enforcement of judgments in civil and commercial matters (recast)
  ('Brussels I recast').. 414
EC/Denmark agreement implementing Regulation (EU) 1215/2012....... 442
Regulation (EU) No 655/2014 establishing a European Account
  Preservation Order procedure to facilitate cross-border debt recovery in
  civil and commercial matters.. 442
Regulation (EU) 2015/848 on insolvency proceedings ('Insolvency
  Regulation recast')... 471

Part V: International Conventions
Hague Convention on the Civil Aspects of International Child Abduction
  1980: *see Child Abduction and Custody Act 1985*
Hague Convention on the Law Applicable to Trusts and on their
  Recognition 1986: *see Recognition of Trusts Act 1987*
Rome Convention on the Law Applicable to Contractual Obligations:
  see Contracts (Applicable Law) Act 1990
Hague Convention in respect of parental responsibility and measures for
  the protection of children (1996) 515
Hague Convention on Choice of Court Agreements (2005)............. 527
Hague Convention on international recovery of child support and family
  maintenance (2007).. 536
Lugano Convention on jurisdiction and the enforcement of judgments 556

Index of Legislation... 575

PART I

STATUTES (UK AND ASP)

FOREIGN MARRIAGE ACT 1892
(1892 c 23)

1 Validity of marriages solemnized abroad in manner provided by Act

[(1) All marriages between parties of whom at least one is a United Kingdom national] solemnized in the manner in this Act provided in any foreign country or place by or before a marriage officer within the meaning of this Act shall be as valid in law as if the same had been solemnized in the United Kingdom with a due observance of all forms required by law.

[(2) In this Act 'United Kingdom national' means a person who is—

(a) a British citizen, a [British overseas territories citizen,] a British Overseas citizen or a British National (Overseas); or

(b) a British subject under the British Nationality Act 1981; or

(c) a British protected person, within the meaning of that Act.]

[4 Consent to marriage and power to forbid marriage

...

(3) No consent shall be required to a marriage under this Act in respect of a party domiciled in Scotland.]

7 Oath before marriage

Before a marriage is solemnized under this Act, each of the parties intending marriage shall appear before the marriage officer, and make, and subscribe in a book kept by the officer for the purpose, an oath—

(a) that he or she believes that there is not any impediment to the marriage by reason of kindred or alliance, or otherwise; and

(b) that both of the parties have for three weeks immediately preceding had their usual residence within the district of the marriage officer; and

[(c) where either party is under the age of eighteen years and domiciled in a country other than Scotland—

(i) that any consent to the marriage which is required in respect of that party has been obtained,

(ii) that the necessity of obtaining any such consent in respect of that party has been dispensed with, or

(iii) if that party is domiciled in England and Wales or in a country outside the United Kingdom, either that he or she is a widow or widower or that there is no person having authority to give any such consent.]

8 Solemnization of marriage at office in presence of marriage officer and two witnesses

(1) After the expiration of fourteen days after the notice of an intended marriage has been entered under this Act, then, if no lawful impediment to the marriage is shown to the satisfaction of the marriage officer, and the marriage has not been forbidden in manner provided by this Act, the marriage may be solemnized under this Act.

[(2) Every such marriage shall be solemnised—

(a) at the official house of the marriage officer, with open doors, between 8 am and 6 pm, in the presence of two or more witnesses;

(b) by the marriage officer or, if the parties so desire, by another person in his presence; and

(c) according to such form and ceremony as the parties see fit to adopt.

(3) Where (apart from this subsection) it would not be stated or otherwise indicated in the course of the ceremony adopted by the parties that neither of them knows of any lawful impediment to their marriage, then, in some part of the ceremony and in the presence of the marriage officer and witnesses, they shall each declare—

'I solemnly declare that I know not of any lawful impediment why A.B. [or C.D.] may not be joined in matrimony to C.D. [or A.B.].'

(4) Where (apart from this subsection) it would not be stated by each of the parties in the course of the ceremony adopted by them that he or she takes the other as wife or husband, then, in some part of the ceremony and in the presence of the marriage officer and witnesses, each of the parties shall say to the other—

'I call upon these persons here present to witness that I A.B. [or C.D.] take thee C.D. [or A.B.] to be my lawful wedded wife or husband'.]

13 Avoidance of objections to marriages on account of want of formalities or authority of officer

(1) After a marriage has been solemnized under this Act it shall not be necessary, in support of the marriage, to give any proof of the residence for the time required by or in pursuance of this Act of either of the parties previous to the marriage, or of the consent of any person whose consent thereto is required by law, nor shall any evidence to prove the contrary be given in any legal proceeding touching the validity of the marriage.

(2) Where a marriage purports to have been solemnized and registered under this Act in the official house of a British ambassador or consul, [...] it shall not be necessary in support of the marriage, to give any proof of the authority of the marriage officer by or before whom the marriage was solemnized and registered, nor shall any evidence to prove his want of authority, whether by reason of his not being a duly authorized marriage officer or of any prohibitions or restrictions under the marriage regulations or otherwise, be given in any legal proceeding touching the validity of the marriage.

18 Registration of marriages solemnized under local law

(1) Subject to the marriage regulations, a British consul, or person authorised to act as British consul, on being satisfied by personal attendance that a marriage between parties, of whom one at least is a [United Kingdom national], has been duly solemnized in a foreign country, in accordance with the local law of the country, and on payment of the proper fee, may register the marriage in accordance with the marriage regulations as having been so solemnized, and thereupon this Act shall apply as if the marriage had been registered in pursuance of this Act, except that nothing in this Act shall affect the validity of the marriage so solemnized.

[(2) In the case of such marriages solemnized as aforesaid at which a British consul, or person authorised to act as British consul, has not attended, His Majesty may by Order in Council provide in such classes of cases, and subject to such conditions, as may be prescribed by the Order—

(a) for the transmission to and receipt by the Registrars General of Births, Deaths and Marriages in England, Scotland and Northern Ireland, respectively, of certificates of such marriages issued in accordance with the local law; and

(b) for the issue by those Registrars-General, on payment of such fees as may be prescribed by the Order, of certified copies of such certificates received by them, and for enabling such certified copies to be received in evidence.

(3) Any Order in Council made under the foregoing provisions of this section may be varied or revoked by a subsequent Order in Council, and any Order in

Council made under this section shall be laid forthwith before each House of Parliament.]

19   Power to refuse solemnization of marriage where marriage inconsistent with international law

A marriage officer shall not be required to solemnize a marriage, or to allow a marriage to be solemnized in his presence, if in his opinion the solemnization thereof would be inconsistent with international law or the comity of nations;

Provided that any person requiring his marriage to be solemnized shall, if the officer refuses to solemnize it or allow it to be solemnized in his presence, have the right to appeal to the Secretary of State given by this Act.

[22   Validity of marriages solemnized by chaplains of HM forces serving abroad and other persons

(1)   A marriage solemnized in any foreign territory by a chaplain serving with any part of the naval, military or air forces of His Majesty serving in that territory or by a person authorised, either generally or in respect of the particular marriage, by the commanding officer of any part of those forces serving in that territory shall, subject as hereinafter provided, be as valid in law as if the marriage had been solemnized in the United Kingdom with a due observance of all forms required by law: [...]

[(1A)   Subsection (1) above shall not apply to a marriage unless—
   (a)   at least one of the parties to the marriage is a person who—
      (i)   is a member of the said forces serving in the foreign territory concerned or is [a relevant civilian who is employed in that territory; or]
      (ii)   is a child of a person falling within sub-paragraph (i) above and has his home with that person in that territory; and
   (b)   such other conditions as may be [prescribed by Order in Council] are complied with.

[(1AA)   In subsection (1A)(a)(i) 'relevant civilian' means a civilian subject to service discipline (within the meaning of the Armed Forces Act 2006) of a description prescribed by Order in Council.]

[(1B)   In determining for the purposes of subsection (1A) above whether one person is the child of another, a person who is or was treated by another as a child of the family in relation to—
   (a)   a marriage to which the other is or was a party, or
   (b)   a civil partnership in which the other is or was a civil partner,
shall be regarded as the other's child.]

(2)   In this section the expression 'foreign territory' means territory other than—
   (a)   any part of His Majesty's dominions;
   (b)   any British protectorate; or
   (c)   any other country or territory under His Majesty's protection or suzerainty or in which His Majesty has for the time being jurisdiction:
Provided that His Majesty may by Order in Council direct that—
      (i)   any British protectorate or any such other country or territory as is referred to in paragraph (c) hereof; or
      (ii)   any part of His Majesty's dominions which has been occupied by a State at war with His Majesty and in which the facilities for marriage in accordance with the local law have not in the opinion of His Majesty been adequately restored;
shall, while the Order remains in force, be treated as foreign territory for the purposes of this section.

(3)   Any reference in this section to foreign territory, to forces serving in foreign territory and to persons employed in foreign territory shall include references to ships which are for the time being in the waters of any foreign territory, to forces serving in any such ship and to persons employed in any such ship, respectively.

(4)   His Majesty may by Order in Council provide for the registration of marriages solemnized under this section [...].

(5)   Where a marriage purports to have been solemnized under this section, it shall not be necessary in any legal proceeding touching the validity of the marriage to prove the authority of the person by or before whom it was solemnized, nor shall any evidence to prove his want of authority be given in any such proceeding.

(6)   Any Order in Council made under the foregoing provisions of this section may be varied or revoked by a subsequent Order in Council, and any Order in Council made under this section shall be laid forthwith before each House of Parliament.]

23   Savings
Nothing in this Act shall confirm or impair or in anywise affect the validity in law of any marriage solemnized beyond the seas, otherwise than as herein provided, and this Act shall not extend to the marriage of any of the Royal family.

ADMINISTRATION OF JUSTICE ACT 1920
(1920 c 81)

PART II
RECIPROCAL ENFORCEMENT OF JUDGMENTS IN THE UNITED KINGDOM AND IN OTHER PARTS OF HIS MAJESTY'S DOMINIONS

9   Enforcement in the United Kingdom of judgments obtained in superior courts in other British dominions
(1)   Where a judgment has been obtained in a superior court in any part of His Majesty's dominions outside the United Kingdom to which this Part of this Act extends, the judgment creditor may apply to the High Court in England or [Northern Ireland] or to the Court of Session in Scotland, at any time within twelve months after the date of the judgment, or such longer period as may be allowed by the court, to have the judgment registered in the court, and on any such application the court may, if in all the circumstances of the case they think it just and convenient that the judgment should be enforced in the United Kingdom, and subject to the provisions of this section, order the judgment to be registered accordingly.

(2)   No judgment shall be ordered to be registered under this section if—
   (a)   the original court acted without jurisdiction; or
   (b)   the judgment debtor, being a person who was neither carrying on business nor ordinarily resident within the jurisdiction of the original court, did not voluntarily appear or otherwise submit or agree to submit to the jurisdiction of that court; or
   (c)   the judgment debtor, being the defendant in the proceedings, was not duly served with the process of the original court and did not appear, notwithstanding that he was ordinarily resident or was carrying on business within the jurisdiction of that court or agreed to submit to the jurisdiction of that court; or
   (d)   the judgment was obtained by fraud; or
   (e)   the judgment debtor satisfies the registering court either that an appeal is pending, or that he is entitled and intends to appeal, against the judgment; or
   (f)   the judgment was in respect of a cause of action which for reasons of public policy or for some other similar reason could not have been entertained by the registering court.

(3)   Where a judgment is registered under this section—
   (a)   the judgment shall, as from the date of registration, be of the same force and effect, and proceedings may be taken thereon, as if it had been a judgment

originally obtained or entered up on the date of registration in the registering court;

(b)   the registering court shall have the same control and jurisdiction over the judgment as it has over similar judgments given by itself, but in so far only as relates to execution under this section;

(c)   the reasonable costs of and incidental to the registration of the judgment (including the costs of obtaining a certified copy thereof from the original court and of the application for registration) shall be recoverable in like manner as if they were sums payable under the judgment.

(4)   [Rules of court shall provide]—

(a)   for service on the judgment debtor of notice of the registration of a judgment under this section; and

(b)   for enabling the registering court on an application by the judgment debtor to set aside the registration of a judgment under this section on such terms as the court thinks fit; and

(c)   for suspending the execution of a judgment registered under this section until the expiration of the period during which the judgment debtor may apply to have the registration set aside.

(5)   In any action brought in any court in the United Kingdom on any judgment which might be ordered to be registered under this section, the plaintiff shall not be entitled to recover any costs of the action unless an application to register the judgment under this section has previously been refused or unless the court otherwise orders.

12   Interpretation

(1)   In this Part of this Act, unless the context otherwise requires—

The expression 'judgment' means any judgment or order given or made by a court in any civil proceedings, whether before or after the passing of this Act, whereby any sum of money is made payable, and includes an award in proceedings on an arbitration if the award has, in pursuance of the law in force in the place where it was made, become enforceable in the same manner as a judgment given by a court in that place:

The expression 'original court' in relation to any judgment means the court by which the judgment was given:

The expression 'registering court' in relation to any judgment means the court by which the judgment was registered:

The expression 'judgment creditor' means the person by whom the judgment was obtained, and includes the successors and assigns of that person:

The expression 'judgment debtor' means the person against whom the judgment was given, and includes any person against whom the judgment is enforceable in the place where it was given.

[(2)   Subject to [rules of court], any of the powers conferred by this Part of this Act on any court may be exercised by a judge of the court.]

14   Extent of Part II of Act

(1)   Where His Majesty is satisfied that reciprocal provisions have been made by the legislature of any part of His Majesty's dominions outside the United Kingdom for the enforcement within that part of His dominions of judgments obtained in the High Court in England, the Court of Session in Scotland, and the [High Court in Northern Ireland], His Majesty may by Order in Council declare that this Part of this Act shall extend to that part of His dominions, and on any such Order being made this Part of this Act shall extend accordingly.

(2)   An Order in Council under this section may be varied or revoked by a subsequent Order.

[(3)   Her Majesty may by Order in Council under this section consolidate any Orders in Council under this section which are in force when the consolidating Order is made.]

FOREIGN JUDGMENTS (RECIPROCAL ENFORCEMENT) ACT 1933
(1933 c 13)

PART I
REGISTRATION OF FOREIGN JUDGMENTS

1 Power to extend Part I of Act to foreign countries giving reciprocal treatment

[(1)   If, in the case of any foreign country, Her Majesty is satisfied that, in the event of the benefits conferred by this Part of this Act being extended to, or to any particular class of, judgments given in the courts of that country or in any particular class of those courts, substantial reciprocity of treatment will be assured as regards the enforcement in that country of similar judgments given in similar courts of the United Kingdom, She may by order in Council direct—

(a)   that this Part of this Act shall extend to that country;

(b)   that such courts of that country as are specified in the Order shall be recognised courts of that country for the purposes of this Part of this Act; and

(c)   that judgments of any such recognised court, or such judgments of any class so specified, shall, if within subsection (2) of this section, be judgments to which this Part of this Act applies.

(2)   Subject to subsection (2A) of this section, a judgment of a recognised court is within this subsection if it satisfies the following conditions, namely—

(a)   it is either final and conclusive as between the judgment debtor and the judgment creditor or requires the former to make an interim payment to the latter; and

(b)   there is payable under it a sum of money, not being a sum payable in respect of taxes or other charges of a like nature or in respect of a fine or other penalty; and

(c)   it is given after the coming into force of the Order in Council which made that court a recognised court.

(2A)   The following judgments of a recognised court are not within subsection (2) of this section—

(a)   a judgment given by that court on appeal from a court which is not a recognised court;

(b)   a judgment or other instrument which is regarded for the purposes of its enforcement as a judgment of that court but which was given or made in another country;

(c)   a judgment given by that court in proceedings founded on a judgment of a court in another country and having as their object the enforcement of that judgment.]

(3)   For the purposes of this section, a judgment shall be deemed to be final and conclusive notwithstanding that an appeal may be pending against it, or that it may still be subject to appeal, in the courts of the country of the original court.

(4)   His Majesty may by a subsequent Order in Council vary or revoke any Order previously made under this section.

[(5)   Any Order in council made under this section before its amendment by the Civil Jurisdiction and Judgments Act 1982 which deems any court of a foreign country to be a superior court of that country for the purposes of this Part of this Act shall (without prejudice to subsection (4) of this section) have effect from the time of that amendment as if it provided for that court to be a recognised court of that country for those purposes, and for any final and conclusive judgment of that court, if within subsection (2) of this section, to be a judgment to which this Part of this Act applies.]

2 Application for, and effect of, registration of foreign judgment

(1)   A person, being a judgment creditor under a judgment to which this Part of this Act applies, may apply to the High Court at any time within six years after

the date of the judgment, or, where there have been proceedings by way of appeal against the judgment, after the date of the last judgment given in those proceedings, to have the judgment registered in the High Court, and on any such application the court shall, subject to proof of the prescribed matters and to the other provisions of this Act, order the judgment to be registered:

Provided that a judgment shall not be registered if at the date of the application—

(a) it has been wholly satisfied; or

(b) it could not be enforced by execution in the country of the original court.

(2) Subject to the provisions of this Act with respect to the setting aside of registration—

(a) a registered judgment shall, for the purposes of execution, be of the same force and effect; and

(b) proceedings may be taken on a registered judgment; and

(c) the sum for which a judgment is registered shall carry interest; and

(d) the registering court shall have the same control over the execution of a registered judgment;

as if the judgment had been a judgment originally given in the registering court and entered on the date of registration:

Provided that execution shall not issue on the judgment so long as, under this Part of this Act and the Rules of Court made thereunder, it is competent for any party to make an application to have the registration of the judgment set aside, or, where such an application is made, until after the application has been finally determined.

[...]

(4) If at the date of the application for registration the judgment of the original court has been partly satisfied, the judgment shall not be registered in respect of the whole sum payable under the judgment of the original court, but only in respect of the balance remaining payable at that date.

(5) If, on an application for the registration of a judgment, it appears to the registering court that the judgment is in respect of different matters and that some, but not all, of the provisions of the judgment are such that if those provisions had been contained in separate judgments those judgments could properly have been registered, the judgment may be registered in respect of the provisions aforesaid but not in respect of any other provisions contained therein.

(6) In addition to the sum of money payable under the judgment of the original court, including any interest which by the law of the country of the original court becomes due under the judgment up to the time of registration, the judgment shall be registered for the reasonable costs of and incidental to registration, including the costs of obtaining a certified copy of the judgment from the original court.

4 Cases in which registered judgments must, or may, be set aside

(1) On an application in that behalf duly made by any party against whom a registered judgment may be enforced, the registration of the judgment—

(a) shall be set aside if the registering court is satisfied—

(i) that the judgment is not a judgment to which this Part of this Act applies or was registered in contravention of the foregoing provisions of this Act; or

(ii) that the courts of the country of the original court had no jurisdiction in the circumstances of the case; or

(iii) that the judgment debtor, being the defendant in the proceedings in the original court, did not (notwithstanding that process may have been duly served on him in accordance with the law of the country of the original court) receive notice of those proceedings in sufficient time to enable him to defend the proceedings and did not appear; or

(iv) that the judgment was obtained by fraud; or

(v) that the enforcement of the judgment would be contrary to public policy in the country of the registering court; or

(vi) that the rights under the judgment are not vested in the person by whom the application for registration was made;

(b)   may be set aside if the registering court is satisfied that the matter in dispute in the proceedings in the original court had previously to the date of the judgment in the original court been the subject of a final and conclusive judgment by a court having jurisdiction in the matter.

(2) For the purposes of this section the courts of the country of the original court shall, subject to the provisions of subsection (3) of this section, be deemed to have had jurisdiction—

(a) in the case of a judgment given in an action in personam—

(i) if the judgment debtor, being a defendant in the original court, submitted to the jurisdiction of that court by voluntarily appearing in the proceedings [...]; or

(ii) if the judgment debtor was plaintiff in, or counter-claimed in, the proceedings in the original court; or

(iii) if the judgment debtor, being a defendant in the original court, had before the commencement of the proceedings agreed, in respect of the subject matter of the proceedings, to submit to the jurisdiction of that court or of the courts of the country of that court; or

(iv) if the judgment debtor, being a defendant in the original court, was at the time when the proceedings were instituted resident in, or being a body corporate had its principal place of business in, the country of that court; or

(v) if the judgment debtor, being a defendant in the original court, had an office or place of business in the country of that court and the proceedings in that court were in respect of a transaction effected through or at that office or place;

(b) in the case of a judgment given in an action of which the subject matter was immovable property or in an action in rem of which the subject matter was movable property, if the property in question was at the time of the proceedings in the original court situate in the country of that court;

(c) in the case of a judgment given in an action other than any such action as is mentioned in paragraph (a) or paragraph (b) of this subsection, if the jurisdiction of the original court is recognised by the law of the registering court.

(3) Notwithstanding anything in subsection (2) of this section, the courts of the country of the original court shall not be deemed to have had jurisdiction—

(a) if the subject matter of the proceedings was immovable property outside the country of the original court; or

[...]

(c) if the judgment debtor, being a defendant in the original proceedings, was a person who under the rules of public international law was entitled to immunity from the jurisdiction of the courts of the country of the original court and did not submit to the jurisdiction of that court.

5   Powers of registering court on application to set aside registration

(1) If, on an application to set aside the registration of a judgment, the applicant satisfies the registering court either that an appeal is pending, or that he is entitled and intends to appeal, against the judgment, the court, if it thinks fit, may, on such terms as it may think just, either set aside the registration or adjourn the application to set aside the registration until after the expiration of such period as appears to the court to be reasonably sufficient to enable the applicant to take the necessary steps to have the appeal disposed of by the competent tribunal.

(2) Where the registration of a judgment is set aside under the last foregoing subsection, or solely for the reason that the judgment was not at the date of the

application for registration enforceable by execution in the country of the original court, the setting aside of the registration shall not prejudice a further application to register the judgment when the appeal has been disposed of or if and when the judgment becomes enforceable by execution in that country, as the case may be.

(3)   Where the registration of a judgment is set aside solely for the reason that the judgment, notwithstanding that it had at the date of the application for registration been partly satisfied, was registered for the whole sum payable thereunder, the registering court shall, on the application of the judgment creditor, order judgment to be registered for the balance remaining payable at that date.

6   Foreign judgments which can be registered not to be enforceable otherwise

No proceedings for the recovery of a sum payable under a foreign judgment, being a judgment to which this Part of this Act applies, other than proceedings by way of registration of the judgment, shall be entertained by any court in the United Kingdom.

7   Power to apply Part I of Act to British dominions, protectorates and mandated territories

(1)   His Majesty may by Order in Council direct that this Part of this Act shall apply to His Majesty's dominions outside the United Kingdom and to judgments obtained in the courts of the said dominions as it applies to foreign countries and judgments obtained in the courts of foreign countries, and, in the event of His Majesty so directing, this Act shall have effect accordingly and Part II of the Administration of Justice Act 1920, shall cease to have effect except in relation to those parts of the said dominions to which it extends at the date of the Order.

(2)   If at any time after His Majesty has directed as aforesaid an Order in Council is made under section one of this Act extending Part I of this Act to any part of His Majesty's dominions to which the said Part II extends as aforesaid, the said Part II shall cease to have effect in relation to that part of His Majesty's dominions.

(3)   References in this section to His Majesty's dominions outside the United Kingdom shall be construed as including references to any territories which are under His Majesty's protection and to any territories in respect of which a mandate under the League of Nations has been accepted by His Majesty.

PART II
MISCELLANEOUS AND GENERAL

8   General effect of certain foreign judgments

(1)   Subject to the provisions of this section, a judgment to which Part I of this Act applies or would have applied if a sum of money had been payable thereunder, whether it can be registered or not, and whether, if it can be registered, it is registered or not, shall be recognised in any court in the United Kingdom as conclusive between the parties thereto in all proceedings founded on the same cause of action and may be relied on by way of defence or counter-claim in any such proceedings.

(2)   This section shall not apply in the case of any judgment—

(a)   where the judgment has been registered and the registration thereof has been set aside on some ground other than—

(i)   that a sum of money was not payable under the judgment; or

(ii)   that the judgment had been wholly or partly satisfied; or

(iii)   that at the date of the application the judgment could not be enforced by execution in the country of the original court; or

(b)   where the judgment has not been registered, it is shown (whether it could have been registered or not) that if it had been registered the registration thereof would have been set aside on an application for that purpose on some ground other than one of the grounds specified in paragraph (a) of this subsection.

(3)   Nothing in this section shall be taken to prevent any court in the United Kingdom recognising any judgment as conclusive of any matter of law or fact decided therein if that judgment would have been so recognised before the passing of this Act.

9   Power to make foreign judgments unenforceable in United Kingdom if no reciprocity

(1)   If it appears to His Majesty that the treatment in respect of recognition and enforcement accorded by the courts of any foreign country to judgments given in the [...] courts of the United Kingdom is substantially less favourable than that accorded by the courts of the United Kingdom to judgments of the [...] courts of that country, His Majesty may by Order in Council apply this section to that country.

(2)   Except in so far as His Majesty may by Order in Council under this section otherwise direct, no proceedings shall be entertained in any court in the United Kingdom for the recovery of any sum alleged to be payable under a judgment given in a court of a country to which this section applies.

(3)   His Majesty may by a subsequent Order in Council vary or revoke any Order previously made under this section.

[10A   Arbitration awards

The provisions of this Act, except sections 1(5) and 6, shall apply, as they apply to a judgment, in relation to an award in proceedings on an arbitration which has, in pursuance of the law in force in the place where it was made, become enforceable in the same manner as a judgment given by a court in that place.]

11   Interpretation

(1)   In this Act, unless the context otherwise requires, the following expressions have the meanings hereby assigned to them respectively, that is to say—

'Appeal' includes any proceeding by way of discharging or setting aside a judgment or an application for a new trial or a stay of execution;

'Country of the original court' means the country in which the original court is situated;

['Court', except in section 10 of this Act, includes a tribunal;]

'Judgment' means a judgment or order given or made by a court in any civil proceedings, or a judgment or order given or made by a court in any criminal proceedings for the payment of a sum of money in respect of compensation or damages to an injured party;

'Judgment creditor' means the person in whose favour the judgment was given and includes any person in whom the rights under the judgment have become vested by succession or assignment or otherwise;

'Judgment debtor' means the person against whom the judgment was given, and includes any person against whom the judgment is enforceable under the law of the original court;

[...]

'Original court' in relation to any judgment means the court by which the judgment was given;

'Prescribed' means prescribed by rules of court;

'Registration' means registration under Part I of this Act, and the expressions 'register' and 'registered' shall be construed accordingly;

'Registering court' in relation to any judgment means the court to which an application to register the judgment is made.

(2)   For the purposes of this Act, the expression 'action in personam' shall not be deemed to include any matrimonial cause or any proceedings in connection with any of the following matters, that is to say, matrimonial matters, administration of the estates of deceased persons, bankruptcy, winding up of companies, lunacy, or guardianship of infants.

12 Application to Scotland
This Act in its application to Scotland shall have effect subject to the following
modifications:—
  (a)   For any reference to the High Court [...] there shall be substituted a reference to the Court of Session:
  (b)   The Court of Session shall, subject to the provisions of subsection (2) of
section three of this Act, have power by Act of Sederunt to make rules for the
purposes specified in subsection (1) of the said section:
  (c)   Registration under Part I of this Act shall be effected by registering in the
Books of Council and Session or in such manner as the Court of Session may by
Act of Sederunt prescribe:
  (d)   [...]
  (e)   For any reference to the entering of a judgment there shall be substituted
a reference to the signing of the interlocutor embodying the judgment.

MAINTENANCE ORDERS ACT 1950
(1950 c 37)

PART II
ENFORCEMENT

16 Application of Part II
  (1)   Any order to which this section applies (in this Part of this Act referred to
as a maintenance order) made by a court in any part of the United Kingdom may,
if registered in accordance with the provisions of this Part of this Act in a court in
another part of the United Kingdom, be enforced in accordance with those provisions in that other part of the United Kingdom.
  (2)   This section applies to the following orders, that is to say—
  (a)   an order for alimony, maintenance or other payments made or deemed
to be made by a court in England under any of the following enactments:—
      (i) [sections 15 to 17, 19 to 22, 30, 34 and 35 of the Matrimonial Causes
    Act 1965 and sections 22, 23(1), (2) and (4) and 27 of the Matrimonial
    Causes Act 1973 and section 14 or 17 of the Matrimonial and Family
    Proceedings Act 1984];
      (ii) [Part I of the Domestic Proceedings and Magistrates' Courts Act 1978];
      (iii) [Schedule 1 to the Children Act 1989];
      [...]
      (v) [paragraph 23 of Schedule 2 to the Children Act 1989] [...];
      [...]
  [(viii) section 106 of the Social Security Administration Act 1992;]
  [(ix) Part 1, 8 or 9 of Schedule 5 to the Civil Partnership Act 2004, Schedule
  6 to that Act or paragraph 5 or 9 of Schedule 7 to that Act];
  (b)   a decree for payment of aliment granted by a court in Scotland, including—
      (i) an order for the payment of an annual or periodical allowance under
    section two of the Divorce (Scotland) Act 1938, [an order for the payment of a
    periodic allowance [or a capital sum] under section 26 of the Succession
    (Scotland) Act 1964 or section 5 of the Divorce (Scotland) Act 1976; or section
    29 of the Matrimonial and Family Proceedings Act 1984; or an order for
    financial provision in the form of a monetary payment under section 8 of the
    Family Law (Scotland) Act 1985];
      (ii) an order for the payment of weekly or periodical sums under sub-
    section (2) of section three or subsection (4) of section five of the Guardianship
    of Infants Act 1925;

(iii) an order for the payment of sums in respect of aliment under sub-section (3) of section one of the Illegitimate Children (Scotland) Act 1930;

(iv) a decree for payment of aliment under section forty-four of the National Assistance Act 1948, or under section twenty-six of the Children Act 1948; and

[...]

[(vi) a contribution order under section 80 of, or a decree or an order made under section 81 of, the Social Work (Scotland) Act 1968;]

[(vii) an order for the payment of weekly or other periodical sums under subsection (3) of section 11 of the Guardianship Act 1973;]

[(viii) an order made on an application under section 18 or 19(8) of the Supplementary Benefits Act 1976;]

[(ix) an order made on an application under section 106 of the Social Security Administration Act 1992;]

[(x) an order made on an application under Schedule 11 to the Civil Partnership Act 2004];

(c) an order for alimony, maintenance or other payments made by a court in Northern Ireland under or by virtue of any of the following enactments:—

(i) subsection (2) of section seventeen, subsections (2) to (7) of section nineteen, subsection (2) of section twenty, section twenty-two or subsection (1) of section twenty-eight of the Matrimonial Causes Act (Northern Ireland) 1939;

(ii) [Schedule 1 to the Children (Northern Ireland) Order 1995;]

[...]

[(iv) Article 41 of the Children (Northern Ireland) Order 1995 or Article 101 of the Health and Personal Social Services (Northern Ireland) Order 1972;]

[(v) any enactment of the Parliament of Northern Ireland containing pro-visions corresponding with section 22(1), 34 or 35 of the Matrimonial Causes Act 1965, with section 22, 23(1), (2) or (4) or 27 of the Matrimonial Causes Act 1973;]

[(vi) Article 23 or 24 of the Supplementary Benefits (Northern Ireland) Order 1977;]

[(vii) the Domestic Proceedings (Northern Ireland) Order 1980;]

[(viii) any enactment applying in Northern Ireland and corresponding to section 106 of the Social Security Administration Act 1992;]

[(ix) Article 18 or 21 of the Matrimonial and Family Proceedings (Northern Ireland) Order 1989;]

[(x) Part 1, 7 or 8 of Schedule 15 to the Civil Partnership Act 2004, Schedule 16 to that Act or paragraph 5 or 9 of Schedule 17 to that Act.]

(3) For the purposes of this section, any order made before the commencement of the Matrimonial Causes Act (Northern Ireland) 1939, being an order which, if that Act had been in force, could have been made under or by virtue of any pro-vision of that Act, shall be deemed to be an order made by virtue of that provision.

17 Procedure for registration of maintenance orders

(1) An application for the registration of a maintenance order under this Part of this Act shall be made in the prescribed manner to the appropriate authority, that is to say—

(a) where the maintenance order was made by a court of summary juris-diction in England, a justice or justices [acting in the same local justice area] as the court which made the order;

(b) where the maintenance order was made by a court of summary juris-diction in Northern Ireland, a resident magistrate acting for the same petty ses-sions district as the court which made the order;

(c) in every other case, the prescribed officer of the court which made the order.

(2)　If upon application made as aforesaid by or on behalf of the person entitled to payments under a maintenance order it appears that the person liable to make those payments resides in another part of the United Kingdom, and that it is convenient that the order should be enforceable there, the appropriate authority shall cause a certified copy of the order to be sent to the prescribed officer of a court in that part of the United Kingdom in accordance with the provisions of the next following subsection.

(3)　The Court to whose officer the certified copy of a maintenance order is sent under this section shall be—

(a)　where the maintenance order was made by a superior court, the [Senior Courts], the Court of Session or the [Court of Judicature], as the case may be;

(b)　in any other case, a court of summary jurisdiction acting for the place in England or Northern Ireland in which the defendant appears to be, or as the case may be, the sheriff court in Scotland within the jurisdiction of which he appears to be.

(4)　Where the prescribed officer of any court receives a certified copy of a maintenance order sent to him under this section, he shall cause the order to be registered in that court in the prescribed manner, and shall give notice of the registration in the prescribed manner to the prescribed officer of the court which made the order.

(5)　The officer to whom any notice is given under the last foregoing subsection shall cause particulars of the notice to be registered in his court in the prescribed manner.

(6)　Where the sums payable under a maintenance order, being an order made by a court of summary jurisdiction in England or Northern Ireland, are payable to or through an officer of any court, that officer shall, if the person entitled to the payments so requests, make an application on behalf of that person for the registration of the order under this Part of this Act; but the person at whose request the application is made shall have the same liability for costs properly incurred in or about the application as if the application had been made by him.

(7)　An order which is for the time being registered under this Part of this Act in any court shall not be registered thereunder in any other court.

18　Enforcement of registered orders

(1)　Subject to the provisions of this section, a maintenance order registered under this Part of this Act in a court in any part of the United Kingdom may be enforced in that part of the United Kingdom in all respects as if it had been made by that court and as if that court had had jurisdiction to make it; and proceedings for or with respect to the enforcement of any such order may be taken accordingly.

[(1A)　Does not apply to Scotland.]

[(1B)　A maintenance order made in Scotland which is registered under this Part of this Act in the [Senior Courts or the Court of Judicature] shall, if interest is by the law of Scotland recoverable under the order, carry the like interest in accordance with subsection (1) of this section.]

...

21　Discharge and variation of maintenance orders registered in superior courts

(1)　The registration of a maintenance order in a superior court under this Part of this Act shall not confer on that court any power to vary or discharge the order, or affect any jurisdiction of the court in which the order was made to vary or discharge the order.

(2)　Where a maintenance order made in Scotland is for the time being—

[(a)　registered under this Part of this Act in a superior court and not registered under Part I of the Maintenance Orders Act 1958 [or under section 36 of the Civil Jurisdiction and Judgments Act 1982], or

(b)   registered in a court in England under that Part of that Act [of 1958] by virtue of section 1(2) of that Act [of 1958],

[(c)   registered in a court in Northern Ireland under section 36 of the Civil Jurisdiction and Judgments Act 1982,]

the person liable to make payments under the order may, upon application made to that court in the prescribed manner, adduce before that court any evidence upon which he would be entitled to rely in any proceedings brought before the court by which the order was made for the variation or discharge of the order.

...

22   Discharge and variation of maintenance orders registered in summary or sheriff courts

(1)   [Subject to subsection (1ZA)] where a maintenance order is for the time being registered under this Part of this Act in a court of summary jurisdiction or sheriff court, that court may, upon application made in the prescribed manner by or on behalf of the person liable to make [periodical] payments under the order or the person entitled to those payments, by order make such variation as the court thinks fit in the rate of the payments under the maintenance order; but no such variation shall impose on the person liable to make payments under the maintenance order a liability to make payments in excess of the maximum rate (if any) authorised by the law for the time being in force in the part of the United Kingdom in which the maintenance order was made.

[(1ZA)   The power under subsection (1) to vary the rate of payments may not be exercised where paragraph 9(2) of Schedule 6 to the Civil Jurisdiction and Judgments (Maintenance) Regulations 2011 applies (restriction on modifying maintenance decision where creditor remains habitually resident in the part of the United Kingdom in which the decision was made).]

...

(2)   For the purposes of subsection (1) of this section, a court in any part of the United Kingdom may take notice of the law in force in any other part of the United Kingdom.

...

(4)   Except as provided by subsection (1) of this section, no variation shall be made in the rate of the payments under a maintenance order which is for the time being registered under this Part of this Act in a court of summary jurisdiction or sheriff court, but without prejudice to any power of the court which made the order to discharge it or vary it otherwise than in respect of the rate of the payments thereunder.

(5)   Where a maintenance order is for the time being registered under this Part of this Act in a court of summary jurisdiction or sheriff court—

(a)   the person entitled to payments under the order or the person liable to make payments under the order may, upon application made in the prescribed manner to the court by which the order was made, or in which the order is registered, as the case may be, adduce in the prescribed manner before the court in which the applications is made any evidence on which he would be entitled to rely in proceedings for the variation or discharge of the order;

(b)   the court in which the application is made shall cause a transcript or summary of that evidence, signed by the deponent, to be sent to the prescribed officer of the court in which the order is registered or of the court by which the order was made, as the case may be; and in any proceedings for the variation or discharge of the order the transcript or summary shall be evidence of the facts stated therein.

PART III
GENERAL

...

27 General provisions as to jurisdiction

(1) Nothing in this Act shall be construed as derogating from any jurisdiction exercisable, apart from the provisions of this Act, by any court in any part of the United Kingdom.

(2) It is hereby declared that any jurisdiction conferred by Part I of this Act, or any enactment therein referred to, upon a court in any part of the United Kingdom is exercisable notwithstanding that any party to the proceedings is not domiciled in that part of the United Kingdom; and any jurisdiction so conferred in affiliation proceedings shall be exercisable notwithstanding that the child to whom the proceedings relate was not born in that part of the United Kingdom.

(3) For the avoidance of doubt it is hereby declared that in relation to proceedings in which the sheriff has jurisdiction by virtue of the provisions of this Act there are the same rights of appeal and of remit to the Court of Session as there are in relation to the like proceedings in which the sheriff has jurisdiction otherwise than by virtue of the said provisions.

WILLS ACT 1963
(1963 c 44)

1 General rule as to formal validity

A will shall be treated as properly executed if its execution conformed to the internal law in force in the territory where it was executed, or in the territory where, at the time of its execution or of the testator's death, he was domiciled or had his habitual residence, or in a state of which, at either of those times, he was a national.

2 Additional rules

(1) Without prejudice to the preceding section, the following shall be treated as properly executed—

(a) a will executed on board a vessel or aircraft of any description, if the execution of the will conformed to the internal law in force in the territory with which, having regard to its registration (if any) and other relevant circumstances, the vessel or aircraft may be taken to have been most closely connected;

(b) a will so far as it disposes of immovable property, if its execution conformed to the internal law in force in the territory where the property was situated;

(c) a will so far as it revokes a will which under this Act would be treated as properly executed or revokes a provision which under this Act would be treated as comprised in a properly executed will, if the execution of the later will conformed to any law by reference to which the revoked will or provision would be so treated;

(d) a will so far as it exercises a power of appointment, if the execution of the will conformed to the law governing the essential validity of the power.

(2) A will so far as it exercises a power of appointment shall not be treated as improperly executed by reason only that its execution was not in accordance with any formal requirements contained in the instrument creating the power.

3 Certain requirements to be treated as formal

Where (whether in pursuance of this Act or not) a law in force outside the United Kingdom falls to be applied in relation to a will, any requirement of that law whereby special formalities are to be observed by testators answering a particular description, or witnesses to the execution of a will are to possess certain qualifications, shall be treated, notwithstanding any rule of that law to the contrary, as a formal requirement only.

4 Construction of wills

The construction of a will shall not be altered by reason of any change in the testator's domicile after the execution of the will.

6 Interpretation

(1) In this Act—

'internal law' in relation to any territory or state means the law which would apply in a case where no question of the law in force in any other territory or state arose;

'state' means a territory or group of territories having its own law of nationality;

'will' includes any testamentary instrument or act, and 'testator' shall be construed accordingly.

(2) Where under this Act the internal law in force in any territory or state is to be applied in the case of a will, but there are in force in that territory or state two or more systems of internal law relating to the formal validity of wills, the system to be applied shall be ascertained as follows—

(a) if there is in force throughout the territory or state a rule indicating which of those systems can properly be applied in the case in question, that rule shall be followed; or

(b) if there is no such rule, the system shall be that with which the testator was most closely connected at the relevant time, and for this purpose the relevant time is the time of the testator's death where the matter is to be determined by reference to circumstances prevailing at his death, and the time of execution of the will in any other case.

(3) In determining for the purposes of this Act whether or not the execution of a will conformed to a particular law, regard shall be had to the formal requirements of that law at the time of execution, but this shall not prevent account being taken of an alteration of law affecting wills executed at that time if the alteration enables the will to be treated as properly executed.

7 Short title, commencement, repeal and extent

(1) This Act may be cited as the Wills Act 1963.

(2) This Act shall come into operation on 1st January 1964.

(3) The Wills Act 1861 is hereby repealed.

(4) This Act shall not apply to a will of a testator who died before the time of the commencement of this Act and shall apply to a will of a testator who dies after that time whether the will was executed before or after that time, but so that the repeal of the Wills Act 1861 shall not invalidate a will executed before that time.

SUCCESSION (SCOTLAND) ACT 1964
(1964 c 41)

PART II
LEGAL AND OTHER PRIOR RIGHTS IN ESTATES OF DECEASED PERSONS

8 Prior rights of surviving spouse [or civil partner], on intestacy, in dwelling house and furniture

(1) Where a person dies intestate leaving a spouse [or civil partner], and the intestate estate includes a relevant interest in a [dwelling house mentioned in subsection (4)(a) of this section,] the surviving spouse [or civil partner] shall be entitled [, subject to subsection (2B) of this section,] to receive out of the intestate estate—

(a) where the value of the relevant interest does not exceed [[£473,000] or such larger amount as may from time to time be fixed by order of the Secretary of State]—

(i) if subsection (2) of this section does not apply, the relevant interest;

(ii) if the said subsection (2) applies, a sum equal to the value of the relevant interest;

(b) in any other case, the sum of [[£473,000] or such larger amount as may from time to time be fixed by order of the Secretary of State].

[...]

(2) This subsection shall apply for the purposes of paragraph (a) of the foregoing subsection if—

(a) the dwelling house forms part only of the subjects comprised in one tenancy or lease under which the intestate was the tenant; or

(b) the dwelling house forms the whole or part of subjects an interest in which is comprised in the intestate estate and which were used by the intestate for carrying on a trade, profession or occupation, and the value of the estate as a whole would be likely to be substantially diminished if the dwelling house were disposed of otherwise than with the assets of the trade, profession or occupation.

[(2A) Where the tenant of a croft dies intestate leaving a spouse or civil partner or, where he dies leaving no spouse or civil partner, leaving a cohabitant, and the intestate estate includes a relevant interest in a dwelling house mentioned in subsection (4)(b) of this section, the surviving spouse, civil partner or, as the case may be, cohabitant shall be entitled, subject to subsection (2B) of this section, to receive out of the intestate estate—

(a) where the value of the relevant interest does not exceed the amount for the time being fixed by order under subsection (1)(a) of this section, the tenancy of the croft;

(b) in any other case, the sum for the time being fixed by order under subsection (1)(b) of this section.

(2B) If the intestate estate comprises—

(a) a relevant interest in two or more dwelling houses mentioned in subsection (4)(a) of this section, subsection (1) of this section shall have effect only in relation to such one of them as the surviving spouse or civil partner may elect for the purposes of subsection (1) within 6 months after the date of death of the intestate;

(b) a relevant interest in two or more dwelling houses mentioned in subsection (4)(b) of this section, subsection (2A) of this section shall have effect only in relation to such one of them as the surviving spouse, civil partner or cohabitant may elect for the purposes of subsection (2A) within 6 months after that date;

(c) a relevant interest in both—

(i) one or more dwelling houses mentioned in subsection (4)(a) of this section; and

(ii) one or more dwelling houses mentioned in subsection (4)(b) of this section,

the surviving spouse or civil partner shall not be entitled to receive both the entitlement under subsection (1) of this section and that under subsection (2A) of this section and must elect within 6 months after that date whether to take the entitlement under the said subsection (1) or under the said subsection (2A).]

(3) Where a person dies intestate leaving a spouse [or civil partner], and the intestate estate includes the furniture and plenishings of a dwelling house to which this section applies (whether or not the dwelling house is comprised in the intestate estate), the surviving spouse [or civil partner] shall be entitled to receive out of the intestate estate—

(a) where the value of the furniture and plenishings does not exceed

[[£29,000] or such larger amount as may from time to time be fixed by order of the Secretary of State], the whole thereof;

(b)   in any other case, such part of the furniture and plenishings, to a value not exceeding [[£29,000] or such larger amount as may from time to time be fixed by order of the Secretary of State], as may be chosen by the surviving spouse [or civil partner]:

Provided that, if the intestate estate comprises the furniture and plenishings of two or more such dwelling houses, this subsection shall have effect only in relation to the furniture and plenishings of such one of them as the surviving spouse [or civil partner] may elect for the purposes of this subsection within six months of the date of death of the intestate.

[(4)   The dwelling house is—

(a)   in a case mentioned in subsection (1) of this section, any dwelling house in which the surviving spouse or civil partner of the intestate was ordinarily resident at the date of death of the intestate and which did not, at that date, form part of a croft of which the intestate was tenant;

(b)   in a case mentioned in subsection (2A) of this section, any dwelling house in which the surviving spouse, civil partner or cohabitant was ordinarily resident at the date of death of the intestate and which, at that date, formed part of a croft of which the intestate was tenant.]

(5)   Where any question arises as to the value of any furniture or plenishings, or of any interest in a dwelling house, for the purposes of any provision of this section the question shall be determined by arbitration by a single arbiter appointed, in default of agreement, by the sheriff of the county in which the intestate was domiciled at the date of his death or, if that county is uncertain or the intestate was domiciled furth of Scotland, the sheriff of the Lothians and Peebles at Edinburgh.

(6)   In this section—

[(za)   'cohabitant' means a person—

(i)   who was living with the intestate as if married to him; or

(ii)   who was living with the intestate as if in civil partnership with him,

and had been so living for at least 2 years.]

(a)   'dwelling house' includes a part of a building occupied (at the date of death of the intestate) as a separate dwelling; and any reference to a dwelling house shall be construed as including any garden or portion of ground attached to, and usually occupied with, the dwelling house or otherwise required for the amenity or convenience of the dwelling house;

(b)   'furniture and plenishings' includes garden effects, domestic animals, plate, plated articles, linen, china, glass, books, pictures, prints, articles of household use and consumable stores; but does not include any article or animal used at the date of death of the intestate for business purposes, or money or securities for money, or any heirloom;

(c)   'heirloom', in relation to an intestate estate, means any article which has associations with the intestate's family of such nature and extent that it ought to pass to some member of that family other than the surviving spouse of the intestate;

(d)   'relevant interest', in relation to a dwelling house, means the interest therein of an owner, or the interest therein of a tenant, subject in either case to any heritable debt secured over the interest; and for the purposes of this definition 'tenant' means a tenant under a tenancy or lease (whether of the dwelling house alone or of the dwelling house together with other subjects) which is not a tenancy to which the Rent and Mortgage Interest Restrictions Acts 1920 to 1939 apply.

9 Prior right of surviving spouse [or civil partner] to financial provision on intestacy

(1) Where a person dies intestate and is survived by a husband, [wife or civil partner the survivor] shall be entitled to receive out of the intestate estate—

(a) if the intestate is survived by issue [...] the sum of [£50,000 or such larger amount as may from time to time be fixed by order of the Secretary of State], or

(b) if the intestate is not survived by issue [...] the sum of [£89,000 or such larger amount as may from time to time be fixed by order of the Secretary of State],

together with, in either case, interest at the rate of 4 per cent. per annum [or, at such rate as may from time to time be fixed by order of the Secretary of State], on such sum from the date of the intestate's death until payment:

Provided that where the surviving spouse [or civil partner] is entitled to receive a legacy out of the estate of the intestate (other than a legacy of any dwelling house to which the last foregoing section applies or of any furniture and plenishings of any such dwelling house), he or she shall, unless he or she renounces the legacy, be entitled under this subsection to receive only such sum, if any, as remains after deducting from the sum [fixed by virtue of paragraph (a) of this subsection or the sum fixed by virtue of paragraph (b) of this subsection], as the case may be, the amount or value of the legacy.

(2) Where the intestate estate is less than the amount which the surviving spouse [or civil partner] is entitled to receive by virtue of subsection (1) of this section the right conferred by the said subsection on the surviving spouse [or civil partner] shall be satisfied by the transfer to him or her of the whole of the intestate estate.

(3) The amount which the surviving spouse [or civil partner] is entitled to receive by virtue of subsection (1) of this section shall be borne by, and paid out of, the parts of the intestate estate consisting of heritable and moveable property respectively in proportion to the respective amounts of those parts.

(4) Where by virtue of subsection (2) of this section a surviving spouse [or civil partner] has right to the whole of the intestate estate, he or she shall have the right to be appointed executor.

(5) The rights conferred by the Intestate Husband's Estate (Scotland) Acts 1911 to 1959 on a surviving spouse in his or her deceased spouse's estate shall not be exigible out of the estate of any person dying after the commencement of this Act.

(6) For the purposes of this section—

(a) the expression 'intestate estate' means so much of the net intestate estate as remains after the satisfaction of any claims under the last foregoing section; and

(b) the expression 'legacy' includes any payment or benefit to which a surviving spouse [or civil partner] becomes entitled by virtue of any testamentary disposition; and the amount or value of any legacy shall be ascertained as at the date of the intestate's death.

ADMINISTRATION OF ESTATES ACT 1971
(1971 c 25)

1 Recognition in England and Wales of Scottish confirmations and Northern Irish grants of representation

(1) Where a person dies domiciled in Scotland—

(a) a confirmation granted in respect of all or part of his estate and noting his Scottish domicile, and

(b) a certificate of confirmation, noting his Scottish domicile and relating to one or more items of his estate,

shall, without being resealed, be treated for the purposes of the law of England and Wales as a grant of representation (in accordance with subsection (2) below) to the executors named in the confirmation or certificate in respect of the property of the deceased of which according to the terms of the confirmation they are executors or, as the case may be, in respect of the item or items of property specified in the certificate of confirmation.

(2)   Where by virtue of subsection (1) above a confirmation or certificate of confirmation is treated for the purposes of the law of England and Wales as a grant of representation to the executors named therein then, subject to subsections (3) and (5) below, the grant shall be treated—

(a)   as a grant of probate where it appears from the confirmation or certificate that the executors so named are executors nominate; and

(b)   in any other case, as a grant of letters of administration.

(3)   Section 7 of the Administration of Estates Act 1925 (executor of executor represents original testator) shall not, by virtue of subsection (2)(a) above, apply on the death of an executor named in a confirmation or certificate of confirmation.

(4)   Subject to subsection (5) below, where a person dies domiciled in Northern Ireland a grant of probate of his will or letters of administration in respect of his estate (or any part of it) made by the High Court in Northern Ireland and noting his domicile there shall, without being resealed, be treated for the purposes of the law of England and Wales as if it had been originally made by the High Court in England and Wales.

(5)   Notwithstanding anything in the preceding provisions of this section, a person who is a personal representative according to the law of England and Wales by virtue only of those provisions may not be required, under section 25 of the Administration of Estates Act 1925, to deliver up his grant to the High Court.

(6)   This section applies in relation to confirmations, probates and letters of administration granted before as well as after the commencement of this Act, and in relation to a confirmation, probate or letters of administration granted before the commencement of this Act, this section shall have effect as if it had come into force immediately before the grant was made.

(7)   In this section 'confirmation' includes an additional confirmation, and the term 'executors', where used in relation to a confirmation or certificate of confirmation, shall be construed according to the law of Scotland.

2   Recognition in Northern Ireland of English grants of representation and Scottish confirmations

(1)   Where a person dies domiciled in England and Wales a grant of probate of his will or letters of administration in respect of his estate (or any part of it) made by the High Court in England and Wales and noting his domicile there shall, without being resealed, be treated for the purposes of the law of Northern Ireland as if it had been originally made by the High Court in Northern Ireland.

(2)   Where a person dies domiciled in Scotland—

(a)   a confirmation granted in respect of all or part of his estate and noting his Scottish domicile, and

(b)   a certificate of confirmation noting his Scottish domicile and relating to one or more items of his estate,

shall, without being resealed, be treated for the purposes of the law of Northern Ireland as a grant of representation (in accordance with subsection (3) below) to the executors named in the confirmation or certificate in respect of the property of the deceased of which according to the terms of the confirmation they are executors or, as the case may be, in respect of the item or items of property specified in the certificate of confirmation.

(3)   Where by virtue of subsection (2) above a confirmation or certificate of confirmation is treated for the purposes of the law of Northern Ireland as a grant of representation to the executors named therein then, subject to subsection (4) below, the grant shall be treated—

(a) as a grant of probate where it appears from the confirmation or certificate that the executors so named are executors nominate; and

(b) in any other case, as a grant of letters of administration.

(4) Notwithstanding anything in any enactment or rule of law, subsection (3)(a) above shall not operate to entitle an executor of a sole or last surviving executor of a testator, whose will has been proved in Scotland only, to act as the executor of that testator.

(5) This section applies in relation to probates, letters of administration and confirmations granted before as well as after the commencement of this Act, and—

(a) in relation to a probate, letters of administration or confirmation granted, and resealed in Northern Ireland, before the commencement of this Act, this section shall have effect as if it had come into force immediately before the grant was so resealed; and

(b) a probate, letters of administration or confirmation granted but not resealed in Northern Ireland before the commencement of this Act shall, for the purposes of this section, be treated as having been granted at the commencement of this Act.

(6) In this section 'confirmation' includes an additional confirmation, and the term 'executors', where used in relation to a confirmation or certificate of confirmation shall be construed according to the law of Scotland.

3 Recognition in Scotland of English and Northern Irish grants of representation

(1) Where a person dies domiciled in England and Wales or in Northern Ireland a grant of probate or letters of administration—

(a) from the High Court in England and Wales and noting his domicile there, or

(b) from the High Court in Northern Ireland and noting his domicile there, shall, without being resealed, be of the like force and effect and have the same operation in relation to property in Scotland as a confirmation given under the seal of office of the Commissariot of Edinburgh to the executor or administrator named in the probate or letters of administration.

(2) This section applies in relation to probates and letters of administration granted before as well as after the commencement of this Act, and in relation to a probate or letters of administration granted before the commencement of this Act, this section shall have effect as if it had come into force immediately before the grant was made.

4 Evidence of grants

(1) In England and Wales and in Northern Ireland—

(a) a document purporting to be a confirmation, additional confirmation or certificate of confirmation given under the seal of office of any commissariot in Scotland shall, except where the contrary is proved, be taken to be such a confirmation, additional confirmation or certificate of confirmation without further proof; and

(b) a document purporting to be a duplicate of such a confirmation or additional confirmation and to be given under such a seal shall be receivable in evidence in like manner and for the like purposes as the confirmation or additional confirmation of which it purports to be a duplicate.

(2) In England and Wales and in Scotland—

(a) a document purporting to be a grant of probate or of letters of administration issued under the seal of the High Court in Northern Ireland or of the principal or district probate registry there shall, except where the contrary is proved, be taken to be such a grant without further proof; and

(b) a document purporting to be a copy of such a grant and to be sealed with such a seal shall be receivable in evidence in like manner and for the like purposes as the grant of which it purports to be a copy.

(3) In Scotland and in Northern Ireland—

(a) a document purporting to be a grant of probate or of letters of administration issued under the seal of the High Court in England and Wales or of the principal or a district probate registry there shall, except where the contrary is proved, be taken to be such a grant without further proof; and

(b) a document purporting to be a copy of such a grant and to be sealed with such a seal shall be receivable in evidence in like manner and for the like purposes as the grant of which it purports to be a copy.

5 Property outside Scotland of which deceased was trustee

(1) A confirmation or additional confirmation granted in respect of property situated in Scotland of a person who died domiciled there, which notes that domicile, may contain or have appended thereto and signed by the sheriff clerk a note or statement of property in England and Wales or in Northern Ireland held by the deceased in trust, being a note or statement which has been set forth in any inventory recorded in the books of the court of which the sheriff clerk is clerk.

(2) Section 1 or, as the case may be, section 2 of this Act shall apply in relation to property specified in such a note or statement as is mentioned in subsection (1) above as it applies in relation to property specified in the confirmation or additional confirmation concerned.

6 Inventory of Scottish estate may include real estate in any part of the United Kingdom

(1) It shall be competent to include in the inventory of the estate of any person who dies domiciled in Scotland any real estate of the deceased situated in England and Wales or Northern Ireland, and accordingly in section 9 of the Confirmation of Executors (Scotland) Act 1858 the word 'personal' wherever it occurs is hereby repealed.

(2) Section 14(2) of the Succession (Scotland) Act 1964 (act of sederunt to provide for description of heritable property) shall apply in relation to such real estate as aforesaid as it applies in relation to heritable property in Scotland.

MAINTENANCE ORDERS (RECIPROCAL ENFORCEMENT) ACT 1972
(1972 c 18)

PART I
RECIPROCAL ENFORCEMENT OF MAINTENANCE ORDERS MADE IN UNITED KINGDOM OR RECIPROCATING COUNTRY

1 Orders in Council designating reciprocating countries*

(1) Her Majesty, if satisfied that, in the event of the benefits conferred by this Part of this Act being applied to, or to particular classes of, maintenance orders made by the courts of any country or territory outside the United Kingdom, similar benefits will in that country or territory be applied to, or to those classes of, maintenance orders made by the courts of the United Kingdom, may by Order in Council designate that country or territory as a reciprocating country for the purposes of this Part of this Act; and, subject to subsection (2) below, in this Part of this Act 'reciprocating country' means a country or territory that is for the time being so designated.

(2) A country or territory may be designated under subsection (1) above as a

---

* In relation to maintenance orders made by courts in the United Kingdom or by courts in a State specified in Sch 1 to SI 1995/2709 section 1 does not apply.

reciprocating country either as regards maintenance orders generally, or as regards maintenance orders other than those of any specified class, or as regards maintenance orders of one or more specified classes only; and a country or territory which is for the time being so designated otherwise than as regards maintenance orders generally shall for the purposes of this Part of this Act be taken to be a reciprocating country only as regards maintenance orders of the class to which the designation extends.

2   Transmission of maintenance order made in United Kingdom for enforcement in reciprocating country

(1)   Subject to subsection (2) below, where the payer under a maintenance order made, whether before or after the commencement of this Part of this Act, by a court in the United Kingdom is residing [or has assets] in a reciprocating country, the payee under the order may apply for the order to be sent to that country for enforcement.

(2)   Subsection (1) above shall not have effect in relation to a provisional order or to an order made by virtue of a provision of Part II of this Act.

(3)   Every application under this section shall be made in the prescribed manner to the prescribed officer of the court which made the maintenance order to which the application relates.

(4)   If, on an application duly made under this section to the prescribed officer of a court in the United Kingdom, that officer is satisfied that the payer under the maintenance order to which the application relates is residing [or has assets] in a reciprocating country, the following documents, that is to say—

(a)   a certified copy of the maintenance order;

(b)   a certificate signed by that officer certifying that the order is enforceable in the United Kingdom;

(c)   a certificate of arrears so signed;

(d)   a statement giving such information as the officer possesses as to the whereabouts of the payer [and the nature and location of his assets in that country];

(e)   a statement giving such information as the officer possesses for facilitating the identification of the payer; and

(f)   where available, a photograph of the payer;

shall be sent by that officer to the Secretary of State with a view to their being transmitted by the Secretary of State to the responsible authority in the reciprocating country if he is satisfied that the statement relating to the whereabouts of the payer [and the nature and location of his assets in that country] gives sufficient information to justify that being done.

(5)   Nothing in this section shall be taken as affecting any jurisdiction of a court in the United Kingdom with respect to a maintenance order to which this section applies, and any such order may be enforced, varied or revoked accordingly.

5   Variation and revocation of maintenance order made in United Kingdom

(1)   This section applies to a maintenance order a certified copy of which has been sent to a reciprocating country in pursuance of section 2 of this Act and to a maintenance order made by virtue of section 3 or 4 thereof which has been confirmed by a competent court in such a country.

(2)   A court in the United Kingdom having power to vary a maintenance order to which this section applies shall have power to vary that order by a provisional order.

(3)   Where the payer under a maintenance order to which this section applies is for the time being residing in a reciprocating country, the court shall not, on an application made by the payee under the order for the variation of the order, vary

the order by increasing the rate of the payments thereunder otherwise than by a provisional order.

[(3A) It shall not be necessary for the payee under a maintenance order to which this section applies to intimate to any person the making by him of an application for a provisional order varying the said maintenance order by increasing the rate of the payments thereunder.]

(4) Where a court in the United Kingdom makes a provisional order varying a maintenance order to which this section applies, the prescribed officer of the court shall send in the prescribed manner to the court in a reciprocating country having power to confirm the provisional order a certified copy of the provisional order together with a document, authenticated in the prescribed manner, setting out or summarising the evidence given in the proceedings.

(5) Where a certified copy of a provisional order made by a court in a reciprocating country, being an order varying or revoking a maintenance order to which this section applies, together with a document, duly authenticated, setting out or summarising the evidence given in the proceedings in which the provisional order was made, is received by the court in the United Kingdom which made the maintenance order, that court may confirm or refuse to confirm the provisional order and, if that order is an order varying the maintenance order, confirm it either without alteration or with such alterations as it thinks reasonable.

(6) Where a certified copy of a provisional order varying or revoking a maintenance order to which this section applies is received by a court as mentioned in subsection (5) above, the prescribed officer of that court shall intimate to the payee under the maintenance order, in the prescribed manner, that the provisional order has been received as aforesaid and that, unless the payee enters appearance within the prescribed period, the court will confirm the provisional order under this section.

(7) Where a maintenance order to which this section applies has been varied by an order (including a provisional order which has been confirmed) made by a court in the United Kingdom or by a competent court in a reciprocating country, the maintenance order shall, as from [the date on which under the provisions of the order the variation is to take effect], have effect as varied by that order and, where that order was a provisional order, as if that order had been made in the form in which it was confirmed and as if it had never been a provisional order.

(8) Where a maintenance order to which this section applies has been revoked by an order made by a court in the United Kingdom or by a competent court in a reciprocating country, including a provisional order made by the last-mentioned court which has been confirmed by a court in the United Kingdom, the maintenance order shall, as from [the date on which under the provisions of the order the revocation is to take effect], be deemed to have ceased to have effect except as respects any arrears due under the maintenance order at that date.

(9) Where before a maintenance order made by virtue of section 3 or 4 of this Act is confirmed a document, duly authenticated, setting out or summarising evidence taken in a reciprocating country for the purpose of proceedings relating to the confirmation of the order is received by the court in the United Kingdom which made the order, or that court, in compliance with a request made to it by a court in such a country, takes the evidence of a person residing in the United Kingdom for the purpose of such proceedings, the court in the United Kingdom which made the order shall consider that evidence and if, having done so, it appears to it that the order ought not to have been made—

(a) it shall, in such manner as may be prescribed, give to the person on whose application the maintenance order was made an opportunity to consider that evidence, to make representations with respect to it and to adduce further evidence; and

(b)   after considering all the evidence and any representations made by that person, it may revoke the maintenance order.

(10)   *[Substitutes subsections (3), (3A) and (6) above for Scotland.]*

6   Registration in United Kingdom court of maintenance order made in reciprocating country

(1)   This section applies to a maintenance order made, whether before or after the commencement of this Part of this Act, by a court in a reciprocating country, including such an order made by such a court which has been confirmed by a court in another reciprocating country but excluding a provisional order which has not been confirmed.

(2)   Where a certified copy of an order to which this section applies is received by the Secretary of State from the responsible authority in a reciprocating country, and it appears to the Secretary of State that the payer under the order is residing [or has assets] in the United Kingdom, he shall send the copy of the order to the prescribed officer of the appropriate court.

(3)   Where the prescribed officer of the appropriate court receives from the Secretary of State a certified copy of an order to which this section applies, he shall, subject to subsection (4) below, register the order in the prescribed manner in that court.

(4)   Before registering an order under this section an officer of a court shall take such steps as he thinks fit for the purpose of ascertaining whether the payer under the order is residing [or has assets] within the jurisdiction of the court, and if after taking those steps he is satisfied that the payer is not [residing and has no assets within the jurisdiction of the court] he shall return the certified copy of the order to the Secretary of State with a statement giving such information as he possesses as to the whereabouts of the payer [and the nature and location of his assets].

7   Confirmation by United Kingdom court of provisional maintenance order made in reciprocating country*

(1)   This section applies to a maintenance order made, whether before or after the commencement of this Part of this Act, by a court in a reciprocating country being a provisional order.

(2)   Where a certified copy of an order to which this section applies together with—

(a)   a document, duly authenticated, setting out or summarising the evidence given in the proceedings in which the order was made; and

(b)   a statement of the grounds on which the making of the order might have been opposed by the payer under the order,

is received by the Secretary of State from the responsible authority in a reciprocating country, and it appears to the Secretary of State that the payer under the order is residing in the United Kingdom, he shall send the copy of the order and documents which accompanied it to the prescribed officer of the appropriate court, and that court shall—

(i)   if the payer under the order establishes [any grounds on which he might have opposed the making of the order] in the proceedings in which the order was made, refuse to confirm the order; and

(ii)   in any other case, confirm the order either without alteration or with such alterations as it thinks reasonable.

(3)   In any proceedings for the confirmation under this section of a provisional order, the statement received from the court which made the order of the grounds

---

*Section 7 is repealed in relation to maintenance orders made by courts in the United States of America, the Republic of Ireland or a Hague Convention country.

on which the making of the order might have been opposed by the payer under the order shall be conclusive evidence that the payer might have [opposed the making of the order on any of those grounds].

(4)   [On receiving a certified copy of a provisional order sent to him in pursuance of subsection (2) above the prescribed officer of the appropriate court shall intimate to the payer under the order, in the prescribed manner, that the order has been received as aforesaid and that, unless the payer enters appearance within the prescribed period, the court will confirm the order under this section.]

(5)   The prescribed officer of a court having power under this section to confirm a provisional order shall, if the court confirms the order, register the order in the prescribed manner in that court, and shall, if the court refuses to confirm the order, return the certified copy of the order and the documents which accompanied it to the Secretary of State.

...

(6)   [If such intimation as is mentioned in subsection (4) above cannot be given to the payer under a provisional order in pursuance of that subsection] the officer by whom the certified copy of the order was received shall return that copy and the documents which accompanied it to the Secretary of State with a statement giving such information as he possesses as to the whereabouts of the payer.

(7)   This section shall apply to Scotland subject to the following modifications:—

(a), (b)   [modify subsections (4) and (6) above]

(c)   in any proceedings for the confirmation under this section of a provisional order made by a court in a reciprocating country, the sheriff shall apply the law in force in that country with respect to the sufficiency of evidence.

(8)   [Applies to Northern Ireland.]

8   Enforcement of maintenance order registered in United Kingdom court

(1)   Subject to subsection (2) below, a registered order may be enforced in the United Kingdom as if it had been made by the registering court and as if that court had had jurisdiction to make it; and proceedings for or with respect to the enforcement of any such order may be taken accordingly.

(2)–(5)   [Do not apply to Scotland.]

(6)   In any proceedings for or with respect to the enforcement of an order which is for the time being registered in any court under this Part of this Act a certificate of arrears sent to the prescribed officer of the court shall be [sufficient evidence] of the facts stated therein.

(7)   Subject to subsection (8) below, sums of money payable under a registered order shall be payable in accordance with the order as from [the date on which they are required to be paid under the provisions of the order].

(8)   The court having power under section 7 of this Act to confirm a provisional order may, if it decides to confirm the order, direct that the sums of money payable under it shall be deemed to have been payable in accordance with the order as from [the date on which they are required to be paid under the provisions of the order or such later date], as it may specify; and subject to any such direction, a maintenance order registered under the said section 7 shall be treated as if it had been made in the form in which it was confirmed and as if it had never been a provisional order.

(9)   In the application of this section to Scotland—

(a)   subsections (2) to (5) shall be omitted; and

(b)   in subsection (6), for the word 'evidence' there shall be substituted the words 'sufficient evidence'.

[...]

9   Variation and revocation of maintenance order registered in United Kingdom court

(1)   Subject to the provisions of this section, the registering court—

(a)   shall have the like power, on an application made by the payer or payee under a registered order, to vary or revoke the order as if it had been made by the registering court and as if that court had had jurisdiction to make it; and

(b)   shall have power to vary or revoke a registered order by a provisional order.

[(1A)   The powers conferred by subsection (1) above are not exercisable in relation to so much of a registered order as provides for the payment of a lump sum.

(1B)   The registering court shall not vary or revoke a registered order if neither the payer nor the payee under the order is resident in the United Kingdom.]

...

21   Interpretation of Part I

(1)   In this Part of this Act—

'affiliation order' means an order (however described) adjudging, finding or declaring a person to be the father of a child, whether or not it also provides for the maintenance of the child;

'the appropriate court' in relation to a person residing [or having assets] in England and Wales or in Northern Ireland means a magistrates' court, and in relation to a person residing [or having assets] in Scotland means [a sheriff court], within the jurisdiction of which that person is residing [or has assets];

'certificate of arrears', in relation to a maintenance order, means a certificate certifying that the sum specified in the certificate is to the best of the information or belief of the officer giving the certificate the amount of the arrears due under the order at the date of the certificate or, as the case may be, that to the best of his information or belief there are no arrears due thereunder at that date;

'certified copy', in relation to an order of a court, means a copy of the order certified by the proper officer of the court to be a true copy;

'court' includes any tribunal or person having power to make, confirm, enforce, vary or revoke a maintenance order;

[...]

'maintenance order' means an order (however described) of any of the following descriptions, that is to say—

(a)   an order (including an affiliation order or order consequent upon an affiliation order) which provides for the [payment of a lump sum or the making of periodical payments] towards the maintenance of any person, being a person whom the person liable to make payments under the order is, according to the law applied in the place where the order was made, liable to maintain;

[(aa)   an order which has been made in Scotland, on or after the granting of a decree of divorce, for the payment of a periodical allowance by one party to the marriage to the other party;] and

(b)   an affiliation order or order consequent upon an affiliation order, being an order which provides for the payment by a person adjudged, found or declared to be a child's father of expenses incidental to the child's birth or, where the child has died, of his funeral expenses,

and, in the case of a maintenance order which has been varied, means that order as varied;

'order', as respects Scotland, includes any interlocutor, and any decree or provision contained in an interlocutor;

'payee', in relation to a maintenance order, means the person entitled to the payments for which the order provides;

'payer', in relation to a maintenance order, means the person liable to make payments under the order;

...

'provisional order' means (according to the context)—

(a)   an order made by a court in the United Kingdom which is provisional only and has no effect unless and until confirmed, with or without alteration, by a competent court in a reciprocating country; or

(b)   an order made by a court in a reciprocating country which is provisional only and has no effect unless and until confirmed, with or without alteration, by a court in the United Kingdom having power under this Part of this Act to confirm it;

'reciprocating country' has the meaning assigned to it by section 1 of this Act;

'registered order' means a maintenance order which is for the time being registered in a court in the United Kingdom under this Part of this Act;

'registering court', in relation to a registered order, means the court in which that order is for the time being registered under this Part of this Act;

'the responsible authority', in relation to a reciprocating country, means any person who in that country has functions similar to those of the Secretary of State under this Part of this Act;

['revoke' and 'revocation' include discharge].

(2)   For the purposes of this Part of this Act an order shall be taken to be a maintenance order so far (but only so far) as it relates to the [payment of a lump sum or the making of periodical payments] as mentioned in paragraph (a) of the definition of 'maintenance order' in subsection (1) above, [to the payment of a periodical allowance as mentioned in paragraph (aa) of that definition] or to the payment by a person adjudged, found or declared to be a child's father of any such expenses as are mentioned in paragraph (b) of that definition.

(3)   Any reference in this Part of this Act to the payment of money for the maintenance of a child shall be construed as including a reference to the payment of money for the child's education.

PART II
RECIPROCAL ENFORCEMENT OF CLAIMS FOR THE RECOVERY OF MAINTENANCE

25   Convention countries

(1)   Her Majesty may by Order in Council declare that any country or territory specified in the Order, being a country or territory outside the United Kingdom to which the Maintenance Convention extends, is a convention country for the purposes of this Part of this Act.

(2)   In this section 'the Maintenance Convention' means the United Nations Convention on the Recovery Abroad of Maintenance done at New York on 20th June 1956.

26   Application by person in United Kingdom for recovery, etc of maintenance in convention country

(1)   Where a person in the United Kingdom ('the applicant') claims to be entitled to recover in a convention country maintenance from another person, and that other person is for the time being subject to the jurisdiction of that country, the applicant may apply to the Secretary of State, in accordance with the provisions of this section, to have his claim for the recovery of maintenance from that other person transmitted to that country.

(2)   Where the applicant seeks to vary any provision made in a convention country for the payment by any other person of maintenance to the applicant, and that other person is for the time being subject to the jurisdiction of that country, the applicant may apply to the Secretary of State, in accordance with the provisions of this section, to have his application for the variation of that provision transmitted to that country.

(3)   An application to the Secretary of State under subsection (1) or (2) above

shall be made through the appropriate officer, and that officer shall assist the applicant in completing an application which will comply with the requirements of the law applied by the convention country and shall send the application to the Secretary of State, together with such other documents, if any, as are required by that law.

[(3A)   An application under subsection (1) or (2) above, for the purpose of recovering maintenance from a person in a specified State within the meaning of the Recovery of Maintenance (United States of America) Order 1993, and a certificate signed by a justice of the peace or, where the applicant is residing in Scotland, the sheriff, to the effect that the application sets forth facts from which it may be determined that the respondent owes a duty to maintain the applicant and any other person named in the application and that a court in the specified State may obtain jurisdiction of the respondent or his property, shall be registered in the court in the prescribed manner by the appropriate officer or, in Scotland, by the sheriff clerk in the Maintenance Orders (Reciprocal Enforcement) Act 1972 register.]

(4)   On receiving an application from the appropriate officer the Secretary of State shall transmit it, together with any accompanying documents, to the appropriate authority in the convention country, unless he is satisfied that the application is not made in good faith or that it does not comply with the requirements of the law applied by that country.

(5)   The Secretary of State may request the appropriate officer to obtain from the court of which he is an officer such information relating to the application as may be specified in the request, and it shall be the duty of the court to furnish the Secretary of State with the information he requires.

[(6)   The appropriate officer for the purposes of this section is—

...

(c)   where the applicant is residing in Scotland, the sheriff clerk or sheriff clerk depute of the sheriff court within the jurisdiction of which the applicant is residing.]

31   Application by person in convention country for recovery of maintenance in Scotland

(1)   Where the [Secretary of the Law Society of Scotland who shall send the application and any accompanying documents to a solicitor practising in the sheriff court within the jurisdiction of which that other person resides or to such other solicitor practising in Scotland as appears to the Secretary to be appropriate, for the purposes of enabling the solicitor to take] on behalf of the applicant such steps as appear to the solicitor appropriate in respect of the application.

[(1A)   Proceedings arising out of an application under subsection (1) above shall be treated as an action for aliment within the meaning of the Family Law (Scotland) Act 1985 and, subject to subsections (1B) to (1D) below, the provisions of that Act relating to aliment shall apply in relation to claims for maintenance in such proceedings and decrees therein.

(1B)   Without prejudice to subsection (2) below, any proceedings mentioned in subsection (1A) above shall be brought in the sheriff court.

(1C)   In its application to proceedings mentioned in subsection (1A) above, section 5 of the said Act of 1985 (power to vary or recall decree of aliment) shall be subject to section 34(1) of this Act.

(1D)   Where an application under subsection (1) above is for the recovery of maintenance from a person who is a former spouse of the applicant—

(a)   then, for the purposes of the said Act of 1985, there shall be assumed to be an obligation of aliment within the meaning of that Act owed by the former spouse to the applicant;

(b)   section 2(7) and (8) of that Act shall not apply; and

(c)   an order for payment of maintenance in proceedings arising out of the application—

(i) shall, if subsisting at the death of the party making the payment, continue to operate against that party's estate, but without prejudice to the power of the court to vary or recall the order; and

(ii) shall cease to have effect on the remarriage or death of the party receiving payment, except in relation to any arrears due under it.]

(2)   Where in any proceedings arising out of such an application as aforesaid the sheriff [, or (on appeal or remit) the Court of Session,] makes an order containing a provision requiring the payment of maintenance, [the order shall be registered forthwith in the prescribed manner in the appropriate sheriff court by the sheriff clerk or sheriff clerk depute of that sheriff court; and where an order of the Court of Session varies or revokes a registered order of the sheriff, the said sheriff clerk or sheriff clerk depute shall amend the register accordingly.]

[(2A)   In subsection (2) above 'the appropriate sheriff court' means the sheriff court making the order or (where the order is an order of the Court of Session) from which the remit or appeal has come.]

(3)   Without prejudice to the generality of the powers conferred on the Court of Session by section 32 of the Sheriff Courts (Scotland) Act 1971 to regulate by act of sederunt the procedure of the sheriff court, the said powers shall include power to prescribe the decrees granted, or other things done, by the sheriff, or an officer of the sheriff court, under this Part of this Act, notice of which is to be given to such persons as the act of sederunt may provide and the manner in which such notice shall be given.

[(4)   Where an application under subsection (1) above is for the recovery of maintenance from a person who is a former spouse of the applicant an order containing a provision requiring the payment of such maintenance for the benefit of the applicant shall not be made in respect of that application unless—

[(i) the marriage between the applicant and the said former spouse has been dissolved by a divorce which has been obtained in a country or territory outside the United Kingdom and which is recognised as valid by the law of Scotland;

(ii) an order for the payment of maintenance for the benefit of the applicant as a divorced person has, in or by reason of, or subsequent to, the divorce proceedings, been made by a court in a convention country;

(iia) in a case where the order mentioned in paragraph (ii) above was made by a court of a different country from that in which the divorce was obtained, either the applicant or the said former spouse was resident in that different country at the time the application for the order so mentioned was made; and]

(iii) the court making the order under this section is satisfied that the former spouse of the applicant has failed to comply with the order mentioned in paragraph (ii) above.

[(4A)   In subsection (4)(i) above the reference to the dissolution of a marriage by divorce shall be construed as including a reference to the annulment of a purported marriage and any reference to a marriage, a divorce, a divorced person, a former spouse or divorce proceedings shall be construed accordingly.]

(5)   [...]

(6)   Section 8 of the Law Reform (Miscellaneous Provisions) (Scotland) Act 1966 (which relates to the variation and recall by the sheriff of certain orders made by the Court of Session) shall not apply to an order of the Court of Session registered under subsection (2) above.]

MATRIMONIAL PROCEEDINGS (POLYGAMOUS MARRIAGES) ACT 1972
(1972 c 38)

2 Matrimonial relief and declarations as to validity in respect of polygamous marriages: Scotland

(1) A court in Scotland shall not be precluded from entertaining proceedings for, or granting, any such decree as is mentioned in subsection (2) below by reason only that [either party to the marriage is, or has during the subsistence of the marriage been, married to more than one person].

(2) The decrees referred to in subsection (1) above are—

    (a) a decree of divorce;

    (b) a decree of nullity of marriage;

    [...]

    [(d) a decree of separation;

    (e) a decree of aliment;]

    (f) a decree of declarator that a marriage is valid or invalid;

    (g) any other decree involving a determination as to the validity of a marriage;

and the reference in subsection (1) above to granting such a decree as aforesaid includes a reference to making any ancillary [or incidental] order which the court has power to make in proceedings for such a decree.

    [(3) Provision may be made by rules of court—

    (a) for requiring notice of proceedings brought by virtue of this section to be served on any additional spouse of a party to the marriage in question; and

    (b) for conferring on any such additional spouse the right to be heard in the proceedings,

in such cases as may be specified in the rules.]

DOMICILE AND MATRIMONIAL PROCEEDINGS ACT 1973
(1973 c 45)

1 Abolition of wife's dependent domicile

(1) Subject to subsection (2) below, the domicile of a married woman as at any time after the coming into force of this section shall, instead of being the same as her husband's by virtue only of marriage, be ascertained by reference to the same factors as in the case of any other individual capable of having an independent domicile.

(2) Where immediately before this section came into force a woman was married and then had her husband's domicile by dependence, she is to be treated as retaining that domicile (as a domicile of choice, if it is not also her domicile of origin) unless and until it is changed by acquisition or revival of another domicile either on or after the coming into force of this section.

(3) This section extends to England and Wales, Scotland and Northern Ireland.

4 Dependent domicile of child not living with his father*

(1) Subsection (2) of this section shall have effect with respect to the dependent domicile of a child as at any time after the coming into force of this section when his father and mother are alive but living apart.

(2) The child's domicile as at that time shall be that of his mother if—

    (a) he then has his home with her and has no home with his father; or

    (b) he has at any time had her domicile by virtue of paragraph (a) above and has not since had a home with his father.

(3) As at any time after the coming into force of this section, the domicile of a child whose mother is dead shall be that which she last had before she died if at

---

* In relation to Scotland s 4 is repealed: Family Law (Scotland) Act 2006, Sch 3, para 1.

her death he had her domicile by virtue of subsection (2) above and he has not since had a home with his father.

(4)   Nothing in this section prejudices any existing rule of law as to the cases in which a child's domicile is regarded as being, by dependence, that of his mother.

(5)   In this section, 'child' means a person incapable of having an independent domicile [...].

(6)   This section extends to England and Wales [...] and Northern Ireland.

7 Jurisdiction of Court of Session

(1)   Subsections [(2A) to (10)] below shall have effect, subject to section 12(6) of this Act, with respect to the jurisdiction of the Court of Session to entertain—

(a)   an action for divorce, separation, declarator of nullity of marriage, or declarator of marriage; and

[(aa)   an action for declarator of recognition, or non-recognition, of a relevant foreign decree.]

[...]

(2)   The Court shall have jurisdiction to entertain an action for [...] declarator of freedom and putting to silence if (and only if) either of the parties to the marriage in question—

(a)   is domiciled in Scotland on the date when the action is begun; or

(b)   was habitually resident in Scotland throughout the period of one year ending with that date.

[(2A)   The Court shall have jurisdiction to entertain an action for divorce or separation if (and only if)—

(a)   the Scottish courts have jurisdiction under the Council Regulation; or

(b)   the action is an excluded action and either of the parties to the marriage in question is domiciled in Scotland on the date when the action is begun.]

(3)   The Court shall have jurisdiction to entertain an action for declarator of marriage [...] if (and only if) either of the parties to the marriage—

(a)   is domiciled in Scotland on the date when the action is begun; or

(b)   was habitually resident in Scotland throughout the period of one year ending with that date; or

(c)   died before that date and either—

(i)   was at death domiciled in Scotland, or

(ii)   had been habitually resident in Scotland throughout the period of one year ending with the date of death.

[(3A)   The Court shall have jurisdiction to entertain an action for declarator of nullity of marriage [or for declarator of recognition, or non-recognition, of a relevant foreign decree] if (and only if)—

(a)   the Scottish courts have jurisdiction under the Council Regulation; or

(b)   the action is one to which subsection (3B) below applies and either of the parties to the marriage—

(a)   is domiciled in Scotland on the date when the action is begun; or

(b)   died before that date and either—

(i)   was at death domiciled in Scotland; or

(ii)   had been habitually resident in Scotland throughout the period of one year ending with the date of death.

(3B)   This subsection applies to an action—

(a)   which is an excluded action; or

(b)   where one of the parties to the marriage died before the date when the action is begun.]

[...]

(5)   The Court shall, at any time when proceedings are pending in respect of which it has jurisdiction by virtue of subsection (2) [, (2A), (3) or (3A) above] (or of this subsection), also have jurisdiction to entertain other proceedings, in respect of the same marriage, for divorce, separation or declarator of marriage, or declarator

of nullity of marriage, notwithstanding that jurisdiction would not be exercisable [under any of those subsections].

[(5A) Subsection (5) does not give the Court jurisdiction to entertain proceedings in contravention of Article 6 of the Council Regulation.]

(6) Nothing in this section affects the rules governing the jurisdiction of the Court of Session to entertain, in an action for divorce, an application for payment by a co-defender of damages or expenses.

(7) The foregoing provisions of this section are without prejudice to any rule of law whereby the Court of Session has jurisdiction in certain circumstances to entertain actions for separation as a matter of necessity and urgency.

(8) No action for divorce in respect of a marriage shall be entertained by the Court of Session by virtue of [this section] while proceedings for divorce or nullity of marriage, begun before the commencement of this Act, are pending (in respect of the same marriage) in England and Wales, Northern Ireland, the Channel Islands or the Isle of Man; and provision may be made by rules of court as to when, for the purposes of this subsection, proceedings are to be treated as begun or pending in any of those places.

[(9) In this section, 'relevant foreign decree' means a decree of divorce, nullity or separation granted outwith a member state of the European Union.

(10) References in subsection (3A) to a marriage shall, in the case of an action for declarator of recognition, or non-recognition, of a relevant foreign decree, be construed as references to the marriage to which the relevant foreign decree relates.]

8 Jurisdiction of sheriff court in respect of actions for separation

(1) Subsections (2) to [(6)] below shall have effect, subject to section 12(6) of this Act, with respect to the jurisdiction of the sheriff court to entertain—

[(za) an action for declarator of marriage;]

[(a) an action for separation or divorce;

(b) an action for declarator of recognition, or non-recognition, of a relevant foreign decree] [; and

(c) an action for declarator of nullity of marriage.]

(2) The court shall have jurisdiction to entertain an action for separation [or divorce [or for declarator of recognition, or non-recognition, of a relevant foreign decree] if (and only if)—

(a) either—

(i) the Scottish courts have jurisdiction under the Council Regulation; or

(ii) the action is an excluded action and either party to the marriage in question is domiciled in Scotland at the date when the action is begun; and

(b) either party to the marriage—

(i) was resident in the sheriffdom for a period of forty days ending with that date, or

(ii) had been resident in the sheriffdom for a period of not less than forty days ending not more than forty days before the said date, and has no known residence in Scotland at that date.

[(2ZA) The court has jurisdiction to entertain an action for declarator of marriage if (and only if)—

(a) either party to the marriage—

(i) was resident in the sheriffdom for a period of 40 days ending with the date on which the action is begun, or

(ii) had been resident in the sheriffdom for a period of not less than 40 days ending not more than 40 days before that date, and has no known residence in Scotland on that date, and

(b) any of the following requirements is met in relation to either of the parties to the marriage—

(i) the party is domiciled in Scotland on the date on which the action is begun,

(ii) the party was habitually resident in Scotland throughout the period of one year ending with that date, or

(iii) the party died before that date and either—

(A) was at death domiciled in Scotland, or

(B) had been habitually resident in Scotland throughout the period of one year ending with the date of death.]

[(2A) The court shall have jurisdiction to entertain an action for declarator of nullity of marriage if (and only if)—

(a) either party to the marriage—

(i) was resident in the sheriffdom for a period of forty days ending with the date when the action is begun; or

(ii) had been resident in the sheriffdom for a period of not less than forty days ending not more than forty days before that date and has no known residence in Scotland at that date; and

(b) either—

(i) the Scottish courts have jurisdiction under the Council Regulation; or

(ii) the action is one to which subsection (2B) below applies and a condition mentioned in either subsection (2C) or (2D) is satisfied.

(2B) This subsection applies to an action—

(a) which is an excluded action; or

(b) where one of the parties to the marriage in question died before the date when the action is begun.

(2C) The condition is that either party to the marriage in question is domiciled in Scotland on the date when the action is begun.

(2D) The condition is that either party to the marriage in question died before the date when the action is begun and either—

(a) was at death domiciled in Scotland; or

(b) had been habitually resident in Scotland throughout the period of one year ending with the date of death.]

(3) In respect of any marriage, the court shall have jurisdiction to entertain an action for separation or divorce [or declarator of [marriage or of] nullity of marriage] (notwithstanding that jurisdiction would not be exercisable under subsection (2) [, (2ZA)] [or (2A)] above) if it is begun at a time when an original action is pending in respect of the marriage; and for this purpose 'original action' means an action in respect of which the court has jurisdiction by virtue of subsection (2), [, (2ZA)] [(2A) or] this subsection.

[(3A) Subsection (3) does not give the court jurisdiction to entertain an action in contravention of Article 7 of the Council Regulation.]

(4) The foregoing provisions of this section are without prejudice to any jurisdiction of a sheriff court to entertain an action of separation [or divorce or declarator of nullity of marriage] remitted to it in pursuance of any enactment or rule of court [, provided that entertaining the action would not contravene Article 7 of the Council Regulation].

[(5) In this section, 'relevant foreign decree' has the meaning given by section 7(9).

(6) References in subsection (2) to a marriage shall, in the case of an action for declarator of recognition, or non-recognition, of a relevant foreign decree, be construed as references to the marriage to which the relevant foreign decree relates.]

[8A Same sex marriages

(1) Sections 7 and 8 do not apply in relation to marriages between persons of the same sex.

(2) Schedule 1B (jurisdiction in relation to same sex marriages (Scotland)) has effect.]

10 Ancillary and collateral orders

(1) [Where after the commencement of this Act an application is competently made to the Court of Session or to a sheriff court for the making, or the variation or recall, of an order which is ancillary or collateral to] an action for any of the following remedies, namely, divorce, separation, declarator of marriage and declarator of nullity of marriage (whether the application is made in the same proceedings or in other proceedings and whether it is made before or after the pronouncement of a final decree in the action), then, if the court has or, as the case may be, had by virtue of this Act or of any enactment or rule of law in force before the commencement of this Act jurisdiction to entertain the action, it shall have jurisdiction to entertain the application [...] whether or not it would have jurisdiction to do so apart from this subsection.

[(1A) For the purposes of subsection (1) above, references to an application for the making, or the variation or recall, of an order are references to the making, or the variation or recall, of an order relating to children, aliment, financial provision on divorce, judicial separation, nullity of marriage or expenses.]

[(1B) Subsection (1) above does not give the Court of Session or a sheriff court jurisdiction to entertain an application in proceedings where—

(a)   the court is exercising jurisdiction in the proceedings by virtue of Article 3 of the Council Regulation; and

(b)   the making or variation of an order in consequence of the application would contravene [Article 6] of the Council Regulation.]

[(1BA) In relation to a marriage between persons of the same sex, subsection (1) does not give the Court of Session or a sheriff court jurisdiction to entertain an application in proceedings where—

(a)   the court is exercising jurisdiction in the proceedings by virtue of regulations under paragraph 2 of Schedule 1B; and

(b)   the making or variation of an order in consequence of the application would contravene the regulations.]

[(1C) If the application or part of it relates to a matter where jurisdiction falls to be determined by reference to the jurisdictional requirements of the Maintenance Regulation and Schedule 6 to the Civil Jurisdiction and Judgments (Maintenance) Regulations 2011, the Court of Session or a sheriff court may not entertain the application or that part of it unless it has jurisdiction to do so by virtue of that Regulation and that Schedule.

(1D) In subsection (1C) 'the Maintenance Regulation' means Council Regulation (EC) No 4/2009 including as applied in relation to Denmark by virtue of the Agreement made on 19th October 2005 between the European Community and the Kingdom of Denmark.]

(2) It is hereby declared that where—

(a)   the Court of Session has jurisdiction by virtue of this section to entertain an application for the variation or recall as respects any person of an order made by it, and

(b)   the order is one to which section 8 (variation and recall by the sheriff of certain orders made by the Court of Session) of the Law Reform (Miscellaneous Provisions) (Scotland) Act 1966 applies,

then, for the purposes of any application under the said section 8 for the variation or recall of the order in so far as it relates to that person, the sheriff, as defined in that section, has jurisdiction as respects that person to exercise the power conferred on him by that section.

11 Sisting of certain actions

[(1)] The provisions of Schedule 3 to this Act shall have effect with respect to the sisting of actions for any of the following remedies, namely, divorce, separation, declarator of marriage or declarator of nullity of marriage, and with respect to the other matters mentioned in that Schedule; but nothing in that Schedule—

(a)   requires or authorises a sist of an action which is pending when this Act comes into force; or

(b)   prejudices any power to sist an action which is exercisable by any court apart from the Schedule.

[(2)   Subsection (1) above and Schedule 3 to this Act and any power mentioned in subsection (1)(b) are subject to Article 19 of the Council Regulation.]

[SCHEDULE 1B
JURISDICTION IN RELATION TO SAME SEX MARRIAGES (SCOTLAND)
(introduced by section 8A)

Introduction

1—(1)   This Schedule has effect with respect to the jurisdiction of the Court of Session and of the sheriff court to entertain, in relation to same sex marriages, proceedings for—

(a)   divorce,
(b)   separation,
(c)   declarator of marriage,
(d)   declarator of nullity of marriage,
(e)   declarator of recognition, or non-recognition, of a relevant foreign decree.

(2)   References in this Schedule to 'relevant proceedings' are to such proceedings as are mentioned in sub-paragraph (1).

(3)   In this Schedule—

'relevant foreign decree' means a decree of divorce, separation or nullity granted outwith a member State,

'same sex marriage' means a marriage between persons of the same sex.

Power to make provision corresponding to EC Regulation 2201/2003

2—(1)   The Scottish Ministers may by regulations make provision—

(a)   as to the jurisdiction of courts in Scotland in relevant proceedings in relation to a same sex marriage where one of the parties to the marriage—

(i)   is or has been habitually resident in a member State,
(ii)   is a national of a member State, or
(iii)   is domiciled in a part of the United Kingdom or in the Republic of Ireland, and

(b)   as to the recognition in Scotland of any judgment of a court of another member State which orders the divorce or separation of the parties to a same sex marriage, or the annulment of a same sex marriage.

(2)   The regulations may in particular make provision corresponding to that made by Council Regulation (EC) No 2201/2003 of 27 November 2003 in relation to jurisdiction and the recognition and enforcement of judgments in matrimonial matters.

(3)   The regulations may provide that for the purposes of this Schedule and the regulations 'member State' means—

(a)   all member States with the exception of such member States as are specified in the regulations, or

(b)   such member States as are specified in the regulations.

(4)   The regulations may make provision under sub-paragraph (1)(b) which applies even in a case where the date of the divorce, separation or annulment is earlier than the date on which this paragraph comes into force.

(5)   The regulations are subject to the affirmative procedure.

Divorce or separation

3—(1) The Court of Session has jurisdiction to entertain proceedings for the divorce or separation of the parties to a same sex marriage if (and only if)—

(a)   the Scottish courts have jurisdiction under regulations under paragraph 2, or

(b)   no court has, or is recognised as having, jurisdiction under those regulations and either party to the marriage is domiciled in Scotland on the date on which the proceedings are begun.

(2)   The sheriff court has jurisdiction to entertain proceedings for the divorce or separation of the parties to a same sex marriage if (and only if)—

(a)   the requirements of paragraph (a) or (b) of sub-paragraph (1) are met, and

(b)   either party to the marriage—

(i)   was resident in the sheriffdom for a period of 40 days ending with the date on which the proceedings are begun, or

(ii)   had been resident in the sheriffdom for a period of not less than 40 days ending not more than 40 days before that date, and has no known residence in Scotland on that date.

(3)   Despite sub-paragraph (2), the sheriff court of the sheriffdom of Lothian and Borders at Edinburgh also has jurisdiction to entertain proceedings for the divorce or separation of the parties to a same sex marriage if the following requirements are met—

(a)   the parties married each other in Scotland,

(b)   no court has, or is recognised as having, jurisdiction under regulations under paragraph 2, and

(c)   it appears to the court to be in the interests of justice to assume jurisdiction in the case.

Declarator of marriage

4—(1) In relation to a same sex marriage, the Court of Session has jurisdiction to entertain proceedings for declarator of marriage if (and only if) either of the parties to the marriage—

(a)   is domiciled in Scotland on the date on which the proceedings are begun,

(b)   was habitually resident in Scotland throughout the period of one year ending with that date, or

(c)   died before that date and either—

(i)   was at death domiciled in Scotland, or

(ii)   had been habitually resident in Scotland throughout the period of one year ending with the date of death.

(2)   In relation to a same sex marriage, the sheriff court has jurisdiction to entertain proceedings for declarator of marriage if (and only if)—

(a)   the requirements of paragraph (a), (b) or (c) of sub-paragraph (1) are met in relation to either party to the marriage, and

(b)   either party of the marriage—

(i)   was resident in the sheriffdom for a period of 40 days ending with the date on which the proceedings are begun, or

(ii)   had been resident in the sheriffdom for a period of not less than 40 days ending not more than 40 days before that date, and has no known residence in Scotland on that date.

Nullity of marriage

5—(1) The Court of Session has jurisdiction to entertain proceedings for declarator of nullity of a same sex marriage if (and only if)—

(a)   the Scottish courts have jurisdiction under regulations under paragraph 2, or

(b)   no court has, or is recognised as having, jurisdiction under those regulations and either party to the marriage—

     (i)   is domiciled in Scotland on the date on which the proceedings are begun, or

     (ii)   died before that date and either was at death domiciled in Scotland or had been habitually resident in Scotland throughout the period of one year ending with the date of death.

(2)   The sheriff court has jurisdiction to entertain proceedings for declarator of nullity of a same sex marriage if (and only if)—

(a)   the requirements of paragraph (a) or (b) of sub-paragraph (1) are met, and

(b)   either party to the marriage—

     (i)   was resident in the sheriffdom for a period of 40 days ending with the date on which the proceedings are begun, or

     (ii)   had been resident in the sheriffdom for a period of not less than 40 days ending not more than 40 days before that date, and has no known residence in Scotland on that date.

(3)   Despite sub-paragraph (2), the sheriff court of the sheriffdom of Lothian and Borders at Edinburgh also has jurisdiction to entertain proceedings for declarator of nullity of a same sex marriage if the following requirements are met—

(a)   the parties married each other in Scotland,

(b)   no court has, or is recognised as having, jurisdiction under regulations under paragraph 2, and

(c)   it appears to the court to be in the interests of justice to assume jurisdiction in the case.

Recognition, or non-recognition, of foreign decrees

6—(1)   The Court of Session has jurisdiction to entertain proceedings for declarator of recognition, or non-recognition, of a relevant foreign decree relating to a same sex marriage if (and only if)—

(a)   the Scottish courts have jurisdiction under regulations under paragraph 2, or

(b)   no court has, or is recognised as having, jurisdiction under those regulations and either party to the marriage—

     (i)   is domiciled in Scotland on the date on which the proceedings are begun, or

     (ii)   died before that date and either was at death domiciled in Scotland or had been habitually resident in Scotland throughout the period of one year ending with the date of death.

(2)   The sheriff court has jurisdiction to entertain proceedings for declarator of recognition, or non-recognition, of a relevant foreign decree relating to a same sex marriage if (and only if)—

(a)   the requirements of paragraph (a) or (b) of sub-paragraph (1) are met, and

(b)   either party to the marriage—

     (i)   was resident in the sheriffdom for a period of 40 days ending with the date on which the proceedings are begun, or

     (ii)   had been resident in the sheriffdom for a period of not less than 40 days ending not more than 40 days before that date, and has no known residence in Scotland on that date.

Supplementary provision

7—(1)   Paragraph 3(1) does not affect any rule of law under which the Court of Session has jurisdiction in certain circumstances to entertain proceedings for separation as a matter of necessity and urgency.

(2)   Paragraphs 3 and 5 do not affect any jurisdiction of a sheriff court to entertain any proceedings for separation, divorce or declarator of nullity of marriage remitted to the court under any enactment or rule of court, if entertaining the proceedings would not contravene regulations under paragraph 2.

(3)   At any time when proceedings are pending in respect of which a court has jurisdiction by virtue of any of paragraphs 3 to 6 (or this paragraph), the court also has jurisdiction to entertain other proceedings, in respect of the same marriage, for divorce, separation or declarator of marriage or of nullity of marriage even though that jurisdiction would not be exercisable under any of paragraphs 2 to 6.]

SCHEDULE 3
SISTING OF CONSISTORIAL ACTIONS (SCOTLAND)

Mandatory sists

8.   Where before the beginning of the proof in any action for divorce which is continuing in the Court of Session [or in the Sheriff Court] it appears to the Court [concerned] on the application of a party to the marriage—

(a)   that in respect of the same marriage proceedings for divorce or nullity of marriage are continuing in a related jurisdiction; and

(b)   that the parties to the marriage have resided together after the marriage was contracted; and

(c)   that the place where they resided together when the action in the Court was begun or, if they did not then reside together, where they last resided together before the date on which that action was begun is in that jurisdiction; and

(d)   that either of the said parties was habitually resident in that jurisdiction throughout the year ending with the date on which they last resided together before the date on which that action was begun;

it shall be the duty of the Court, subject to paragraph 10(2) below, to sist the action before it.

9.—(1)   Where before the beginning of the proof in any consistorial action which is continuing in the Court of Session or in a sheriff court, it appears to the court concerned—

(a)   that any other proceedings in respect of the marriage in question or capable of affecting its validity are continuing in another jurisdiction, and

(b)   that the balance of fairness (including convenience) as between the parties to the marriage is such that it is appropriate for those other proceedings to be disposed of before further steps are taken in the action in the said court,

the court may then if it thinks fit sist that action.

(2)   In considering the balance of fairness and convenience for the purposes of sub-paragraph (1)(b) above, the court shall have regard to all factors appearing to be relevant, including the convenience of witnesses and any delay or expense which may result from the proceedings being sisted, or not being sisted.

(3)   Sub-paragraph (1) above is without prejudice to the duty imposed [...] by paragraph 8 above.

(4)   If, at any time after the beginning of the proof in any consistorial action which is pending in the Court of Session or a sheriff court, the court concerned is satisfied that a person has failed to perform the duty imposed on him in respect of the action and any such other proceedings as aforesaid by paragraph 7 above, sub-

paragraph (1) of this paragraph shall have effect in relation to that action and to the other proceedings as if the words 'before the beginning of the proof' were omitted; but no action in respect of the failure of a person to perform such a duty shall be competent.

PRESCRIPTION AND LIMITATION (SCOTLAND) ACT 1973
(1973 c 52)

[23A   Private international law application*
(1)   Where the substantive law of a country other than Scotland falls to be applied by a Scottish court as the law governing an obligation, the court shall apply any relevant rules of law of that country relating to the extinction of the obligation or the limitation of time within which proceedings may be brought to enforce the obligation to the exclusion of any corresponding rule of Scots law.

(2)   This section shall not apply where it appears to the court that the application of the relevant foreign rule of law would be incompatible with the principles of public policy applied by the court.

(3)   This section shall not apply in any case where the application of the corresponding rule of Scots law has extinguished the obligation, or barred the bringing of proceedings prior to the coming into force of the Prescription and Limitation (Scotland) Act 1984.

[(4)   This section shall not apply in any case where the law of a country other than Scotland falls to be applied by virtue of any choice of law rule contained in [the Rome I Regulation or] the Rome II Regulation.]

[(5)   In subsection (4)

[(a)   'the Rome I Regulation' means Regulation (EC) No 593/2008 of the European Parliament and of the Council on the law applicable to contractual obligations (Rome I), including that Regulation as applied by regulation 4 of the Law Applicable to Contractual Obligations (Scotland) Regulations 2009 (conflicts falling within Article 22(2) of Regulation (EC) No 593/2008), and

(b)]   'the Rome II Regulation' means Regulation (EC) No 864/2007 of the European Parliament and of the Council on the law applicable to non-contractual obligations (Rome II), including that Regulation as applied by regulation 4 of the Law Applicable to Non-Contractual Obligations (Scotland) Regulations 2008 (conflicts falling within Article 25(2) of Regulation (EC) No 864/2007).]]

* As amended by SSIs 2008/404 and 2009/410.

EVIDENCE (PROCEEDINGS IN OTHER JURISDICTIONS) ACT 1975
(1975 c 34)

1   Application to United Kingdom court for assistance in obtaining evidence for civil proceedings in other court

Where an application is made to the High Court, the Court of Session or the High Court of Justice in Northern Ireland for an order for evidence to be obtained in the part of the United Kingdom in which it exercises jurisdiction, and the court is satisfied—

(a)   that the application is made in pursuance of a request issued by or on behalf of a court or tribunal ('the requesting court') exercising jurisdiction in any other part of the United Kingdom or in a country or territory outside the United Kingdom; and

(b)   that the evidence to which the application relates is to be obtained for the purposes of civil proceedings which either have been instituted before the requesting court or whose institution before that court is contemplated,

the High Court, Court of Session or High Court of Justice in Northern Ireland, as the case may be, shall have the powers conferred on it by the following provisions of this Act.

DIVORCE (SCOTLAND) ACT 1976
(1976 c 39)

[3A   Postponement of decree of divorce where religious impediment to remarry exists

(1)   Notwithstanding that irretrievable breakdown of a marriage has been established in an action for divorce, the court may—

(a)   on the application of a party ('the applicant'); and

(b)   if satisfied—

(i)   that subsection (2) applies; and

(ii)   that it is just and reasonable to do so,

postpone the grant of decree in the action until it is satisfied that the other party has complied with subsection (3).

(2)   This subsection applies where—

(a)   the applicant is prevented from entering into a religious marriage by virtue of a requirement of the religion of that marriage; and

(b)   the other party can act so as to remove, or enable or contribute to the removal of, the impediment which prevents that marriage.

(3)   A party complies with this subsection by acting in the way described in subsection (2)(b).

(4)   The court may, whether or not on the application of a party and notwithstanding that subsection (2) applies, recall a postponement under subsection (1).

(5)   The court may, before recalling a postponement under subsection (1), order the other party to produce a certificate from a relevant religious body confirming that the other party has acted in the way described in subsection 2(b).

(6)   For the purposes of subsection (5), a religious body is 'relevant' if the applicant considers the body competent to provide the confirmation referred to in that subsection.

(7)   In this section—

'religious marriage' means a marriage solemnised by a marriage celebrant of a prescribed religious body, and 'religion of that marriage' shall be construed accordingly;

'prescribed' means prescribed by regulations made by the Scottish Ministers.

(8)   Any reference in this section to a marriage celebrant of a prescribed religious body is a reference to—

(a)   a minister, clergyman, pastor or priest of such a body;

(b)   a person who has, on the nomination of such a body, been registered under section 9 of the Marriage (Scotland) Act 1977 (c 15) as empowered to solemnise marriages; or

(c)   any person who is recognised by such a body as entitled to solemnise marriages on its behalf.

(9)   Regulations under subsection (7) shall be made by statutory instrument; and any such instrument shall be subject to annulment in pursuance of a resolution of the Scottish Parliament.]

MARRIAGE (SCOTLAND) ACT 1977
(1977 c 15)

1   Minimum age for marriage

(1)   No person domiciled in Scotland may marry before he attains the age of 16.

(2)   A marriage solemnised in Scotland between persons either of whom is under the age of 16 shall be void.

3   Notice of intention to marry

...

(5)   A party to a marriage intended to be solemnised in Scotland who is not domiciled in any part of the United Kingdom is required, if practicable, to submit under subsection (1)(c) above a certificate, issued by a competent authority in the state in which the party is domiciled, to the effect that he is not known to be subject to any legal incapacity (in terms of the law of that state) which would prevent his marrying:

Provided that such a party—

(i)   may, where under the law of the state in which he is domiciled his personal law is that of another foreign state, submit in lieu of the said certificate a like certificate issued by a competent authority in that other state;

(ii)   need not submit a certificate under paragraph (c) of subsection (1) above,

(a)   if he has been resident in the United Kingdom for a period of 2 or more years immediately before the date on which he submits a marriage notice under that subsection in respect of the said marriage; or

(b)   [if no such certificate has been issued only by reason of the fact that the validity of a divorce or annulment granted by a court of civil jurisdiction in Scotland or entitled to recognition in Scotland under section 44 or 45 of the Family Law Act 1986 is not recognised in the state in which the certificate would otherwise have been issued.]

[3A   Additional information if party not relevant national

(1)   This section applies to a marriage notice submitted to a district registrar in accordance with section 3 if one, or each, of the parties to the proposed marriage is not a relevant national.

(2)   But this section does not apply if the parties are in a qualifying civil partnership (within the meaning of section 5(6)(1)) with each other.

(3)   For each party to the proposed marriage who is not a relevant national, the notice shall be accompanied by whichever of statements A, B or C is applicable to that person.

(4)   Statement A is a statement that the person has the appropriate immigration status.

(5)   Statement B is a statement that the person holds a relevant visa in respect of the proposed marriage.

(6)   Statement C is a statement that the person neither—

(a)   has the appropriate immigration status, nor

(b)   holds a relevant visa in respect of the proposed marriage.

(7) If the notice is accompanied by the statement referred to in the first column of an entry in this table, the notice shall also be accompanied by the information and photographs referred to in the second column of that entry (insofar as that entry is applicable to the parties to the proposed marriage)—

If the notice is accompanied by this statement ...	... the notice shall also be accompanied by ...
Statement A (in respect of one or both of the parties to the proposed marriage)	For each party in respect of whom statement A is made, details of the particular immigration status which that party has
Statement B (in respect of one or both of the parties to the proposed marriage)	1. For each party, a specified photograph of that party 2. For each party in respect of whom statement B is made, details of the relevant visa which that party has
Statement C (in respect of one or both of the parties to the proposed marriage)	1. For each party, a specified photograph of that party 2. For each party, the usual address of that party 3. For each party who has previously used any name or names other than the person's name stated in the marriage notice, a statement of the other name or names 4. For each party who currently uses, or has previously used, an alias or aliases, a statement of the alias or aliases

(8) If the notice is accompanied by more than one of statements A, B and C, subsection (7) shall be complied with in relation to each of those statements; but where the notice is accompanied by statements B and C, subsection (7) does not require the notice to be accompanied by more than one specified photograph of each party.

(9) If the notice is accompanied by statement C for a party to the proposed marriage—

(a) the notice may also be accompanied by a statement ('statement D') of that person's immigration position in the United Kingdom;

(b) if the notice is accompanied by statement D for a party to the proposed marriage, the person may provide the district registrar with details of his immigration position in the United Kingdom; and

(c) if any such details are provided, the district registrar shall record them.

(10) In this section and section 3B—

(a) a reference—

(i) to a person having the appropriate immigration status, or

(ii) to a person holding a relevant visa,

is to be construed in accordance with section 49 of the 2014 Act;

(b) a reference to the particular immigration status which a person has is a reference to the immigration status set out in any of paragraphs (a) to (c) of section 49(2) of that Act which the person has;

(c) a reference to a person's immigration position in the United Kingdom includes a reference to the person's not being entitled to be in the United Kingdom.

(11) In this section 'specified photograph' means a photograph that is in accordance with regulations made by the Secretary of State under section 54(2) of, and

paragraph 3 of Schedule 5 to, the 2014 Act (and for this purpose 'photograph' includes other kinds of images).]

[3B   Additional evidence if party not relevant national

(1)   If a marriage notice to which section 3A(1) applies ('the notice') is accompanied by statement A (referred to in section 3A(4)) and accordingly is also accompanied by details of the particular immigration status which a party to the proposed marriage has, the notice shall also be accompanied by specified evidence of that status.

(2)   If the notice is accompanied by statement B (referred to in section 3A(5)), the notice shall also be accompanied by specified evidence of the holding of the relevant visa by the party to the proposed marriage.

(3)   If, in accordance with section 3A(7), the notice is accompanied by the usual address of a party to the proposed marriage, the notice shall also be accompanied by specified evidence that it is that party's usual address.

(4)   If the notice is accompanied by statement D (referred to in section 3A(9)), the notice may also be accompanied by evidence of the person's immigration position in the United Kingdom.

(5)   If subsection (1) or (2) applies to the notice, and the notice is not accompanied by the specified evidence required by that subsection, the notice shall be accompanied by—

(a)   photographs and addresses of the kinds referred to in paragraphs 1 and 2 in the relevant entry in section 3A(7);

(b)   as respects the usual address of each party that is provided in accordance with paragraph (a), specified evidence that the address provided is that party's usual address; and

(c)   names and aliases of the kinds referred to in paragraphs 3 and 4 in the relevant entry in section 3A(7) (insofar as those paragraphs are applicable to the parties to the proposed marriage).

(6)   In this section—

'relevant entry in section 3A(7)' means the second column of the last entry in the table in section 3A(7);

'specified evidence' means evidence that is in accordance with regulations made by the Secretary of State under section 54(2) of, and paragraph 3 of Schedule 5 to, the 2014 Act.]

5   Objections to marriage

...

(4)   For the purposes of [this section] and section 6 of this Act, there is a legal impediment to a marriage where—

(a)   that marriage would be void by virtue of section 2(1) of this Act;

(b)   one of the parties is, or both are, already married [or in civil partnership other than a qualifying civil partnership with each other];

(c)   one or both of the parties will be under the age of 16 on the date of solemnisation of the intended marriage;

(d)   one or both of the parties is or are incapable of understanding the nature of a marriage ceremony or of consenting to marriage;

[...]

(f)   one or both of the parties is, or are, not domiciled in Scotland and, on a ground other than—

[(i)   one mentioned in paragraphs (a) to (d) above; or

(ii)   the ground that the parties are of the same sex,]

a marriage in Scotland between the parties would be void ab initio according to the law of the domicile of the party or parties as the case may be.

(5)   A person who has submitted an objection in accordance with subsection (1) above may at any time withdraw it:

Provided that the Registrar General shall be entitled to have regard to that objection notwithstanding such withdrawal.

[(6) For the purposes of subsection (4)(b) a 'qualifying civil partnership' is a civil partnership which—

(a) was registered in Scotland; and

(b) has not been dissolved, annulled or ended by death.

(7) A civil partnership which was registered outside the United Kingdom under an Order in Council made under Chapter 1 of Part 5 of the Civil Partnership Act 2004 is to be treated for the purposes of subsection (6)(a) as having been registered in Scotland if—

(a) the parties to the civil partnership elected Scotland as the relevant part of the United Kingdom under the Order; and

(b) details of the civil partnership have been sent to the Registrar General of Births, Deaths and Marriages for Scotland.]

...

7 Marriage outside Scotland where a party resides in Scotland

(1) Where a person residing in Scotland is a party to a marriage intended to be solemnised in—

(a) England or Wales with a party residing in England or Wales and desires; or

(b) any country, territory or place outside Great Britain, and, for the purpose of complying with the law in force in that country, territory or place, is required to obtain from a competent authority in Scotland,

a certificate in respect of his legal capacity to marry, he may submit, in the form and with the fee and documents specified in [section 3(1)(a), (b) and (d)] of this Act, notice of intention to marry to the district registrar for the district in which he resides (the said registrar being in this section referred to as the 'appropriate registrar') as if it were intended that the marriage should be solemnised in that district, and sections 3(2) [, (3) and (4A) to (4C)] and 4 of this Act shall apply accordingly.

(2) The appropriate registrar shall, if satisfied (after consultation, if the appropriate registrar considers it necessary, with the Registrar General) that a person who has by virtue of subsection (1) above submitted a marriage notice to him is not subject to any legal incapacity (in terms of Scots law) which would prevent his marrying, issue to that person a certificate in the prescribed form that he is not known to be subject to any such incapacity:

Provided that the certificate shall not be issued earlier than [28 days] after the date of receipt (as entered by the appropriate registrar in the marriage notice book) of the marriage notice.

(3) Any person may, at any time before a certificate is issued under subsection (2) above, submit to the appropriate registrar an objection in writing to such issue; and the objection shall be taken into account by the appropriate registrar in deciding whether, in respect of the person to whom the certificate would be issued, he is satisfied as mentioned in the said subsection (2).

[(4) For the purpose of subsection (3) above, an objection which is submitted by electronic means is to be treated as in writing if it is received in a form which is legible and capable of being used for subsequent reference.]

20 Second marriage ceremony

(1) Where two persons have gone through a marriage ceremony with each other outside the United Kingdom, whether before or after the commencement of this Act, but they are not, or are unable to prove that they are, validly married to each other in Scots law, an authorised registrar, on an application made to him by those persons, may, subject to the approval of the Registrar General and to subsection (2) below, solemnise their marriage as if they had not already gone through a marriage ceremony with each other.

(2) Sections 3 to 6 and 18 and 19 of this Act shall apply for the purpose of solemnising a marriage under this section except that—
(a) there shall be submitted to the authorised registrar a statutory declaration by both parties—
(i) stating that they have previously gone through a marriage ceremony with each other; and
(ii) specifying the date and place at which, and the circumstances in which, they went through that ceremony;
(b) section 5(4)(b) of this Act shall not apply in respect of the parties already being married to each other;
(c) the Marriage Schedule shall contain such modifications as the Registrar General may direct to indicate that the parties have previously gone through a marriage ceremony with each other; and
...

[20A Grounds on which marriage void
(1) Where subsection (2) or (3) applies in relation to a marriage solemnised in Scotland, the marriage shall be void.
(2) This subsection applies if at the time of the marriage ceremony a party to the marriage who was capable of consenting to the marriage purported to give consent but did so by reason only of duress or error.
(3) This subsection applies if at the time of the marriage ceremony a party to the marriage was incapable of—
(a) understanding the nature of marriage; and
(b) consenting to the marriage.
(4) If a party to a marriage purported to give consent to the marriage other than by reason only of duress or error, the marriage shall not be void by reason only of that party's having tacitly withheld consent to the marriage at the time when it was solemnised.
(5) In this section 'error' means—
(a) error as to the nature of the ceremony; or
(b) a mistaken belief held by a person ('A') that the other party at the ceremony with whom A purported to enter into a marriage was the person whom A had agreed to marry.]

22 Interpreters at marriage ceremony
(1) Where the person by whom a marriage is to be solemnised under this Act considers that it is necessary or desirable, he may use the services of an interpreter (not being a party or a witness to the marriage) at the marriage ceremony.
(2) The interpreter shall—
(a) before the marriage ceremony, sign a written statement that he understands, and is able to converse in, any language in respect of which he is to act as interpreter at that ceremony; and
(b) immediately after the marriage ceremony, furnish the person solemnising the marriage with a certificate written in English and signed by the interpreter that he has faithfully acted as interpreter at that ceremony.
(3) Any fee for the services of the interpreter shall be paid by the parties to the marriage.

UNFAIR CONTRACT TERMS ACT 1977
(1977 c 50)

27 Choice of law clauses

(1)   Where the [law applicable to] a contract is the law of any part of the United Kingdom only by choice of the parties (and apart from that choice would be the law of some country outside the United Kingdom) sections 2 to 7 and 16 to 21 of this Act do not operate as part [of the law applicable to the contract].

(2)   This Act has effect notwithstanding any contract term which applies or purports to apply the law of some country outside the United Kingdom, where [...]—

(a)   the term appears to the court, or arbitrator or arbiter to have been imposed wholly or mainly for the purpose of enabling the party imposing it to evade the operation of this Act; or

[(b)   the contract is a consumer contract as defined in Part II of this Act, and the consumer at the date when the contract was made was habitually resident in the United Kingdom, and the essential steps necessary for the making of the contract were taken there, whether by him or by others on his behalf.]*

*Section 27(2)(b) repealed by Consumer Rights Act 2015, Sch 4 para 24 in respect of contracts post-dating 1 October 2015.

ADOPTION (SCOTLAND) ACT 1978
(1978 c 28)

PART IV
STATUS OF ADOPTED CHILDREN

38 Meaning of 'adoption order' in Part IV

(1)   In this Part 'adoption order' means—

(a)   an adoption order within the meaning of section 65(1);

(b)   an adoption order under the Children Act 1975, the Adoption Act 1958, the Adoption Act 1950 or any enactment repealed by the Adoption Act 1950;

(c)   an order effecting an adoption made in England, Wales, Northern Ireland, the Isle of Man or any of the Channel Islands;

[(cc)   a Convention adoption;]

(d)   an 'overseas adoption' within the meaning of section 65(2); or

(e)   any other adoption recognised by the law of Scotland; and cognate expressions shall be construed accordingly.

(2)   The definition of adoption order includes, where the context admits, an adoption order which took effect before the commencement of the Children Act 1975.

39 Status conferred by adoption

(1)   [A child who is the subject of an adoption order shall be treated in law—

(a)   where the adopters are a married couple, as if—

(i)   he had been born as a [...] child of the marriage (whether or not he was in fact born after the marriage was constituted); and

(ii)   [subject to subsection (2A)] he were not the child of any person other than the adopters;

(b)   where the adoption order is made by virtue of section 15(1)(aa) as if—

(i)   he had been born as a [...] child of the marriage between the adopter and the natural parent to whom the adopter is married (whether or not he was in fact born after the marriage was constituted); and

(ii) [subject to subsection (2A)] he were not the child of any person other than the adopter and that natural parent; and
(c)   in any other case, as if—
(i)   he had been born as a [...] child of the adopter; and
(ii) [subject to subsection (2A)] he were not the child of any person other than the adopter.]

(2)   Where [a] child has been adopted by one of his natural parents as sole adoptive parent and the adopter thereafter marries the other natural parent, sub-section (1) shall not affect any enactment or rule of law whereby, by virtue of the marriage, the child is rendered the [...] child of both natural parents.

[(2A) Where, in the case of a child adopted under a Convention adoption, the Court of Session is satisfied, on an application under this subsection—
(a)   that under the law of the country in which the adoption was effected the adoption is not a full adoption;
(b)   that the consents referred to in Article 4(c) and (d) of the Convention have not been given for a full adoption, or that the United Kingdom is not the receiving State (within the meaning of Article 2 of the Convention); and
(c)   that it would be more favourable to the child for a direction to be given under this subsection,
the Court may direct that sub-paragraph (ii) of, as the case may be, paragraph (a), (b) or (c) of subsection (1) shall not apply, or shall not apply to such extent as may be specified in the direction: and in this subsection 'full adoption' means an adoption by virtue of which the child falls to be treated in law as if he were not the child of any person other than the adopters or adopter.]

(3)   This section has effect—
(a)   in the case of an adoption before 1st January 1976, from that date, and
(b)   in the case of any other adoption, from the date of the adoption.
(4)   Subject to the provisions of this Part, this section—
(a)   applies for the construction of enactments or instruments passed or made before or after the commencement of this Act so far as the context admits; and
(b)   does not affect things done or events occurring before the adoption or, where the adoption took place before 1st January 1976, before that date.
(5)   This section has effect subject to the provisions of section 44.

[...]

41   Miscellaneous enactments

(1)   Section 39 does not apply in determining the forbidden degrees of con-sanguinity and affinity in respect of the law relating to marriage [, to the eligibility of persons to register as civil partners of each other] or in respect of the crime of incest, except that, on the making of an adoption order, the adopter and the child shall be deemed, for all time coming, to be within the said forbidden degrees in respect of the law relating to marriage and incest [, to such eligibility and to incest].

(2)   [S]ection 39 does not apply for the purposes of any provision of—
(a)   [the British Nationality Act 1981],
(b)   the Immigration Act 1971,
(c)   any instrument having effect under an enactment within paragraph (a) or (b), or
(d)   any other law for the time being in force which determines [British citizen-ship, British Overseas Territories citizenship, [the status of a British National (Overseas)] or British Overseas citizenship].

42   Pensions

Section 39(1) does not affect entitlement to a pension which is payable to or for the benefit of a child and is in payment at the time of his adoption.

43 Insurance
Where a child is adopted whose natural parent has effected an insurance with a friendly society or a collecting society or an industrial insurance company for the payment on the death of the child of money for funeral expenses, the rights and liabilities under the policy shall by virtue of the adoption be transferred to the adoptive parents who shall for the purposes of the enactments relating to such societies and companies be treated as the person who took out the policy.

44 Effect of s 39 on succession and *inter vivos* deed
Section 39 (status conferred by adoption) does not affect the existing law relating to adopted persons in respect of—
    (a)   the succession to a deceased person (whether testate or intestate), and
    (b)   the disposal of property by virtue of any *inter vivos* deed.

STATE IMMUNITY ACT 1978
(1978 c 33)

PART I
PROCEEDINGS IN UNITED KINGDOM BY OR AGAINST OTHER STATES

1 General immunity from jurisdiction
(1)   A State is immune from the jurisdiction of the courts of the United Kingdom except as provided in the following provisions of this Part of this Act.
(2)   A court shall give effect to the immunity conferred by this section even though the State does not appear in the proceedings in question.

2 Submission to jurisdiction
(1)   A State is not immune as respects proceedings in respect of which it has submitted to the jurisdiction of the courts of the United Kingdom.
(2)   A State may submit after the dispute giving rise to the proceedings has arisen or by a prior written agreement; but a provision in any agreement that it is to be governed by the law of the United Kingdom is not to be regarded as a submission.
(3)   A State is deemed to have submitted—
    (a)   if it has instituted the proceedings; or
    (b)   subject to subsections (4) and (5) below, if it has intervened or taken any step in the proceedings.
(4)   Subsection (3)(b) above does not apply to intervention or any step taken for the purpose only of—
    (a)   claiming immunity; or
    (b)   asserting an interest in property in circumstances such that the State would have been entitled to immunity if the proceedings had been brought against it.
(5)   Subsection (3)(b) above does not apply to any step taken by the State in ignorance of facts entitling it to immunity if those facts could not reasonably have been ascertained and immunity is claimed as soon as reasonably practicable.
(6)   A submission in respect of any proceedings extends to any appeal but not to any counter-claim unless it arises out of the same legal relationship or facts as the claim.
(7)   The head of a State's diplomatic mission in the United Kingdom, or the person for the time being performing his functions, shall be deemed to have authority to submit on behalf of the State in respect of any proceedings; and any person who has entered into a contract on behalf of and with the authority of a State shall be deemed to have authority to submit on its behalf in respect of proceedings arising out of the contract.

3   Commercial transactions and contracts to be performed in United Kingdom

(1)   A State is not immune as respects proceedings relating to—

(a)   a commercial transaction entered into by the State; or

(b)   an obligation of the State which by virtue of a contract (whether a commercial transaction or not) falls to be performed wholly or partly in the United Kingdom.

(2)   This section does not apply if the parties to the dispute are States or have otherwise agreed in writing; and subsection (1)(b) above does not apply if the contract (not being a commercial transaction) was made in the territory of the State concerned and the obligation in question is governed by its administrative law.

(3)   In this section 'commercial transaction' means—

(a)   any contract for the supply of goods or services;

(b)   any loan or other transaction for the provision of finance and any guarantee or indemnity in respect of any such transaction or of any other financial obligation; and

(c)   any other transaction or activity (whether of a commercial, industrial, financial, professional or other similar character) into which a State enters or in which it engages otherwise than in the exercise of sovereign authority;

but neither paragraph of subsection (1) above applies to a contract of employment between a State and an individual.

4   Contracts of employment

(1)   A State is not immune as respects proceedings relating to a contract of employment between the State and an individual where the contract was made in the United Kingdom or the work is to be wholly or partly performed there.

(2)   Subject to subsection (3) and (4) below, this section does not apply if—

(a)   at the time when the proceedings are brought the individual is a national of the State concerned; or

(b)   at the time when the contract was made the individual was neither a national of the United Kingdom nor habitually resident there; or

(c)   the parties to the contract have otherwise agreed in writing.

(3)   Where the work is for an office, agency or establishment maintained by the State in the United Kingdom for commercial purposes, subsection (2)(a) and (b) above do not exclude the application of this section unless the individual was, at the time when the contract was made, habitually resident in that State.

(4)   Subsection (2)(c) above does not exclude the application of this section where the law of the United Kingdom requires the proceedings to be brought before a court of the United Kingdom.

(5)   In subsection (2)(b) above 'national of the United Kingdom' [means—

(a)   a British citizen, [a British overseas territories citizen, a British National (Overseas)] or a British Overseas citizen; or

(b)   a person who under the British Nationality Act 1981 is a British subject; or

(c)   a British protected person (within the meaning of that Act)].

(6)   In this section 'proceedings relating to a contract of employment' includes proceedings between the parties to such a contract in respect of any statutory rights or duties to which they are entitled or subject as employer or employee.

5   Personal injuries and damage to property

A State is not immune as respects proceedings in respect of—

(a)   death or personal injury; or

(b)   damage to or loss of tangible property,

caused by an act or omission in the United Kingdom.

6   Ownership, possession and use of property

(1)   A State is not immune as respects proceedings relating to—

(a)   any interest of the State in, or its possession or use of, immovable property in the United Kingdom; or

(b)   any obligation of the State arising out of its interest in, or its possession or use of, any such property.

(2)   A State is not immune as respects proceedings relating to any interest of the State in movable or immovable property, being an interest arising by way of succession, gift or bona vacantia.

(3)   The fact that a State has or claims an interest in any property shall not preclude any court from exercising in respect of it any jurisdiction relating to the estates of deceased persons or persons of unsound mind or to insolvency, the winding up of companies or the administration of trusts.

(4)   A court may entertain proceedings against a person other than a State notwithstanding that the proceedings relate to property—

(a)   which is in the possession or control of a State; or

(b)   in which a State claims an interest,

if the State would not have been immune had the proceedings been brought against it or, in a case within paragraph (b) above, if the claim is neither admitted nor supported by prima facie evidence.

9   Arbitrations

(1)   Where a State has agreed in writing to submit a dispute which has arisen, or may arise, to arbitration, the State is not immune as respects proceedings in the courts of the United Kingdom which relate to the arbitration.

(2)   This section has effect subject to any contrary provision in the arbitration agreement and does not apply to any arbitration agreement between States.

14   States entitled to immunities and privileges

(1)   The immunities and privileges conferred by this Part of this Act apply to any foreign or commonwealth State other than the United Kingdom; and references to a State include references to—

(a)   the sovereign or other head of that State in his public capacity;

(b)   the government of that State; and

(c)   any department of that government,

but not to any entity (hereafter referred to as a 'separate entity') which is distinct from the executive organs of the government of the State and capable of suing or being sued.

(2)   A separate entity is immune from the jurisdiction of the courts of the United Kingdom if, and only if—

(a)   the proceedings relate to anything done by it in the exercise of sovereign authority; and

(b)   the circumstances are such that a State (or, in the case of proceedings to which section 10 above applies, a State which is not a party to the Brussels Convention) would have been so immune.

(3)   If a separate entity (not being a State's central bank or other monetary authority) submits to the jurisdiction in respect of proceedings in the case of which it is entitled to immunity by virtue of subsection (2) above, subsections (1) to (4) of section 13 above shall apply to it in respect of those proceedings as if references to a State were references to that entity.

(4)   Property of a State's central bank or other monetary authority shall not be regarded for the purposes of subsection (4) of section 13 above as in use or intended for use for commercial purposes; and where any such bank or authority is a separate entity subsections (1) to (3) of that section shall apply to it as if references to a State were references to the bank or authority.

(5)   Section 12 above applies to proceedings against the constituent territories of a federal State; and Her Majesty may by Order in Council provide for the other provisions of this Part of this Act to apply to any such constituent territory specified in the Order as they apply to a State.

(6)   Where the provisions of this Part of this Act do not apply to a constituent territory by virtue of any such Order subsections (2) and (3) above shall apply to it as if it were a separate entity.

CIVIL JURISDICTION AND JUDGMENTS ACT 1982*
(1982 c 27)

PART I
IMPLEMENTATION OF THE CONVENTIONS

Main implementing provisions

1   Interpretation of references to the Conventions and Contracting States
(1)   In this Act—

'the 1968 Convention' means the Convention on jurisdiction and the enforcement of judgments in civil and commercial matters (including the Protocol annexed to that Convention), signed at Brussels on 27th September 1968;

'the 1971 Protocol' means the Protocol on the interpretation of the 1968 Convention by the European Court, signed at Luxembourg on 3rd June 1971;

'the Accession Convention' means the Convention on the accession to the 1968 Convention and the 1971 Protocol of Denmark, the Republic of Ireland and the United Kingdom, signed at Luxembourg on 9th October 1978;

['the 1982 Accession Convention' means the Convention on the accession of the Hellenic Republic to the 1968 Convention and the 1971 Protocol, with the adjustments made to them by the Accession Convention, signed at Luxembourg on 25th October 1982;]

['the 1989 Accession Convention' means the Convention on the accession of the Kingdom of Spain and the Portuguese Republic to the 1968 Convention and the 1971 Protocol, with the adjustments made to them by the Accession Convention and the 1982 Accession Convention, signed at Donostia–San Sebastián on 26th May 1989;]

['the 1996 Accession Convention' means the Convention on the accession of the Republic of Austria, the Republic of Finland and the Kingdom of Sweden to the 1968 Convention and the 1971 Protocol, with the adjustments made to them by the Accession Convention, the 1982 Accession Convention and the 1989 Accession Convention, signed at Brussels on 29th November 1996;]

['the 2005 Hague Convention' means the Convention on Choice of Court Agreements concluded on 30th June 2005 at The Hague;]

['the 2007 Hague Convention' means the Convention on the International Recovery of Child Support and other forms of Family Maintenance done at The Hague on 23 November 2007;]

['the [Brussels Conventions'] means the 1968 Convention, the 1971 Protocol, the Accession Convention, the 1982 Accession Convention, the 1989 Accession Convention [and the 1996 Accession Convention];]

['the Lugano Convention' means the Convention on jurisdiction and the recognition and enforcement of judgments in civil and commercial matters, between the European Community and the Republic of Iceland, the Kingdom of Norway, the Swiss Confederation and the Kingdom of Denmark signed on behalf of the European Community on 30th October 2007;]

['the Maintenance Regulation' means Council Regulation (EC) No 4/2009 including as applied in relation to Denmark by virtue of the Agreement made on

---

* As amended by SI 2009/3131, in consequence of Lugano II.

19th October 2005 between the European Community and the Kingdom of Denmark;]

['the Regulation' means Regulation (EU) No 1215/2012 of the European Parliament and of the Council of 12 December 2012 on jurisdiction and the recognition and enforcement of judgments in civil and commercial matters (recast) as amended from time to time and as applied by the Agreement made on 19 October 2005 between the European Community and the Kingdom of Denmark on jurisdiction and the recognition and enforcement of judgments in civil and commercial matters].

(2) In this Act, unless the context otherwise requires—

(a) references to, or to any provision of, the 1968 Convention or the 1971 Protocol are references to that Convention, Protocol or provision as amended by the Accession Convention [, the 1982 Accession Convention, the 1989 Accession Convention and the 1996 Accession Convention]; and

[...]

(b) [any reference in any provision to a numbered Article without more is a reference—

(i) to the Article so numbered of the 1968 Convention, in so far as the provision applies in relation to that Convention, and

(ii) to the Article so numbered of the Lugano Convention, in so far as the provision applies in relation to that Convention,]

and any reference to a sub-division of a numbered Article shall be construed accordingly.

(3) [In this Act—

['2005 Hague Convention State,' in any provision, in the application of that provision in relation to the 2005 Hague Convention, means a State bound by that Convention;]

['2007 Hague Convention State', in any provision, in the application of that provision in relation to the 2007 Hague Convention, means a State bound by that Convention;]

'Contracting State', without more, in any provision means—

(a) in the application of the provision in relation to the Brussels Conventions, a Brussels Contracting State;

(b) in the application of the provision in relation to the Lugano Convention, a [State bound by the Lugano Convention]; [and

(c) in the application of the provision in relation to the 2005 Hague Convention, a 2005 Hague Convention State;]

['Brussels Contracting State' means a state which is one of the original parties to the 1968 Convention or one of the parties acceding to that Convention under the Accession Convention, or under the 1982 Accession Convention, or under the 1989 Accession Convention, but only with respect to any territory—

(a) to which the Brussels Conventions apply; and

(b) which is excluded from the scope of the Regulation pursuant to [Articles 349 and 355 of the Treaty on the Functioning of the European Union];]

['Maintenance Regulation State', in any provision, in the application of that provision in relation to the Maintenance Regulation means a Member State;]

[...]

['Regulation State' in any provision, in the application of that provision in relation to the Regulation, means a 'Member State'].

['State bound by the Lugano Convention' in any provision, in the application of that provision in relation to the Lugano Convention has the same meaning as in Article 1(3) of that Convention;]

[(4) Any question arising as to whether it is the Regulation, any of [the Brussels Conventions, the Lugano Convention or the 2005 Hague Convention] which applies in the circumstances of a particular case shall be determined as follows—

(a) in accordance with [Article 64] of the Lugano Convention (which determines the relationship between the Brussels Conventions and the Lugano Convention);

(b)   in accordance with Article 68 of the Regulation (which determines the relationship between the Brussels Conventions and the Regulation) [; and

(c)   in accordance with Article 26 of the 2005 Hague Convention (which determines the relationship between the Brussels Conventions, the Lugano Convention, the Regulation and the 2005 Hague Convention).]

2   The [Brussels Conventions] to have the force of law

(1)   The [Brussels Conventions] shall have the force of law in the United Kingdom, and judicial notice shall be taken of them.

(2)   [For convenience of reference there are set out in Schedules 1, 2, 3, 3A, 3B and 3C respectively the English texts of—

(a)   the 1968 Convention as amended by Titles II and III of the Accession Convention, by Titles II and III of the 1982 Accession Convention, by Titles II and III of, and Annex I(d) to, the 1989 Accession Convention and by Titles II and III of the 1996 Accession Convention;

(b)   the 1971 Protocol as amended by Title IV of the Accession Convention, by Title IV of the 1982 Accession Convention, by Title IV of the 1989 Accession Convention and by Title IV of the 1996 Accession Convention;

(c)   Titles V and VI of the Accession Convention (transitional and final provisions) as amended by Title V of the 1989 Accession Convention;

(d)   Titles V and VI of the 1982 Accession Convention (transitional and final provisions); and

(e)   Titles VI and VII of the 1989 Accession Convention (transitional and final provisions),

(f)   Titles V and VI of the 1996 Accession Convention (transitional and final provisions),

being texts prepared from the authentic English texts referred to in Articles 37 and 41 of the Accession Convention [, in Article 17 of the 1982 Accession Convention, in Article 34 of the 1989 Accession Convention and in Article 18 of the 1996 Accession Convention.]

3   Interpretation of the [Brussels Conventions]

(1)   Any question as to the meaning or effect of any provision of the [Brussels Conventions] shall, if not referred to the European Court in accordance with the 1971 Protocol, be determined in accordance with the principles laid down by and any relevant decision of the European Court.

(2)   Judicial notice shall be taken of any decision of, or expression of opinion by, the European Court on any such question.

(3)   Without prejudice to the generality of subsection (1), the following reports (which are reproduced in the Official Journal of the Communities), namely—

(a)   the reports by Mr P Jenard on the 1968 Convention and the 1971 Protocol; and

(b)   the report by Professor Peter Schlosser on the Accession Convention; and

(c)   [the report by Professor Demetrios I Evrigenis and Professor K D Kerameus on the 1982 Accession Convention; and

(d)   the report by Mr Martinho de Almeida Cruz, Mr Manuel Desantes Real and Mr P Jenard on the 1989 Accession Convention,]

may be considered in ascertaining the meaning or effect of any provision of the [Brussels Conventions] and shall be given such weight as is appropriate in the circumstances.

[...]

Supplementary provisions as to recognition and enforcement of judgments

4   Enforcement of judgments other than maintenance orders

(1)   A judgment, other than a maintenance order, which is the subject of an application under Article 31 [of the 1968 Convention ...] for its enforcement in any part of the United Kingdom shall, to the extent that its enforcement is authorised by the appropriate court, be registered in the prescribed manner in that court.

In this subsection 'the appropriate court' means the court to which the application is made in pursuance of Article 32 (that is to say, the High Court or the Court of Session).

(2)   Where a judgment is registered under this section, the reasonable costs or expenses of and incidental to its registration shall be recoverable as if they were sums recoverable under the judgment.

(3)   A judgment registered under this section shall, for the purposes of its enforcement, be of the same force and effect, the registering court shall have in relation to its enforcement the same powers, and proceedings for or with respect to its enforcement may be taken, [as if it was a judgment which had been originally given] by the registering court and had (where relevant) been entered.

(4)   Subsection (3) is subject to Article 39 (restriction of enforcement where appeal pending or time for appeal unexpired), to section 7 and to any provision made by rules of court as to the manner in which and conditions subject to which a judgment registered under this section may be enforced.

[4A   Enforcement of judgments, other than maintenance orders, under the Lugano Convention

(1)   Where a judgment, other than a maintenance order, is registered under the Lugano Convention, the reasonable costs or expenses of and incidental to its registration shall be recoverable as if they were sums recoverable under the judgment.

(2)   A judgment other than a maintenance order registered under the Lugano Convention shall, for the purposes of its enforcement, be of the same force and effect, the registering court shall have in relation to its enforcement the same powers, and proceedings for or with respect to its enforcement may be taken, as if the judgment had been originally given by the registering court and had (where relevant) been entered.

(3)   Subsection (2) is subject to Article 47(3) of the Lugano Convention (restriction on enforcement where appeal pending or time for appeal unexpired), to section 7 (interest on registered judgments) and to any provision made by rules of court as to the manner in which and conditions subject to which a judgment registered under the Lugano Convention may be enforced.]

[4B   Registration and enforcement of judgments under the 2005 Hague Convention

(1)   A judgment which is required to be recognised and enforced under the 2005 Hague Convention in any part of the United Kingdom must be registered in the prescribed manner in the appropriate court, on the application of any interested party.

(2)   In subsection (1) 'the appropriate court' means—

  (a)   in England and Wales or Northern Ireland, the High Court;
  (b)   in Scotland, the Court of Session.

(3)   A judgment which is required to be recognised and enforced under the 2005 Hague Convention must be registered without delay on completion of the formalities in Article 13 of the 2005 Hague Convention if the registering court considers that it meets the condition for recognition in Article 8(3) of the 2005 Hague Convention, without any review of whether a ground for refusal under Article 9 applies.

(4)   The party against whom enforcement is sought shall not be entitled to make any submission on the application for registration.

(5)   Where a judgment which is required to be recognised and enforced under the 2005 Hague Convention has been registered, the reasonable costs or expenses of and incidental to its registration shall be recoverable as if they were sums recoverable under the judgment.

(6)   A judgment which is required to be recognised and enforced under the 2005 Hague Convention shall, for the purposes of its enforcement, be of the same force and effect, the registering court shall have in relation to its enforcement the same powers, and proceedings for or with respect to its enforcement may be taken, as if the judgment had been originally given by the registering court and had (where relevant) been entered.

(7)   Subsection (6) is subject to section 7 (interest on registered judgments) and to any provision made by rules of court as to the manner in which and conditions subject to which a judgment registered under the 2005 Hague Convention may be enforced.]

5   Recognition and enforcement of maintenance orders

(1)   The function of transmitting to the appropriate court an application under Article 31 [of the 1968 Convention ...] for the recognition or enforcement in the United Kingdom of a maintenance order shall be discharged—

(a)   [as respects England and Wales ..., by the Lord Chancellor; and

(b)   as respects Scotland, by the Secretary of State] [; and

(c)   as respects Northern Ireland, by the Department of Justice in Northern Ireland.]

In this subsection 'the appropriate court' means the magistrates' court or sheriff court having jurisdiction in the matter in accordance with the second paragraph of Article 32.

(2)   Such an application shall be determined in the first instance by the prescribed officer of that court.

(3)   Where on such an application the enforcement of the order is authorised to any extent, the order shall to that extent be registered in the prescribed manner in that court.

(4)   A maintenance order registered under this section shall, for the purposes of its enforcement, be of the same force and effect, the registering court shall have in relation to its enforcement the same powers, and proceedings for or with respect to its enforcement may be taken, as if it was an order which had been originally made by the registering court.

(5)   Subsection (4) is subject to Article 39 (restriction on enforcement where appeal pending or time for appeal unexpired), to section 7 and to any provision made by rules of court as to the manner in which and conditions subject to which an order registered under this section may be enforced.

(6)   A maintenance order which by virtue of this section is enforceable by a magistrates' court in Northern Ireland [shall, subject to the modifications of Article 98 of the Magistrates' Courts (Northern Ireland) Order 1981 specified in subsection (6A) below, be enforceable as an order made by that court to which that article applies].

(6A)   [*Applies to Northern Ireland.*]

(7)   The payer under a maintenance order registered under this section in a magistrates' court in England and Wales or Northern Ireland shall give notice of any change of address to the [proper officer] of that court.

A person who without reasonable excuse fails to comply with this subsection shall be guilty of an offence and liable on summary conviction to a fine not exceeding [level 2 on the standard scale].

[(8)   In subsection (7) 'proper officer' means—

(a)   in relation to a magistrates' court in England and Wales, the [designated officer]

for the court; and

(b)   in relation to a magistrates' court in Northern Ireland, the clerk of the court.]

[5A   Recognition and enforcement of maintenance orders under the Lugano Convention

(1)   The Secretary of State's function (under Article 39 and Annex II of the Lugano Convention) of transmitting to the appropriate court an application for the recognition or enforcement in the United Kingdom of a maintenance order (made under Article 38 of the Lugano Convention) shall be discharged—

(a)   as respects England and Wales ..., by the Lord Chancellor; and

(b)   as respects Scotland, by the Scottish Ministers] [; and

(c)   as respects Northern Ireland, by the Department of Justice in Northern Ireland.]

In this subsection 'the appropriate court' means the magistrates' court or sheriff court having jurisdiction in the matter in accordance with the second paragraph of Article 39.

(2)   Such an application shall be determined in the first instance by the prescribed officer of the court having jurisdiction in the matter.

(3)   A maintenance order registered under the Lugano Convention shall, for the purposes of its enforcement, be of the same force and effect, the registering court shall have in relation to its enforcement the same powers, and proceedings for or with respect to its enforcement may be taken, as if the order had been made by the registering court.

(4)   Subsection (3) is subject to Article 47 of the Lugano Convention (restriction on enforcement where appeal pending or time for appeal unexpired), to subsection (6) and to any provision made by rules of court as to the manner in which and conditions subject to which an order registered under the Lugano Convention may be enforced.

(5)   A maintenance order which by virtue of the Lugano Convention is enforceable by a magistrates' court in England and Wales shall, subject to the modifications of sections 76 and 93 of the Magistrates' Courts Act 1980 specified in sections 5(5B) and 5(5C) of the Act, be enforceable in the same manner as a magistrates' court maintenance order made by that court.

In this subsection 'magistrates' court maintenance order' has the same meaning as in section 150(1) of the Magistrates' Courts Act 1980.

(6)   A maintenance order which by virtue of the Lugano Convention is enforceable by a magistrates' court in Northern Ireland shall, subject to the modifications of Article 98 of the Magistrates' Courts (Northern Ireland) Order 1981 specified in section 5(6A) of this Act, be enforceable as an order made by that court to which that Article applies.

(7)   The payer under a maintenance order registered under the Lugano Convention in a magistrates' court in England and Wales or Northern Ireland shall give notice of any change of address to the proper officer of that court.

(8)   A person who without reasonable excuse fails to comply with subsection (7) shall be guilty of an offence and liable on summary conviction to a fine not exceeding level 2 on the standard scale.

(9)   In subsection (7) 'proper officer' means—

(a)   in relation to a magistrates' court in England and Wales, the designated officer; and

(b)   in relation to a magistrates' court in Northern Ireland, the clerk of the court.]

6   Appeals under Article 37, second paragraph and Article 41

(1)   The single further appeal on a point of law referred to in the 1968 Convention [...] Article 37, second paragraph and Article 41 in relation to the recognition or enforcement of a judgment other than a maintenance order lies—

(a)   in England and Wales or Northern Ireland, to the Court of Appeal or to

the House of Lords in accordance with Part II of the Administration of Justice
Act 1969 (appeals direct from the High Court to the House of Lords);
    (b)   in Scotland, to the Inner House of the Court of Session.
(2)   Paragraph (a) of subsection (1) has effect notwithstanding section 15(2)
of the Administration of Justice Act 1969 (exclusion of direct appeal to the
House of Lords in cases where no appeal to that House lies from a decision of the
Court of Appeal).
(3)   The single further appeal on a point of law referred to in [the 1968 Con-
vention] Article 37, second paragraph and Article 41 in relation to the recognition
or enforcement of a maintenance order lies—
    (a)   in England and Wales, [to a county court in accordance with section
111A] of the Magistrates' Courts Act 1980;
    (b)   in Scotland, to the Inner House of the Court of Session;
    (c)   in Northern Ireland, to the Court of Appeal.

[6A   Appeals under Article 44 and Annex IV of the Lugano Convention

(1)   The single further appeal on a point of law referred to in Article 44 and
Annex IV of the Lugano Convention in relation to the recognition or enforcement
of a judgment other than a maintenance order lies—
    (a)   in England and Wales or Northern Ireland, to the Court of Appeal or to
the Supreme Court in accordance with Part II of the Administration of Justice
Act 1969 (appeals direct from the High Court to the Supreme Court);
    (b)   in Scotland, to the Inner House of the Court of Session.
(2)   Paragraph (a) of subsection (1) has effect notwithstanding section 15(2) of
the Administration of Justice Act 1969 (exclusion of direct appeal to the Supreme
Court in cases where no appeal to that House lies from a decision of the Court of
Appeal).
(3)   The single further appeal on a point of law referred to in Article 44 and
Annex IV of the Lugano Convention in relation to the recognition or enforcement
of a maintenance order lies—
    (a)   in England and Wales, to a county court in accordance with section 111A
of the Magistrates' Courts Act 1980;
    (b)   in Scotland, to the Inner House of the Court of Session;
    (c)   in Northern Ireland, to the Court of Appeal.]

[6B   Appeals in relation to registration of judgments under the 2005 Hague Convention

(1)   A decision on the application for registration of a judgment required to be
recognised and enforced under the 2005 Hague Convention may be appealed
against by either party.
(2)   The appeal referred to in subsection (1) lies—
    (a)   in England and Wales or Northern Ireland, to the High Court;
    (b)   in Scotland, to the Court of Session.
(3)   The court to which an appeal referred to in subsection (1) is brought must
refuse or revoke registration only if—
    (a)   the condition for recognition in Article 8(3) of the 2005 Hague Conven-
tion is not met;
    (b)   the ground for postponement or refusal of recognition in Article 8(4) of
the 2005 Hague Convention applies; or
    (c)   one or more of the grounds specified in Article 9 of the 2005 Hague Con-
vention apply.
(4)   A single further appeal on a point of law against the judgment given on the
appeal referred to in subsection (1) lies—
    (a)   in England and Wales or Northern Ireland, to the Court of Appeal or to
the Supreme Court in accordance with Part II of the Administration of Justice
Act 1969 (appeals direct from the High Court to the Supreme Court);
    (b)   in Scotland, to the Inner House of the Court of Session.

(5)   Paragraph (a) of subsection (4) has effect notwithstanding section 15(2) of the Administration of Justice Act 1969 (exclusion of direct appeal to the Supreme Court in cases where no appeal to that Court lies from a decision of the Court of Appeal).]

7 Interest on registered judgments

(1)   Subject to subsection (4), where in connection with an application for registration of a judgment under section [4, 4A, 4B, 5 or 5A] the applicant shows—

(a)   that the judgment provides for the payment of a sum of money; and

(b)   that in accordance with the law of the Contracting State in which the judgment was given interest on that sum is recoverable under the judgment from a particular date of time, the rate of interest and the date or time from which it is so recoverable shall be registered with the judgment and, subject to any provision made under subsection (2), the debt resulting, apart from section 4(2), from the registration of the judgment shall carry interest in accordance with the registered particulars.

(2)   Provision may be made by rules of court as to the manner in which and the periods by reference to which any interest payable by virtue of subsection (1) is to be calculated and paid, including provision for such interest to cease to accrue as from a prescribed date.

(3)   Costs or expenses recoverable by virtue of section 4(2) shall carry interest as if they were the subject of an order for the payment of costs or expenses made by the registering court on the date of registration.

(4)   Interest on arrears of sums payable under a maintenance order registered under section 5 in a magistrates' court in England and Wales or Northern Ireland shall not be recoverable in that court, but without prejudice to the operation in relation to any such order of section 2A of the Maintenance Orders Act 1958 or section 11A of the Maintenance and Affiliation Orders Act (Northern Ireland) 1966 (which enable interest to be recovered if the order is re-registered for enforcement in the High Court).

(5)   Except as mentioned in subsection (4), debts under judgments registered under section [4, 4A, 4B, 5 or 5A] shall carry interest only as provided by this section.

8 Currency of payment under registered maintenance orders

(1)   Sums payable in the United Kingdom under a maintenance order by virtue of its registration under section 5 [or 5A], including any arrears so payable, shall be paid in the currency of the United Kingdom.

(2)   Where the order is expressed in any other currency, the amounts shall be converted on the basis of the exchange rate prevailing on the date of registration of the order.

(3)   For the purposes of this section, a written certificate purporting to be signed by an officer of any bank in the United Kingdom and stating the exchange rate prevailing on a specified date shall be evidence, and in Scotland sufficient evidence, of the facts stated.

Other supplementary provisions

9 Provisions supplementary to Title VII of 1968 Convention

(1)   The provisions of Title VII of the 1968 Convention [and, apart from [Article 64], of Title VII of the Lugano Convention and Article 26 of the 2005 Hague Convention] (relationship between [the Convention in question] and other conventions to which Contracting States are or may become parties) shall have effect in relation to—

(a)   any statutory provision, whenever passed or made, implementing any such other convention in the United Kingdom; and

(b)   any rule of law so far as it has the effect of so implementing any such other convention,
as they have effect in relation to that other convention itself.
[...]

10   Allocation within UK of jurisdiction with respect to trusts and consumer contracts

(1)   The provisions of this section have effect for the purpose of allocating within the United Kingdom jurisdiction in certain proceedings in respect of which the 1968 Convention [or the Lugano Convention] confers jurisdiction on the courts of the United Kingdom generally and to which section 16 does not apply.

(2)   Any proceedings which by virtue of Article 5(6) (trusts) are brought in the United Kingdom shall be brought in the courts of the part of the United Kingdom in which the trust is domiciled.

(3)   Any proceedings which by virtue of the first paragraph of Article 14 [of the 1968 Convention or Article 16(1) of the Lugano Convention] (consumer contracts) are brought in the United Kingdom by a consumer on the ground that he is himself domiciled there shall be brought in the courts of the part of the United Kingdom in which he is domiciled.

11   Proof and admissibility of certain judgments and related documents

(1)   For the purposes of the 1968 Convention [...]—

(a)   a document, duly authenticated, which purports to be a copy of a judgment given by a court of a Contracting State other than the United Kingdom shall without further proof be deemed to be a true copy, unless the contrary is shown; and

(b)   the original or a copy of any such document as is mentioned in Article 46(2) or 47 (supporting documents to be produced by a party seeking recognition or enforcement of a judgment) shall be evidence, and in Scotland sufficient evidence, of any matter to which it relates.

[(2)   A document purporting to be a copy of an authentic instrument drawn up or registered, and enforceable, in a Contracting State other than the United Kingdom is duly authenticated for the purposes of this section if it purports to be certified to be a true copy of such an instrument by a person duly authorised in that Contracting State to do so.]

(3)   Nothing in this section shall prejudice the admission in evidence of any document which is admissible apart from this section.

[11A   Proof and admissibility of certain judgments and related documents for the purposes of the Lugano Convention

(1)   For the purposes of the Lugano Convention—

(a)   a document, duly authenticated, which purports to be a copy of a judgment given by a court of a State bound by the Lugano Convention other than the United Kingdom shall without further proof be deemed to be a true copy, unless the contrary is shown; and

(b)   a certificate obtained in accordance with Article 54 and Annex V shall be evidence, and in Scotland sufficient evidence, that the judgment is enforceable in the State of origin which is bound by the Lugano Convention.

(2)   A document purporting to be a copy of a judgment given by any such court as is mentioned in subsection (1)(a) is duly authenticated for the purposes of this section if it purports—

(a)   to bear the seal of that court; or

(b)   to be certified by any person in his capacity as a judge or officer of that court to be a true copy of a judgment given by that court.

(3)   Nothing in this section shall prejudice the admission in evidence of any document which is admissible apart from this section.]

[11B Proof and admissibility of certain judgments and related documents for the purposes of the 2005 Hague Convention

(1) For the purposes of the 2005 Hague Convention—

(a) a document, duly authenticated, which purports to be a copy of a judgment given by a court of a 2005 Hague Convention State other than the United Kingdom shall without further proof be deemed to be a true copy, unless the contrary is shown; and

(b) a certificate issued by the court of the 2005 Hague Convention State of origin, in the form recommended for use under the 2005 Hague Convention and published by the Hague Conference on Private International Law, as referred to in Article 13(3) of the 2005 Hague Convention, shall be evidence, and in Scotland sufficient evidence, as to whether the judgment has effect or is enforceable in the 2005 Hague Convention State of origin.

(2) A document purporting to be a copy of a judgment given by any such court as is mentioned in subsection (1)(a) is duly authenticated for the purposes of this section if it purports—

(a) to bear the seal of that court; or

(b) to be certified by any person in their capacity as judge or officer of that court to be a true copy of a judgment given by that court.

(3) Nothing in this section shall prejudice the admission in evidence of any document which is admissible apart from this section.]

12 Provision for issue of copies of, and certificated in connection with, UK Judgments

The Court of Session may by Act of Sederunt make provision for enabling any interested party wishing to secure under the 1968 Convention [, the Lugano Convention [or the 2005 Hague Convention]] the recognition or enforcement in another Contracting State of a judgment within section 18(2)(c) to obtain, subject to any conditions specified in the rules—

(a) a copy of the judgment; and

(b) a certificate giving particulars relating to the judgment [...].

13 Modifications to cover authentic instruments and court settlements.

(1) Her Majesty may by Order in Council provide that—

(a) any provision of this Act relating to the recognition or enforcement in the United Kingdom or elsewhere of judgments to which the 1968 Convention [...] applies; and

(b) any other statutory provision, whenever passed or made, so relating,

shall apply, with such modifications as may be specified in the Order, in relation to documents and settlements within Title IV of the 1968 Convention [...] (authentic instruments and court settlements enforceable in the same manner as judgments) as if they were judgments to which [the Convention in question] applies.

(2) An Order in Council under this section may make different provision in relation to different descriptions of documents and settlements.

(3) Any Order in Council under this section shall be subject to annulment in pursuance of a resolution of either House of Parliament.

14 Modifications consequential on revision of the Conventions

(1) If at any time it appears to Her Majesty in Council that Her Majesty's Government in the United Kingdom have agreed to a revision of [the Lugano Convention or any of the Brussels Conventions], including in particular any revision connected with the accession to [...] the 1968 Convention of one or more further states, Her Majesty may by Order in Council make such modifications of this Act or any other statutory provision, whenever passed or made, as Her Majesty considers appropriate in consequence of the revision.

(2) An Order in Council under this section shall not be made unless a draft of

the Order has been laid before Parliament and approved by a resolution of each House of Parliament.

(3)   In this section 'revision' means an omission from, addition to or alteration of [...] any of the Brussels Conventions] and includes replacement of any of the Conventions to any extent by another convention, protocol or other description of international agreement.

15   Interpretation of Part I and consequential amendments

(1)   In this Part, unless the context otherwise requires—

'judgment' has the meaning given by Article 25 [of the 1968 Convention or, as the case may be, Article 32 of the Lugano Convention [or Article 4(1) of the 2005 Hague Convention]];

'maintenance order' means a maintenance judgment within the meaning of the 1968 Convention [or, as the case may be, the Lugano Convention];

'payer', in relation to a maintenance order, means the person liable to make payments for which the order provides;

'prescribed' means prescribed by rules of court.

(2)   References in this Part to a judgment registered under [sections 4, 4A, 4B, 5 or 5A] include, to the extent of its registration, references to a judgment so registered to a limited extent only.

(3)   Anything authorised or required by the 1968 Convention, [the Lugano Convention] or this Part to be done by, to or before a particular magistrates' court may be done by, to or before any magistrates' court acting [in the same local justice area (or, in Northern Ireland, for the same] petty sessions district) as that court.

PART II
JURISDICTION, AND RECOGNITION AND ENFORCEMENT OF JUDGMENTS, WITHIN UNITED KINGDOM

16   Allocation within UK of jurisdiction in certain civil proceedings

(1)   The provisions set out in Schedule 4 (which contains a modified version of [Chapter II of the Regulation]) shall have effect for determining, for each part of the United Kingdom, whether the courts of law of that part, or any particular court of law in that part, have or has jurisdiction in proceedings where—

(a)   [the subject-matter of the proceedings is within the scope of the Regulation as determined by Article 1 of the Regulation (whether or not the Regulation has effect in relation to the proceedings); and]

(b)   the defendant or defender is domiciled in the United Kingdom or the proceedings are of a kind mentioned in [Article [24] of the Regulation] (exclusive jurisdiction regardless of domicile).

[...]

(3)   In determining any question as to the meaning or effect of any provision contained in Schedule 4—

(a)   regard shall be had to any relevant principles laid down by the European Court in connection with Title II of the 1998 Convention [or Chapter II of the Regulation] and to any relevant decision of that court as to the meaning or effect of any provision of that Title [or that Chapter]; and

(b)   without prejudice to the generality of paragraph (a), the reports mentioned in section 3(3) may be considered and shall, so far as relevant, be given such weight as is appropriate in the circumstances.

(4)   The provisions of this section and Schedule 4 shall have effect subject to [the Regulation, Schedule 6 to the Civil Jurisdiction and Judgments (Maintenance) Regulations 2011,] the 1968 Convention [, the Lugano Convention [and the 2005 Hague Convention]] and to the provisions of section 17.

...

17 Exclusion of certain proceedings from Schedule 4

(1) Schedule 4 shall not apply to proceedings of any description listed in Schedule 5 or to proceedings in Scotland under any enactment which confers jurisdiction on a Scottish court in respect of a specific subject-matter on specific grounds.

(2) Her Majesty may by Order in Council—

(a) add to the list in Schedule 5 any description of proceedings in any part of the United Kingdom; and

(b) remove from that list any description of proceedings in any part of the United Kingdom (whether included in the list as originally enacted or added by virtue of this subsection).

(3) An Order in Council under subsection (2)—

(a) may make different provisions for different descriptions of proceedings, for the same description of proceedings in different courts or for different parts of the United Kingdom; and

(b) may contain such transitional and other incidental provisions as appear to Her Majesty to be appropriate.

(4) An Order in Council under subsection (2) shall not be made unless a draft of the Order has been laid before parliament and approved by a resolution of each House of Parliament.

18 Enforcement of UK judgments in other parts of UK

(1) In relation to any judgment to which this section applies—

(a) Schedule 6 shall have effect for the purpose of enabling any money provisions contained in the judgments to be enforced in a part of the United Kingdom other than the part in which the judgment was given; and

(b) Schedule 7 shall have effect for the purpose of enabling any non-money provisions so contained to be so enforced.

(2) In this section 'judgment' means any of the following (references to the giving of a judgment being construed accordingly)—

(a) any judgment or order (by whatever name called) given or made by a court of law in the United Kingdom;

(b) any judgment or order not within paragraph (a) which has been entered in England and Wales or Northern Ireland in the High Court or a county court;

(c) any document which the Scotland has been registered for execution in the Books of Council and Session or in the sheriff court books kept for any sheriffdom;

(d) any award or order made by a tribunal in any part of the United Kingdom which is enforceable in that part without an order of a court of law;

(e) an arbitration award which has become enforceable in the part of the United Kingdom in which it was given in the same manner as a judgment given by a court of law in that part;

[(f) an order made, or a warrant issued, under Part 8 of the Proceeds of Crime Act 2002 for the purposes of a civil recovery investigation [or a detained cash investigation] within the [meanings] given by section 341 of that Act;]

and, subject to the following provisions of this section, this section applies to all such judgments.

(3) Subject to subsection (4), this section does not apply to—

(a) a judgment given in proceedings in a magistrates' court in England and Wales or Northern Ireland;

(b) a judgment given in proceedings other the civil proceedings;

[(ba) a judgment given in the exercise of jurisdiction in relation to insolvency law, within the meaning of section 426 of the Insolvency Act 1986;]

(c) a judgment given in proceedings relating to—

[...]

(iii) the obtaining of title to administer the estate of a deceased person;

(d) an order made under Part 2, 3 or 4 of the Proceeds of Crime Act 2002 (confiscation).

(4) This section applies, whatever the nature of the proceedings in which it is made, to—

(a) a decree issued under section 13 of the Court of Exchequer (Scotland) Act 1856 (recovery of certain rent-charges and penalties by process of the Court of Session);

(b) an order which is enforceable in the same manner as a judgment of the High Court in England and Wales by virtue of section 16 of the Contempt of Court Act 1981 or section 140 of the Supreme Court Act 1981 (which relate to fines for contempt of court and forfeiture of recognisances).

[(4A) This section does not apply as respects—

(a) the enforcement in Scotland of orders made by the High Court or a county court in England and Wales under or for the purposes of Part VI of the Criminal Justice Act 1988 or the Drug Trafficking Act 1994 (confiscation of the proceeds of certain offences or of drug trafficking); or

(b) the enforcement in England and Wales of orders made by the Court of Session or by the sheriff under or for the purposes of the Proceeds of Crime (Scotland) Act 1995.]

(5) This section does not apply to so much of any judgment as—

(a) is an order to which section 16 of the Maintenance Orders Act 1950 applies (and is therefore an order for whose enforcement in another part of the United Kingdom provision is made by Part II of that Act);

(b) concerns the status or legal capacity of an individual;

(c) relates to the management of the affairs of a person not capable of managing his own affairs;

(d) is a provisional (including protective) measure other than an order for the making of an interim payment;

and except where otherwise stated references to a judgment to which this section applies are to such a judgment exclusive of any such provisions.

(6) The following are within subsection (5)(b), but without prejudice to the generality of that provision—

(a) a decree of judicial separation or of separation;

(b) [any order which is a Part I order for the purposes of the Family Law Act 1986].

[(6A) In subsection (5)(d), 'an interim order made in connection with the civil recovery of proceeds of unlawful conduct' means any of the following made under Chapter 2 of Part 5 of the Proceeds of Crime Act 2002—

(a) a property freezing order or prohibitory property order;

(b) an order under section 245E or 245F of that Act (order relating to receivers in connection with property freezing order);

(c) an interim receiving order or interim administration order;]

[(d) an order under section 255G or 255H of that Act (order relating to PPO receivers in connection with prohibitory property order).]

(7) This section does not apply to a judgment of a court outside the United Kingdom which falls to be treated for the purposes of its enforcement as a judgments of a court of law in the United Kingdom by virtue of registration under Part II of the Administration of Justice Act 1920, Part I of the Foreign Judgments (Reciprocal Enforcement) Act 1933, Part I of the Maintenance Orders (Reciprocal Enforcement) Act 1972 or section 4 or 5 of this Act [or by virtue of the Civil Jurisdiction and Judgments (Maintenance) Regulations 2011].

(8) A judgment to which this section applies, other than a judgment within paragraph (e) of subsection (2), shall not be enforced in another part of the United Kingdom except by way of registration under Schedule 6 or 7.

19 Recognition of UK judgments in other parts of UK

(1) A judgment to which this section applies given in one part of the United Kingdom shall not be refused recognition in another part of the United Kingdom solely on the ground that, in relation to that judgment, the court which gave it was not a court of competent jurisdiction according to the rules of private international law in force in that other part.

(2) Subject to subsection (3), this section applies to any judgment to which section 18 applies.

(3) This section does not apply to—

(a) the documents mentioned in paragraph (c) of the definition of 'judgment' in section 18(2);

(b) the awards and orders mentioned in paragraphs (d) and (e) of that definition;

(c) the decrees and orders referred to in section 18(4).

PART III
JURISDICTION IN SCOTLAND

20 Rules as to jurisdiction in Scotland

(1) Subject to [the Regulation, to] Parts I and II and to the following provisions of this Part, Schedule 8 has effect to determine in what circumstances a person may be sued in civil proceedings in the Court of Session or in a sheriff court.

(2) Nothing in Schedule 8 affects the competence as respects subject-matter or value of the Court of Session or of the sheriff court.

(3) Section 6 of the Sheriff Courts (Scotland) Act 1907 shall cease to have effect—

[(a)] to the extent that it determines jurisdiction in relation to any matter to which Schedule 8 applies [; and

(b) to the extent that it relates to any matter where jurisdiction falls to be determined by reference to the jurisdictional requirements of the Maintenance Regulation and Schedule 6 to the Civil Jurisdiction and Judgments (Maintenance) Regulations 2011.]

[...]

(5) In determining any question as to the meaning or effect of any provision contained in Schedule 8—

(a) regard shall be had to any relevant principles laid down by the European Court in connection with Title II of the 1968 Convention [or Chapter II of the Regulation] and to any relevant decision of that court as to the meaning or effect of any provision of that Title [or that Chapter]; and

(b) without prejudice to the generality of paragraph (a), the reports mentioned in section 3(3) may be considered and shall, so far as relevant, be given such weight as is appropriate in the circumstances.

21 Continuance of certain existing jurisdictions

(1) Schedule 8 does not affect—

(a) the operation of any enactment which confers jurisdiction on a Scottish court in respect of a specific subject-matter on specific grounds;

(b) without prejudice to the foregoing generality, the jurisdiction of any court in respect of any matter mentioned in Schedule 9.

(2) Her Majesty may by Order in Council—

(a) add to the list in Schedule 9 any description of proceedings; and

(b) remove from that list any description of proceedings (whether included in the list as originally enacted or added by virtue of this subsection).

(3) An Order in Council under subsection (2) may—

(a) make different provision for different descriptions of proceedings or for the same description of proceedings in different courts; and

(b)   contain such transitional and other incidental provisions as appear to Her Majesty to be appropriate.

(4)   An Order in Council under subsection (2) shall not be made unless a draft of the Order has been laid before Parliament and approved by a resolution of each House of Parliament.

22   Supplementary provision

(1)   Nothing in Schedule 8 shall prevent a court from declining jurisdiction on the ground of forum non conveniens.

(2)   Nothing in Schedule 8 affects the operation of any enactment or rule of law under which a court may decline to exercise jurisdiction because of the prorogation by parties of the jurisdiction of another court.

(3)   For the avoidance of doubt, it is declared that nothing in Schedule 8 affects the nobile officium of the Court of Session.

(4)   Where a court has jurisdiction in any proceedings by virtue of Schedule 8, that court shall also have jurisdiction to determine any matter which—

(a)   is ancillary or incidental to the proceedings; or

(b)   requires to be determined for the purposes of a decision in the proceedings.

23   Savings and consequential amendments

(1)   Nothing in Schedule 8 shall affect—

(a)   the power of any court to vary or recall a maintenance order granted by the court;

(b)   the power of a sheriff court under section 22 of the Maintenance Orders Act 1950 (discharge and variation of maintenance orders registered in sheriff courts) to very or discharge a maintenance order registered in that court under Part II of that Act; or

(c)   the power of a sheriff court under section 9 of the Maintenance Orders (Reciprocal Enforcement) Act 1972 (variation and revocation of maintenance orders registered in United Kingdom courts) to vary or revoke a registered order within the meaning of Part I of that Act.

(2)   [Amending provisions.]

PART IV
MISCELLANEOUS PROVISIONS

Provisions relating to jurisdiction

...

27   Provisional and protective measures in Scotland in the absence of substantive proceedings

(1)   The Court of Session may, in any case to which this subsection applies—

(a)   subject to subsection (2)(c), grant a warrant for the arrestment of any assets situated in Scotland;

(b)   subject to subsection (2)(c), grant a warrant of inhibition over any property situated in Scotland; and

[(ba)   subject to subsection (2)(c) below, grant a warrant for the interim attachment of corporeal moveable property situated in Scotland;]

(c)   grant interim interdict.

(2)   Subsection (1) applies to any case in which—

(a)   proceedings have been commenced but not concluded, or, in relation to paragraph (c) of that subsection, are to be commenced, in another [Brussels or Lugano Contracting State], in another Regulation State [, in another Maintenance Regulation State [, in another Hague Convention State]] or in England and Wales or Northern Ireland;

(b)   [the subject-matter of the proceedings is within the scope of the Regulation as determined by Article 1 of the Regulation [, is within scope of the Maintenance Regulation as determined by Article 1 of that Regulation [or is within
the scope of the 2005 Hague Convention as determined by Articles 1 and 2 of
that Convention]]; and]
(c)   in relation to paragraphs (a) [, (b) and (ba)] of subsection (1), such a
warrant could competently have been granted in equivalent proceedings before
a Scottish court;
but it shall not be necessary, in determining whether proceedings have been commenced for the purpose of paragraph (a) of this subsection, to show that any document has been served on or notice given to the defender.
(3)   Her Majesty may by Order in Council confer on the Court of Session power
to do anything mentioned in subsection (1) or in section 28 in relation to proceedings of any of the following descriptions, namely—
(a)   proceedings commenced otherwise than in a [Brussels, Lugano Contracting State [, Regulation State or Maintenance Regulation State [or a 2005 Hague
Convention State]]];
(b)   [proceedings whose subject-matter is not within the scope of the Regulation as determined by Article 1 of the Regulation [or the Maintenance Regulation
as determined by Article 1 of that Regulation [or the 2005 Hague Convention as
determined by Articles 1 and 2 of that Convention]];]
(c)   arbitration proceedings;
(d)   in relation to subsection (1)(c) or section 28, proceedings which are to be
commenced otherwise than in a [Brussels or Lugano Contracting State [, Regulation State, Maintenance Regulation State [or a 2005 Hague Convention State]]].
(4)   An Order in Council under subsection (3)—
(a)   may confer power to do only certain of the things mentioned in subsection (1) or in section 28;
(b)   may make different provision for different classes of proceedings, for
proceedings pending in different countries or courts outside the United Kingdom or in different parts of the United Kingdom, and for other different circumstances; and
(c)   may impose conditions or restrictions on the exercise of any power
conferred by the Order.
(5)   Any Order in Council under subsection (3) shall be subject to annulment in
pursuance of a resolution of either House of Parliament.

28   Application of s 1 of Administration of Justice (Scotland) Act 1972

[(1)]   When any proceedings have been brought, or are likely to be brought, in
another [Brussels or Lugano Contracting State, in a Regulation State [, in a 2005
Hague Convention State]] or in England and Wales or Northern Ireland in respect
of any matter which is within the scope of the [Regulation] as determined in
Article 1, the Court of Session shall have the like power to make an order under
section 1 of the Administration of Justice (Scotland) Act 1972 [as amended by the
Law Reform (Miscellaneous Provisions)(Scotland) Act 1985] as if the proceedings
in question had been brought, or were likely to be brought, in that court.
[(2)   When any proceedings have been brought or are likely to be brought in
another Maintenance Regulation State or in England and Wales or Northern
Ireland in respect of any matter which is within the scope of the Maintenance
Regulation as determined by Article 1 of that Regulation, the Court of Session has
the like power to make an order under section 1 of the Administration of Justice
(Scotland) Act 1972 as if the proceedings in question had been brought, or were
likely to be brought, in that court.]

30   Proceedings in England and Wales or Northern Ireland for torts to immovable property

(1)   The jurisdiction of any court in England and Wales or Northern Ireland to

entertain proceedings for trespass to, or any other tort affecting, immovable property shall extend to cases in which the property in question is situated outside that part of the United Kingdom unless the proceedings are principally concerned with a question of the title to, or the right to possession of, that property.

(2) Subsection (1) has effect subject to the 1968 Convention [and the Lugano Convention and the Regulation] and to the provisions set out in Schedule 4.

Provisions relating to recognition and enforcement of judgments

31   Overseas judgments given against states, etc

(1) A judgment given by a court of an overseas country against a state other than the United Kingdom or the state to which that court belongs shall be recognised and enforced in the United Kingdom if, and only if—

(a) it would be so recognised and enforced if it had not been given against a state; and

(b) that court would have had jurisdiction in the matter if it had applied rules corresponding to those applicable to such matters in the United Kingdom in accordance with sections 2 to 11 of the State Immunity Act 1978.

(2) References in subsection (1) to a judgment given against a state include references to judgments of any of the following descriptions given in relation to a state—

(a) judgments against the government, or a department of the government, of the state but not (except as mentioned in paragraph (c)) judgments against an entity which is distinct from the executive organs of government;

(b) judgments against the sovereign or head of state in his public capacity;

(c) judgments against any such separate entity as is mentioned in paragraph (a) given in proceedings relating to anything done by it in the exercise of the sovereign authority of the state.

(3) Nothing in subsection (1) shall affect the recognition or enforcement in the United Kingdom of a judgment to which Part I of the Foreign Judgments (Reciprocal Enforcement) Act 1933 applies by virtue of section 4 of the Carriage of Goods by Road Act 1965, section 17(4) of the Nuclear Installations Act 1965, section [166(4) of the Merchant Shipping Act 1995, regulation 8 of the Railways (Convention on International Carriage by Rail Regulations 2005] or section 5 of the Carriage of Passengers by Road Act 1974.

(4) Sections 12, 13 and 14(3) and (4) of the State Immunity Act 1978 (service of process and procedural privileges) shall apply to proceedings for the recognition or enforcement in the United Kingdom of a judgment given by a court of an overseas country (whether or not that judgment is within subsection (1) of this section) as they apply to other proceedings.

(5) In this section 'state', in the case of a federal state, includes any of its constituent territories.

32   Overseas judgments given in proceedings brought in breach of agreement for settlement of disputes

(1) Subject to the following provisions of this section, a judgment given by a court of an overseas country in any proceedings shall not be recognised or enforced in the United Kingdom if—

(a) the bringing of those proceedings in that court was contrary to an agreement under which the dispute in question was to be settled otherwise than by proceedings in the courts of that country; and

(b) those proceedings were not brought in that court by, or with the agreement of, the person against whom the judgment was given; and

(c) that person did not counter claim in the proceedings or otherwise submit to the jurisdiction of that court.

(2) Subsection (1) does not apply where the agreement referred to in paragraph (a) of the subsection was illegal, void or unenforceable or was incapable of being

performed for reasons not attributable to the fault of the party bringing the proceedings in which the judgment was given.

(3) In determining whether a judgment given by a court of an overseas country should be recognised or enforced in the United Kingdom, a court in the United Kingdom shall not be bound by any decision of the overseas court relating to any of the matters mentioned in subsection (1) or (2).

(4) Nothing in subsection (1) shall affect the recognition or enforcement in the United Kingdom of—

(a) a judgment which is required to be recognised or enforced there under [the 2005 Hague Convention,] the 1968 Convention [or the Lugano Convention or the Regulation [or the Maintenance Regulation]];

(b) a judgment to which Part I of the Foreign Judgments (Reciprocal Enforcement) Act 1933 applies by virtue of section 4 of the Carriage of Goods by Road Act 1965, section 17(4) of the Nuclear Installations Act 1965, [regulation 8 of the Railways (Convention on International Carriage by Rail) Regulations 2005] or section 5 of the Carriage of Passengers by Road Act 1974 or section 177(4) of the Merchant Shipping Act 1995.

33 Certain steps not to amount to submission to jurisdiction of overseas court

(1) For the purposes of determining whether a judgments given by a court of an overseas country should be recognised or enforced in England and Wales or Northern Ireland, the person against whom the judgment was given shall not be regarded as having submitted to the jurisdiction of the court by reason only of the fact that he appeared (conditionally or otherwise) in the proceedings for all or any one or more of the following purposes, namely—

(a) to contest the jurisdiction of the court;

(b) to ask the court to dismiss or stay the proceedings on the ground that the dispute in question should be submitted to arbitration or to the determination of the courts of another country;

(c) to protect, or obtain the release of, property seized or threatened with seizure in the proceedings.

(2) Nothing in this section shall affect the recognition or enforcement in England and Wales or Northern Ireland of a judgment which is required to be recognised or enforced there under the 1968 Convention [or the Lugano Convention or the Regulation [or the Maintenance Regulation [or the 2005 Hague Convention]]].

34 Certain judgments a bar to further proceedings on the same cause of action

No proceedings may be brought by a person in England and Wales or Northern Ireland on a cause of action in respect of which a judgment has been given in his favour in proceedings between the same parties, or their privies, in a court in another part of the United Kingdom or in a court of an overseas country, unless that judgment is not enforceable or entitled to recognition in England and Wales or, as the case may be, in Northern Ireland.

35 Minor amendments relating to overseas judgments

(1) The Foreign Judgments (Reciprocal Enforcement) Act 1933 shall have effect with the amendments specified in Schedule 10, being amendments whose main purpose is to enable Part I of that Act to be applied to judgments of courts other than superior courts, to judgments providing for interim payments and to certain arbitration awards.

...

PART V
SUPPLEMENTARY AND GENERAL PROVISIONS

Domicile

41 Domicile of individuals

(1)   Subject to Article 52 (which contains provisions for determining whether a party is domiciled in a Contracting State), the following provisions of this section determine, for the purposes of the 1968 Convention [...] and this Act, whether an individual is domiciled in the United Kingdom or in a particular part of, or place in, the United Kingdom or in a state other than a Contracting State.

(2)   An individual is domiciled in the United Kingdom if and only if—
(a)   he is resident in the United Kingdom; and
(b)   the nature and circumstances of this residence indicate that he has a substantial connection with the United Kingdom.

(3)   Subject to subsection (5), an individual is domiciled in a particular part of the United Kingdom if and only if—
(a)   he is resident in that part; and
(b)   the nature and circumstances of his residence indicate that he has a substantial connection with that part.

(4)   An individual is domiciled in a particular place in the United Kingdom if and only if he—
(a)   is domiciled in the part of the United Kingdom in which that place is situated; and
(b)   is resident in that place.

(5)   An individual who is domiciled in the United Kingdom but in whose case the requirements of subsection (3)(b) are not satisfied in relation to any particular part of the United Kingdom shall be treated as domiciled in the part of the United Kingdom in which he is resident.

(6)   In the case of an individual who—
(a)   is resident in the United Kingdom, or in a particular part of the United Kingdom; and
(b)   has been so resident for the last three months or more,
the requirements of subsection (2)(b) or, as the case may be, subsection (3)(b) shall be presumed to be fulfilled unless the contrary is proved.

(7)   An individual is domiciled in a state other than a Contracting State if and only if—
(a)   he is resident in that state; and
(b)   the nature and circumstances of his residence indicate that he has a substantial connection with that state.

[41A Domicile of individuals for the purposes of the Lugano Convention

(1)   Subject to Article 59 of the Lugano Convention (which contains provisions for determining whether a party is domiciled in a State bound by the Lugano Convention), the following provisions of this section determine, for the purposes of the Lugano Convention, whether an individual is domiciled in the United Kingdom or in a particular part of, or place in, the United Kingdom or in a state other than a State bound by the Lugano Convention.

(2)   An individual is domiciled in the United Kingdom if and only if—
(a)   he is resident in the United Kingdom; and
(b)   the nature and circumstances of his residence indicate that he has a substantial connection with the United Kingdom.

(3)   Subject to subsection (5), an individual is domiciled in a particular part of the United Kingdom if and only if—
(a)   he is resident in that part; and
(b)   the nature and circumstances of his residence indicate that he has a substantial connection with that part.

(4)   An individual is domiciled in a particular place in the United Kingdom if and only if he—

(a)   is domiciled in the part of the United Kingdom in which that place is situated; and

(b)   is resident in that place.

(5)   An individual who is domiciled in the United Kingdom but in whose case the requirements of subsection (3)(b) are not satisfied in relation to any particular part of the United Kingdom shall be treated as domiciled in the part of the United Kingdom in which he is resident.

(6)   In the case of an individual who—

(a)   is resident in the United Kingdom, or in a particular part of the United Kingdom; and

(b)   has been so resident for the last three months or more,

the requirements of subsection (2)(b) or, as the case may be, subsection (3)(b) shall be presumed to be fulfilled unless the contrary is proved.

(7)   An individual is domiciled in a state other than a State bound by the Lugano Convention if and only if—

(a)   he is resident in that state; and

(b)   the nature and circumstances of his residence indicate that he has a substantial connection with that state.]

42   Domicile and seat of corporation or association

(1)   For the purposes of this Act the seat of a corporation or association (as determined by this section) shall be treated as its domicile.

(2)   The following provisions of this section determine where a corporation or association has its seat—

(a)   for the purpose of Article 53 (which for the purposes of the 1968 Convention [...] equates the domicile of such a body with its seat); and

(b)   for the purposes of this Act other than the provisions mentioned in section 43(1)(b) and (c).

(3)   A corporation or association has its seat in the United Kingdom, if and only if—

(a)   it was incorporated or formed under the law of a part of the United Kingdom and has its registered office or some other official address in the United Kingdom; or

(b)   its central management and control is exercised in the United Kingdom.

(4)   A corporation or association has its seat in a particular part of the United Kingdom if and only if it has its seat in the United Kingdom and—

(a)   it has its registered office or some other official address in that part; or

(b)   its central management and control is exercised in that part; or

(c)   it has a place of business in that part.

(5)   A corporation or association has its seat in a particular place in the United Kingdom if and only if it has its seat in the part of the United Kingdom in which that place is situated and—

(a)   it has its registered office or some other official address in that place; or

(b)   its central management and control is exercised in that place; or

(c)   it has a place of business in that place.

(6)   Subject to subsection (7), a corporation or association has its seat in a state other than the United Kingdom if and only if—

(a)   it was incorporated or formed under the law of that state and has its registered office or some other official address there; or

(b)   its central management and control is exercised in that state.

(7)   A corporation or association shall not be regarded as having its seat in a Contracting State other than the United Kingdom if it is shown that the courts of that state would not regard it as having its seat there.

(8)   In this section—

'business' includes any activity carried on by a corporation or association, and 'place of business' shall be construed accordingly;

'official address', in relation to a corporation or association, means an address which it is required by law to register, notify or maintain for the purpose of receiving notices or other communications.

43   Seat of corporation or association for purposes of Article 16(2) and related provisions

(1)   The following provisions of this section determine where a corporation or association has its seat for the purposes of—

    (a)   Article 16(2) [of the 1968 Convention ...] (which confers exclusive jurisdiction over proceedings relating to the formation or dissolution of such bodies, or to the decisions of their organs);

    (b)   [rules 4 and 11(b)] in Schedule 4; and

    (c)   [rules 2(1) and 5(1)(b)] in Schedule 8.

(2)   A corporation or association has its seat in the United Kingdom if and only if—

    (a)   it was incorporated or formed under the law of a part of the United Kingdom; or

    (b)   its central management and control is exercised in the United Kingdom.

(3)   A corporation or association has its seat in a particular part of the United Kingdom if and only if it has its seat in the United Kingdom and—

    (a)   subject to subsection (5), it was incorporated or formed under the law of that part; or

    (b)   being incorporated or formed under the law of a state other than the United Kingdom, its central management and control is exercised in that part.

(4)   A corporation or association has its seat in a particular place in Scotland if and only if it has its seat in Scotland and—

    (a)   it has its registered office or some other official address in that place; or

    (b)   it has no registered office or other official address in Scotland, but its central management and control is exercised in that place.

(5)   A corporation or association incorporated or formed under—

    (a)   an enactment forming part of the law of more than one part of the United Kingdom; or

    (b)   an instrument having effect in the domestic law of more than one part of the United Kingdom,

shall, if it has a registered office, be taken to have its seat in the part of the United Kingdom in which that office is situated, and not in any other part of the United Kingdom.

(6)   Subject to subsection (7), a corporation or association has its seat in a Contracting State other than the United Kingdom if and only if—

    (a)   it was incorporated or formed under the law of that state; or

    (b)   its central management and control is exercised in that state.

(7)   A corporation or association shall not be regarded as having its seat in a Contracting State other than the United Kingdom if—

    (a)   it has its seat in the United Kingdom by virtue of subsection (2)(a); or

    (b)   it is shown that the courts of that other state would not regard it for the purposes of Article 16(2) as having its seat there.

(8)   In this section 'official address' has the same meaning as in section 42.

[43A   Seat of companies or other legal persons, or of associations, for the purposes of Article 22(2) of the Lugano Convention

(1)   The following provisions of this section determine where a company, or other legal person or an association of natural or legal persons, has its seat for the purposes of Article 22(2) of the Lugano Convention (which confers exclusive juris-

diction over proceedings relating to the validity of the constitution, the nullity or the dissolution of such bodies, or to the validity of the decisions of their organs).

(2) A company, legal person or association has its seat in the United Kingdom if and only if—

(a) it was incorporated or formed under the law of a part of the United Kingdom; or

(b) its central management and control is exercised in the United Kingdom.

(3) Subject to subsection (4), a company, legal person or association has its seat in a State bound by the Lugano Convention other than the United Kingdom if and only if—

(a) it was incorporated or formed under the law of that state; or

(b) its central management and control is exercised in that state.

(4) A company, legal person or association shall not be regarded as having its seat in a State bound by the Lugano Convention other than the United Kingdom if—

(a) it has its seat in the United Kingdom by virtue of subsection (2)(a); or

(b) it is shown that the courts of that other state would not regard it for the purposes of Article 22(2) as having its seat there.]

44 Persons deemed to be domiciled in the United Kingdom for certain purposes

(1) This section applies to—

(a) proceedings within Section 3 of Title II of the 1968 Convention [...] (insurance contracts), and

(b) proceedings within Section 4 of [Title II of [the 1968 Convention]] (consumer contracts).

(2) A person who, for the purposes of proceedings to which this section applies arising out of the operations of a branch, agency or other establishment in the United Kingdom, is deemed for the purposes of the 1968 Convention [...] to be domiciled in the United Kingdom by virtue of—

(a) Article 8, second paragraph (insurers); or

(b) Article 13, second paragraph (suppliers of goods, services or credit to consumers),

shall, for the purposes of those proceedings, be treated for the purposes of this Act as so domiciled and as domiciled in the part of the United Kingdom in which the branch, agency or establishment in question is situated.

[44A Persons deemed to be domiciled in the United Kingdom for certain purposes of the Lugano Convention

(1) This section applies to—

(a) proceedings within Section 3 of Title II of the Lugano Convention (insurance contracts);

(b) proceedings within Section 4 of Title II of the Lugano Convention (consumer contracts); and

(c) proceedings within Section 5 of Title II of the Lugano Convention (employment contracts).

(2) A person who, for the purposes of proceedings to which this section applies arising out of the operations of a branch, agency or other establishment in the United Kingdom, is deemed for the purposes of the Lugano Convention to be domiciled in the United Kingdom by virtue of —

(a) Article 9(2) (insurers); or

(b) Article 15(2) (suppliers of goods, services or credit to consumers); or

(c) Article 18(2) (employers),

shall, for the purposes of those proceedings, be treated as so domiciled and as domiciled in the part of the United Kingdom in which the branch, agency or establishment in question is situated.]

45 Domicile of trusts

(1) The following provisions of this section determine, for the purposes of the 1968 Convention [, the Lugano Convention] and this Act, where a trust is domiciled.

(2) A trust is domiciled in the United Kingdom if and only if it is by virtue of subsection (3) domiciled in a part of the United Kingdom.

(3) A trust is domiciled in a part of the United Kingdom if and only if the system of law of that part is the system of law with which the trust has its closest and most real connection.

...

Other supplementary provisions

...

49 Saving for powers to stay, sist, strike out or dismiss proceedings

Nothing in this Act shall prevent any court in the United Kingdom from staying, sisting, striking out or dismissing any proceedings before it, on the ground of forum non conveniens or otherwise, where to do so is not inconsistent with the 1968 Convention [or, as the case may be, the Lugano Convention [or the 2005 Hague Convention]].

General

50 Interpretation: general

In this Act, unless the context otherwise requires—

['the Accession Convention', 'the 1982 Accession Convention', 'the 1989 Accession Convention' and 'the 1996 Accession' Convention have the meaning given by section 1(1);]

'Article' and references to sub-divisions of numbered Articles are to be construed in accordance with section 1(2)(b);

'association' means an unincorporated body of persons;

['Brussels Contracting State' has the meaning given by section 1(3);

'the Brussels Conventions' has the meaning given by section 1(1);]

'Contracting State' has the meaning given by section 1(3);

'the 1968 Convention' has the meaning given by section 1(1), and references to that Convention and to provisions of it are to be construed in accordance with section 1(2)(a);

'corporation' means a body corporate, and includes a partnership subsisting under the law of Scotland;

'court', without more, includes a tribunal;

'court of law', in relation to the United Kingdom, means any of the following courts, namely—

[(a) the Supreme Court,]

(b) in England and Wales or Northern Ireland, the Court of Appeal, the High Court, the Crown Court, a county court and a magistrates' court,

(c) in Scotland, the Court of Session and a sheriff court;

'the Crown' is to be construed in accordance with section 51(2);

'enactment' includes an enactment comprised in Northern Ireland legislation;

['the 2005 Hague Convention' has the meaning given by section 1(1);

'2005 Hague Convention State' has the meaning given by section 1(3);]

['the 2007 Hague Convention' has the meaning given by section 1(1);

'2007 Hague Convention State' has the meaning given by section 1(3);]

'judgment', subject to sections 15(1) and 18(2) and to paragraph 1 of Schedules 6 and 7, means any judgment or order (by whatever name called) given or made by a court in any civil proceedings;

[...

'the Lugano Convention' has the meaning given by section 1(i);]

'magistrates' court', in relation to Northern Ireland, means a court of summary jurisdiction;

'modifications' includes additions, omissions and alterations;

'overseas country' means any country or territory outside the United Kingdom;

'part of the United Kingdom' means England and Wales, Scotland or Northern Ireland;

'the 1971 Protocol' has the meaning given by section 1(1), and references to that Protocol and to provisions of it are to be construed in accordance with section 1(2)(a);

['the Regulation' has the meaning given by section 1(1);

'Regulation State' has the meaning given by section 1(3);]

'rules of court', in relation to any court, means rules, orders or regulations made by the authority having power to make rules, orders or regulations regulating the procedure of that court, and includes—

(a)   in Scotland, Acts of Sederunt;

(b)   in Northern Ireland, Judgment Enforcement Rules;

['State bound by the Lugano Convention' has the meaning given by section 1(3);]

'statutory provision' means any provisions contained in an Act, or in any Northern Ireland legislation, or in—

(a)   subordinate legislation (as defined in section 21(1) of the Interpretation Act 1978); or

(b)   any instrument of a legislative character made under any Northern Ireland legislation;

'tribunal' —

(a)   means a tribunal of any description other than a court of law;

(b)   in relation to an overseas country, includes, as regards matters relating to maintenance within the meaning of the 1968 Convention, any authority having power to give, enforce, vary or revoke a maintenance order.

SCHEDULES

SCHEDULE 2
TEXT OF 1971 PROTOCOL, AS AMENDED

Article 1

The Court of Justice of the [European Union] shall have jurisdiction to give rulings on the interpretation of the Convention on jurisdiction and the enforcement of judgments in civil and commercial matters and of the Protocol annexed to that Convention, signed at Brussels on 27th September 1968, and also on the interpretation of the present Protocol.

The Court of Justice of the [European Union] shall also have jurisdiction to give rulings on the interpretation of the Convention on the accession of the Kingdom of Denmark, Ireland and the United Kingdom of Great Britain and Northern Ireland to the Convention of 27 September 1968 and to this Protocol.

The Court of Justice of the [European Union] shall also have jurisdiction to give rulings on the interpretation of the Convention on the accession of the Hellenic Republic to the Convention of 27 September 1968 and to this Protocol, as adjusted by the 1978 Convention.

The Court of Justice of the [European Union] shall also have jurisdiction to give rulings on the interpretation of the Convention on the accession of the Kingdom of Spain and the Portuguese Republic to the Convention of 27 September 1968 and to this Protocol, as adjusted by the 1978 Convention and the 1982 Convention.

The Court of Justice of the [European Union] shall also have jurisdiction to give rulings on the interpretation of the Convention on the accession of the Republic of Austria, the Republic of Finland and the Kingdom of Sweden to the Convention of

27 September 1968 and to this Protocol, as adjusted by the 1978 Convention, the 1982 Convention and the 1989 Convention.

Article 2
The following courts may request the Court of Justice to give preliminary rulings on questions of interpretation—
    1.   ... .
    – in the United Kingdom: the House of Lords and courts to which application has been made under the second paragraph of Article 37 or under Article 41 of the Convention.
    2.   The courts of the Contracting States when they are sitting in an appellate capacity.
    3.   In the cases provided for in Article 37 of the Convention, the courts referred to in that Article.

Article 3
    1.   Where a question of interpretation of the Convention or of one of the other instruments referred to in Article 1 is raised in a case pending before one of the courts listed in point 1 of Article 2, that court shall, if it considers that a decision on the question is necessary to enable it to give judgment, request the Court of Justice to give a ruling thereon.
    2.   Where such a question is raised before any court referred to in point 2 or 3 of Article 2, that court may, under the conditions laid down in paragraph 1, request the Court of Justice to give a ruling thereon.

Article 4
    1.   The competent authority of a Contracting State may request the Court of Justice to give a ruling on a question of interpretation of the Convention or of one of the other instruments referred to in Article 1 if judgments given by courts of that State conflict with the with the interpretation given either by the Court of Justice or in a judgment of one of the courts of another Contracting State referred to in point 1 or 2 of Article 2.The provisions of this paragraph shall apply only to judgments which have become res judicata.
    2.   The interpretation given by the Court of Justice in response to such a request shall not affect the judgments which gave rise to the request for interpretation.
    3.   The Procurators-General of the Courts of Cassation of the Contracting States, or any other authority designated by a Contracting State, shall be entitled to request the Court of Justice for a ruling on interpretation in accordance with paragraph 1.
    4.   The Registrar of the Court of Justice shall give notice of the request to the Contracting States, to the Commission and to the Council of the [European Union]; they shall then be entitled within two months of the notification to submit statements of case or written observations to the Court.
    5.   No fees shall be levied or any costs or expenses awarded in respect of the proceedings provided for in this Article.

Article 5
    1.   Except where this Protocol otherwise provides, the provisions of the Treaty establishing the European Economic Community and those of the Protocol on the Statute of the Court of Justice annexed thereto, which are applicable when the Court is requested to give a preliminary ruling, shall also apply to any proceedings for the interpretation of the Convention and the other instruments referred to in Article 1.
    2.   The Rules of Procedure of the Court of Justice shall, if necessary, be adjusted and supplemented in accordance with Article 188 of the Treaty establishing the European Economic Community.
    ...

[SCHEDULE 4
CHAPTER II OF THE REGULATION AS MODIFIED: RULES FOR
ALLOCATION OF JURISDICTION WITHIN UK

General

1.   Subject to the rules of this Schedule, persons domiciled in a part of the United Kingdom shall be sued in the courts of that part.

2.   Persons domiciled in a part of the United Kingdom may be sued in the courts of another part of the United Kingdom only by virtue of rules 3 to 13 of this Schedule.

Special jurisdiction

3.   A person domiciled in a part of the United Kingdom may, in another part of the United Kingdom, be sued—
   (a)   in matters relating to a contract, in the courts for the place of performance of the obligation in question;
   [...]
   (c)   in matters relating to tort, delict or quasi-delict, in the courts for the place where the harmful event occurred or may occur;
   (d)   as regards a civil claim for damages or restitution which is based on an act giving rise to criminal proceedings, in the court seised of those proceedings, to the extent that that court has jurisdiction under its own law to entertain civil proceedings;
   (e)   as regards a dispute arising out of the operations of a branch, agency or other establishment, in the courts for the place in which the branch, agency or other establishment is situated;
   (f)   as settlor, trustee or beneficiary of a trust created by the operation of a statute, or by a written instrument, or created orally and evidenced in writing, in the courts of the part of the United Kingdom in which the trust is domiciled;
   (g)   as regards a dispute concerning the payment of remuneration claimed in respect of the salvage of a cargo or freight, in the court under the authority of which the cargo or freight in question—
      (i)   has been arrested to secure such payment; or
      (ii)   could have been so arrested, but bail or other security has been given;
provided that this provision shall apply only if it is claimed that the defendant has an interest in the cargo or freight or had such an interest at the time of salvage;
   (h)   in proceedings—
      (i)   concerning a debt secured on immovable property; or
      (ii)   which are brought to assert, declare or determine proprietary or possessory rights, or rights of security, in or over movable property, or to obtain authority to dispose of movable property;
in the courts of the part of the United Kingdom in which the property is situated.

4.   Proceedings which have as their object a decision of an organ of a company or other legal person or of an association of natural or legal persons may, without prejudice to the other provisions of this Schedule, be brought in the courts of the part of the United Kingdom in which that company, legal person or association has its seat.

5.   A person domiciled in a part of the United Kingdom may, in another part of the United Kingdom, also be sued—
   (a)   where he is one of a number of defendants, in the courts for the place where any one of them is domiciled, provided the claims are so closely connected that it is expedient to hear and determine them together to avoid the risk of irreconcilable judgments resulting from separate proceedings;

(b)   as a third party in an action on a warranty or guarantee or in any other third party proceedings, in the court seised of the original proceedings, unless these were instituted solely with the object of removing him from the jurisdiction of the court which would be competent in his case;

(c)   on a counter-claim arising from the same contract or facts on which the original claim was based, in the court in which the original claim is pending;

(d)   in matters relating to a contract, if the action may be combined with an action against the same defendant in matters relating to rights in rem in immovable property, in the court of the part of the United Kingdom in which the property is situated.

6.   Where by virtue of this Schedule a court of a part of the United Kingdom has jurisdiction in actions relating to liability arising from the use or operation of a ship, that court, or any other court substituted for this purpose by the internal law of that part, shall also have jurisdiction over claims for limitation of such liability.

Jurisdiction over consumer contracts

7.—(1)   In matters relating to a contract concluded by a person, the consumer, for a purpose which can be regarded as being outside his trade or profession, jurisdiction shall be determined by this rule and rules 8 and 9, without prejudice to rule 3(e) and (h)(ii), if—

(a)   it is a contract for the sale of goods on instalment credit terms; or

(b)   it is a contract for a loan repayable by instalments, or for any other form of credit, made to finance the sale of goods; or

(c)   in all other cases, the contract has been concluded with a person who pursues commercial or professional activities in the part of the United Kingdom in which the consumer is domiciled or, by any means, directs such activities to that part or to other parts of the United Kingdom including that part, and the contract falls within the scope of such activities.

(2)   This rule shall not apply to a contract of transport other than a contract which, for an inclusive price, provides for a combination of travel and accommodation, or to a contract of insurance.

8.—(1)   A consumer may bring proceedings against the other party to a contract either in the courts of the part of the United Kingdom in which that party is domiciled or in the courts of the part of the United Kingdom in which the consumer is domiciled.

(2)   Proceedings may be brought against a consumer by the other party to the contract only in the courts of the part of the United Kingdom in which the consumer is domiciled.

(3)   The provisions of this rule shall not affect the right to bring a counter-claim in the court in which, in accordance with this rule and rules 7 and 9, the original claim is pending.

9.   The provisions of rules 7 and 8 may be departed from only by an agreement—

(a)   which is entered into after the dispute has arisen; or

(b)   which allows the consumer to bring proceedings in courts other than those indicated in those rules; or

(c)   which is entered into by the consumer and the other party to the contract, both of whom are at the time of conclusion of the contract domiciled or habitually resident in the same part of the United Kingdom, and which confers jurisdiction on the courts of that part, provided that such an agreement is not contrary to the law of that part.

Jurisdiction over individual contracts of employment

10.—(1) In matters relating to individual contracts of employment, jurisdiction shall be determined by this rule, without prejudice to rule 3(e).

(2) An employer may be sued—

(a) in the courts of the part of the United Kingdom in which he is domiciled; or

(b) in the courts of the part of the United Kingdom where the employee habitually carries out his work or in the courts of that part where he last did so; or

(c) if the employee does not or did not habitually carry out his work in any one place, in the courts of the part of the United Kingdom where the business which engaged the employee is or was situated.

(3) An employer may bring proceedings only in the courts of the part of the United Kingdom in which the employee is domiciled.

(4) The provisions of this rule shall not affect the right to bring a counter-claim in the court in which, in accordance with this rule, the original claim is pending.

(5) The provisions of this rule may be departed from only by an agreement on jurisdiction—

(a) which is entered into after the dispute has arisen; or

(b) which allows the employee to bring proceedings in courts other than those indicated in this rule.

Exclusive jurisdiction

11. The following courts shall have exclusive jurisdiction, regardless of domicile:—

(a)—(i) in proceedings which have as their object rights in rem in immovable property or tenancies of immovable property, the courts of the part of the United Kingdom in which the property is situated;

(ii) however, in proceedings which have as their object tenancies of immovable property concluded for temporary private use for a maximum period of six consecutive months, the courts of the part of the United Kingdom in which the defendant is domiciled shall also have jurisdiction, provided that the tenant is a natural person and that the landlord and the tenant are domiciled in the same part of the United Kingdom;

(b) in proceedings which have as their object the validity of the constitution, the nullity or the dissolution of companies or other legal persons or associations of natural or legal persons, the courts of the part of the United Kingdom in which the company, legal person or association has its seat;

(c) in proceedings which have as their object the validity of entries in public registers, the courts of the part of the United Kingdom in which the register is kept;

(d) in proceedings concerned with the enforcement of judgments, the courts of the part of the United Kingdom in which the judgment has been or is to be enforced.

Prorogation of jurisdiction

12.—(1) If the parties have agreed that a court or the courts of a part of the United Kingdom are to have jurisdiction to settle any disputes which have arisen or which may arise in connection with a particular legal relationship, and, apart from this Schedule, the agreement would be effective to confer jurisdiction under the law of that part, that court or those courts shall have jurisdiction.

(2) The court or courts of a part of the United Kingdom on which a trust instrument has conferred jurisdiction shall have jurisdiction in any proceedings

brought against a settlor, trustee or beneficiary, if relations between these persons or their rights or obligations under the trust are involved.

(3)   Agreements or provisions of a trust instrument conferring jurisdiction shall have no legal force if they are contrary to the provisions of rule 9, or if the courts whose jurisdiction they purport to exclude have exclusive jurisdiction by virtue of rule 11.

13.—(1)   Apart from jurisdiction derived from other provisions of this Schedule, a court of a part of the United Kingdom before which a defendant enters an appearance shall have jurisdiction.

(2)   This rule shall not apply where appearance was entered to contest the jurisdiction, or where another court has exclusive jurisdiction by virtue of rule 11.

Examination as to jurisdiction and admissibility

14.   Where a court of a part of the United Kingdom is seised of a claim which is principally concerned with a matter over which the courts of another part of the United Kingdom have exclusive jurisdiction by virtue of rule 11, it shall declare of its own motion that it has no jurisdiction.

15.—(1)   Where a defendant domiciled in one part of the United Kingdom is sued in a court of another part of the United Kingdom and does not enter an appearance, the court shall declare of its own motion that it has no jurisdiction unless its jurisdiction is derived from the provisions of this Schedule.

(2)   The court shall stay the proceedings so long as it is not shown that the defendant has been able to receive the document instituting the proceedings or an equivalent document in sufficient time to enable him to arrange for his defence, or that all necessary steps have been taken to this end.

Provisional, including protective, measures

16.   Application may be made to the courts of a part of the United Kingdom for such provisional, including protective, measures as may be available under the law of that part, even if, under this Schedule, the courts of another part of the United Kingdom have jurisdiction as to the substance of the matter.]

SCHEDULE 6
ENFORCEMENT OF UK JUDGMENTS (MONEY PROVISIONS)

Preliminary

1.   In this Schedule—
'judgment' means any judgment to which section 18 applies and references to the giving of a judgment shall be construed accordingly;
'money provision' means a provision for the payment of one or more sums of money;
'prescribed' means prescribed by rules of court.

Certificates in respect of judgments

2.—(1)   Any interested party who wishes to secure the enforcement in another part of the United Kingdom of any money provisions contained in a judgment may apply for a certificate under this Schedule.

(2)   The application shall be made in the prescribed manner to the proper officer of the original court, that is to say—
(a)   in relation to a judgment within paragraph (a) of the definition of 'judg-

ment' in section 18(2), the court by which the judgment or order was given or made;

    (b)   in relation to a judgment within paragraph (b) of that definition, the court in which the judgment or order is entered;

    (c)   in relation to a judgment within paragraph (c) of that definition, the court in whose books the document is registered;

    (d)   in relation to a judgment within paragraph (d) of the definition, the tribunal by which the award or order was made;

    (e)   in relation to a judgment within paragraph (e) of that definition, the court which gave the judgment or made the order by virtue of which the award has become enforceable as mentioned in that paragraph.

3.   A certificate shall not be issued under this Schedule in respect of a judgment unless under the law of the part of the United Kingdom in which the judgement was given—

    (a)   either—

        (i)   the time for bringing an appeal against the judgment has expired, no such appeal having been brought within that time; or

        (ii)   such an appeal having been brought within that time, that appeal has been finally disposed of; and

    (b)   enforcement of the judgment is not for the time being stayed or suspended, and the time available for its enforcement has not expired.

4.—(1)   Subject to paragraph 3, on an application under paragraph 2 the proper officer shall issue to the applicant a certificate in the prescribed form—

    (a)   stating the sum or aggregate of the sums (including any costs or expenses) payable under the money provisions contained in the judgment, the rate of interest, if any, payable thereon and the date or time from which any such interest began to accrue;

    (b)   stating that the conditions specified in paragraph 3(a) and (b) are satisfied in relation to the judgment; and

    (c)   containing such other particulars as may be prescribed.

(2)   More than one certificate may be issued under this Schedule (simultaneously or at different times) in respect of the same judgment.

Registration of certificates

5.—(1)   Where a certificate has been issued under this Schedule in any part of the United Kingdom, any interested party may, within six months from the date of its issue, apply in the prescribed manner to the proper officer of the superior court in any other part of the United Kingdom for the certificate to be registered in that court.

(2)   In this paragraph 'superior court' means, in relation to England and Wales or Northern Ireland, the High Court and, in relation to Scotland, the Court of Session.

(3)   Where an application is duly made under this paragraph to the proper officer of a superior court, he shall register the certificate in that court in the prescribed manner.

General effect of registration

6.—(1)   A certificate registered under this Schedule shall, for the purposes of its enforcement, be of the same force and effect, the registering court shall have in relation to its enforcement the same powers, and proceedings for or with respect to its enforcement may be taken, as if the certificate had been a judgment originally given in the registering court and had (where relevant) been entered.

(2)   Sub-paragraph (1) is subject to the following provisions of this Schedule and to any provision made by rules of court as to the manner in which and the conditions subject to which a certificate registered under this Schedule may be enforced.

Costs or expenses

7.   Where a certificate is registered under this Schedule, the reasonable costs or expenses of and incidental to the obtaining of the certificate and its registration shall be recoverable as if they were costs or expenses stated in the certificate to be payable under a money provision contained in the original judgment.

Interest

8.—(1)   Subject to any provision made under sub-paragraph (2), the debt resulting, apart from paragraph 7, from the registration of the certificate shall carry interest at the rate, if any, stated in the certificate from the date or time so stated.

(2)   Provision may be made by rules of court as to the manner in which and the periods by reference to which any interest payable by virtue of sub-paragraph (1) is to be calculated and paid, including provision for such interest to cease to accrue as from a prescribed date.

(3)   All such sums as are recoverable by virtue of paragraph 7 carry interest as if they were the subject of an order for costs or expenses made by the registering court on the date of registration of the certificate.

(4)   Except as provided by this paragraph sums payable by virtue of the registration of a certificate under this Schedule shall not carry interest.

Stay or sisting of enforcement in certain cases

9.   Where a certificate in respect of a judgment has been registered under this Schedule, the registering court may, if it is satisfied that any person against whom it is sought to enforce the certificate is entitled and intends to apply under the law of the part of the United Kingdom in which the judgment was given for any remedy which would result in the setting aside or quashing of the judgment, stay (or, in Scotland, sist) proceedings for the enforcement of the certificate, on such terms as it thinks fit, for such period as appears to the court to be reasonably sufficient to enable the application to be disposed of.

Cases in which registration of a certificate must or may be set aside

10.   Where a certificate has been registered under this Schedule, the registering court—

(a)   shall set aside the registration if, on an application made by any interested party, it is satisfied that the registration was contrary to the provisions of this Schedule;

(b)   may set aside the registration if, on an application so made, it is satisfied that the matter in dispute in the proceedings in which the judgment in question was given had previously been the subject of a judgment by another court or tribunal having jurisdiction in the matter.

SCHEDULE 7
ENFORCEMENT OF UK JUDGMENTS (NON-MONEY PROVISIONS)

Preliminary

1.   In this Schedule—

'judgment' means any judgment to which section 18 applies and references to the giving of a judgment shall be construed accordingly;

'non-money provision' means a provision for any relief or remedy not requiring payment of a sum of money;

'prescribed' means prescribed by rules of court.

Certified copy of judgments

2.—(1)   Any interested party who wishes to secure the enforcement in another part of the United Kingdom of any non-money provisions contained in a judgment may apply for a certified copy of the judgment.

(2)   The application shall be made in the prescribed manner to the proper officer of the original court, that is to say—

(a)   in relation to a judgment within paragraph (a) of the definition of 'judgment' in section 18(2), the court by which the judgment or order was given or made;

(b)   in relation to a judgment within paragraph (b) of that definition, the court in which the judgment or order is entered;

(c)   in relation to a judgment within paragraph (c) of that definition, the court in whose books the document is registered;

(d)   in relation to a judgment within paragraph (d) of that definition, the tribunal by which the award for order was made;

(e)   in relation to a judgment within paragraph (e) of that definition, the court which gave the judgment or made the order by virtue of which the award has become enforceable as mentioned in that paragraph.

3.   A certified copy of a judgment shall not be issued under this Schedule unless under the law of the part of the United Kingdom in which the judgment was given—

(a)   either—

(i)   the time for bringing an appeal against the judgment has expired, no such appeal having been brought within that time; or

(ii)   such an appeal having been brought within that time, that appeal has been finally disposed of; and

(b)   enforcement of the judgment is not for the time being stayed or suspended, and the time available for its enforcement has not expired.

4.—(1)   Subject to paragraph 3, on an application under paragraph 2 the proper officer shall issue to the applicant—

(a)   a certified copy of the judgment (including any money provisions or excepted provisions which it may contain); and

(b)   a certificate stating that the conditions specified in paragraph 3(a) and (b) are satisfied in relation to the judgment.

(2)   In sub-paragraph (1)(a) 'excepted provision' means any provision of a judgment which is excepted from the application of section 18 by subsection (5) of that section.

(3)   There may be issued under this Schedule (simultaneously or at different times)—

(a)   more than one certified copy of the same judgment; and

(b)   more than one certificate in respect of the same judgment.

Registration of judgments

5.—(1)   Where a certified copy of a judgment has been issued under this Schedule in any part of the United Kingdom, any interested party may apply in the pre-scribed manner to the superior court in any other part of the United Kingdom for the judgment to be registered in that court.

(2)   In this paragraph 'superior court' means, in relation to England and Wales or Northern Ireland, the High Court and, in relation to Scotland, the Court of Session.

(3)   An application under this paragraph for the registration of a judgment must be accompanied by—

(a)   a certified copy of the judgment issued under this Schedule; and

(b)   a certificate issued under paragraph 4(1)(b) in respect of the judgment not more than six months before the date of the application.

(4)   Subject to sub-paragraph (5), where an application under this paragraph is duly made to a superior court, the court shall order the whole of the judgment as set out in the certified copy to be registered in that court in the prescribed manner.

(5)   A judgment shall not be registered under this Schedule by the superior court in any part of the United Kingdom if compliance with the non-money pro-visions contained in the judgment would involve a breach of the law of that part of the United Kingdom.

General effect of registration

6.—(1)   The non-money provisions contained in a judgment registered under this Schedule shall, for the purposes of their enforcement, be of the same force and effect, the registering court shall have in relation to their enforcement the same powers, and proceedings for or with respect to their enforcement may be taken, as if the judgment containing them had been originally given in the registering court and had (where relevant) been entered.

(2)   Sub-paragraph (1) is subject to the following provisions of this Schedule and to any provision made by rules of court as to the manner in which and con-ditions subject to which the non-money provisions contained in a judgment regis-tered under this Schedule may be enforced.

Costs of expenses

7.—(1)   Where a judgment is registered under this Schedule, the reasonable costs or expenses of and incidental to—

(a)   the obtaining of the certified copy of the judgment and of the necessary certificate under paragraph 4(1)(b) in respect of it; and

(b)   the registration of the judgment,

shall be recoverable as if on the date of registration there had also been registered in the registering court a certificate under Schedule 6 in respect of the judgment and as if those costs or expenses were costs or expenses stated in that certificate to be payable under a money provision contained in the judgment.

(2)   All such sums as are recoverable by virtue of sub-paragraph (1) shall carry interest as if they were the subject of an order for costs or expenses made by the registering court on the date of registration of the judgment.

Stay or sisting of enforcement in certain cases

8.   Where a judgment has been registered under this Schedule, the registering court may, if it is satisfied that any person against whom it is sought to enforce the judgment is entitled and intends to apply under the law of the part of the United Kingdom in which the judgment was given for any remedy which would result in

the setting aside or quashing of the judgment, stay (or, in Scotland, sist) proceedings for the enforcement of the judgment, on such terms as it thinks fit, for such period as appears to the court to be reasonably sufficient to enable the application to be disposed of.

Cases in which registered judgment may be set aside

9.   Where a judgment has been registered under this Schedule, the registering court—
(a)   shall set aside the registration if, on an application made by any interested party, it is satisfied that the registration was contrary to the provisions of this Schedule;
(b)   may set aside the registration if, on an application so made, it is satisfied that the matter in dispute in the proceedings in which the judgment was given had previously been the subject of a judgment by another court or tribunal having jurisdiction in the matter.

[SCHEDULE 8
RULES AS TO JURISDICTION IN SCOTLAND

General

1.   Subject to the following rules, persons shall be sued in the courts for the place where they are domiciled.

Special jurisdiction

2.   Subject to rules 3 (jurisdiction over consumer contracts), 4 (jurisdiction over individual contracts of employment), 5 (exclusive jurisdiction) and 6 (prorogation), a person may also be sued—
(a)   where he has no fixed residence, in a court within whose jurisdiction he is personally cited;
(b)   in matters relating to a contract, in the courts for the place of performance of the obligation in question;
(c)   in matters relating to delict or quasi-delict, in the courts for the place where the harmful event occurred or may occur;
(d)   as regards a civil claim for damages or restitution which is based on an act giving rise to criminal proceedings, in the court seised of those proceedings to the extent that the court has jurisdiction to entertain civil proceedings;
[...]
(f)   as regards a dispute arising out of the operations of a branch, agency or other establishment, in the courts for the place in which the branch, agency or other establishment is situated;
(g)   in his capacity as settlor, trustee or beneficiary of a trust domiciled in Scotland created by the operation of a statute, or by a written instrument, or created orally and evidenced in writing, in the Court of Session, or the appropriate sheriff court within the meaning of section 24A of the Trusts (Scotland) Act 1921;
[(ga) in the person's capacity as an executor (where confirmation has been obtained in Scotland)—
(i)   in the Court of Session, or
(ii)   before a sheriff of the sheriffdom in which confirmation was obtained.]
(h)   where he is not domiciled in the United Kingdom, in the courts for any place where—
(i)   any movable property belonging to him has been arrested; or

(ii) any immovable property in which he has any beneficial interest is situated;

(i)   in proceedings which are brought to assert, declare or determine proprietary or possessory rights, or rights of security, in or over movable property, or to obtain authority to dispose of movable property, in the courts for the place where the property is situated;

(j)   in proceedings for interdict, in the courts for the place where it is alleged that the wrong is likely to be committed;

(k)   in proceedings concerning a debt secured over immovable property, in the courts for the place where the property is situated;

(l)   in proceedings which have as their object a decision of an organ of a company or other legal person or of an association of natural or legal persons, in the courts for the place where that company, legal person or association has its seat;

(m)   in proceedings concerning an arbitration which is conducted in Scotland or in which the procedure is governed by Scots law, in the Court of Session;

(n)   in proceedings principally concerned with the registration in the United Kingdom or the validity in the United Kingdom of patents, trade marks, designs or other similar rights required to be deposited or registered, in the Court of Session;

(o) (i)   where he is one of a number of defenders, in the courts for the place where any one of them is domiciled, provided the claims are so closely connected that it is expedient to hear and determine them together to avoid the risk of irreconcilable judgments resulting from separate proceedings;

(ii) as a third party in an action on a warranty or guarantee or in any other third party proceedings, in the court seised of the original proceedings, unless these were instituted solely with the object of removing him from the jurisdiction of the court which would be competent in his case;

(iii) on a counterclaim arising from the same contract or facts on which the original claim was based, in the court in which the original claim is pending;

(p)   in matters relating to a contract, if the action may be combined with an action against the same defender in matters relating to rights in rem in immovable property, in the courts for the place where the property is situated;

(q)   as regards a claim for limitation of liability arising from the use or operation of a ship, in the court having jurisdiction in the action relating to such liability.

Jurisdiction over consumer contracts

3.—(1)   In matters relating to a contract concluded by a person, the consumer, for a purpose which can be regarded as being outside his trade or profession, subject to rule 5, jurisdiction shall be determined by this rule if—

(a)   it is a contract for the sale of goods on instalment credit terms; or

(b)   it is a contract for a loan repayable by instalments, or for any other form of credit, made to finance the sale of goods; or

(c)   in all other cases, the contract has been concluded with a person who pursues commercial or professional activities in Scotland or, by any means, directs such activities to Scotland or to several places including Scotland, and the contract falls within the scope of such activities.

(2)   This rule shall not apply to a contract of transport other than a contract which, for an inclusive price, provides for a combination of travel and accommodation.

(3)   A consumer may bring proceedings against the other party to a contract only in—

(a)   the courts for the place in which that party is domiciled;

(b)   the courts for the place in which he is himself domiciled; or

(c)   any court having jurisdiction by virtue of rule 2(f) or (i).

(4)   Proceedings may be brought against a consumer by the other party to the contract only in the courts for the place where the consumer is domiciled or any court having jurisdiction under rule 2(i).

(5)   The provisions of this rule shall not affect the right to bring a counterclaim in the court in which, in accordance with this rule, the original claim is pending.

(6)   The provisions of this rule may be departed from only by an agreement—

(a)   which is entered into after the dispute has arisen; or

(b)   which allows the consumer to bring proceedings in courts other than those indicated in this rule; or

(c)   which is entered into by the consumer and the other party to the contract, both of whom are at the time of conclusion of the contract domiciled or habitually resident in the same Regulation State, and which confers jurisdiction on the courts of that Regulation State, provided that such an agreement is not contrary to the law of that Regulation State.

Jurisdiction over individual contracts of employment

4.—(1)   In matters relating to individual contracts of employment, jurisdiction shall be determined by this rule, without prejudice to rule 2(f).

(2)   An employer may be sued—

(a)   in the courts for the place where he is domiciled; or

(b)   in the courts for the place where the employee habitually carries out his work or in the courts for the last place where he did so; or

(c)   if the employee does not or did not habitually carry out his work in any one place, in the courts for the place where the business which engaged the employee is or was situated.

(3)   An employer may bring proceedings only in the courts for the place in which the employee is domiciled.

(4)   The provisions of this rule shall not affect the right to bring a counter-claim in the court in which, in accordance with this rule, the original claim is pending.

(5)   The provisions of this rule may be departed from only by an agreement on jurisdiction—

(a)   which is entered into after the dispute has arisen; or

(b)   which allows the employee to bring proceedings in courts other than those indicated in this rule.

Exclusive jurisdiction

5.—(1)   Notwithstanding anything contained in any of rules 1 to 4 above or 6 to 9 below but subject to paragraph (3) below, the following courts shall have exclusive jurisdiction:—

(a)   in proceedings which have as their object rights in rem in, or tenancies of, immovable property, the courts for the place where the property is situated;

(b)   in proceedings which have as their object the validity of the constitution, the nullity or the dissolution of companies or other legal persons or associations of natural or legal persons, the courts for the place where the company, legal person or association has its seat;

(c)   in proceedings which have as their object the validity of entries in public registers, the courts for the place where the register is kept;

(d)   in proceedings concerned with the enforcement of judgments, the courts for the place where the judgment has been or is to be enforced.

(2)   No court shall exercise jurisdiction in a case where immovable property, the seat of a body mentioned in paragraph (1)(b) above, a public register or the place where a judgment has been or is to be enforced is situated outside Scotland and

where paragraph (1) would apply if the property, seat, register or, as the case may be, place of enforcement were situated in Scotland.

(3)   In proceedings which have as their object tenancies of immovable property concluded for temporary private use for a maximum period of six consecutive months, the courts for the place in which the defender is domiciled shall also have jurisdiction, provided that the tenant is a natural person and that the landlord and tenant are domiciled in Scotland.

Prorogation of jurisdiction

6.—(1)   If the parties have agreed that a court is to have jurisdiction to settle any disputes which have arisen or which may arise in connection with a particular legal relationship, that court shall have jurisdiction.

(2)   Such an agreement conferring jurisdiction shall be either—

(a)   in writing or evidenced in writing; or

(b)   in a form which accords with practices which the parties have established between themselves; or

(c)   in international trade or commerce, in a form which accords with a usage of which the parties are or ought to have been aware and which in such trade or commerce is widely known to, and regularly observed by, parties to contracts of the type involved in the particular trade or commerce concerned.

(3)   Any communication by electronic means which provides a durable record of the agreement shall be equivalent to 'writing'.

(4)   The court on which a trust instrument has conferred jurisdiction shall have exclusive jurisdiction in any proceedings brought against a settlor, trustee or beneficiary, if relations between these persons or their rights or obligations under the trust are involved.

(5)   Where an agreement or a trust instrument confers jurisdiction on the courts of the United Kingdom or of Scotland, proceedings to which paragraph (1) or, as the case may be, (4) above applies may be brought in any court in Scotland.

(6)   Agreements or provisions of a trust instrument conferring jurisdiction shall have no legal force if the courts whose jurisdiction they purport to exclude have exclusive jurisdiction by virtue of rule 5 or where rule 5(2) applies.

7.—(1)   Apart from jurisdiction derived from other provisions of this Schedule, a court before whom a defender enters an appearance shall have jurisdiction.

(2)   This rule shall not apply where appearance was entered to contest jurisdiction, or where another court has exclusive jurisdiction by virtue of rule 5 or where rule 5(2) applies.

Examination as to jurisdiction and admissibility

8.   Where a court is seised of a claim which is principally concerned with a matter over which another court has exclusive jurisdiction by virtue of rule 5, or where it is precluded from exercising jurisdiction by rule 5(2), it shall declare of its own motion that it has no jurisdiction.

9.   Where in any case a court has no jurisdiction which is compatible with this Schedule, and the defender does not enter an appearance, the court shall declare of its own motion that it has no jurisdiction.]

MATRIMONIAL AND FAMILY PROCEEDINGS ACT 1984
(1984 c 42)

PART IV
FINANCIAL PROVISION IN SCOTLAND AFTER OVERSEAS DIVORCE ETC

28 Circumstances in which a Scottish court may entertain application for financial provision

(1) Where parties to a marriage have been divorced in an overseas country, then, subject to subsection (4) below, if the jurisdictional requirements and the conditions set out in subsections (2) and (3) below respectively are satisfied, the court may entertain an application by one of the parties for an order for financial provision.

(2) The jurisdictional requirements mentioned in subsection (1) above are that—

(a) the applicant was domiciled or habitually resident in Scotland on the date when the application was made; and

(b) the other party to the marriage—

(i) was domiciled or habitually resident in Scotland on the date when the application was made; or

(ii) was domiciled or habitually resident in Scotland when the parties last lived together as husband and wife; or

(iii) on the date when the application was made, was an owner or tenant of, or had a beneficial interest in, property in Scotland which had at some time been a matrimonial home of the parties; and

(c) where the court is the sheriff court, either—

(i) one of the parties was, on the date when the application was made, habitually resident in the sheriffdom; or

(ii) paragraph (b)(iii) above is satisfied in respect of property wholly or partially within the sheriffdom.

(3) The conditions mentioned in subsection (1) above are that—

(a) the divorce falls to be recognised in Scotland;

(b) the other party to the marriage initiated the proceedings for divorce;

(c) the application was made within five years after the date when the divorce took effect;

(d) a court in Scotland would have had jurisdiction to entertain an action for divorce between the parties if such an action had been brought in Scotland immediately before the foreign divorce took effect;

(e) the marriage had a substantial connection with Scotland; and

(f) both parties are living at the time of the application.

[(3A) If an application or part of an application relates to a matter where jurisdiction falls to be determined by reference to the jurisdictional requirements of the Maintenance Regulation and Schedule 6 to the Civil Jurisdiction and Judgments (Maintenance) Regulations 2011—

(a) those requirements are to be satisfied in respect of the application, or that part of it, instead of the requirements set out in subsection (2), and

(b) the condition mentioned in subsection (3)(e) does not apply.]

(4) Where the jurisdiction of the court to entertain proceedings under this Part of this Act would fall to be determined by reference to the jurisdictional requirements imposed by virtue of Part I of the Civil Jurisdiction and Judgments Act 1982 (implementation of certain European conventions) then—

(a) satisfaction of the requirements of subsection (2) above shall not obviate the need to satisfy the requirements imposed by virtue of Part I of that Act; and

(b) satisfaction of the requirements imposed by virtue of Part I of that Act shall obviate the need to satisfy the requirements of subsection (2) above;

and the court shall entertain or not entertain the proceedings accordingly.

[(5) 'The Maintenance Regulation' means Council Regulation (EC) No 4/2009 including as applied in relation to Denmark by virtue of the Agreement made on 19th October 2005 between the European Community and the Kingdom of Denmark.]

29 Disposal of application in Scotland

(1) Subject to subsections (2) to (5) below, Scots law shall apply, with any necessary modifications, in relation to an application under section 28 above as it would apply if the application were being made in an action for divorce in Scotland.

(2) In disposing of an application entertained by it under the said section 28, the court shall exercise its powers so as to place the parties, in so far as it is reasonable and practicable to do so, in the financial position in which they would have been if the application had been disposed of, in an action for divorce in Scotland, on the date on which the foreign divorce took effect.

(3) In determining what is reasonable and practicable for the purposes of subsection (2) above, the court shall have regard in particular to—

(a) the parties' resources, present and foreseeable at the date of disposal of the application;

(b) any order made by a foreign court in or in connection with the divorce proceedings for the making of financial provision in whatever form, or the transfer of property, by one of the parties to the other; and

(c) subsection (5) below.

(4) Except where subsection (5) below applies, the court may make an order for an interim award of a periodical allowance where—

(a) it appears from the applicant's averments that in the disposal of the application an order for financial provision is likely to be made; and

(b) the court considers that such an interim award is necessary to avoid hardship to the applicant.

(5) Where but for section 28(2)(b)(iii) above the court would not have jurisdiction to entertain the application, the court may make an order—

(a) relating to the former matrimonial home or its furniture and plenishings; or

(b) that the other party to the marriage shall pay to the applicant a capital sum not exceeding the value of that other party's interest in the former matrimonial home and its furniture and plenishings,

but shall not be entitled to make any other order for financial provision.

[29A Application of Part IV to annulled marriages

This Part of this Act shall apply to an annulment, of whatever nature, of a purported marriage, as it applies to a divorce and references to marriage and divorce shall be construed accordingly.]

CHILD ABDUCTION AND CUSTODY ACT 1985
(1985 c 60)

PART I
INTERNATIONAL CHILD ABDUCTION

1 The Hague Convention

(1) In this Part of this Act 'the Convention' means the Convention on the Civil Aspects of International Child Abduction which was signed at The Hague on 25th October 1980.

(2) Subject to the provisions of this Part of this Act, the provisions of that Convention set out in Schedule 1 to this Act shall have the force of law in the United Kingdom.

[(3) But—

  (a) those provisions of the Convention,

  (b) this Part of this Act, and

  (c) rules of court under section 10 of this Act,

are subject to Article 60 of the Council Regulation (by virtue of which the Regulation takes precedence over the Hague Convention, in so far as it concerns matters governed by the Regulation).

(4) 'The Council Regulation' means Council Regulation (EC) No 2201/2003 of 27th November 2003 concerning jurisdiction and the recognition and enforcement of judgments in matrimonial matters and matters of parental responsibility.]

2 Contracting States

(1) For the purposes of the Convention as it has effect under this Part of this Act the Contracting States other than the United Kingdom shall be those for the time being specified by an Order in Council under this section.

(2) An Order in Council under this section shall specify the date of the coming into force of the Convention as between the United Kingdom and any State specified in the Order; and, except where the Order otherwise provides, the Convention shall apply as between the United Kingdom and that State only in relation to wrongful removals or retentions occurring on or after that date.

(3) Where the Convention applies, or applies only, to a particular territory or particular territories specified in a declaration made by a Contracting State under Article 39 or 40 of the Convention references to that State in subsections (1) and (2) above shall be construed as references to that territory or those territories.

3 Central Authorities

(1) Subject to subsection (2) below, the functions under the Convention of a Central Authority shall be discharged—

  (a) in England and Wales [...] by the Lord Chancellor; and

  (b) in Scotland by the Secretary of State [; and

  (c) in Northern Ireland by the Department of Justice in Northern Ireland.]

(2) Any application made under the Convention by or on behalf of a person outside the United Kingdom may be addressed to the Lord Chancellor as the Central Authority in the United Kingdom.

[(3) Where any such application relates to a function to be discharged under subsection (1) above by an authority ('the responsible authority') other than the authority to which the application is addressed, the authority to which the application is addressed shall transmit it to the responsible authority.]

4 Judicial authorities

The courts having jurisdiction to entertain applications under the Convention shall be—

  (a) in England and Wales or in Northern Ireland the High Court; and

  (b) in Scotland the Court of Session.

5 Interim powers

Where an application has been made to a court in the United Kingdom under the Convention, the court may, at any time before the application is determined, give such interim directions as it thinks fit for the purpose of securing the welfare of the child concerned or of preventing changes in the circumstances relevant to the determination of the application.

6 Reports

Where the Lord Chancellor [, the Department of Justice in Northern Ireland] or the Secretary of State is requested to provide information relating to a child under Article 7(d) of the Convention he may—

(a)   request a local authority or [an officer of the Service] to make a report to him in writing with respect to any matter which appears to him to be relevant;

(b)   request the Department of Health and Social Services for Northern Ireland to arrange for a suitably qualified person to make such a report to him;

(c)   request any court to which a written report relating to the child has been made to send him a copy of the report;

and such a request shall be duly complied with.

7 Proof of documents and evidence

(1)   For the purposes of Article 14 of the Convention a decision or determination of a judicial or administrative authority outside the United Kingdom may be proved by a duly authenticated copy of the decision or determination; and any document purporting to be such a copy shall be deemed to be a true copy unless the contrary is shown.

(2)   For the purposes of subsection (1) above a copy is duly authenticated if it bears the seal, or is signed by a judge or officer, of the authority in question.

(3)   For the purposes of Articles 14 and 30 of the Convention any such document as is mentioned in Article 8 of the Convention, or a certified copy of any such document, shall be sufficient evidence of anything stated in it.

8 Declarations by United Kingdom courts

The High Court or Court of Session may, on an application made for the purposes of Article 15 of the Convention by any person appearing to the court to have an interest in the matter, make a declaration or declarator that the removal of any child from, or his retention outside, the United Kingdom was wrongful within the meaning of Article 3 of the Convention.

9 Suspension of court's powers in cases of wrongful removal

The reference in Article 16 of the Convention to deciding on the merits of rights of custody shall be construed as a reference to—

(a)   making, varying or revoking a custody order, or [a supervision order under section 31 of the Children Act 1989 or Article 50 of the Children Order (Northern Ireland) 1995 (not being a custody order)];

[(aa)   enforcing under section 29 of the Family Law Act 1986 a custody order within the meaning of Chapter V of Part I of that Act;]

(b)   registering or enforcing a decision under Part II of this Act;

[(ba)   registering or enforcing a decision under the Convention on Jurisdiction, Applicable Law, Recognition, Enforcement and Co-Operation in respect of Parental Responsibility and Measures for the Protection of Children that was signed at The Hague on 19 October 1996 ('the 1996 Convention'), except where provisions of the 1996 Convention are invoked in accordance with Article 50 of the 1996 Convention;]

[...]

[(d)   making, varying, amending or revoking a permanence order under section 80 of the Adoption and Children (Scotland) Act 2007 (including a deemed permanence order having effect by virtue of article 13(1) or 14(2) of the Adop-

tion and Children (Scotland) Act 2007 (Commencement No 4, Transitional and Savings Provisions) Order 2009 (SSI 2009/267))]
  [...]

PART II
RECOGNITION AND ENFORCEMENT OF CUSTODY DECISIONS

...

[24A   Power to order disclosure of child's whereabouts
  (1)   Where—
    (a)   in proceedings for the return of a child under Part I of this Act; or
    (b)   on an application for the recognition, registration or enforcement of a decision in respect of a child under Part II of this Act,
there is not available to the court adequate information as to where the child is, the court may order any person who it has reason to believe may have relevant information to disclose it to the court.
  (2)   A person shall not be excused from complying with an order under subsection (1) above by reason that to do so may incriminate him or his spouse [or civil partner] of an offence; but a statement or admission made in compliance with such an order shall not be admissible in evidence against either of them in proceedings for any offence other than perjury.]

PART III
SUPPLEMENTARY

25   Termination of existing custody orders, etc
  (1)   Where—
    (a)   an order is made for the return of a child under Part I of this Act; or
    (b)   a decision with respect to a child (other than a decision mentioned in subsection (2) below) is registered under section 16 of this Act,
any custody order relating to him shall cease to have effect.
  (2)   The decision referred to in subsection (1)(b) above is a decision which is only a decision relating to custody within the meaning of section 16 of this Act by virtue of being a decision relating to rights of access.
  [...]

Section 1(2)   SCHEDULE 1
        CONVENTION ON THE CIVIL ASPECTS OF INTERNATIONAL CHILD
                                ABDUCTION

CHAPTER 1 – SCOPE OF THE CONVENTION

Article 3
The removal or the retention of a child is to be considered wrongful where—
    (a)   it is in breach of rights of custody attributed to a person, an institution or any other body, either jointly or alone, under the law of the State in which the child was habitually resident immediately before the removal or retention; and
    (b)   at the time of removal or retention those rights were actually exercised, either jointly or alone, or would have been so exercised but for the removal or retention.
The rights of custody mentioned in sub-paragraph (a) above may arise in particular by operation of law or by reason of a judicial or administrative decision, or by reason of an agreement having legal effect under the law of that State.

Article 4

The Convention shall apply to any child who was habitually resident in a Contracting State immediately before any breach of custody or access rights. The Convention shall cease to apply when the child attains the age of sixteen years.

Article 5

For the purposes of this Convention—

(a) 'rights of custody' shall include rights relating to the care of the person of the child and, in particular, the right to determine the child's place of residence;

(b) 'rights of access' shall include the right to take a child for a limited period of time to a place other than the child's habitual residence.

CHAPTER II – CENTRAL AUTHORITIES

Article 7

Central Authorities shall co-operate with each other and promote co-operation amongst the competent authorities in their respective States to secure the prompt return of children and to achieve the other objects of this Convention.

In particular, either directly or through any intermediary, they shall take all appropriate measures—

(a) to discover the whereabouts of a child who has been wrongfully removed or retained;

(b) to prevent further harm to the child or prejudice to interested parties by taking or causing to be taken provisional measures;

(c) to secure the voluntary return of the child or to bring about an amicable resolution of the issues;

(d) to exchange, where desirable, information relating to the social background of the child;

(e) to provide information of a general character as to the law of their State in connection with the application of the Convention;

(f) to initiate or facilitate the institution of judicial or administrative proceedings with a view to obtaining the return of the child and, in a proper case, to make arrangements for organizing or securing the effective exercise of rights of access;

(g) where the circumstances so require, to provide or facilitate the provision of legal aid and advice, including the participation of legal counsel and advisers;

(h) to provide such administrative arrangements as may be necessary and appropriate to secure the safe return of the child;

(i) to keep each other informed with respect to the operation of this Convention and, as far as possible, to eliminate any obstacles to its application.

CHAPTER III – RETURN OF CHILDREN

Article 8

Any person, institution or other body claiming that a child has been removed or retained in breach of custody rights may apply either to the Central Authority of the child's habitual residence or to the Central Authority of any other Contracting State for assistance in securing the return of the child.

The application shall contain—

(a) information concerning the identity of the applicant, of the child and of the person alleged to have removed or retained the child;

(b) where available, the date of birth of the child;

(c) the grounds on which the applicant's claim for return of the child is based;

(d) all available information relating to the whereabouts of the child and the identity of the person with whom the child is presumed to be.

The application may be accompanied or supplemented by—

(e)   an authenticated copy of any relevant decision or agreement;

(f)   a certificate or an affidavit emanating from a Central Authority, or other competent authority of the State of the child's habitual residence, or from a qualified person, concerning the relevant law of that State;

(g)   any other relevant document.

Article 9

If the Central Authority which receives an application referred to in Article 8 has reason to believe that the child is in another Contracting State, it shall directly and without delay transmit the application to the Central Authority of that Contracting State and inform the requesting Central Authority, or the applicant, as the case may be.

Article 10

The Central Authority of the State where the child is shall take or cause to be taken all appropriate measures in order to obtain the voluntary return of the child.

Article 11

The judicial or administrative authorities of Contracting States shall act expeditiously in proceedings for the return of children.

If the judicial or administrative authority concerned has not reached a decision within six weeks from the date of commencement of the proceedings, the applicant or the Central Authority of the requested State, on its own initiative or if asked by the Central Authority of the requesting State, shall have the right to request a statement of the reasons for the delay. If a reply is received by the Central Authority of the requested State, that Authority shall transmit the reply to the Central Authority of the requesting State, or to the applicant, as the case may be.

Article 12

Where a child has been wrongfully removed or retained in terms of Article 3 and, at the date of the commencement of the proceedings before the judicial or administrative authority of the Contracting State where the child is, a period of less than one year has elapsed from the date of the wrongful removal or retention, the authority concerned shall order the return of the child forthwith.

The judicial or administrative authority, even where the proceedings have been commenced after the expiration of the period of one year referred to in the preceding paragraph, shall also order the return of the child, unless it is demonstrated that the child is now settled in its new environment.

Where the judicial or administrative authority in the requested state has reason to believe that the child has been taken to another State, it may stay the proceedings or dismiss the application for the return of the child.

Article 13

Notwithstanding the provisions of the preceding Article, the judicial or administrative authority of the requested State is not bound to order the return of the child if the person, institution or other body which opposes its return establishes that—

(a)   the person, institution or other body having the care of the person of the child was not actually exercising the custody rights at the time of removal or retention, or had consented to or subsequently acquiesced in the removal or retention; or

(b)   there is a grave risk that his or her return would expose the child to physical or psychological harm or otherwise place the child in an intolerable situation.

The judicial or administrative authority may also refuse to order the return of the child if it finds that the child objects to being returned and has attained an age and degree of maturity at which it is appropriate to take account of its views.

In considering the circumstances referred to in this Article, the judicial and administrative authorities shall take into account the information relating to the social background of the child provided by the Central Authority or other competent authority of the child's habitual residence.

Article 14
In ascertaining whether there has been a wrongful removal or retention within the meaning of Article 3, the judicial or administrative authorities of the requested State may take notice directly of the law of, and of judicial or administrative decisions, formally recognised or not in the State of the habitual residence of the child, without recourse to the specific procedures for the proof of that law or for the recognition of foreign decisions which would otherwise be applicable.

Article 15
The judicial or administrative authorities of a Contracting State may, prior to the making of an order for the return of the child, request that the applicant obtain from the authorities of the State of the habitual residence of the child a decision or other determination that the removal or retention was wrongful within the meaning of Article 3 of the Convention, where such a decision or determination may be obtained in that State. The Central Authorities of the Contracting States shall so far as practicable assist applicants to obtain such a decision or determination.

Article 16
After receiving notice of a wrongful removal or retention of a child in the sense of Article 3, the judicial or administrative authorities of the Contracting State to which the child has been removed or in which it has been retained shall not decide on the merits of rights of custody until it has been determined that the child is not to be returned under this Convention or unless an application under this Convention is not lodged within a reasonable time following receipt of the notice.

Article 17
The sole fact that a decision relating to custody has been given in or is entitled to recognition in the requested State shall not be a ground for refusing to return a child under this Convention, but the judicial or administrative authorities of the requested State may take account of the reasons for that decision in applying this Convention.

Article 18
The provisions of this Chapter do not limit the power of a judicial or administrative authority to order the return of the child at any time.

Article 19
A decision under this Convention concerning the return of the child shall not be taken to be a determination on the merits of any custody issue.

CHAPTER IV – RIGHTS OF ACCESS

Article 21
An application to make arrangements for organising or securing the effective exercise of rights of access may be presented to the Central Authorities of the Contracting States in the same way as an application for the return of a child.

The Central Authorities are bound by the obligations of co-operation which are set forth in Article 7 to promote the peaceful enjoyment of access rights and the fulfilment of any conditions to which the exercise of those rights may be subject. The Central Authorities shall take steps to remove, as far as possible, all obstacles to the exercise of such rights. The Central Authorities, either directly or through intermediaries, may initiate or assist in the institution of proceedings with a view to organising or protecting these rights and securing respect for the conditions to which the exercise of these rights may be subject.

CHAPTER V – GENERAL PROVISIONS

Article 22

No security, bond or deposit, however described, shall be required to guarantee the payment of costs and expenses in the judicial or administrative proceedings falling within the scope of this Convention.

Article 24

Any application, communication or other document sent to the Central Authority of the requested State shall be in the original language, and shall be accompanied by a translation into the official language or one of the official languages of the requested State or, where that is not feasible, a translation into French or English.

Article 26

Each Central Authority shall bear its own costs in applying this Convention.

Central Authorities and other public services of Contracting States shall not impose any charges in relation to applications submitted under this Convention. In particular, they may not require any payment from the applicant towards the costs and expenses of the proceedings or, where applicable, those arising from the participation of legal counsel or advisers. However, they may require the payment of the expenses incurred or to be incurred in implementing the return of the child.

However, a Contracting State may, by making a reservation in accordance with Article 42, declare that it shall not be bound to assume any costs referred to in the preceding paragraph resulting from the participation of legal counsel or advisers or from court proceedings, except insofar as those costs may be covered by its system of legal aid and advice.

Upon ordering the return of a child or issuing an order concerning rights of access under this Convention, the judicial or administrative authorities may, where appropriate, direct the person who removed or retained the child, or who prevented the exercise of rights of access, to pay necessary expenses incurred by or on behalf of the applicant, including travel expenses, any costs incurred or payments made for locating the child, the costs of legal representation of the applicant, and those of returning the child.

Article 27

When it is manifest that the requirements of this Convention are not fulfilled or that the application is otherwise not well founded, a Central Authority is not bound to accept the application. In that case, the Central Authority shall forthwith inform the applicant or the Central Authority through which the application was submitted, as the case may be, of its reasons.

Article 28

A Central Authority may require that the application be accompanied by a written authorisation empowering it to act on behalf of the applicant, or to designate a representative so to act.

Article 29

This Convention shall not preclude any person, institution or body who claims that there has been a breach of custody or access rights within the meaning of Article 3 or 21 from applying directly to the judicial or administrative authorities of a Contracting State, whether or not under the provisions of this Convention.

Article 30

Any application submitted to the Central Authorities or directly to the judicial or administrative authorities of a Contracting State in accordance with the terms of this Convention, together with documents and any other information appended thereto or provided by a Central Authority, shall be admissible in the courts or administrative authorities of the Contracting States.

Article 31

In relation to a State which in matters of custody of children has two or more systems of law applicable in different territorial units—

(a) any reference to habitual residence in that State shall be construed as referring to habitual residence in a territorial unit of that State;

(b) any reference to the law of the State of habitual residence shall be construed as referring to the law of the territorial unit in that State where the child habitually resides.

Article 32

In relation to a State which in matters of custody of children has two or more systems of law applicable to different categories of persons, any reference to the law of that State shall be construed as referring to the legal system specified by the law of that State.

FAMILY LAW ACT 1986
(1986 c 55)

PART I
CHILD CUSTODY

CHAPTER III – JURISDICTION OF COURTS IN SCOTLAND

8 Jurisdiction in independent proceedings

A court in Scotland may entertain an application for a [Part I order] otherwise than in matrimonial [or civil partnership] proceedings only if it has jurisdiction under section 9, 10, 12 or 15(2) of this Act.

9 Habitual residence

Subject to section 11 of this Act, an application for a [Part I order] otherwise than in matrimonial [or civil partnership] proceedings may be entertained by—

(a) the Court of Session if, on the date of the application, the child concerned is habitually resident in Scotland;

(b) the sheriff if, on the date of the application, the child concerned is habitually resident in the sheriffdom.

10 Presence of child

Subject to section 11 of this Act, an application for a [Part I order] otherwise than in matrimonial [or civil partnership] proceedings may be entertained by—

(a) the Court of Session if, on the date of the application, the child concerned—

(i) is present in Scotland; and

(ii) is not habitually resident in any part of the United Kingdom;

(b) the sheriff if, on the date of the application,—

(i) the child is present in Scotland;

(ii) the child is not habitually resident in any part of the United Kingdom; and

(iii) either the pursuer or the defender in the application is habitually resident in the sheriffdom.

11 Provisions supplementary to sections 9 and 10

(1) Subject to subsection (2) below, the jurisdiction of the court to entertain an application for a [Part I order] with respect to a child by virtue of section 9, 10 or 15(2) of this Act is excluded if, on the date of the application, matrimonial or civil partnership proceedings are continuing in a court in any part of the United Kingdom in respect of the marriage or civil partnership of the parents of the child.

(2)   Subsection (1) above shall not apply in relation to an application for a [Part I order] if the court in which the matrimonial [or civil partnership] proceedings are continuing has made one of the following orders, that is to say—

(a)   an order under section 2A(4), 13(6) or 19A(4) of this Act (not being an order made by virtue of section 13(6)(a)(ii)); or

(b)   an order under section 5(2), 14(2) or 22(2) of this Act which is recorded as made for the purpose of enabling [Part I proceedings with respect to] the child concerned to be taken in Scotland or, as the case may be, in another court in Scotland,

and that order is in force.

12   Emergency jurisdiction

Notwithstanding that any other court, whether within or outside Scotland, has jurisdiction to entertain an application for a [Part I order], the Court of Session or the sheriff shall have jurisdiction to entertain such an application if—

(a)   the child concerned is present in Scotland or, as the case may be, in the sheriffdom on the date of the application; and

(b)   the Court of Session or sheriff considers that, for the protection of the child, it is necessary to make such an order immediately.

13   Jurisdiction ancillary to matrimonial proceedings

(1)   The jurisdiction of a court in Scotland to entertain an application for a [Part I order] in matrimonial or civil partnership proceedings shall be modified by the following provisions of this section.

(2)   A court in Scotland shall not have jurisdiction—

[(a)] after the dismissal of matrimonial proceedings or after decree of absolvitor is granted therein; [or

(b)   after the dismissal of civil partnership proceedings,]

to entertain an application for a [Part I order] in those proceedings unless the application therefor was made on or before such dismissal or the granting of the decree of absolvitor.

(3)   Where, after a decree of separation has been granted, an application is made in the separation process for a [Part I order], a court in Scotland shall not have jurisdiction to entertain that application if, on the date of the application, proceedings for divorce or nullity of marriage or proceedings for dissolution or nullity of civil partnership in respect of the marriage or civil partnership concerned are continuing in another court in the United Kingdom.

(4)   A court in Scotland shall not have jurisdiction to entertain an application for the variation of a [Part I order] made in [matrimonial or civil partnership proceedings where the court has refused to grant the principal remedy sought in the proceedings] if, on the date of the application, matrimonial or civil partnership proceedings in respect of the marriage or civil partnership concerned are continuing in another court in the United Kingdom.

(5)   Subsections (3) and (4) above shall not apply if the court in which the other proceedings there referred to are continuing has made—

(a)   an order under section [2A(4) or 19A(4)] of this Act or under subsection (6) below (not being an order made by virtue of paragraph (a)(ii) of that subsection), or

(b)   an order under section 5(2), 14(2) or 22(2) of this Act which is recorded as made for the purpose of enabling [Part I proceedings with respect to] the child concerned to be taken in Scotland or, as the case may be, in another court in Scotland,

and that order is in force.

(6)   A court in Scotland which has jurisdiction in matrimonial [or civil partnership] proceedings to entertain an application for a [Part I order] with respect to a child may make an order declining such jurisdiction if—

(a) it appears to the court with respect to that child that—

(i) but for section 11(1) of this Act, another court in Scotland would have jurisdiction to entertain an application for a [Part I order], or

(ii) but for section 3(2), 6(3), 20(2) or 23(3) of this Act, a court in another part of the United Kingdom would have jurisdiction to make a [Part I order] or an order varying a [Part I order]; and

(b) the court considers that it would be more appropriate for [Part I matters relating to] that child to be determined in that other court or part.

(7) The court may recall an order made under subsection (6) above.

14 Power of court to refuse application or sist proceedings

(1) A court in Scotland which has jurisdiction to entertain an application for a [Part I order] may refuse the application in any case where the matter in question has already been determined in other proceedings.

(2) Where, at any stage of the proceedings on an application made to a court in Scotland for a [Part I order], it appears to the court—

(a) that proceedings with respect to the matters to which the application relates are continuing outside Scotland or in another court in Scotland;

(b) that it would be more appropriate for those matters to be determined in proceedings outside Scotland or in another court in Scotland and that such proceedings are likely to be taken there [; ...

(c) that it should exercise its powers under Article 15 of the Council Regulation (transfer to a court better placed to hear the case),] [or

(d) that it should exercise its powers under Article 8 of the Hague Convention (request to authority in another Contracting State to assume jurisdiction),]

the court may sist the proceedings on that application [or (as the case may be) exercise its powers under Article 15 [of the Council Regulation or Article 8 of the Hague Convention]].

[(3) The court may recall a sist granted in order for it to exercise its powers under Article 8 of the Hague Convention, and withdraw any request made by it to an authority in another Contracting State to assume jurisdiction, if—

(a) the authority in the other Contracting State does not assume jurisdiction within the period for which the court granted the sist, or

(b) the parties do not, within the period specified by the court, request the authority in the other Contracting State to assume jurisdiction.]

15 Duration, variation and recall of orders

(1) Where, after the making by a court in Scotland of a [Part I order] ('the existing order') with respect to a child,—

(a) a [Part I order], or an order varying a [Part I order], competently made by another court in any part of the United Kingdom with respect to that child; or

(b) an order [relating to the parental responsibilities or parental rights in relation to] that child which is made outside the United Kingdom and recognised in Scotland by virtue of section 26 of this Act [or by virtue of the Council Regulation],

comes into force, the existing order shall cease to have effect so far as it makes provision for any matter for which the same or different provision is made by the order of the other court in the United Kingdom or, as the case may be, the order so recognised.

(2) Subject to sections 11(1) and 13(3) and (4) of this Act, a court in Scotland which has made a [Part I order] ('the original order') may, notwithstanding that it would no longer have jurisdiction to make the original order, make an order varying or recalling the original order; but if the original order has by virtue of subsection (1) above ceased to have effect so far as it makes provision for any matter, the court shall not have power to vary that order under this subsection so as to make provision for that matter.

(3) In subsection (2) above, an order varying an original order means any [Part I order] made with respect to the same child as the original order was made.

(4) [Where, by virtue of subsection (1) above, a child is to live with a different person], then, if there is in force an order made by a court in Scotland providing for the supervision of that child by a local authority, that order shall cease to have effect.

17 Orders for delivery of child

(1) [...] An application by one parent of a child for an order for the delivery of the child from the other parent, where the order is not sought to implement a [Part I order], may be entertained by the Court of Session or a sheriff if, but only if, the Court of Session or, as the case may be, the sheriff would have jurisdiction under this Chapter to make a [Part I order] with respect to the child concerned.

[...]

(3) Subsection (1) above shall apply to an application by one party to a marriage for an order for the delivery of the child concerned from the other party where the child, [although not a child of both parties to the marriage, is a child of the family of those parties] as it applies to an application by one parent of a child for an order for the delivery of the child from the other parent.

[(4) In subsection (3) above, 'child of the family' means any child who has been treated by both parties as a child of their family, except a child who has been placed with those parties as foster parents by a local authority or a voluntary organisation.]

[17A The provisions of this Chapter are subject to Sections 2 and 3 of Chapter II of the Council Regulation [and are subject to the Hague Convention].]

18 Interpretation of Chapter III

(1) In this Chapter—
'child' means a person who has not attained the age of sixteen;
['civil partnership proceedings' means proceedings for dissolution or nullity of a civil partnership or for the separation of the partners in a civil partnership;]
'matrimonial proceedings' means proceedings for divorce, nullity of marriage or judicial separation.

(2) In this Chapter, 'the date of the application' means, where two or more applications are pending, the date of the first of those applications; and, for the purposes of this subsection, an application is pending until a [Part I order] or, in the case of an application mentioned in section 16(1) of this Act, an order relating to the [guardianship of a child], has been granted in pursuance of the application or the court has refused to grant such an order.

CHAPTER V – RECOGNITION AND ENFORCEMENT

25 Recognition of Part I orders: general

(1) Where a [Part I order] made by a court in any part of the United Kingdom is in force with respect to a child who has not attained the age of sixteen, then, subject to subsection (2) below, the order shall be recognised in any other part of the United Kingdom as having the same effect in that other part as if it had been made by the appropriate court in that other part and as if that court had had jurisdiction to make it.

(2) Where a [Part I order] includes provision as to the means by which rights conferred by the order are to be enforced, subsection (1) above shall not apply to that provision.

(3) A court in a part of the United Kingdom in which a [Part I order] is recognised in accordance with subsection (1) above shall not enforce the order unless it has been registered in that part of the United Kingdom under section 27 of this Act and proceedings for enforcement are taken in accordance with section 29 of this Act.

26   Recognition: special Scottish rule

[(1)   An order relating to parental responsibilities or parental rights in relation to a child which is made outside the United Kingdom shall be recognised in Scotland if the order was made in the country where the child was habitually resident.]

[(2)   Subsection (1) above shall not apply to an order as regards which provision as to recognition is made by [Articles 21 to 27, 41(1) and 42(1)] of the Council Regulation.]

27   Registration

[(1)   Any person on whom any rights are conferred by a [Part I order] may apply to the court which made it for the order to be registered in another part of the United Kingdom under this section.]

[(2)   An application under this section shall be made in the prescribed manner and shall contain the prescribed information and be accompanied by such documents as may be prescribed.]

(3)   On receiving an application under this section the court which made the [Part I order] shall, unless it appears to the court that the order is no longer in force, cause the following documents to be sent to the appropriate court in the part of the United Kingdom specified in the application, namely—

(a)   a certified copy of the order, and

(b)   where the order has been varied, prescribed particulars of any variation which is in force, and

(c)   a copy of the application and of any accompanying documents.

(4)   Where the prescribed officer of the appropriate court receives a certified copy of a [Part I order] under subsection (3) above, he shall forthwith cause the order, together with particulars of any variation, to be registered in that court in the prescribed manner.

(5)   An order shall not be registered under this section in respect of a child who has attained the age of sixteen, and the registration of an order in respect of a child who has not attained the age of sixteen shall cease to have effect on the attainment by the child of that age.

28   Cancellation and variation of registration

(1)   A court which revokes, recalls or varies an order registered under section 27 of this Act shall cause notice of the revocation, recall or variation to be given in the prescribed manner to the prescribed officer of the court in which it is registered and, on receiving the notice, the prescribed officer—

(a)   in the case of the revocation or recall of the order, shall cancel the registration, and

(b)   in the case of the variation of the order, shall cause particulars of the variation to be registered in the prescribed manner.

(2)   Where—

(a)   an order registered under section 27 of this Act ceases (in whole or in part) to have effect in the part of the United Kingdom in which it was made, otherwise than because of its revocation, recall or variation, or

(b)   an order registered under section 27 of this Act in Scotland ceases (in whole or in part) to have effect there as a result of the making of an order in proceedings outside the United Kingdom.

the court in which the order is registered may, of its own motion or on the application of any person who appears to the court to have an interest in the matter, cancel the registration (or, if the order has ceased to have effect in part, cancel the registration so far as it relates to the provisions which have ceased to have effect).

29   Enforcement

(1)   Where a [Part I order] has been registered under section 27 of this Act, the court in which it is registered shall have the same powers for the purpose of enforcing the order as it would have if it had itself made the order and had juris-

diction to make it; and proceedings for or with respect to enforcement may be taken accordingly.

(2)   Where an application has been made to any court for the enforcement of an order registered in that court under section 27 of this Act, the court may, at any time before the application is determined, give such interim directions as it thinks fit for the purpose of securing the welfare of the child concerned or of preventing changes in the circumstances relevant to the determination of the application.

(3)   The references in subsection (1) above to a [Part I order] do not include references to any provision of the order as to the means by which rights conferred by the order are to be enforced.

30   Staying or sisting of enforcement proceedings

(1)   Where in accordance with section 29 of this Act proceedings are taken in any court for the enforcement of an order registered in that court, any person who appears to the court to have an interest in the matter may apply for the proceedings to be stayed or sisted on the ground that he has taken or intends to take other proceedings (in the United Kingdom or elsewhere) as a result of which the order may cease to have effect, or may have a different effect, in the part of the United Kingdom in which it is registered.

[(1A)   No application may be made under subsection (1) for proceedings to be stayed or sisted if the proceedings are proceedings on an application for an order under section 110(2) of the Children Act 1989.]

(2)   If after considering an application under subsection (1) above the court considers that the proceedings for enforcement should be stayed or sisted in order that other proceedings may be taken or concluded, it shall stay or sist the proceedings for enforcement accordingly.

(3)   The court may remove a stay or recall a sist granted in accordance with subsection (2) above if it appears to the court—

(a)   that there has been unreasonable delay in the taking or prosecution of the other proceedings referred to in that subsection, or

(b)   that those other proceedings are concluded and that the registered order, or a relevant part of it, is still in force.

(4)   Nothing in this section shall affect any power exercisable apart from this section to grant, remove or recall a stay or sist.

31   Dismissal of enforcement proceedings

(1)   Where in accordance with section 29 of this Act proceedings are taken in any court for the enforcement of an order registered in that court, any person who appears to the court to have an interest in the matter may apply for those proceedings to be dismissed on the ground that the order has (in whole or in part) ceased to have effect in the part of the United Kingdom in which it was made.

[(1A)   No application may be made under subsection (1) for proceedings to be dismissed if the proceedings are proceedings on an application for an order under section 110(2) of the Children Act 1989.]

(2)   Where in accordance with section 29 of this Act proceedings are taken in the Court of Session for the enforcement of an order registered in that court, any person who appears to the court to have an interest in the matter may apply for those proceedings to be dismissed on the ground that the order has (in whole or in part) ceased to have effect in Scotland as a result of the making of an order in proceedings outside the United Kingdom.

(3)   If, after considering an application under subsection (1) or (2) above, the court is satisfied that the registered order has ceased to have effect, it shall dismiss the proceedings for enforcement (or, if it is satisfied that the order has ceased to have effect in part, it shall dismiss the proceedings so far as they relate to the enforcement of provisions which have ceased to have effect).

32 Interpretation of Chapter V

(1) In this Chapter—

'the appropriate court', in relation to England and Wales or Northern Ireland, means the High Court and, in relation to Scotland, means the Court of Session;

['Part I order'] includes (except where the context otherwise requires) any order within section 1(3) of this Act which, on the assumptions mentioned in subsection (3) below—

(a)   could have been made notwithstanding the provisions of this Part;

(b)   would have been a [Part I order] for the purposes of this Part; and

(c)   would not have ceased to have effect by virtue of section 6, 15 or 23 of this Act.

(2) In the application of this Chapter to Scotland, ['Part I order'] also includes (except where the context otherwise requires) any order within section 1(3) of this Act which, on the assumptions mentioned in subsection (3) below—

(a)   would have been a [Part I order] for the purposes of this Part; and

(b)   would not have ceased to have effect by virtue of section 6 or 23 of this Act,

and which, but for the provisions of this Part, would be recognised in Scotland under any rule of law.

(3) The said assumptions are—

(a)   that this Part had been in force at all material times; and

(b)   that any reference in section 1 of this Act to any enactment included a reference to any corresponding enactment previously in force.

CHAPTER VI – MISCELLANEOUS AND SUPPLEMENTAL

33 Power to order disclosure of child's whereabouts

(1) Where in proceedings for or relating to a [Part I order] in respect of a child there is not available to the court adequate information as to where the child is, the court may order any person who it has reason to believe may have relevant information to disclose it to the court.

(2) A person shall not be excused from complying with an order under subsection (1) above by reason that to do so may incriminate him or his spouse [or civil partner] of an offence; but a statement or admission made in compliance with such an order shall not be admissible in evidence against either of them in proceedings for any offence other than perjury.

(3) A court in Scotland before which proceedings are pending for the enforcement of an order [relating to parental responsibilities or parental rights in relation to] a child made outside the United Kingdom which is recognised in Scotland shall have the same powers as it would have under subsection (1) above if the order were its own.

34 Power to order recovery of child

(1) Where—

(a)   a person is required by a [Part I order], or an order for the enforcement of a [Part I order], to give up a child to another person ('the person concerned'), and

(b)   the court which made the order imposing the requirement is satisfied that the child has not been given up in accordance with the order,

the court may make an order authorising an officer of the court or a constable to take charge of the child and deliver him to the person concerned.

(2) The authority conferred by subsection (1) above includes authority—

(a)   to enter and search any premises where the person acting in pursuance of the order has reason to believe the child may be found, and

(b)   to use such force as may be necessary to give effect to the purpose of the order.

(3)   Where by virtue of—
    (a)   [section 14 of the Children Act 1989, or]
    (b)   [Article 14 (enforcement of residence orders) of the Children (Northern Ireland) Order 1995,]
a [Part I order] (or a provision of a [Part I order]) may be enforced as if it were an order requiring a person to give up a child to another person, subsection (1) above shall apply as if the [Part I order] had included such a requirement.

(4)   This section is without prejudice to any power conferred on a court by or under any other enactment or rule of law.

35   Powers to restrict removal of child from jurisdiction
[...]
(3)   A court in Scotland—
    (a)   at any time after the commencement of proceedings in connection with which the court would have jurisdiction to make [a Part I] order, or
    (b)   in any proceedings in which it would be competent for the court to grant an interdict prohibiting the removal of a child from its jurisdiction,
may, on an application by any of the persons mentioned in subsection (4) below, grant interdict or interim interdict prohibiting the removal of the child from the United Kingdom or any part of the United Kingdom, or out of the control of the person in [whose care] the child is.

(4)   The said persons are—
    (a)   any party to the proceedings,
    (b)   the [guardian] of the child concerned, and
    (c)   any other person who has or wishes to obtain the [...] care of the child.

(5)   In subsection (3) above 'the court' means the Court of Session or the sheriff; and for the purposes of subsection (3)(a) above, proceedings shall be held to commence—
    (a)   in the Court of Session, when a summons is signeted or a petition is presented;
    (b)   in the sheriff court, when the warrant of citation is signed.

36   Effect of orders restricting removal
(1)   This section applies to any order made by a court in the United Kingdom prohibiting the removal of a child from the United Kingdom or from any specified part of it.

(2)   An order to which this section applies shall have effect in each part of the United Kingdom other than the part in which it was made—
    (a)   as if it had been made by the appropriate court in that other part, and
    (b)   in the case of an order which has the effect of prohibiting the child's removal to that other part, as if it had included a prohibition on his further removal to any place except one to which he could be removed consistently with the order.

(3)   The references in subsections (1) and (2) above to prohibitions on a child's removal include references to prohibitions subject to exceptions; and in a case where removal is prohibited except with the consent of the court, nothing in subsection (2) above shall be construed as affecting the identity of the court whose consent is required.

(4)   In this section 'child' means a person who has not attained the age of sixteen; and this section shall cease to apply to an order relating to a child when he attains the age of sixteen.

37   Surrender of passports
(1)   Where there is in force an order prohibiting or otherwise restricting the removal of a child from the United Kingdom or from any specified part of it, the court by which the order was in fact made, or by which it is treated under section 36 of this Act as having been made, may require any person to surrender any

United Kingdom passport which has been issued to, or contains particulars of, the child.

(2)   In this section 'United Kingdom passport' means a current passport issued by the Government of the United Kingdom.

38   Automatic restriction on removal of wards of court

(1)   The rule of law which (without any order of the court) restricts the removal of a ward of court from the jurisdiction of the court shall, in a case to which this section applies, have effect subject to the modifications in subsection (3) below.

(2)   This section applies in relation to a ward of court if—

(a)   proceedings for divorce, nullity or judicial separation in respect of the marriage of his parents are continuing in a court in another part of the United Kingdom (that is to say, in a part of the United Kingdom outside the jurisdiction of the court of which he is a ward),

[(aa)   proceedings for dissolution or annulment or legal separation in respect of the civil partnership of his parents are continuing in a court in another part of the United Kingdom (that is to say, in a part of the United Kingdom outside the jurisdiction of the court of which he is a ward), or]

(b)   he is habitually resident in another part of the United Kingdom, except where that other part is Scotland and he has attained the age of sixteen.

(3)   Where this section applies, the rule referred to in subsection (1) above shall not prevent—

(a)   the removal of the ward of court, without the consent of any court, to the other part of the United Kingdom mentioned in subsection (2) above, or

(b)   his removal to any other place with the consent of either the appropriate court in that other part of the United Kingdom or the court mentioned in subsection (2)(a) [or (aa)] above.

39   Duty to furnish particulars of other proceedings

Parties to proceedings for or relating to a [Part I order] shall, to such extent and in such manner as may be prescribed, give particulars of other proceedings known to them which relate to the child concerned (including proceedings instituted abroad and proceedings which are no longer continuing).

40   Interpretation of Chapter VI

(1)   In this Chapter—

'the appropriate court' has the same meaning as in Chapter V;

['Part I order'] includes (except where the context otherwise requires) any such order as is mentioned in section 32(1) of this Act.

(2)   In the application of this Chapter to Scotland, ['Part I order'] also includes (except where the context otherwise requires) any such order as is mentioned in section 32(2) of this Act.

41   Habitual residence after removal without consent, etc

(1)   Where a child who—

(a)   has not attained the age of sixteen, and

(b)   is habitually resident in a part of the United Kingdom, becomes habitually resident outside that part of the United Kingdom in consequence of circumstances of the kind specified in subsection (2) below, he shall be treated for the purposes of this Part as continuing to be habitually resident in that part of the United Kingdom for the period of one year beginning with the date on which those circumstances arise.

(2)   The circumstances referred to in subsection (1) above exist where the child is removed from or retained outside, or himself leaves or remains outside, the part of the United Kingdom in which he was habitually resident before his change of residence—

(a)   without the agreement of the person or all the persons having, under the law of that part of the United Kingdom, the right to determine where he is to reside, or

(b)   in contravention of an order made by a court in any part of the United Kingdom.

(3)   A child shall cease to be treated by virtue of subsection (1) above as habitually resident in a part of the United Kingdom if, during the period there mentioned—

(a)   he attains the age of sixteen, or

(b)   he becomes habitually resident outside that part of the United Kingdom with the agreement of the person or persons mentioned in subsection (2)(a) above and not in contravention of an order made by a court in any part of the United Kingdom.

42   General interpretation of Part I

(1)   In this Part—

'certified copy', in relation to an order of any court, means a copy certified by the prescribed officer of the court to be a true copy of the order or of the official record of the order;

['parental responsibilities' and 'parental rights' have the meanings respectively given by sections 1(3) and 2(4) of the Children (Scotland) Act 1995;]

'part of the United Kingdom' means England and Wales, Scotland or Northern Ireland;

'prescribed' means prescribed by rules of court or act of sederunt;

['the Council Regulation' means Council Regulation (EC) No 2201/2003 of 27th November 2003 concerning jurisdiction and the recognition and enforcement of judgments in matrimonial matters and matters of parental responsibility.]

['the Hague Convention' means the Convention on Jurisdiction, Applicable Law, Recognition, Enforcement and Co-Operation in respect of Parental Responsibility and Measures for the Protection of Children that was signed at The Hague on 19 October 1996.]

(2)   For the purposes of this Part proceedings in England and Wales or in Northern Ireland for divorce, nullity or judicial separation in respect of the marriage of the parents of a child shall, unless they have been dismissed, be treated as continuing until the child concerned attains the age of eighteen (whether or not a decree has been granted and whether or not, in the case of a decree of divorce or nullity of marriage, that decree has been made absolute).

[(2A)   For the purposes of this Part proceedings in England and Wales or in Northern Ireland for dissolution, annulment or legal separation in respect of the civil partnership of the parents of the child shall, unless they have been dismissed, be treated as continuing until the child concerned attains the age of eighteen (whether or not a dissolution, nullity or separation order has been made and whether or not, in the case of a dissolution or nullity order, that order has been made final).]

(3)   For the purposes of this Part, matrimonial proceedings [or civil partnership proceedings] in a court in Scotland which has jurisdiction in those proceedings to make a [Part I order] with respect to a child shall, unless they have been dismissed or decree of absolvitor has been granted therein, be treated as continuing until the child concerned attains the age of sixteen.

(4)   Any reference in this Part to proceedings in respect of the marriage of the parents of a child shall, in relation to a child who, although not a child of both parties to the marriage, is a child of the family of those parties, be construed as a reference to proceedings in respect of that marriage; and for this purpose 'child of the family'—

(a)   if the proceedings are in England and Wales, means any child who has been treated by both parties as a child of their family, except a child who [is placed with those parties as foster parents] by a local authority or a voluntary organisation;

(b) if the proceedings are in Scotland, means any child [who has been treated by both parties as a child of their family, except a child who has been placed with those parties as foster parents by a local authority or a voluntary organisation];

(c) if the proceedings are in Northern Ireland, means any child who has been treated by both parties as a child of their family, except a child who [is placed with those parties as foster parents by an authority within the meaning of the Children (Northern Ireland) Order 1995] or a voluntary organisation.

[(4A) Any reference in this Part to proceedings in respect of the civil partnership of the parents of a child shall, in relation to a child who, although not a child of the civil partners, is a child of the family of the civil partners, be construed as a reference to proceedings in respect of that civil partnership; and for this purpose 'child of the family' has the meaning given in paragraphs (a) to (c) of subsection (4) (but substituting references to the civil partners for references to the parties to the marriage).]

(5) References in this Part to Part I orders include (except where the context otherwise requires) references to Part I orders as varied.

(6) For the purposes of this Part each of the following orders shall be treated as varying the [Part I order] to which it relates—

(a) an order which provides for a person [to be allowed contact with or] to be given access to a child who is the subject of a [Part I order], or which makes provision for the education of such a child.

[...]

(7) [In this Part—

(a) references to Part I proceedings in respect of a child are references to any proceedings for a Part I order or an order corresponding to a Part I order and include, in relation to proceedings outside the United Kingdom, references to proceedings before a tribunal or other authority having power under the law having effect there to determine Part I matters; and

(b) references to Part I matters are references to matters that might be determined by a Part I order or an order corresponding to a Part I order.]

PART II
RECOGNITION OF DIVORCES, ANNULMENTS AND LEGAL SEPARATIONS
DIVORCES, ANNULMENTS AND JUDICIAL SEPARATIONS GRANTED IN THE BRITISH ISLANDS

44 Recognition in United Kingdom of divorces, annulments and judicial separations granted in the British Islands

(1) Subject to section 52(4) and (5)(a) of this Act, no divorce or annulment obtained in any part of the British Islands shall be regarded as effective in any part of the United Kingdom unless granted by a court of civil jurisdiction.

(2) Subject to section 51 of this Act, the validity of any divorce, annulment or judicial separation granted by a court of civil jurisdiction in any part of the British Islands shall be recognised throughout the United Kingdom.

45 Recognition in the United Kingdom of overseas divorces, annulments and legal separations

[(1) Subject to subsection (2) of this section] and sections 51 and 52 of this Act, the validity of a divorce, annulment or legal separation obtained in a country outside the British Islands (in this Part referred to as an overseas divorce, annulment or legal separation) shall be recognised in the United Kingdom if, and only if, it is entitled to recognition—

(a) by virtue of sections 46 to 49 of this Act, or

(b) by virtue of any enactment other than this Part.

[(2)   Subsection (1) and the following provisions of this Part do not apply to an overseas divorce, annulment or legal separation as regards which provision as to recognition is made by [Articles 21 to 27, 41(1) and 42(1)] of the Council Regulation.]

46   Grounds for recognition

(1)   The validity of an overseas divorce, annulment or legal separation obtained by means of proceedings shall be recognised if—

(a)   the divorce, annulment or legal separation is effective under the law of the country in which it was obtained; and

(b)   at the relevant date either party to the marriage—

(i)   was habitually resident in the country in which the divorce, annulment or legal separation was obtained; or

(ii)   was domiciled in that country; or

(iii)   was a national of that country.

(2)   The validity of an overseas divorce, annulment or legal separation obtained otherwise than by means of proceedings shall be recognised if—

(a)   the divorce, annulment or legal separation is effective under the law of the country in which it was obtained;

(b)   at the relevant date—

(i)   each party to the marriage was domiciled in that country; or

(ii)   either party to the marriage was domiciled in that country and the other party was domiciled in a country under whose law the divorce, annulment or legal separation is recognised as valid; and

(c)   neither party to the marriage was habitually resident in the United Kingdom throughout the period of one year immediately preceding that date.

(3)   In this section 'the relevant date' means—

(a)   in the case of an overseas divorce, annulment or legal separation obtained by means of proceedings, the date of the commencement of the proceedings;

(b)   in the case of an overseas divorce, annulment or legal separation obtained otherwise than by means of proceedings, the date on which it was obtained.

(4)   Where in the case of an overseas annulment, the relevant date fell after the death of either party to the marriage, any reference in subsection (1) or (2) above to that date shall be construed in relation to that party as a reference to the date of death.

(5)   For the purpose of this section, a party to a marriage shall be treated as domiciled in a country if he was domiciled in that country either according to the law of that country in family matters or according to the law of the part of the United Kingdom in which the question of recognition arises.

47   Cross-proceedings and divorces following legal separations

(1)   Where there have been cross-proceedings, the validity of an overseas divorce, annulment or legal separation obtained either in the original proceedings or in the cross-proceedings shall be recognised if—

(a)   the requirements of section 46(1)(b)(i), (ii) or (iii) of this Act are satisfied in relation to the date of the commencement either of the original proceedings or of the cross-proceedings, and

(b)   the validity of the divorce, annulment or legal separation is otherwise entitled to recognition by virtue of the provisions of this Part.

(2)   Where a legal separation, the validity of which is entitled to recognition by virtue of the provisions of section 46 of this Act or of subsection (1) above is converted, in the country in which it was obtained, into a divorce which is effective under the law of that country, the validity of the divorce shall be recognised whether or not it would itself be entitled to recognition by virtue of those provisions.

48   Proof of facts relevant to recognition

(1)   For the purpose of deciding whether an overseas divorce, annulment or legal separation obtained by means of proceedings is entitled to recognition by virtue of section 46 and 47 of this Act, any finding of fact made (whether expressly or by implication) in the proceedings and on the basis of which jurisdiction was assumed in the proceedings shall—

(a)   if both parties to the marriage took part in the proceedings, be conclusive evidence of the fact found; and

(b)   in any other case, be sufficient proof of that fact unless the contrary is shown.

(2)   In this section 'finding of fact' includes a finding that either party to the marriage—

(a)   was habitually resident in the country in which the divorce, annulment or legal separation was obtained; or

(b)   was under the law of that country domiciled there; or

(c)   was a national of that country.

(3)   For the purposes of subsection (1)(a) above, a party to the marriage who has appeared in judicial proceedings shall be treated as having taken part in them.

49   Modifications of Part II in relation to countries comprising territories having different systems of law

(1)   In relation to a country comprising territories in which different systems of law are in force in matters of divorce, annulment or legal separation, the provisions of this Part mentioned in subsections (2) to (5) below shall have effect subject to the modifications there specified.

(2)   In the case of a divorce, annulment or legal separation the recognition of the validity of which depends on whether the requirements of subsection (1)(b)(i) or (ii) of section 46 of this Act are satisfied, that section and, in the case of a legal separation, section 47(2) of this Act shall have effect as if each territory were a separate country.

(3)   In the case of a divorce, annulment or legal separation the recognition of the validity of which depends on whether the requirements of subsection (1)(b)(iii) of section 46 of this Act are satisfied—

(a)   that section shall have effect as if for paragraph (a) of subsection (1) there were substituted the following paragraph—

'(a)   the divorce, annulment or legal separation is effective throughout the country in which it was obtained;'; and

(b)   in the case of a legal separation, section 47(2) of this Act shall have effect as if for the words 'is effective under the law of that country' there were substituted the words 'is effective throughout that country'.

(4)   In the case of a divorce, annulment or legal separation the recognition of the validity of which depends on whether the requirements of subsection (2)(b) of section 46 of this Act are satisfied, that section and section 52(3) and (4) of this Act and, in the case of a legal separation, section 47(2) of this Act shall have effect as if each territory were a separate country.

(5)   Paragraphs (a) and (b) of section 48(2) of this Act shall each have effect as if each territory were a separate country.

50   Non-recognition of divorce or annulment in another jurisdiction no bar to remarriage

Where, in any part of the United Kingdom—

(a)   a divorce or annulment has been granted by a court of civil jurisdiction, or

(b)   the validity of a divorce or annulment is recognised by virtue of this Part,

the fact that the divorce or annulment would not be recognised elsewhere shall not preclude either party to the marriage from [forming a subsequent marriage or civil partnership in that part of the United Kingdom or cause the subsequent marriage or civil partnership of either party (wherever it takes place) to be treated as invalid in that part.]

51 Refusal of recognition

(1) Subject to section 52 of this Act, recognition of the validity of—

(a) a divorce, annulment or judicial separation granted by a court of civil jurisdiction in any part of the British Islands, or

(b) an overseas divorce, annulment or legal separation,

may be refused in any part of the United Kingdom if the divorce, annulment or separation was granted or obtained at a time when it was irreconcilable with a decision determining the question of the subsistence or validity of the marriage of the parties previously given (whether before or after the commencement of this Part) by a court of civil jurisdiction in that part of the United Kingdom or by a court elsewhere and recognised or entitled to be recognised in that part of the United Kingdom.

(2) Subject to section 52 of this Act, recognition of the validity of—

(a) a divorce or judicial separation granted by a court of civil jurisdiction in any part of the British Islands, or

(b) an overseas divorce or legal separation,

may be refused in any part of the United Kingdom if the divorce or separation was granted or obtained at a time when, according to the law of that part of the United Kingdom (including its rules of private international law and the provisions of this Part), there was no subsisting marriage between the parties.

(3) Subject to section 52 of this Act, recognition by virtue of section 45 of this Act of the validity of an overseas divorce, annulment or legal separation may be refused if—

(a) in the case of a divorce, annulment or legal separation obtained by means of proceedings, it was obtained—

(i) without such steps having been taken for giving notice of the proceedings to a party to the marriage as, having regard to the nature of the proceedings and all the circumstances, should reasonably have been taken; or

(ii) without a party to the marriage having been given (for any reason other than lack of notice) such opportunity to take part in the proceedings as, having regard to those matters, he should reasonably have been given; or

(b) in the case of a divorce, annulment or legal separation obtained otherwise than by means of proceedings—

(i) there is no official document certifying that the divorce, annulment or legal separation is effective under the law of the country in which it was obtained; or

(ii) where either party to the marriage was domiciled in another country at the relevant date, there is no official document certifying that the divorce, annulment or legal separation is recognised as valid under the law of that other country; or

(c) in either case, recognition of the divorce, annulment or legal separation would be manifestly contrary to public policy.

(4) In this section—

'official', in relation to a document certifying that a divorce, annulment or legal separation is effective, or is recognised as valid, under the law of any country, means issued by a person or body appointed or recognised for the purpose under that law;

'the relevant date' has the same meaning as in section 46 of this Act;

and subsection (5) of that section shall apply for the purposes of this section as it applies for the purposes of that section.

(5)   Nothing in this Part shall be construed as requiring the recognition of any finding of fault made in any proceedings for divorce, annulment or separation or of any maintenance, custody or other ancillary order made in any such proceedings.

52   Provisions as to divorces, annulments etc obtained before commencement of Part II

(1)   The provisions of this Part shall apply—

(a)   to a divorce, annulment or judicial separation granted by a court of civil jurisdiction in the British Islands before the date of the commencement of this Part, and

(b)   to an overseas divorce, annulment or legal separation obtained before that date,

as well as to one granted or obtained on or after that date.

(2)   In the case of such a divorce, annulment or separation as is mentioned in subsection (1)(a) or (b) above, the provisions of this Part shall require or, as the case may be, preclude the recognition of its validity in relation to any time before that date as well as in relation to any subsequent time, but those provisions shall not—

(a)   affect any property to which any person became entitled before that date, or

(b)   affect the recognition of the validity of the divorce, annulment or separation if that matter has been decided by any competent court in the British Islands before that date.

(3)   Subsections (1) and (2) above shall apply in relation to any divorce or judicial separation granted by a court of civil jurisdiction in the British Islands before the date of the commencement of this Part whether granted before or after the commencement of section 1 of the Recognition of Divorces and Legal Separations Act 1971.

(4)   The validity of any divorce, annulment or legal separation mentioned in subsection (5) below shall be recognised in the United Kingdom whether or not it is entitled to recognition by virtue of any of the foregoing provisions of this Part.

(5)   The divorces, annulments and legal separations referred to in subsection (4) above are—

(a)   a divorce which was obtained in the British Islands before 1st January 1974 and was recognised as valid under rules of law applicable before that date;

(b)   an overseas divorce which was recognised as valid under the Recognition of Divorces and Legal Separations Act 1971 and was not affected by section 16(2) of the Domicile and Matrimonial Proceedings Act 1973 (proceedings otherwise than in a court of law where both parties resident in United Kingdom);

(c)   a divorce of which the decree was registered under section 1 of the Indian and Colonial Divorce Jurisdiction Act 1926;

(d)   a divorce or annulment which-was recognised as valid under section 4 of the Matrimonial Causes (War Marriages) Act 1944; and

(e)   an overseas legal separation which was recognised as valid under the Recognition of Divorces and Legal Separations Act 1971.

54   Interpretation of Part II

(1)   In this Part—

'annulment' includes any decree or declarator of nullity of marriage, however expressed;

['the Council Regulation' means Council Regulation (EC) No 2201/2003 of 27th November 2003 concerning jurisdiction and the recognition and enforcement of judgments in matrimonial matters and matters of parental responsibility;]

'part of the United Kingdom' means England and Wales, Scotland or Northern Ireland;

'proceedings' means judicial or other proceedings.

(2) In this Part 'country' includes a colony or other dependent territory of the United Kingdom but for the purposes of this Part a person shall be treated as a national of such a territory only if it has a law of citizenship or nationality separate from that of the United Kingdom and he is a citizen or national of that territory under that law.

RECOGNITION OF TRUSTS ACT 1987
(1987 c 14)

1 Applicable law and recognition of trusts

(1) The provisions of the Convention set out in the Schedule to this Act shall have the force of law in the United Kingdom.

(2) Those provisions shall, so far as applicable, have effect not only in relation to the trusts described in Articles 2 and 3 of the Convention but also in relation to any other trusts of property arising under the law of any part of the United Kingdom or by virtue of a judicial decision whether in the United Kingdom or elsewhere.

(3) In accordance with Articles 15 and 16 such provisions of the law as are there mentioned shall, to the extent there specified, apply to the exclusion of the other provisions of the Convention.

(4) In Article 17 the reference to a State includes a reference to any country or territory (whether or not a party to the Convention and whether or not forming part of the United Kingdom) which has its own system of law.

(5) Article 22 shall not be construed as affecting the law to be applied in relation to anything done or omitted before the coming into force of this Act.

Section 1   SCHEDULE
CONVENTION ON THE LAW APPLICABLE TO TRUSTS AND ON THEIR
RECOGNITION

CHAPTER I – SCOPE

Article 1

This Convention specifies the law applicable to trusts and governs their recognition.

Article 2

For the purposes of this Convention, the term 'trust' refers to the legal relationship created – inter vivos or on death – by a person, the settlor, when assets have been placed under the control of a trustee for the benefit of a beneficiary or for a specified purpose.

A trust has the following characteristics—

(a) the assets constitute a separate fund and are not a part of the trustee's own estate;

(b) title to the trust assets stands in the name of the trustee or in the name of another person on behalf of the trustee;

(c) the trustee has the power and the duty, in respect of which he is accountable, to manage, employ or dispose of the assets in accordance with the terms of the trust and the special duties imposed upon him by law.

The reservation by the settlor of certain rights and powers, and the fact that the trustee may himself have rights as a beneficiary, are not necessarily inconsistent with the existence of a trust.

Article 3

The Convention applies only to trusts created voluntarily and evidenced in writing.

Article 4
The Convention does not apply to preliminary issues relating to the validity of wills or of other acts by virtue of which assets are transferred to the trustee.

Article 5
The Convention does not apply to the extent that the law specified by Chapter II does not provide for trusts or the category of trusts involved.

CHAPTER II – APPLICABLE LAW

Article 6
A trust shall be governed by the law chosen by the settlor. The choice must be express or be implied in the terms of the instrument creating or the writing evidencing the trust, interpreted, if necessary, in the light of the circumstances of the case.

Where the law chosen under the previous paragraph does not provide for trusts or the category of trust involved, the choice shall not be effective and the law specified in Article 7 shall apply.

Article 7
Where no applicable law has been chosen, a trust shall be governed by the law with which it is most closely connected.

In ascertaining the law with which a trust is most closely connected reference shall be made in particular to—
    (a)   the place of administration of the trust designated by the settlor;
    (b)   the situs of the assets of the trust;
    (c)   the place of residence or business of the trustee;
    (d)   the objects of the trust and the places where they are to be fulfilled.

Article 8
The law specified by Article 6 or 7 shall govern the validity of the trust, its construction, its effects and the administration of the trust.

In particular that law shall govern—
    (a)   the appointment, resignation and removal of trustees, the capacity to act as a trustee, and the devolution of the office of trustee;
    (b)   the rights and duties of trustees among themselves;
    (c)   the right of trustees to delegate in whole or in part the discharge of their duties or the exercise of their powers;
    (d)   the power of trustees to administer or to dispose of trust assets, to create security interests in the trust assets, or to acquire new assets;
    (e)   the powers of investment of trustees;
    (f)   restrictions upon the duration of the trust, and upon the power to accumulate the income of the trust;
    (g)   the relationships between the trustees and the beneficiaries including the personal liability of the trustees to the beneficiaries;
    (h)   the variation or termination of the trust;
    (i)   the distribution of the trust assets;
    (j)   the duty of trustees to account for their administration.

Article 9
In applying this Chapter a severable aspect of the trust, particularly matters of administration, may be governed by a different law.

Article 10
The law applicable to the validity of the trust shall determine whether that law or the law governing a severable aspect of the trust may be replaced by another law.

CHAPTER III – RECOGNITION

Article 11

A trust created in accordance with the law specified by the preceding Chapter shall be recognised as a trust.

Such recognition shall imply, as a minimum, that the trust property constitutes a separate fund, that the trustee may sue and be sued in his capacity as trustee, and that he may appear or act in this capacity before a notary or any person acting in an official capacity.

In so far as the law applicable to the trust requires or provides, such recognition shall imply in particular—

(a)   that personal creditors of the trustee shall have no recourse against the trust assets;

(b)   that the trust assets shall not form part of the trustee's estate upon his insolvency or bankruptcy;

(c)   that the trust assets shall not form part of the matrimonial property of the trustee or his spouse nor part of the trustee's estate upon his death;

(d)   that the trust assets may be recovered when the trustee, in breach of trust, has mingled trust assets with his own property or has alienated trust assets. However, the rights and obligations of any third party holder of the assets shall remain subject to the law determined by the choice of law rules of the forum.

Article 12

Where the trustee desires to register assets, movable or immovable, or documents of title to them, he shall be entitled, in so far as this is not prohibited by or inconsistent with the law of the State where registration is sought, to do so in his capacity as trustee or in such other way that the existence of the trust is disclosed.

Article 14

The Convention shall not prevent the application of rules of law more favourable to the recognition of trusts.

CHAPTER IV – GENERAL CLAUSES

Article 15

The Convention does not prevent the application of provisions of the law designated by the conflicts rules of the forum, in so far as those provisions cannot be derogated from by voluntary act, relating in particular to the following matters—

(a)   the protection of minors and incapable parties;

(b)   the personal and proprietary effects of marriage;

(c)   succession rights, testate and intestate, especially the indefeasible shares of spouses and relatives;

(d)   the transfer of title to property and security interests in property;

(e)   the protection of creditors in matters of insolvency;

(f)   the protection, in other respects, of third parties acting in good faith.

If recognition of a trust is prevented by application of the preceding paragraph, the court shall try to give effect to the objects of the trust by other means.

Article 16

The Convention does not prevent the application of those provisions of the law of the forum which must be applied even to international situations, irrespective of rules of conflict of laws.

Article 17

In the Convention the word 'law' means the rules of law in force in a State other than its rules of conflict of laws.

Article 18
The provisions of the Convention may be disregarded when their application would be manifestly incompatible with public policy.

Article 22
The Convention applies to trusts regardless of the date on which they were created.

CONTRACTS (APPLICABLE LAW) ACT 1990
(1990 c 36)

SCHEDULE 1
THE ROME CONVENTION

The High Contracting Parties to the Treaty establishing the European Economic Community,

Anxious to continue in the field of private international law the work of unification of law which has already been done within the Community, in particular in the field of jurisdiction and enforcement of judgments,

Wishing to establish uniform rules concerning the law applicable to contractual obligations,

Have agreed as follows:

...

TITLE II – UNIFORM RULES

Article 3. Freedom of choice
1. A contract shall be governed by the law chosen by the parties. The choice must be express or demonstrated with reasonable certainty by the terms of the contract or the circumstances of the case. By their choice the parties can select the law applicable to the whole or a part only of the contract.
2. The parties may at any time agree to subject the contract to a law other than that which previously governed it, whether as a result of an earlier choice under this Article or of other provisions of this Convention. Any variation by the parties of the law to be applied made after the conclusion of the contract shall not prejudice its formal validity under Article 9 or adversely affect the rights of third parties.
3. The fact that the parties have chosen a foreign law, whether or not accompanied by the choice of a foreign tribunal, shall not, where all the other elements relevant to the situation at the time of the choice are connected with one country only, prejudice the application of rules of the law of that country which cannot be derogated from by contract, hereinafter called 'mandatory rules'.
4. The existence and validity of the consent of the parties as to the choice of the applicable law shall be determined in accordance with the provisions of Articles 8, 9 and 11.

Article 4. Applicable law in the absence of choice
1. To the extent that the law applicable to the contract has not been chosen in accordance with Article 3, the contract shall be governed by the law of the country with which it is most closely connected. Nevertheless, a severable part of the contract which has a closer connection with another country may by way of exception be governed by the law of that other country.
2. Subject to the provisions of paragraph 5 of this Article, it shall be presumed that the contract is most closely connected with the country where the party who is to effect the performance which is characteristic of the contract has, at the time of conclusion of the contract, his habitual residence, or, in the case of a body cor-

porate or unincorporate, its central administration. However, if the contract is entered into in the course of that party's trade or profession, that country shall be the country in which the principal place of business is situated or, where under the terms of the contract the performance is to be effected through a place of business other than the principal place of business, the country in which that other place of business is situated.

3. Notwithstanding the provisions of paragraph 2 of this Article, to the extent that the subject matter of the contract is a right in immovable property or a right to use immovable property it shall be presumed that the contract is most closely connected with the country where the immovable property is situated.

4. A contract for the carriage of goods shall not be subject to the presumption in paragraph 2. In such a contract if the country in which, at the time the contract is concluded, the carrier has his principal place of business is also the country in which the place of loading or the place of discharge or the principal place of business of the consignor is situated, it shall be presumed that the contract is most closely connected with that country. In applying this paragraph single voyage charter-parties and other contracts the main purpose of which is the carriage of goods shall be treated as contracts for the carriage of goods.

5. Paragraph 2 shall not apply if the characteristic performance cannot be determined, and the presumptions in paragraphs 2, 3 and 4 shall be disregarded if it appears from the circumstances as a whole that the contract is more closely connected with another country.

Article 5. Certain consumer contracts

1. This Article applies to a contract the object of which is the supply of goods or services to a person ('the consumer') for a purpose which can be regarded as being outside his trade or profession, or a contract for the provision of credit for that object.

2. Notwithstanding the provisions of Article 3, a choice of law made by the parties shall not have the result of depriving the consumer of the protection afforded to him by the mandatory rules of the law of the country in which he has his habitual residence:

– if in that country the conclusion of the contract was preceded by a specific invitation addressed to him or by advertising, and he had taken in that country all the steps necessary on his part for the conclusion of the contract, or

– if the other party or his agent received the consumer's order in that country, or

– if the contract is for the sale of goods and the consumer travelled from that country to another country and there gave his order, provided that the consumer's journey was arranged by the seller for the purpose of inducing the consumer to buy.

3. Notwithstanding the provisions of Article 4, a contract to which this Article applies shall, in the absence of choice in accordance with Article 3, be governed by the law of the country in which the consumer has his habitual residence if it is entered into in the circumstances described in paragraph 2 of this Article.

4. This Article shall not apply to:
(a)   a contract of carriage;
(b)   a contract for the supply of services where the services are to be supplied to the consumer exclusively in a country other than that in which he has his habitual residence.

5. Notwithstanding the provisions of paragraph 4, this Article shall apply to a contract which, for an inclusive price, provides for a combination of travel and accommodation.

Article 6. Individual employment contracts

1. Notwithstanding the provisions of Article 3, in a contract of employment a

choice of law made by the parties shall not have the result of depriving the employee of the protection afforded to him by the mandatory rules of the law which would be applicable under paragraph 2 in the absence of choice.

2.   Notwithstanding the provisions of Article 4, a contract of employment shall, in the absence of choice in accordance with Article 3, be governed:

(a)   by the law of the country in which the employee habitually carries out his work in performance of the contract, even if he is temporarily employed in another country; or

(b)   if the employee does not habitually carry out his work in any one country, by the law of the country in which the place of business through which he was engaged is situated;

unless it appears from the circumstances as a whole that the contract is more closely connected with another country, in which case the contract shall be governed by the law of that country.

Article 7. Mandatory rules

1.   *When applying under this Convention the law of a country, effect may be given to the mandatory rules of the law of another country with which the situation has a close connection, if and in so far as, under the law of the latter country, those rules must be applied whatever the law applicable to the contract. In considering whether to give effect to these mandatory rules, regard shall be had to their nature and purpose and to the consequences of their application or non-application.**

2.   Nothing in this Convention shall restrict the application of the rules of the law of the forum in a situation where they are mandatory irrespective of the law otherwise applicable to the contract.

* The UK entered a reservation disapplying Arts 7(1) and 10(1)(e) in UK courts.

...

SCHEDULE 3
THE BRUSSELS PROTOCOL

The High Contracting Parties to the Treaty establishing the European Economic Community,

Having regard to the Joint Declaration annexed to the Convention on the law applicable to contractual obligations, opened for signature in Rome on 19 June 1980,

Have decided to conclude a Protocol conferring jurisdiction on the Court of Justice of the European Communities to interpret that Convention, and to this end have designated as their Plenipotentiaries:

(Designation of plenipotentiaries)

Who, meeting within the Council of the European Communities, having exchanged their full powers, found in good and due form,

Have agreed as follows:

Article 1

The Court of Justice of the European Communities shall have jurisdiction to give rulings on the interpretation of—

(a)   the Convention on the law applicable to contractual obligations, opened for signature in Rome on 19 June 1980, hereinafter referred to as 'the Rome Convention';

(b)   the Convention on accession to the Rome Convention by the States which have become Members of the European Communities since the date on which it was opened for signature;

(c)   this Protocol.

Article 2
Any of the courts referred to below may request the Court of Justice to give a pre-liminary ruling on a question raised in a case pending before it and concerning interpretation of the provisions contained in the instruments referred to in Article 1 if that court considers that a decision on the question is necessary to enable it to give judgment:
    (a)   ...
        – in the United Kingdom:
        the House of Lords and other courts from which no further appeal is possible;
    (b)   the courts of the Contracting States when acting as appeal courts.

Article 3
    1.   The competent authority of a Contracting State may request the Court of Justice to give a ruling on a question of interpretation of the provisions contained in the instruments referred to in Article 1 if judgments given by courts of that State conflict with the interpretation given either by the Court of Justice or in a judg-ment of one of the courts of another Contracting State referred to in Article 2. The provisions of this paragraph shall apply only to judgments which have become res judicata.
    2.   The interpretation given by the Court of Justice in response to such a request shall not affect the judgments which gave rise to the request for interpretation.
    3.   The Procurators-General of the Supreme Courts of Appeal of the Contracting States, or any other authority designated by a Contracting State, shall be entitled to request the Court of Justice for a ruling on interpretation in accordance with para-graph 1.
    4.   The Registrar of the Court of Justice shall give notice of the request to the Contracting States, to the Commission and to the Council of the European Com-munities; they shall then be entitled within two months of the notification to sub-mit statements of case or written observations to the Court.
    5.   No fees shall be levied or any costs or expenses awarded in respect of the proceedings provided for in this Article.

...

Article 9
This Protocol shall have effect for as long as the Rome Convention remains in force under the conditions laid down in Article 30 of that Convention.

Article 10
Any Contracting State may request the revision of this Protocol. In this event, a revision conference shall be convened by the President of the Council of the Euro-pean Communities.

FOREIGN CORPORATIONS ACT 1991
(1991 c 44)

1 Recognition of corporate status of certain foreign corporations

(1) If at any time—

(a) any question arises whether a body which purports to have or, as the case may be, which appears to have lost corporate status under the laws of a territory which is not at that time a recognised State should or should not be regarded as having legal personality as a body corporate under the law of any part of the United Kingdom, and

(b) it appears that the laws of that territory are at that time applied by a settled court system in that territory,

that question and any other material question relating to the body shall be determined (and account shall be taken of those laws) as if that territory were a recognised State.

(2) For the purposes of subsection (1) above—

(a) 'a recognised State' is a territory which is recognised by Her Majesty's Government in the United Kingdom as a State;

(b) the laws of a territory which is so recognised shall be taken to include the laws of any part of the territory which are ac-knowledged by the federal or other central government of the territory as a whole; and

(c) a material question is a question (whether as to capacity, constitution or otherwise) which, in the case of a body corporate, falls to be determined by reference to the laws of the territory under which the body is incorporated.

(3) Any registration or other thing done at a time before the coming into force of this section shall be regarded as valid if it would have been valid at that time, had subsections (1) and (2) above then been in force.

CHILDREN (SCOTLAND) ACT 1995
(1995 c 36)

14 Jurisdiction and choice of law in relation to certain matters

(1) The Court of Session shall have jurisdiction to entertain an application for an order relating to the administration of a child's property if the child is habitually resident in, or the property is situated in, Scotland.

(2) A sheriff shall have jurisdiction to entertain such an application if the child is habitually resident in, or the property is situated in, the sheriffdom.

(3) Subject to subsection (4) below, any question arising under this Part of this Act—

(a) concerning—

(i) parental responsibilities or parental rights; or

(ii) the responsibilities or rights of a guardian,

in relation to a child shall, in so far as it is not also a question such as is mentioned in paragraph (b) below, be determined by the law of the place of the child's habitual residence at the time when the question arises;

(b) concerning the immediate protection of a child shall be determined by the law of the place where the child is when the question arises; and

(c) as to whether a person is validly appointed or constituted guardian of a child's shall be determined by the law of the place of the child's habitual residence on the date when the appointment was made (the date of death of the testator being taken to be the date of appointment where an appointment was made by will), or the event constituting the guardianship occurred.

(4) Nothing in any provision of law in accordance with which, under subsection (3) above, a question which arises in relation to an application for, or the making of, an order under subsection (1) of section 11 of this Act falls to be determined, shall affect the application of subsection (7) of that section.

[(5)   The provisions of sections 9, 11, 13 and this section are subject to Sections 2 and 3 of Chapter II of Council Regulation (EC) No 2201/2003 of 27th November 2003 concerning jurisdiction and the recognition and enforcement of judgments in matrimonial matters and matters of parental responsibility.]

PRIVATE INTERNATIONAL LAW (MISCELLANEOUS PROVISIONS) ACT 1995*
(1995 c 42)

*As amended by SSI 2008/404.

PART II
VALIDITY OF MARRIAGES UNDER A LAW WHICH PERMITS POLYGAMY

7   Validity and effect in Scots law of potentially polygamous marriages

(1)   A person domiciled in Scotland does not lack capacity to enter into a marriage by reason only that the marriage is entered into under a law which permits polygamy.

(2)   For the avoidance of doubt, a marriage valid by the law of Scotland and entered into—

  (a) under a law which permits polygamy; and
  (b) at a time when neither party to the marriage is already married,

has, so long as neither party marries a second spouse during the subsistence of the marriage, the same effects for all purposes of the law of Scotland as a marriage entered into under a law which does not permit polygamy.

PART III
CHOICE OF LAW IN TORT AND DELICT

9   Purpose of Part III

(1)   The rules in this Part apply for choosing the law (in this Part referred to as 'the applicable law') to be used for determining issues relating to tort or (for the purposes of the law of Scotland) delict.

(2)   The characterisation for the purposes of private international law of issues arising in a claim as issues relating to tort or delict is a matter for the courts of the forum.

(3)   The rules in this Part do not apply in relation to issues arising in any claim excluded from the operation of this Part by section 13 below.

(4)   The applicable law shall be used for determining the issues arising in a claim, including in particular the question whether an actionable tort or delict has occurred.

(5)   The applicable law to be used for determining the issues arising in a claim shall exclude any choice of law rules forming part of the law of the country or countries concerned.

(6)   For the avoidance of doubt (and without prejudice to the operation of section 14 below) this Part applies in relation to events occurring in the forum as it applies in relation to events occurring in any other country.

(7)   In this Part as it extends to any country within the United Kingdom, 'the forum' means England and Wales, Scotland or Northern Ireland, as the case may be.

(8)   In this Part 'delict' includes quasi-delict.

10   Abolition of certain common law rules

The rules of the common law, in so far as they—

(a)   require actionability under both the law of the forum and the law of another country for the purpose of determining whether a tort or delict is actionable; or

(b)   allow (as an exception from the rules falling within paragraph (a) above) for the law of a single country to be applied for the purpose of determining the issues, or any of the issues, arising in the case in question,

are hereby abolished so far as they apply to any claim in tort or delict which is not excluded from the operation of this Part by section 13 below.

11   Choice of applicable law: the general rule

(1)   The general rule is that the applicable law is the law of the country in which the events constituting the tort or delict in question occur.

(2)   Where elements of those events occur in different countries, the applicable law under the general rule is to be taken as being—

(a)   for a cause of action in respect of personal injury caused to an individual or death resulting from personal injury, the law of the country where the individual was when he sustained the injury;

(b)   for a cause of action in respect of damage to property, the law of the country where the property was when it was damaged; and

(c)   in any other case, the law of the country in which the most significant element or elements of those events occurred.

(3)   In this section 'personal injury' includes disease or any impairment of physical or mental condition.

12   Choice of applicable law: displacement of general rule

(1)   If it appears, in all the circumstances, from a comparison of—

(a)   the significance of the factors which connect a tort or delict with the country whose law would be the applicable law under the general rule; and

(b)   the significance of any factors connecting the tort or delict with another country,

that it is substantially more appropriate for the applicable law for determining the issues arising in the case, or any of those issues, to be the law of the other country, the general rule is displaced and the applicable law for determining those issues or that issue (as the case may be) is the law of that other country.

(2)   The factors that may be taken into account as connecting a tort or delict with a country for the purposes of this section include, in particular, factors relating to the parties, to any of the events which constitute the tort or delict in question or to any of the circumstances or consequences of those events.

13   Exclusion of defamation claims from Part III

(1)   Nothing in this Part applies to affect the determination of issues arising in any defamation claim.

(2)   For the purposes of this section 'defamation claim' means —

(a)   any claim under the law of any part of the United Kingdom for libel or slander or for slander of title, slander of goods or other malicious falsehood and any claim under the law of Scotland for verbal injury; and

(b)   any claim under the law of any other country corresponding to or otherwise in the nature of a claim mentioned in paragraph (a) above.

14   Transitional provision and savings

(1)   Nothing in this Part applies to acts or omissions giving rise to a claim which occur before the commencement of this Part.

(2)   Nothing in this Part affects any rules of law (including rules of private international law) except those abolished by section 10 above.

(3)   Without prejudice to the generality of subsection (2) above, nothing in this Part—

(a)   authorises the application of the law of a country outside the forum as the applicable law for determining issues arising in any claim in so far as to do so—

(i)   would conflict with principles of public policy; or

(ii)   would give effect to such a penal, revenue or other public law as would not otherwise be enforceable under the law of the forum; or

(b)   affects any rules of evidence, pleading or practice or authorises questions of procedure in any proceedings to be determined otherwise than in accordance with the law of the forum.

(4)   This Part has effect without prejudice to the operation of any rule of law which either has effect notwithstanding the rules of private international law applicable in the particular circumstances or modifies the rules of private international law that would otherwise be so applicable.

15   Crown application

(1)   This Part applies in relation to claims by or against the Crown as it applies in relation to claims to which the Crown is not a party.

(2)   In subsection (1) above a reference to the Crown does not include a reference to Her Majesty in Her private capacity or to Her Majesty in right of Her Duchy of Lancaster or to the Duke of Cornwall.

(3)   Without prejudice to the generality of section 14(2) above, nothing in this section affects any rule of law as to whether proceedings of any description may be brought against the Crown.

[15A   *Applies to England and Wales and Northern Ireland.*]

[15B   Disapplication of Part III where the rules in the Rome II Regulation apply: Scotland

(1)   Nothing in this Part applies to affect the determination of issues relating to delict which fall to be determined under the Rome II Regulation.

(2)   In subsection (1) 'the Rome II Regulation' means Regulation (EC) No 864/ 2007 of the European Parliament and of the Council on the law applicable to non-contractual obligations (Rome II) including that Regulation as applied by regulation 4 of the Law Applicable to Non-Contractual Obligations (Scotland) Regulations 2008 (conflicts falling within Article 25(2) of Regulation (EC) No 864/2007).

(3)   This section extends to Scotland only.]

SCOTLAND ACT 1998
(1998 c 46)

Legislation

29 Legislative competence

(1)   An Act of the Scottish Parliament is not law so far as any provision of the Act is outside the legislative competence of the Parliament.

(2)   A provision is outside that competence so far as any of the following paragraphs apply—

(a)   it would form part of the law of a country or territory other than Scotland, or confer or remove functions exercisable otherwise than in or as regards Scotland,

(b)   it relates to reserved matters,

(c)   it is in breach of the restrictions in Schedule 4,

(d)   it is incompatible with any of the Convention rights or with Community law,

(e)   it would remove the Lord Advocate from his position as head of the systems of criminal prosecution and investigation of deaths in Scotland.

(3)   For the purposes of this section, the question whether a provision of an Act of the Scottish Parliament relates to a reserved matter is to be determined, subject to subsection (4), by reference to the purpose of the provision, having regard (among other things) to its effect in all the circumstances.

(4)   A provision which—

(a)   would otherwise not relate to reserved matters, but

(b)   makes modifications of Scots private law, or Scots criminal law, as it applies to reserved matters,

is to be treated as relating to reserved matters unless the purpose of the provision is to make the law in question apply consistently to reserved matters and otherwise.

[(5)   Subsection 1 is subject to section 30(6).]

30 Legislative competence; supplementary

(1)   Schedule 5 (which defines reserved matters) shall have effect.

(2)   Her Majesty may by Order in Council make any modifications of Schedule 4 or 5 which She considers necessary or expedient.

(3)   Her Majesty may by Order in Council specify functions which are to be treated, for such purposes of this Act as may be specified, as being, or as not being, functions which are exercisable in or as regards Scotland.

(4)   An Order in Council under this section may also make such modifications of—

(a)   any enactment or prerogative instrument (including any enactment comprised in or made under this Act), or

(b)   any other instrument or document,

as Her Majesty considers necessary or expedient in connection with other provision made by the Order.

[(5)   Subsection (6) applies where any alteration is made—

(a)   to the matters which are reserved matters, or

(b)   to Schedule 4,

(whether by virtue of the making, revocation or expiry of an Order in Council under this section or otherwise).

(6)   Where the effect of the alteration is that a provision of an Act of the Scottish Parliament ceases to be within the legislative competence of the Parliament, the provision does not for that reason cease to have effect (unless an enactment provides otherwise).]

Ministerial functions

57 [EU] law and Convention rights

(1)   Despite the transfer to the Scottish Ministers by virtue of section 53 of functions in relation to observing and implementing obligations under Community law, any function of a Minister of the Crown in relation to any matter shall continue to be exercisable by him as regards Scotland for the purposes specified in section 2(2) of the European Communities Act 1972.

(2)   A member of the [Scottish Government] has no power to make any subordinate legislation, or to do any other act, so far as the legislation or act is incompatible with any of the Convention rights or with [EU] law.

(3)   Subsection (2) does not apply to an act of the Lord Advocate—

(a)   in prosecuting any offence, or

(b)   in his capacity as head of the systems of criminal prosecution and investigation of deaths in Scotland,

which, because of subsection (2) of section 6 of the Human Rights Act 1998, is not unlawful under subsection (1) of that section.

Final provisions

126 Interpretation

...

(4)   References in this Act to Scots private law are to the following areas of the civil law of Scotland—

(a)   the general principles of private law (including private international law),

(b)   the law of persons (including natural persons, legal persons and unincorporated bodies),

(c)   the law of obligations (including obligations arising from contract, unilateral promise, delict, unjustified enrichment and negotiorum gestio),

(d)   the law of property (including heritable and moveable property, trusts and succession), and

(e)   the law of actions (including jurisdiction, remedies, evidence, procedure, diligence, recognition and enforcement of court orders, limitation of actions and arbitration), and include references to judicial review of administrative action.

...

(9)   In this Act—

(a)   all those rights, powers, liabilities, obligations and restrictions from time to time created or arising by or under the Community Treaties, and

(b)   all those remedies and procedures from time to time provided for by or under the Community Treaties,

are referred to as 'Community law.'

(10)   In this Act, 'international obligations' means any international obligations of the United Kingdom other than obligations to observe and implement Community law or the Convention rights.

...

SCHEDULE 5
RESERVED MATTERS

Foreign affairs etc

7.—(1) International relations, including relations with territories outside the United Kingdom, the [European Union] (and their institutions) and other international organisations, regulation of international trade, and international development assistance and co-operation are reserved matters.

(2) Sub-paragraph (1) does not reserve—

(a) observing and implementing international obligations, obligations under the Human Rights Convention and obligations under [EU] law,

(b) assisting Ministers of the Crown in relation to any matter to which that sub-paragraph applies.

ADOPTION (INTERCOUNTRY ASPECTS) ACT 1999
(1999 c 18)

Implementation of Convention

1 Regulations giving effect to Convention

(1) Subject to the provisions of this Act, regulations made by the Secretary of State may make provision for giving effect to the Convention on Protection of Children and Co-operation in respect of Intercountry Adoption, concluded at the Hague on 29th May 1993 ('the Convention').

(2) The text of the Convention (so far as material) is set out in Schedule 1 to this Act.

(3) Regulations under this section may—

(a) apply, with or without modifications, any provision of the enactments relating to adoption;

(b) provide that any person who contravenes or fails to comply with any provision of the regulations is to be guilty of an offence and liable on summary conviction to imprisonment for a term not exceeding three months, or a fine not exceeding level 5 on the standard scale, or both;

(c) make different provision for different purposes or areas; and

(d) make such incidental, supplementary, consequential or transitional provision as appears to the Secretary of State to be expedient.

(4) Regulations under this section shall be made by statutory instrument which shall be subject to annulment in pursuance of a resolution of either House of Parliament.

(5) Subject to subsection (6), any power to make subordinate legislation under or for the purposes of the enactments relating to adoption includes power to do so with a view to giving effect to the provisions of the Convention.

(6) Subsection (5) does not apply in relation to any power which is exercisable by the National Assembly for Wales.

[(7) References in this section to enactments include references to Acts of the Scottish Parliament.]

2 Central Authorities and accredited bodies

(1) The functions under the Convention of the Central Authority are to be discharged—

(a) separately in relation to England and Scotland by the Secretary of State; and

(b) in relation to Wales by the National Assembly for Wales.

[...]

[(2A) [A registered adoption society] is an accredited body for the purposes of the Convention if, in accordance with the conditions of the registration, the

[society may provide facilities in respect of Convention adoptions and adoptions effected by Convention adoption orders.]

[(2B)   A registered adoption service is an accredited body for the purpose of the Convention if, in accordance with the conditions of its registration, the service may provide facilities in respect of Convention adoptions and adoptions effected by Convention adoption orders.]

(3)   An approved adoption society is an accredited body for the purposes of the Convention if the approval extends to the provision of facilities in respect of Convention adoptions and adoptions effected by Convention adoption orders.

(4)   The functions under Article 9(a) to (c) of the Convention are to be discharged by local authorities and accredited bodies on behalf of the Central Authority.

[(5)   In this section, 'registered adoption society' has the same meaning as in section 2 of the Adoption and Children Act 2002 (basic definitions); and expressions used in this section in its application to England and Wales which are also used in that Act have the same meanings as in that Act.]

(6)   [In this section in its application to Scotland, 'registered adoption service' means an adoption service provided as mentioned in section 2(11)(b) of the Regulation of Care (Scotland) Act 2001 (asp 8) and registered under Part 1 of that Act; and 'registration' shall be construed accordingly.]

Miscellaneous and supplemental

17   Savings for adoptions etc under 1965 Convention

(1)   In relation to—
   (a)   a 1965 Convention adoption order or an application for such an order; or
   (b)   a 1965 Convention adoption,
the 1976 and 1978 Acts shall have effect without the amendments made by sections 3 to 6 and 8 and Schedule 2 to this Act and the associated repeals made by Schedule 3 to this Act.

(2)   In subsection (1) in its application to the 1976 or 1978 Act—
'1965 Convention adoption order' has the meaning which 'Convention adoption order' has in that Act as it has effect without the amendments and repeals mentioned in that subsection;
'1965 Convention adoption' has the meaning which 'regulated adoption' has in that Act as it so has effect.

18   Short title, interpretation, commencement and extent

(1)   This Act may be cited as the Adoption (Intercountry Aspects) Act 1999.

[...]

(3)   This Act, except this section, shall come into force on such day as the Secretary of State may by order made by statutory instrument appoint and different days may be appointed for different purposes.

(4)   Subject to subsection (5), this Act extends to Great Britain only.

(5)   Any amendment of an enactment which extends to any other part of the British Islands or any colony also extends to that part or colony.

CONVENTION ON PROTECTION OF CHILDREN AND CO-OPERATION IN
RESPECT OF INTERCOUNTRY ADOPTION

The States signatory to the present Convention.

Recognizing that the child, for the full and harmonious development of his or her personality, should grow up in a family environment, in an atmosphere of happiness, love and understanding,

Recalling that each State should take, as a matter of priority, appropriate measures to enable the child to remain in the care of his or her family of origin,

Recognizing that intercountry adoption may offer the advantage of a permanent family to a child for whom a suitable family cannot be found in his or her State of origin,

Convinced of the necessity to take measures to ensure that intercountry adoptions are made in the best interests of the child and with respect for his or her fundamental rights, and to prevent the abduction, the sale of, or traffic in children,

Desiring to establish common provisions to this effect, taking into account the principles set forth in international instruments, in particular the United Nations Convention on the Rights of the Child, of 20 November 1989, and the United Nations Declaration on Social and Legal Principles relating to the Protection and Welfare of Children, with Special Reference to Foster Placement and Adoption Nationally and Internationally (General Assembly Resolution 41/85, of 3 December 1986),

Have agreed upon the following provisions—

CHAPTER 1 – SCOPE OF THE CONVENTION

Article 1

The objects of the present Convention are—

(a)   to establish safeguards to ensure that intercountry adoptions take place in the best interests of the child and with respect for his or her fundamental rights as recognised in international law;

(b)   to establish a system of co-operation amongst Contracting States to ensure that those safeguards are respected and thereby prevent the abduction, the sale of, or traffic in children;

(c)   to secure the recognition in Contracting States of adoptions made in accordance with the Convention.

Article 2

1.   The Convention shall apply where a child habitually resident in one Contracting State ('the State of origin') has been, is being, or is to be moved to another Contracting State ('the receiving State') either after his or her adoption in the State of origin by spouses or a person habitually resident in the receiving State, or for the purposes of such an adoption in the receiving State or in the State of origin.

2.   The Convention covers only adoptions which create a permanent parent-child relationship.

Article 3

The Convention ceases to apply if the agreements mentioned in Article 17, sub-paragraph (c), have not been given before the child attains the age of eighteen years.

CHAPTER II – REQUIREMENTS FOR INTERCOUNTRY ADOPTIONS

Article 4

An adoption within the scope of the Convention shall take place only if the competent authorities of the State of origin—

(a)   have established that the child is adoptable;

(b)   have determined, after possibilities for placement of the child within the

State of origin have been given due consideration, that an intercountry adoption is in the child's best interests;

(c) have ensured that—

(i) the persons, institutions and authorities whose consent is necessary for adoption, have been counselled as may be necessary and duly informed of the effects of their consent, in particular whether or not an adoption will result in the termination of the legal relationship between the child and his or her family of origin,

(ii) such persons, institutions and authorities have given their consent freely, in the required legal form, and expressed or evidenced in writing,

(iii) the consents have not been induced by payment or compensation of any kind and have not been withdrawn, and

(iv) the consent of the mother, where required, has been given only after the birth of the child; and

(d) have ensured, having regard to the age and degree of maturity of the child, that—

(i) he or she has been counselled and duly informed of the effects of the adoption and of his or her consent to the adoption, where such consent is required,

(ii) consideration has been given to the child's wishes and opinions,

(iii) the child's consent to the adoption, where such consent is required, has been given freely, in the required legal form, and expressed or evidenced in writing, and

(iv) such consent has not been induced by payment or compensation of any kind.

Article 5

An adoption within the scope of the Convention shall take place only if the competent authorities of the receiving State—

(a) have determined that the prospective adoptive parents are eligible and suited to adopt;

(b) have ensured that the prospective adoptive parents have been counselled as may be necessary; and

(c) have determined that the child is or will be authorised to enter and reside permanently in that State.

CHAPTER III – CENTRAL AUTHORITIES AND ACCREDITED BODIES

Article 6

1. A Contracting State shall designate a Central Authority to discharge the duties which are imposed by the Convention upon such authorities.

2. Federal States, States with more than one system of law or States having autonomous territorial units shall be free to appoint more than one Central Authority and to specify the territorial or personal extent of their functions. Where a State has appointed more than one Central Authority, it shall designate the Central Authority to which any communication may be addressed for transmission to the appropriate Central Authority within that State.

Article 7

1. Central Authorities shall co-operate with each other and promote co-operation amongst the competent authorities in their States to protect children and to achieve the other objects of the Convention.

2. They shall take directly all appropriate measures to—

(a) provide information as to the laws of their States concerning adoption and other general information, such as statistics and standard forms;

(b) keep one another informed about the operation of the Convention and, as far as possible, eliminate any obstacles to its application.

Article 8

Central Authorities shall take, directly or through public authorities, all appropriate measures to prevent improper financial or other gain in connection with an adoption and to deter all practices contrary to the objects of the Convention.

Article 9

Central Authorities shall take, directly or through public authorities or other bodies duly accredited in their State, all appropriate measures, in particular to—

    (a)   collect, preserve and exchange information about the situation of the child and the prospective adoptive parents, so far as is necessary to complete the adoption;

    (b)   facilitate, follow and expedite proceedings with a view to obtaining the adoption;

    (c)   promote the development of adoption counselling and post-adoption services in their States;

    (d)   provide each other with general evaluation reports about experience with intercountry adoption;

    (e)   reply, in so far as is permitted by the law of their State, to justified requests from other Central Authorities or public authorities for information about a particular adoption situation.

Article 10

Accreditation shall only be granted to and maintained by bodies demonstrating their competence to carry out properly the tasks with which they may be entrusted.

Article 11

An accredited body shall—

    (a)   pursue only non-profit objectives according to such conditions and within such limits as may be established by the competent authorities of the State of accreditation;

    (b)   be directed and staffed by persons qualified by their ethical standards and by training or experience to work in the field of intercountry adoption; and

    (c)   be subject to supervision by competent authorities of that State as to its composition, operation and financial situation.

Article 12

A body accredited in one Contracting State may act in another Contracting State only if the competent authorities of both States have authorised it to do so.

Article 13

The designation of the Central Authorities and, where appropriate, the extent of their functions, as well as the names and addresses of the accredited bodies shall be communicated by each Contracting State to the Permanent Bureau of the Hague Conference on Private International Law.

CHAPTER IV – PROCEDURAL REQUIREMENTS IN INTERCOUNTRY
ADOPTION

Article 14

Persons habitually resident in a Contracting State, who wish to adopt a child habitually resident in another Contracting State, shall apply to the Central Authority in the State of their habitual residence.

Article 15

    1.   If the Central Authority of the receiving State is satisfied that the applicants are eligible and suited to adopt, it shall prepare a report including information about their identity, eligibility and suitability to adopt, background, family and medical history, social environment, reasons for adoption, ability to undertake an

intercountry adoption, as well as the characteristics of the children for whom they would be qualified to care.

2.   It shall transmit the report to the Central Authority of the State of origin.

Article 16

1.   If the Central Authority of the State of origin is satisfied that the child is adoptable, it shall—

(a)   prepare a report including information about his or her identity, adoptability, background, social environment, family history, medical history including that of the child's family, and any special needs of the child;

(b)   give due consideration to the child's upbringing and to his or her ethnic, religious and cultural background;

(c)   ensure that consents have been obtained in accordance with Article 4; and

(d)   determine, on the basis in particular of the reports relating to the child and the prospective adoptive parents, whether the envisaged placement is in the best interests of the child.

2.   It shall transmit to the Central Authority of the receiving State its report on the child, proof that the necessary consents have been obtained and the reasons for its determination on the placement, taking care not to reveal the identity of the mother and the father if, in the State of origin, these identities may not be disclosed.

Article 17

Any decision in the State of origin that a child should be entrusted to prospective adoptive parents may only be made if—

(a)   the Central Authority of that State has ensured that the prospective adoptive parents agree;

(b)   the Central Authority of the receiving State has approved such decision, where such approval is required by the law of that State or by the Central Authority of the State of origin;

(c)   the Central Authorities of both States have agreed that the adoption may proceed; and

(d)   it has been determined, in accordance with Article 5, that the prospective adoptive parents are eligible and suited to adopt and that the child is or will be authorised to enter and reside permanently in the receiving State.

Article 18

The Central Authorities of both States shall take all necessary steps to obtain permission for the child to leave the State of origin and to enter and reside permanently in the receiving State.

Article 19

1.   The transfer of the child to the receiving State may only be carried out if the requirements of Article 17 have been satisfied.

2.   The Central Authorities of both States shall ensure that this transfer takes place in secure and appropriate circumstances and, if possible, in the company of the adoptive or prospective adoptive parents.

3.   If the transfer of the child does not take place, the reports referred to in Articles 15 and 16 are to be sent back to the authorities who forwarded them.

Article 20

The Central Authorities shall keep each other informed about the adoption process and the measures taken to complete it, as well as about the progress of the placement if a probationary period is required.

Article 21

1.   Where the adoption is to take place after the transfer of the child to the receiving State and it appears to the Central Authority of that State that the con-

tinued placement of the child with the prospective adoptive parents is not in the child's best interests, such Central Authority shall take the measures necessary to protect the child, in particular—

(a)   to cause the child to be withdrawn from the prospective adoptive parents and to arrange temporary care;

(b)   in consultation with the Central Authority of the State of origin, to arrange without delay a new placement of the child with a view to adoption or, if this is not appropriate, to arrange alternative long-term care; an adoption shall not take place until the Central Authority of the State of origin has been duly informed concerning the new prospective adoptive parents;

(c)   as a last resort, to arrange the return of the child, if his or her interests so require.

2.   Having regard in particular to the age and degree of maturity of the child, he or she shall be consulted and, where appropriate, his or her consent obtained in relation to measures to be taken under this Article.

Article 22

1.   The functions of a Central Authority under this Chapter may be performed by public authorities or by bodies accredited under Chapter III, to the extent permitted by the law of its State.

2.   Any Contracting State may declare to the depositary of the Convention that the functions of the Central Authority under Articles 15 to 21 may be performed in that State, to the extent permitted by the law and subject to the supervision of the competent authorities of that State, also by bodies or persons who—

(a)   meet the requirements of integrity, professional competence, experience and accountability of that State; and

(b)   are qualified by their ethical standards and by training or experience to work in the field of intercountry adoption.

3.   A Contracting State which makes the declaration provided for in paragraph 2 shall keep the Permanent Bureau of the Hague Conference on Private International Law informed of the names and addresses of these bodies and persons.

4.   Any Contracting State may declare to the depositary of the Convention that adoptions of children habitually resident in its territory may only take place if the functions of the Central Authorities are performed in accordance with paragraph 1.

5.   Notwithstanding any declaration made under paragraph 2, the reports provided for in Articles 15 and 16 shall, in every case, be prepared under the responsibility of the Central Authority or other authorities or bodies in accordance with paragraph 1.

CHAPTER V – RECOGNITION AND EFFECTS OF THE ADOPTION

Article 23

1.   An adoption certified by the competent authority of the State of the adoption as having been made in accordance with the Convention shall be recognised by operation of law in the other Contracting States. The certificate shall specify when and by whom the agreements under Article 17, sub-paragraph c, were given.

2.   Each Contracting State shall, at the time of signature, ratification, acceptance, approval or accession, notify the depositary of the Convention of the identity and the functions of the authority or the authorities which, in that State, are competent to make the certification. It shall also notify the depositary of any modification in the designation of these authorities.

Article 24

The recognition of an adoption may be refused in a contracting State only if the adoption is manifestly contrary to its public policy, taking into account the best interests of the child.

Article 25
Any Contracting State may declare to the depositary of the convention that it will not be bound under this Convention to recognise adoptions made in accordance with an agreement concluded by application of Article 39, paragraph 2.

Article 26
1.   The recognition of an adoption includes recognition of—
    (a)   The legal parent-child relationship between the child and his or her adoptive parents;
    (b)   parental responsibility of the adoptive parents for the child;
    (c)   the termination of a pre-existing legal relationship between the child and his or her mother and father, if the adoption has this effect in the Contracting State where it was made.
2.   In the case of an adoption having the effect of terminating a pre-existing legal parent-child relationship, the child shall enjoy in the receiving State, and in any other Contracting State where the adoption is recognised, rights equivalent to those resulting from adoptions having this effect in each such State.
3.   The preceding paragraphs shall not prejudice the application of any provision more favourable for the child, in force in the Contracting State which recognises the adoption.

Article 27
1.   Where an adoption granted in the State of origin does not have the effect of terminating a pre-existing legal parent-child relationship, it may, in the receiving State which recognises the adoption under the Convention, be converted into an adoption having such an effect—
    (a)   if the law of the receiving State so permits; and
    (b)   if the consents referred to in Article 4, sub-paragraphs c and d, have been or are given for the purpose of such an adoption.
2.   Article 23 applies to the decision converting the adoption.

CHAPTER VI – GENERAL PROVISIONS

Article 28
The Convention does not affect any law of a State of origin which requires that the adoption of a child habitually resident within that State take place in that State or which prohibits the child's placement in, or transfer to, the receiving State prior to adoption.

Article 29
There shall be no contact between the prospective adoptive parents and the child's parents or any other person who has care of the child until the requirements of Article 4, sub-paragraphs a to c, and Article 5, sub-paragraph a, have been met, unless the adoption takes place within a family or unless the contact is in compliance with the conditions established by the competent authority of the State of origin.

Article 30
1.   The competent authorities of a Contracting State shall ensure that information held by them concerning the child's origin, in particular information concerning the identity of his or her parents, as well as the medical history, is preserved.
2.   They shall ensure that the child or his or her representative has access to such information, under appropriate guidance, in so far as is permitted by the law of that State.

Article 31
Without prejudice to Article 30, personal data gathered or transmitted under the Convention, especially data referred to in Articles 15 and 16, shall be used only for the purposes for which they were gathered or transmitted.

Article 32

1.   No one shall derive improper financial or other gain from an activity related to an intercountry adoption.

2.   Only costs and expenses, including reasonable professional fees of persons involved in the adoption, may be charged or paid.

3.   The directors, administrators and employees of bodies involved in an adoption shall not receive remuneration which is unreasonably high in relation to services rendered.

Article 33

A competent authority which finds that any provision of the Convention has not been respected or that there is a serious risk that it may not be respected, shall immediately inform the Central Authority of its State. This Central Authority shall be responsible for ensuring that appropriate measures are taken.

Article 34

If the competent authority of the State of destination of a document so requests, a translation certified as being in conformity with the original must be furnished. Unless otherwise provided, the costs of such translation are to be borne by the prospective adoptive parents.

Article 35

The competent authorities of the contracting States shall act expeditiously in the process of adoption.

Article 36

In relation to a State which has two or more systems of law with regard to adoption applicable in different territorial units—

(a)   any reference to habitual residence in that State shall be construed as referring to habitual residence in a territorial unit of that State;

(b)   any reference to the law of that State shall be construed as referring to the law in force in the relevant territorial unit;

(c)   any reference to the competent authorities or to the public authorities of that State shall be construed as referring to those authorised to act in the relevant territorial unit;

(d)   any reference to the accredited bodies of that State shall be construed as referring to bodies accredited in the relevant territorial unit.

Article 37

In relation to a State which with regard to adoption has two or more systems of law applicable to different categories of persons, any reference to the law of that State shall be construed as referring to the legal system specified by the law of that State.

Article 38

A State within which different territorial units have their own rules of law in respect of adoption shall not be bound to apply the Convention where a State with a unified system of law would not be bound to do so.

Article 39

1.   The convention does not affect any international instrument to which Contracting States are Parties and which contains provisions on matters governed by the Convention, unless a contrary declaration is made by the States parties to such instrument.

2.   Any Contracting State may enter into agreements with one or more other Contracting States, with a view to improving the application of the Convention in their mutual relations. These agreements may derogate only from the provisions of Articles 14 to 16 and 18 to 21. The States which have concluded such an agreement shall transmit a copy to the depositary of the Convention.

Article 40
No reservation to the Convention shall be permitted.

Article 41
The Convention shall apply in every case where an application pursuant to Article 14 has been received after the Convention has entered into force in the receiving State and the State of origin.

Article 42
The Secretary General of the Hague Conference on Private International Law shall at regular intervals convene a Special Commission in order to review the practical operation of the Convention.

IMMIGRATION AND ASYLUM ACT 1999
(1999 c 33)

24 Duty to report suspicious marriages
(1) Subsection (3) applies if—
  (a)   a superintendent registrar to whom a notice of marriage has been given under section 27 of the Marriage Act 1949,
  [(aa) a superintendent registrar, or registrar of births, deaths and marriages, who receives information in advance of a person giving such a notice,]
  (b)   any other person who, under section 28(2) of that Act, has attested a declaration accompanying such a notice,
  (c)   a district registrar to whom a marriage notice or an approved certificate has been submitted under section 3 of the Marriage (Scotland) Act 1977,
  [(ca) a district registrar who receives information in advance of a person submitting such a notice or certificate,]
  (d)   a registrar or deputy registrar to whom notice has been given under section 13 of the Marriages (Ireland) Act 1844 or section 4 of the Marriage Law (Ireland) Amendment Act 1863, [or
  (da) a registrar or deputy registrar who receives information in advance of a person giving such a notice,]
has reasonable grounds for suspecting that the marriage will be a sham marriage.
(2) Subsection (3) also applies if—
  (a)   a marriage is solemnized in the presence of a registrar of marriages or, in relation to Scotland, an authorised registrar (within the meaning of the Act of 1977); and
  (b)   before, during or immediately after solemnization of the marriage, the registrar has reasonable grounds for suspecting that the marriage will be, or is, a sham marriage.
(3) The person concerned must report his suspicion to the Secretary of State without delay and in such form and manner as may be prescribed by regulations.
(4) The regulations are to be made—
  (a)   in relation to England and Wales, by the Registrar General for England and Wales with the approval of [the Secretary of State];
  (b)   in relation to Scotland, by the Secretary of State after consulting the Registrar General of Births, Deaths and Marriages for Scotland;
  (c)   in relation to Northern Ireland, by the Secretary of State after consulting the Registrar General in Northern Ireland.
[(5) A marriage (whether or not it is void) is a 'sham marriage' if—
  (a)   either, or both, of the parties to the marriage is not a relevant national,
  (b)   there is no genuine relationship between the parties to the marriage, and
  (c)   either, of both, of the parties to the marriage enter into the marriage for one or more of these purposes—
    (i)   avoiding the effect of one or more provisions of United Kingdom immigration law or the immigration rules;

(ii) enabling a party to the marriage to obtain a right conferred by that law or those rules to reside in the United Kingdom.]
[(6) in subsection (5)—
'relevant national' means—
(a) a British citizen,
(b) a national of an EEA State other than the United Kingdom, or
(c) a national of Switzerland;
'United Kingdom immigration law' includes any subordinate legislation concerning the right of relevant nationals to move between and reside in member States.]

[24A Duty to report suspicious civil partnerships

(1) Subsection (3) applies if—
(a) a registration authority to whom a notice of proposed civil partnership has been given under section 8 of the Civil Partnership Act 2004,
[(aa) a registration authority that receives information in advance of a person giving such a notice,]
(b) any person who, under section 8 of the 2004 Act, has attested a declaration accompanying such a notice,
(c) a district registrar to whom a notice of proposed civil partnership has been given under section 88 of the 2004 Act,
[(ca) a district registrar who receives information in advance of a person giving such a notice,]
(d) a registrar to whom a civil partnership notice has been given under section 139 of the 2004 Act, [or
(da) a registrar who receives information in advance of a person giving such a notice,]
has reasonable grounds for suspecting that the civil partnership will be a sham civil partnership.
(2) Subsection (3) also applies if—
(a) two people register as civil partners of each other under Part 2, 3 or 4 of the 2004 Act in the presence of the registrar, and
(b) before, during or immediately after they do so, the registrar has reasonable grounds for suspecting that the civil partnership will be, or is, a sham civil partnership.
(3) The person concerned must report his suspicion to the Secretary of State without delay and in such form and manner as may be prescribed by regulations.
(4) The regulations are to be made—
(a) in relation to England and Wales, by the Registrar General for England and Wales with the approval of [the Secretary of State];
(b) in relation to Scotland, by the Secretary of State after consulting the Registrar General of Births, Deaths and Marriages for Scotland;
(c) in relation to Northern Ireland, by the Secretary of State after consulting the Registrar General in Northern Ireland.
[(5) A civil partnership (whether or not it is void) is a 'sham civil partnership' if—
(a) either, or both, of the parties to the civil partnership is not a relevant national,
(b) there is no genuine relationship between the parties to the civil partnership, and
(c) either, of both, of the parties to the civil partnership enter into the civil partnership for one or more of these purposes—
(i) avoiding the effect of one or more provisions of United Kingdom immigration law or the immigration rules;
(ii) enabling a party to the civil partnership to obtain a right conferred by that law or those rules to reside in the United Kingdom.]

[(6)   in subsection (5)—
'relevant national' means—
    (a)   a British citizen,
    (b)   a national of an EEA State other than the United Kingdom, or
    (c)   a national of Switzerland;
'United Kingdom immigration law' includes any subordinate legislation concerning the right of relevant nationals to move between and reside in member States.]]

ADOPTION AND CHILDREN ACT 2002
(2002 c 38)

Bringing children into and out of the United Kingdom

83   Restriction on bringing children in

   (1)   This section applies where a person who is habitually resident in the British Islands (the 'British resident')—
    (a)   brings, or causes another to bring, a child who is habitually resident outside the British Islands into the United Kingdom for the purpose of adoption by the British resident, or
    (b)   at any time brings, or causes another to bring, into the United Kingdom a child adopted by the British resident under an external adoption effected within the period of six months ending with that time.
The references to adoption, or to a child adopted, by the British resident include a reference to adoption, or to a child adopted, by the British resident and another person.
   (2)   But this section does not apply if the child is intended to be adopted under a Convention adoption order.
   (3)   An external adoption means an adoption, other than a Convention adoption, of a child effected under the law of any country or territory outside the British Islands, whether or not the adoption is—
    (a)   an adoption within the meaning of Chapter 4, or
    (b)   a full adoption (within the meaning of section 88(3)).
   (4)   Regulations may require a person intending to bring, or to cause another to bring, a child into the United Kingdom in circumstances where this section applies—
    (a)   to apply to an adoption agency (including a Scottish or Northern Irish adoption agency) in the prescribed manner for an assessment of his suitability to adopt the child, and
    (b)   to give the agency any information it may require for the purpose of the assessment.
   (5)   Regulations may require prescribed conditions to be met in respect of a child brought into the United Kingdom in circumstances where this section applies.
   (6)   In relation to a child brought into the United Kingdom for adoption in circumstances where this section applies, regulations may—
    (a)   provide for any provision of Chapter 3 to apply with modifications or not to apply,
    (b)   if notice of intention to adopt has been given, impose functions in respect of the child on the local authority to which the notice was given.
   (7)   If a person brings, or causes another to bring, a child into the United Kingdom at any time in circumstances where this section applies, he is guilty of an offence if—
    (a)   he has not complied with any requirement imposed by virtue of subsection (4), or

(b)   any condition required to be met by virtue of subsection (5) is not met,
before that time, or before any later time which may be prescribed.

(8)   A person guilty of an offence under this section is liable—

(a)   on summary conviction to imprisonment for a term not exceeding six
months, or a fine not exceeding the statutory maximum, or both,

(b)   on conviction on indictment, to imprisonment for a term not exceeding
twelve months, or a fine, or both.

(9)   In this section, 'prescribed' means prescribed by regulations and 'regulations' means regulations made by the Secretary of State, after consultation with the
Assembly.

84   Giving parental responsibility prior to adoption abroad

(1)   The High Court may, on an application by persons who the court is satisfied intend to adopt a child under the law of a country or territory outside the
British Islands, make an order giving parental responsibility for the child to them.

(2)   An order under this section may not give parental responsibility to persons
who the court is satisfied meet those requirements as to domicile, or habitual residence, in England and Wales which have to be met if an adoption order is to be
made in favour of those persons.

(3)   An order under this section may not be made unless any requirements prescribed by regulations are satisfied.

(4)   An application for an order under this section may not be made unless at
all times during the preceding ten weeks the child's home was with the applicant
or, in the case of an application by two people, both of them.

(5)   Section 46(2) to (4) has effect in relation to an order under this section as it
has effect in relation to adoption orders.

(6)   Regulations may provide for any provision of this Act which refers to
adoption orders to apply, with or without modifications, to orders under this
section.

(7)   In this section, 'regulations' means regulations made by the Secretary of
State, after consultation with the Assembly.

85   Restriction on taking children out

(1)   A child who—

(a)   is a Commonwealth citizen, or

(b)   is habitually resident in the United Kingdom,

must not be removed from the United Kingdom to a place outside the British
Islands for the purpose of adoption unless the condition in subsection (2) is met.

(2)   The condition is that—

(a)   the prospective adopters have parental responsibility for the child by
virtue of an order under section 84, or

(b)   the child is removed under the authority of an order under [section 59 of
the Adoption and Children (Scotland) Act 2007 (asp 4)] or Article 57 of the
Adoption (Northern Ireland) Order 1987 (SI 1987/2203 (NI 22)).

(3)   Removing a child from the United Kingdom includes arranging to do so;
and the circumstances in which a person arranges to remove a child from the
United Kingdom include those where he—

(a)   enters into an arrangement for the purpose of facilitating such a removal
of the child,

(b)   initiates or takes part in any negotiations of which the purpose is the
conclusion of an arrangement within paragraph (a), or

(c)   causes another person to take any step mentioned in paragraph (a) or (b).
An arrangement includes an agreement (whether or not enforceable).

(4)   A person who removes a child from the United Kingdom in contravention
of subsection (1) is guilty of an offence.

(5)   A person is not guilty of an offence under subsection (4) of causing a
person to take any step mentioned in paragraph (a) or (b) of subsection (3) unless

it is proved that he knew or had reason to suspect that the step taken would contravene subsection (1).

But this subsection only applies if sufficient evidence is adduced to raise an issue as to whether the person had the knowledge or reason mentioned.

(6) A person guilty of an offence under this section is liable—

(a) on summary conviction to imprisonment for a term not exceeding six months, or a fine not exceeding the statutory maximum, or both,

(b) on conviction on indictment, to imprisonment for a term not exceeding twelve months, or a fine, or both.

(7) In any proceedings under this section—

(a) a report by a British consular officer or a deposition made before a British consular officer and authenticated under the signature of that officer is admissible, upon proof that the officer or the deponent cannot be found in the United Kingdom, as evidence of the matters stated in it, and

(b) it is not necessary to prove the signature or official character of the person who appears to have signed any such report or deposition.

86 Power to modify sections 83 and 85

(1) Regulations may provide for section 83 not to apply if—

(a) the adopters or (as the case may be) prospective adopters are natural parents, natural relatives or guardians of the child in question (or one of them is), or

(b) the British resident in question is a partner of a parent of the child, and any prescribed conditions are met.

(2) Regulations may provide for section 85(1) to apply with modifications, or not to apply, if—

(a) the prospective adopters are parents, relatives or guardians of the child in question (or one of them is), or

(b) the prospective adopter is a partner of a parent of the child, and any prescribed conditions are met.

(3) On the occasion of the first exercise of the power to make regulations under this section—

(a) the statutory instrument containing the regulations is not to be made unless a draft of the instrument has been laid before, and approved by a resolution of, each House of Parliament, and

(b) accordingly section 140(2) does not apply to the instrument.

(4) In this section, 'prescribed' means prescribed by regulations and 'regulations' means regulations made by the Secretary of State after consultation with the Assembly.

Overseas adoptions

87 Overseas adoptions

(1) In this Act, 'overseas adoption'—

(a) means an adoption of a description specified in an order made by the Secretary of State, being a description of adoptions effected under the law of any country or territory outside the British Islands, but

(b) does not include a Convention adoption.

(2) Regulations may prescribe the requirements that ought to be met by an adoption of any description effected after the commencement of the regulations for it to be an overseas adoption for the purposes of this Act.

(3) At any time when such regulations have effect, the Secretary of State must exercise his powers under this section so as to secure that subsequently effected adoptions of any description are not overseas adoptions for the purposes of this Act if he considers that they are not likely within a reasonable time to meet the prescribed requirements.

(4) In this section references to this Act include the Adoption Act 1976 (c 36).

(5)   An order under this section may contain provision as to the manner in which evidence of any overseas adoption may be given.

(6)   In this section—

'adoption' means an adoption of a child or of a person who was a child at the time the adoption was applied for,

'regulations' means regulations made by the Secretary of State after consultation with the Assembly.

Miscellaneous

88   Modification of section 67 for Hague Convention adoptions

(1)   If the High Court is satisfied, on an application under this section, that each of the following conditions is met in the case of a Convention adoption, it may direct that section 67(3) does not apply, or does not apply to any extent specified in the direction.

(2)   The conditions are—

(a)   that under the law of the country in which the adoption was effected, the adoption is not a full adoption,

(b)   that the consents referred to in Article 4(c) and (d) of the Convention have not been given for a full adoption or that the United Kingdom is not the receiving State (within the meaning of Article 2 of the Convention),

(c)   that it would be more favourable to the adopted child for a direction to be given under subsection (1).

(3)   A full adoption is an adoption by virtue of which the child is to be treated in law as not being the child of any person other than the adopters or adopter.

(4)   In relation to a direction under this section and an application for it, sections 59 and 60 of the Family Law Act 1986 (c 55) (declarations under Part 3 of that Act as to marital status) apply as they apply in relation to a direction under that Part and an application for such a direction.

89   Annulment etc of overseas or Hague Convention adoptions

(1)   The High Court may, on an application under this subsection, by order annul a Convention adoption or Convention adoption order on the ground that the adoption is contrary to public policy.

(2)   The High Court may, on an application under this subsection—

(a)   by order provide for an overseas adoption or a determination under section 91 to cease to be valid on the ground that the adoption or determination is contrary to public policy or that the authority which purported to authorise the adoption or make the determination was not competent to entertain the case, or

(b)   decide the extent, if any, to which a determination under section 91 has been affected by a subsequent determination under that section.

(3)   The High Court may, in any proceedings in that court, decide that an overseas adoption or a determination under section 91 is to be treated, for the purposes of those proceedings, as invalid on either of the grounds mentioned in subsection (2)(a).

(4)   Subject to the preceding provisions, the validity of a Convention adoption, Convention adoption order or overseas adoption or a determination under section 91 cannot be called in question in proceedings in any court in England and Wales.

91   Overseas determinations and orders

(1)   Subsection (2) applies where any authority of a Convention country (other than the United Kingdom) or of the Channel Islands, the Isle of Man or any British overseas territory has power under the law of that country or territory—

(a)   to authorise, or review the authorisation of, an adoption order made in that country or territory, or

(b)   to give or review a decision revoking or annulling such an order or a Convention adoption.

(2)   If the authority makes a determination in the exercise of that power, the determination is to have effect for the purpose of effecting, confirming or terminating the adoption in question or, as the case may be, confirming its termination.

(3)   Subsection (2) is subject to section 89 and to any subsequent determination having effect under that subsection.

105   Effect of certain Scottish orders and provisions

(1)   A Scottish adoption order or an order under section 25 of the Adoption (Scotland) Act 1978 (c 28) (interim adoption orders) has effect in England and Wales as it has in Scotland, but as if references to the parental responsibilities and the parental rights in relation to a child were to parental responsibility for the child.

(2)   [A Scottish permanence order which includes provision granting authority for the child to be adopted has the same effect in England and Wales as it has in Scotland], but as if references to the parental responsibilities and the parental rights in relation to a child were to parental responsibility for the child.

[(3)   Any person who contravenes any of the provisions of the Adoption and Children (Scotland) Act 2007 mentioned in subsection (3A) is guilty of an offence and is liable on summary conviction to imprisonment for a term not exceeding 3 months, or a fine not exceeding level 5 on the standard scale or both.

(3A)   The provisions are—
   (a)   section 20 (restrictions on removal: child placed for adoption);
   (b)   section 21 (restrictions on removal: notice of intention to adopt given);
   (c)   section 22 (restrictions on removal: application for adoption order pending).]

(4)   Orders made under [section 24 of the Adoption and Children (Scotland) Act 2007 (return of child removed in breach of certain provisions)] are to have effect in England and Wales as if they were orders of the High Court under section 41 of this Act.

[(5)   In this section, 'Scottish permanence order' means a permanence order under section 80 of the Adoption and Children (Scotland) Act 2007 (asp 4) (including a deemed permanence order having effect by virtue of article 13(1), 14(2), 17(1) or 19(2) of the Adoption and Children (Scotland) Act 2007 (Commencement No 4, Transitional and Savings Provisions Order 2009 (SSI 2009/267)).]

CIVIL PARTNERSHIP ACT 2004
(2004, c 33)

PART 1
INTRODUCTION

1 Civil partnership
(1)   A civil partnership is a relationship between two people of the same sex ('civil partners')—
  (a)   which is formed when they register as civil partners of each other—
      (i)   in England or Wales (under Part 2),
      (ii)   in Scotland (under Part 3),
      (iii)   in Northern Ireland (under Part 4), or
      (iv)   outside the United Kingdom under an Order in Council made under Chapter 1 of Part 5 (registration at British consulates etc or by armed forces personnel), or
  (b)   which they are treated under Chapter 2 of Part 5 as having formed (at the time determined under that Chapter) by virtue of having registered an overseas relationship.
(2)   Subsection (1) is subject to the provisions of this Act under or by virtue of which a civil partnership is void.
(3)   A civil partnership ends only
  (a)   on death, dissolution or annulment [, or
  (b)   in the case of a civil partnership formed as mentioned in subsection (1)(a)(i) or (iv), on the conversion of the civil partnership into a marriage under section 9 of the Marriage (Same Sex Couples) Act 2013.]
[(3A)   Subsection (3) is subject to section 11(2)(a) of the Marriage and Civil Partnership (Scotland) Act 2014 (ending of certain civil partnerships on marriage under Scots law).]
(4)   The references in subsection (3) to dissolution and annulment are to dissolution and annulment having effect under or recognised in accordance with this Act.
(5)   References in this Act to an overseas relationship are to be read in accordance with Chapter 2 of Part 5.

PART 3
CIVIL PARTNERSHIP: SCOTLAND

85 Formation of civil partnership by registration
(1)   For the purposes of section 1, two people are to be regarded as having registered as civil partners of each other once each of them has signed the civil partnership schedule, in the presence of—
  (a)   each other,
  (b)   two witnesses both of whom have attained the age of 16, and
  [(c)   the approved celebrant or, as the case may be, the authorised registrar].
(2)   But the two people must be eligible to be so registered.
(3)   Subsection (1) applies regardless of whether subsection (4) is complied with.
(4)   After the civil partnership schedule has been signed under subsection (1), it must also be signed, in the presence of the civil partners and each other by—
  (a)   each of the two witnesses, and
  (b)   [the approved celebrant or, as the case may be,] the authorised registrar.

86 Eligibility
(1)   Two people are not eligible to register in Scotland as civil partners of each other if—
  (a)   they are not of the same sex,

(b)   they are related in a forbidden degree,
(c)   either has not attained the age of 16,
(d)   either is married or already in civil partnership, or
(e)   either is incapable of—
    (i)   understanding the nature of civil partnership, or
    (ii)   validly consenting to its formation.

[(2)   Subject to subsection (3), a person is related to another person in a forbidden degree if related to that person in a degree specified in Schedule 10.]

(3)   [A person who is related to another person in a degree specified in paragraph 2 of Schedule 10 (relations by affinity) is not related to that person] in a forbidden degree if—
(a)   both persons have attained the age of 21, and
(b)   the younger has not at any time before attaining the age of 18 lived in the same household as the elder and been treated by the elder as a child of the elder's family.

[(3A)   For the purposes of paragraph 2 of Schedule 10, 'spouse' means—
(a)   in the case of a marriage between persons of different sexes, a wife in relation to her husband or a husband in relation to his wife, and
(b)   in the case of a marriage between persons of the same sex, one of the parties to the marriage in relation to the other.]

[(4)   Paragraph 2 of Schedule 10 has effect subject to the modifications specified in subsection (5) in the case of a person (here the 'relevant person') whose gender has become the acquired gender under the Gender Recognition Act 2004 (c 7).

(5)   The reference in [subsection (3A)(a) as it applies to] that paragraph to—
(a)   a [...] wife of the relevant person includes any [...] husband of the relevant person, and
(b)   a [...] husband of the relevant person includes any [...] wife of the relevant person.]

[(5A)   This section and Schedule 10 have effect as if any reference in that Schedule to a [parent] within any of the degrees of relationship specified [...] included a woman who is a parent of a child by virtue of section 42 or 43 of the Human Fertilisation and Embryology Act 2008 (c 22).]

[...]

(8)   References in this section and in Schedule 10 to relationships and degrees of relationship are to be construed in accordance with section 1(1) of the Law Reform (Parent and Child) (Scotland) Act 1986 (c 9).

(9)   For the purposes of this section, a degree of relationship specified in paragraph 1 of Schedule 10 exists whether it is of the full blood or the half blood.

(10)   [Amends Adoption (Scotland) Act 1978.]

125   Financial provision after overseas dissolution or annulment
Schedule 11 relates to applications for financial provision in Scotland after a civil partnership has been dissolved or annulled in a country or territory outside the British Islands.

PART 5
CIVIL PARTNERSHIPS FORMED OR DISSOLVED ABROAD ETC

Chapter 1
Registration outside UK under Order in Council

210   Registration at British consulates etc
(1)   Her Majesty may by Order in Council make provision for two people to register as civil partners of each other—
(a)   in prescribed countries or territories outside the United Kingdom, and
(b)   in the presence of [a registration officer],
in cases where the officer is satisfied that the conditions in subsection (2) are met.

(2)   The conditions are that—

(a)   at least one of the proposed civil partners is a United Kingdom national,

(b)   the proposed civil partners would have been eligible to register as civil partners of each other in such part of the United Kingdom as is determined in accordance with the Order,

(c)   the authorities of the country or territory in which it is proposed that they register as civil partners will not object to the registration, and

(d)   insufficient facilities exist for them to enter into an overseas relationship under the law of that country or territory.

(3)   [A registration officer] is not required to allow two people to register as civil partners of each other if in his opinion the formation of a civil partnership between them would be inconsistent with international law or the comity of nations.

(4)   An Order in Council under this section may make provision for appeals against a refusal, in reliance on subsection (3), to allow two people to register as civil partners of each other.

(5)   An Order in Council under this section may provide that two people who register as civil partners of each other under such an Order are to be treated for the purposes of sections 221(1)(c)(i) and (2)(c)(i), 222(c), 224(b), 225(1)(c)(i) and (3)(c)(i), 229(1)(c)(i) and (2)(c)(i) [and section 232(b)] and section 1(3)(c)(i) of the Presumption of Death (Scotland) Act 1977 (c 27) as if they had done so in the part of the United Kingdom determined as mentioned in subsection (2)(b).

[(6)   'Registration officer' means—

(a)   a consular officer in the service of Her Majesty's government in the United Kingdom, or

(b)   in the case of registration of a country [or territory] in which Her Majesty's government in the United Kingdom has for the time being no consular representative, a person authorised by the Secretary of State in respect of registration of civil partnerships in that country [or territory].]

211   Registration by armed forces personnel

(1)   Her Majesty may by Order in Council make provision for two people to register as civil partners of each other—

(a)   in prescribed countries or territories outside the United Kingdom, and

(b)   in the presence of an officer appointed by virtue of the Registration of Births, Deaths and Marriages (Special Provisions) Act 1957 (c 58),

in cases where the officer is satisfied that the conditions in subsection (2) are met.

(2)   The conditions are that—

(a)   at least one of the proposed civil partners—

(i)   is a member of a part of Her Majesty's forces serving in the country or territory,

(ii)   is employed in the country or territory in such other capacity as may be prescribed, or

(iii)   is a child of a person falling within sub-paragraph (i) or (ii) and has his home with that person in that country or territory,

(b)   the proposed civil partners would have been eligible to register as civil partners of each other in such part of the United Kingdom as is determined in accordance with the Order, and

(c)   such other requirements as may be prescribed are complied with.

(3)   In determining for the purposes of subsection (2) whether one person is the child of another, a person who is or was treated by another as a child of the family in relation to—

(a)   a marriage to which the other is or was a party, or

(b)   a civil partnership in which the other is or was a civil partner,

is to be regarded as the other's child.

(4)   An Order in Council under this section may provide that two people who

register as civil partners of each other under such an Order are to be treated for the purposes of section 221(1)(c)(i) and (2)(c)(i), 222(c), 224(b), 225(1)(c)(i) and (3)(c)(i), 229(1)(c)(i) and (2)(c)(i) [and section 232(b)] and section 1(3)(c)(i) of the Presumption of Death (Scotland) Act 1977 (c 27) as if they had done so in the part of the United Kingdom determined in accordance with subsection (2)(b).

(5)   Any references in this section—
    (a)   to a country or territory outside the United Kingdom,
    (b)   to forces serving in such a country or territory, and
    (c)   to persons employed in such a country or territory,
include references to ships which are for the time being in the waters of a country or territory outside the United Kingdom, to forces serving in any such ship and to persons employed in any such ship.

Chapter 2
Overseas relationships treated as civil partnerships

212   Meaning of 'overseas relationship'

(1)   For the purposes of this Act an overseas relationship is a relationship which—
    (a)   is either a specified relationship or a relationship which meets the general conditions, and
    (b)   is registered (whether before or after the passing of this Act) with a responsible authority in a country or territory outside the United Kingdom, by two people—
        (i)   who under the relevant law are of the same sex at the time when they do so, and
        (ii)   neither of whom is already a civil partner or lawfully married.
[(1A)   But, for the purposes of the application of this Act to England and Wales marriage is not an overseas relationship.]
(2)   In this Chapter, 'the relevant law' means the law of the country or territory where the relationship is registered (including its rules of private international law).

213   Specified relationships

(1)   A specified relationship is a relationship which is specified for the purposes of section 212 by Schedule 20.
[(1A)   But, for the purposes of the application of this Act to England and Wales, marriage is not an overseas relationship.]
(2)   The [Secretary of State] may by order amend Schedule 20 by—
    (a)   adding a relationship,
    (b)   amending the description of a relationship, or
    (c)   omitting a relationship.
(3)   No order may be made under this section without the consent of the Scottish Ministers and the Department of Finance and Personnel.
(4)   The power to make an order under this section is exercisable by statutory instrument.
(5)   An order which contains any provision (whether alone or with other provisions) amending Schedule 20 by—
    (a)   amending the description of a relationship, or
    (b)   omitting a relationship,
may not be made unless a draft of the statutory instrument containing the order is laid before, and approved by a resolution of, each House of Parliament.
(6)   A statutory instrument containing any other order under this section is subject to annulment in pursuance of a resolution of either House of Parliament.

214   The general conditions

The general conditions are that, under the relevant law—

(a)   the relationship may not be entered into if either of the parties is already a party to a relationship of that kind or lawfully married,

(b)   the relationship is of indeterminate duration,

[(ba)   the relationship is not one of marriage,

(c)   the effect of entering into it is that the parties are—

(i)   treated as a couple either generally or for specified purposes,

(ii)   [but are not treated as married].

215   Overseas relationships treated as civil partnerships: the general rule

(1)   Two people are to be treated as having formed a civil partnership as a result of having registered an overseas relationship if, under the relevant law, they—

(a)   had capacity to enter into the relationship, and

(b)   met all requirements necessary to ensure the formal validity of the relationship.

(2)   Subject to subsection (3), the time when they are to be treated as having formed the civil partnership is the time when the overseas relationship is registered (under the relevant law) as having been entered into.

(3)   If the overseas relationship is registered (under the relevant law) as having been entered into before this section comes into force, the time when they are to be treated as having formed a civil partnership is the time when this section comes into force.

(4)   But if—

(a)   before this section comes into force, a dissolution or annulment of the overseas relationship was obtained outside the United Kingdom, and

(b)   the dissolution or annulment would be recognised under Chapter 3 if the overseas relationship had been treated as a civil partnership at the time of the dissolution or annulment,

subsection (3) does not apply and subsections (1) and (2) have effect subject to subsection (5).

(5)   The overseas relationship is not to be treated as having been a civil partnership for the purposes of any provisions except—

(a)   Schedules 7, 11 and 17 (financial relief in United Kingdom after dissolution or annulment obtained outside the United Kingdom);

(b)   such provisions as are specified (with or without modifications) in an order under section 259;

(c)   Chapter 3 (so far as necessary for the purposes of paragraphs (a) and (b)).

(6)   This section is subject to sections 216, 217 and 218.

216   The same-sex requirement

(1)   Two people are not to be treated as having formed a civil partnership as a result of having registered an overseas relationship if, at the critical time, they were not of the same sex under United Kingdom law.

(2)   But if a full gender recognition certificate is issued under the 2004 Act to a person who has registered an overseas relationship which is within subsection (4), after the issue of the certificate the relationship is no longer prevented from being treated as a civil partnership on the ground that, at the critical time, the parties were not of the same sex.

(3)   However, subsection (2) does not apply to an overseas relationship which is within subsection (4) if either of the parties has formed a subsequent civil partnership or lawful marriage.

(4)   An overseas relationship is within this subsection if (and only if), at the time mentioned in section 215(2)—

(a)   one of the parties ('A') was regarded under the relevant law as having changed gender (but was not regarded under United Kingdom law as having done so), and

(b) the other party was (under United Kingdom law) of the gender to which A had changed under the relevant law.

(5) In this section—

'the critical time' means the time determined in accordance with section 215(2) or (as the case may be) (3);

'the 2004 Act' means the Gender Recognition Act 2004 (c 7);

'United Kingdom law' means any enactment or rule of law applying in England and Wales, Scotland and Northern Ireland.

(6) Nothing in this section prevents the exercise of any enforceable [EU] right.

217 Person domiciled in a part of the United Kingdom

(1) Subsection (2) applies if an overseas relationship has been registered by a person who was at the time mentioned in section 215(2) domiciled in England and Wales.

(2) The two people concerned are not to be treated as having formed a civil partnership if, at the time mentioned in section 215(2)—

(a) either of them was under 16, or

(b) they would have been within prohibited degrees of relationship under Part 1 of Schedule 1 if they had been registering as civil partners of each other in England and Wales.

(3) Subsection (4) applies if an overseas relationship has been registered by a person who at the time mentioned in section 215(2) was domiciled in Scotland.

(4) The two people concerned are not to be treated as having formed a civil partnership if, at the time mentioned in section 215(2), they were not eligible by virtue of paragraph (b), (c) or (e) of section 86(1) to register in Scotland as civil partners of each other.

(5) Subsection (6) applies if an overseas relationship has been registered by a person who at the time mentioned in section 215(2) was domiciled in Northern Ireland.

(6) The two people concerned are not to be treated as having formed a civil partnership if, at the time mentioned in section 215(2)—

(a) either of them was under 16, or

(b) they would have been within prohibited degrees of relationship under Schedule 12 if they had been registering as civil partners of each other in Northern Ireland.

218 The public policy exception

Two people are not to be treated as having formed a civil partnership as a result of having entered into an overseas relationship if it would be manifestly contrary to public policy to recognise the capacity, under the relevant law, of one or both of them to enter into the relationship.

Chapter 3
Dissolution etc: jurisdiction and recognition

Introduction

219 Power to make provision corresponding to EC Regulation 2201/2003

(1) The Lord Chancellor may by regulations make provision—

(a) as to the jurisdiction of courts in England and Wales [...] in proceedings for the dissolution or annulment of a civil partnership or for legal separation of the civil partners in cases where a civil partner—

(i) is or has been habitually resident in a member State,

(ii) is a national of a member State, or

(iii) is domiciled in a part of the United Kingdom or the Republic of Ireland, and

(b) as to the recognition in England and Wales [...] of any judgment of a court of another member State which orders the dissolution or annulment of a civil partnership or the legal separation of the civil partners.

[(1A)   The Department of Justice in Northern Ireland may by regulations make provision—

(a)   as to the jurisdiction of courts in Northern Ireland in proceedings for the dissolution or annulment of a civil partnership or for legal separation of the civil partners in such cases as are mentioned in subsection (1)(a), and

(b)   as to the recognition in Northern Ireland of any such judgment as is mentioned in subsection (1)(b).]

(2)   The Scottish Ministers may by regulations make provision—

(a)   as to the jurisdiction of courts in Scotland in proceedings for the dissolution or annulment of a civil partnership or for legal separation of the civil partners in such cases as are mentioned in subsection (1)(a), and

(b)   as to the recognition in Scotland of any such judgment as is mentioned in subsection (1)(b).

(3)   The regulations may in particular make provision corresponding to that made by Council Regulation (EC) No 2201/2003 of 27th November 2003 in relation to jurisdiction and the recognition and enforcement of judgments in matrimonial matters.

(4)   The regulations may provide that for the purposes of this Part and the regulations 'member State' means—

(a)   all member States with the exception of such member States as are specified in the regulations, or

(b)   such member States as are specified in the regulations.

(5)   The regulations may make provision under subsections (1)(b) [, (1A)(b)] and (2)(b) which applies even if the date of the dissolution, annulment or legal separation is earlier than the date on which this section comes into force.

(6)   Regulations under subsection (1) are to be made by statutory instrument and may only be made if a draft has been laid before and approved by resolution of each House of Parliament.

[(6A)   Regulations under subsection (1A) are to be made by statutory rule for the purposes of the Statutory Rules (Northern Ireland) Order 1979.

(6B)   No regulations shall be made under subsection (1A) unless a draft has been laid before and approved by resolution of the Northern Ireland Assembly.

(6C)   Section 41(3) of the Interpretation Act (Northern Ireland) 1954 applies for the purposes of subsection (6B) in relation to the laying of a draft as it applies in relation to the laying of a statutory document under an enactment.]

(7)   Regulations under subsection (2) are to be made by statutory instrument and may only be made if a draft has been laid before and approved by resolution of the Scottish Parliament.

(8)   In this Part 'section 219 regulations' means regulations made under this section.

Jurisdiction of Scottish courts

225   Jurisdiction of Scottish courts

(1)   The Court of Session has jurisdiction to entertain an action for the dissolution of a civil partnership or for separation of civil partners if (and only if)—

(a)   the court has jurisdiction under section 219 regulations,

(b)   no court has, or is recognised as having, jurisdiction under section 219 regulations and either civil partner is domiciled in Scotland on the date when the proceedings are begun, or

(c)   the following conditions are met—

(i)   the two people concerned registered as civil partners of each other in Scotland,

(ii) no court has, or is recognised as having, jurisdiction under section 219 regulations, and

(iii) it appears to the court to be in the interests of justice to assume jurisdiction in the case.

(2) The sheriff has jurisdiction to entertain an action for the dissolution of a civil partnership or for separation of civil partners if (and only if) the requirements of paragraph (a) or (b) of subsection (1) are met and either civil partner—

(a) was resident in the sheriffdom for a period of 40 days ending with the date when the action is begun, or

(b) had been resident in the sheriffdom for a period of not less than 40 days ending not more than 40 days before that date and has no known residence in Scotland at that date.

(3) The Court of Session has jurisdiction to entertain an action for declarator of nullity of a civil partnership if (and only if)—

(a) the Court has jurisdiction under section 219 regulations,

(b) no court has, or is recognised as having, jurisdiction under section 219 regulations and either of the ostensible civil partners—

(i) is domiciled in Scotland on the date when the proceedings are begun, or

(ii) died before that date and either was at death domiciled in Scotland or had been habitually resident in Scotland throughout the period of 1 year ending with the date of death, or

(c) the following conditions are met—

(i) the two people concerned registered as civil partners of each other in Scotland,

(ii) no court has, or is recognised as having, jurisdiction under section 219 regulations, and

(iii) it appears to the court to be in the interests of justice to assume jurisdiction in the case.

(4) At any time when proceedings are pending in respect of which a court has jurisdiction by virtue of any of subsections (1) to (3) (or this subsection) it also has jurisdiction to entertain other proceedings, in respect of the same civil partnership (or ostensible civil partnership), for dissolution, separation or (but only where the court is the Court of Session) declarator of nullity, even though that jurisdiction would not be exercisable under any of subsections (1) to (3).

226 Sisting of proceedings

(1) Rules of court may make provision in relation to civil partnerships corresponding to the provision made in relation to marriages by Schedule 3 to the Domicile and Matrimonial Proceedings Act 1973 (c 45) (sisting of Scottish consistorial actions).

(2) The rules may in particular make provision—

(a) for the provision of information by the pursuer and by any other person who has entered appearance in an action where proceedings relating to the same civil partnership (or ostensible civil partnership) are continuing in another jurisdiction, and

(b) for an action to be sisted where there are concurrent proceedings elsewhere in respect of the same civil partnership (or ostensible civil partnership).

227 Scottish ancillary and collateral orders

(1) This section applies where after the commencement of this Act an application is competently made to the Court of Session or the sheriff for the making, or the variation or recall, of an order which is ancillary or collateral to an action for—

(a) the dissolution of a civil partnership,

(b) the separation of civil partners, or

(c) declarator of nullity of a civil partnership.

(2) And the section applies whether the application is made in the same pro-

ceedings or in other proceedings and whether it is made before or after the pronouncement of a final decree in the action.

(3)   [Subject to subsections (3A) and (3B), if] the court has or, as the case may be, had jurisdiction to entertain the action, it has jurisdiction to entertain [the application.

(3A)   The court may not entertain the application if—]

(a)   jurisdiction to entertain the action was under section 219 regulations, and

(b)   to make, vary or recall the order to which the application relates would contravene the regulations.

[(3B)   If the application or part of it relates to a matter where jurisdiction falls to be determined by reference to the jurisdictional requirements of the Maintenance Regulation and Schedule 6 to the Civil Jurisdiction and Judgments (Maintenance) Regulations 2011, the court may not entertain the application or that part of it unless it has jurisdiction to do so by virtue of that Regulation and that Schedule.]

(4)   Where the Court of Session has jurisdiction by virtue of this section to entertain an application for the variation or recall, as respects any person, of an order made by it and the order is one to which section 8 (variation and recall by the sheriff of certain orders made by the Court of Session) of the Law Reform (Miscellaneous Provisions) (Scotland) Act 1966 (c 19) applies, then for the purposes of any application under that section for the variation or recall of the order in so far as it relates to the person, the sheriff (as defined in that section) has jurisdiction to exercise the power conferred on him by that section.

(5)   The reference in subsection (1) to an order which is ancillary or collateral is to an order relating to children, aliment, financial provision or expenses.

[(6)   In this section 'the Maintenance Regulation' means Council Regulation (EC) No 4/2009 including as applied in relation to Denmark by virtue of the Agreement made on 19th October 2005 between the European Community and the Kingdom of Denmark.]

Recognition of dissolution, annulment and separation

233   Effect of dissolution, annulment or separation obtained in the UK

(1)   No dissolution or annulment of a civil partnership obtained in one part of the United Kingdom is effective in any part of the United Kingdom unless obtained from a court of civil jurisdiction.

(2)   Subject to subsections (3) and (4), the validity of a dissolution or annulment of a civil partnership or a legal separation of civil partners which has been obtained from a court of civil jurisdiction in one part of the United Kingdom is to be recognised throughout the United Kingdom.

(3)   Recognition of the validity of a dissolution, annulment or legal separation obtained from a court of civil jurisdiction in one part of the United Kingdom may be refused in any other part if the dissolution, annulment or separation was obtained at a time when it was irreconcilable with a decision determining the question of the subsistence or validity of the civil partnership—

(a)   previously given by a court of civil jurisdiction in the other part, or

(b)   previously given by a court elsewhere and recognised or entitled to be recognised in the other part.

(4)   Recognition of the validity of a dissolution or legal separation obtained from a court of civil jurisdiction in one part of the United Kingdom may be refused in any other part if the dissolution or separation was obtained at a time when, according to the law of the other part, there was no subsisting civil partnership.

234   Recognition in the UK of overseas dissolution, annulment or separation

(1)   Subject to subsection (2), the validity of an overseas dissolution, annulment

or legal separation is to be recognised in the United Kingdom if, and only if, it is entitled to recognition by virtue of sections 235 to 237.

(2)   This section and sections 235 to 237 do not apply to an overseas dissolution, annulment or legal separation as regards which provision as to recognition is made by section 219 regulations.

(3)   For the purposes of subsections (1) and (2) and sections 235 to 237, an overseas dissolution, annulment or legal separation is a dissolution or annulment of a civil partnership or a legal separation of civil partners which has been obtained outside the United Kingdom (whether before or after this section comes into force).

235   Grounds for recognition

(1)   The validity of an overseas dissolution, annulment or legal separation obtained by means of proceedings is to be recognised if—

  (a)   the dissolution, annulment or legal separation is effective under the law of the country in which it was obtained, and

  (b)   at the relevant date either civil partner—

    (i)   was habitually resident in the country in which the dissolution, annulment or legal separation was obtained,

    (ii)   was domiciled in that country, or

    (iii)   was a national of that country.

(2)   The validity of an overseas dissolution, annulment or legal separation obtained otherwise than by means of proceedings is to be recognised if—

  (a)   the dissolution, annulment or legal separation is effective under the law of the country in which it was obtained,

  (b)   at the relevant date—

    (i)   each civil partner was domiciled in that country, or

    (ii)   either civil partner was domiciled in that country and the other was domiciled in a country under whose law the dissolution, annulment or legal separation is recognised as valid, and

  (c)   neither civil partner was habitually resident in the United Kingdom throughout the period of 1 year immediately preceding that date.

(3)   In this section 'the relevant date' means—

  (a)   in the case of an overseas dissolution, annulment or legal separation obtained by means of proceedings, the date of the commencement of the proceedings;

  (b)   in the case of an overseas dissolution, annulment or legal separation obtained otherwise than by means of proceedings, the date on which it was obtained.

(4)   Where in the case of an overseas annulment the relevant date fell after the death of either civil partner, any reference in subsection (1) or (2) to that date is to be read in relation to that civil partner as a reference to the date of death.

236   Refusal of recognition

(1)   Recognition of the validity of an overseas dissolution, annulment or legal separation may be refused in any part of the United Kingdom if the dissolution, annulment or separation was obtained at a time when it was irreconcilable with a decision determining the question of the subsistence or validity of the civil partnership—

  (a)   previously given by a court of civil jurisdiction in that part of the United Kingdom, or

  (b)   previously given by a court elsewhere and recognised or entitled to be recognised in that part of the United Kingdom.

(2)   Recognition of the validity of an overseas dissolution or legal separation may be refused in any part of the United Kingdom if the dissolution or separation was obtained at a time when, according to the law of that part of the United Kingdom, there was no subsisting civil partnership.

(3)   Recognition of the validity of an overseas dissolution, annulment or legal separation may be refused if—

(a)   in the case of a dissolution, annulment or legal separation obtained by means of proceedings, it was obtained—

(i)   without such steps having been taken for giving notice of the proceedings to a civil partner as, having regard to the nature of the proceedings and all the circumstances, should reasonably have been taken, or

(ii)   without a civil partner having been given (for any reason other than lack of notice) such opportunity to take part in the proceedings as, having regard to those matters, he should reasonably have been given, or

(b)   in the case of a dissolution, annulment or legal separation obtained otherwise than by means of proceedings—

(i)   there is no official document certifying that the dissolution, annulment or legal separation is effective under the law of the country in which it was obtained, or

(ii)   where either civil partner was domiciled in another country at the relevant date, there is no official document certifying that the dissolution, annulment or legal separation is recognised as valid under the law of that other country, or

(c)   in either case, recognition of the dissolution, annulment or legal separation would be manifestly contrary to public policy.

(4)   In this section—

'official', in relation to a document certifying that a dissolution, annulment or legal separation is effective, or is recognised as valid, under the law of any country, means issued by a person or body appointed or recognised for the purpose under that law;

'the relevant date' has the same meaning as in section 235.

237   Supplementary provisions relating to recognition of dissolution etc

(1)   For the purposes of sections 235 and 236, a civil partner is to be treated as domiciled in a country if he was domiciled in that country—

(a)   according to the law of that country in family matters, or

(b)   according to the law of the part of the United Kingdom in which the question of recognition arises.

(2)   The Lord Chancellor [, the Department of Justice in Northern Ireland] or the Scottish Ministers may by regulations make provision—

(a)   applying sections 235 and 236 and subsection (1) with modifications in relation to any country whose territories have different systems of law in force in matters of dissolution, annulment or legal separation;

(b)   applying sections 235 and 236 with modifications in relation to—

(i)   an overseas dissolution, annulment or legal separation in the case of an overseas relationship (or an apparent or alleged overseas relationship);

(ii)   any case where a civil partner is domiciled in a country or territory whose law does not recognise legal relationships between two people of the same sex;

(c)   with respect to recognition of the validity of an overseas dissolution, annulment or legal separation in cases where there are cross-proceedings;

(d)   with respect to cases where a legal separation is converted under the law of the country or territory in which it is obtained into a dissolution which is effective under the law of that country or territory;

(e)   with respect to proof of findings of fact made in proceedings in any country or territory outside the United Kingdom.

(3)   The power [of the Lord Chancellor or the Scottish Ministers] to make regulations under subsection (2) is exercisable by statutory instrument.

(4)   A statutory instrument containing such regulations—

(a) if made by the Lord Chancellor, is subject to annulment in pursuance of a resolution of either House of Parliament;

(b) if made by the Scottish Ministers, is subject to annulment in pursuance of a resolution of the Scottish Parliament.

[(4A) The power of the Department of Justice in Northern Ireland to make regulations under subsection (2) is exercisable by statutory rule for the purposes of the Statutory Rules (Northern Ireland) Order 1979.

(4B) Regulations made by the Department of Justice under subsection (2) are subject to negative resolution within the meaning of section 41(6) of the Interpretation Act (Northern Ireland) 1954.]

(5) In this section (except subsection (4)) and sections 233 to 236 and 238—

'annulment' includes any order annulling a civil partnership, however expressed;

'part of the United Kingdom' means England and Wales, Scotland or Northern Ireland;

'proceedings' means judicial or other proceedings.

(6) Nothing in this Chapter is to be read as requiring the recognition of any finding of fault made in proceedings for dissolution, annulment or legal separation or of any maintenance, custody or other ancillary order made in any such proceedings.

238 Non-recognition elsewhere of dissolution or annulment

(1) This section applies where, in any part of the United Kingdom—

(a) a dissolution or annulment of a civil partnership has been granted by a court of civil jurisdiction, or

(b) the validity of a dissolution or annulment of a civil partnership is recognised by virtue of this Chapter.

(2) The fact that the dissolution or annulment would not be recognised outside the United Kingdom does not—

(a) preclude either party from forming a subsequent civil partnership or marriage in that part of the United Kingdom, or

(b) cause the subsequent civil partnership or marriage of either party (wherever it takes place) to be treated as invalid in that part.

FAMILY LAW (SCOTLAND) ACT 2006
(2006 asp 2)

2 *[Inserts s 20A into the Marriage (Scotland) Act 1977]*

4 Extension of jurisdiction of sheriff

In subsection (1) of section 5 of the Sheriff Courts (Scotland) Act 1907 (c 51) (extension of jurisdiction), the words '(except declarators of marriage or nullity of marriage)' shall be repealed.

22 Domicile of persons under 16

(1) Subsection (2) applies where—

(a) the parents of a child are domiciled in the same country as each other; and

(b) the child has a home with a parent or a home (or homes) with both of them.

(2) The child shall be domiciled in the same country as the child's parents.

(3) Where subsection (2) does not apply, the child shall be domiciled in the country with which the child has for the time being the closest connection.

(4) In this section, 'child' means a person under 16 years of age.

Cohabitation

25 Meaning of 'cohabitant' in sections 26 to 29

(1) In sections 26 to 29, 'cohabitant' means either member of a couple consisting of—

(a) a man and a woman who are (or were) living together as if they were husband and wife; or

(b) two persons of the same sex who are (or were) living together as if they were civil partners.

(2) In determining for the purposes of any of sections 26 to 29 whether a person ('A') is a cohabitant of another person ('B'), the court shall have regard to—

(a) the length of the period during which A and B have been living together (or lived together);

(b) the nature of their relationship during that period; and

(c) the nature and extent of any financial arrangements subsisting, or which subsisted, during that period.

(3) In subsection (2) and section 28, 'court' means Court of Session or sheriff.

26 Rights in certain household goods

(1) Subsection (2) applies where any question arises (whether during or after the cohabitation) as to the respective rights of ownership of cohabitants in any household goods.

(2) It shall be presumed that each cohabitant has a right to an equal share in household goods acquired (other than by gift or succession from a third party) during the period of cohabitation.

(3) The presumption in subsection (2) shall be rebuttable.

(4) In this section, 'household goods' means any goods (including decorative or ornamental goods) kept or used at any time during the cohabitation in any residence in which the cohabitants are (or were) cohabiting for their joint domestic purposes; but does not include—

(a) money;

(b) securities;

(c) any motor car, caravan or other road vehicle; or

(d) any domestic animal.

27 Rights in certain money and property

(1) Subsection (2) applies where, in relation to cohabitants, any question arises (whether during or after the cohabitation) as to the right of a cohabitant to—

(a) money derived from any allowance made by either cohabitant for their joint household expenses or for similar purposes; or

(b) any property acquired out of such money.

(2) Subject to any agreement between the cohabitants to the contrary, the money or property shall be treated as belonging to each cohabitant in equal shares.

(3) In this section 'property' does not include a residence used by the cohabitants as the sole or main residence in which they live (or lived) together.

28 Financial provision where cohabitation ends otherwise than by death

(1) Subsection (2) applies where cohabitants cease to cohabit otherwise than by reason of the death of one (or both) of them.

(2) On the application of a cohabitant (the 'applicant'), the appropriate court may, after having regard to the matters mentioned in subsection (3)—

(a) make an order requiring the other cohabitant (the 'defender') to pay a capital sum of an amount specified in the order to the applicant;

(b) make an order requiring the defender to pay such amount as may be specified in the order in respect of any economic burden of caring, after the end of the cohabitation, for a child of whom the cohabitants are the parents;

(c) make such interim order as it thinks fit.

(3) Those matters are—

(a)   whether (and, if so, to what extent) the defender has derived economic advantage from contributions made by the applicant; and

(b)   whether (and, if so, to what extent) the applicant has suffered economic disadvantage in the interests of—

(i)   the defender; or

(ii)   any relevant child.

(4)   In considering whether to make an order under subsection (2)(a), the appropriate court shall have regard to the matters mentioned in subsections (5) and (6).

(5)   The first matter is the extent to which any economic advantage derived by the defender from contributions made by the applicant is offset by any economic disadvantage suffered by the defender in the interests of—

(a)   the applicant; or

(b)   any relevant child.

(6)   The second matter is the extent to which any economic disadvantage suffered by the applicant in the interests of—

(a)   the defender; or

(b)   any relevant child,

is offset by any economic advantage the applicant has derived from contributions made by the defender.

(7)   In making an order under paragraph (a) or (b) of subsection (2), the appropriate court may specify that the amount shall be payable—

(a)   on such date as may be specified;

(b)   in instalments.

(8)   [Subject to section 29A,] any application under this section shall be made not later than one year after the day on which the cohabitants cease to cohabit.

(9)   In this section—

'appropriate court' means—

(a)   where the cohabitants are a man and a woman, the court which would have jurisdiction to hear an action of divorce in relation to them if they were married to each other;

(b)   where the cohabitants are of the same sex, the court which would have jurisdiction to hear an action for the dissolution of the civil partnership if they were civil partners of each other;

'child' means a person under 16 years of age;

'contributions' includes indirect and non-financial contributions (and, in particular, any such contribution made by looking after any relevant child or any house in which they cohabited); and

'economic advantage' includes gains in—

(a)   capital;

(b)   income; and

(c)   earning capacity;

and 'economic disadvantage' shall be construed accordingly.

(10)   For the purposes of this section, a child is 'relevant' if the child is—

(a)   a child of whom the cohabitants are the parents;

(b)   a child who is or was accepted by the cohabitants as a child of the family.

29   Application to court by survivor for provision on intestacy

(1)   This section applies where—

(a)   a cohabitant (the 'deceased') dies intestate; and

(b)   immediately before the death the deceased was—

(i)   domiciled in Scotland; and

(ii)   cohabiting with another cohabitant (the 'survivor').

(2)   Subject to subsection (4), on the application of the survivor, the court may—

(a)   after having regard to the matters mentioned in subsection (3), make an order—

    (i) for payment to the survivor out of the deceased's net intestate estate of
a capital sum of such amount as may be specified in the order;
    (ii) for transfer to the survivor of such property (whether heritable or
moveable) from that estate as may be so specified;
    (b) make such interim order as it thinks fit.
(3) Those matters are—
    (a) the size and nature of the deceased's net intestate estate;
    (b) any benefit received, or to be received, by the survivor—
        (i) on, or in consequence of, the deceased's death; and
        (ii) from somewhere other than the deceased's net intestate estate;
    (c) the nature and extent of any other rights against, or claims on, the de-
ceased's net intestate estate; and
    (d) any other matter the court considers appropriate.
(4) An order or interim order under subsection (2) shall not have the effect of
awarding to the survivor an amount which would exceed the amount to which the
survivor would have been entitled had the survivor been the spouse or civil
partner of the deceased.
(5) An application under this section may be made to—
    (a) the Court of Session;
    (b) a sheriff in the sheriffdom in which the deceased was habitually resident
at the date of death;
    (c) if at the date of death it is uncertain in which sheriffdom the deceased
was habitually resident, the sheriff at Edinburgh.
(6) [Subject to section 29A,] any application under this section shall be made
before the expiry of the period of 6 months beginning with the day on which the
deceased died.
(7) In making an order under paragraph (a)(i) of subsection (2), the court may
specify that the capital sum shall be payable—
    (a) on such date as may be specified;
    (b) in instalments.
(8) In making an order under paragraph (a)(ii) of subsection (2), the court may
specify that the transfer shall be effective on such date as may be specified.
(9) If the court makes an order in accordance with subsection (7), it may, on an
application by any party having an interest, vary the date or method of payment
of the capital sum.
(10) In this section—
'intestate' shall be construed in accordance with section 36(1) of the Succession
(Scotland) Act 1964 (c 41);
'legal rights' has the meaning given by section 36(1) of the Succession (Scotland)
Act 1964 (c 41);
'net intestate estate' means so much of the intestate estate as remains after provision for the satisfaction of—
    (a) inheritance tax;
    (b) other liabilities of the estate having priority over legal rights and the
prior rights of a surviving spouse or surviving civil partner; and
    (c) the legal rights, and the prior rights, of any surviving spouse or surviv-
ing civil partner; and
'prior rights' has the meaning given by section 36(1) of the Succession (Scotland)
Act 1964 (c 41).

**[29A Extension of time limits for applications under sections 28 and 29:
cross-border mediation**
    (1) This section applies to the calculation of—
    (a) the one year period for the purposes of section 28(8) in relation to a
relevant cross-border dispute; and

(b)   the 6 month period for the purposes of section 29(6) in relation to a relevant cross-border dispute.

(2)   A period referred to in subsection (1) is extended where it would, apart from this subsection, expire—

(a)   in the 8 weeks after the date that a mediation in relation to the dispute ends;

(b)   on the date that a mediation in relation to the dispute ends; or

(c)   after the date when all of the parties to the dispute agree to participate in a mediation in relation to the dispute but before the date that such mediation ends.

(3)   Where subsection (2) applies, the period is extended so that it expires on the date falling 8 weeks after the date on which the mediation ends.

(4)   For the purposes of this section, mediation in relation to a relevant cross-border dispute ends when any of the following occurs—

(a)   all of the parties reach an agreement in resolution of the dispute;

(b)   all of the parties agree to end the mediation;

(c)   a party withdraws from the mediation, which is the date on which—

(i)   a party informs all of the other parties of that party's withdrawal,

(ii)   in the case of a mediation involving 2 parties, 14 days expire after a request made by one party to the other party for confirmation of whether the other party has withdrawn, if the other party does not respond in that period, or

(iii)   in the case of a mediation involving more than 2 parties, a party informs all of the remaining parties that the party received no response in the 14 days after a request to another party for confirmation of whether the other party had withdrawn; or

(d)   a period of 14 days expires after the date on which the mediator's tenure ends (by reason of death, resignation or otherwise), if a replacement mediator has not been appointed.

(5)   In this section—

'the Directive means Directive 2008/52/EC of the European Parliament and of the Council of 21st May 2008 on certain aspects of mediation in civil and commercial matters;

'mediation' and 'mediator' have the meanings given by Article 3 of the Directive; and

'relevant cross-border dispute' means a cross-border dispute within the meaning given by Article 2 of the Directive which is about—

(a)   a sum which a court may order to be paid under section 28(2);

(b)   a sum which a court may order to be paid under section 29(2); or

(c)   property which a court may order to be transferred under section 29(2).]

37   [Amends the Domicile and Matrimonial Proceedings Act 1973]

38   Validity of marriages

(1)   Subject to [section 13(1) of, and Schedule 6 to, the Marriage (Same Sex Couples) Act 2013 and to any orders in Council made under that Schedule], the question whether a marriage is formally valid shall be determined by the law of the place where the marriage was celebrated.

(2)   The question whether a person who enters into a marriage—

(a)   had capacity; or

(b)   consented,

to enter into it shall, subject to subsections (3) and (4) and to section 50 of the Family Law Act 1986 (c 55) (non-recognition of divorce or annulment in another jurisdiction no bar to remarriage), be determined by the law of the place where, immediately before the marriage, that person was domiciled.

(3) If a marriage entered into in Scotland is void under a rule of Scots internal law, then, notwithstanding subsection (2), that rule shall prevail over any law under which the marriage would be valid.

(4) The capacity of the person to enter into the marriage shall not be determined under the law of the place where, immediately before the marriage, the person was domiciled in so far as it would be contrary to public policy in Scotland for such capacity to be so determined.

(5) If the law of the place in which a person is domiciled requires a person under a certain age to obtain parental consent before entering into a marriage, that requirement shall not be taken to affect the capacity of a person to enter into a marriage in Scotland unless failure to obtain such consent would render invalid any marriage that the person purported to enter into in any form anywhere in the world.

39 Matrimonial property

(1) Any question in relation to the rights of spouses to each other's immoveable property arising by virtue of the marriage shall be determined by the law of the place in which the property is situated.

(2) Subject to subsections (4) and (5), if spouses are domiciled in the same country, any question in relation to the rights of the spouses to each other's moveable property arising by virtue of the marriage shall be determined by the law of that country.

(3) Subject to subsections (4) and (5), if spouses are domiciled in different countries then, for the purposes of any question in relation to the rights of the spouses to each other's moveable property arising by virtue of the marriage, the spouses shall be taken to have the same rights to such property as they had immediately before the marriage.

(4) Any question in relation to—

    (a) the use or occupation of a matrimonial home which is moveable; or

    (b) the use of the contents of a matrimonial home (whether the home is moveable or immoveable),

shall be determined by the law of the country in which the home is situated.

(5) A change of domicile by a spouse (or both spouses) shall not affect a right in moveable property which, immediately before the change, has vested in either spouse.

(6) This section shall not apply—

    (a) in relation to the law on aliment, financial provision on divorce, transfer of property on divorce or succession;

    (b) to the extent that spouses agree otherwise.

(7) In this section, 'matrimonial home' has the same meaning as in section 22 of the 1981 Act.

40 Aliment

Subject to the Maintenance Orders (Reciprocal Enforcement) Act 1972 (c 18), a court in Scotland shall apply Scots internal law in any action for aliment which comes before it.

41 Effect of parents' marriage in determining status to depend on law of domicile

Any question arising as to the effect on a person's status of—

    (a) the person's parents being, or having been, married to each other; or

    (b) the person's parents not being, or not having been, married to each other,

shall be determined by the law of the country in which the person is domiciled at the time at which the question arises.

ADOPTION AND CHILDREN (SCOTLAND) ACT 2007
(2007 asp 4)

PART 1
ADOPTION

CHAPTER 3 – STATUS OF ADOPTED CHILDREN

39   Meaning of 'adoption' in Chapter 3

(1)   In this Chapter, 'adoption' means—

(a)   adoption by an adoption order,

(b)   adoption by an adoption order as defined in section 46(1) of the 2002 Act,

(c)   adoption by an order made, or having effect as if made, under Article 12 of the Northern Ireland Order,

(d)   adoption by an order made in the Isle of Man or any of the Channel Islands,

(e)   a Convention adoption,

(f)   an overseas adoption, or

(g)   an adoption recognised by the law of Scotland and effected under the law of any other country;

and related expressions are to be interpreted accordingly.

(2)   References in this Chapter to adoption do not include an adoption effected before the day on which this Chapter comes into force.

(3)   Any reference in an enactment to an adopted person within the meaning of this Chapter includes a reference to an adopted child within the meaning of Part IV of the Adoption (Scotland) Act 1978 (c 28).

40   Status conferred by adoption

(1)   An adopted person is to be treated in law as if born as the child of the adopters or adopter.

(2)   If an adopted person is adopted—

(a)   by a relevant couple, or

(b)   by virtue of section 30(3), by a member of a relevant couple,

the adopted person is to be treated as the child of the couple concerned.

(3)   An adopted person adopted by virtue of section 30(3) by a member of a relevant couple is to be treated in law as not being the child of any person other than the adopter and the other member of the couple.

(4)   Otherwise, an adopted person is to be treated in law as not being the child of any person other than the adopters or adopter.

(5)   Subsections (3) and (4) do not affect any reference in this Act to a person's natural parent or to any other natural relationship.

(6)   Subsection (7) applies where, in the case of a person adopted under a Convention adoption, the Court of Session is satisfied, on an application under this section—

(a)   that under the law of the country in which the adoption was effected the adoption is not a full adoption,

(b)   that—

(i)   the consents mentioned in Article 4(c) and (d) of the Convention have not been given for a full adoption, or

(ii)   the United Kingdom is not the receiving State (within the meaning of Article 2 of the Convention), and

(c)   that it would be more favourable to the person for a direction to be given under that subsection.

(7)   The court may direct that subsection (4)—

(a)   is not to apply, or

(b)   is not to apply to such extent as may be specified in the direction.

(8)   In subsection (6), 'full adoption' means an adoption by virtue of which the person falls to be treated in law as if the person were not the child of any person other than the adopters or adopter.

(9)   This section has effect from the date of the adoption.

(10)   Subject to the provisions of this Chapter, this section—

(a)   applies for the interpretation of enactments or instruments passed or made before as well as after the adoption and so applies subject to any contrary indication, and

(b)   has effect as respects things done, or events occurring, on or after the adoption.

CHAPTER 6 – ADOPTIONS WITH A FOREIGN ELEMENT

58   Restriction on bringing children into the United Kingdom

(1)   This section applies where a person who is habitually resident in the British Islands (the 'British resident')—

(a)   brings, or causes another to bring, a child who is habitually resident outwith the British Islands into the United Kingdom for the purpose of adoption by the British resident, or

(b)   at any time brings, or causes another to bring, into the United Kingdom a child adopted by the British resident under an external adoption effected within the period of 12 months ending with that time.

(2)   In subsection (1), the references to adoption, or a child adopted, by the British resident include a reference to adoption, or a child adopted, by the British resident and another person.

(3)   This section does not apply if the child is intended to be adopted under a Convention adoption order.

(4)   An external adoption means an adoption, other than a Convention adoption, of a child effected under the law of any country or territory outwith the British Islands, whether or not the adoption is—

(a)   an adoption within the meaning of Chapter 3, or

(b)   a full adoption (as defined in section 40(8)).

(5)   Regulations may require a person intending to bring, or to cause another to bring, a child into the United Kingdom in circumstances where this section applies—

(a)   to apply to an adoption agency in the prescribed manner for an assessment of the person's suitability to adopt the child, and

(b)   to give the agency any information it may require for the purpose of the assessment.

(6)   Regulations may require prescribed conditions to be met in respect of a child brought into the United Kingdom in circumstances where this section applies.

(7)   In relation to a child brought into the United Kingdom for adoption in circumstances where this section applies, regulations may provide for any provision of Chapter 2 to apply with modifications or not to apply.

(8)   Regulations may provide for this section not to apply if—

(a)   the adopters or, as the case may be, prospective adopters of the child in question are—

(i)   natural parents,

(ii)   natural relatives, or

(iii)   guardians,

of the child (or one of them is), or

(b)   the British resident in question is a step-parent of the child,

and any prescribed conditions are met.

(9)   On the occasion of the first exercise of the power to make regulations under subsection (8)—

(a)   the regulations must not be made unless a draft of the regulations has been approved by a resolution of the Scottish Parliament, and

(b)   accordingly section 117(4) does not apply to the statutory instrument containing the regulations.

(10)   In this section, 'prescribed' means prescribed by regulations and 'regulations' means regulations made by the Scottish Ministers.

59   Preliminary order where child to be adopted abroad

(1)   The appropriate court may, on an application by persons ('the prospective adopters') who the court is satisfied intend to adopt a child under the law of a country or territory outwith the British Islands, make an order vesting parental responsibilities and parental rights in relation to the child in the prospective adopters.

(2)   If the court is satisfied that the prospective adopters would meet the requirements as to domicile, or habitual residence, in Scotland which they would require to meet if an adoption order were to be made on their application, the court may not make an order under this section.

(3)   An order under this section may not be made unless any requirements prescribed by regulations by the Scottish Ministers are satisfied.

(4)   An application for an order under this section may not be made unless at all times during the period of 10 weeks immediately preceding the application the child's home was with the prospective adopters.

(5)   Section 35 has effect in relation to an order under this section as it has effect in relation to adoption orders.

(6)   The Scottish Ministers may by regulations provide for any provision of this Act which relates to adoption orders to apply, with or without modifications, to orders under this section.

60   Restriction on removal of children for adoption outwith Great Britain

(1)   A person who takes or sends a protected child out of Great Britain to any place outwith the British Islands with a view to the adoption of the child by any person commits an offence.

(2)   A person who makes or takes part in any arrangements for transferring the care of a protected child to another person, knowing that the other person intends to take or send the child out of Great Britain in circumstances which would constitute an offence under subsection (1), commits an offence.

(3)   No offence is committed under subsection (1) if the child is taken or sent out of Great Britain under the authority of an order under—

(a)   section 59,

(b)   section 84 of the 2002 Act, or

(c)   Article 57 of the Northern Ireland Order.

(4)   A person is deemed to take part in arrangements for transferring the care of a child to another person for the purpose mentioned in subsection (2) if the person—

(a)   facilitates the placing of the child in the care of the other person,

(b)   initiates or takes part in negotiations the purpose or effect of which is—

(i)   the making of such arrangements, or

(ii)   the conclusion of an agreement to transfer the care of the child,

for the purpose mentioned in that subsection, or

(c)   causes any person to initiate or take part in any such negotiations.

(5)   The Scottish Ministers may by regulations provide for subsections (1) to (3) to apply with modifications, or not to apply, if—

(a)   the prospective adopters are—

(i)   parents,

     (ii) relatives, or

     (iii) guardians,

of the child (or one of them is), or

    (b)   the prospective adopter is a step-parent of the child,

and any conditions prescribed by the regulations are met.

    (6)   On the occasion of the first exercise of the power to make regulations under subsection (5)—

    (a)   the regulations must not be made unless a draft of the regulations has been approved by a resolution of the Scottish Parliament, and

    (b)   accordingly section 117(4) does not apply to the statutory instrument containing the regulations.

    (7)   In any proceedings under this section—

    (a)   a report by a British consular officer or a deposition made before, and authenticated under the signature of, such an officer is (if proved that the officer or deponent cannot be found in the United Kingdom) sufficient evidence of the matters stated in the report or deposition, and

    (b)   it is not necessary to prove the signature or official character of the person who bears to have signed the report or deposition.

    (8)   A person who commits an offence under this section is liable on summary conviction to imprisonment for a term not exceeding 3 months or a fine not exceeding level 5 on the standard scale or both.

    (9)   In subsections (1) and (2), 'protected child' means a child who is—

    (a)   habitually resident in the United Kingdom, or

    (b)   a Commonwealth citizen.

61   Regulations under section 58: offences

    (1)   If a person brings, or causes another to bring, a child into the United Kingdom at any time in circumstances where section 58 applies, the person commits an offence—

    (a)   if the person has not complied with any requirement imposed by virtue of subsection (5) of that section, or

    (b)   if the person has not met any condition which the person is required to meet by virtue of subsection (6) of that section,

before that time, or before any later time which may be prescribed by regulations made by the Scottish Ministers.

    (2)   A person who commits an offence under subsection (1) is liable—

    (a)   on summary conviction to imprisonment for a term not exceeding 6 months or a fine not exceeding the statutory maximum or both,

    (b)   on conviction on indictment to imprisonment for a term not exceeding 12 months, or a fine or both.

62   Declaration of special restrictions on adoptions from abroad

    (1)   This section applies if the Scottish Ministers have reason to believe that, because of practices taking place in a country or territory outwith the British Islands (the 'relevant country') in connection with the adoption of children, it would be contrary to public policy to further the bringing of children into the United Kingdom in the cases mentioned in subsection (2).

    (2)   Those cases are—

    (a)   that a British resident wishes to bring, or cause another to bring, a child who is not a British resident into the United Kingdom for the purpose of adoption by the British resident and, in connection with the proposed adoption, there have been, or would have to be, proceedings in the relevant country or dealings with authorities or agencies there, or

    (b)   that a British resident wishes to bring, or cause another to bring, into the United Kingdom a child adopted by the British resident under an adoption effected, within the period of 12 months ending with the date of the bringing in, under the law of the relevant country.

(3)   The Scottish Ministers may by order declare, in relation to any relevant country, that special restrictions are to apply for the time being in relation to the bringing in of children in the cases mentioned in subsection (2).

(4)   The Scottish Ministers must, as respects each relevant country in relation to which such a declaration has effect for the time being (a 'restricted country'), publish reasons for making the declaration in relation to the country.

(5)   The Scottish Ministers must publish a list of restricted countries ('the restricted list') and keep the list up to date.

(6)   The reasons and the restricted list are to be published in whatever way the Scottish Ministers think appropriate for bringing them to the attention of adoption agencies and members of the public.

(7)   In this section, 'British resident' means a person habitually resident in the British Islands.

(8)   Any reference in this section to adoption by a British resident includes adoption by a British resident and another person.

63   Review

(1)   The Scottish Ministers must keep under review, in relation to each restricted country, whether it should continue to be a restricted country.

(2)   If the Scottish Ministers determine, in relation to a restricted country, that there is no longer a reason to believe what is mentioned in subsection (1) of section 62, they must by order revoke the order containing the declaration made in relation to it under subsection (3) of that section.

(3)   In this section, 'restricted country' has the same meaning as in section 62.

64   The special restrictions

(1)   The special restrictions mentioned in subsection (3) of section 62 are that the Scottish Ministers are not to take any step which they might otherwise have taken in connection with furthering the bringing of a child into the United Kingdom in the cases mentioned in subsection (2) of that section (whether or not that step is provided for by virtue of any enactment).

(2)   Nothing in subsection (1) prevents the Scottish Ministers from taking those steps if, in any particular case, the prospective adopters or, as the case may be, the adopters satisfy the Scottish Ministers that they should take those steps despite the special restrictions.

(3)   The Scottish Ministers may make regulations providing for—

(a)   the procedure to be followed by them in determining whether or not they are satisfied as mentioned in subsection (2),

(b)   matters which they are to take into account when making such a determination (whether or not they also take other matters into account).

65   Imposition of extra conditions in certain cases

(1)   The Scottish Ministers may make regulations providing—

(a)   for them to specify in the restricted list, in relation to any restricted country, a step which is not otherwise provided for by virtue of any enactment but which, by virtue of the arrangements between the United Kingdom and that country, the Scottish Ministers normally take in connection with the bringing in of a child where that country is concerned, and

(b)   that, if such a step has been so specified in relation to a restricted country, one or more conditions specified in the regulations are to be met in respect of a child brought into the United Kingdom in either of the cases mentioned in section 62(2) (reading the reference there to the 'relevant country' as being to the restricted country in question).

(2)   Those conditions are in addition to any provided for by virtue of—

(a)   section 58, or

(b)   any other enactment.

(3)   A person who brings, or causes another to bring, a child into the United

Kingdom commits an offence if the person has not met any condition which the person is required to meet by virtue of subsection (1)(b).

(4)   Subsection (3) does not apply if the step specified in the restricted list in relation to any country had already been taken before the publication of the restricted list.

(5)   A person who commits an offence under subsection (3) is liable—

(a)   on summary conviction to imprisonment for a term not exceeding 6 months or a fine not exceeding the statutory maximum or both,

(b)   on conviction on indictment to imprisonment for a term not exceeding 12 months or a fine or both.

(6)   In this section, 'restricted country' and 'restricted list' have the same meanings as in section 62.

66   Power to charge

(1)   This section applies to adoptions to which—

(a)   section 58 applies, or

(b)   regulations made under section 1 of the Adoption (Intercountry Aspects) Act 1999 (c 18) apply.

(2)   The Scottish Ministers may charge a fee to adopters for services provided or to be provided by them in relation to adoptions to which this section applies.

(3)   The Scottish Ministers may determine the level of fee as they see fit and may, in particular—

(a)   charge a flat fee or charge different fees in different cases or descriptions of case,

(b)   in any case or description of case, waive a fee.

(4)   The Scottish Ministers must secure that, taking one financial year with another, the income from fees under this section does not exceed the total cost to them of providing the services in relation to which the fees are imposed.

(5)   In this section, 'financial year' means a period of 12 months ending with 31 March.

(6)   Any references in this section—

(a)   to adoptions include prospective adoptions, and

(b)   to adopters include prospective adopters.

67   Meaning of 'overseas adoption'

(1)   In this Act, 'overseas adoption'—

(a)   means an adoption of a description specified in regulations made by the Scottish Ministers (being a description of adoptions effected under the law of any country or territory outwith the British Islands), but

(b)   does not include a Convention adoption.

(2)   The Scottish Ministers may by regulations prescribe the requirements that ought to be met by an adoption of any description effected after the coming into force of the regulations for it to be an overseas adoption for the purposes of this Act.

(3)   At any time when regulations under subsection (2) are in force, the Scottish Ministers must exercise their power under subsection (1) so as to secure that adoptions of any description effected after the coming into force of the regulations are not overseas adoptions for the purposes of this Act if they consider that such adoptions are not likely, within a reasonable time, to meet the requirements prescribed under subsection (2).

(4)   Regulations under subsection (1) may contain provision as to the manner in which evidence of any overseas adoption may be given.

(5)   In this section, 'adoption' means the adoption of a child or of a person who was a child at the time the adoption was applied for.

68   Annulment and recognition

(1)   The Court of Session may, on an application under this subsection, by order

annul a Convention adoption or a Convention adoption order on the ground that the adoption or, as the case may be, order is contrary to public policy.

(2) The Court of Session may, on an application under this subsection—

(a) order that an overseas adoption or a determination is to cease to be valid in Great Britain on the ground that the adoption or, as the case may be, determination is contrary to public policy or that the authority which purported to authorise the adoption or make the determination was not competent to entertain the case,

(b) decide the extent, if any, to which a determination has been affected by a subsequent determination.

(3) The Court of Session may, in any proceedings in that court, decide that an overseas adoption or a determination is, for the purposes of those proceedings, to be treated as invalid in Great Britain on either of the grounds mentioned in subsection (2)(a).

(4) An order or decision of the High Court on an application under section 89(2) of the 2002 Act is to be recognised and to have effect as if it were an order or decision of the Court of Session on an application under subsection (2).

(5) Except as provided by this section, the validity of a Convention adoption, a Convention adoption order, an overseas adoption or a determination is not to be questioned in proceedings in any court in Scotland.

(6) In this section 'determination' means such a determination as is mentioned in section 70.

69 Section 68: supplementary provision

(1) Any application for—

(a) an order under section 68, or

(b) a decision under subsection (2)(b) of that section,

is to be made in the manner prescribed in regulations made by the Scottish Ministers and within such period as may be so prescribed.

(2) No application is to be made under section 68(1) in respect of an adoption unless immediately before the application is made—

(a) the person adopted was habitually resident in Scotland, or

(b) the persons on whose application the adoption order was made were habitually resident there.

(3) In deciding in pursuance of section 68 whether such an authority as is mentioned in section 70 was competent to hear a particular case, a court is to be bound by any finding of fact made by the authority and stated by the authority to be so made for the purpose of determining whether the authority was competent to hear the case.

70 Effect of determinations and orders made outwith Scotland

(1) Subsection (2) applies where—

(a) an authority of a Convention country (other than the United Kingdom) having power under the law of that country—

(i) to authorise, or review the authorisation of, a Convention adoption, or

(ii) to give or review a decision revoking or annulling such an adoption or a Convention adoption order, or

(b) an authority of a relevant territory having power under the law of that territory—

(i) to authorise, or review the authorisation of, a Convention adoption or an adoption effected in that territory, or

(ii) to give or review a decision revoking or annulling such an adoption or a Convention adoption order,

makes a determination ('the relevant determination') in the exercise of that power.

(2) Subject to section 68 and any subsequent determination having effect under this subsection, the relevant determination has effect in Scotland for the purpose of

effecting, confirming or terminating the adoption in question or confirming its termination as the case may be.

(3) In subsection (1), 'relevant territory' means—

(a) any of the Channel Islands,

(b) the Isle of Man, or

(c) any British overseas territory (within the meaning of the British Nationality Act 1981 (c 61)).

(4) Section 35 applies in relation to an order under Article 17 (freeing child for adoption with parental agreement) or 18 (freeing child for adoption without parental agreement) of the Northern Ireland Order as if it were an adoption order.

(5) Sections 35(2) and (3) and 43 apply in relation to a child who is the subject of an order which—

(a) is similar to an order under section 59, and

(b) is made (whether before or after this Act has effect) in a part of the British Islands,

as those sections apply in relation to a child who is the subject of an adoption order.

119 Interpretation

(1) In this Act, unless the context otherwise requires—

...

'the Convention' means the Convention on Protection of Children and Co-operation in respect of Intercountry Adoption, concluded at the Hague on 29th May 1993,

'Convention adoption' means an adoption effected under the law of a Convention country outwith the British Islands and certified in pursuance of Article 23(1) of the Convention,

'Convention adoption order' means an adoption order which, by virtue of regulations under section 1 of the Adoption (Intercountry Aspects) Act 1999 (c 18), is made as a Convention adoption order,

'Convention country' means any country or territory in which the Convention is in force,

(2) In this Act, unless the context otherwise requires, references to adoption are to the adoption of children, wherever they may be habitually resident, effected under the law of any country or territory, whether within or outwith the British Islands.

HUMAN FERTILISATION AND EMBRYOLOGY ACT 2008
(2008 c 22)

54 Parental orders

(1) On an application made by two people ('the applicants'), the court may make an order providing for a child to be treated in law as the child of the applicants if—

(a) the child has been carried by a woman who is not one of the applicants, as a result of the placing in her of an embryo or sperm and eggs or her artificial insemination,

(b) the gametes of at least one of the applicants were used to bring about the creation of the embryo, and

(c) the conditions in subsections (2) to (8) are satisfied.

(2) The applicants must be—

(a) husband and wife,

(b) civil partners of each other, or

(c) two persons who are living as partners in an enduring family relationship and are not within prohibited degrees of relationship in relation to each other.

(3) Except in a case falling within subsection (11), the applicants must apply for the order during the period of 6 months beginning with the day on which the child is born.

(4) At the time of the application and the making of the order—

(a) the child's home must be with the applicants, and

(b) either or both of the applicants must be domiciled in the United Kingdom or in the Channel Islands or the Isle of Man.

(5) At the time of the making of the order both the applicants must have attained the age of 18.

(6) The court must be satisfied that both—

(a) the woman who carried the child, and

(b) any other person who is a parent of the child but is not one of the applicants (including any man who is the father by virtue of section 35 or 36 or any woman who is a parent by virtue of section 42 or 43),

have freely, and with full understanding of what is involved, agreed unconditionally to the making of the order.

(7) Subsection (6) does not require the agreement of a person who cannot be found or is incapable of giving agreement; and the agreement of the woman who carried the child is ineffective for the purpose of that subsection if given by her less than six weeks after the child's birth.

(8) The court must be satisfied that no money or other benefit (other than for expenses reasonably incurred) has been given or received by either of the applicants for or in consideration of—

(a) the making of the order,

(b) any agreement required by subsection (6),

(c) the handing over of the child to the applicants, or

(d) the making of arrangements with a view to the making of the order,

unless authorised by the court.

(9) For the purposes of an application under this section—

(a) in relation to England and Wales [—

(i) 'the court' means the High Court or the family court, and

(ii) proceedings on the application are to be 'family proceedings' for the purposes of the Children Act 1989,]

(b) in relation to Scotland, 'the court' means the Court of Session or the sheriff court of the sheriffdom within which the child is, and

(c) in relation to Northern Ireland, 'the court' means the High Court or any county court within whose division the child is.

(10)   Subsection (1)(a) applies whether the woman was in the United Kingdom or elsewhere at the time of the placing in her of the embryo or the sperm and eggs or her artificial insemination.

(11)   An application which—

(a)   relates to a child born before the coming into force of this section, and

(b)   is made by two persons who, throughout the period applicable under subsection (2) of section 30 of the 1990 Act, were not eligible to apply for an order under that section in relation to the child as husband and wife,

may be made within the period of six months beginning with the day on which this section comes into force.

FORCED MARRIAGE ETC (PROTECTION AND JURISDICTION) (SCOTLAND) ACT 2011
(2011 asp 15)

PART 1
FORCED MARRIAGE PROTECTION ORDERS

Forced marriage protection orders

1   Forced marriage protection orders

(1)   The court may make an order for the purposes of protecting a person (a 'protected person')—

(a)   from being forced into a marriage or from any attempt to force the person into a marriage, or

(b)   who has been forced into a marriage.

(2)   In deciding whether to make such an order and, if so, what order to make, the court must have regard to all the circumstances including the need to secure the health, safety and well-being of the protected person.

(3)   In ascertaining the protected person's well-being, the court must, in particular, have such regard to the person's wishes and feelings (so far as they are reasonably ascertainable) as the court considers appropriate on the basis of the person's age and understanding.

(4)   For the purposes of this Part, a person ('A') is forced into a marriage if another person ('B') forces A to enter into a marriage (whether with B or another person) without A's free and full consent.

(5)   For the purposes of subsection (4), it does not matter whether the conduct of B which forces A to enter into a marriage is directed against A, B or another person.

(6)   In this Part—

'force' includes—

(a)   coerce by physical, verbal or psychological means, threatening conduct, harassment or other means,

(b)   knowingly take advantage of a person's incapacity to consent to marriage or to understand the nature of the marriage,

and related expressions are to be read accordingly,

'forced marriage protection order' means an order under subsection (1).

2   Contents of orders

(1)   A forced marriage protection order may contain such—

(a)   prohibitions, restrictions or requirements, and

(b)   other terms,

as the court considers appropriate for the purposes of the order.

(2)   The terms of such an order may, in particular, relate to—

(a)   conduct outwith (as well as, or instead of, conduct within) Scotland,

(b)   persons who force or attempt to force, or may force or attempt to force, a protected person to enter into a marriage,

(c)   persons who are, or may become, involved in other respects.

(3)   A forced marriage protection order may, among other things, require a person—

(a)   to take the protected person to a place of safety designated in the order,

(b)   to bring the protected person to a court at such time and place as the court making the order may specify,

(c)   to refrain from violent, threatening or intimidating conduct (whether against the protected person or any other person),

(d)   who is a person such as is mentioned in subsection (2)(b) or (c), to appear in court,

(e)   to disclose, if known, the whereabouts of such a person,

(f)   to refrain from taking the protected person from, or to, such place as the court may specify,

(g)   to facilitate or otherwise enable the protected person or another person to return or go to such place (whether in Scotland or another part of the United Kingdom) as the court may specify within such period as may be so specified,

(h)   to submit to the court such documents (including passports, birth certificates or other documents identifying the person and travel documents) as the court may specify,

(i)   to provide the court with such other information as it may specify.

(4)   For the purposes of subsection (2)(c), examples of involvement in other respects are—

(a)   aiding, abetting, counselling, procuring, encouraging or assisting another person to force, or to attempt to force, a person to enter into a marriage,

(b)   conspiring to force, or to attempt to force, a person to enter into a marriage.

3   Applications for orders

(1)   The court may make a forced marriage protection order on an application being made to it by—

(a)   the protected person, or

(b)   a relevant third party.

(2)   An application may be made by any other person only with the leave of the court.

(3)   In deciding whether to grant such leave, the court must have regard to all the circumstances including—

(a)   the applicant's connection with the protected person,

(b)   the applicant's knowledge of the circumstances of the protected person, and

(c)   the wishes and feelings of the protected person so far as they are reasonably ascertainable.

(4)   But the court need only have regard to those wishes and feelings so far as it considers it appropriate, on the basis of the protected person's age and understanding, to do so.

(5)   An application made to the sheriff under this section is to be made by summary application.

(6)   An application made to the sheriff under this section is to be made—

(a)   to the sheriff in whose sheriffdom the protected person is ordinarily resident, or

(b)   where the protected person is not ordinarily resident in Scotland, to the sheriff of the sheriffdom of Lothian and Borders at Edinburgh.

(7)   In this section, 'a relevant third party' means—

(a)   a local authority,

(b)   the Lord Advocate,

    (c)   a person specified, or falling within a description of persons specified, by order made by the Scottish Ministers.

4 Power to make orders without application, etc

(1)   The court may make a forced marriage protection order without an application being made to it where—

    (a)   civil proceedings are before the court,

    (b)   the court considers that a forced marriage protection order should be made to protect a person (whether or not a party to the civil proceedings), and

    (c)   a person who would be a party to any proceedings for the forced marriage protection order (other than as the protected person) is a party to the civil proceedings.

(2)   Subsection (3) applies where—

    (a)   criminal proceedings are before the sheriff or the High Court, and

    (b)   the sheriff or the High Court considers that a forced marriage protection order should be made to protect a person (whether or not a party to the criminal proceedings).

(3)   The sheriff or, as the case may be, the High Court may refer the matter to the Lord Advocate who may—

    (a)   apply under section 3 for a forced marriage protection order,

    (b)   take such other steps as the Lord Advocate considers appropriate.

Interim orders

5 Interim orders

(1)   The court may, in a case where it considers that it is equitable to do so, make a forced marriage protection order in the absence of a person who is, or would be, a party to proceedings for the order (and may do so whether or not the person has been given such notice of the application for the order as would otherwise be required by rules of court).

(2)   An order made by virtue of subsection (1) is an 'interim forced marriage protection order'.

(3)   In deciding whether to make an interim order by virtue of subsection (1), the court must have regard to all the circumstances including any risk of significant harm to the protected person or to another person if the order is not made immediately.

(4)   In this Part (unless the context otherwise requires), references to forced marriage protection orders include references to interim forced marriage protection orders.

Duration, variation, recall and extension

6 Duration of orders

A forced marriage protection order has effect—

    (a)   where the order specifies a period for which it is to have effect, until the expiry of that period (unless the order is recalled under section 7 or extended under section 8),

    (b)   where no such period is specified, until the order is recalled under section 7.

7 Variation and recall of orders

(1)   The court may vary or recall a forced marriage protection order on an application by—

    (a)   any person who was or, in the case of an order made by virtue of section 4(1) or 5(1), would have been a party to the proceedings for the order,

    (b)   the protected person (if not such a person),

(c)   any other person affected by the order, or

(d)   with the leave of the court only, any person not falling within paragraphs (a) to (c).

(2)   In deciding whether to grant leave under subsection (1)(d), the court must have regard to all the circumstances including—

(a)   the applicant's connection with the protected person,

(b)   the applicant's knowledge of the circumstances of the protected person, and

(c)   the wishes and feelings of the protected person so far as they are reasonably ascertainable.

(3)   But the court need only have regard to those wishes and feelings so far as it considers it appropriate, on the basis of the protected person's age and understanding, to do so.

(4)   In addition, the court may vary or recall a forced marriage protection order made by virtue of section 4(1) even though no application under subsection (1) of this section has been made to the court.

(5)   Section 5 applies to the variation of a forced marriage protection order as it applies to the making of an interim forced marriage protection order; and accordingly the references in that section to the making of such an interim order are to be read for the purposes of this subsection as references to varying a forced marriage protection order.

(6)   In this Part, where a forced marriage protection order specifies a period for which it is to have effect, references to varying an order do not include extending any such period.

8   Extension of orders

(1)   This section applies where a forced marriage protection order specifies a period for which it is to have effect.

(2)   Before the expiry of the period, a person mentioned in subsection (3) may apply to the court for an extension of the order.

(3)   The persons are—

(a)   any person who was or, in the case of an order made by virtue of section 4(1) or 5(1), would have been a party to the proceedings for the order,

(b)   the protected person (if not such a person),

(c)   any other person affected by the order, or

(d)   with the leave of the court only, any person not falling within paragraphs (a) to (c).

(4)   In deciding whether to grant leave under subsection (3)(d), the court must have regard to all the circumstances including—

(a)   the applicant's connection with the protected person,

(b)   the applicant's knowledge of the circumstances of the protected person, and

(c)   the wishes and feelings of the protected person so far as they are reasonably ascertainable.

(5)   But the court need only have regard to those wishes and feelings so far as it considers it appropriate, on the basis of the protected person's age and understanding, to do so.

(6)   In addition, where the order was made by virtue of section 4(1), the court may before the expiry of the period extend the order even though no application has been made to the court.

(7)   An order may be extended on more than one occasion.

(8)   Section 5 applies to the extension of a forced marriage protection order as it applies to the making of an interim forced marriage protection order; and accordingly the references in that section to the making of such an interim order are to be read for the purposes of this subsection as references to extending such an order.

Offence

9   Offence of breaching order

(1)   Any person who, knowingly and without reasonable excuse, breaches a forced marriage protection order commits an offence.

(2)   A constable may arrest without warrant any person the constable reasonably believes is committing or has committed an offence under subsection (1).

(3)   Subsection (2) is without prejudice to any power of arrest conferred by law apart from that subsection.

(4)   A person guilty of an offence under subsection (1) is liable—

    (a)   on summary conviction, to imprisonment for a period not exceeding 12 months, to a fine not exceeding the statutory maximum, or to both,

    (b)   on conviction on indictment, to imprisonment for a period not exceeding 2 years, to a fine, or to both.

(5)   Where a person is convicted of an offence under subsection (1) in respect of any conduct, that conduct is not punishable as a contempt of court.

Power to apply Part to civil partnerships

10   Power to apply Part to civil partnerships

(1)   The Scottish Ministers may by order make provision applying this Part (or particular provisions of it) to civil partnerships as it applies (or as the particular provisions of it apply) to marriages.

(2)   An order under subsection (1) may, for the purposes of the application mentioned in that subsection, make such modifications of enactments (including of this Act) as the Scottish Ministers consider necessary.

Supplementary

11   Guidance

(1)   The Scottish Ministers must, no later than the day on which section 1 comes into force, give guidance to such persons or descriptions of persons as Ministers consider appropriate about the effect of this Part or any provision of it.

(2)   The Scottish Ministers may give guidance to such persons or descriptions of persons as Ministers consider appropriate about matters (other than that mentioned in subsection (1)) relating to forced marriages.

(3)   A person exercising public functions to whom guidance is given under this section must have regard to it in the exercise of those functions.

(4)   The Scottish Ministers may not give guidance under this section to any court or tribunal.

12   Other protection or assistance against forced marriage

(1)   This Part does not affect any other protection or assistance available to a person who—

    (a)   is being, or may be, forced into a marriage,

    (b)   is being, or may be, subjected to an attempt to force the person into a marriage, or

    (c)   has been forced into a marriage.

(2)   In particular, it does not affect—

    (a)   the equitable jurisdiction of the High Court or the Court of Session,

    (b)   any criminal liability,

    (c)   any civil remedies under the Protection from Harassment Act 1997 (c 40),

    (d)   any right to—

       (i)   an order under the Matrimonial Homes (Family Protection) (Scotland) Act 1981 (c 59) relating to occupancy rights,

       (ii)   an exclusion order under that Act,

(e)   any protection or assistance under the Children (Scotland) Act 1995 (c 36) or the Children's Hearings (Scotland) Act 2011 (asp 1),

(f) any claim in delict, or

(g)   the law of marriage.

13   [*Amends Children's Hearings (Scotland) Act 2011.*]

14   Interpretation of Part

In this Part (except where the context otherwise requires)—

'court' means the Court of Session or the sheriff,

'force' and related expressions have the meanings given by section 1(6),

'forced marriage protection order' has the meaning given by section 1(6),

'interim forced marriage protection order' has the meaning given by section 5(2),

'marriage' means any religious or civil ceremony of marriage (wherever carried out and whether or not legally binding under the law of Scotland or any other place),

'protected person' has the meaning given by section 1(1).

13   [*Amends s 8 of Domicile and Matrimonial Proceedings Act 1973.*]

PART 3
GENERAL

16   Ancillary provision

(1)   The Scottish Ministers may by order make such incidental, consequential, transitional, transitory or saving provision as they consider appropriate for the purposes, or in consequence, of any provision of this Act.

(2)   An order under subsection (1) may modify any enactment (including this Act).

17   Subordinate legislation

(1)   Any power conferred by this Act on the Scottish Ministers to make orders is exercisable by statutory instrument.

(2)   Subject to subsection (3), a statutory instrument containing an order under this Act (other than one under section 19(2)) is subject to annulment in pursuance of a resolution of the Scottish Parliament.

(3)   No order under—

(a)   section 10(1),

(b)   section 16(1) containing provisions which add to, replace or omit any part of the text of any Act,

may be made unless a draft of the statutory instrument containing the order has been laid before, and approved by resolution of, the Scottish Parliament.

18   Crown application

(1)   No contravention by the Crown of—

(a)   section 9(1), or

(b)   any provision made by virtue of section 10,

makes the Crown criminally liable.

(2)   But the Court of Session may, on the application of any public body or office holder having responsibility for enforcing section 9(1) or any provision made by virtue of section 10, declare unlawful any act or omission of the Crown which constitutes such a contravention.

(3)   Despite subsection (1), section 9(1) and any provision made by virtue of section 10 apply to persons in the public service of the Crown as they apply to other persons.

(4)   Nothing in this Act affects Her Majesty in Her private capacity.

19   Short title and commencement

(1)   The short title of this Act is the Forced Marriage etc (Protection and Jurisdiction) (Scotland) Act 2011.

(2)   This Act (other than this section) comes into force on such day as the Scottish Ministers may by order appoint.

DEFAMATION ACT 2013
(2013 c 26)

9   Action against a person not domiciled in the UK or a Member State etc

(1)   This section applies to an action for defamation against a person who is not domiciled—

(a)   in the United Kingdom;

(b)   in another Member State; or

(c)   in a state which is for the time being a contracting party to the Lugano Convention.

(2)   A court does not have jurisdiction to hear and determine an action to which this section applies unless the court is satisfied that, of all the places in which the statement complained of has been published, England and Wales is clearly the most appropriate place in which to bring an action in respect of the statement.

(3)   The references in subsection (2) to the statement complained of include references to any statement which conveys the same, or substantially the same, imputation as the statement complained of.

(4)   For the purposes of this section—

(a)   a person is domiciled in the United Kingdom or in another Member State if the person is domiciled there for the purposes of the Brussels Regulation;

(b)   a person is domiciled in a state which is a contracting party to the Lugano Convention if the person is domiciled in the state for the purposes of that Convention.

(5)   In this section—

'the Brussels Regulation' means [Regulation (EU)   No 1215/2012 of the European Parliament and of the Council of 12 December 2012 on jurisdiction and the recognition and enforcement of judgments in civil and commercial matters (recast), as amended from time to time and as applied by virtue of the Agreement made on 19 October 2005 between the European Community and the Kingdom of Denmark on jurisdiction and the recognition and enforcement of judgments in civil and commercial matters;]

'the Lugano Convention' means the Convention on jurisdiction and the recognition and enforcement of judgments in civil and commercial matters, between the European Community and the Republic of Iceland, the Kingdom of Norway, the Swiss Confederation and the Kingdom of Denmark signed on behalf of the European Community on 30th October 2007.

MARRIAGE (SAME SEX COUPLES) ACT 2013
(2013 c 30)

PART 1
MARRIAGE OF SAME SEX COUPLES IN ENGLAND AND WALES

1 Extension of marriage to same sex couples

(1) Marriage of same sex couples is lawful.

(2) The marriage of a same sex couple may only be solemnized in accordance with—

(a) Part 3 of the Marriage Act 1949,

(b) Part 5 of the Marriage Act 1949,

(c) the Marriage (Registrar General's Licence) Act 1970, or

(d) an Order in Council made under Part 1 or 3 of Schedule 6.

(3) No Canon of the Church of England is contrary to section 3 of the Submission of the Clergy Act 1533 (which provides that no Canons shall be contrary to the Royal Prerogative or the customs, laws or statutes of this realm) by virtue of its making provision about marriage being the union of one man with one woman.

(4) Any duty of a member of the clergy to solemnize marriages (and any corresponding right of persons to have their marriages solemnized by members of the clergy) is not extended by this Act to marriages of same sex couples.

(5) A 'member of the clergy' is—

(a) a clerk in Holy Orders of the Church of England, or

(b) a clerk in Holy Orders of the Church in Wales.

9 Conversion of civil partnership into marriage

(1) The parties to an England and Wales civil partnership may convert their civil partnership into a marriage under a procedure established by regulations made by the Secretary of State.

(2) The parties to a civil partnership within subsection (3) may convert their civil partnership into a marriage under a procedure established by regulations made by the Secretary of State.

(3) A civil partnership is within this subsection if—

(a) it was formed outside the United Kingdom under an Order in Council made under Chapter 1 of Part 5 of the Civil Partnership Act 2004 (registration at British consulates etc or by armed forces personnel), and

(b) the part of the United Kingdom that was relevant for the purposes of section 210(2)(b) or (as the case may be) section 211(2)(b) of that Act was England and Wales.

(4) Regulations under this section may in particular make—

(a) provision about the making by the parties to a civil partnership of an application to convert their civil partnership into a marriage;

(b) provision about the information to be provided in support of an application to convert;

(c) provision about the making of declarations in support of an application to convert;

(d) provision for persons who have made an application to convert to appear before any person or attend at any place;

(e) provision conferring functions in connection with applications to convert on relevant officials, relevant armed forces personnel, the Secretary of State, or any other persons;

(f) provision for fees, of such amounts as are specified in or determined in accordance with the regulations, to be payable in respect of—

(i) the making of an application to convert;

(ii) the exercise of any function conferred by virtue of paragraph (e).

(5) Functions conferred by virtue of paragraph (e) of subsection (4) may include functions relating to—

    (a)   the recording of information on the conversion of civil partnerships;

    (b)   the issuing of certified copies of any information recorded;

    [(ba)   the carrying out, on request, of searches of any information recorded and the provision, on request, of records of any information recorded (otherwise than in the form of certified copies);]

    (c)   the conducting of services or ceremonies (other than religious services or ceremonies) following the conversion of a civil partnership.

    (6)   Where a civil partnership is converted into a marriage under this section—

    (a)   the civil partnership ends on the conversion, and

    (b)   the resulting marriage is to be treated as having subsisted since the date the civil partnership was formed.

    (7)   In this section—

'England and Wales civil partnership' means a civil partnership which is formed by two people registering as civil partners of each other in England or Wales (see Part 2 of the Civil Partnership Act 2004);

'relevant armed forces personnel' means—

    (a)   a member of Her Majesty's forces;

    (b)   a civilian subject to service discipline (within the meaning of the Armed Forces Act 2006);

and for this purpose 'Her Majesty's forces' has the same meaning as in the Armed Forces Act 2006;

'relevant official' means—

    (a)   the Registrar General;

    (b)   a superintendent registrar;

    (c)   a registrar;

    (d)   a consular officer in the service of Her Majesty's government in the United Kingdom;

    (e)   a person authorised by the Secretary of State in respect of the solemnization of marriages or formation of civil partnerships in a country or territory in which Her Majesty's government in the United Kingdom has for the time being no consular representative.

10   Extra-territorial matters

    (1)   A marriage under—

    (a)   the law of any part of the United Kingdom (other than England and Wales), or

    (b)   the law of any country or territory outside the United Kingdom,

is not prevented from being recognised under the law of England and Wales only because it is the marriage of a same sex couple.

    (2)   For the purposes of this section it is irrelevant whether the law of a particular part of the United Kingdom, or a particular country or territory outside the United Kingdom—

    (a)   already provides for marriage of same sex couples at the time when this section comes into force, or

    (b)   provides for marriage of same sex couples from a later time.

    (3)   Schedule 2 (extra-territorial matters) has effect.

11   Effect of extension of marriage

    (1)   In the law of England and Wales, marriage has the same effect in relation to same sex couples as it has in relation to opposite sex couples.

    (2)   The law of England and Wales (including all England and Wales legislation whenever passed or made) has effect in accordance with subsection (1).

    (3)   Schedule 3 (interpretation of legislation) has effect.

    (4)   Schedule 4 (effect of extension of marriage: further provision) has effect.

    (5)   For provision about limitations on the effects of subsections (1) and (2) and Schedule 3, see Part 7 of Schedule 4.

(6)   Subsections (1) and (2) and Schedule 3 do not have any effect in relation to—

(a)   Measures and Canons of the Church of England (whenever passed or made),

(b)   subordinate legislation (whenever made) made under a Measure or Canon of the Church of England, or

(c)   other ecclesiastical law (whether or not contained in England and Wales legislation, and, if contained in England and Wales legislation, whenever passed or made).

(7)   In Schedules 3 and 4—

'existing England and Wales legislation' means—

(a)   in the case of England and Wales legislation that is primary legislation, legislation passed before the end of the Session in which this Act is passed (excluding this Act), or

(b)   in the case of England and Wales legislation that is subordinate legislation, legislation made on or before the day on which this Act is passed (excluding legislation made under this Act);

'new England and Wales legislation' means—

(a)   in the case of England and Wales legislation that is primary legislation, legislation passed after the end of the Session in which this Act is passed, or

(b)   in the case of England and Wales legislation that is subordinate legislation, legislation made after the day on which this Act is passed.

13   Marriage overseas

(1)   Schedule 6 (marriage overseas) has effect.

(2)   The Foreign Marriage Act 1892 is repealed.

15   Review of civil partnership

(1)   The Secretary of State must arrange—

(a)   for the operation and future of the Civil Partnership Act 2004 in England and Wales to be reviewed, and

(b)   for a report on the outcome of the review to be produced and published.

(2)   Subsection (1) does not prevent the review from also dealing with other matters relating to civil partnership.

(3)   The arrangements made by the Secretary of State must provide for the review to begin as soon as practicable and include a full public consultation.

20   Extent

(1)   This Act extends to England and Wales.

(2)   These provisions of this Act also extend to Scotland—

(a)   in Part 1, section 10(3) and Schedule 2;

(b)   Part 2, except for sections 14 and 15;

(c)   Part 3.

(3)   These provisions of this Act also extend to Northern Ireland—

(a)   in Part 1, section 10(3) and Schedule 2;

(b)   Part 2, except for sections 14 to 16 and paragraphs 4, 5, 10 and 11 of Schedule 6;

(c)   Part 3.

(4)   Subsections (1) to (3) do not apply to an amendment or repeal or revocation made by this Act.

(5)   An amendment or repeal or revocation made by this Act has the same extent as the provision amended or repealed or revoked.

(6)   Subsection (5) is subject to subsections (7) to (9).

(7)   Any amendment of the following Acts extends to England and Wales only—

(a)   the Social Security Contributions and Benefits Act 1992;

(b)   the Pension Schemes Act 1993;

(c) the Human Fertilisation and Embryology Act 2008.

(8) The repeal of the Foreign Marriage Act 1892 made by section 13(2) does not extend to Northern Ireland.

(9) Any amendment made by Part 2 of Schedule 5 does not extend to Northern Ireland.

ANTI-SOCIAL BEHAVIOUR, CRIME AND POLICING ACT 2014
(2014 c 12)

121 Offence of forced marriage: England and Wales

(1) A person commits an offence under the law of England and Wales if he or she—

(a) uses violence, threats or any other form of coercion for the purpose of causing another person to enter into a marriage, and

(b) believes, or ought reasonably to believe, that the conduct may cause the other person to enter into the marriage without free and full consent.

(2) In relation to a victim who lacks capacity to consent to marriage, the offence under subsection (1) is capable of being committed by any conduct carried out for the purpose of causing the victim to enter into a marriage (whether or not the conduct amounts to violence, threats or any other form coercion).

(3) A person commits an offence under the law of England and Wales if he or she—

(a) practises any form of deception with the intention of causing another person to leave the United Kingdom, and

(b) intends the other person to be subjected to conduct outside the United Kingdom that is an offence under subsection (1) or would be an offence under that subsection if the victim were in England or Wales.

(4) 'Marriage' means any religious or civil ceremony of marriage (whether or not legally binding).

(5) 'Lacks capacity' means lacks capacity within the meaning of the Mental Capacity Act 2005.

(6) It is irrelevant whether the conduct mentioned in paragraph (a) of subsection (1) is directed at the victim of the offence under that subsection or another person.

(7) A person commits an offence under subsection (1) or (3) only if, at the time of the conduct or deception—

(a) the person or the victim or both of them are in England or Wales,

(b) neither the person nor the victim is in England or Wales but at least one of them is habitually resident in England and Wales, or

(c) neither the person nor the victim is in the United Kingdom but at least one of them is a UK national.

(8) 'UK national' means an individual who is—

(a) a British citizen, a British overseas territories citizen, a British National (Overseas) or a British Overseas citizen;

(b) a person who under the British Nationality Act 1981 is a British subject; or

(c) a British protected person within the meaning of that Act.

(9) A person guilty of an offence under this section is liable—

(a) on summary conviction, to imprisonment for a term not exceeding 12 months or to a fine or both;

(b) on conviction on indictment, to imprisonment for a term not exceeding 7 years.

(10) In relation to an offence committed before the commencement of section 154(1) of the Criminal Justice Act 2003, the reference to 12 months in subsection (9)(a) is to be read as a reference to six months.

122   Offence of forced marriage: Scotland

(1)   A person commits an offence under the law of Scotland if he or she—

(a)   uses violence, threats or any other form of coercion for the purpose of causing another person to enter into a marriage, and

(b)   believes, or ought reasonably to believe, that the conduct may cause the other person to enter into the marriage without free and full consent.

(2)   In relation to a victim who is incapable of consenting to marriage by reason of mental disorder, the offence under subsection (1) is capable of being committed by any conduct carried out for the purpose of causing the victim to enter into a marriage (whether or not the conduct amounts to violence, threats or any other form coercion).

(3)   A person commits an offence under the law of Scotland if he or she—

(a)   practises any form of deception with the intention of causing another person to leave the United Kingdom, and

(b)   intends the other person to be subjected to conduct outside the United Kingdom that is an offence under subsection (1) or would be an offence under that subsection if the victim were in Scotland.

(4)   'Marriage' means any religious or civil ceremony of marriage (whether or not legally binding).

(5)   'Mental disorder' has the meaning given by section 328 of the Mental Health (Care and Treatment) (Scotland) Act 2003.

(6)   It is irrelevant whether the conduct mentioned in paragraph (a) of subsection (1) is directed at the victim of the offence under that subsection or another person.

(7)   A person commits an offence under subsection (1) or (3) only if, at the time of the conduct or deception—

(a)   the person or the victim or both of them are in Scotland,

(b)   neither the person nor the victim is in Scotland but at least one of them is habitually resident in Scotland, or

(c)   neither the person nor the victim is in the United Kingdom but at least one of them is a UK national.

(8)   'UK national' means an individual who is—

(a)   a British citizen, a British overseas territories citizen, a British National (Overseas) or a British Overseas citizen;

(b)   a person who under the British Nationality Act 1981 is a British subject; or

(c)   a British protected person within the meaning of that Act.

(9)   A person guilty of an offence under this section is liable—

(a)   on summary conviction, to imprisonment for a term not exceeding 12 months or to a fine not exceeding the statutory maximum or both;

(b)   on conviction on indictment, to imprisonment for a term not exceeding 7 years or to a fine or both.

MARRIAGE AND CIVIL PARTNERSHIP (SCOTLAND) ACT 2014
(2014 asp 5)

PART 1
MARRIAGE

Chapter 1
Same Sex Marriage

2 [*Amends Marriage (Scotland) Act 1977, s 5(4).*]

4 Meaning of marriage and related expressions in enactments and documents

(1)   References (however expressed) in any enactment to—

(a)   marriage (including a marriage that has ended),

(b)   a person who is (or was) married to another person, and

(c)   two people who are (or were) married to each other,

are references to marriage whether between persons of different sexes or persons of the same sex and to a party (or former party), or as the case may be the parties (or former parties), to such a marriage.

(2)   Subsection (3) applies to references (however expressed) in any enactment to two people who—

(a)   are (or were) not married to each other, but

(b)   are (or were) living together as if they were husband and wife.

(3)   The references include two people of the same sex who are (or were) not married to, nor in civil partnership with, each other but who are (or were) living together as if they were married to each other.

(4)   References (however expressed) in any enactment to two people of the same sex who are (or were) living together as if they were in a civil partnership cease to have effect.

(5)   Subsections (1) to (4)—

(a)   apply to enactments (other than private Acts) passed or made before the commencement of this section, and

(b)   do not apply in so far as the enactment, or any other enactment, provides otherwise.

(6)   In so far as being (or having been) married or in a purported marriage is relevant for the operation of any rule of law, the rule of law applies equally in relation to marriage or purported marriage to a person of a different sex and marriage or purported marriage to a person of the same sex.

(7)   Subsections (1) to (6) are subject to an order under subsection (8).

(8)   The Scottish Ministers may by order provide for any of subsections (1) to (6)—

(a)   to have effect subject to provision made by the order, or

(b)   not to apply in cases specified in the order.

(9)   An order under subsection (8)—

(a)   may make different provision for different purposes,

(b)   may include consequential, supplementary, incidental, transitional, transitory or saving provision,

(c)   may modify any enactment (including this Act),

(d)   is (except where subsection (10) applies) subject to the negative procedure.

(10)   An order under subsection (8) which adds to, replaces or omits any part of the text of an Act is subject to the affirmative procedure.

(11)   References (however expressed) in any document to—

(a)   marriage (including a marriage that has ended),

(b)   a person who is (or was) married to another person, and

(c)   two people who are (or were) married to each other,

are references to marriage whether between persons of different sexes or persons of the same sex and to a party (or former party), or as the case may be the parties (or former parties), to such a marriage.

(12)   The following expressions in any document have the meanings given—

(a)   'widow' includes a woman whose marriage to another woman ended with the other woman's death,

(b)   'widower' includes a man whose marriage to another man ended with the other man's death.

(13)   Subsections (11) and (12)—

(a)   apply to documents executed on or after the commencement of this section, and

(b)   do not apply in so far as the document provides otherwise.

(14)   In section 26(2) of the 1977 Act (interpretation), after the definition of 'authorised registrar' insert—

"'marriage' means marriage between persons of different sexes and marriage between persons of the same sex;'.

(15)   In schedule 1 to the Interpretation and Legislative Reform (Scotland) Act 2010 (definitions of words and expressions), insert at the appropriate place in alphabetical order—

"'marriage' means marriage between persons of different sexes and marriage between persons of the same sex (and any reference to a person being (or having been) married to another person, or to two people being (or having been) married to each other, is to be read accordingly),',

"'widow' includes a woman whose marriage to another woman ended with the other woman's death,',

"'widower' includes a man whose marriage to another man ended with the other man's death,'.

Chapter 2
Marriage Between Civil Partners in Qualifying Civil Partnerships

9   Power to modify meaning of 'qualifying civil partnership'

(1)   The Scottish Ministers may by order modify the meaning of 'qualifying civil partnership' given by section 5(6) of the 1977 Act (inserted by section 8(3)(b) of this Act) so as to include civil partnerships registered outside Scotland.

(2)   An order under subsection (1)—

(a)   may make different provision for different purposes,

(b)   may include consequential, supplementary, incidental, transitional, transitory or saving provision,

(c)   may modify any enactment (including this Act),

(d)   is subject to the affirmative procedure.

(3)   Before laying a draft of an order under subsection (1) before the Scottish Parliament, the Scottish Ministers must consult the following persons on a copy of the proposed draft order—

(a)   the Registrar General of Births, Deaths and Marriages for Scotland, and

(b)   such other persons as the Scottish Ministers consider appropriate.

10   Change of qualifying civil partnership into marriage

(1)   The Scottish Ministers may by regulations make provision to establish a procedure for the parties to a qualifying civil partnership to change their civil partnership into a marriage.

(2)   Regulations under subsection (1) may in particular make provision—

(a)   about the making by the parties to a qualifying civil partnership of an application to change their civil partnership into a marriage,

(b)   about the information to be provided in support of an application,

(c)   about the provision of evidence in support of an application,

(d) for persons who have made an application to appear before any person or appear at any place,

(e) conferring functions on persons in relation to applications,

(f) for fees, of such amounts as are specified in or determined in accordance with the regulations, to be payable in respect of—

(i) the making of an application,

(ii) the exercise of any function conferred by virtue of paragraph (e).

(3) Functions conferred by virtue of subsection (2)(e) may include functions relating to—

(a) the recording of information relating to qualifying civil partnerships changing into marriages,

(b) the issuing of certified copies of any information recorded.

(4) Before making regulations under subsection (1), the Scottish Ministers must consult the Registrar General of Births, Deaths and Marriages for Scotland.

(5) Regulations under subsection (1)—

(a) may make different provision for different purposes,

(b) may include consequential, supplementary, incidental, transitional, transitory or saving provision,

(c) may modify any enactment (including this Act),

(d) are (except where subsection (6) applies) subject to the negative procedure.

(6) Regulations under subsection (1) which add to, replace or omit any part of the text of an Act are subject to the affirmative procedure.

(7) In this section 'qualifying civil partnership' has the meaning given by [section 5(6)(i)(A) of the 1977 Act].

11   Effect of marriage between civil partners in a qualifying civil partnership

(1) This section applies where civil partners in a qualifying civil partnership (within the meaning of section 5(6) of the 1977 Act)—

(a) marry in accordance with that Act, or

(b) change their civil partnership into a marriage in accordance with provision made under section 10(1).

(2) Where this section applies—

(a) the qualifying civil partnership ends on the date on which—

(i) the marriage was solemnised, or

(ii) the change took effect, and

(b) the civil partners are to be treated as having been married to each other since the date on which the qualifying civil partnership was registered.

(3) For the purposes of subsection (2)(b)—

(a) a civil partnership registered under an Order in Council made under section 210 of the 2004 Act is to be treated as having been registered when it is entered in the Register Book maintained under the Order,

(b) a civil partnership registered under an Order in Council made under section 211 of the 2004 Act is to be treated as having been registered when the civil partnership register is signed in accordance with the Order.

(4) Subsection (2)(b) is subject to—

(a) any provision to the contrary made by or under any enactment,

(b) an order under subsection (5).

(5) The Scottish Ministers may by order provide for subsection (2)(b)—

(a) to have effect subject to provision made by the order, or

(b) not to apply in cases specified in the order.

(6) An order under subsection (5)—

(a) may include consequential, supplementary, incidental, transitional, transitory or saving provision,

(b) is subject to the negative procedure.

(7) If a decree of aliment under section 3 of the Family Law (Scotland) Act 1985

(powers of court in action for aliment) requiring one of the civil partners to make payments to the other is in force at the time the qualifying civil partnership ends by virtue of subsection (2)(a) of this section, the decree continues to have effect despite the ending of the civil partnership.

(8)   If an order under section 103(3) or (4) of the 2004 Act (regulation by court of rights of occupancy of family home) is in force at the time the qualifying civil partnership ends by virtue of subsection (2)(a) of this section the order has effect from that time as if made under section 3(3) or, as the case may be, 3(4) of the Matrimonial Homes (Family Protection) (Scotland) Act 1981 (regulation by court of rights of occupancy of matrimonial home).

(9)   [Amends Civil Partnership Act 2004.]

PART 3
MARRIAGE AND CIVIL PARTNERSHIP: OTHER PROVISION

28   Bigamy

...

(3)   The common law offence of bigamy is abolished.

...

SUCCESSION (SCOTLAND) ACT 2016
(2016 ASP 7)

1   Effect of divorce, dissolution or annulment on will
(1)   This section applies where—
  (a)   a person ('the testator') by a will—
    (i)   confers a benefit or power of appointment on a person, or
    (ii)   appoints a person as a trustee or executor,
  (b)   that person ('P') is, or becomes, the testator's spouse or civil partner,
  (c)   the marriage or civil partnership is terminated, and
  (d)   the testator then dies.
(2)   P is to be treated as having died before the testator for the purposes of the will except for the purposes of any appointment of P or another person as a guardian.
(3)   Subsection (2) does not apply if the will expressly provides that P is to—
  (a)   have the benefit or power of appointment, or
  (b)   be so appointed as a trustee or executor,
even if the marriage or civil partnership is terminated.
(4)   For the purposes of this section, a marriage is terminated in the event of divorce or annulment and a civil partnership is terminated in the event of dissolution or annulment.
(5)   In this section, references to 'divorce', 'dissolution' and 'annulment' are to divorce, dissolution or annulment—
  (a)   obtained from a court of civil jurisdiction in the United Kingdom, the Channel Islands or the Isle of Man, or
  (b)   if not so obtained, the validity of which is recognised in Scotland.

2   Effect of divorce, dissolution or annulment on special destination
(1)   This section applies where—
  (a)   property is held in the name of—
    (i)   a person ('A') and A's spouse or civil partner ('B') and the survivor of them,
    (ii)   A, B and another person or other persons and the survivor or survivors of them,

      (iii) A with a special destination, on A's death, in favour of B,

    (b)   A and B's marriage or civil partnership is terminated, and

    (c)   A then dies.

(2)   In relation to the succession to the property mentioned in subsection (1)(a) on A's death, B is to be treated as having died before A.

(3)   Subsection (2) does not apply if the document under which the property is held expressly provides that succession to the property is to be unaffected by A and B's marriage or civil partnership being terminated.

(4)   If a person has in good faith and for value (whether by purchase or otherwise) acquired title to the property, that title is not to be challengeable on the ground that, by virtue of subsection (2), the property falls to A's estate.

(5)   For the purposes of this section, a marriage is terminated in the event of divorce or annulment and a civil partnership is terminated in the event of dissolution or annulment.

(6)   In this section, references to 'divorce', 'dissolution' and 'annulment' are to divorce, dissolution or annulment—

    (a)   obtained from a court of civil jurisdiction in the United Kingdom, the Channel Islands or the Isle of Man, or

    (b)   if not so obtained, the validity of which is recognised in Scotland.

9　Uncertainty of survivorship treated as failure to survive

(1)   Where two persons die simultaneously or in circumstances in which it is uncertain who survived whom, each is to be treated as having failed to survive the other for all purposes affecting title or succession to property.

(2)   Where a person mentioned in subsection (1) ('the testator') by a will confers a benefit on a person on the condition that the other person mentioned in subsection (1) dies before the testator, the condition that the person dies before the testator (however it is expressed) is to be read as a condition that the person fails to survive the testator.

(3)   This section is subject to section 10.

27   *[Amends Civil Jurisdiction and Judgments Act 1982, Sch 8 para 2.]*

BANKRUPTCY (SCOTLAND) ACT 2016
(2016 asp 21)

15　Jurisdiction

(1)   Where a petition is presented for the sequestration of the estate of a debtor (whether living or deceased), the sheriff has jurisdiction if, at the relevant time, the debtor—

    (a)   had an established place of business in the sheriffdom, or

    (b)   was habitually resident in the sheriffdom.

(2)   AiB may determine a debtor application for the sequestration of the estate of a living or deceased debtor if, at the relevant time, the debtor—

    (a)   had an established place of business in Scotland, or

    (b)   was habitually resident in Scotland.

(3)   Where a petition is presented for the sequestration of the estate of an entity which may be sequestrated by virtue of section 6, the sheriff has jurisdiction if the entity—

    (a)   had at the relevant time an established place of business in the sheriffdom, or

    (b)   was constituted or formed under Scots law and at any time carried on business in the sheriffdom.

(4)   AiB may determine a debtor application for the sequestration of the estate of such an entity if the entity—

    (a)   had at the relevant time an established place of business in Scotland, or

(b)   was constituted or formed under Scots law and at any time carried on business in Scotland.

(5)   Even where a person (whether living or deceased) does not fall within subsection (1), the sheriff has jurisdiction in respect of the sequestration of that person's estate if—

(a)   a petition has been presented for the sequestration of the estate of a partnership of which the person is, or was at the relevant time before dying, a partner, and

(b)   the process of that sequestration is still current.

(6)   Subsection (7) applies as regards any proceedings under this Act which—

(a)   may be brought before a sheriff, and

(b)   relate either to a debtor application or to the sequestration of a debtor's estate following any such application.

(7)   The proceedings are to be brought before the sheriff who, under subsection (1) or (3), would have jurisdiction in respect of a petition for sequestration of the debtor's estate.

(8)   References in this section to 'the relevant time' are to any time in the year immediately preceding (as the case may be)—

(a)   the date of presentation of the petition,

(b)   the date the debtor application is made, or

(c)   the debtor's date of death.

(9)   This section is subject to Article 3 of the EC insolvency proceedings regulation.

PART II

STATUTORY INSTRUMENTS

CIVIL JURISDICTION AND JUDGMENTS ACT 1982 (PROVISIONAL AND PROTECTIVE MEASURES) (SCOTLAND) ORDER 1997
(SI 1997/2780)

2. The Court of Session shall have power to do anything mentioned in section 27(1) or 28 of the Civil Jurisdiction and Judgments Act 1982 in relation to proceedings of the following descriptions, namely:—

    (a) proceedings commenced otherwise than in a Brussels or [State bound by the Lugano Convention];

    (b) proceedings whose subject-matter is not within the scope of the 1968 Convention as determined by Article 1 thereof.

3. The Court of Session shall have power—

    (a) to grant interim interdict under subsection (1)(c) of section 27 of the Civil Jurisdiction and Judgments Act 1982;

    (b) to act as described in section 28 of that Act,

in relation to proceedings which are to be commenced otherwise than in a Brussels or [State bound by the Lugano Convention].

CIVIL JURISDICTION AND JUDGMENTS ORDER 2001
(SI 2001/3929)

Interpretation

2.—(1) In this Order—

'the Act' means the Civil Jurisdiction and Judgments Act 1982;

['the 2005 Agreement' means the Agreement made on 19th October 2005 between the European Community and the Kingdom of Denmark on jurisdiction and the recognition and enforcement of judgments in civil and commercial matters;]

['the Regulation' means Regulation (EU) No 1215/2012 of the European Parliament and of the Council of 12 December 2012 on jurisdiction and the recognition and enforcement of judgments in civil and commercial matters (recast) as amended from time to time and as applied by virtue of the Agreement made on 19 October 2005 between the European Community and the Kingdom of Denmark on jurisdiction and the recognition and enforcement of judgments in civil and commercial matters;]

'Regulation State' in any provision, in the application of that provision in relation to the Regulation, means a Member State.]

The Regulation

3. Schedule 1 to this Order (which applies certain provisions of the Act with modifications for the purposes of the Regulation) shall have effect.

[The 2005 Agreement

3A. The Regulation shall have effect as regards Denmark in accordance with the 2005 Agreement.]

SCHEDULE 1
THE REGULATION

Interpretation

1.—(1)   In this Schedule—
'court', without more, includes a tribunal;
'judgment' has the meaning given by [Article 2] of the Regulation;
'maintenance order' means a maintenance judgment within the meaning of the Regulation;
'part of the United Kingdom' means England and Wales, Scotland or Northern Ireland;
'payer', in relation to a maintenance order, means the person liable to make the payments for which the order provides;
'prescribed' means prescribed by rules of court.

Enforcement of judgments other than maintenance orders (section 4)

2.—(1)   Where a judgment is [enforced] under the Regulation, the reasonable costs or expenses of and incidental to its [enforcement] shall be recoverable as if they were sums recoverable under the judgment.
[(2)   A judgment to be enforced under the Regulation shall for the purposes of its enforcement be of the same force and effect, the enforcing court shall have in relation to its enforcement the same powers, and proceedings for or with respect to its enforcement may be taken, as if the judgment had been originally given by the enforcing court.]
[(2A)   Where a judgment to be enforced under the Regulation would, if it had been given by a court in Northern Ireland, be enforced by the Enforcement of Judgments Office pursuant to the Judgments Enforcement (Northern Ireland) Order 1981, that judgment shall for the purposes of its enforcement be of the same force and effect, the Enforcement of Judgments Office shall have in relation to its enforcement the same powers, and proceedings for or with respect to its enforce-ment may be taken, as if the judgment had been originally given by a court in Northern Ireland.]
(3)   Sub-paragraph (2) is subject to [Articles 41(2) and 46], to paragraph 5 and to any provision made by rules of court as to the manner in which and conditions subject to which a judgment registered under the Regulation may be enforced.

[...]

Appeals under [Articles 50 and 75C]

4.—(1)   The single further appeal on a point of law referred to under [Articles 50 and 75C] in relation to the recognition or enforcement of a judgment other than a maintenance order lies—
(a)   in England and Wales or Northern Ireland, to the Court of Appeal or to the House of Lords in accordance with Part II of the Administration of Justice Act 1969 (appeals direct from the High Court to the House of Lords);
(b)   in Scotland, to the Inner House of the Court of Session.
(2)   Paragraph (a) of sub-paragraph (1) has effect notwithstanding section 15(2) of the Administration of Justice Act 1969 (exclusion of direct appeal to the House of Lords in cases where no appeal to that House lies from a decision of the Court of Appeal).
(3)   The single further appeal on a point of law referred to in Article 44 and Annex IV in relation to the recognition or enforcement of a maintenance order lies—

(a)   in England and Wales, [to a county court in accordance with section 111A] of the Magistrates' Courts Act 1980;

(b)   in Scotland, to the Inner House of the Court of Session;

(c)   in Northern Ireland, to the Court of Appeal.

...

Allocation within United Kingdom of jurisdiction with respect to trusts and consumer contracts (section 10)

7.—(1)   The provisions of this paragraph have effect for the purpose of allocating within the United Kingdom jurisdiction in certain proceedings in respect of which the Regulation confers jurisdiction on the courts of the United Kingdom generally and to which section 16 of the Act does not apply.

(2)   Any proceedings which by virtue of [Article 7(6)] (trusts) are brought in the United Kingdom shall be brought in the courts of the part of the United Kingdom in which the trust is domiciled.

(3)   Any proceedings which by virtue of the [Article 18(1)] (consumer contracts) are brought in the United Kingdom by a consumer on the ground that he is himself domiciled there shall be brought in the courts of the part of the United Kingdom in which he is domiciled.

Proof and admissibility of certain judgments and related documents (section 11)

8.—(1)   For the purposes of the Regulation—

(a)   a document, duly authenticated, which purports to be a copy of a judgment given by a court of a Regulation State other than the United Kingdom shall without further proof be deemed to be a true copy, unless the contrary is shown; and

(b)   a certificate obtained in accordance with [Article 53 and Annex I] shall be evidence, and in Scotland sufficient evidence, that the judgment is enforceable in the Regulation State of origin.

(2)   A document purporting to be a copy of a judgment given by any such court as is mentioned in sub-paragraph (1)(a) is duly authenticated for the purposes of this paragraph if it purports—

(a)   to bear the seal of that court; or

(b)   to be certified by any person in his capacity as a judge or officer of that court to be a true copy of a judgment given by that court.

(3)   Nothing in this paragraph shall prejudice the admission in evidence of any document which is admissible apart from this paragraph.

Domicile of individuals (section 41)

9.—(1)   Subject to [Article 62] (which contains provisions for determining whether a party is domiciled in a Regulation State), the following provisions of this paragraph determine, for the purposes of the Regulation, whether an individual is domiciled in the United Kingdom or in a particular part of, or place in, the United Kingdom or in a state other than a Regulation State.

(2)   An individual is domiciled in the United Kingdom if and only if—

(a)   he is resident in the United Kingdom; and

(b)   the nature and circumstances of his residence indicate that he has a substantial connection with the United Kingdom.

(3)   Subject to sub-paragraph (5), an individual is domiciled in a particular part of the United Kingdom if and only if—

(a)   he is resident in that part; and

(b)   the nature and circumstances of his residence indicate that he has a substantial connection with that part.

(4)   An individual is domiciled in a particular place in the United Kingdom if and only if he—

(a)   is domiciled in the part of the United Kingdom in which that place is situated; and

(b)   is resident in that place.

(5)   An individual who is domiciled in the United Kingdom but in whose case the requirements of sub-paragraph (3)(b) are not satisfied in relation to any particular part of the United Kingdom shall be treated as domiciled in the part of the United Kingdom in which he is resident.

(6)   In the case of an individual who—

(a)   is resident in the United Kingdom, or in a particular part of the United Kingdom; and

(b)   has been so resident for the last three months or more,

the requirements of sub-paragraph (2)(b) or, as the case may be, sub-paragraph (3)(b) shall be presumed to be fulfilled unless the contrary is proved.

(7)   An individual is domiciled in a state other than a Regulation State if and only if—

(a)   he is resident in that state; and

(b)   the nature and circumstances of his residence indicate that he has a substantial connection with that state.

Seat of company, or other legal person or association for purposes of [Article 24(2)]
(section 43)

10.—(1)   The following provisions of this paragraph determine where a company, legal person or association has its seat for the purposes of [Article 24(2)] (which confers exclusive jurisdiction over proceedings relating to the formation or dissolution of such bodies, or to the decisions of their organs).

(2)   A company, legal person or association has its seat in the United Kingdom if and only if—

(a)   it was incorporated or formed under the law of a part of the United Kingdom; or

(b)   its central management and control is exercised in the United Kingdom.

(3)   Subject to sub-paragraph (4), a company, legal person or association has its seat in a Regulation State other than the United Kingdom if and only if—

(a)   it was incorporated or formed under the law of that state; or

(b)   its central management and control is exercised in that state.

(4)   A company, legal person or association shall not be regarded as having its seat in a Regulation State other than the United Kingdom if—

(a)   it has its seat in the United Kingdom by virtue of sub-paragraph (2)(a); or

(b)   it is shown that the courts of that other state would not regard it for the purposes of [Article 24(2)] as having its seat there.

Persons deemed to be domiciled in the United Kingdom for certain purposes (section 44)

11.—(1)   This paragraph applies to—

(a)   proceedings within Section 3 of Chapter II of the Regulation (insurance contracts),

(b)   proceedings within Section 4 of Chapter II of the Regulation (consumer contracts), and

(c)   proceedings within Section 5 of Chapter II of the Regulation (employment contracts).

(2)   A person who, for the purposes of proceedings to which this paragraph

applies arising out of the operations of a branch, agency or other establishment in the United Kingdom, is deemed for the purposes of the Regulation to be domiciled in the United Kingdom by virtue of—

(a) [Article 11(2)] (insurers); or

(b) [Article 17(2)] (suppliers of goods, services or credit to consumers), or

(c) [Article 20(2)] (employers),

shall, for the purposes of those proceedings, be treated as so domiciled and as domiciled in the part of the United Kingdom in which the branch, agency or establishment in question is situated.

Domicile of trusts (section 45)

12.—(1) The following provisions of this paragraph determine for the purposes of the Regulation where a trust is domiciled.

(2) A trust is domiciled in the United Kingdom if and only if it is by virtue of sub-paragraph (3) domiciled in a part of the United Kingdom.

(3) A trust is domiciled in a part of the United Kingdom if and only if the system of law of that part is the system of law with which the trust has its closest and most real connection.

CROSS–BORDER INSOLVENCY REGULATIONS 2006
(SI 2006/1030)

Citation, commencement and interpretation

1.—(1) These Regulations may be cited as the Cross-Border Insolvency Regulations 2006 and shall come into force on the day after the day on which they are made.

(2) In these Regulations 'the UNCITRAL Model Law' means the Model Law on cross-border insolvency as adopted by the United Nations Commission on International Trade Law on 30th May 1997.

UNCITRAL Model Law to have force of law

2.—(1) The UNCITRAL Model Law shall have the force of law in Great Britain in the form set out in Schedule 1 to these Regulations (which contains the UNCITRAL Model Law with certain modifications to adapt it for application in Great Britain).

(2) Without prejudice to any practice of the courts as to the matters which may be considered apart from this paragraph, the following documents may be considered in ascertaining the meaning or effect of any provision of the UNCITRAL Model Law as set out in Schedule 1 to these Regulations—

(a) the UNCITRAL Model Law;

(b) any documents of the United Nations Commission on International Trade Law and its working group relating to the preparation of the UNCITRAL Model Law; and

(c) the Guide to Enactment of the UNCITRAL Model Law (UNCITRAL document A/CN9/442) prepared at the request of the United Nations Commission on International Trade Law made in May 1997.

Modification of British insolvency law

3.—(1) British insolvency law (as defined in article 2 of the UNCITRAL Model Law as set out in Schedule 1 to these Regulations) and Part 3 of the Insolvency Act 1986 shall apply with such modifications as the context requires for the purpose of giving effect to the provisions of these Regulations.

(2) In the case of any conflict between any provision of British insolvency law

or of Part 3 of the Insolvency Act 1986 and the provisions of these Regulations, the latter shall prevail.

Procedural matters in England and Wales
4.   Schedule 2 to these Regulations (which makes provision about procedural matters in England and Wales in connection with the application of the UNCITRAL Model Law as set out in Schedule 1 to these Regulations) shall have effect.

Procedural matters in Scotland
5.   Schedule 3 to these Regulations (which makes provision about procedural matters in Scotland in connection with the application of the UNCITRAL Model Law as set out in Schedule 1 to these Regulations) shall have effect.

Notices delivered to the registrar of companies
6.   Schedule 4 to these Regulations (which makes provision about notices delivered to the registrar of companies under these Regulations) shall have effect.

Co-operation between courts exercising jurisdiction in relation to cross-border insolvency
7.—(1)   An order made by a court in either part of Great Britain in the exercise of jurisdiction in relation to the subject matter of these Regulations shall be enforced in the other part of Great Britain as if it were made by a court exercising the corresponding jurisdiction in that other part.
   (2)   However, nothing in paragraph (1) requires a court in either part of Great Britain to enforce, in relation to property situated in that part, any order made by a court in the other part of Great Britain.
   (3)   The courts having jurisdiction in relation to the subject matter of these Regulations in either part of Great Britain shall assist the courts having the corresponding jurisdiction in the other part of Great Britain.

Disapplication of section 388 of the Insolvency Act 1986
8.   Nothing in section 388 of the Insolvency Act 1986 applies to anything done by a foreign representative—
   (a)   under or by virtue of these Regulations;
   (b)   in relation to relief granted or cooperation or coordination provided under these Regulations.

SCHEDULE 1
UNCITRAL MODEL LAW ON CROSS-BORDER INSOLVENCY

CHAPTER I
GENERAL PROVISIONS

Article 1. Scope of Application
1.   This Law applies where—
   (a)   assistance is sought in Great Britain by a foreign court or a foreign representative in connection with a foreign proceeding; or
   (b)   assistance is sought in a foreign State in connection with a proceeding under British insolvency law; or
   (c)   a foreign proceeding and a proceeding under British insolvency law in respect of the same debtor are taking place concurrently; or
   (d)   creditors or other interested persons in a foreign State have an interest in requesting the commencement of, or participating in, a proceeding under British insolvency law.
2.   This Law does not apply to a proceeding concerning—
   (a)   a company holding an appointment under Chapter 1 of Part 2 of the Water Industry Act 1991 (water and sewage undertakers) or a qualifying licensed water supplier within the meaning of section 23(6) of that Act (meaning and effect of special administration order);

(b)   Scottish Water established under section 20 of the Water Industry (Scotland) Act 2002 (Scottish Water);

(c)   a protected railway company within the meaning of section 59 of the Railways Act 1993 (railway administration order) (including that section as it has effect by virtue of section 19 of the Channel Tunnel Rail Link Act 1996 (administration));

(d)   a licence company within the meaning of section 26 of the Transport Act 2000 (air traffic services);

(e)   a public private partnership company within the meaning of section 210 of the Greater London Authority Act 1999 (public-private partnership agreement);

(f)   a protected energy company within the meaning of section 154(5) of the Energy Act 2004 (energy administration orders);

(g)   a building society within the meaning of section 119 of the Building Societies Act 1986 (interpretation);

(h)   a UK credit institution or an EEA credit institution or any branch of either such institution as those expressions are defined by regulation 2 of the Credit Institutions (Reorganisation and Winding Up) Regulations 2004 (interpretation);

(i)   a third country credit institution within the meaning of regulation 36 of the Credit Institutions (Reorganisation and Winding Up) Regulations 2004 (interpretation of this Part);

(j)   a person who has permission under or by virtue of Parts 4 or 19 of the Financial Services and Markets Act 2000 to effect or carry out contracts of insurance;

(k)   an EEA insurer within the meaning of regulation 2 of the Insurers (Reorganisation and Winding Up) Regulations 2004 (interpretation);

(l)   a person (other than one included in paragraph 2(j)) pursuing the activity of reinsurance who has received authorisation for that activity from a competent authority within an EEA State; or

(m)   any of the Concessionaires within the meaning of section 1 of the Channel Tunnel Act 1987.

3.   In paragraph 2 of this article—

(a)   in sub-paragraph (j) the reference to 'contracts of insurance' must be construed in accordance with—

(i)   section 22 of the Financial Services and Markets Act 2000 (classes of regulated activity and categories of investment);

(ii)   any relevant order under that section; and

(iii)   Schedule 2 to that Act (regulated activities);

(b)   in sub-paragraph (1) 'EEA State' means a State, other than the United Kingdom, which is a contracting party to the agreement on the European Economic Area signed at Oporto on 2 May 1992.

4.   The court shall not grant any relief, or modify any relief already granted, or provide any cooperation or coordination, under or by virtue of any of the provisions of this Law if and to the extent that such relief or modified relief or cooperation or coordination would—

(a)   be prohibited under or by virtue of—

(i)   Part 7 of the Companies Act 1989;

(ii)   Part 3 of the Financial Markets and Insolvency (Settlement Finality) Regulations 1999; or

(iii)   Part 3 of the Financial Collateral Arrangements (No 2) Regulations 2003;

in the case of a proceeding under British insolvency law; or

(b)   interfere with or be inconsistent with any rights of a collateral taker under Part 4 of the Financial Collateral Arrangements (No 2) Regulations 2003 which could be exercised in the case of such a proceeding.

5. Where a foreign proceeding regarding a debtor who is an insured in accordance with the provisions of the Third Parties (Rights against Insurers) Act 1930 is recognised under this Law, any stay and suspension referred to in article 20(1) and any relief granted by the court under article 19 or 21 shall not apply to or affect—

(a) any transfer of rights of the debtor under that Act; or

(b) any claim, action, cause or proceeding by a third party against an insurer under or in respect of rights of the debtor transferred under that Act.

6. Any suspension under this Law of the right to transfer, encumber or otherwise dispose of any of the debtor's assets—

(a) is subject to section 26 of the Land Registration Act 2002 where owner's powers are exercised in relation to a registered estate or registered charge;

(b) is subject to section 52 of the Land Registration Act 2002, where the powers referred to in that section are exercised by the proprietor of a registered charge; and

(c) in any other case, shall not bind a purchaser of a legal estate in good faith for money or money's worth unless the purchaser has express notice of the suspension.

7. In paragraph 6—

(a) 'owner's powers' means the powers described in section 23 of the Land Registration Act 2002 and 'registered charge' and 'registered estate' have the same meaning as in section 132(1) of that Act; and

(b) 'legal estate' and 'purchaser' have the same meaning as in section 17 of the Land Charges Act 1972.

Article 2. Definitions

For the purposes of this Law—

(a) 'British insolvency law' means—

(i) in relation to England and Wales, provision extending to England and Wales and made by or under the Insolvency Act 1986 (with the exception of Part 3 of that Act) or by or under that Act as extended or applied by or under any other enactment (excluding these Regulations); and

(ii) in relation to Scotland, provision extending to Scotland and made by or under the Insolvency Act 1986 (with the exception of Part 3 of that Act), the Bankruptcy (Scotland) Act 1985 or by or under those Acts as extended or applied by or under any other enactment (excluding these Regulations);

(b) 'British insolvency officeholder' means—

(i) the official receiver within the meaning of section 399 of the Insolvency Act 1986 when acting as liquidator, provisional liquidator, trustee, interim receiver or nominee or supervisor of a voluntary arrangement;

(ii) a person acting as an insolvency practitioner within the meaning of section 388 of that Act but shall not include a person acting as an administrative receiver; and

(iii) the Accountant in Bankruptcy within the meaning of section 1 of the Bankruptcy (Scotland) Act 1985 when acting as interim or permanent trustee;

(c) the court except as otherwise provided in articles 14(4) and 23(6)(b), means in relation to any matter the court which in accordance with the provisions of article 4 of this Law has jurisdiction in relation to that matter;

(d) 'the EC Insolvency Regulation' means Council Regulation (EC) No 1346/2000 of 29 May 2000 on Insolvency Proceedings;

(e) 'establishment' means any place of operations where the debtor carries out a non-transitory economic activity with human means and assets or services;

(f) 'foreign court' means a judicial or other authority competent to control or supervise a foreign proceeding;

(g) 'foreign main proceeding' means a foreign proceeding taking place in the State where the debtor has the centre of its main interests;

(h) 'foreign non-main proceeding' means a foreign proceeding, other than a foreign main proceeding, taking place in a State where the debtor has an establishment within the meaning of sub-paragraph (e) of this article;

(i) 'foreign proceeding' means a collective judicial or administrative proceeding in a foreign State, including an interim proceeding, pursuant to a law relating to insolvency in which proceeding the assets and affairs of the debtor are subject to control or supervision by a foreign court, for the purpose of re-organisation or liquidation;

(j) 'foreign representative' means a person or body, including one appointed on an interim basis, authorised in a foreign proceeding to administer the reorganisation or the liquidation of the debtor's assets or affairs or to act as a representative of the foreign proceeding;

(k) 'hire-purchase agreement' includes a conditional sale agreement, a chattel leasing agreement and a retention of title agreement;

(l) 'section 426 request' means a request for assistance in accordance with section 426 of the Insolvency Act 1986 made to a court in any part of the United Kingdom;

(m) 'secured creditor' in relation to a debtor, means a creditor of the debtor who holds in respect of his debt a security over property of the debtor;

(n) 'security' means—
    (i) in relation to England and Wales, any mortgage, charge, lien or other security; and
    (ii) in relation to Scotland, any security (whether heritable or moveable), any floating charge and any right of lien or preference and any right of retention (other than a right of compensation or set off);

(o) in the application of Articles 20 and 23 to Scotland, 'an individual' means any debtor within the meaning of the Bankruptcy (Scotland) Act 1985;

(p) in the application of this Law to Scotland, references howsoever expressed to—
    (i) 'filing' an application or claim are to be construed as references to lodging an application or submitting a claim respectively;
    (ii) 'relief' and 'standing' are to be construed as references to 'remedy' and 'title and interest' respectively; and
    (iii) a 'stay' are to be construed as references to restraint, except in relation to continuation of actions or proceedings when they shall be construed as a reference to sist; and

(q) references to the law of Great Britain include a reference to the law of either part of Great Britain (including its rules of private international law).

Article 3. International obligations of Great Britain under the EC Insolvency Regulation

To the extent that this Law conflicts with an obligation of the United Kingdom under the EC Insolvency Regulation, the requirements of the EC Insolvency Regulation prevail.

Article 4. Competent court

1. The functions referred to in this Law relating to recognition of foreign proceedings and cooperation with foreign courts shall be performed by the High Court and assigned to the Chancery Division, as regards England and Wales and the Court of Session as regards Scotland.

2. Subject to paragraph 1 of this article, the court in either part of Great Britain shall have jurisdiction in relation to the functions referred to in that paragraph if—
    (a) the debtor has—
        (i) a place of business; or

      (ii) in the case of an individual, a place of residence; or
      (iii) assets,
situated in that part of Great Britain; or
    (b)   the court in that part of Great Britain considers for any other reason that it is the appropriate forum to consider the question or provide the assistance requested.

3.   In considering whether it is the appropriate forum to hear an application for recognition of a foreign proceeding in relation to a debtor, the court shall take into account the location of any court in which a proceeding under British insolvency law is taking place in relation to the debtor and the likely location of any future proceedings under British insolvency law in relation to the debtor.

Article 5. Authorisation of British insolvency officeholders to act in a foreign State

A British insolvency officeholder is authorised to act in a foreign State on behalf of a proceeding under British insolvency law, as permitted by the applicable foreign law.

Article 6. Public policy exception

Nothing in this Law prevents the court from refusing to take an action governed by this Law if the action would be manifestly contrary to the public policy of Great Britain or any part of it.

Article 7. Additional assistance under other laws

Nothing in this Law limits the power of a court or a British insolvency officeholder to provide additional assistance to a foreign representative under other laws of Great Britain.

Article 8. Interpretation

In the interpretation of this Law, regard is to be had to its international origin and to the need to promote uniformity in its application and the observance of good faith.

CHAPTER II

ACCESS OF FOREIGN REPRESENTATIVES AND CREDITORS TO COURTS IN GREAT BRITAIN

Article 9. Right of direct access

A foreign representative is entitled to apply directly to a court in Great Britain.

Article 10. Limited jurisdiction

The sole fact that an application pursuant to this Law is made to a court in Great Britain by a foreign representative does not subject the foreign representative or the foreign assets and affairs of the debtor to the jurisdiction of the courts of Great Britain or any part of it for any purpose other than the application.

Article 11. Application by a foreign representative to commence a proceeding under British insolvency law

A foreign representative appointed in a foreign main proceeding or foreign non-main proceeding is entitled to apply to commence a proceeding under British insolvency law if the conditions for commencing such a proceeding are otherwise met.

Article 12. Participation of a foreign representative in a proceeding under British insolvency law

Upon recognition of a foreign proceeding, the foreign representative is entitled to participate in a proceeding regarding the debtor under British insolvency law.

Article 13. Access of foreign creditors to a proceeding under British insolvency law

1. Subject to paragraph 2 of this article, foreign creditors have the same rights regarding the commencement of, and participation in, a proceeding under British insolvency law as creditors in Great Britain.

2. Paragraph 1 of this article does not affect the ranking of claims in a proceeding under British insolvency law, except that the claim of a foreign creditor shall not be given a lower priority than that of general unsecured claims solely because the holder of such a claim is a foreign creditor.

3. A claim may not be challenged solely on the grounds that it is a claim by a foreign tax or social security authority but such a claim may be challenged—

(a)   on the ground that it is in whole or in part a penalty, or

(b)   on any other ground that a claim might be rejected in a proceeding under British insolvency law.

Article 14. Notification to foreign creditors of a proceeding under British insolvency law

1. Whenever under British insolvency law notification is to be given to creditors in Great Britain, such notification shall also be given to the known creditors that do not have addresses in Great Britain. The court may order that appropriate steps be taken with a view to notifying any creditor whose address is not yet known.

2. Such notification shall be made to the foreign creditors individually, unless—

(a)   the court considers that under the circumstances some other form of notification would be more appropriate; or

(b)   the notification to creditors in Great Britain is to be by advertisement only, in which case the notification to the known foreign creditors may be by advertisement in such foreign newspapers as the British insolvency officeholder considers most appropriate for ensuring that the content of the notification comes to the notice of the known foreign creditors.

3. When notification of a right to file a claim is to be given to foreign creditors, the notification shall—

(a)   indicate a reasonable time period for filing claims and specify the place for their filing;

(b)   indicate whether secured creditors need to file their secured claims; and

(c)   contain any other information required to be included in such a notification to creditors pursuant to the law of Great Britain and the orders of the court.

4. In this article 'the court' means the court which has jurisdiction in relation to the particular proceeding under British insolvency law under which notification is to be given to creditors.

CHAPTER III

RECOGNITION OF A FOREIGN PROCEEDING AND RELIEF

Article 15. Application for recognition of a foreign proceeding

1. A foreign representative may apply to the court for recognition of the foreign proceeding in which the foreign representative has been appointed.

2. An application for recognition shall be accompanied by—

(a)   a certified copy of the decision commencing the foreign proceeding and appointing the foreign representative; or

(b)   a certificate from the foreign court affirming the existence of the foreign proceeding and of the appointment of the foreign representative; or

(c)   in the absence of evidence referred to in sub-paragraphs (a) and (b), any other evidence acceptable to the court of the existence of the foreign proceeding and of the appointment of the foreign representative.

3. An application for recognition shall also be accompanied by a statement

identifying all foreign proceedings, proceedings under British insolvency law and section 426 requests in respect of the debtor that are known to the foreign representative.

4.   The foreign representative shall provide the court with a translation into English of documents supplied in support of the application for recognition.

Article 16. Presumptions concerning recognition

1.   If the decision or certificate referred to in paragraph 2 of article 15 indicates that the foreign proceeding is a proceeding within the meaning of sub-paragraph (i) of article 2 and that the foreign representative is a person or body within the meaning of sub-paragraph (j) of article 2, the court is entitled to so presume.

2.   The court is entitled to presume that documents submitted in support of the application for recognition are authentic, whether or not they have been legalised.

3.   In the absence of proof to the contrary, the debtor's registered office, or habitual residence in the case of an individual, is presumed to be the centre of the debtor's main interests.

Article 17. Decision to recognise a foreign proceeding

1.   Subject to article 6, a foreign proceeding shall be recognised if—

   (a)   it is a foreign proceeding within the meaning of sub-paragraph (i) of article 2;

   (b)   the foreign representative applying for recognition is a person or body within the meaning of sub-paragraph (j) of article 2;

   (c)   the application meets the requirements of paragraphs 2 and 3 of article 15; and

   (d)   the application has been submitted to the court referred to in article 4.

2.   The foreign proceeding shall be recognised—

   (a)   as a foreign main proceeding if it is taking place in the State where the debtor has the centre of its main interests; or

   (b)   as a foreign non-main proceeding if the debtor has an establishment within the meaning of sub-paragraph (e) of article 2 in the foreign State.

3.   An application for recognition of a foreign proceeding shall be decided upon at the earliest possible time.

4.   The provisions of articles 15 to 16, this article and article 18 do not prevent modification or termination of recognition if it is shown that the grounds for granting it were fully or partially lacking or have fully or partially ceased to exist and in such a case, the court may, on the application of the foreign representative or a person affected by recognition, or of its own motion, modify or terminate recognition, either altogether or for a limited time, on such terms and conditions as the court thinks fit.

Article 18. Subsequent information

From the time of filing the application for recognition of the foreign proceeding, the foreign representative shall inform the court promptly of—

   (a)   any substantial change in the status of the recognised foreign proceeding or the status of the foreign representative's appointment; and

   (b)   any other foreign proceeding, proceeding under British insolvency law or section 426 request regarding the same debtor that becomes known to the foreign representative.

Article 19. Relief that may be granted upon application for recognition of a foreign proceeding

1.   From the time of filing an application for recognition until the application is decided upon, the court may, at the request of the foreign representative, where relief is urgently needed to protect the assets of the debtor or the interests of the creditors, grant relief of a provisional nature, including—

   (a)   staying execution against the debtor's assets;

   (b)   entrusting the administration or realisation of all or part of the debtor's assets located in Great Britain to the foreign representative or another person designated by the court, in order to protect and preserve the value of assets that, by their nature or because of other circumstances, are perishable, susceptible to devaluation or otherwise in jeopardy; and

   (c)   any relief mentioned in paragraph 1 (c), (d) or (g) of article 21.

2.   Unless extended under paragraph 1(f) of article 21, the relief granted under this article terminates when the application for recognition is decided upon.

3.   The court may refuse to grant relief under this article if such relief would interfere with the administration of a foreign main proceeding.

Article 20. Effects of recognition of a foreign main proceeding

1.   Upon recognition of a foreign proceeding that is a foreign main proceeding, subject to paragraph 2 of this article—

   (a)   commencement or continuation of individual actions or individual proceedings concerning the debtor's assets, rights, obligations or liabilities is stayed;

   (b)   execution against the debtor's assets is stayed; and

   (c)   the right to transfer, encumber or otherwise dispose of any assets of the debtor is suspended.

2.   The stay and suspension referred to in paragraph 1 of this article shall be—

   (a)   the same in scope and effect as if the debtor, in the case of an individual, had been adjudged bankrupt under the Insolvency Act 1986 or had his estate sequestrated under the Bankruptcy (Scotland) Act 1985, or, in the case of a debtor other than an individual, had been made the subject of a winding-up order under the Insolvency Act 1986; and

   (b)   subject to the same powers of the court and the same prohibitions, limitations, exceptions and conditions as would apply under the law of Great Britain in such a case,

and the provisions of paragraph 1 of this article shall be interpreted accordingly.

3.   Without prejudice to paragraph 2 of this article, the stay and suspension referred to in paragraph 1 of this article, in particular, does not affect any right—

   (a)   to take any steps to enforce security over the debtor's property;

   (b)   to take any steps to repossess goods in the debtor's possession under a hire-purchase agreement;

   (c)   exercisable under or by virtue of or in connection with the provisions referred to in article 1(4); or

   (d)   of a creditor to set off its claim against a claim of the debtor,

being a right which would have been exercisable if the debtor, in the case of an individual, had been adjudged bankrupt under the Insolvency Act 1986 or had his estate sequestrated under the Bankruptcy (Scotland) Act 1985, or, in the case of a debtor other than an individual, had been made the subject of a winding-up order under the Insolvency Act 1986.

4.   Paragraph 1(a) of this article does not affect the right to—

   (a)   commence individual actions or proceedings to the extent necessary to preserve a claim against the debtor; or

   (b)   commence or continue any criminal proceedings or any action or proceedings by a person or body having regulatory, supervisory or investigative functions of a public nature, being an action or proceedings brought in the exercise of those functions.

5.   Paragraph 1 of this article does not affect the right to request or otherwise initiate the commencement of a proceeding under British insolvency law or the right to file claims in such a proceeding.

6.   In addition to and without prejudice to any powers of the court under or by virtue of paragraph 2 of this article, the court may, on the application of the foreign representative or a person affected by the stay and suspension referred to in paragraph 1 of this article, or of its own motion, modify or terminate such stay

and suspension or any part of it, either altogether or for a limited time, on such terms and conditions as the court thinks fit.

Article 21. Relief that may be granted upon recognition of a foreign proceeding

1.   Upon recognition of a foreign proceeding, whether main or non-main, where necessary to protect the assets of the debtor or the interests of the creditors, the court may, at the request of the foreign representative, grant any appropriate relief, including—

(a)   staying the commencement or continuation of individual actions or individual proceedings concerning the debtor's assets, rights, obligations or liabilities, to the extent they have not been stayed under paragraph 1(a) of article 20;

(b)   staying execution against the debtor's assets to the extent it has not been stayed under paragraph 1(b) of article 20;

(c)   suspending the right to transfer, encumber or otherwise dispose of any assets of the debtor to the extent this right has not been suspended under paragraph 1(c) of article 20;

(d)   providing for the examination of witnesses, the taking of evidence or the delivery of information concerning the debtor's assets, affairs, rights, obligations or liabilities;

(e)   entrusting the administration or realisation of all or part of the debtor's assets located in Great Britain to the foreign representative or another person designated by the court;

(f)   extending relief granted under paragraph 1 of article 19; and

(g)   granting any additional relief that may be available to a British insolvency officeholder under the law of Great Britain, including any relief provided under paragraph 43 of Schedule B1 to the Insolvency Act 1986.

2.   Upon recognition of a foreign proceeding, whether main or non-main, the court may, at the request of the foreign representative, entrust the distribution of all or part of the debtor's assets located in Great Britain to the foreign representative or another person designated by the court, provided that the court is satisfied that the interests of creditors in Great Britain are adequately protected.

3.   In granting relief under this article to a representative of a foreign non-main proceeding, the court must be satisfied that the relief relates to assets that, under the law of Great Britain, should be administered in the foreign non-main proceeding or concerns information required in that proceeding.

4.   No stay under paragraph 1(a) of this article shall affect the right to commence or continue any criminal proceedings or any action or proceedings by a person or body having regulatory, supervisory or investigative functions of a public nature, being an action or proceedings brought in the exercise of those functions.

Article 22. Protection of creditors and other interested persons

1.   In granting or denying relief under article 19 or 21, or in modifying or terminating relief under paragraph 3 of this article or paragraph 6 of article 20, the court must be satisfied that the interests of the creditors (including any secured creditors or parties to hire-purchase agreements) and other interested persons, including if appropriate the debtor, are adequately protected.

2.   The court may subject relief granted under article 19 or 21 to conditions it considers appropriate, including the provision by the foreign representative of security or caution for the proper performance of his functions.

3.   The court may, at the request of the foreign representative or a person affected by relief granted under article 19 or 21, or of its own motion, modify or terminate such relief.

Article 23. Actions to avoid acts detrimental to creditors

1.   Subject to paragraphs 6 and 9 of this article, upon recognition of a foreign proceeding, the foreign representative has standing to make an application to the

court for an order under or in connection with sections 238, 239, 242, 243, 244, 245, 339, 340, 342A, 343, and 423 of the Insolvency Act 1986 and sections 34, 35, 36, 36A and 61 of the Bankruptcy (Scotland) Act 1985.

2.   Where the foreign representative makes such an application ('an article 23 application'), the sections referred to in paragraph 1 of this article and sections 240, 241, 341, 342, 342B to 342F, 424 and 425 of the Insolvency Act 1986 and sections 36B and 36C of the Bankruptcy (Scotland) Act 1985 shall apply—

(a)   whether or not the debtor, in the case of an individual, has been adjudged bankrupt or had his estate sequestrated, or, in the case of a debtor other than an individual, is being wound up or is in administration, under British insolvency law; and

(b)   with the modifications set out in paragraph 3 of this article.

3.   The modifications referred to in paragraph 2 of this article are as follows—

(a)   for the purposes of sections 241(2A)(a) and 342(2A)(a) of the Insolvency Act 1986, a person has notice of the relevant proceedings if he has notice of the opening of the relevant foreign proceeding;

(b)   for the purposes of sections 240(1) and 245(3) of that Act, the onset of insolvency shall be the date of the opening of the relevant foreign proceeding;

(c)   the periods referred to in sections 244(2), 341(1)(a) to (c) and 343(2) of that Act shall be periods ending with the date of the opening of the relevant foreign proceeding;

(d)   for the purposes of sections 242(3)(a), (3)(b) and 243(1) of that Act, the date on which the winding up of the company commences or it enters administration shall be the date of the opening of the relevant foreign proceeding; and

(e)   for the purposes of sections 34(3)(a), (3)(b), 35(1)(c), 36(1)(a) and (1)(b) and 61(2) of the Bankruptcy (Scotland) Act 1985, the date of sequestration or granting of the trust deed shall be the date of the opening of the relevant foreign proceeding.

4.   For the purposes of paragraph 3 of this article, the date of the opening of the foreign proceeding shall be determined in accordance with the law of the State in which the foreign proceeding is taking place, including any rule of law by virtue of which the foreign proceeding is deemed to have opened at an earlier time.

5.   When the foreign proceeding is a foreign non-main proceeding, the court must be satisfied that the article 23 application relates to assets that, under the law of Great Britain, should be administered in the foreign non-main proceeding.

6.   At any time when a proceeding under British insolvency law is taking place regarding the debtor—

(a)   the foreign representative shall not make an article 23 application except with the permission of—

(i)   in the case of a proceeding under British insolvency law taking place in England and Wales, the High Court; or

(ii)   in the case of a proceeding under British insolvency law taking place in Scotland, the Court of Session; and

(b)   references to 'the court' in paragraphs 1, 5 and 7 of this article are references to the court in which that proceeding is taking place.

7.   On making an order on an article 23 application, the court may give such directions regarding the distribution of any proceeds of the claim by the foreign representative, as it thinks fit to ensure that the interests of creditors in Great Britain are adequately protected.

8.   Nothing in this article affects the right of a British insolvency officeholder to make an application under or in connection with any of the provisions referred to in paragraph 1 of this article.

9.   Nothing in paragraph 1 of this article shall apply in respect of any preference given, floating charge created, alienation, assignment or relevant contributions (within the meaning of section 342A(5) of the Insolvency Act 1986) made or other transaction entered into before the date on which this Law comes into force.

Article 24. Intervention by a foreign representative in proceedings in Great Britain
Upon recognition of a foreign proceeding, the foreign representative may, provided the requirements of the law of Great Britain are met, intervene in any proceedings in which the debtor is a party.

CHAPTER IV
COOPERATION WITH FOREIGN COURTS AND FOREIGN REPRESENTATIVES

Article 25. Cooperation and direct communication between a court of Great Britain and foreign courts or foreign representatives
1.   In matters referred to in paragraph 1 of article 1, the court may cooperate to the maximum extent possible with foreign courts or foreign representatives, either directly or through a British insolvency officeholder.
2.   The court is entitled to communicate directly with, or to request information or assistance directly from, foreign courts or foreign representatives.

Article 26. Cooperation and direct communication between the British insolvency officeholder and foreign courts or foreign representatives
1.   In matters referred to in paragraph 1 of article 1, a British insolvency officeholder shall to the extent consistent with his other duties under the law of Great Britain, in the exercise of his functions and subject to the supervision of the court, cooperate to the maximum extent possible with foreign courts or foreign representatives.
2.   The British insolvency officeholder is entitled, in the exercise of his functions and subject to the supervision of the court, to communicate directly with foreign courts or foreign representatives.

Article 27. Forms of cooperation
Cooperation referred to in articles 25 and 26 may be implemented by any appropriate means, including—
    (a)   appointment of a person to act at the direction of the court;
    (b)   communication of information by any means considered appropriate by the court;
    (c)   coordination of the administration and supervision of the debtor's assets and affairs;
    (d)   approval or implementation by courts of agreements concerning the coordination of proceedings;
    (e)   coordination of concurrent proceedings regarding the same debtor.

CHAPTER V
CONCURRENT PROCEEDINGS

Article 28. Commencement of a proceeding under British insolvency law after recognition of a foreign main proceeding
After recognition of a foreign main proceeding, the effects of a proceeding under British insolvency law in relation to the same debtor shall, insofar as the assets of that debtor are concerned, be restricted to assets that are located in Great Britain and, to the extent necessary to implement cooperation and coordination under articles 25, 26 and 27, to other assets of the debtor that, under the law of Great Britain, should be administered in that proceeding.

Article 29. Coordination of a proceeding under British insolvency law and a foreign proceeding
Where a foreign proceeding and a proceeding under British insolvency law are taking place concurrently regarding the same debtor, the court may seek cooperation and coordination under articles 25, 26 and 27, and the following shall apply—

(a)   when the proceeding in Great Britain is taking place at the time the application for recognition of the foreign proceeding is filed—
        (i)   any relief granted under article 19 or 21 must be consistent with the proceeding in Great Britain; and
        (ii)   if the foreign proceeding is recognised in Great Britain as a foreign main proceeding, article 20 does not apply;
(b)   when the proceeding in Great Britain commences after the filing of the application for recognition of the foreign proceeding—
        (i)   any relief in effect under article 19 or 21 shall be reviewed by the court and shall be modified or terminated if inconsistent with the proceeding in Great Britain;
        (ii)   if the foreign proceeding is a foreign main proceeding, the stay and suspension referred to in paragraph 1 of article 20 shall be modified or terminated pursuant to paragraph 6 of article 20, if inconsistent with the proceeding in Great Britain; and
        (iii) any proceedings brought by the foreign representative by virtue of paragraph 1 of article 23 before the proceeding in Great Britain commenced shall be reviewed by the court and the court may give such directions as it thinks fit regarding the continuance of those proceedings; and
(c)   in granting, extending or modifying relief granted to a representative of a foreign non-main proceeding, the court must be satisfied that the relief relates to assets that, under the law of Great Britain, should be administered in the foreign non-main proceeding or concerns information required in that proceeding.

Article 30. Coordination of more than one foreign proceeding

In matters referred to in paragraph 1 of article 1, in respect of more than one foreign proceeding regarding the same debtor, the court may seek cooperation and coordination under articles 25, 26 and 27, and the following shall apply—
(a)   any relief granted under article 19 or 21 to a representative of a foreign non-main proceeding after recognition of a foreign main proceeding must be consistent with the foreign main proceeding;
(b)   if a foreign main proceeding is recognised after the filing of an application for recognition of a foreign non-main proceeding, any relief in effect under article 19 or 21 shall be reviewed by the court and shall be modified or terminated if inconsistent with the foreign main proceeding; and
(c)   if, after recognition of a foreign non-main proceeding, another foreign non-main proceeding is recognised, the court shall grant, modify or terminate relief for the purpose of facilitating coordination of the proceedings.

Article 31. Presumption of insolvency based on recognition of a foreign main proceeding

In the absence of evidence to the contrary, recognition of a foreign main proceeding is, for the purpose of commencing a proceeding under British insolvency law, proof that the debtor is unable to pay its debts or, in relation to Scotland, is apparently insolvent within the meaning given to those expressions under British insolvency law.

Article 32. Rule of payment in concurrent proceedings

Without prejudice to secured claims or rights in rem, a creditor who has received part payment in respect of its claim in a proceeding pursuant to a law relating to insolvency in a foreign State may not receive a payment for the same claim in a proceeding under British insolvency law regarding the same debtor, so long as the payment to the other creditors of the same class is proportionately less than the payment the creditor has already received.

SCHEDULE 2
[Applies to England and Wales only]

SCHEDULE 3
PROCEDURAL MATTERS IN SCOTLAND

PART 1
INTERPRETATION

Interpretation
1.—(1) In this Schedule—
'the 1986 Act' means the Insolvency Act 1986;
'article 21 remedy application' means an application to the court by a foreign representative under article 21(1) or (2) of the Model Law for remedy;
'business day' means any day other than a Saturday, a Sunday, Christmas Day, Good Friday or a day which is a bank holiday in Scotland under or by virtue of the Banking and Financial Dealings Act 1971;
'the Gazette' means the Edinburgh Gazette;
'main proceedings' means proceedings opened in accordance with Article 3(1) of the EC Insolvency Regulation and falling within the definition of insolvency proceedings in Article 2(a) of the EC Insolvency Regulation;
'member State liquidator' means a person falling within the definition of liquidator in Article 2(b) of the EC Insolvency Regulation appointed in proceedings to which it applies in a member State other than the United Kingdom;
'the Model Law' means the UNCITRAL Model Law as set out in Schedule 1 to these Regulations;
'modification or termination order' means an order by the court pursuant to its powers under the Model Law modifying or terminating recognition of a foreign proceeding, the sist, restraint or suspension referred to in article 20(1) or any part of it or any remedy granted under article 19 or 21 of the Model Law;
'recognition application' means an application to the court by a foreign representative in accordance with article 15 of the Model Law for an order recognising the foreign proceeding in which he has been appointed;
'recognition order' means an order by the court recognising a proceeding the subject of a recognition application as a foreign main proceeding or foreign non-main proceeding, as appropriate;
'relevant company' means a company within the meaning of section 735(1) of the Companies Act 1985 or an unregistered company within the meaning of Part 5 of the 1986 Act which is subject to a requirement imposed by virtue of section 690A, 691(1) or 718 of the Companies Act 1985;
'review application' means an application to the court for a modification or termination order.
(2) Expressions defined in the Model Law have the same meaning when used in this Schedule.
(3) References in this Schedule to a debtor who is of interest to the Financial Services Authority are references to a debtor who—
(a) is, or has been, an authorised person within the meaning of section 31 of the Financial Services and Markets Act 2000 (authorised persons);
(b) is, or has been, an appointed representative within the meaning of section 39 (exemption of appointed representatives) of that Act; or
(c) is carrying, or has carried on, a regulated activity in contravention of the general prohibition.
(4) In sub-paragraph (3) 'the general prohibition' has the meaning given by section 19 of the Financial Services and Markets Act 2000 and the reference to a 'regulated activity' must be construed in accordance with—

(a)   section 22 of that Act (classes of regulated activity and categories of investment);

(b)   any relevant order under that section; and

(c)   Schedule 2 to that Act (regulated activities).

(5)   References in this Schedule to a numbered form are to the form that bears that number in Schedule 5.

PART 2
THE FOREIGN REPRESENTATIVE

Application for confirmation of status of replacement foreign representative

2.—(1)   This paragraph applies where following the making of a recognition order the foreign representative dies or for any other reason ceases to be the foreign representative in the foreign proceedings in relation to the debtor.

(2)   In this paragraph 'the former foreign representative' means the foreign representative referred to in sub-paragraph (1).

(3)   If a person has succeeded the former foreign representative or is otherwise holding office as foreign representative in the foreign proceeding in relation to the debtor, that person may apply to the court for an order confirming his status as replacement foreign representative for the purpose of proceedings under these Regulations.

(4)   If the court dismisses an application under sub-paragraph (3) then it may also, if it thinks fit, make an order terminating recognition of the foreign proceeding and—

(a)   such an order may include such provision as the court thinks fit with respect to matters arising in connection with the termination; and

(b)   paragraph 5 shall not apply to such an order.

Misfeasance by a foreign representative

3.—(1)   The court may examine the conduct of a person who—

(a)   is or purports to be the foreign representative in relation to a debtor, or

(b)   has been or has purported to be the foreign representative in relation to a debtor.

(2)   An examination under this paragraph may be held only on the application of—

(a)   a British insolvency officeholder acting in relation to the debtor,

(b)   a creditor of the debtor, or

(c)   with the permission of the court, any other person who appears to have an interest justifying an application.

(3)   An application under sub-paragraph (2) must allege that the foreign representative—

(a)   has misapplied or retained money or other property of the debtor,

(b)   has become accountable for money or other property of the debtor,

(c)   has breached a fiduciary duty or other duty in relation to the debtor, or

(d)   has been guilty of misfeasance.

(4)   On an examination under this paragraph into a person's conduct the court may order him—

(a)   to repay, restore or account for money or property;

(b)   to pay interest;

(c)   to contribute a sum to the debtor's property by way of compensation for breach of duty or misfeasance.

(5)   In sub-paragraph (3), 'foreign representative' includes a person who purports or has purported to be a foreign representative in relation to a debtor.

PART 3
COURT PROCEDURE AND PRACTICE

Preliminary and interpretation
4.—(1) This Part applies to—
(a) any of the following applications made to the court under these Regulations—
(i) a recognition application;
(ii) an article 21 remedy application;
(iii) an application under paragraph 2(3) for an order confirming the status of a replacement foreign representative;
(iv) a review application; and
(b) any of the following orders made by the court under these Regulations—
(i) a recognition order;
(ii) an order granting interim remedy under article 19 of the Model Law;
(iii) an order granting remedy under article 21 of the Model Law;
(iv) an order confirming the status of a replacement foreign representative; or
(v) a modification or termination order.

Reviews of court orders—where court makes order of its own motion
5.—(1) The court shall not of its own motion make a modification or termination order unless the foreign representative and the debtor have either—
(a) had an opportunity of being heard on the question, or
(b) consented in writing to such an order.
(2) If the court makes a modification or termination order, the order may include such provision as the court thinks fit with respect to matters arising in connection with the modification or termination.

The hearing
6.—(1) At the hearing of the application, the applicant and any of the following persons (not being the applicant) may appear or be represented—
(a) the foreign representative;
(b) the debtor and, in the case of any debtor other than an individual, any one or more directors or other officers of the debtor, including—
(i) where applicable, any person registered under Part 23 of the Companies Act 1985 as authorised to represent the debtor in respect of its business in Scotland;
(ii) in the case of a debtor which is a partnership, any person who is a member of the partnership;
(c) if a British insolvency officeholder is acting in relation to the debtor, that person;
(d) if any person has been appointed an administrative receiver of the debtor or as a receiver or manager of the property of the debtor, that person;
(e) if a member State liquidator has been appointed in main proceedings in relation to the debtor, that person;
(f) if a foreign representative has been appointed in any other foreign proceeding regarding the debtor, that person;
(g) any person who has presented a petition for the winding up or sequestration of the debtor in Scotland;
(h) any person who is or may be entitled to appoint an administrator of the debtor under paragraph 14 of Schedule B1 to the 1986 Act (appointment of administrator by holder of qualifying floating charge);
(i) if the debtor is a debtor who is of interest to the Financial Services Authority, that Authority; and
(j) with the permission of the court, any other person who appears to have an interest justifying his appearance.

Notification and advertisement of order

7.—(1) This paragraph applies where the court makes any of the orders referred to in paragraph 4(1)(b).

(2) The foreign representative shall send a certified copy of the interlocutor as soon as reasonably practicable to the debtor.

(3) The foreign representative shall, as soon as reasonably practicable after the date of the order, give notice of the making of the order—

(a) if a British insolvency officeholder is acting in relation to the debtor, to him;

(b) if any person has been appointed an administrative receiver of the debtor or, to the knowledge of the foreign representative, as a receiver or manager of the property of the debtor, to him;

(c) if a member State liquidator has been appointed in main proceedings in relation to the debtor, to him;

(d) if to his knowledge a foreign representative has been appointed in any other foreign proceeding regarding the debtor, that person;

(e) if there is pending in Scotland a petition for the winding up or sequestration of the debtor, to the petitioner;

(f) to any person who to his knowledge is or may be entitled to appoint an administrator of the debtor under paragraph 14 of Schedule B1 to the 1986 Act (appointment of administrator by holder of qualifying floating charge);

(g) if the debtor is a debtor who is of interest to the Financial Services Authority, to that Authority; and

(h) to such persons as the court may direct.

(4) Where the debtor is a relevant company, the foreign representative shall send notice of the making of the order to the registrar of companies before the end of the period of 5 business days beginning with the date of the order. The notice to the registrar of companies shall be in Form ML 7.

(5) The foreign representative shall advertise the making of the following orders once in the Gazette and once in such newspaper as he thinks most appropriate for ensuring that the making of the order comes to the notice of the debtor's creditors—

(a) a recognition order,

(b) an order confirming the status of a replacement foreign representative, and

(c) a modification or termination order which modifies or terminates recognition of a foreign proceeding,

and the advertisement shall be in Form ML 8.

Registration of court order

8.—(1) Where the court makes a recognition order in respect of a foreign main proceeding or an order suspending the right to transfer, encumber or otherwise dispose of any assets of the debtor being heritable property, the clerk of the court shall send forthwith a certified copy of the order to the keeper of the register of inhibitions and adjudications for recording in that register.

(2) Recording under sub-paragraph (1) or (3) shall have the effect as from the date of the order of an inhibition and of a citation in an adjudication of the debtor's heritable estate at the instance of the foreign representative.

(3) Where the court makes a modification or termination order, the clerk of the court shall send forthwith a certified copy of the order to the keeper of the register of inhibitions and adjudications for recording in that register.

(4) The effect mentioned in sub-paragraph (2) shall expire—

(a) on the recording of a modification or termination order under sub-paragraph (3); or

(b) subject to sub-paragraph (5), if the effect has not expired by virtue of paragraph (a), at the end of the period of 3 years beginning with the date of the order.

(5) The foreign representative may, if recognition of the foreign proceeding has not been modified or terminated by the court pursuant to its powers under the Model Law, before the end of the period of 3 years mentioned in sub-paragraph (4)(b), send a memorandum in a form prescribed by the Court of Session by act of sederunt to the keeper of the register of inhibitions and adjudications for recording in that register, and such recording shall renew the effect mentioned in sub-paragraph (2); and thereafter the said effect shall continue to be preserved only if such memorandum is so recorded before the expiry of every subsequent period of 3 years.

Right to inspect court process

9.—(1) In the case of any proceedings under these Regulations, the following have the right, at all reasonable times, to inspect the court process of the proceedings—

(a) the Secretary of State;

(b) the person who is the foreign representative in relation to the proceedings;

(c) if a foreign representative has been appointed in any other foreign proceeding regarding the debtor, that person;

(d) if a British insolvency officeholder is acting in relation to the debtor, that person;

(e) any person stating himself in writing to be a creditor of the debtor to which the proceedings under these Regulations relate;

(f) if a member State liquidator has been appointed in relation to a debtor which is subject to proceedings under these Regulations, that person; and

(g) the debtor to which the proceedings under these Regulations relate, or, if that debtor is a company, corporation or partnership, every person who is, or at any time has been—

(i) director or officer of the debtor,

(ii) a member of the debtor, or

(iii) where applicable, a person registered under Part 23 of the Companies Act 1985 as authorised to represent the debtor in respect of its business in Scotland.

(2) The right of inspection conferred as above on any person may be exercised on his behalf by a person properly authorised by him.

Copies of court orders

10.—(1) In any proceedings under these Regulations, any person who under paragraph 9 has a right to inspect documents in the court process also has the right to require the foreign representative in relation to those proceedings to furnish him with a copy of any court order in the proceedings.

(2) Sub-paragraph (1) does not apply if a copy of the court order has been served on that person or notice of the making of the order has been given to that person under other provisions of these Regulations.

Transfer of proceedings—actions to avoid acts detrimental to creditors

11. If, in accordance with article 23(6) of the Model Law, the court grants a foreign representative permission to make an application in accordance with paragraph (1) of that article, it may also order the relevant proceedings under British insolvency law taking place regarding the debtor to be transferred to the Court of Session if those proceedings are taking place in Scotland and are not already in that court.

PART 3
GENERAL

Giving of notices, etc

12.—(1)   All notices required or authorised by or under these Regulations to be given, sent or delivered must be in writing, unless it is otherwise provided, or the court allows the notice to be sent or given in some other way.

(2)   Any reference in these Regulations to giving, sending or delivering a notice or any such document means, without prejudice to any other way and unless it is otherwise provided, that the notice or document may be sent by post, and that, subject to paragraph 13, any form of post may be used. Personal service of the notice or document is permissible in all cases.

(3)   Where under these Regulations a notice or other document is required or authorised to be given, sent or delivered by a person ('the sender') to another ('the recipient'), it may be given, sent or delivered by any person duly authorised by the sender to do so to any person duly authorised by the recipient to receive or accept it.

(4)   Where two or more persons are acting jointly as the British insolvency officeholder in proceedings under British insolvency law, the giving, sending or delivering of a notice or document to one of them is to be treated as the giving, sending or delivering of a notice or document to each or all.

Sending by post

13.—(1)   For a document to be properly sent by post, it must be contained in an envelope addressed to the person to whom it is to be sent, and pre-paid for either first or second class post.

(2)   Any document to be sent by post may be sent to the last known address of the person to whom the document is to be sent.

(3)   Where first class post is used, the document is to be deemed to be received on the second business day after the date of posting, unless the contrary is shown.

(4)   Where second class post is used, the document is to be deemed to be received on the fourth business day after the date of posting, unless the contrary is shown.

Certificate of giving notice, etc

14.—(1)   Where in any proceedings under these Regulations a notice or document is required to be given, sent or delivered by any person, the date of giving, sending or delivery of it may be proved by means of a certificate by that person that he gave, posted or otherwise sent or delivered the notice or document on the date stated in the certificate, or that he instructed another person (naming him) to do so.

(2)   A certificate under this paragraph may be endorsed on a copy of the notice to which it relates.

(3)   A certificate purporting to be signed by or on behalf of the person mentioned in sub-paragraph (1) shall be deemed, unless the contrary is shown, to be sufficient evidence of the matters stated therein.

Forms for use in proceedings under these Regulations

15.—(1)   Forms ML 7 and ML 8 contained in Schedule 5 to these Regulations shall be used in, and in connection with, proceedings under these Regulations.

(2)   The forms shall be used with such variations, if any, as the circumstances may require.

ADOPTION (RECOGNITION OF OVERSEAS ADOPTIONS) ORDER 2013
(SI 2013/1801)

Citation and commencement

1. This Order may be cited as the Adoption (Recognition of Overseas Adoptions) Order 2013 and comes into force on 3rd January 2014.

Overseas adoptions

2.—(1) An adoption of a child is specified as an overseas adoption if it is an adoption effected under the law of a country or territory listed in the Schedule after the coming into force of this Order and is not a Convention adoption(3).

(2) In this Article "law" does not include customary or common law.

Evidence of an overseas adoption

3.—(1) The following documents may be provided as evidence that an overseas adoption has been effected—

    (a) a certified copy of an entry made, in accordance with the law of the country or territory concerned, in a public register relating to the recording of adoptions and showing that the adoption has been effected; or

    (b) a certificate that the adoption has been effected, signed or purporting to be signed by a person authorised by the law of the country or territory concerned to sign such a certificate, or a certified copy of such a certificate.

(2) Where a document produced by virtue of paragraph (1) is not in English, the Registrar General may require the production of an English translation of the document before being satisfied of the matters specified in paragraph 3 of Schedule 1 to the Adoption and Children Act 2002.

(3) Nothing in this Article may be construed as precluding proof, in accordance with the Evidence (Foreign, Dominion and Colonial Documents) Act 1933, or the Oaths and Evidence (Overseas Authorities and Countries) Act 1963, or otherwise, that an overseas adoption has been effected.

Revocations and savings provision

4.—(1) The Adoption (Designation of Overseas Adoptions) Order 1973 ('the 1973 Order') and the Adoption (Designation of Overseas Adoptions) (Variation) Order 1993 are revoked.

(2) The revocations do not affect any adoption designated as an overseas adoption by virtue of the 1973 Order prior to the coming into force of this Order.

Article 2(1)

SCHEDULE

Albania	Chile
Andorra	The People's Republic of China
Armenia	Colombia
Australia	Costa Rica
Austria	Cuba
Azerbaijan	The Republic of Cyprus
Belarus	Czech Republic
Belgium	Denmark (including the Faroe Islands and
Belize	Greenland)
Bolivia	Dominican Republic
Brazil	Ecuador
Bulgaria	El Salvador
Burkina Faso	Estonia
Burundi	Fiji
Canada	Finland
Cape Verde	France

Georgia
Germany
Greece
Guinea
Hungary
Iceland
India
The Republic of Ireland
Israel
Italy
Kazakhstan
Kenya
Latvia
Lesotho
Liechtenstein
Lithuania
Luxembourg
The Former Yugoslav Republic of Macedonia
Madagascar
Mali
Malta
Mauritius
Mexico
The Republic of Moldova
Monaco
Mongolia
Montenegro
The Netherlands (including the Caribbean
    part of the Netherlands (the islands of
    Bonaire, Sint Eustatius and Saba)

New Zealand
Norway
Panama
Paraguay
Peru
Philippines
Poland
Portugal
Romania
Rwanda
San Marino
Senegal
Seychelles
Slovakia
Slovenia
South Africa
Spain
Sri Lanka
Swaziland
Sweden
Switzerland
Thailand
Togo
Turkey
The United States of America
Uruguay
Venezuela
Vietnam

PART III

SCOTTISH STATUTORY INSTRUMENTS

REGISTRATION OF FOREIGN ADOPTIONS (SCOTLAND) REGULATIONS 2003
(SSI 2003/67)

Citation and commencement
1. These Regulations may be cited as the Registration of Foreign Adoptions (Scotland) Regulations 2003, and shall come into force on 1st June 2003.

Interpretation
2. In these Regulations—
'the 1978 Act' means the Adoption (Scotland) Act 1978;
'the Adopted Children Register' has the same meaning as in section 45 of the 1978 Act;
'central authority' has the same meaning as in the Convention;
'the Convention' means the Convention on Protection of Children and Co-operation in respect of Intercountry Adoption, concluded at the Hague on 29th May 1993;
'Convention adoption' means an adoption effected under the law of any country or territory outside the British Islands in which the Convention is in force, and certified in pursuance of Article 23(1) of the Convention; and
'overseas adoption' has the same meaning as in section 65(2) of the 1978 Act.

Requirements for registration
7.—(1) An application for an entry to be made in the Adopted Children Register in respect of a Convention adoption may be made only if the person making the application provides—
   (a) the Article 23 certificate made under the Convention by the central authority of the appropriate Convention country or territory in respect of the adoption, or a copy of that certificate certified as a true copy of the original by a notary public or equivalent officer; and
   (b) where appropriate, a translation of that certificate into English certified by the translator as a correct translation.
(2) An application for an entry to be made in the Adopted Children Register in respect of an overseas adoption may be made only if the person making the application provides—
   (a) either—
      (i) a certified copy of the adoption order made in respect of the adopted child; or
      (ii) a certified copy of an entry made in respect of the adopted child, in accordance with the law of the country or territory concerned, in a public register relating to the recording of adoptions, and showing that the adoption has been effected; and
   (b) where appropriate, a translation of that order or entry into English certified by the translator as a correct translation.
(3) In paragraph (2)(a) above a copy is certified if it is certified as a true copy of the original order or entry by the court or other competent authority that made that order or entry.

EUROPEAN COMMUNITIES (MATRIMONIAL AND PARENTAL RESPONSIBILITY JURISDICTION AND JUDGMENTS) (SCOTLAND) REGULATIONS 2005
(SSI 2005/42)

Citation, commencement and extent

1.—(1)   These Regulations may be cited as the European Communities (Matrimonial and Parental Responsibility Jurisdiction and Judgments) (Scotland) Regulations 2005 and shall come into force on 1st March 2005.

(2)   These Regulations extend to Scotland only.

...

Transitional

6.   Proceedings started under Council Regulation (EC) No 1347/2000 of 29th May 2000 on jurisdiction and the recognition and enforcement of judgments in matrimonial matters and in matters of parental responsibility for children of both spouses may continue under that Regulation until decree as if these Regulations had not been made.

...

Application

7.   The amendments to—
    (a)   the Domicile and Matrimonial Proceedings Act 1973 made by regulation 2;
    (b)   the Family Law Act 1986 made by regulation 4; and
    (c)   the Children (Scotland) Act 1995 made by regulation 5,
shall apply only in respect of proceedings commenced on or after 1st March 2005.

DIVORCE (RELIGIOUS BODIES) (SCOTLAND) REGULATIONS 2006
(SSI 2006/253)

Citation and commencement

1.   These Regulations may be cited as the Divorce (Religious Bodies) (Scotland) Regulations 2006 and shall come into force on 3rd June 2006.

Religious body

2.   Any Hebrew Congregation is prescribed as a religious body for the purposes of section 3A(7) of the Divorce (Scotland) Act 1976.

ADOPTIONS WITH A FOREIGN ELEMENT (SPECIAL RESTRICTIONS ON ADOPTIONS FROM ABROAD) (SCOTLAND) REGULATIONS 2008
(SSI 2008/303)

Citation and commencement

1.   These Regulations may be cited as the Adoptions with a Foreign Element (Special Restrictions on Adoptions from Abroad) (Scotland) Regulations 2008 and come into force on 7th October 2008.

2.—(1)   In these Regulations—
    'the Act' means the Adoption and Children (Scotland) Act 2007;
    'request' means a request that is made in writing by the prospective adopters stating that the Scottish Ministers should take any step as mentioned in section 64(1) of the Act despite an order having been made under section 62(3) of the Act in relation to the State of origin; and
    'the State of origin' means the country or territory from which the prospective adopters wish to bring a child into the United Kingdom.

(2)   For the purposes of these Regulations the Scottish Ministers are 'satisfied that the case is exceptional' if they are satisfied that they should take any step as mentioned in section 64(1) of the Act despite an order having been made under section 62(3) of the Act in relation to the State of origin.

(3)   Any reference in these Regulations to anything done in writing or produced in written form includes a reference to an electronic communication as defined in the Electronic Communications Act 2000 which has been recorded and is consequently capable of reproduction.

(4)   An electronic communication may only be sent to a person if that person has consented in writing to the use of that method of communication and transmission is to an email address provided by the recipient.

(5)   An electronic communication shall be taken to be received on the day after the day of its transmission.

Receipt of a request
3.—(1)   On receipt of a request, the Scottish Ministers must—
(a)   acknowledge receipt of the request in writing as soon as is practicable;
(b)   make such enquiries of the prospective adopters as appear necessary to clarify—
(i)   the reasons why the prospective adopters consider that the Scottish Ministers should be satisfied that the case is exceptional; or
(ii)   any other information that has been submitted by the prospective adopters;
(c)   make such further enquiries as they consider appropriate; and
(d)   ask the prospective adopters whether there is any further information that they have not submitted but that they consider relevant to the request.
(2)   The Scottish Ministers may defer making a determination in accordance with regulation 4 until—
(a)   the prospective adopters confirm that there is no further information that they consider relevant to the request; or
(b)   where the prospective adopters indicate that there is further information that they consider relevant to the request, that information has been received.

Determining whether an exception to the special restrictions should be made
4.—(1)   In determining whether they are satisfied that the case is exceptional, the Scottish Ministers must—
(a)   consider all the information they hold that is relevant to the request; and
(b)   take into account the matters referred to in regulation 6.
(2)   After making a determination, the Scottish Ministers must—
(a)   notify the prospective adopters in writing as to whether they are satisfied that the case is exceptional; and
(b)   where they are not so satisfied, give reasons.

Further requests
5.—(1)   This regulation applies where the Scottish Ministers have made a determination in accordance with regulation 4 and the prospective adopters submit a further request.
(2)   The Scottish Ministers must consider that further request if they consider that it contains—
(a)   new information; or
(b)   information that might have led to them being satisfied that the case was exceptional if it had been available at the time they made the determination.

Matters to be taken into account
6.—(1)   In determining under regulation 4 whether or not they are satisfied that a case is exceptional, the Scottish Ministers must take the following matters into account (whether or not they also take other matters into account)—

(a)   where the prospective adopters wish to adopt a particular child—

(i)   the circumstances leading to the child becoming available for adoption;

(ii)   whether any competent authority in the State of origin has made a decision in relation to the adoption or availability for adoption of the child;

(iii)   the relationship of the child to the prospective adopters, including how and when it was formed;

(iv)   the child's particular needs and the capacity of the prospective adopters to meet those needs; and

(v)   the reasons why the State of origin was placed on the restricted list; or

(b)   in any other case, the reasons why the State of origin was placed on the restricted list.

(2)   In this regulation, a 'competent authority' means a court or a person who performs functions which correspond to the functions of an adoption agency or to the functions of the Scottish Ministers in respect of intercountry adoption.

Imposition of extra conditions

7.—(1)   The Scottish Ministers may specify in the restricted list, in relation to any restricted country, a step which is not otherwise provided for by virtue of any enactment but which, by virtue of the arrangements between the United Kingdom and that country or territory, the Scottish Ministers normally take in connection with the bringing in of a child where that country or territory is concerned.

(2)   If a step has been specified under paragraph (1), the condition which is to be met for the purposes of section 65(1)(b) of the Act is that the Scottish Ministers have notified the prospective adopters in writing that the adoption may proceed.

(3)   A notification for the purpose of paragraph (2) must state that it is given for the purpose of that paragraph.

ADOPTIONS WITH A FOREIGN ELEMENT (SCOTLAND) REGULATIONS 2009
(SSI 2009/182)

PART 1
GENERAL

Citation and commencement

1.—(1)   These Regulations may be cited as the Adoptions with a Foreign Element (Scotland) Regulations 2009 and come into force on 28th September 2009.

(2)   These regulations extend to Scotland only.

Interpretation

2.   In these Regulations—

'the Act' means the Adoption and Children (Scotland) Act 2007;

'the Adoption Agencies Regulations' means—

(a)   in Part 2, the Adoptions Agencies (Scotland) Regulations 2009; and

(b)   in Part 3, those Regulations subject to the modifications set out in regulation 62;

'adoption agency' in Part 3 means a local authority or a registered adoption service which is an accredited body for the purposes of the Convention;

'adoption panel', in relation to an adoption agency, means an adoption panel appointed by the agency under regulation 3 of the Adoption Agencies Regulations, and includes a joint adoption panel (within the meaning of that regulation) established by the agency jointly with any other adoption agency;

'CA of the receiving State' means, in relation to a Convention country other than the United Kingdom, the Central Authority of the receiving State;

'CA of the State of origin' means, in relation to a Convention country other than the United Kingdom, the Central Authority of the State of origin;

'Central Authority' means the Scottish Executive;

'competent authority', in relation to a function under the Convention, means an authority in a Contracting State which is entitled to carry out that function;

'Convention prospective adopter' is to be construed in accordance with regulation 45(1);

'eligible to adopt' in Part 3, except in regulations 16(4)(b) and 50(3)(a)(ii), is to be construed in accordance with regulation 12(1);

'prospective adopters'—

(a) in Chapter 1 of Part 2 means a person who makes, or persons who make, an application under regulation 3; and

(b) in Chapter 1 of Part 3 means a person or, as the case may be, a relevant couple who makes an application under regulation 11;

'receiving State' is to be construed in accordance with Article 2 of the Convention;

'relevant foreign authority' means a person or body outwith the British Islands performing functions in the country in which the child, or the prospective adopter, is habitually resident which correspond to the functions of an adoption agency or to the functions of the Scottish Ministers in respect of adoptions with a foreign element;

'relevant local authority', in relation to prospective adopters, means—

(a) the local authority within whose area the prospective adopters have their home; or

(b) in the case where the prospective adopters no longer have a home in Scotland, the local authority for the area in which they last had their home; and

'State of origin' is to be construed in accordance with Article 2 of the Convention.

PART 2
BRINGING CHILDREN INTO, AND TAKING CHILDREN OUT OF, THE
UNITED KINGDOM

Chapter 1
Bringing Children into the United Kingdom

Requirements applicable in respect of bringing, or causing another to bring, a child into the United Kingdom

3. A person intending to bring, or to cause another to bring, a child into the United Kingdom in circumstances where section 58 of the Act applies must—

(a) apply in writing to an adoption agency for an assessment of the person's suitability to adopt a child; and

(b) give the adoption agency any information it may require for the purpose of the assessment.

Conditions applicable in respect of a child brought into the United Kingdom

4.—(1) This regulation prescribes the conditions for the purposes of section 58(6) of the Act in respect of a child brought into the United Kingdom in circumstances where section 58 applies.

(2) Prior to the child's entry into the United Kingdom, the prospective adopters must—

(a) receive from the [Scottish Ministers] notification in writing that the [Scottish Ministers have] issued a certificate confirming to the relevant foreign authority—

(i) that the prospective adopters have been assessed and approved as eligible and suitable to be adoptive parents in accordance with the Adoption Agencies Regulations; and

(ii) that if entry clearance and leave to enter and remain, as may be necessary, is granted and not revoked or curtailed, and an adoption order is made or an overseas adoption is effected, the child will be authorised to enter and reside permanently in the United Kingdom;

(b)   before visiting the child in the State of origin—

(i)   notify the adoption agency of the details of the child to be adopted;

(ii)   provide the adoption agency with any information and reports received from the relevant foreign authority; and

(iii)   discuss with the adoption agency the proposed adoption and any information and reports so received;

(c)   visit the child in the State of origin (and, where the prospective adopters are a couple, each of them must so visit the child); and

(d)   after that visit—

(i)   confirm in writing to the adoption agency that the prospective adopters have done so and wish to proceed with the adoption;

(ii)   provide the adoption agency with any additional reports and information received on or after that visit; and

(iii)   notify the adoption agency of the date the prospective adopters expect to enter the United Kingdom with the child.

(3)   On entering the United Kingdom, the child must be accompanied by the prospective adopters (and, where the prospective adopters are a couple, the child must be accompanied by both members of the couple unless the adoption agency and the relevant foreign authority have agreed that it is necessary for only one of them to do so).

(4)   Except where an overseas adoption is, or is to be, effected, the prospective adopters must within the period of 14 days beginning with the date on which the child is brought into the United Kingdom give notice to the relevant local authority—

(a)   of the child's arrival in the United Kingdom; and

(b)   of the prospective adopters' intention—

(i)   to apply for an adoption order in accordance with section 18(2) of the Act; or

(ii)   not to give the child a home.

(5)   In a case where the prospective adopters have given notice in accordance with paragraph (4) and subsequently move their home into the area of another local authority, they must within 14 days of so moving confirm in writing to that authority—

(a)   the child's arrival in the United Kingdom; and

(b)   that notice of the prospective adopters' intention has been given in accordance with paragraph (4)(b).

(6)   In this regulation, 'entry clearance' has the same meaning as in the Immigration Act 1971.

Functions imposed on the local authority

5.—(1)   This regulation applies where—

(a)   a child is brought into the United Kingdom in circumstances where section 58 of the Act applies; and

(b)   notice has been given by the prospective adopters to the relevant local authority in accordance with section 18(2) of the Act of their intention to apply for an adoption order.

(2)   The local authority must—

(a)   if it has not already done so, set up a case record in respect of the child and place on it any information received from—

(i)   the relevant foreign authority;

(ii)   the adoption agency (if it is not the local authority);

(iii)   the prospective adopters;

(iv)   the entry clearance officer; and

(v)   the [...] Scottish Ministers;

(b)   send to the Scottish Ministers written notification of the child's arrival in the United Kingdom;

(c)   send the prospective adopters' registered medical practitioner (and, where required in cases where the prospective adopters are a relevant couple, the registered medical practitioner of each member of the couple) written notification of the child's arrival in the United Kingdom and send with that notification a written report of the child's health history and current state of health (so far as is known);

(d)   send to the Health Board constituted under section 2 of the National Health Service (Scotland) Act 1978 in whose area the prospective adopters have their home written notification of the child's arrival in the United Kingdom;

(e)   where the child is of school age (as defined in section 31 of the Education (Scotland) Act 1980), send to the education authority in whose area the prospective adopters have their home written notification of the child's arrival in the United Kingdom and information, if known, about—

(i)   the child's educational history; and

(ii)   whether the child has additional support needs (within the meaning of the Education (Additional Support for Learning) (Scotland) Act 2004);

(f)   ensure that the child and the prospective adopters are visited within one week of receipt of the notice mentioned in paragraph (1)(b) and thereafter not less than once a week until the review mentioned in sub-paragraph (g) and thereafter at such frequency as the local authority may (subject to sub-paragraphs (g) and (h)) decide;

(g)   unless the child no longer has a home with the prospective adopters or an adoption order is made in respect of the child—

(i)   carry out a review of the child's case not more than 4 weeks after receipt of the notice mentioned in paragraph (1)(b);

(ii)   within 3 months of that review, visit the child and prospective adopters and, if the local authority considers it necessary, carry out a further review of the child's case; and

(iii)   thereafter at intervals not exceeding 6 months, visit the child and prospective adopters and, if the local authority considers it necessary, carry out a further review of the child's case;

(h)   when carrying out a review, consider—

(i)   the child's needs, welfare and development and whether any changes need to be made to meet those needs or assist that development;

(ii)   the arrangements for the provision of adoption support services and whether there should be any re-assessment of the need for those services; and

(iii)   the need for further visits and reviews; and

(i)   ensure that—

(i)   where necessary, advice is given to the prospective adopters as to the child's needs, welfare and development;

(ii)   written reports are made of all visits and reviews of the case and placed on the child's case record; and

(iii)   during visits carried out in accordance with this paragraph, advice is given, where appropriate, to the prospective adopters and the child as to the availability of adoption support services.

(3)   Part VIII of the Adoption Agencies (Scotland) Regulations applies to any case record set up in respect of the child as a consequence of this regulation as if that record had been created under those Regulations.

(4)   In a case where the prospective adopters fail, within 2 years of the local authority's receiving the notice mentioned in paragraph (1)(b), to make an application under section 29 or section 30 of the Act, the authority must review the case.

(5)   For the purposes of the review referred to in paragraph (4), the local authority must consider—

(a)   the child's needs, welfare and development and whether any changes need to be made to meet those needs or assist that development;

(b)   the arrangements, if any, in relation to the exercise of parental responsibilities and parental rights in relation to the child;

(c)   the terms upon which leave to enter the United Kingdom is granted and the immigration status of the child;

(d)   the arrangements for the provision of adoption support services and whether there should be any re-assessment of the need for those services; and

(e)   in conjunction with the appropriate agencies, the arrangements for meeting the child's health care and educational needs.

(6)   In a case where a local authority ('the original authority') receives the notice mentioned in paragraph (1)(b) and is further notified by the prospective adopters that they intend to move, or have moved, their home into the area of another local authority ('the new authority'), the original authority must, within 14 days of receipt of such further notification, notify the new authority of—

(a)   the name, sex, date of birth and place of birth of the child;

(b)   the name, sex and date of birth of the prospective adopters;

(c)   the date of the child's arrival in the United Kingdom;

(d)   the date the original authority received the notice mentioned in paragraph (1)(b);

(e)   (if known), whether an application for an adoption order in respect of the child has been made and the stage of those proceedings; and

(f)   any other relevant information.

(7)   In this regulation, 'entry clearance officer' means a person responsible for the grant or refusal of entry clearance; and 'entry clearance' has the same meaning as in the Immigration Act 1971.

Application of Chapter 2 of Part 1 of the Act

6.—(1)   This regulation applies in the case of a child brought into the United Kingdom in circumstances where section 58 of the Act applies.

(2)   Subsection (6) of section 21 of the Act (restrictions on removal: notice of intention to adopt given) does not apply.

(3)   Section 25 of the Act (return of child placed for adoption by adoption agency) applies as if—

(a)   for paragraphs (a) and (b) of subsection (1) there were substituted 'a child is brought into the United Kingdom in circumstances where section 58 applies';

(b)   in subsection (2)—

(i)   after 'adopters' there were inserted 'of the child in question'; and

(ii)   for 'agency or society' there were substituted 'local authority for the area in which they have their home ('the authority')';

(c)   for 'agency or society' in subsection (3) there were substituted 'authority';

(d)   in subsection (6)—

(i)   for 'return' there were substituted 'deliver';

(ii)   in each of paragraphs (a) and (b), for 'agency or, as the case may be, society' there were substituted 'authority';

(e)   in subsection (8) for 'return' there were substituted 'deliver'; and

(f)   in subsection (9)—

(i)   for 'returned' there were substituted 'delivered'; and

(ii)   for the words from 'child's' to the end of that subsection there were substituted 'authority'.

Chapter 2
Taking Children out of the United Kingdom

Orders under section 59 of the Act: requirements

7.—(1)   This regulation prescribes, for the purposes of subsection (3) of section 59 of the Act (preliminary order where child to be adopted abroad), the requirements to be satisfied before an order under that section may be made in the case where the prospective adopters (within the meaning of that section) intend to adopt a child otherwise than under a Convention adoption.

(2)　This regulation applies in the case of a child placed for adoption with the prospective adopters by an adoption agency.

(3)　The requirements are—

(a)　that the adoption agency has—

(i)　confirmed to the court that it has complied with the requirements imposed on it under Parts IV and V of the Adoption Agencies Regulations; and

(ii)　submitted to the court the things mentioned in regulation 8;

(b)　that the relevant foreign authority has—

(i)　confirmed in writing to the adoption agency that the prospective adopters have been counselled and that the legal implications of adoption have been explained to them;

(ii)　prepared a report on the suitability of the prospective adopters to be adoptive parents;

(iii)　determined and confirmed in writing to the adoption agency that the prospective adopters are eligible and suitable to adopt in the country or territory in which the adoption is to be effected; and

(iv)　confirmed to the adoption agency that the child is or will be authorised to enter and reside permanently in that country or territory;

(c)　in a case where there is only one prospective adopter, that the prospective adopter has confirmed in writing to the adoption agency that the prospective adopter will accompany the child out of Great Britain and into the country or territory where the adoption is to be effected; and

(d)　in a case where there are two prospective adopters, that they have confirmed in writing to the adoption agency—

(i)　that both will so accompany the child; or

(ii)　if the adoption agency and the relevant foreign authority have confirmed that it is necessary for only one so to accompany the child, that one of them will do so.

Matters to be submitted to the court under regulation 7

8.　The things to be submitted to the court under regulation 7(3)(a)(ii) are—

(a)　a copy of the recommendations of the adoption panel under regulation 6(2) of the Adoption Agencies Regulations;

(b)　if regulation 6(4) of those Regulations applies, a copy of the report of the adoption panel mentioned in that regulation;

(c)　a copy of the report on the health of the child mentioned in regulation 18(1)(d) of those Regulations and any report obtained in accordance with regulation 18(2) of those Regulations;

(d)　a copy of the report and information mentioned in regulation 18(1)(i) of those Regulations; and

(e)　a copy of the written reports mentioned in regulation 25(1)(b) of those Regulations.

Application of the Act in respect of orders under section 59

9.—(1)　Subject to paragraphs (2), (3) and (4) the provisions of Chapter 2 of Part 1 of the Act, as they relate to adoption orders, apply to orders under section 59 of the Act so far as the nature of the provision permits and unless the contrary intention is shown.

(2)　The following provisions of the Act which relate to adoption orders apply to orders under section 59 of the Act subject to the following:—

(a)　in section 28, omit subsections (1), (3), (4), (5) and (6);

(b)　in section 29, omit subsections (1)(c) and (2); and

(c)　in section 30, omit subsections (1)(c), (3)(d) and (6).

(3)   For the purposes of section 14(1) of the Act, a court considering an application for an order under section 59 in respect of a child is to be treated as a court coming to a decision relating to the adoption of a child.

(4)   The following provisions of Chapter 2 of Part 1 of the Act do not apply to orders under section 59 of the Act:—
   (a)   section 15;
   (b)   section 21;
   (c)   section 22;
   (d)   section 24;
   (e)   section 25;
   (f)   section 26;
   (g)   section 34.

(5)   Sections 53 to 55 and paragraphs 1 to 4 of schedule 1 to the Act, as they relate to adoption orders, apply to orders made under section 59 of the Act as if—
   (a)   in each place where the words 'adoption order' appear there were substituted 'order under section 59';
   (b)   in each place where the words 'adopted person' appear there were substituted 'person subject to an order made under section 59';
   (c)   in section 55(1) and paragraph 3 of schedule 1 where the words 'Adopted' appear there were substituted 'Proposed foreign adoption'; and
   (d)   in paragraph 3 of schedule 1 where the words 'Re-adopted' appear there were substituted 'Proposed foreign re-adoption'.

PART 3
ADOPTIONS UNDER THE CONVENTION

Chapter 1
Procedure in Scotland where the United Kingdom in the Receiving State

Application of Chapter 1
10.   The provisions of this Chapter apply where—
   (a)   a person; or
   (b)   a relevant couple,
habitually resident in the British Islands wishes to adopt, in accordance with the Convention, a child who is habitually resident outwith the British Islands.

Application: eligibility, and suitability, to adopt
11.   Such a person or couple must—
   (a)   apply in writing to an adoption agency for—
      (i)   a determination of their eligibility to adopt; and
      (ii)   an assessment of their suitability to be adoptive parents; and
   (b)   provide the agency with such information as it may require for the purposes of the assessment.

Determination of eligibility to adopt
12.—(1)   An adoption agency is not to consider prospective adopters eligible to adopt unless at the date of the application under regulation 11 the person or, as the case may be, each member of the relevant couple making the application—
   (a)   has attained the age of 21 years; and
   (b)   has been habitually resident in a part of the British Islands for a period of not less than one year ending with the date of application.

(2)   An adoption agency must notify prospective adopters in writing as soon as possible after becoming aware that the prospective adopters are not eligible to adopt because they do not meet the requirements of paragraph (1).

Provision of information
13.—(1)   Where an application is made under regulation 11, the adoption agency must—

(a)   explain to the prospective adopters the procedure in relation to, and the legal implications of, adopting a child from the State of origin from which the prospective adopters wish to adopt in accordance with the Convention; and

(b)   provide the prospective adopters with written information about the matters referred to in sub-paragraph (a).

(2)   Paragraph (1) does not apply if the adoption agency is satisfied that the requirements in that paragraph have been met in respect of the prospective adopters by another adoption agency.

Case records and counselling

14.—(1)   Paragraph (2) applies to an adoption agency which—

(a)   has determined that the prospective adopters are eligible to adopt;

(b)   has satisfied the requirements in regulation 13; and

(c)   considers that the prospective adopters' suitability to be adoptive parents should be assessed.

(2)   The adoption agency must—

(a)   if it has not already done so, set up a case record in respect of the prospective adopters and place on it any information obtained under regulations 15 and 16; and

(b)   ensure that such counselling as may be necessary in connection with the proposed adoption is made available to the prospective adopters.

(3)   Part VIII of the Adoption Agencies Regulations applies to any case record set up in respect of the prospective adopters as a consequence of this regulation as if that record had been created under that Part.

Criminal record checks

15.—(1)   This regulation applies to an adoption agency to which regulation 14(2) applies.

(2)   The adoption agency must so far as is reasonably practicable obtain information about—

(a)   any criminal convictions of the prospective adopters and any other member of the prospective adopters' household aged 16 or over; and

(b)   any police cautions issued to such persons in England, Wales or Northern Ireland in respect of an offence which was admitted at the time the caution was issued.

(3)   In paragraph (2)(a), the reference to criminal convictions includes a reference to convictions in England, Wales or Northern Ireland.

(4)   The adoption agency is not to consider prospective adopters to be suitable to be adoptive parents if the prospective adopters or any member of their household aged 16 or over—

(a)   have been convicted of an offence specified in Schedule 1;

(b)   have been convicted of—

(i)   a specified offence (within the meaning of regulation 23(3) of the Adoption Agencies Regulations 2005 (requirement to carry out police checks)), other than an offence mentioned in paragraphs 2 to 11 of Part I of Schedule 3 to those Regulations (offences in Scotland and Northern Ireland); or

(ii)   an offence mentioned in Part 2 of Schedule 3 to those Regulations (repealed statutory offences) notwithstanding its repeal; or

(c)   have received a police caution in England, Wales or Northern Ireland in respect of an offence mentioned in sub-paragraph (a) or (b) which, at the time the caution was given, the prospective adopters or, as the case may be, the member of their household, admitted.

(5)   The adoption agency must—

(a)   as soon as possible after becoming aware that the prospective adopters are not suitable to be adoptive parents by virtue of paragraph (4), notify the prospective adopters in writing of that fact; and

(b)   where the conviction or police caution in question relates to the prospective adopters, specify in the notification the conviction or, as the case may be, the police caution.

Duties of adoption agency prior to decision on suitability

16.—(1) This regulation applies to an adoption agency to which regulation 14(2) applies.

(2) The adoption agency must so far as is reasonably practicable obtain—

(a) such information in relation to the prospective adopters as is referred to in Part I of Schedule 1 to the Adoption Agencies Regulations; and

(b) any other relevant information which may be requested by the adoption panel.

(3) Where the adoption agency is not the local authority in whose area the prospective adopters have their home—

(a) the agency must request the authority to provide any relevant information relating to the prospective adopters of which the authority is aware; and

(b) the authority must provide the information.

(4) The adoption agency must prepare a written report which—

(a) identifies the Convention country from which the prospective adopters wish to adopt a child;

(b) confirms the prospective adopters are eligible to adopt a child under the law of that Convention country;

(c) provides any other information obtained as a consequence of the requirements of that Convention country;

(d) includes the adoption agency's assessment of the prospective adopters' suitability to be adoptive parents;

(e) includes any other observations of the adoption agency on the matters referred to in this regulation and regulations 12, 14 and 15; and

(f) includes any other information about the prospective adopters of the type specified in Article 15(1) of the Convention.

(5) The adoption agency must notify the prospective adopters that their application is to be referred to an adoption panel and, at the same time—

(a) send the prospective adopters a copy of the written report referred to in paragraph (4) (excluding any information from third parties given in confidence); and

(b) invite the prospective adopters to send any observations on the report in writing to the agency within a period of 14 days beginning with the date on which the notification was sent.

(6) At the end of the period of 14 days referred to in paragraph (5) (or earlier if any observations of the prospective adopters are received before that period has expired), the adoption agency must refer the prospective adopters' case to the adoption panel and pass to the panel—

(a) the written report referred to in paragraph (4);

(b) all relevant information obtained by the agency under this regulation and regulations 14 and 15; and

(c) any observations of the prospective adopters on the written report.

Functions of the adoption panel

17.—(1) The adoption panel must—

(a) consider the case of the prospective adopters referred to it by the adoption agency; and

(b) make a recommendation to the agency as to whether the prospective adopters are suitable to be adoptive parents.

(2) In considering what recommendation to make, the adoption panel—

(a) must take into account all information and reports passed to it under regulation 16(6);

(b) must give the prospective adopters the opportunity to meet with the adoption panel to discuss the information and reports;

(c)   may request the adoption agency to obtain any other relevant information which the panel considers necessary; and

(d)   may obtain legal advice in relation to the case.

Adoption agency decision, notification and request for review

18.—(1)   The adoption agency must—

(a)   take into account the recommendation of the adoption panel in coming to a decision (in this regulation, 'the decision') on the prospective adopters' suitability to be adoptive parents; and

(b)   make the decision within 14 days of the date the recommendation was made.

(2)   No member of the adoption panel which made the recommendation is to take part in the decision.

(3)   Where the decision is that the prospective adopters are suitable to be adoptive parents, the adoption agency must notify the prospective adopters in writing of the decision within 14 days of making the decision.

(4)   Where the decision is that the prospective adopters are not suitable to be adoptive parents (other than by virtue of regulation 15(4)), the adoption agency must—

(a)   notify the prospective adopters in writing of the decision within 7 days of making the decision;

(b)   send with the notification—

(i)   its reasons for the decision; and

(ii)   where the adoption panel's recommendation was that the prospective adopters were suitable to be adoptive parents, a copy of the recommendation;

(c)   inform the prospective adopters in writing that they may require the decision to be reviewed within 28 days of the date of the notification (the '28 day period'); and

(d)   invite the prospective adopters to submit to the adoption agency any representations regarding the decision within the 28 day period.

(5)   Where the prospective adopters have, within the 28 day period, required a review of the decision (whether or not they have also submitted any representations under paragraph (4)(d)), the adoption agency must refer the case to the adoption panel and pass any such representations and any other relevant information to the panel for further consideration.

(6)   The adoption panel must reconsider any case referred to it under paragraph (5) and make a fresh recommendation to the adoption agency as to whether the prospective adopters are suitable to be adoptive parents.

(7)   The adoption agency must, having taken into account the adoption panel's fresh recommendation, make a decision (the 'reviewed decision') on the case within 14 days of the date the fresh recommendation was made.

(8)   The adoption agency must, within 7 days of making the reviewed decision, notify the prospective adopters of the reviewed decision.

(9)   Where the reviewed decision is that the prospective adopters are not suitable to be adoptive parents, the notification under paragraph (8) must—

(a)   state the reasons for the reviewed decision; and

(b)   where the adoption panel's fresh recommendation was that the prospective adopters were suitable to be adoptive parents, include a copy of the adoption panel's fresh recommendation.

Review without request

19.—(1)   Where an adoption agency has decided that prospective adopters are suitable to be adoptive parents, the agency must review that decision in accordance with this regulation unless the agency has received written notification from the Central Authority that the agreement under Article 17(c) of the Convention has been made.

(2)   A review under this regulation must be carried out whenever the adoption agency considers it necessary but otherwise not more than one year after the decision and thereafter at intervals of not more than one year.

(3)   When undertaking such a review the adoption agency must—

(a)   make such enquiries and obtain such information as it considers necessary in order to review whether the prospective adopters continue to be suitable to be adoptive parents; and

(b)   seek and take into account the views of the prospective adopters.

(4)   If following the review, the adoption agency considers that the prospective adopters may no longer be suitable to be adoptive parents it must—

(a)   prepare a written report (the 'review report') setting out the agency's reasons for its view;

(b)   notify the prospective adopters that the case is to be referred to the adoption panel;

(c)   send the prospective adopters a copy of the review report; and

(d)   invite the prospective adopters to submit any representations to the adoption agency within 14 days of the report's being sent.

(5)   At the end of the period of 14 days referred to in paragraph (4)(d) (or earlier if any representations of the prospective adopters are received before that period has expired), the adoption agency must send the review report, together with any such representations, to the adoption panel.

(6)   The adoption agency must obtain, so far as is reasonably practicable, any other relevant information which may be required by the adoption panel and send that information to the panel.

(7)   The adoption panel must consider the review report, the prospective adopters' representations (if any) and any other information passed to it by the adoption agency and make a recommendation to the agency as to whether the prospective adopters continue to be suitable to be adoptive parents.

(8)   The adoption agency must, having taken into account the adoption panel's recommendation under paragraph (7), make a decision as to whether the prospective adopters continue to be suitable to be adoptive parents; and paragraphs (2) to (9) of regulation 18 apply to that recommendation or, as the case may be, decision as if—

(a)   references to the recommendation of the adoption panel were references to a recommendation under paragraph (7); and

(b)   references to the decision were to a decision under this paragraph.

Procedure following decision that prospective adopters are suitable to adopt

20.—(1)   Paragraph (2) applies where an adoption agency—

(a)   has determined that the prospective adopters are eligible to adopt; and

(b)   has made a decision that the prospective adopters are suitable to be adoptive parents.

(2)   The adoption agency must send to the Central Authority within 7 days of the date the decision mentioned in paragraph (1)(b) is made—

(a)   written confirmation of the decision; and

(b)   a copy of the written report prepared under regulation 16(4).

(3)   The Central Authority may, if it considers it appropriate, require further information from the adoption agency.

(4)   If the Central Authority is satisfied that the adoption agency has—

(a)   complied with these Regulations; and

(b)   supplied all the information required under paragraph (2) and, where appropriate and available to the Authority, under paragraph (3),

the Authority must send to the CA of the State of origin the documents mentioned in paragraph (5).

(5)   The documents are—

(a)   a certificate in the form set out in Schedule 2 confirming that—

(i) the prospective adopters are eligible to adopt;

(ii) the prospective adopters have been assessed in accordance with these Regulations;

(iii) the prospective adopters have been approved as suitable to be adoptive parents; and

(iv) the child will be authorised to enter and reside permanently in the United Kingdom if either of the conditions mentioned in paragraph (6) are met;

(b) the information required under paragraph (2)(a) and (b); and

(c) the documents (if any) containing information required under paragraph (3).

(6) The conditions are that—

(a) the requirements specified in section 1(5A) of the British Nationality Act 1981 are met;

(b) entry clearance and leave to enter and remain, as may be necessary, is granted and not revoked or curtailed and a Convention adoption order or Convention adoption is made.

(7) The Central Authority must notify the adoption agency and the prospective adopters in writing that the certificate and documents have been sent to the CA of the State of origin.

Procedure following receipt of Article 16 Information

21.—(1) Where the Central Authority receives from the CA of the State of origin the Article 16 Information relating to the child who the CA of the State of origin considers should be placed for adoption with the prospective adopters, the Central Authority must send that information to the adoption agency.

(2) The adoption agency must consider the Article 16 Information and—

(a) send the Information to the prospective adopters;

(b) meet with the prospective adopters to discuss the Information, the proposed placement and the availability of adoption support services; and

(c) if appropriate, offer—

(i) such counselling as may be necessary in connection with the proposed adoption; and

(ii) further information as required.

[(3) Where—

(a) the procedure in paragraph (2) has been followed; and

(b) the prospective adopters have confirmed in writing to the adoption agency that they wish to proceed to adopt the child,

the adoption agency must notify the Central Authority in writing that the requirements specified in sub-paragraphs (a) and (b) have been satisfied and, at the same time, confirm that it is satisfied that there are no impediments to the adoption proceeding.]

(4) Where the Central Authority has received notification from the adoption agency under paragraph (3), the Authority must—

(a) notify the CA of the State of origin that—

(i) the prospective adopters wish to proceed to adopt the child; and

(ii) it is prepared to agree with the CA of the State of origin that the adoption may proceed; and

(b) confirm to the CA of the State of origin that—

(i) in the case where the requirements specified in section 1(5A) of the British Nationality Act 1981 are met, that the child will be authorised to enter and reside permanently in the United Kingdom; or

(ii) in any other case, if entry clearance and leave to enter and remain, as may be necessary, is granted and not revoked or curtailed and a Convention adoption order or a Convention adoption is made, the child will be authorised to enter and reside permanently in the United Kingdom.

(5)   The Central Authority must inform the adoption agency and the prospective adopters when the agreement under Article 17(c) of the Convention has been made.

[(5A)   Where the prospective adopters visit the child in the State of origin they must, no later than 3 working days after visiting the child—

(a)   notify the adoption agency—

(i)   that they have visited the child; and

(ii)   as to whether they wish to proceed to adopt the child; and

(b)   provide the adoption agency with any additional reports and information received on or after that visit.

(5B)   Where the adoption agency receives notice under paragraph (5A) the agency must notify the Central Authority in writing—

(a)   that the prospective adopters have visited the child; and

(b)   as to whether the prospective adopters wish to proceed to adopt the child.]

(6)   For the purposes of this regulation, regulation 22 and regulation 34, 'the Article 16 Information' means—

(a)   the report referred to in Article 16 of the Convention including information about the child's identity, adoptability, background, social environment, family history, medical history including that of the child's family and any special needs of the child;

(b)   proof of confirmation that the consents of the persons, institutions and authorities whose consents are necessary for adoption have been obtained in accordance with Article 4 of the Convention; and

(c)   the reasons for the CA of the State of origin's determination on the placement.

Procedure where proposed adoption not to proceed

22.—(1)   If, at any time before the agreement under Article 17(c) of the Convention is made, the CA of the State of origin notifies the Central Authority that it has decided that the proposed placement should not proceed—

(a)   the Central Authority must inform the adoption agency of the CA of the State of origin's decision;

(b)   the agency must then inform the prospective adopters and return the Article 16 Information to the Central Authority; and

(c)   the Central Authority must then return the Article 16 Information to the CA of the State of origin.

(2)   Where, at any time before the adoption agency receives notification of the agreement under Article 17(c) of the Convention, the agency's decision that the prospective adopters are suitable to be adoptive parents is reviewed under regulation 19 and, as a consequence, the agency determines that the prospective adopters are no longer suitable to be adoptive parents—

(a)   the agency must inform the Central Authority and return the Article 16 Information; and

(b)   the Central Authority must then notify the CA of the State of origin and return that Information.

(3)   If, at any time before [any Convention adoption is made in the State of origin or, if none is made, before the child's entry into the United Kingdom], the prospective adopters notify the adoption agency that they do not wish to proceed with the adoption of the child—

(a)   the agency must inform the Central Authority and return the Article 16 Information to that Authority; and

(b)   the Central Authority must then notify the CA of the State of origin of the prospective adopters' decision and return the Information to the CA of the State of origin.

Child's entry into the United Kingdom
23.—(1) Following any agreement under Article 17(c) of the Convention, the prospective adopters must—
    (a) notify the adoption agency of their expected date of entry into the United Kingdom with the child;
    (b) confirm to the agency when the child is placed with them by the competent authority in the State of origin; and
    (c) accompany the child on entering the United Kingdom unless, in the case of a relevant couple, the adoption agency and the CA of the State of origin have agreed that it is necessary for only one member of the couple to do so.
(2) In exceptional circumstances, a nominee of the prospective adopters who has been approved by the adoption agency may accompany the child as mentioned in paragraph (1)(c) instead of the prospective adopters; and in such a case the word 'their' in paragraph (1)(a) is to be read as 'the nominee's'.

Notifications to be given prior to child's entry into the United Kingdom
24. Where the adoption agency is informed by the Central Authority that the agreement under Article 17(c) of the Convention has been made and the adoption may proceed, before the child enters the United Kingdom the agency must—
    (a) send to the Central Authority written notification of the proposed arrival of the child into Scotland;
    (b) send the prospective adopters' registered medical practitioner (and, where required in cases where the prospective adopters are a relevant couple, the registered medical practitioner of each member of the couple) written notification of the proposed placement and send with that notification a written report of the child's health history, so far as it is known;
    (c) send the local authority (if that authority is not the adoption agency), and the Health Board constituted under section 2 of the National Health Service (Scotland) Act 1978, in whose areas the prospective adopters have their home written notification of the proposed arrival of the child into Scotland; and
    (d) where the child is of school age (within the meaning of section 31 of the Education (Scotland) Act 1980), send the education authority in whose area the prospective adopters have their home written notification of the proposed arrival of the child into Scotland and information about the child's educational history (if known) including whether the child is likely to have additional support needs (within the meaning of the Education (Additional Support for Learning) (Scotland) Act 2004).

Child's entry into the United Kingdom where no Convention adoption made: applicable provisions
25. Regulations 26 to 30 apply where—
    (a) following the agreement between the Central Authority and the CA of the State of origin under Article 17(c) of the Convention that the adoption may proceed—
        (i) no Convention adoption is made, or applied for, in the State of origin; or
        (ii) in the case of regulations 29 and 30, a Convention adoption is applied for in the State of origin and regulation 32(2) applies; and
    (b) the child is placed with the prospective adopters who then return (or whose nominee mentioned in regulation 23(2) then returns) to Scotland with the child.

Duty of prospective adopters to notify local authority
26.—(1) The prospective adopters must, within the period of 14 days beginning with the date on which the child enters the United Kingdom, give notice to the relevant local authority—
    (a) of the child's entry into the United Kingdom; and

(b) of their intention—

    (i) to apply for an adoption order in accordance with section 18(2) of the Act; or

    (ii) not to give the child a home.

(2) In a case where prospective adopters have given notice in accordance with paragraph (1) and subsequently move their home into the area of another local authority, they must within 14 days of so moving confirm in writing to that authority—

(a) the child's entry into the United Kingdom; and

(b) that notice of the prospective adopters' intention has been given in accordance with paragraph (1)(b).

Functions of the local authority following child's entry into the United Kingdom

27.—(1) Where notice is given to a local authority in accordance with regulation 26, the functions imposed on the authority by virtue of regulation 5 apply subject to the modifications in paragraph (2).

(2) Paragraph (2) of regulation 5 applies as if—

(a) in sub-paragraph (a)—

    (i) in paragraph (i) for 'relevant foreign authority' there were substituted 'CA of the State of origin and competent authorities of the State of origin';

    (ii) for paragraph (v) there were substituted—

        '(v) the Central Authority'; and

(b) sub-paragraphs (b) to (d) were omitted.

Duty of prospective adopters

28.—(1) The prospective adopters are not obliged to allow the child to visit or stay with any person, or otherwise to allow contact between the child and any person except under and in terms of a contact order within the meaning of section 11(2)(d) of the Children (Scotland) Act 1995.

(2) Subject to paragraphs (3) and (4), the prospective adopters must not cause or permit the child—

(a) to be known by a new surname;

(b) to be removed from the United Kingdom,

unless the court consents or each parent or guardian of the child gives written consent.

(3) Paragraph (2)(a) does not apply if the competent authority of the State of origin has agreed that the child may be known by a new surname.

(4) Paragraph (2)(b) does not prevent the removal of the child by the prospective adopters for a period of less than one month.

(5) In paragraph (2), 'the court' means—

(a) the Court of Session; or

(b) the sheriff court of the sheriffdom within which the child is.

Prospective adopters not wishing to proceed with adoption

29.—(1) Where the prospective adopters give notice to the relevant local authority that they do not wish to proceed with the adoption and no longer wish to give the child a home, the prospective adopters must deliver the child to that authority before the end of the period of 7 days beginning with the giving of the notice.

(2) Where a relevant local authority receives a notice in accordance with paragraph (1), that authority must give notice to the Central Authority of the decision of the prospective adopters not to proceed with the adoption.

Withdrawal of child from prospective adopters

30.—(1) Where the relevant local authority is of the opinion that the continued placement of the child is not in the child's best interests—

(a) the authority must give notice to the prospective adopters of its opinion and request that the child be delivered to the authority; and

(b)   subject to paragraph (3), the prospective adopters must, no later than the end of the period of 7 days beginning with the date on which notice was given, deliver the child to the authority.

(2)   When giving notice under paragraph (1)(a) the relevant local authority must notify the Central Authority that it has requested the delivery of the child.

(3)   Where notice has been given under paragraph (1)(a) but—

(a)   an application for a Convention adoption order was made prior to the giving of the notice; and

(b)   the application has not been disposed of,

the prospective adopters are not required by virtue of paragraph (1) to deliver the child unless the court so orders.

(4)   This regulation does not affect the exercise by any local authority or other person of any power conferred by any enactment or the exercise of any power of arrest.

Breakdown of placement

31.—(1)   This regulation applies where—

(a)   notification is given by the prospective adopters under regulation 29 that they do not wish to proceed with the adoption;

(b)   the child is withdrawn from the prospective adopters under regulation 30 or is otherwise removed by the relevant local authority under any other power competent to it;

(c)   an application for a Convention adoption order is refused;

(d)   a Convention adoption which is subject to a probationary period cannot be made; or

(e)   a Convention adoption order or a Convention adoption is annulled pursuant to section 68(1) of the Act.

(2)   Where the relevant local authority is satisfied that it would be in the child's best interests to be placed for adoption with other prospective adopters habitually resident in the United Kingdom, the authority must take the necessary measures to identify suitable adoptive parents for the child.

(3)   Where the relevant local authority has identified and approved other prospective adopters who are eligible to adopt and who have been assessed as suitable to be adoptive parents in accordance with these Regulations, or their equivalent applying elsewhere in the British Islands, the authority must notify the Central Authority in writing that—

(a)   other prospective adopters have been identified; and

(b)   regulations 13 to 18, 20 and 21 have been complied with in respect of the other prospective adopters.

(4)   Where the Central Authority has been notified in accordance with paragraph (3)(a), the Authority must—

(a)   inform the CA of the State of origin of the proposed placement; and

(b)   seek to reach agreement under Article 17(c) of the Convention with the CA of the State of origin in accordance with the provisions in this Chapter.

(5)   Where the relevant local authority—

(a)   is not satisfied as mentioned in paragraph (2); or

(b)   is so satisfied but is unable to identify and approve other prospective adopters as mentioned in paragraph (3),

the authority must liaise with the Central Authority to arrange for the return of the child to the child's State of origin.

(6)   Before coming to any decision under this regulation, the relevant local authority must—

(a)   have regard to the wishes and feelings of the child (taking into account the child's age and understanding); and

(b)   where appropriate, obtain the child's consent in relation to measures to be taken under this regulation.

Convention adoptions subject to a probationary period

32.—(1) Paragraph (2) applies where—

    (a) the child has been placed with the prospective adopters by the competent authority of the State of origin in that State and a Convention adoption has been applied for by the prospective adopters in the State of origin, but the placement is subject to a probationary period before the Convention adoption is made; and

    (b) the prospective adopters return to Scotland with the child before the probationary period is completed and before the Convention adoption is made in the State of origin.

(2) The relevant local authority must, if requested by the competent authority of the State of origin, submit a report about the placement to the competent authority; and such a report must be prepared within such timescales, and contain such information, as the competent authority may reasonably require.

(3) The reference in paragraph (1)(b) to prospective adopters includes a reference to any nominee mentioned in regulation 23(2).

Report of local authority investigation

33. The report of the investigation which a local authority must submit to the court in accordance with section 19(2) of the Act must include—

    (a) confirmation that the certificate of eligibility and approval mentioned in paragraph (5)(a) of regulation 20 has been sent to the CA of the State of origin in accordance with paragraph (4) of that regulation;

    (b) the date on which the agreement under Article 17(c) of the Convention was made; and

    (c) details of the reports of the visits and reviews made in accordance with regulation 5 as modified by regulation 27.

Convention adoption order

34. An adoption order may not be made as a Convention adoption order unless—

    (a) in the case of—

      (i) an application for the order by a relevant couple, both members of the couple have been habitually resident in any part of the British Islands for a period of not less than one year ending with the date of the application; or

      (ii) an application for the order by one person, the applicant has been habitually resident in any part of the British Islands for a period of not less than one year ending with the date of the application;

    (b) the child to be adopted was, on the date on which the agreement under Article 17(c) of the Convention was made, habitually resident in a Convention country outwith the British Islands;

    (c) copies of the Article 16 Information and the agreement under Article 17(c) of the Convention are made available to the court; and

    (d) in a case where one member of a relevant couple (in the case of an application by a relevant couple) or the applicant (in the case of an application by one person) is not a British citizen, the Home Office has confirmed that the child is authorised to enter and reside permanently in the United Kingdom.

Requirements following a Convention adoption order or a Convention adoption

35.—(1) Where a Convention adoption order is made by a court in Scotland, the court must send a copy of the order to the Central Authority.

(2) On receipt of a copy of the order under paragraph (1), the Central Authority must issue a certificate in the form set out in Schedule 3 certifying that the adoption has been made in accordance with the Convention.

(3) A copy of the certificate issued under paragraph (2) must be sent to—

    (a) the CA of the State of origin;

(b)   the adoptive parents; and
(c)   the adoption agency and, if different, the relevant local authority.
(4)   Where a Convention adoption is made and the Central Authority receives a certificate under Article 23(17) of the Convention in respect of that Convention adoption, the Central Authority must send a copy of that certificate to—
(a)   the adoptive parents; and
(b)   the adoption agency and, if different, the relevant local authority.

Convention adoption order: refusal or withdrawal

36.—(1)   Where an application for a Convention adoption order is refused by the court, the prospective adopters must deliver the child to the relevant local authority within the period determined by the court.
(2)   Paragraphs (3) and (4) apply where an application for a Convention adoption order in respect of a child is withdrawn by the prospective adopters.
(3)   Where the prospective adopters do not submit a fresh application for a Convention adoption order in respect of the child within 28 days of the withdrawal (or such longer period as the relevant local authority may agree in writing) they must deliver the child to the relevant local authority within 7 days of the expiry of the 28 day period or, as the case may be, such longer period.
(4)   But where the prospective adopters notify the adoption agency that they do not intend to submit a fresh application for a Convention adoption order in respect of the child, they must deliver the child to the relevant local authority within 7 days of such notification.

Annulment of Convention adoption order or Convention adoption

37.   Where a Convention adoption order or a Convention adoption is annulled under section 68(1) of the Act—
(a)   the court must send a copy of the order effecting the annulment to the Central Authority; and
(b)   the Central Authority must then send a copy of the order to the CA of the State of origin.

Chapter 2
Procedure in Scotland where the United Kingdom is the State of Origin

Application of Chapter 2

38.   The provisions of this Chapter apply to—
(a)   a child who is habitually resident in the British Islands;
(b)   a person, or a relevant couple, habitually resident outwith the British Islands who wishes to adopt such a child in accordance with the Convention.

Counselling and information for the child

39.—(1)   Where an adoption agency is considering whether a child is suitable for an adoption in accordance with the Convention, it must so far as reasonably practicable—
(a)   ensure that such counselling as may be necessary in connection with such an adoption is made available to the child;
(b)   explain to the child in an appropriate manner the procedure in relation to, and the legal implications of, adoption in accordance with the Convention for the child by prospective adopters habitually resident in the receiving State; and
(c)   provide the child with written information about the matters referred to in sub-paragraph (b).
(2)   Paragraph (1) does not apply if the adoption agency is satisfied that the requirements in that paragraph have been met in respect of the child by another adoption agency.

Counselling and information for parent or guardian and counselling for others
40.—(1)   Where an adoption agency is considering whether a child is suitable for an adoption in accordance with the Convention, it must—
    (a)   ensure that such counselling as may be necessary in connection with an adoption in accordance with the Convention is made available to—
        (i)   the parent or guardian of the child; and
        (ii)   any individual who has any parental responsibilities or parental rights in relation to the child;
    (b)   explain to the parent or guardian the procedure in relation to, and the legal implications of, adoption in accordance with the Convention by prospective adopters habitually resident in the receiving State; and
    (c)   provide the parent or guardian with written information about the matters referred to in sub-paragraph (b).
(2)   Paragraph (1) does not apply—
    (a)   if the adoption agency is satisfied that the requirements in that paragraph have been met in respect of the parent, guardian or, as the case may be, individual mentioned in sub-paragraph (a)(ii) of that paragraph by another adoption agency;
    (b)   to the father of the child if, after reasonable steps have been taken by the adoption agency, his identity cannot be ascertained.

Information for inclusion in report and for adoption panel
41.—(1)   The report mentioned in regulation 18(1)(i) of the Adoption Agencies Regulations must include—
    (a)   a summary of the possibilities (if any) for placement of the child for adoption within the United Kingdom; and
    (b)   an assessment of whether an adoption by a person in a particular receiving State is in the child's best interests.
(2)   The adoption agency must refer the child's case to the adoption panel and send to the panel—
    (a)   if received, the report from the CA of the receiving State which has been prepared for the purposes of Article 15 of the Convention (in this Chapter, the 'Article 15 Report');
    (b)   the agency's observations on any Article 15 report; and
    (c)   copies of—
        (i)   the report on the health of the child mentioned in regulation 18(1)(d) of the Adoption Agencies Regulations and any report obtained in accordance with regulation 18(2) of those Regulations; and
        (ii)   the report mentioned in regulation 18(1)(i) of those Regulations.

Function of the adoption panel in assessing the child
42.—(1)   The adoption panel must consider the case of the child and make a recommendation to the adoption agency as to whether adoption by a person, or a relevant couple, habitually resident in a Convention country outwith the British Islands is in the best interests of the child.
(2)   In considering what recommendation to make under paragraph (1), the adoption panel must—
    (a)   have regard to the duties imposed on an adoption agency by section 14 of the Act (considerations applying to the exercise of powers);
    (b)   take into account all the information and reports passed to it under regulation 41;
    (c)   request the adoption agency to obtain any other relevant information which the panel considers necessary; and
    (d)   obtain such legal advice in relation to the case as may be necessary.

Decision and notification

43.—(1) The adoption agency must—

(a) take into account the recommendation of the adoption panel in coming to a decision ('the decision') on whether adoption by a person, or a relevant couple, habitually resident in a Convention country outwith the British Islands is in the best interests of the child; and

(b) make the decision within 14 days of the date the recommendation was made.

(2) No member of the adoption panel which made the recommendation is to take part in the decision.

(3) Where the decision is that adoption is in the best interests of the child, the adoption agency must, within 7 days of making the decision, notify the Central Authority of—

(a) the name and age of the child;

(b) the reasons why the agency considers that the child may be suitable for adoption by a person, or a relevant couple, habitually resident in a Convention country outside the British Islands; and

(c) any other information that the Central Authority may require.

(4) The adoption agency must within 7 days of the day on which the decision is made notify in writing the parent or guardian of the child, and any individual who has any parental responsibilities or parental rights in relation to the child, that the child has been approved in principle for adoption in a Convention country outwith the British Islands.

(5) Paragraph (4) does not apply if, after reasonable steps have been taken by the adoption agency, the identity of the parent, guardian or individual cannot be ascertained.

Convention list

44.—(1) The Central Authority must—

(a) maintain a list of children (in this Chapter, the 'Convention list') in respect of whom it is given notification under regulation 43(3); and

(b) make the contents of the Convention list available for inspection by the other Central Authorities within the British Islands on request.

(2) Where an adoption agency—

(a) places for adoption a child in respect of whom notification under regulation 43(3) has been given to the Central Authority; or

(b) determines that an adoption in accordance with the Convention is no longer in the best interests of the child,

the agency must notify the Central Authority accordingly and the Authority must remove the details relating to that child from the Convention list.

Receipt of Article 15 Report

45.—(1) This regulation applies where—

(a) the Central Authority receives from the CA of the receiving State an Article 15 Report which relates to a prospective adopter who is habitually resident in that receiving State (a 'Convention prospective adopter'); and

(b) the Convention prospective adopter wishes to adopt a child who is habitually resident in the British Islands.

(2) Subject to paragraph (3), if the Central Authority is satisfied that the Convention prospective adopter meets—

(a) the age requirements specified in section 29 of the Act (in the case of a relevant couple) or section 30 of the Act (in the case of adoption by one person); and

(b) in the case of adoption by a relevant couple, both members of the couple are, or in the case of adoption by one person, that person is, habitually resident in a Convention country outwith the British Islands,

the Central Authority must consult the Convention list and may, if the Authority considers it appropriate, consult any list of children notified to any other Central Authority within the British Islands in accordance with provisions which correspond to regulation 44(1) (a 'Convention list equivalent').

(3)   Where a Convention prospective adopter has already been identified in relation to a proposed adoption of a particular child and the Central Authority is satisfied that the Convention prospective adopter meets the requirements in paragraph (2)(a) and (b), the Authority—

(a)   need not consult the Convention list; and

(b)   must send the Article 15 Report to the adoption agency which notified the Central Authority of the child's details.

(4)   The Central Authority may pass a copy of the Article 15 Report to any other Central Authority within the British Islands for the purpose of enabling the other Central Authority to consult its Convention list equivalent.

(5)   Where the Central Authority identifies a child on the Convention list who may be suitable for adoption by the Convention prospective adopter, the Authority must send the Article 15 Report to the adoption agency which notified the Authority of the child's details.

(6)   In considering whether it is appropriate to place the child for adoption with the Convention prospective adopter, the adoption agency must take into account the Article 15 Report.

(7)   Where the adoption agency considers such a placement appropriate, it must refer the proposed placement to the adoption panel together with—

(a)   the Article 15 Report;

(b)   the documents referred to in sub-paragraphs (b) and (c) of regulation 41(2);

(c)   its observations on the proposed adoption; and

(d)   any other relevant information about the child.

Proposed placement: functions of adoption panel and adoption agency

46.—(1)   The adoption panel must consider the proposed placement referred to it by an adoption agency under regulation 45(7) and make a recommendation to the agency as to whether—

(a)   the Convention prospective adopter is suitable to be an adoptive parent for the child; and

(b)   the proposed placement is in the best interests of the child.

(2)   In considering what recommendation to make under paragraph (1), the adoption panel—

(a)   must have regard to—

(i)   the child's upbringing and ethnic, religious and cultural background;

(ii)   the duties imposed on the adoption agency by section 14 of the Act (considerations applying to the exercise of powers); and

(iii)   the documents referred to it under regulation 45(7);

(b)   may ask the adoption agency to obtain any other relevant information which the panel considers necessary; and

(c)   may obtain legal advice in relation to the case.

(3)   The adoption agency must—

(a)   take into account the recommendation of the adoption panel in coming to a decision ('the decision') about whether the proposed placement should proceed or not; and

(b)   make the decision within 14 days of the date the recommendation was made.

(4)   No member of the adoption panel which made the recommendation is to take part in the decision.

(5)   Paragraphs (6) to (8) apply where the decision is that the proposed placement should proceed.

(6)   The adoption agency must, if practicable, within 7 days of making the deci-

sion, notify in writing the parent or guardian of the child, and any individual who has any parental responsibilities or parental rights in relation to the child, that the child has been or, as the case may be, is to be placed for adoption in a Convention country outwith the British Islands.

(7)   Where the adoption agency is a local authority it must—

(a)   make an application to the appropriate court for a permanence order; and

(b)   in the application, request that the order include—

(i) ancillary provisions vesting in the local authority the parental responsibilities and parental rights referred to in paragraph (a) of subsection (1) of section 82 of the Act (permanence orders: ancillary provisions); and

(ii) provision granting authority for the child to be adopted.

(8)   Where the adoption agency is not a local authority, the agency must notify the local authority for the area where the child has a home of its decision; and that local authority must make an application and request as mentioned in paragraph (7).

(9)   An application under paragraph (7) must be made—

(a)   where notification is given under paragraph (6), within 28 days of the adoption agency giving such notification;

(b)   where notification is not given under that paragraph, within 28 days of the adoption agency making the decision.

(10)   An application under paragraph (8) must be made within 28 days of the local authority being notified under that paragraph.

Adoption agency's decision: notification and return of documents

47.—(1)   As soon as possible after the adoption agency makes a decision under regulation 46(3), it must notify the Central Authority of the decision.

(2)   If the proposed placement is not to proceed—

(a)   the adoption agency must return the Article 15 Report and any other documents or information sent to it by the Central Authority to that Authority; and

(b)   the Central Authority must then send the Article 15 Report and any such documents or information to the CA of the receiving State.

Preparation of the Article 16 Report

48.—(1)   If the adoption agency decides that the proposed adoption should proceed, it must prepare a report for the purposes of Article 16 of the Convention (the 'Article 16 Report') which must include—

(a)   the information about the child specified in Part II of Schedule 1 to the Adoption Agencies Regulations; and

(b)   the reasons for the agency's decision.

(2)   Where a permanence order including provision granting authority for the child to be adopted is made the adoption agency must, within 14 days of the order being made, send to the Central Authority—

(a)   the Article 16 Report;

(b)   details of the permanence order; and

(c)   where known, details of any other orders made by the courts in relation to the child.

(3)   The Central Authority must then send to the CA of the receiving State—

(a)   the Article 16 Report; and

(b)   the other information sent to it by virtue of paragraph (2).

(4)   Where a court does not grant an application for a permanence order as mentioned in paragraph (2) the adoption agency must, within 14 days of the decision of the court, notify the Central Authority of the decision.

Requirements to be met before child placed with Convention prospective adopter

49.—(1)   The Central Authority may notify the CA of the receiving State that it is prepared to agree that the proposed adoption should proceed provided the CA of the receiving State has confirmed that—

(a)   the Convention prospective adopter has agreed to adopt the child and has received such counselling as may be necessary;

(b)   the Convention prospective adopter has confirmed that—

(i) the Convention prospective adopter will accompany the child to the receiving State unless, in the case of a relevant couple, the adoption agency and the CA of the receiving State have agreed that it is necessary for only one member of the relevant couple to do so; or

(ii) in exceptional circumstances, the child will be accompanied to the receiving State by a nominee of the Convention prospective adopter who has been approved by the adoption agency;

(c)   it is content for the proposed adoption to proceed;

(d)   in the case where a Convention adoption is to be effected, it has explained to the Convention prospective adopter the need to make an application under section 59(1) of the Act; and

(e)   the child is or will be authorised to enter and reside permanently in the Convention country if a Convention adoption is effected or a Convention adoption order is made.

(2)   The Central Authority may not make an agreement with the CA of the receiving State under Article 17(c) of the Convention unless—

(a)   confirmation has been received in respect of the matters referred to in paragraph (1);

(b)   the adoption agency has confirmed to the Central Authority that—

(i) it has met the Convention prospective adopter and explained the requirement to make an application under section 59(1) of the Act before the child can be taken or sent out of Great Britain;

(ii) the Convention prospective adopter or, where the Convention prospective adopter is a relevant couple and there are exceptional circumstances, one member of the couple has visited the child; and

(iii) the Convention prospective adopter is content for the proposed adoption to proceed.

(3)   The adoption agency may not place the child for adoption with the Convention prospective adopter unless the agreement under Article 17(c) of the Convention has been made; and the Central Authority must advise the agency when the agreement has been made.

Requirements for order under section 59 of the Act prior to proposed Convention adoption

50.—(1)   This regulation prescribes, for the purposes of subsection (3) of section 59 of the Act (preliminary order where child to be adopted abroad), the requirements to be satisfied before an order under that section may be made in the case where the prospective adopters (within the meaning of that section) intend to adopt a child under a Convention adoption.

(2)   This regulation applies in the case of a child placed for adoption with the prospective adopters by an adoption agency.

(3)   The requirements are that—

(a)   the competent authorities of the receiving State have—

(i) prepared an Article 15 report;

(ii) determined and confirmed in writing that the prospective adopters are eligible and suitable to adopt;

(iii) ensured and confirmed in writing that the prospective adopters have been counselled as may be necessary; and

(iv) determined and confirmed in writing that the child is or will be authorised to enter and reside permanently in the receiving State;

(b)   the report required for the purposes of Article 16(1) of the Convention has been prepared by the adoption agency;

(c)   the adoption agency confirms in writing to the court that it has complied with the requirements imposed on it under Parts IV and V of the Adoption Agencies Regulations;

(d)   the adoption agency has obtained and made available to the court—

(i)   a copy of the recommendations of the adoption panel under regulation 46(1);

(ii)   a copy of the report on the health of the child mentioned in regulation 18(1)(d) of the Adoption Agencies Regulations and any report obtained in accordance with regulation 18(2) of those Regulations;

(iii)   a copy of the report and information mentioned in regulation 18(1)(i) of those Regulations; and

(iv)   a copy of the permanence order including provision granting authority for the child to be adopted;

(e)   the adoption agency includes in any report submitted to the court in accordance with subsection (2) of section 17 of the Act (reports where child placed by agency), or subsection (2) of section 19 of the Act (notice under section 18: local authority's duties) (as those sections fall to be construed by virtue of the modifications in regulation 9), details of—

(i)   visits carried out under regulation 25(1) of the Adoption Agencies Regulations; and

(ii)   any reviews carried out under regulation 26(2) of those Regulations;

(f)   in a case where there is only one prospective adopter, the prospective adopter has confirmed in writing to the adoption agency that the prospective adopter will accompany the child out of Great Britain and into the receiving State; and

(g)   in a case where the prospective adopters are a relevant couple, they have confirmed in writing to the adoption agency—

(i)   that both members of the relevant couple will so accompany the child; or

(ii)   if the adoption agency and the competent authority of the receiving State have confirmed that it is necessary for only one such member so to accompany the child, that one such member will do so.

Convention adoption order

51.   An adoption order may not be made as a Convention adoption order unless—

(a)   in the case of—

(i)   an application for the order by a relevant couple, both members of the couple have been habitually resident in a Convention country outwith the British Islands for a period of not less than one year ending with the date of the application;

(ii)   an application for the order by one person, the applicant has been habitually resident in a Convention country outwith the British Islands for a period of not less than one year ending with the date of the application;

(b)   the child to be adopted was, on the date on which the agreement under Article 17(c) of the Convention was made, habitually resident in any part of the British Islands;

(c)   copies of the Article 16 Report (within the meaning of regulation 48) and the agreement under Article 17(c) of the Convention are made available to the court; and

(d)   the competent authority of the receiving State has confirmed that the child is authorised to enter and remain permanently in the Convention country in which the applicant is or, as the case may be, the applicants are habitually resident.

Requirements following a Convention adoption order or a Convention adoption

52.—(1)　Where a Convention adoption order is made by a court in Scotland, the court must send a copy of the order to the Central Authority.

(2)　On receipt of a copy of the order under paragraph (1), the Central Authority must issue a certificate in the form set out in Schedule 3 certifying that the adoption has been made in accordance with the Convention.

(3)　A copy of the certificate issued under paragraph (2) must be sent to—
    (a)　the CA of the receiving State; and
    (b)　the relevant local authority.

(4)　Where a Convention adoption is made and the Central Authority receives a certificate under Article 23 of the Convention in respect of that Convention adoption, the Central Authority must send a copy of that certificate to—
    (a)　the adoption agency which sent the Central Authority the Article 16 Report under regulation 48(2); and
    (b)　the Registrar General of Births, Deaths and Marriages for Scotland.

Chapter 3
Miscellaneous Provisions

Application of the Act to, and making of, Convention adoption orders

53.—(1)　Subject to the modifications provided for in this Chapter, the provisions of the Act apply to Convention adoption orders so far as the nature of the provision permits and unless the contrary intention is shown.

(2)　Without prejudice to paragraph (1), an adoption order is to be made as a Convention adoption order if—
    (a)　the application is for a Convention adoption order; and
    (b)　the requirements specified in regulation 34 or, as the case may be, regulation 51 are complied with.

Notification to local authority of adoption application

54.　Section 18(1) of the Act applies as if for the words 'not placed for adoption with the applicants by an adoption agency' there were substituted 'entrusted to the applicants by a competent authority within the meaning of the Convention (other than an adoption agency which placed the child for adoption with the applicants).'.

Prohibition on removal where Convention adoption order pending

55.　Section 20 of the Act applies as if—
    (a)　for subsection (1) there were substituted—
    '(1) Where an application for a Convention adoption order in respect of a child has been made but not disposed of, a parent or guardian of the child is not entitled to remove the child from the care of the applicant except with the consent of the court.'; and
    (b)　subsection (2) were omitted.

Removal of children

56.—(1)　In a case falling within Chapter 1 of this Part, sections 21 to 23 of the Act do not apply.

(2)　In a case falling within Chapter 2 of this Part, section 21 of the Act applies as if—
    (a)　in subsection (4), references to an adoption order were references to a Convention adoption order; and
    (b)　subsection (6) were omitted.

Return or delivery of child

57.　As respects Convention adoption orders, the Act applies as if sections 25 and 26 were omitted.

Age of person in respect of whom Convention adoption order may be made
58.   Section 28(4) of the Act applies as if 'or over' were omitted.

Application for Convention adoption order by relevant couple
59.   Section 29 of the Act applies as if—
   (a)   in subsection (1)—
      (i)   'and' were inserted at the end of paragraph (a);
      (ii)   paragraph (c) and 'and' immediately preceding it were omitted; and
   (b)   subsection (2) were omitted.

Application for Convention adoption order by one person
60.   Section 30 of the Act applies as if subsections (1)(c), (3)(d) and (6) were omitted.

Convention adoption orders: consent
61.   As respects Convention adoption orders, the Act applies as if section 31 were omitted.

Application and modification of the Adoption Agencies Regulations
62.—(1)   Subject to paragraphs (2) and (3), the provisions of the Adoption Agencies Regulations apply to adoptions to be effected by a Convention adoption order or a Convention adoption, so far as the nature of the provision permits and unless the contrary intention is shown.
   (2)   In their application to such adoptions, the Adoption Agencies Regulations apply as if—
   (a)   regulations 6, 7, 8, 9, 10, 11, 14, 15, and 21 were omitted;
   (b)   in regulation 13—
      (i)   paragraphs (1) and (2) were omitted;
      (ii)   in paragraph (3) the references to a decision were to a decision mentioned in regulation 18(1) of these Regulations;
      (iii)   in that paragraph the reference to a recommendation were to a recommendation under regulation 17(1)(b) of these Regulations;
      (iv)   in paragraph (4) the reference to the decision under paragraph (1) of regulation 13 were a reference to a decision mentioned in regulation 18(1) of these Regulations; and
      (v)   in each of paragraphs (5) and (6) the references to a recommendation under regulation 6(2) were references to a recommendation under regulation 17(1)(b) of these Regulations; and
   (c)   in each of regulations 16(1) and 17(1), the references to a decision under regulation 13(1) were references to a decision mentioned in regulation 18(1) of these Regulations.
   (3)   In a case falling within Chapter 1 of this Part, the Adoption Agencies Regulations apply as if regulations 24 and 25 of those Regulations were omitted.

Offences
63.—(1)   Any person who contravenes or fails to comply with any of the regulations mentioned in paragraph (2) commits an offence and is liable on summary conviction to imprisonment for a term not exceeding three months, or a fine not exceeding level 5 on the standard scale, or both.
   (2)   The regulations are—
   (a)   regulation 26;
   (b)   regulation 29(1);
   (c)   regulation 30(1)(b);
   (d)   regulation 30(3); and
   (e)   regulation 36.

PART 4
REVOCATION

Revocation
64. The Intercountry Adoption (Hague Convention) (Scotland) Regulations 2003 are revoked.

PARENTAL RESPONSIBILITY AND MEASURES FOR THE PROTECTION OF CHILDREN (INTERNATIONAL OBLIGATIONS) (SCOTLAND) REGULATIONS 2010
(SSI 2010/213)*

For England and Wales, and Northern Ireland, see SI 2010/1898.

Citation, commencement and extent
1.—(1) These Regulations may be cited as the Parental Responsibility and Measures for the Protection of Children (International Obligations) (Scotland) Regulations 2010.

(2) These Regulations come into force on the day on which the Convention enters into force for the United Kingdom, which date will be notified in the London, Edinburgh and Belfast Gazettes.

(3) These Regulations extend to Scotland.

Interpretation
2. In these Regulations—

'Children's Hearing' has the meaning given by section 93(1) of the Children (Scotland) Act 1995;

'Contracting State' means a state party to the Convention;

'the Convention' means the Convention on Jurisdiction, Applicable Law, Recognition, Enforcement and Co-Operation in respect of Parental Responsibility and Measures for the Protection of Children that was signed at The Hague on 19 October 1996;

'the Council Regulation' means Council Regulation (EC) No. 2201/2003 concerning jurisdiction and the recognition and enforcement of judgments in matrimonial matters and the matters of parental responsibility;

'local authority' means a council constituted by section 2 of the Local Government etc. (Scotland) Act 1994;

'member State' means a member State of the European Union which is bound by the Council Regulation;

'the Principal Reporter' means the Principal Reporter within the meaning given in section 93(1) of the Children (Scotland) Act 1995;

'public authority' means a body whose functions are wholly or mainly of a public nature.

Power of court to recall sist under Article 8
3.—(1) This regulation applies where—

(a) a court has exercised its power under Article 8 of the Convention to request an authority of another Contracting State to assume jurisdiction in relation to an application, and

(b) the court has sisted proceedings on the application, and

(c) Part 1 of the Family Law Act 1986 does not apply in relation to the application.

(2) The court may recall a sist granted in order for it to exercise its powers under Article 8 of the Convention, and withdraw any request made by it under

that Article to an authority in another Contracting State to assume jurisdiction, if—

(a)   the authority in the other Contracting State does not assume jurisdiction within the period for which the court granted the sist, or

(b)   the parties do not, within the period specified by the court, request the authority in the other Contracting State to assume jurisdiction.

Local authorities: application to court to make request under Article 9

4.—(1)   This regulation applies where—

(a)   a local authority in Scotland wishes to make an application for a permanence order in respect of a child under section 80 of the Adoption and Children(Scotland)Act 2007; and

(b)   the authorities of another Contracting State have jurisdiction in respect of the child under the Convention.

(2)   The local authority must make an application to the court requesting the court to exercise its power under Article 9 of the Convention (request to competent authority of the Contracting State of the habitual residence of the child for authorisation to exercise jurisdiction).

Principal Reporters: application to refer a child to Children's Hearing

5.—(1)   This regulation applies where—

(a)   the Principal Reporter is obliged to refer a child to a Children's Hearing under section 65(1) of the Children (Scotland) Act 1995; and

(b)   the authorities of another Contracting State have jurisdiction in respect of the child under the Convention.

(2)   The Principal Reporter must through the Central Authority in Scotland make an application to the competent authority of the Contracting State in exercise of his power under Article 9 of the Convention (request to competent authority of the Contracting State of the habitual residence of the child for authorisation to exercise jurisdiction).

Application of Article 15

6.   The reference to Chapter II of the Convention in Article 15(1) of the Convention is to be read as including a reference to Chapter II of the Council Regulation.

Judicial authorities

7.—(1)   The Court of Session is to have jurisdiction to entertain an application under Article 24 of the Convention for recognition, or non-recognition, of a measure taken in another Contracting State.

(2)   But where the recognition or non-recognition of a measure is raised as an incidental question in another court, that court may determine the issue.

(3)   The Court of Session is also to have jurisdiction—

(a)   to register a measure taken in another Contracting State for enforcement under Article 26 of the Convention, and

(b)   to entertain an application for a declarator—

(i)   that a person has, or does not have, parental responsibility for a child by virtue of Article 16 of the Convention, or

(ii)   as to the extent of a person's parental responsibility for a child by virtue of that Article.

Central Authority in Scotland

8.—(1)   The functions under the Convention of a Central Authority in Scotland are to be discharged by the Scottish Ministers.

(2)   If a person outside the United Kingdom does not know to which Central Authority in the United Kingdom a communication should be addressed, the person may address it to the Lord Chancellor.

Information sharing

9.—(1)   Paragraph (2) applies if the Central Authority in Scotland receives a request for assistance under Article 31(c) of the Convention (either directly or via another Central Authority in the United Kingdom).

(2)   The Scottish Ministers may request information from—

(a)   a local authority in Scotland, or

(b)   a Health Board or Special Health Board (constituted by Order under section 2 of the National Health Service (Scotland) Act 1978).

(3)   A person who receives a request for information under this regulation must comply with the request as soon as reasonably practicable (but this is subject to Article 37 of the Convention).

Requests for information under Council Regulation

10.—(1)   This regulation applies if the designated Central Authority in Scotland under Article 53 of the Council Regulation receives a request for information from another member State under Article 55(a)(i) of the Council Regulation.

(2)   The designated Central Authority in Scotland may request information from—

(a)   a local authority in Scotland,

(b)   the Principal Reporter,

(c)   a safeguarder in respect of the child appointed under section 41(1)(b) of the Children (Scotland) Act 1995, or

(d)   a Health Board or Special Health Board (constituted by Order under section 2 of the National Health Service (Scotland) Act 1978).

(3)   A person who receives a request for information under this regulation must comply with the request as soon as reasonably practicable.

Power to request report on child's situation

11.—(1)   This regulation applies where a Central Authority thinks it appropriate to provide a report on the situation of a child under Article 32(a) of the Convention.

(2)   The Scottish Ministers may—

(a)   request a written report on the situation of the child from a local authority in Scotland, or

(b)   if a written report has been provided to a court in relation to the child, request a copy of the report from the court.

(3)   A person in Scotland who receives a request for a report under this regulation must comply with the request as soon as reasonably practicable (but this is subject to Article 37 of the Convention).

Local authorities and Children's Hearings: placement of child in another Contracting State

12.—(1)   This regulation applies if a local authority or Children's Hearing in Scotland is contemplating—

(a)   placing a child in another Contracting State, within the meaning given by Article 33 of the Convention, or

(b)   placing a child in another member State, within the meaning given by Article 56 of the Council Regulation.

(2)   This regulation applies if a Children's Hearing is contemplating—

(a)   making a supervision requirement under section 70(3)(a) of the Children (Scotland) Act 1995 requiring a child to reside in another Contracting State, within the meaning given by Article 33 of the Convention, or

(b)   making a supervision requirement under section 70(3)(a) of the Children (Scotland) Act 1995 requiring a child to reside in another member State, within the meaning given by Article 56 of the Council Regulation.

(3)   The local authority, or in the case of the Children's Hearing the Principal Reporter, whichever has jurisdiction under Articles 5 to 10 of the Convention or Articles 8 to 14 of the Council Regulation, as the case may be ('the authority')—

(a)   must provide through the Central Authority in Scotland a report to the

Central Authority, or other competent authority, of the other Contracting State in accordance with Article 33(1) of the Convention, if the authority is exercising jurisdiction under the Convention, or

(b)   must consult the Central Authority, or other competent authority, of the other member State in accordance with Article 56 of the Council Regulation, if the authority is exercising jurisdiction under the Council Regulation.

Power to respond to a request under Article 34

13.   A public authority in Scotland may provide information in response to a request communicated to it by the Central Authority under Article 34 of the Convention.

Services under Article 35

14.—(1)   The Scottish Ministers may charge a reasonable fee in respect of the provision of a service under Article 35 (1) or (2) of the Convention.

(2)   A request under Article 35(2) of the Convention is to be made to the local authority in whose area the parent making the request resides.

(3)   A local authority in Scotland may charge a reasonable fee for the provision of information or evidence under Article 35(2).

(4)   A fee is 'reasonable' for the purposes of this regulation if the income from fees of that kind equates as nearly as possible to the costs of providing the service to which the fees relate (including a reasonable share of expenditure which is referable only partly or only indirectly to the provision of that service).

...

INTERNATIONAL RECOVERY OF MAINTENANCE (HAGUE CONVENTION 2007) (SCOTLAND) REGULATIONS 2012 (SSI 2012/301)*

*See, for England and Wales, SI 2012/2814, and for Northern Ireland, NI 2012/413. For rules of court provision, see SI 2012/1770.

Citation, commencement and extent

1.—These Regulations—

(a)   may be cited as the International Recovery of Maintenance (Hague Convention 2007) (Scotland) Regulations 2012;

(b)   come into force on the day on which the Convention enters into force in respect of the European Union, which day is to be notified in the Edinburgh Gazette; and

(c)   extend to Scotland only.

Interpretation

2.—(1)   In these Regulations—

'Contracting State' means a State bound by the Convention other than an EU Member State;

'the Convention' means the Convention on the International Recovery of Child Support and other forms of Family Maintenance done at The Hague on 23rd November 2007;

'court', in relation to a maintenance decision given in a Contracting State, includes a tribunal, and any administrative authority (within the meaning of Article 19(3)) with competence to make a decision of a maintenance obligation; and

'maintenance decision' means a decision, or part of a decision, made by a court in a Contracting State, to which Chapter V of the Convention applies by virtue of Article 19(1).

(2)   In these Regulations, any reference to a numbered Article is a reference to the Article so numbered in the Convention and any reference to a sub-division of a numbered Article is to be construed accordingly.

Central Authority in relation to Scotland
3.—The Scottish Ministers are designated for the purposes of Article 4 as the Central Authority in relation to Scotland.

Recognition and enforcement in Scotland of maintenance decisions made by courts in Contracting States
4.—(1)   The court in Scotland to which an application for registration of a maintenance decision under the Convention is to be made is the sheriff court.

(2)   Jurisdiction in relation to an application for registration of a maintenance decision lies with the courts of Scotland if—

(a)   the person against whom enforcement is sought is resident in Scotland; or

(b)   assets belonging to that person and which are susceptible to enforcement are situated or held in Scotland.

(3)   Where jurisdiction in relation to an application for registration of a maintenance decision lies with the courts of Scotland, the Scottish Ministers are to transmit it to the sheriff court having jurisdiction in Scotland in accordance with Schedule 8 to the Civil Jurisdiction and Judgments Act 1982.

(4)   An application for registration is to be determined by the sheriff clerk of the registering court.

(5)   The determination of the sheriff clerk under paragraph (4) may be appealed to the sheriff by way of summary application.

(6)   The determination of the sheriff of a summary application under paragraph (5) may be subject to a final appeal on a point of law to the Inner House of the Court of Session.

(7)   For the purposes of enforcement of a maintenance decision registered under the Convention in the registering court—

(a)   the decision is of the same force and effect;

(b)   the registering court has in relation to its enforcement the same powers; and

(c)   proceedings for or with respect to its enforcement may be taken,

as if the decision had originally been made by the registering court.

(8)   Paragraph (7) is subject to—

(a)   regulation 5 (interest on debts under a maintenance decision); and

(b)   any provision made by rules of court as to the procedure for the enforcement of maintenance decisions registered in accordance with this regulation.

Interest on debts under a maintenance decision
5.—(1)   Where a person applying for registration of a maintenance decision shows that—

(a)   the decision provides for the payment of money; and

(b)   in accordance with the law of the Contracting State in which the maintenance decision was given and the terms of the decision, interest on that sum is recoverable at a particular rate and from a particular date or time,

the debt resulting from registration of the decision is to carry interest at that rate and from that date or time.

(2)   Interest is not recoverable under paragraph (1) unless the rate of interest and the date or time referred to in paragraph (1)(b) are registered with the decision.

(3)   Debts under a maintenance decision registered in a court in Scotland under the Convention are to carry interest only as provided for in this regulation.

Currency of payments under a maintenance decision
6.—(1)   Sums payable under a maintenance decision registered in a court in

Scotland under the Convention, including any arrears so payable, are to be paid in sterling.

(2)   Where the maintenance decision is expressed in any other currency, the amounts are to be converted on the basis of the exchange rate prevailing on the date on which the application for registration was received by the Scottish Ministers for transmission to a court.

(3)   For the purposes of this regulation, a written certificate purporting to be signed by an officer in any bank in Scotland and stating the exchange rate prevailing on a specified date is sufficient evidence of those facts.

Proof and admissibility of certain maintenance decisions and related documents

7.—(1)   For the purposes of proceedings relating to the Convention, a document that is duly authenticated and which purports to be a copy of a maintenance decision given by a court in a Contracting State is without further proof deemed to be a true copy, unless the contrary is shown.

(2)   A document purporting to be a copy of a maintenance decision given by a court in a Contracting State is duly authenticated for the purposes of this paragraph if it purports—

(a)   to bear the seal of that court; or

(b)   to be certified by any person in that person's capacity as a judge or officer of that court to be a true copy of a maintenance decision given by that court.

(3)   Nothing in this regulation is to prejudice the admission in evidence of any document which is admissible apart from this regulation.

Maintenance arrangements

8.—(1)   References in this regulation to maintenance arrangements are to those maintenance arrangements (as defined in Article 3(e)) which are to be recognised and enforceable in the same way as maintenance decisions by virtue of Article 30.

(2)   In relation to a maintenance arrangement which is enforceable as a maintenance decision in the Contracting State of origin, these Regulations apply, subject to the modifications in paragraph (3), as if that maintenance arrangement was a maintenance decision given by a court of that State.

(3)   The modifications are as follows—

(a)   regulation 4 (recognition and enforcement in Scotland of maintenance decisions made by courts in Contracting States) applies to maintenance arrangements as if—

(i)   in paragraph (7), for 'as if the decision had originally' there were substituted 'as if it were a decision which had originally'; and

(ii)   after paragraph (8)(b), there were inserted—

'(c)   Article 30(6) (restriction on enforcement where there is a challenge to a maintenance arrangement in the Contracting State of origin).';

(b)   regulation 5 (interest on debts under a maintenance decision) applies to maintenance arrangements as if, in paragraph (1)(b), for the word 'given' there were substituted 'concluded'; and

(c)   regulation 7 (proof and admissibility of certain maintenance decisions and related documents) applies to maintenance arrangements as if—

(i)   in paragraph (1), for 'given by a court' there were substituted 'formally drawn up or registered as an authentic instrument by, or authenticated by, or concluded, registered or filed with a competent authority'; and

(ii)   for paragraph (2) there were substituted—

'(2)   A document purporting to be a copy of a maintenance arrangement drawn up or registered as an authentic instrument by, or authenticated by, or concluded, registered or filed with a competent authority in a Contracting State is duly authenticated for the purposes of this paragraph if it purports to be certified to be a true copy of such an arrangement by a person duly authorised in that State to do so.'.

(4)   Section 18 (enforcement of UK judgments in other parts of UK) of the Civil Jurisdiction and Judgments Act 1982 does not apply to maintenance arrangements.

...

ADOPTION (RECOGNITION OF OVERSEAS ADOPTIONS) (SCOTLAND) REGULATIONS 2013
(SSI 2013/310)

Citation and commencement
1.   These Regulations may be cited as the Adoption (Recognition of Overseas Adoptions) (Scotland) Regulations 2013 and come into force on 3rd January 2014.

Interpretation
2.   In these Regulations 'law' does not include customary or common law.

Overseas adoptions
3.   An adoption of a child is specified as an overseas adoption if—
    (a)   it is an adoption effected under the law of a country or territory listed in the Schedule to these Regulations; and
    (b)   it is not a Convention adoption.

Evidence of an overseas adoption
4.—(1)   The following documents may be provided as evidence that an overseas adoption has been effected—
    (a)   a certified copy of an entry made, in accordance with the law of the country or territory concerned, in a public register relating to the recording of adoptions and showing that the adoption has been effected; or
    (b)   a certificate that the adoption has been effected, signed or purporting to be signed by a person authorised by the law of the country or territory concerned to sign a certificate, or a certified copy of such a certificate.

(2)   Where a document produced by virtue of paragraph (1) is not in English, the Registrar General may require the production of an English translation of the document before being satisfied of the matters specified in paragraph 6 of schedule 1 to the Adoption and Children (Scotland) Act 2007.

(3)   Nothing in this regulation may be construed as precluding proof, in accordance with the Evidence (Foreign, Dominion and Colonial Documents) Act 1933(2) or the Oaths and Evidence (Overseas Authorities and Countries) Act 1963(3) or otherwise, that an overseas adoption has been effected.

Revocation and saving
5.—(1)   Subject to paragraph (2), the following instruments are revoked—
    (a)   The Adoption (Designation of Overseas Adoptions) Order 1973(4); and
    (b)   The Adoption (Designation of Overseas Adoptions) (Variation) (Scotland) Order 1995.

(2)   The revocation of the Adoption (Designation of Overseas Adoptions) Order 1973 does not affect any adoption designated as an overseas adoption by virtue of that Order prior to the coming into force of these Regulations.

Regulation 3(a)

SCHEDULE

Albania
Andorra
Armenia
Australia
Austria
Azerbaijan
Belarus
Belgium
Belize
Bolivia
Brazil
Bulgaria
Burkina Faso
Burundi
Canada
Cape Verde
Chile
The People's Republic of China
Colombia
Costa Rica
Cuba
The Republic of Cyprus
Czech Republic
Denmark (including the Faroe Islands and
   Greenland)
Dominican Republic
Ecuador
El Salvador
Estonia
Fiji
Finland
France
Georgia
Germany
Greece
Guinea
Hungary
Iceland
India
The Republic of Ireland
Israel
Italy
Kazakhstan
Kenya
Latvia

Lesotho
Liechtenstein
Lithuania
Luxembourg
The Former Yugoslav Republic of Macedonia
Madagascar
Mali
Malta
Mauritius
Mexico
The Republic of Moldova
Monaco
Mongolia
Montenegro
The Netherlands (including the Caribbean
   part of the Netherlands (the islands of
   Bonaire, Sint Eustatius and Saba))
New Zealand
Norway
Panama
Paraguay
Peru
Philippines
Poland
Portugal
Romania
Rwanda
San Marino
Senegal
Seychelles
Slovakia
Slovenia
South Africa
Spain
Sri Lanka
Swaziland
Sweden
Switzerland
Thailand
Togo
Turkey
The United States of America
Uruguay
Venezuela
Vietnam

MARRIAGE (SAME SEX COUPLES) (JURISDICTION AND RECOGNITION OF JUDGMENTS) (SCOTLAND) REGULATIONS 2014
(SSI 2014/362)

Citation, commencement, extent and interpretation

1.—(1) These Regulations may be cited as the Marriage (Same Sex Couples) (Jurisdiction and Recognition of Judgments) (Scotland) Regulations 2014 and come into force on 16th December 2014.

(2) These Regulations extend to Scotland only.

(3) In these Regulations 'member State' means a member State of the European Union.

PART 1
JURISDICTION

Jurisdiction

2.—(1) In this Part—

'relevant foreign decree' means a decree of divorce of, nullity of the marriage of, or judicial separation of a married same sex couple granted outwith a member State.

(2) The courts in Scotland have jurisdiction in proceedings for the declarator of recognition, or non-recognition, of a relevant foreign decree and in proceedings for the divorce of, declarator of nullity of the marriage of, or judicial separation of a married same sex couple where—

(a) both spouses are habitually resident in Scotland;

(b) both spouses were last habitually resident in Scotland and one of the spouses continues to reside there;

(c) the defender is habitually resident in Scotland;

(d) the pursuer is habitually resident in Scotland and has resided there for at least one year immediately preceding the date on which the action is begun;

(e) the pursuer is domiciled and habitually resident in Scotland and has resided there for at least six months immediately preceding the date on which the action is begun; or

(f) both spouses are domiciled in Scotland.

PART 2
RECOGNITION AND REFUSAL OF RECOGNITION OF A JUDGMENT OF A COURT OF A MEMBER STATE

Interpretation and application

3.—(1) In this Part 'judgment' means a judgment of a court of a member State other than the United Kingdom which orders the divorce of, annulment of the marriage of, or the judicial separation of a married same sex couple.

(2) In paragraph (1) a 'court of a member State' means any authority, whether judicial or administrative, in a member State with jurisdiction in those matters falling within the scope of these Regulations.

(3) This Part applies to all judgments even if the date of the judgment is earlier than the date on which paragraph 2 of Schedule 1B to the Domicile and Matrimonial Proceedings Act 1973 and these Regulations come into force.

Recognition of a judgment

4.—(1) Subject to regulation 5, where a judgment is (or has been) given in respect of a marriage of a same sex couple, that judgment is to be recognised.

(2) Any interested party may apply to either the Court of Session or the sheriff court for a declarator of recognition or non-recognition of a judgment.

(3) Where the recognition of a judgment is raised as an incidental issue in proceedings before a court, that court may determine the issue.

Refusal of recognition of judgment

5.—(1) Recognition of the validity of a judgment may be refused if the judgment was obtained at a time when it was irreconcilable with a decision determining the question of the subsistence or validity of the marriage—

(a) previously given by a court of civil jurisdiction in Scotland; or

(b) previously given by a court elsewhere and recognised or entitled to be recognised in Scotland.

(2) Recognition of the validity of a judgment may be refused if the judgment was obtained at a time when the law of Scotland did not recognise marriages of same sex couples.

(3) Paragraph (2) does not prevent the recognition of a judgment if, at the time the judgment was obtained, the marriage would have been treated as a subsisting civil partnership according to the law of Scotland.

(4) Recognition of the validity of a judgment may be refused if—

(a) in the case of a judgment obtained by means of proceedings, it was obtained—

(i) without such steps having been taken for giving notice of the proceedings to a spouse as, having regard to the nature of the proceedings and all the circumstances, should reasonably have been taken; or

(ii) without a spouse having been given (for any reason other than lack of notice) such opportunity to take part in the proceedings as, having regard to those matters, that spouse should reasonably have been given; or

(b) in the case of a judgment obtained otherwise than by means of proceedings, there is no official document certifying the judgment is effective under the law of the country in which it was obtained; or

(c) in either case, recognition of the judgment would be manifestly contrary to public policy.

(5) In this regulation 'official', in relation to a document certifying that a judgment is effective under the law of any country, means issued by a person or a body appointed or recognised for the purpose under that law.

Jurisdiction and review

6.—(1) The court may not review the jurisdiction of the court which issued the judgment.

(2) A judgment may not be reviewed as to its substance.

Differences in applicable law

7. The recognition of a judgment may not be refused because the law of Scotland would not allow divorce, declarator of nullity or judicial separation on the same facts.

Sist of proceedings

8. Where recognition is sought of a judgment given in a member State and an appeal against that judgment has been lodged in that member State, the court may sist the proceedings.

PART IV

EU MATERIALS

CONSOLIDATED VERSION OF THE TREATY ON THE FUNCTIONING OF THE EUROPEAN UNION

OJ 2008 C115/47

PART THREE: UNION POLICIES AND INTERNAL ACTIONS; TITLE V: AREA OF FREEDOM, SECURITY AND JUSTICE

CHAPTER 3:
JUDICIAL COOPERATION IN CIVIL MATTERS

Article 81 (ex Article 65 TEC)

1.   The Union shall develop judicial cooperation in civil matters having cross-border implications, based on the principle of mutual recognition of judgments and of decisions in extrajudicial cases. Such cooperation may include the adoption of measures for the approximation of the laws and regulations of the Member States.

2.   For the purposes of paragraph 1, the European Parliament and the Council, acting in accordance with the ordinary legislative procedure, shall adopt measures, particularly when necessary for the proper functioning of the internal market, aimed at ensuring:

(a)   the mutual recognition and enforcement between Member States of judgments and of decisions in extrajudicial cases;

(b)   the cross-border service of judicial and extrajudicial documents;

(c)   the compatibility of the rules applicable in the Member States concerning conflict of laws and of jurisdiction;

(d)   cooperation in the taking of evidence;

(e)   effective access to justice;

(f)   the elimination of obstacles to the proper functioning of civil proceedings, if necessary by promoting the compatibility of the rules on civil procedure applicable in the Member States;

(g)   the development of alternative methods of dispute settlement;

(h)   support for the training of the judiciary and judicial staff.

3.   Notwithstanding paragraph 2, measures concerning family law with cross-border implications shall be established by the Council, acting in accordance with a special legislative procedure. The Council shall act unanimously after consulting the European Parliament.

The Council, on a proposal from the Commission, may adopt a decision determining those aspects of family law with cross-border implications which may be the subject of acts adopted by the ordinary legislative procedure. The Council shall act unanimously after consulting the European Parliament.

The proposal referred to in the second subparagraph shall be notified to the national Parliaments. If a national Parliament makes known its opposition within six months of the date of such notification, the decision shall not be adopted. In the absence of opposition, the Council may adopt the decision.

TREATY ESTABLISHING THE EUROPEAN COMMUNITY (AMSTERDAM CONSOLIDATED VERSION)

These provisions have been replaced by Article 81 of the Treaty on the Functioning of the European Union and are included for comparative purposes only.

OJ 1997 C340/173

TITLE IV(ex Title IIIa) VISAS, ASYLUM, IMMIGRATION AND OTHER POLICIES RELATED TO FREE MOVEMENT OF PERSONS

Article 61 (ex Article 73i)
In order to establish progressively an area of freedom, security and justice, the Council shall adopt:

...
   (c)   measures in the field of judicial cooperation in civil matters as provided for in Article 65;

...

Article 65 (ex Article 73m)
Measures in the field of judicial cooperation in civil matters having cross-border implications, to be taken in accordance with Article 67 and insofar as necessary for the proper functioning of the internal market, shall include:
   (a)   improving and simplifying:
   – the system for cross-border service of judicial and extrajudicial documents;
   – cooperation in the taking of evidence;
   – the recognition and enforcement of decisions in civil and commercial cases, including decisions in extrajudicial cases;
   (b)   promoting the compatibility of the rules applicable in the Member States concerning the conflict of laws and of jurisdiction;
   (c)   eliminating obstacles to the good functioning of civil proceedings, if necessary by promoting the compatibility of the rules on civil procedure applicable in the Member States.

CONSOLIDATED VERSIONS OF THE TREATY ON EUROPEAN UNION AND THE TREATY ON THE FUNCTIONING OF THE EUROPEAN UNION: PROTOCOLS—PROTOCOL (NO 21) ON THE POSITION OF THE UNITED KINGDOM AND IRELAND IN RESPECT OF THE AREA OF FREEDOM, SECURITY AND JUSTICE

Official Journal C 115, 09/05/2008 p 295

THE HIGH CONTRACTING PARTIES,
   DESIRING to settle certain questions relating to the United Kingdom and Ireland,
   HAVING REGARD to the Protocol on the application of certain aspects of Article 26 of the Treaty on the Functioning of the European Union to the United Kingdom and to Ireland,
   HAVE AGREED UPON the following provisions, which shall be annexed to the Treaty on European Union and the Treaty on the Functioning of the European Union:

Article 1
Subject to Article 3, the United Kingdom and Ireland shall not take part in the adoption by the Council of proposed measures pursuant to Title V of Part Three of the Treaty on the Functioning of the European Union. The unanimity of the

members of the Council, with the exception of the representatives of the governments of the United Kingdom and Ireland, shall be necessary for decisions of the
Council which must be adopted unanimously.

For the purposes of this Article, a qualified majority shall be defined in accordance with Article 238(3) of the Treaty on the Functioning of the European Union.

Article 2

In consequence of Article 1 and subject to Articles 3, 4 and 6, none of the provisions of Title V of Part Three of the Treaty on the Functioning of the European
Union, no measure adopted pursuant to that Title, no provision of any international agreement concluded by the Union pursuant to that Title, and no decision
of the Court of Justice interpreting any such provision or measure shall be binding
upon or applicable in the United Kingdom or Ireland; and no such provision, measure or decision shall in any way affect the competences, rights and obligations of
those States; and no such provision, measure or decision shall in any way affect
the Community or Union acquis nor form part of Union law as they apply to the
United Kingdom or Ireland.

Article 3

1.   The United Kingdom or Ireland may notify the President of the Council in
writing, within three months after a proposal or initiative has been presented to
the Council pursuant to Title V of Part Three of the Treaty on the Functioning of
the European Union, that it wishes to take part in the adoption and application of
any such proposed measure, whereupon that State shall be entitled to do so.

The unanimity of the members of the Council, with the exception of a member
which has not made such a notification, shall be necessary for decisions of the
Council which must be adopted unanimously. A measure adopted under this
paragraph shall be binding upon all Member States which took part in its
adoption.

Measures adopted pursuant to Article 70 of the Treaty on the Functioning of the
European Union shall lay down the conditions for the participation of the United
Kingdom and Ireland in the evaluations concerning the areas covered by Title V of
Part Three of that Treaty.

For the purposes of this Article, a qualified majority shall be defined in accordance with Article 238(3) of the Treaty on the Functioning of the European Union.

2.   If after a reasonable period of time a measure referred to in paragraph 1 cannot be adopted with the United Kingdom or Ireland taking part, the Council may
adopt such measure in accordance with Article 1 without the participation of the
United Kingdom or Ireland. In that case Article 2 applies.

Article 4

The United Kingdom or Ireland may at any time after the adoption of a measure
by the Council pursuant to Title V of Part Three of the Treaty on the Functioning
of the European Union notify its intention to the Council and to the Commission
that it wishes to accept that measure. In that case, the procedure provided for in
Article 331(1) of the Treaty on the Functioning of the European Union shall apply
mutatis mutandis.

Article 4a

1.   The provisions of this Protocol apply for the United Kingdom and Ireland
also to measures proposed or adopted pursuant to Title V of Part Three of the
Treaty on the Functioning of the European Union amending an existing measure
by which they are bound.

2.   However, in cases where the Council, acting on a proposal from the Commission, determines that the non-participation of the United Kingdom or Ireland
in the amended version of an existing measure makes the application of that
measure inoperable for other Member States or the Union, it may urge them to
make a notification under Article 3 or 4. For the purposes of Article 3, a further

period of two months starts to run as from the date of such determination by the Council.

If at the expiry of that period of two months from the Council's determination the United Kingdom or Ireland has not made a notification under Article 3 or Article 4, the existing measure shall no longer be binding upon or applicable to it, unless the Member State concerned has made a notification under Article 4 before the entry into force of the amending measure. This shall take effect from the date of entry into force of the amending measure or of expiry of the period of two months, whichever is the later.

For the purpose of this paragraph, the Council shall, after a full discussion of the matter, act by a qualified majority of its members representing the Member States participating or having participated in the adoption of the amending measure. A qualified majority of the Council shall be defined in accordance with Article 238(3)(a) of the Treaty on the Functioning of the European Union.

3. The Council, acting by a qualified majority on a proposal from the Commission, may determine that the United Kingdom or Ireland shall bear the direct financial consequences, if any, necessarily and unavoidably incurred as a result of the cessation of its participation in the existing measure.

4. This Article shall be without prejudice to Article 4.

Article 5
A Member State which is not bound by a measure adopted pursuant to Title V of Part Three of the Treaty on the Functioning of the European Union shall bear no financial consequences of that measure other than administrative costs entailed for the institutions, unless all members of the Council, acting unanimously after consulting the European Parliament, decide otherwise.

Article 6
Where, in cases referred to in this Protocol, the United Kingdom or Ireland is bound by a measure adopted by the Council pursuant to Title V of Part Three of the Treaty on the Functioning of the European Union, the relevant provisions of the Treaties shall apply to that State in relation to that measure.

Article 6a
The United Kingdom and Ireland shall not be bound by the rules laid down on the basis of Article 16 of the Treaty on the Functioning of the European Union which relate to the processing of personal data by the Member States when carrying out activities which fall within the scope of Chapter 4 or Chapter 5 of Title V of Part Three of that Treaty where the United Kingdom and Ireland are not bound by the rules governing the forms of judicial cooperation in criminal matters or police cooperation which require compliance with the provisions laid down on the basis of Article 16.

Article 7
Articles 3, 4 and 4a shall be without prejudice to the Protocol on the Schengen acquis integrated into the framework of the European Union.

Article 8
Ireland may notify the Council in writing that it no longer wishes to be covered by the terms of this Protocol. In that case, the normal treaty provisions will apply to Ireland.

Article 9
With regard to Ireland, this Protocol shall not apply to Article 75 of the Treaty on the Functioning of the European Union.

COUNCIL REGULATION (EC) NO 44/2001 OF 22 DECEMBER 2000 ON JURISDICTION AND THE RECOGNITION AND ENFORCEMENT OF JUDGMENTS IN CIVIL AND COMMERCIAL MATTERS ('BRUSSELS I REGULATION')

Official Journal L 12, 16/01/2001 p 1

THE COUNCIL OF THE EUROPEAN UNION,

Having regard to the Treaty establishing the European Community, and in particular Article 61(c) and Article 67(1) thereof,
   Having regard to the proposal from the Commission,
   Having regard to the opinion of the European Parliament,
   Having regard to the opinion of the Economic and Social Committee,

Whereas:
   (1)   The Community has set itself the objective of maintaining and developing an area of freedom, security and justice, in which the free movement of persons is ensured. In order to establish progressively such an area, the Community should adopt, amongst other things, the measures relating to judicial cooperation in civil matters which are necessary for the sound operation of the internal market.
   (2)   Certain differences between national rules governing jurisdiction and recognition of judgments hamper the sound operation of the internal market. Provisions to unify the rules of conflict of jurisdiction in civil and commercial matters and to simplify the formalities with a view to rapid and simple recognition and enforcement of judgments from Member States bound by this Regulation are essential.
   (3)   This area is within the field of judicial cooperation in civil matters within the meaning of Article 65 of the Treaty.
   (4)   In accordance with the principles of subsidiarity and proportionality as set out in Article 5 of the Treaty, the objectives of this Regulation cannot be sufficiently achieved by the Member States and can therefore be better achieved by the Community. This Regulation confines itself to the minimum required in order to achieve those objectives and does not go beyond what is necessary for that purpose.
   (5)   On 27 September 1968 the Member States, acting under Article 293, fourth indent, of the Treaty, concluded the Brussels Convention on Jurisdiction and the Enforcement of Judgments in Civil and Commercial Matters, as amended by Conventions on the Accession of the New Member States to that Convention (hereinafter referred to as the 'Brussels Convention'). On 16 September 1988 Member States and EFTA States concluded the Lugano Convention on Jurisdiction and the Enforcement of Judgments in Civil and Commercial Matters, which is a parallel Convention to the 1968 Brussels Convention. Work has been undertaken for the revision of those Conventions, and the Council has approved the content of the revised texts. Continuity in the results achieved in that revision should be ensured.
   (6)   In order to attain the objective of free movement of judgments in civil and commercial matters, it is necessary and appropriate that the rules governing jurisdiction and the recognition and enforcement of judgments be governed by a Community legal instrument which is binding and directly applicable.
   (7)   The scope of this Regulation must cover all the main civil and commercial matters apart from certain well-defined matters.
   (8)   There must be a link between proceedings to which this Regulation applies and the territory of the Member States bound by this Regulation. Accordingly common rules on jurisdiction should, in principle, apply when the defendant is domiciled in one of those Member States.
   (9)   A defendant not domiciled in a Member State is in general subject to national rules of jurisdiction applicable in the territory of the Member State of the court seised, and a defendant domiciled in a Member State not bound by this Regulation must remain subject to the Brussels Convention.

(10)   For the purposes of the free movement of judgments, judgments given in a Member State bound by this Regulation should be recognised and enforced in another Member State bound by this Regulation, even if the judgment debtor is domiciled in a third State.

(11)   The rules of jurisdiction must be highly predictable and founded on the principle that jurisdiction is generally based on the defendant's domicile and jurisdiction must always be available on this ground save in a few well-defined situations in which the subject-matter of the litigation or the autonomy of the parties warrants a different linking factor. The domicile of a legal person must be defined autonomously so as to make the common rules more transparent and avoid conflicts of jurisdiction.

(12)   In addition to the defendant's domicile, there should be alternative grounds of jurisdiction based on a close link between the court and the action or in order to facilitate the sound administration of justice.

(13)   In relation to insurance, consumer contracts and employment, the weaker party should be protected by rules of jurisdiction more favourable to his interests than the general rules provide for.

(14)   The autonomy of the parties to a contract, other than an insurance, consumer or employment contract, where only limited autonomy to determine the courts having jurisdiction is allowed, must be respected subject to the exclusive grounds of jurisdiction laid down in this Regulation.

(15)   In the interests of the harmonious administration of justice it is necessary to minimise the possibility of concurrent proceedings and to ensure that irreconcilable judgments will not be given in two Member States. There must be a clear and effective mechanism for resolving cases of lis pendens and related actions and for obviating problems flowing from national differences as to the determination of the time when a case is regarded as pending. For the purposes of this Regulation that time should be defined autonomously.

(16)   Mutual trust in the administration of justice in the Community justifies judgments given in a Member State being recognised automatically without the need for any procedure except in cases of dispute.

(17)   By virtue of the same principle of mutual trust, the procedure for making enforceable in one Member State a judgment given in another must be efficient and rapid. To that end, the declaration that a judgment is enforceable should be issued virtually automatically after purely formal checks of the documents supplied, without there being any possibility for the court to raise of its own motion any of the grounds for non-enforcement provided for by this Regulation.

(18)   However, respect for the rights of the defence means that the defendant should be able to appeal in an adversarial procedure, against the declaration of enforceability, if he considers one of the grounds for non-enforcement to be present. Redress procedures should also be available to the claimant where his application for a declaration of enforceability has been rejected.

(19)   Continuity between the Brussels Convention and this Regulation should be ensured, and transitional provisions should be laid down to that end. The same need for continuity applies as regards the interpretation of the Brussels Convention by the Court of Justice of the European Communities and the 1971 Protocol should remain applicable also to cases already pending when this Regulation enters into force.

(20)   The United Kingdom and Ireland, in accordance with Article 3 of the Protocol on the position of the United Kingdom and Ireland annexed to the Treaty on European Union and to the Treaty establishing the European Community, have given notice of their wish to take part in the adoption and application of this Regulation.

(21)   Denmark, in accordance with Articles 1 and 2 of the Protocol on the position of Denmark annexed to the Treaty on European Union and to the Treaty

establishing the European Community, is not participating in the adoption of this Regulation, and is therefore not bound by it nor subject to its application.*

(22)   Since the Brussels Convention remains in force in relations between Denmark and the Member States that are bound by this Regulation, both the Convention and the 1971 Protocol continue to apply between Denmark and the Member States bound by this Regulation.

(23)   The Brussels Convention also continues to apply to the territories of the Member States which fall within the territorial scope of that Convention and which are excluded from this Regulation pursuant to Article 299 of the Treaty.

(24)   Likewise for the sake of consistency, this Regulation should not affect rules governing jurisdiction and the recognition of judgments contained in specific Community instruments.

(25)   Respect for international commitments entered into by the Member States means that this Regulation should not affect conventions relating to specific matters to which the Member States are parties.

(26)   The necessary flexibility should be provided for in the basic rules of this Regulation in order to take account of the specific procedural rules of certain Member States. Certain provisions of the Protocol annexed to the Brussels Convention should accordingly be incorporated in this Regulation.

(27)   In order to allow a harmonious transition in certain areas which were the subject of special provisions in the Protocol annexed to the Brussels Convention, this Regulation lays down, for a transitional period, provisions taking into consideration the specific situation in certain Member States.

(28)   No later than five years after entry into force of this Regulation the Commission will present a report on its application and, if need be, submit proposals for adaptations.

(29)   The Commission will have to adjust Annexes I to IV on the rules of national jurisdiction, the courts or competent authorities and redress procedures available on the basis of the amendments forwarded by the Member State concerned; amendments made to Annexes V and VI should be adopted in accordance with Council Decision 1999/468/EC of 28 June 1999 laying down the procedures for the exercise of implementing powers conferred on the Commission,

HAS ADOPTED THIS REGULATION:

CHAPTER I
SCOPE

Article 1

1.   This Regulation shall apply in civil and commercial matters whatever the nature of the court or tribunal. It shall not extend, in particular, to revenue, customs or administrative matters.

2.   The Regulation shall not apply to:

   (a)   the status or legal capacity of natural persons, rights in property arising out of a matrimonial relationship, wills and succession;

   (b)   bankruptcy, proceedings relating to the winding-up of insolvent companies or other legal persons, judicial arrangements, compositions and analogous proceedings;

   (c)   social security;

   (d)   arbitration.

3.   In this Regulation, the term 'Member State' shall mean Member States with the exception of Denmark.

CHAPTER II
JURISDICTION

Section 1
General provisions

Article 2

1. Subject to this Regulation, persons domiciled in a Member State shall, whatever their nationality, be sued in the courts of that Member State.

2. Persons who are not nationals of the Member State in which they are domiciled shall be governed by the rules of jurisdiction applicable to nationals of that State.

Article 3

1. Persons domiciled in a Member State may be sued in the courts of another Member State only by virtue of the rules set out in Sections 2 to 7 of this Chapter.

2. In particular the rules of national jurisdiction set out in Annex I shall not be applicable as against them.

Article 4

1. If the defendant is not domiciled in a Member State, the jurisdiction of the courts of each Member State shall, subject to Articles 22 and 23, be determined by the law of that Member State.

2. As against such a defendant, any person domiciled in a Member State may, whatever his nationality, avail himself in that State of the rules of jurisdiction there in force, and in particular those specified in Annex I, in the same way as the nationals of that State.

Section 2
Special jurisdiction

Article 5

A person domiciled in a Member State may, in another Member State, be sued:

1. (a) in matters relating to a contract, in the courts for the place of performance of the obligation in question;

(b) for the purpose of this provision and unless otherwise agreed, the place of performance of the obligation in question shall be:

– in the case of the sale of goods, the place in a Member State where, under the contract, the goods were delivered or should have been delivered,

– in the case of the provision of services, the place in a Member State where, under the contract, the services were provided or should have been provided,

(c) if subparagraph (b) does not apply then subparagraph (a) applies;

2. in matters relating to maintenance, in the courts for the place where the maintenance creditor is domiciled or habitually resident or, if the matter is ancillary to proceedings concerning the status of a person, in the court which, according to its own law, has jurisdiction to entertain those proceedings, unless that jurisdiction is based solely on the nationality of one of the parties;

3. in matters relating to tort, delict or quasi-delict, in the courts for the place where the harmful event occurred or may occur;

4. as regards a civil claim for damages or restitution which is based on an act giving rise to criminal proceedings, in the court seised of those proceedings, to the extent that that court has jurisdiction under its own law to entertain civil proceedings;

5. as regards a dispute arising out of the operations of a branch, agency or other establishment, in the courts for the place in which the branch, agency or other establishment is situated;

6. as settlor, trustee or beneficiary of a trust created by the operation of a

statute, or by a written instrument, or created orally and evidenced in writing, in the courts of the Member State in which the trust is domiciled;

7. as regards a dispute concerning the payment of remuneration claimed in respect of the salvage of a cargo or freight, in the court under the authority of which the cargo or freight in question:

(a) has been arrested to secure such payment, or

(b) could have been so arrested, but bail or other security has been given; provided that this provision shall apply only if it is claimed that the defendant has an interest in the cargo or freight or had such an interest at the time of salvage.

Article 6

A person domiciled in a Member State may also be sued:

1. where he is one of a number of defendants, in the courts for the place where any one of them is domiciled, provided the claims are so closely connected that it is expedient to hear and determine them together to avoid the risk of irreconcilable judgments resulting from separate proceedings;

2. as a third party in an action on a warranty or guarantee or in any other third party proceedings, in the court seised of the original proceedings, unless these were instituted solely with the object of removing him from the jurisdiction of the court which would be competent in his case;

3. on a counter-claim arising from the same contract or facts on which the original claim was based, in the court in which the original claim is pending;

4. in matters relating to a contract, if the action may be combined with an action against the same defendant in matters relating to rights in rem in immovable property, in the court of the Member State in which the property is situated.

Article 7

Where by virtue of this Regulation a court of a Member State has jurisdiction in actions relating to liability from the use or operation of a ship, that court, or any other court substituted for this purpose by the internal law of that Member State, shall also have jurisdiction over claims for limitation of such liability.

Section 3
Jurisdiction in matters relating to insurance

Article 8

In matters relating to insurance, jurisdiction shall be determined by this Section, without prejudice to Article 4 and point 5 of Article 5.

Article 9

1. An insurer domiciled in a Member State may be sued:

(a) in the courts of the Member State where he is domiciled, or

(b) in another Member State, in the case of actions brought by the policyholder, the insured or a beneficiary, in the courts for the place where the plaintiff is domiciled,

(c) if he is a co-insurer, in the courts of a Member State in which proceedings are brought against the leading insurer.

2. An insurer who is not domiciled in a Member State but has a branch, agency or other establishment in one of the Member States shall, in disputes arising out of the operations of the branch, agency or establishment, be deemed to be domiciled in that Member State.

Article 10

In respect of liability insurance or insurance of immovable property, the insurer may in addition be sued in the courts for the place where the harmful event occurred. The same applies if movable and immovable property are covered by the same insurance policy and both are adversely affected by the same contingency.

Article 11

1. In respect of liability insurance, the insurer may also, if the law of the court permits it, be joined in proceedings which the injured party has brought against the insured.

2. Articles 8, 9 and 10 shall apply to actions brought by the injured party directly against the insurer, where such direct actions are permitted.

3. If the law governing such direct actions provides that the policyholder or the insured may be joined as a party to the action, the same court shall have jurisdiction over them.

Article 12

1. Without prejudice to Article 11(3), an insurer may bring proceedings only in the courts of the Member State in which the defendant is domiciled, irrespective of whether he is the policyholder, the insured or a beneficiary.

2. The provisions of this Section shall not affect the right to bring a counterclaim in the court in which, in accordance with this Section, the original claim is pending.

Article 13

The provisions of this Section may be departed from only by an agreement:

1. which is entered into after the dispute has arisen, or

2. which allows the policyholder, the insured or a beneficiary to bring proceedings in courts other than those indicated in this Section, or

3. which is concluded between a policyholder and an insurer, both of whom are at the time of conclusion of the contract domiciled or habitually resident in the same Member State, and which has the effect of conferring jurisdiction on the courts of that State even if the harmful event were to occur abroad, provided that such an agreement is not contrary to the law of that State, or

4. which is concluded with a policyholder who is not domiciled in a Member State, except in so far as the insurance is compulsory or relates to immovable property in a Member State, or

5. which relates to a contract of insurance in so far as it covers one or more of the risks set out in Article 14.

Article 14

The following are the risks referred to in Article 13(5):

1. any loss of or damage to:

(a) seagoing ships, installations situated offshore or on the high seas, or aircraft, arising from perils which relate to their use for commercial purposes;

(b) goods in transit other than passengers' baggage where the transit consists of or includes carriage by such ships or aircraft.

2. any liability, other than for bodily injury to passengers or loss of or damage to their baggage:

(a) arising out of the use or operation of ships, installations or aircraft as referred to in point 1(a) in so far as, in respect of the latter, the law of the Member State in which such aircraft are registered does not prohibit agreements on jurisdiction regarding insurance of such risks;

(b) for loss or damage caused by goods in transit as described in point 1(b).

3. any financial loss connected with the use or operation of ships, installations or aircraft as referred to in point 1(a), in particular loss of freight or charter-hire;

4. any risk or interest connected with any of those referred to in points 1 to 3;

5. notwithstanding points 1 to 4, all 'large risks' as defined in Council Directive 73/239/EEC, as amended by Council Directives 88/357/EEC and 90/618/EEC, as they may be amended.

Section 4
Jurisdiction over consumer contracts

Article 15

1. In matters relating to a contract concluded by a person, the consumer, for a purpose which can be regarded as being outside his trade or profession, jurisdiction shall be determined by this Section, without prejudice to Article 4 and point 5 of Article 5, if:

    (a)   it is a contract for the sale of goods on instalment credit terms; or

    (b)   it is a contract for a loan repayable by instalments, or for any other form of credit, made to finance the sale of goods; or

    (c)   in all other cases, the contract has been concluded with a person who pursues commercial or professional activities in the Member State of the consumer's domicile or, by any means, directs such activities to that Member State or to several States including that Member State, and the contract falls within the scope of such activities.

2. Where a consumer enters into a contract with a party who is not domiciled in the Member State but has a branch, agency or other establishment in one of the Member States, that party shall, in disputes arising out of the operations of the branch, agency or establishment, be deemed to be domiciled in that State.

3. This Section shall not apply to a contract of transport other than a contract which, for an inclusive price, provides for a combination of travel and accommodation.

Article 16

1. A consumer may bring proceedings against the other party to a contract either in the courts of the Member State in which that party is domiciled or in the courts for the place where the consumer is domiciled.

2. Proceedings may be brought against a consumer by the other party to the contract only in the courts of the Member State in which the consumer is domiciled.

3. This Article shall not affect the right to bring a counter-claim in the court in which, in accordance with this Section, the original claim is pending.

Article 17

The provisions of this Section may be departed from only by an agreement:

    1.   which is entered into after the dispute has arisen; or

    2.   which allows the consumer to bring proceedings in courts other than those indicated in this Section; or

    3.   which is entered into by the consumer and the other party to the contract, both of whom are at the time of conclusion of the contract domiciled or habitually resident in the same Member State, and which confers jurisdiction on the courts of that Member State, provided that such an agreement is not contrary to the law of that Member State.

Section 5
Jurisdiction over individual contracts of employment

Article 18

1. In matters relating to individual contracts of employment, jurisdiction shall be determined by this Section, without prejudice to Article 4 and point 5 of Article 5.

2. Where an employee enters into an individual contract of employment with an employer who is not domiciled in a Member State but has a branch, agency or other establishment in one of the Member States, the employer shall, in disputes arising out of the operations of the branch, agency or establishment, be deemed to be domiciled in that Member State.

Article 19

An employer domiciled in a Member State may be sued:

1.   in the courts of the Member State where he is domiciled; or
2.   in another Member State:
   (a)   in the courts for the place where the employee habitually carries out his
work or in the courts for the last place where he did so, or
   (b)   if the employee does not or did not habitually carry out his work in any
one country, in the courts for the place where the business which engaged the
employee is or was situated.

Article 20

1.   An employer may bring proceedings only in the courts of the Member State
in which the employee is domiciled.
2.   The provisions of this Section shall not affect the right to bring a counter-
claim in the court in which, in accordance with this Section, the original claim is
pending.

Article 21

The provisions of this Section may be departed from only by an agreement on
jurisdiction:
   1.   which is entered into after the dispute has arisen; or
   2.   which allows the employee to bring proceedings in courts other than those
indicated in this Section.

Section 6
Exclusive jurisdiction

Article 22

The following courts shall have exclusive jurisdiction, regardless of domicile:
   1.   in proceedings which have as their object rights in rem in immovable property or tenancies of immovable property, the courts of the Member State in which
the property is situated.
   However, in proceedings which have as their object tenancies of immovable
property concluded for temporary private use for a maximum period of six consecutive months, the courts of the Member State in which the defendant is domiciled shall also have jurisdiction, provided that the tenant is a natural person and
that the landlord and the tenant are domiciled in the same Member State;
   2.   in proceedings which have as their object the validity of the constitution, the
nullity or the dissolution of companies or other legal persons or associations of
natural or legal persons, or of the validity of the decisions of their organs, the
courts of the Member State in which the company, legal person or association has
its seat. In order to determine that seat, the court shall apply its rules of private
international law;
   3.   in proceedings which have as their object the validity of entries in public
registers, the courts of the Member State in which the register is kept;
   4.   in proceedings concerned with the registration or validity of patents, trade
marks, designs, or other similar rights required to be deposited or registered, the
courts of the Member State in which the deposit or registration has been applied
for, has taken place or is under the terms of a Community instrument or an international convention deemed to have taken place.
   Without prejudice to the jurisdiction of the European Patent Office under the
Convention on the Grant of European Patents, signed at Munich on 5 October
1973, the courts of each Member State shall have exclusive jurisdiction, regardless
of domicile, in proceedings concerned with the registration or validity of any
European patent granted for that State;
   5.   in proceedings concerned with the enforcement of judgments, the courts of
the Member State in which the judgment has been or is to be enforced.

Section 7
Prorogation of jurisdiction

Article 23

1.   If the parties, one or more of whom is domiciled in a Member State, have agreed that a court or the courts of a Member State are to have jurisdiction to settle any disputes which have arisen or which may arise in connection with a particular legal relationship, that court or those courts shall have jurisdiction. Such jurisdiction shall be exclusive unless the parties have agreed otherwise. Such an agreement conferring jurisdiction shall be either:

(a)   in writing or evidenced in writing; or

(b)   in a form which accords with practices which the parties have established between themselves; or

(c)   in international trade or commerce, in a form which accords with a usage of which the parties are or ought to have been aware and which in such trade or commerce is widely known to, and regularly observed by, parties to contracts of the type involved in the particular trade or commerce concerned.

2.   Any communication by electronic means which provides a durable record of the agreement shall be equivalent to 'writing'.

3.   Where such an agreement is concluded by parties, none of whom is domiciled in a Member State, the courts of other Member States shall have no jurisdiction over their disputes unless the court or courts chosen have declined jurisdiction.

4.   The court or courts of a Member State on which a trust instrument has conferred jurisdiction shall have exclusive jurisdiction in any proceedings brought against a settlor, trustee or beneficiary, if relations between these persons or their rights or obligations under the trust are involved.

5.   Agreements or provisions of a trust instrument conferring jurisdiction shall have no legal force if they are contrary to Articles 13, 17 or 21, or if the courts whose jurisdiction they purport to exclude have exclusive jurisdiction by virtue of Article 22.

Article 24

Apart from jurisdiction derived from other provisions of this Regulation, a court of a Member State before which a defendant enters an appearance shall have jurisdiction. This rule shall not apply where appearance was entered to contest the jurisdiction, or where another court has exclusive jurisdiction by virtue of Article 22.

Section 8
Examination as to jurisdiction and admissibility

Article 25

Where a court of a Member State is seised of a claim which is principally concerned with a matter over which the courts of another Member State have exclusive jurisdiction by virtue of Article 22, it shall declare of its own motion that it has no jurisdiction.

Article 26

1.   Where a defendant domiciled in one Member State is sued in a court of another Member State and does not enter an appearance, the court shall declare of its own motion that it has no jurisdiction unless its jurisdiction is derived from the provisions of this Regulation.

2.   The court shall stay the proceedings so long as it is not shown that the defendant has been able to receive the document instituting the proceedings or an equivalent document in sufficient time to enable him to arrange for his defence, or that all necessary steps have been taken to this end.

3.   Article 19 of Council Regulation (EC) No 1348/2000 of 29 May 2000 on the service in the Member States of judicial and extrajudicial documents in civil or

commercial matters shall apply instead of the provisions of paragraph 2 if the document instituting the proceedings or an equivalent document had to be transmitted from one Member State to another pursuant to this Regulation.

4.   Where the provisions of Regulation (EC) No 1348/2000 are not applicable, Article 15 of the Hague Convention of 15 November 1965 on the Service Abroad of Judicial and Extrajudicial Documents in Civil or Commercial Matters shall apply if the document instituting the proceedings or an equivalent document had to be transmitted pursuant to that Convention.

Section 9
Lis pendens—related actions

Article 27

1.   Where proceedings involving the same cause of action and between the same parties are brought in the courts of different Member States, any court other than the court first seised shall of its own motion stay its proceedings until such time as the jurisdiction of the court first seised is established.

2.   Where the jurisdiction of the court first seised is established, any court other than the court first seised shall decline jurisdiction in favour of that court.

Article 28

1.   Where related actions are pending in the courts of different Member States, any court other than the court first seised may stay its proceedings.

2.   Where these actions are pending at first instance, any court other than the court first seised may also, on the application of one of the parties, decline jurisdiction if the court first seised has jurisdiction over the actions in question and its law permits the consolidation thereof.

3.   For the purposes of this Article, actions are deemed to be related where they are so closely connected that it is expedient to hear and determine them together to avoid the risk of irreconcilable judgments resulting from separate proceedings.

Article 29

Where actions come within the exclusive jurisdiction of several courts, any court other than the court first seised shall decline jurisdiction in favour of that court.

Article 30

For the purposes of this Section, a court shall be deemed to be seised:

1.   at the time when the document instituting the proceedings or an equivalent document is lodged with the court, provided that the plaintiff has not subsequently failed to take the steps he was required to take to have service effected on the defendant, or

2.   if the document has to be served before being lodged with the court, at the time when it is received by the authority responsible for service, provided that the plaintiff has not subsequently failed to take the steps he was required to take to have the document lodged with the court.

Section 10
Provisional, including protective, measures

Article 31

Application may be made to the courts of a Member State for such provisional, including protective, measures as may be available under the law of that State, even if, under this Regulation, the courts of another Member State have jurisdiction as to the substance of the matter.

CHAPTER III
RECOGNITION AND ENFORCEMENT

Article 32
For the purposes of this Regulation, 'judgment' means any judgment given by a court or tribunal of a Member State, whatever the judgment may be called, including a decree, order, decision or writ of execution, as well as the determination of costs or expenses by an officer of the court.

Section 1
Recognition

Article 33
1.   A judgment given in a Member State shall be recognised in the other Member States without any special procedure being required.
2.   Any interested party who raises the recognition of a judgment as the principal issue in a dispute may, in accordance with the procedures provided for in Sections 2 and 3 of this Chapter, apply for a decision that the judgment be recognised.
3.   If the outcome of proceedings in a court of a Member State depends on the determination of an incidental question of recognition that court shall have jurisdiction over that question.

Article 34
A judgment shall not be recognised:
1.   if such recognition is manifestly contrary to public policy in the Member State in which recognition is sought;
2.   where it was given in default of appearance, if the defendant was not served with the document which instituted the proceedings or with an equivalent document in sufficient time and in such a way as to enable him to arrange for his defence, unless the defendant failed to commence proceedings to challenge the judgment when it was possible for him to do so;
3.   if it is irreconcilable with a judgment given in a dispute between the same parties in the Member State in which recognition is sought;
4.   if it is irreconcilable with an earlier judgment given in another Member State or in a third State involving the same cause of action and between the same parties, provided that the earlier judgment fulfils the conditions necessary for its recognition in the Member State addressed.

Article 35
1.   Moreover, a judgment shall not be recognised if it conflicts with Sections 3, 4 or 6 of Chapter II, or in a case provided for in Article 72.
2.   In its examination of the grounds of jurisdiction referred to in the foregoing paragraph, the court or authority applied to shall be bound by the findings of fact on which the court of the Member State of origin based its jurisdiction.
3.   Subject to the paragraph 1, the jurisdiction of the court of the Member State of origin may not be reviewed. The test of public policy referred to in point 1 of Article 34 may not be applied to the rules relating to jurisdiction.

Article 36
Under no circumstances may a foreign judgment be reviewed as to its substance.

Article 37
1.   A court of a Member State in which recognition is sought of a judgment given in another Member State may stay the proceedings if an ordinary appeal against the judgment has been lodged.

2. A court of a Member State in which recognition is sought of a judgment given in Ireland or the United Kingdom may stay the proceedings if enforcement is suspended in the State of origin, by reason of an appeal.

Section 2
Enforcement

Article 38

1. A judgment given in a Member State and enforceable in that State shall be enforced in another Member State when, on the application of any interested party, it has been declared enforceable there.

2. However, in the United Kingdom, such a judgment shall be enforced in England and Wales, in Scotland, or in Northern Ireland when, on the application of any interested party, it has been registered for enforcement in that part of the United Kingdom.

Article 39

1. The application shall be submitted to the court or competent authority indicated in the list in Annex II.

2. The local jurisdiction shall be determined by reference to the place of domicile of the party against whom enforcement is sought, or to the place of enforcement.

Article 40

1. The procedure for making the application shall be governed by the law of the Member State in which enforcement is sought.

2. The applicant must give an address for service of process within the area of jurisdiction of the court applied to. However, if the law of the Member State in which enforcement is sought does not provide for the furnishing of such an address, the applicant shall appoint a representative ad litem.

3. The documents referred to in Article 53 shall be attached to the application.

Article 41

The judgment shall be declared enforceable immediately on completion of the formalities in Article 53 without any review under Articles 34 and 35. The party against whom enforcement is sought shall not at this stage of the proceedings be entitled to make any submissions on the application.

Article 42

1. The decision on the application for a declaration of enforceability shall forthwith be brought to the notice of the applicant in accordance with the procedure laid down by the law of the Member State in which enforcement is sought.

2. The declaration of enforceability shall be served on the party against whom enforcement is sought, accompanied by the judgment, if not already served on that party.

Article 43

1. The decision on the application for a declaration of enforceability may be appealed against by either party.

2. The appeal is to be lodged with the court indicated in the list in Annex III.

3. The appeal shall be dealt with in accordance with the rules governing procedure in contradictory matters.

4. If the party against whom enforcement is sought fails to appear before the appellate court in proceedings concerning an appeal brought by the applicant, Article 26(2) to (4) shall apply even where the party against whom enforcement is sought is not domiciled in any of the Member States.

5. An appeal against the declaration of enforceability is to be lodged within one month of service thereof. If the party against whom enforcement is sought is domiciled in a Member State other than that in which the declaration of enforce-

ability was given, the time for appealing shall be two months and shall run from the date of service, either on him in person or at his residence. No extension of time may be granted on account of distance.

Article 44
The judgment given on the appeal may be contested only by the appeal referred to in Annex IV.

Article 45
1.   The court with which an appeal is lodged under Article 43 or Article 44 shall refuse or revoke a declaration of enforceability only on one of the grounds specified in Articles 34 and 35. It shall give its decision without delay.

2.   Under no circumstances may the foreign judgment be reviewed as to its substance.

Article 46
1.   The court with which an appeal is lodged under Article 43 or Article 44 may, on the application of the party against whom enforcement is sought, stay the proceedings if an ordinary appeal has been lodged against the judgment in the Member State of origin or if the time for such an appeal has not yet expired; in the latter case, the court may specify the time within which such an appeal is to be lodged.

2.   Where the judgment was given in Ireland or the United Kingdom, any form of appeal available in the Member State of origin shall be treated as an ordinary appeal for the purposes of paragraph 1.

3.   The court may also make enforcement conditional on the provision of such security as it shall determine.

Article 47
1.   When a judgment must be recognised in accordance with this Regulation, nothing shall prevent the applicant from availing himself of provisional, including protective, measures in accordance with the law of the Member State requested without a declaration of enforceability under Article 41 being required.

2.   The declaration of enforceability shall carry with it the power to proceed to any protective measures.

3.   During the time specified for an appeal pursuant to Article 43(5) against the declaration of enforceability and until any such appeal has been determined, no measures of enforcement may be taken other than protective measures against the property of the party against whom enforcement is sought.

Article 48
1.   Where a foreign judgment has been given in respect of several matters and the declaration of enforceability cannot be given for all of them, the court or competent authority shall give it for one or more of them.

2.   An applicant may request a declaration of enforceability limited to parts of a judgment.

Article 49
A foreign judgment which orders a periodic payment by way of a penalty shall be enforceable in the Member State in which enforcement is sought only if the amount of the payment has been finally determined by the courts of the Member State of origin.

Article 50
An applicant who, in the Member State of origin has benefited from complete or partial legal aid or exemption from costs or expenses, shall be entitled, in the procedure provided for in this Section, to benefit from the most favourable legal aid or the most extensive exemption from costs or expenses provided for by the law of the Member State addressed.

Article 51

No security, bond or deposit, however described, shall be required of a party who in one Member State applies for enforcement of a judgment given in another Member State on the ground that he is a foreign national or that he is not domiciled or resident in the State in which enforcement is sought.

Article 52

In proceedings for the issue of a declaration of enforceability, no charge, duty or fee calculated by reference to the value of the matter at issue may be levied in the Member State in which enforcement is sought.

Section 3
Common provisions

Article 53

1. A party seeking recognition or applying for a declaration of enforceability shall produce a copy of the judgment which satisfies the conditions necessary to establish its authenticity.

2. A party applying for a declaration of enforceability shall also produce the certificate referred to in Article 54, without prejudice to Article 55.

Article 54

The court or competent authority of a Member State where a judgment was given shall issue, at the request of any interested party, a certificate using the standard form in Annex V to this Regulation.

Article 55

1. If the certificate referred to in Article 54 is not produced, the court or competent authority may specify a time for its production or accept an equivalent document or, if it considers that it has sufficient information before it, dispense with its production.

2. If the court or competent authority so requires, a translation of the documents shall be produced. The translation shall be certified by a person qualified to do so in one of the Member States.

Article 56

No legalisation or other similar formality shall be required in respect of the documents referred to in Article 53 or Article 55(2), or in respect of a document appointing a representative ad litem.

CHAPTER IV
AUTHENTIC INSTRUMENTS AND COURT SETTLEMENTS

Article 57

1. A document which has been formally drawn up or registered as an authentic instrument and is enforceable in one Member State shall, in another Member State, be declared enforceable there, on application made in accordance with the procedures provided for in Articles 38, et seq. The court with which an appeal is lodged under Article 43 or Article 44 shall refuse or revoke a declaration of enforceability only if enforcement of the instrument is manifestly contrary to public policy in the Member State addressed.

2. Arrangements relating to maintenance obligations concluded with administrative authorities or authenticated by them shall also be regarded as authentic instruments within the meaning of paragraph 1.

3. The instrument produced must satisfy the conditions necessary to establish its authenticity in the Member State of origin.

4. Section 3 of Chapter III shall apply as appropriate. The competent authority of a Member State where an authentic instrument was drawn up or registered

shall issue, at the request of any interested party, a certificate using the standard form in Annex VI to this Regulation.

Article 58

A settlement which has been approved by a court in the course of proceedings and is enforceable in the Member State in which it was concluded shall be enforceable in the State addressed under the same conditions as authentic instruments. The court or competent authority of a Member State where a court settlement was approved shall issue, at the request of any interested party, a certificate using the standard form in Annex V to this Regulation.

CHAPTER V
GENERAL PROVISIONS

Article 59

1. In order to determine whether a party is domiciled in the Member State whose courts are seised of a matter, the court shall apply its internal law.

2. If a party is not domiciled in the Member State whose courts are seised of the matter, then, in order to determine whether the party is domiciled in another Member State, the court shall apply the law of that Member State.

Article 60

1. For the purposes of this Regulation, a company or other legal person or association of natural or legal persons is domiciled at the place where it has its:
   (a)   statutory seat, or
   (b)   central administration, or
   (c)   principal place of business.

2. For the purposes of the United Kingdom and Ireland 'statutory seat' means the registered office or, where there is no such office anywhere, the place of incorporation or, where there is no such place anywhere, the place under the law of which the formation took place.

3. In order to determine whether a trust is domiciled in the Member State whose courts are seised of the matter, the court shall apply its rules of private international law.

Article 61

Without prejudice to any more favourable provisions of national laws, persons domiciled in a Member State who are being prosecuted in the criminal courts of another Member State of which they are not nationals for an offence which was not intentionally committed may be defended by persons qualified to do so, even if they do not appear in person. However, the court seised of the matter may order appearance in person; in the case of failure to appear, a judgment given in the civil action without the person concerned having had the opportunity to arrange for his defence need not be recognised or enforced in the other Member States.

...

CHAPTER VI
TRANSITIONAL PROVISIONS

Article 66

1. This Regulation shall apply only to legal proceedings instituted and to documents formally drawn up or registered as authentic instruments after the entry into force thereof.

2. However, if the proceedings in the Member State of origin were instituted before the entry into force of this Regulation, judgments given after that date shall be recognised and enforced in accordance with Chapter III,
   (a)   if the proceedings in the Member State of origin were instituted after the

entry into force of the Brussels or the Lugano Convention both in the Member State or origin and in the Member State addressed;

(b)   in all other cases, if jurisdiction was founded upon rules which accorded with those provided for either in Chapter II or in a convention concluded between the Member State of origin and the Member State addressed which was in force when the proceedings were instituted.

CHAPTER VII
RELATIONS WITH OTHER INSTRUMENTS

Article 67
This Regulation shall not prejudice the application of provisions governing jurisdiction and the recognition and enforcement of judgments in specific matters which are contained in Community instruments or in national legislation harmonised pursuant to such instruments.

Article 68
1.   This Regulation shall, as between the Member States, supersede the Brussels Convention, except as regards the territories of the Member States which fall within the territorial scope of that Convention and which are excluded from this Regulation pursuant to Article 299 of the Treaty.

2.   In so far as this Regulation replaces the provisions of the Brussels Convention between Member States, any reference to the Convention shall be understood as a reference to this Regulation.

...

Article 71
1.   This Regulation shall not affect any conventions to which the Member States are parties and which in relation to particular matters, govern jurisdiction or the recognition or enforcement of judgments.

2.   With a view to its uniform interpretation, paragraph 1 shall be applied in the following manner:

(a)   this Regulation shall not prevent a court of a Member State, which is a party to a convention on a particular matter, from assuming jurisdiction in accordance with that convention, even where the defendant is domiciled in another Member State which is not a party to that convention. The court hearing the action shall, in any event, apply Article 26 of this Regulation;

(b)   judgments given in a Member State by a court in the exercise of jurisdiction provided for in a convention on a particular matter shall be recognised and enforced in the other Member States in accordance with this Regulation.

Where a convention on a particular matter to which both the Member State of origin and the Member State addressed are parties lays down conditions for the recognition or enforcement of judgments, those conditions shall apply. In any event, the provisions of this Regulation which concern the procedure for recognition and enforcement of judgments may be applied.

Article 72
This Regulation shall not affect agreements by which Member States undertook, prior to the entry into force of this Regulation pursuant to Article 59 of the Brussels Convention, not to recognise judgments given, in particular in other Contracting States to that Convention, against defendants domiciled or habitually resident in a third country where, in cases provided for in Article 4 of that Convention, the judgment could only be founded on a ground of jurisdiction specified in the second paragraph of Article 3 of that Convention.

CHAPTER VIII
FINAL PROVISIONS

Article 76
This Regulation shall enter into force on 1 March 2002.

This Regulation is binding in its entirety and directly applicable in the Member States in accordance with the Treaty establishing the European Community.

Done at Brussels, 22 December 2000.

COUNCIL REGULATION (EC) NO 1206/2001 OF 28 MAY 2001 ON COOPERATION BETWEEN THE COURTS OF THE MEMBER STATES IN THE TAKING OF EVIDENCE IN CIVIL OR COMMERCIAL MATTERS

Official Journal L 174, 27/06/2001 p 1

THE COUNCIL OF THE EUROPEAN UNION,

Having regard to the Treaty establishing the European Community, and in particular Article 61(c) and Article 67(1) thereof,
   Having regard to the initiative of the Federal Republic of Germany,
   Having regard to the opinion of the European Parliament,
   Having regard to the opinion of the Economic and Social Committee,

Whereas:
   (1)   The European Union has set itself the objective of maintaining and developing the European Union as an area of freedom, security and justice in which the free movement of persons is ensured. For the gradual establishment of such an area, the Community is to adopt, among others, the measures relating to judicial cooperation in civil matters needed for the proper functioning of the internal market.
   (2)   For the purpose of the proper functioning of the internal market, cooperation between courts in the taking of evidence should be improved, and in particular simplified and accelerated.
   (3)   At its meeting in Tampere on 15 and 16 October 1999, the European Council recalled that new procedural legislation in cross-border cases, in particular on the taking of evidence, should be prepared.
   (4)   This area falls within the scope of Article 65 of the Treaty.
   (5)   The objectives of the proposed action, namely the improvement of cooperation between the courts on the taking of evidence in civil or commercial matters, cannot be sufficiently achieved by the Member States and can therefore be better achieved at Community level. The Community may adopt measures in accordance with the principle of subsidiarity as set out in Article 5 of the Treaty. In accordance with the principle of proportionality, as set out in that Article, this Regulation does not go beyond what is necessary to achieve those objectives.
   (6)   To date, there is no binding instrument between all the Member States concerning the taking of evidence. The Hague Convention of 18 March 1970 on the taking of evidence abroad in civil or commercial matters applies between only 11 Member States of the European Union.
   (7)   As it is often essential for a decision in a civil or commercial matter pending before a court in a Member State to take evidence in another Member State, the Community's activity cannot be limited to the field of transmission of judicial and extrajudicial documents in civil or commercial matters which falls within the scope of Council Regulation (EC) No 1348/2000 of 29 May 2000 on the serving in the Member States of judicial and extrajudicial documents in civil or commercial matters. It is therefore necessary to continue the improvement of cooperation between courts of Member States in the field of taking of evidence.

(8)   The efficiency of judicial procedures in civil or commercial matters requires that the transmission and execution of requests for the performance of taking of evidence is to be made directly and by the most rapid means possible between Member States' courts.

(9)   Speed in transmission of requests for the performance of taking of evidence warrants the use of all appropriate means, provided that certain conditions as to the legibility and reliability of the document received are observed. So as to ensure the utmost clarity and legal certainty the request for the performance of taking of evidence must be transmitted on a form to be completed in the language of the Member State of the requested court or in another language accepted by that State. For the same reasons, forms should also be used as far as possible for further communication between the relevant courts.

(10)   A request for the performance of the taking of evidence should be executed expeditiously. If it is not possible for the request to be executed within 90 days of receipt by the requested court, the latter should inform the requesting court accordingly, stating the reasons which prevent the request from being executed swiftly.

(11)   To secure the effectiveness of this Regulation, the possibility of refusing to execute the request for the performance of taking of evidence should be confined to strictly limited exceptional situations.

(12)   The requested court should execute the request in accordance with the law of its Member State.

(13)   The parties and, if any, their representatives, should be able to be present at the performance of the taking of evidence, if that is provided for by the law of the Member State of the requesting court, in order to be able to follow the proceedings in a comparable way as if evidence were taken in the Member State of the requesting court. They should also have the right to request to participate in order to have a more active role in the performance of the taking of evidence. However, the conditions under which they may participate should be determined by the requested court in accordance with the law of its Member State.

(14)   The representatives of the requesting court should be able to be present at the performance of the taking of evidence, if that is compatible with the law of the Member State of the requesting court, in order to have an improved possibility of evaluation of evidence. They should also have the right to request to participate, under the conditions laid down by the requested court in accordance with the law of its Member State, in order to have a more active role in the performance of the taking of evidence.

(15)   In order to facilitate the taking of evidence it should be possible for a court in a Member State, in accordance with the law of its Member State, to take evidence directly in another Member State, if accepted by the latter, and under the conditions determined by the central body or competent authority of the requested Member State.

(16)   The execution of the request, according to Article 10, should not give rise to a claim for any reimbursement of taxes or costs. Nevertheless, if the requested court requires reimbursement, the fees paid to experts and interpreters, as well as the costs occasioned by the application of Article 10(3) and (4), should not be borne by that court. In such a case, the requesting court is to take the necessary measures to ensure reimbursement without delay. Where the opinion of an expert is required, the requested court may, before executing the request, ask the requesting court for an adequate deposit or advance towards the costs.

(17)   This Regulation should prevail over the provisions applying to its field of application, contained in international conventions concluded by the Member States. Member States should be free to adopt agreements or arrangements to further facilitate cooperation in the taking of evidence.

(18)   The information transmitted pursuant to this Regulation should enjoy protection. Since Directive 95/46/EC of the European Parliament and of the Council

of 24 October 1995 on the protection of individuals with regard to the processing of personal data and on the free movement of such data, and Directive 97/66/EC of the European Parliament and of the Council of 15 December 1997 concerning the processing of personal data and the protection of privacy in the tele-communications sector, are applicable, there is no need for specific provisions on data protection in this Regulation.

(19)   The measures necessary for the implementation of this Regulation should be adopted in accordance with Council Decision 1999/468/EC of 28 June 1999 lay-ing down the procedures for the exercise of implementing powers conferred on the Commission.

(20)   For the proper functioning of this Regulation, the Commission should review its application and propose such amendments as may appear necessary.

(21)   The United Kingdom and Ireland, in accordance with Article 3 of the Protocol on the position of the United Kingdom and Ireland annexed to the Treaty on the European Union and to the Treaty establishing the European Community, have given notice of their wish to take part in the adoption and application of this Regulation.

(22)   Denmark, in accordance with Articles 1 and 2 of the Protocol on the posi-tion of Denmark annexed to the Treaty on European Union and to the Treaty establishing the European Community, is not participating in the adoption of this Regulation, and is therefore not bound by it nor subject to its application,

HAS ADOPTED THIS REGULATION:

CHAPTER I
GENERAL PROVISIONS

Article 1. Scope

1.   This Regulation shall apply in civil or commercial matters where the court of a Member State, in accordance with the provisions of the law of that State, requests:

(a)   the competent court of another Member State to take evidence; or

(b)   to take evidence directly in another Member State.

2.   A request shall not be made to obtain evidence which is not intended for use in judicial proceedings, commenced or contemplated.

3.   In this Regulation, the term 'Member State' shall mean Member States with the exception of Denmark.

Article 2. Direct transmission between the courts

1.   Requests pursuant to Article 1(1)(a), hereinafter referred to as 'requests', shall be transmitted by the court before which the proceedings are commenced or contemplated, hereinafter referred to as the 'requesting court', directly to the com-petent court of another Member State, hereinafter referred to as the 'requested court', for the performance of the taking of evidence.

2.   Each Member State shall draw up a list of the courts competent for the per-formance of taking of evidence according to this Regulation. The list shall also indicate the territorial and, where appropriate, the special jurisdiction of those courts.

Article 3. Central body

1.   Each Member State shall designate a central body responsible for:

(a)   supplying information to the courts;

(b)   seeking solutions to any difficulties which may arise in respect of a request;

(c)   forwarding, in exceptional cases, at the request of a requesting court, a request to the competent court.

2.   A federal State, a State in which several legal systems apply or a State with

autonomous territorial entities shall be free to designate more than one central body.

3.   Each Member State shall also designate the central body referred to in paragraph 1 or one or several competent authority(ies) to be responsible for taking decisions on requests pursuant to Article 17.

CHAPTER II
TRANSMISSION AND EXECUTION OF REQUESTS

Section 1
Transmission of the request

Article 4. Form and content of the request
1.   The request shall be made using form A or, where appropriate, form I in the Annex. It shall contain the following details:
   (a)   the requesting and, where appropriate, the requested court;
   (b)   the names and addresses of the parties to the proceedings and their representatives, if any;
   (c)   the nature and subject matter of the case and a brief statement of the facts;
   (d)   a description of the taking of evidence to be performed;
   (e)   where the request is for the examination of a person:
   – the name(s) and address(es) of the person(s) to be examined,
   – the questions to be put to the person(s) to be examined or a statement of the facts about which he is (they are) to be examined,
   – where appropriate, a reference to a right to refuse to testify under the law of the Member State of the requesting court,
   – any requirement that the examination is to be carried out under oath or affirmation in lieu thereof, and any special form to be used,
   – where appropriate, any other information that the requesting court deems necessary;
   (f)   where the request is for any other form of taking of evidence, the documents or other objects to be inspected;
   (g)   where appropriate, any request pursuant to Article 10(3) and (4), and Articles 11 and 12 and any information necessary for the application thereof.
2.   The request and all documents accompanying the request shall be exempted from authentication or any equivalent formality.
3.   Documents which the requesting court deems it necessary to enclose for the execution of the request shall be accompanied by a translation into the language in which the request was written.

Article 5. Language
The request and communications pursuant to this Regulation shall be drawn up in the official language of the requested Member State or, if there are several official languages in that Member State, in the official language or one of the official languages of the place where the requested taking of evidence is to be performed, or in another language which the requested Member State has indicated it can accept. Each Member State shall indicate the official language or languages of the institutions of the European Community other than its own which is or are acceptable to it for completion of the forms.

Article 6. Transmission of requests and other communications
Requests and communications pursuant to this Regulation shall be transmitted by the swiftest possible means, which the requested Member State has indicated it can accept. The transmission may be carried out by any appropriate means, provided that the document received accurately reflects the content of the document forwarded and that all information in it is legible.

Section 2
Receipt of request

Article 7. Receipt of request

1.   Within seven days of receipt of the request, the requested competent court shall send an acknowledgement of receipt to the requesting court using form B in the Annex. Where the request does not comply with the conditions laid down in Articles 5 and 6, the requested court shall enter a note to that effect in the acknowledgement of receipt.

2.   Where the execution of a request made using form A in the Annex, which complies with the conditions laid down in Article 5, does not fall within the jurisdiction of the court to which it was transmitted, the latter shall forward the request to the competent court of its Member State and shall inform the requesting court thereof using form A in the Annex.

Article 8. Incomplete request

1.   If a request cannot be executed because it does not contain all of the necessary information pursuant to Article 4, the requested court shall inform the requesting court thereof without delay and, at the latest, within 30 days of receipt of the request using form C in the Annex, and shall request it to send the missing information, which should be indicated as precisely as possible.

2.   If a request cannot be executed because a deposit or advance is necessary in accordance with Article 18(3), the requested court shall inform the requesting court thereof without delay and, at the latest, within 30 days of receipt of the request using form C in the Annex and inform the requesting court how the deposit or advance should be made. The requested Court shall acknowledge receipt of the deposit or advance without delay, at the latest within 10 days of receipt of the deposit or the advance using form D.

Article 9. Completion of the request

1.   If the requested court has noted on the acknowledgement of receipt pursuant to Article 7(1) that the request does not comply with the conditions laid down in Articles 5 and 6 or has informed the requesting court pursuant to Article 8 that the request cannot be executed because it does not contain all of the necessary information pursuant to Article 4, the time limit pursuant to Article 10 shall begin to run when the requested court received the request duly completed.

2.   Where the requested court has asked for a deposit or advance in accordance with Article 18(3), this time limit shall begin to run when the deposit or the advance is made.

Section 3
Taking of evidence by the requested court

Article 10. General provisions on the execution of the request

1.   The requested court shall execute the request without delay and, at the latest, within 90 days of receipt of the request.

2.   The requested court shall execute the request in accordance with the law of its Member State.

3.   The requesting court may call for the request to be executed in accordance with a special procedure provided for by the law of its Member State, using form A in the Annex. The requested court shall comply with such a requirement unless this procedure is incompatible with the law of the Member State of the requested court or by reason of major practical difficulties. If the requested court does not comply with the requirement for one of these reasons it shall inform the requesting court using form E in the Annex.

4.   The requesting court may ask the requested court to use communications technology at the performance of the taking of evidence, in particular by using videoconference and teleconference.

The requested court shall comply with such a requirement unless this is incompatible with the law of the Member State of the requested court or by reason of major practical difficulties.

If the requested court does not comply with the requirement for one of these reasons, it shall inform the requesting court, using form E in the Annex.

If there is no access to the technical means referred to above in the requesting or in the requested court, such means may be made available by the courts by mutual agreement.

Article 11. Performance with the presence and participation of the parties

1.   If it is provided for by the law of the Member State of the requesting court, the parties and, if any, their representatives, have the right to be present at the performance of the taking of evidence by the requested court.

2.   The requesting court shall, in its request, inform the requested court that the parties and, if any, their representatives, will be present and, where appropriate, that their participation is requested, using form A in the Annex. This information may also be given at any other appropriate time.

3.   If the participation of the parties and, if any, their representatives, is requested at the performance of the taking of evidence, the requested court shall determine, in accordance with Article 10, the conditions under which they may participate.

4.   The requested court shall notify the parties and, if any, their representatives, of the time when, the place where, the proceedings will take place, and, where appropriate, the conditions under which they may participate, using form F in the Annex.

5.   Paragraphs 1 to 4 shall not affect the possibility for the requested court of asking the parties and, if any their representatives, to be present at or to participate in the performance of the taking of evidence if that possibility is provided for by the law of its Member State.

Article 12. Performance with the presence and participation of representatives of the requesting court

1.   If it is compatible with the law of the Member State of the requesting court, representatives of the requesting court have the right to be present in the performance of the taking of evidence by the requested court.

2.   For the purpose of this Article, the term 'representative' shall include members of the judicial personnel designated by the requesting court, in accordance with the law of its Member State. The requesting court may also designate, in accordance with the law of its Member State, any other person, such as an expert.

3.   The requesting court shall, in its request, inform the requested court that its representatives will be present and, where appropriate, that their participation is requested, using form A in the Annex. This information may also be given at any other appropriate time.

4.   If the participation of the representatives of the requesting court is requested in the performance of the taking of evidence, the requested court shall determine, in accordance with Article 10, the conditions under which they may participate.

5.   The requested court shall notify the requesting court, of the time when, and the place where, the proceedings will take place, and, where appropriate, the conditions under which the representatives may participate, using form F in the Annex.

Article 13. Coercive measures

Where necessary, in executing a request the requested court shall apply the appropriate coercive measures in the instances and to the extent as are provided for by the law of the Member State of the requested court for the execution of a request made for the same purpose by its national authorities or one of the parties concerned.

Article 14. Refusal to execute

1.   A request for the hearing of a person shall not be executed when the person concerned claims the right to refuse to give evidence or to be prohibited from giving evidence,

(a)   under the law of the Member State of the requested court; or

(b)   under the law of the Member State of the requesting court, and such right has been specified in the request, or, if need be, at the instance of the requested court, has been confirmed by the requesting court.

2.   In addition to the grounds referred to in paragraph 1, the execution of a request may be refused only if:

(a)   the request does not fall within the scope of this Regulation as set out in Article 1; or

(b)   the execution of the request under the law of the Member State of the requested court does not fall within the functions of the judiciary; or

(c)   the requesting court does not comply with the request of the requested court to complete the request pursuant to Article 8 within 30 days after the requested court asked it to do so; or

(d)   a deposit or advance asked for in accordance with Article 18(3) is not made within 60 days after the requested court asked for such a deposit or advance.

3.   Execution may not be refused by the requested court solely on the ground that under the law of its Member State a court of that Member State has exclusive jurisdiction over the subject matter of the action or that the law of that Member State would not admit the right of action on it.

4.   If execution of the request is refused on one of the grounds referred to in paragraph 2, the requested court shall notify the requesting court thereof within 60 days of receipt of the request by the requested court using form H in the Annex.

Article 15. Notification of delay

If the requested court is not in a position to execute the request within 90 days of receipt, it shall inform the requesting court thereof, using form G in the Annex. When it does so, the grounds for the delay shall be given as well as the estimated time that the requested court expects it will need to execute the request.

Article 16. Procedure after execution of the request

The requested court shall send without delay to the requesting court the documents establishing the execution of the request and, where appropriate, return the documents received from the requesting court. The documents shall be accompanied by a confirmation of execution using form H in the Annex.

Section 4
Direct taking of evidence by the requesting court

Article 17

1.   Where a court requests to take evidence directly in another Member State, it shall submit a request to the central body or the competent authority referred to in Article 3(3) in that State, using form I in the Annex.

2.   Direct taking of evidence may only take place if it can be performed on a voluntary basis without the need for coercive measures.

Where the direct taking of evidence implies that a person shall be heard, the requesting court shall inform that person that the performance shall take place on a voluntary basis.

3.   The taking of evidence shall be performed by a member of the judicial personnel or by any other person such as an expert, who will be designated, in accordance with the law of the Member State of the requesting court.

4.   Within 30 days of receiving the request, the central body or the competent authority of the requested Member State shall inform the requesting court if the

request is accepted and, if necessary, under what conditions according to the law of its Member State such performance is to be carried out, using form J.

In particular, the central body or the competent authority may assign a court of its Member State to take part in the performance of the taking of evidence in order to ensure the proper application of this Article and the conditions that have been set out.

The central body or the competent authority shall encourage the use of communications technology, such as videoconferences and teleconferences.

5.   The central body or the competent authority may refuse direct taking of evidence only if:

(a)   the request does not fall within the scope of this Regulation as set out in Article 1;

(b)   the request does not contain all of the necessary information pursuant to Article 4; or

(c)   the direct taking of evidence requested is contrary to fundamental principles of law in its Member State.

6.   Without prejudice to the conditions laid down in accordance with paragraph 4, the requesting court shall execute the request in accordance with the law of its Member State.

Section 5

Costs

Article 18

1.   The execution of the request, in accordance with Article 10, shall not give rise to a claim for any reimbursement of taxes or costs.

2.   Nevertheless, if the requested court so requires, the requesting court shall ensure the reimbursement, without delay, of:

– the fees paid to experts and interpreters, and

– the costs occasioned by the application of Article 10(3) and (4).

The duty for the parties to bear these fees or costs shall be governed by the law of the Member State of the requesting court.

3.   Where the opinion of an expert is required, the requested court may, before executing the request, ask the requesting court for an adequate deposit or advance towards the requested costs. In all other cases, a deposit or advance shall not be a condition for the execution of a request.

The deposit or advance shall be made by the parties if that is provided for by the law of the Member State of the requesting court.

...

CHAPTER III

FINAL PROVISIONS

Article 22. Communication
By 1 July 2003 each Member State shall communicate to the Commission the following:

(a)   the list pursuant to Article 2(2) indicating the territorial and, where appropriate, the special jurisdiction of the courts;

(b)   the names and addresses of the central bodies and competent authorities pursuant to Article 3, indicating their territorial jurisdiction;

(c)   the technical means for the receipt of requests available to the courts on the list pursuant to Article 2(2);

(d)   the languages accepted for the requests as referred to in Article 5.

Member States shall inform the Commission of any subsequent changes to this information.

Article 23. Review
No later than 1 January 2007, and every five years thereafter, the Commission shall present to the European Parliament, the Council and the Economic and Social Committee a report on the application of this Regulation, paying special attention to the practical application of Article 3(1)(c) and 3, and Articles 17 and 18.

Article 24. Entry into force
1.   This Regulation shall enter into force on 1 July 2001.
2.   This Regulation shall apply from 1 January 2004, except for Articles 19, 21 and 22, which shall apply from 1 July 2001.

This Regulation shall be binding in its entirety and directly applicable in the Member States in accordance with the Treaty establishing the European Community.

Done at Brussels, 28 May 2001.

COUNCIL REGULATION (EC) NO 2201/2003 OF 27 NOVEMBER 2003 CONCERNING JURISDICTION AND THE RECOGNITION AND ENFORCEMENT OF JUDGMENTS IN MATRIMONIAL MATTERS AND THE MATTERS OF PARENTAL RESPONSIBILITY, REPEALING REGULATION (EC) NO 1347/2000 ('BRUSSELS II *BIS*')

Official Journal L 338, 23/12/2003 p 1

THE COUNCIL OF THE EUROPEAN UNION,

Having regard to the Treaty establishing the European Community, and in particular Article 61(c) and Article 67(1) thereof,
   Having regard to the proposal from the Commission,
   Having regard to the opinion of the European Parliament,
   Having regard to the opinion of the European Economic and Social Committee,

Whereas:
   (1)   The European Community has set the objective of creating an area of freedom, security and justice, in which the free movement of persons is ensured. To this end, the Community is to adopt, among others, measures in the field of judicial cooperation in civil matters that are necessary for the proper functioning of the internal market.
   (2)   The Tampere European Council endorsed the principle of mutual recognition of judicial decisions as the cornerstone for the creation of a genuine judicial area, and identified visiting rights as a priority.
   (3)   Council Regulation (EC) No 1347/2000 sets out rules on jurisdiction, recognition and enforcement of judgments in matrimonial matters and matters of parental responsibility for the children of both spouses rendered on the occasion of the matrimonial proceedings. The content of this Regulation was substantially taken over from the Convention of 28 May 1998 on the same subject matter.
   (4)   On 3 July 2000 France presented an initiative for a Council Regulation on the mutual enforcement of judgments on rights of access to children.
   (5)   In order to ensure equality for all children, this Regulation covers all decisions on parental responsibility, including measures for the protection of the child, independently of any link with a matrimonial proceeding.
   (6)   Since the application of the rules on parental responsibility often arises in the context of matrimonial proceedings, it is more appropriate to have a single instrument for matters of divorce and parental responsibility.

(7)   The scope of this Regulation covers civil matters, whatever the nature of the court or tribunal.

(8)   As regards judgments on divorce, legal separation or marriage annulment, this Regulation should apply only to the dissolution of matrimonial ties and should not deal with issues such as the grounds for divorce, property consequences of the marriage or any other ancillary measures.

(9)   As regards the property of the child, this Regulation should apply only to measures for the protection of the child, i.e. (i) the designation and functions of a person or body having charge of the child's property, representing or assisting the child, and (ii) the administration, conservation or disposal of the child's property. In this context, this Regulation should, for instance, apply in cases where the parents are in dispute as regards the administration of the child's property. Measures relating to the child's property which do not concern the protection of the child should continue to be governed by Council Regulation (EC) No 44/2001 of 22 December 2000 on jurisdiction and the recognition and enforcement of judgments in civil and commercial matters.

(10)   This Regulation is not intended to apply to matters relating to social security, public measures of a general nature in matters of education or health or to decisions on the right of asylum and on immigration. In addition it does not apply to the establishment of parenthood, since this is a different matter from the attribution of parental responsibility, nor to other questions linked to the status of persons. Moreover, it does not apply to measures taken as a result of criminal offences committed by children.

(11)   Maintenance obligations are excluded from the scope of this Regulation as these are already covered by Council Regulation No 44/2001. The courts having jurisdiction under this Regulation will generally have jurisdiction to rule on maintenance obligations by application of Article 5(2) of Council Regulation No 44/2001.

(12)   The grounds of jurisdiction in matters of parental responsibility established in the present Regulation are shaped in the light of the best interests of the child, in particular on the criterion of proximity. This means that jurisdiction should lie in the first place with the Member State of the child's habitual residence, except for certain cases of a change in the child's residence or pursuant to an agreement between the holders of parental responsibility.

(13)   In the interest of the child, this Regulation allows, by way of exception and under certain conditions, that the court having jurisdiction may transfer a case to a court of another Member State if this court is better placed to hear the case. However, in this case the second court should not be allowed to transfer the case to a third court.

(14)   This Regulation should have effect without prejudice to the application of public international law concerning diplomatic immunities. Where jurisdiction under this Regulation cannot be exercised by reason of the existence of diplomatic immunity in accordance with international law, jurisdiction should be exercised in accordance with national law in a Member State in which the person concerned does not enjoy such immunity.

(15)   Council Regulation (EC) No 1348/2000 of 29 May 2000 on the service in the Member States of judicial and extrajudicial documents in civil or commercial matters should apply to the service of documents in proceedings instituted pursuant to this Regulation.

(16)   This Regulation should not prevent the courts of a Member State from taking provisional, including protective measures, in urgent cases, with regard to persons or property situated in that State.

(17)   In cases of wrongful removal or retention of a child, the return of the child should be obtained without delay, and to this end the Hague Convention of 25 October 1980 would continue to apply as complemented by the provisions of this Regulation, in particular Article 11. The courts of the Member State to or in which

the child has been wrongfully removed or retained should be able to oppose his or her return in specific, duly justified cases. However, such a decision could be replaced by a subsequent decision by the court of the Member State of habitual residence of the child prior to the wrongful removal or retention. Should that judgment entail the return of the child, the return should take place without any special procedure being required for recognition and enforcement of that judgment in the Member State to or in which the child has been removed or retained.

(18)   Where a court has decided not to return a child on the basis of Article 13 of the 1980 Hague Convention, it should inform the court having jurisdiction or central authority in the Member State where the child was habitually resident prior to the wrongful removal or retention. Unless the court in the latter Member State has been seised, this court or the central authority should notify the parties. This obligation should not prevent the central authority from also notifying the relevant public authorities in accordance with national law.

(19)   The hearing of the child plays an important role in the application of this Regulation, although this instrument is not intended to modify national procedures applicable.

(20)   The hearing of a child in another Member State may take place under the arrangements laid down in Council Regulation (EC) No 1206/2001 of 28 May 2001 on cooperation between the courts of the Member States in the taking of evidence in civil or commercial matters.

(21)   The recognition and enforcement of judgments given in a Member State should be based on the principle of mutual trust and the grounds for non-recognition should be kept to the minimum required.

(22)   Authentic instruments and agreements between parties that are enforceable in one Member State should be treated as equivalent to 'judgments' for the purpose of the application of the rules on recognition and enforcement.

(23)   The Tampere European Council considered in its conclusions (point 34) that judgments in the field of family litigation should be 'automatically recognised throughout the Union without any intermediate proceedings or grounds for refusal of enforcement'. This is why judgments on rights of access and judgments on return that have been certified in the Member State of origin in accordance with the provisions of this Regulation should be recognised and enforceable in all other Member States without any further procedure being required. Arrangements for the enforcement of such judgments continue to be governed by national law.

(24)   The certificate issued to facilitate enforcement of the judgment should not be subject to appeal. It should be rectified only where there is a material error, i.e. where it does not correctly reflect the judgment.

(25)   Central authorities should cooperate both in general matter and in specific cases, including for purposes of promoting the amicable resolution of family disputes, in matters of parental responsibility. To this end central authorities shall participate in the European Judicial Network in civil and commercial matters created by Council Decision 2001/470/EC of 28 May 2001 establishing a European Judicial Network in civil and commercial matters.

(26)   The Commission should make publicly available and update the lists of courts and redress procedures communicated by the Member States.

(27)   The measures necessary for the implementation of this Regulation should be adopted in accordance with Council Decision 1999/468/EC of 28 June 1999 laying down the procedures for the exercise of implementing powers conferred on the Commission.

(28)   This Regulation replaces Regulation (EC) No 1347/2000 which is consequently repealed.

(29)   For the proper functioning of this Regulation, the Commission should review its application and propose such amendments as may appear necessary.

(30)   The United Kingdom and Ireland, in accordance with Article 3 of the Protocol on the position of the United Kingdom and Ireland annexed to the Treaty

on European Union and the Treaty establishing the European Community, have given notice of their wish to take part in the adoption and application of this Regulation.

(31) Denmark, in accordance with Articles 1 and 2 of the Protocol on the position of Denmark annexed to the Treaty on European Union and the Treaty establishing the European Community, is not participating in the adoption of this Regulation and is therefore not bound by it nor subject to its application.

(32) Since the objectives of this Regulation cannot be sufficiently achieved by the Member States and can therefore be better achieved at Community level, the Community may adopt measures, in accordance with the principle of subsidiarity as set out in Article 5 of the Treaty. In accordance with the principle of proportionality, as set out in that Article, this Regulation does not go beyond what is necessary in order to achieve those objectives.

(33) This Regulation recognises the fundamental rights and observes the principles of the Charter of Fundamental Rights of the European Union. In particular, it seeks to ensure respect for the fundamental rights of the child as set out in Article 24 of the Charter of Fundamental Rights of the European Union,

HAS ADOPTED THE PRESENT REGULATION:

CHAPTER I
SCOPE AND DEFINITIONS

Article 1. Scope
1. This Regulation shall apply, whatever the nature of the court or tribunal, in civil matters relating to:
    (a) divorce, legal separation or marriage annulment;
    (b) the attribution, exercise, delegation, restriction or termination of parental responsibility.
2. The matters referred to in paragraph 1(b) may, in particular, deal with:
    (a) rights of custody and rights of access;
    (b) guardianship, curatorship and similar institutions;
    (c) the designation and functions of any person or body having charge of the child's person or property, representing or assisting the child;
    (d) the placement of the child in a foster family or in institutional care;
    (e) measures for the protection of the child relating to the administration, conservation or disposal of the child's property.
3. This Regulation shall not apply to:
    (a) the establishment or contesting of a parent-child relationship;
    (b) decisions on adoption, measures preparatory to adoption, or the annulment or revocation of adoption;
    (c) the name and forenames of the child;
    (d) emancipation;
    (e) maintenance obligations;
    (f) trusts or succession;
    (g) measures taken as a result of criminal offences committed by children.

Article 2. Definitions
For the purposes of this Regulation:
1. the term 'court' shall cover all the authorities in the Member States with jurisdiction in the matters falling within the scope of this Regulation pursuant to Article 1;
2. the term 'judge' shall mean the judge or an official having powers equivalent to those of a judge in the matters falling within the scope of the Regulation;
3. the term 'Member State' shall mean all Member States with the exception of Denmark;
4. the term 'judgment' shall mean a divorce, legal separation or marriage

annulment, as well as a judgment relating to parental responsibility, pronounced by a court of a Member State, whatever the judgment may be called, including a decree, order or decision;

5.   the term 'Member State of origin' shall mean the Member State where the judgment to be enforced was issued;

6.   the term 'Member State of enforcement' shall mean the Member State where enforcement of the judgment is sought;

7.   the term 'parental responsibility' shall mean all rights and duties relating to the person or the property of a child which are given to a natural or legal person by judgment, by operation of law or by an agreement having legal effect. The term shall include rights of custody and rights of access;

8.   the term 'holder of parental responsibility' shall mean any person having parental responsibility over a child;

9.   the term 'rights of custody' shall include rights and duties relating to the care of the person of a child, and in particular the right to determine the child's place of residence;

10. the term 'rights of access' shall include in particular the right to take a child to a place other than his or her habitual residence for a limited period of time;

11. the term 'wrongful removal or retention' shall mean a child's removal or retention where:

(a)   it is in breach of rights of custody acquired by judgment or by operation of law or by an agreement having legal effect under the law of the Member State where the child was habitually resident immediately before the removal or retention; and

(b)   provided that, at the time of removal or retention, the rights of custody were actually exercised, either jointly or alone, or would have been so exercised but for the removal or retention. Custody shall be considered to be exercised jointly when, pursuant to a judgment or by operation of law, one holder of parental responsibility cannot decide on the child's place of residence without the consent of another holder of parental responsibility.

CHAPTER II
JURISDICTION

Section 1
Divorce, legal separation and marriage annulment

Article 3. General jurisdiction

1.   In matters relating to divorce, legal separation or marriage annulment, jurisdiction shall lie with the courts of the Member State

(a)   in whose territory:

– the spouses are habitually resident, or

– the spouses were last habitually resident, insofar as one of them still resides there, or

– the respondent is habitually resident, or

– in the event of a joint application, either of the spouses is habitually resident, or

– the applicant is habitually resident if he or she resided there for at least a year immediately before the application was made, or

– the applicant is habitually resident if he or she resided there for at least six months immediately before the application was made and is either a national of the Member State in question or, in the case of the United Kingdom and Ireland, has his or her 'domicile' there;

(b)   of the nationality of both spouses or, in the case of the United Kingdom and Ireland, of the 'domicile' of both spouses.

2. For the purpose of this Regulation, 'domicile' shall have the same meaning as it has under the legal systems of the United Kingdom and Ireland.

Article 4. Counterclaim
The court in which proceedings are pending on the basis of Article 3 shall also have jurisdiction to examine a counterclaim, insofar as the latter comes within the scope of this Regulation.

Article 5. Conversion of legal separation into divorce
Without prejudice to Article 3, a court of a Member State that has given a judgment on a legal separation shall also have jurisdiction for converting that judgment into a divorce, if the law of that Member State so provides.

Article 6. Exclusive nature of jurisdiction under Articles 3, 4 and 5
A spouse who:
    (a)   is habitually resident in the territory of a Member State; or
    (b)   is a national of a Member State, or, in the case of the United Kingdom and Ireland, has his or her 'domicile' in the territory of one of the latter Member States,
may be sued in another Member State only in accordance with Articles 3, 4 and 5.

Article 7. Residual jurisdiction
1. Where no court of a Member State has jurisdiction pursuant to Articles 3, 4 and 5, jurisdiction shall be determined, in each Member State, by the laws of that State.
2. As against a respondent who is not habitually resident and is not either a national of a Member State or, in the case of the United Kingdom and Ireland, does not have his 'domicile' within the territory of one of the latter Member States, any national of a Member State who is habitually resident within the territory of another Member State may, like the nationals of that State, avail himself of the rules of jurisdiction applicable in that State.

Section 2
Parental responsibility

Article 8. General jurisdiction
1. The courts of a Member State shall have jurisdiction in matters of parental responsibility over a child who is habitually resident in that Member State at the time the court is seised.
2. Paragraph 1 shall be subject to the provisions of Articles 9, 10 and 12.

Article 9. Continuing jurisdiction of the child's former habitual residence
1. Where a child moves lawfully from one Member State to another and acquires a new habitual residence there, the courts of the Member State of the child's former habitual residence shall, by way of exception to Article 8, retain jurisdiction during a three-month period following the move for the purpose of modifying a judgment on access rights issued in that Member State before the child moved, where the holder of access rights pursuant to the judgment on access rights continues to have his or her habitual residence in the Member State of the child's former habitual residence.
2. Paragraph 1 shall not apply if the holder of access rights referred to in paragraph 1 has accepted the jurisdiction of the courts of the Member State of the child's new habitual residence by participating in proceedings before those courts without contesting their jurisdiction.

Article 10. Jurisdiction in cases of child abduction
In case of wrongful removal or retention of the child, the courts of the Member State where the child was habitually resident immediately before the wrongful

removal or retention shall retain their jurisdiction until the child has acquired a habitual residence in another Member State and:

(a) each person, institution or other body having rights of custody has acquiesced in the removal or retention; or

(b) the child has resided in that other Member State for a period of at least one year after the person, institution or other body having rights of custody has had or should have had knowledge of the whereabouts of the child and the child is settled in his or her new environment and at least one of the following conditions is met:

(i) within one year after the holder of rights of custody has had or should have had knowledge of the whereabouts of the child, no request for return has been lodged before the competent authorities of the Member State where the child has been removed or is being retained;

(ii) a request for return lodged by the holder of rights of custody has been withdrawn and no new request has been lodged within the time limit set in paragraph (i);

(iii) a case before the court in the Member State where the child was habitually resident immediately before the wrongful removal or retention has been closed pursuant to Article 11(7);

(iv) a judgment on custody that does not entail the return of the child has been issued by the courts of the Member State where the child was habitually resident immediately before the wrongful removal or retention.

Article 11. Return of the child

1. Where a person, institution or other body having rights of custody applies to the competent authorities in a Member State to deliver a judgment on the basis of the Hague Convention of 25 October 1980 on the Civil Aspects of International Child Abduction (hereinafter 'the 1980 Hague Convention'), in order to obtain the return of a child that has been wrongfully removed or retained in a Member State other than the Member State where the child was habitually resident immediately before the wrongful removal or retention, paragraphs 2 to 8 shall apply.

2. When applying Articles 12 and 13 of the 1980 Hague Convention, it shall be ensured that the child is given the opportunity to be heard during the proceedings unless this appears inappropriate having regard to his or her age or degree of maturity.

3. A court to which an application for return of a child is made as mentioned in paragraph 1 shall act expeditiously in proceedings on the application, using the most expeditious procedures available in national law.

Without prejudice to the first subparagraph, the court shall, except where exceptional circumstances make this impossible, issue its judgment no later than six weeks after the application is lodged.

4. A court cannot refuse to return a child on the basis of Article 13b of the 1980 Hague Convention if it is established that adequate arrangements have been made to secure the protection of the child after his or her return.

5. A court cannot refuse to return a child unless the person who requested the return of the child has been given an opportunity to be heard.

6. If a court has issued an order on non-return pursuant to Article 13 of the 1980 Hague Convention, the court must immediately either directly or through its central authority, transmit a copy of the court order on non-return and of the relevant documents, in particular a transcript of the hearings before the court, to the court with jurisdiction or central authority in the Member State where the child was habitually resident immediately before the wrongful removal or retention, as determined by national law. The court shall receive all the mentioned documents within one month of the date of the non-return order.

7. Unless the courts in the Member State where the child was habitually resident immediately before the wrongful removal or retention have already been

seised by one of the parties, the court or central authority that receives the information mentioned in paragraph 6 must notify it to the parties and invite them to make submissions to the court, in accordance with national law, within three months of the date of notification so that the court can examine the question of custody of the child.

Without prejudice to the rules on jurisdiction contained in this Regulation, the court shall close the case if no submissions have been received by the court within the time limit.

8.   Notwithstanding a judgment of non-return pursuant to Article 13 of the 1980 Hague Convention, any subsequent judgment which requires the return of the child issued by a court having jurisdiction under this Regulation shall be enforceable in accordance with Section 4 of Chapter III below in order to secure the return of the child.

Article 12. Prorogation of jurisdiction

1.   The courts of a Member State exercising jurisdiction by virtue of Article 3 on an application for divorce, legal separation or marriage annulment shall have jurisdiction in any matter relating to parental responsibility connected with that application where:

(a)   at least one of the spouses has parental responsibility in relation to the child; and

(b)   the jurisdiction of the courts has been accepted expressly or otherwise in an unequivocal manner by the spouses and by the holders of parental responsibility, at the time the court is seised, and is in the superior interests of the child.

2.   The jurisdiction conferred in paragraph 1 shall cease as soon as:

(a)   the judgment allowing or refusing the application for divorce, legal separation or marriage annulment has become final;

(b)   in those cases where proceedings in relation to parental responsibility are still pending on the date referred to in (a), a judgment in these proceedings has become final;

(c)   the proceedings referred to in (a) and (b) have come to an end for another reason.

3.   The courts of a Member State shall also have jurisdiction in relation to parental responsibility in proceedings other than those referred to in paragraph 1 where:

(a)   the child has a substantial connection with that Member State, in particular by virtue of the fact that one of the holders of parental responsibility is habitually resident in that Member State or that the child is a national of that Member State; and

(b)   the jurisdiction of the courts has been accepted expressly or otherwise in an unequivocal manner by all the parties to the proceedings at the time the court is seised and is in the best interests of the child.

4.   Where the child has his or her habitual residence in the territory of a third State which is not a contracting party to the Hague Convention of 19 October 1996 on jurisdiction, applicable law, recognition, enforcement and cooperation in respect of parental responsibility and measures for the protection of children, jurisdiction under this Article shall be deemed to be in the child's interest, in particular if it is found impossible to hold proceedings in the third State in question.

Article 13. Jurisdiction based on the child's presence

1.   Where a child's habitual residence cannot be established and jurisdiction cannot be determined on the basis of Article 12, the courts of the Member State where the child is present shall have jurisdiction.

2.   Paragraph 1 shall also apply to refugee children or children internationally displaced because of disturbances occurring in their country.

Article 14. Residual jurisdiction
Where no court of a Member State has jurisdiction pursuant to Articles 8 to 13, jurisdiction shall be determined, in each Member State, by the laws of that State.

Article 15. Transfer to a court better placed to hear the case
1. By way of exception, the courts of a Member State having jurisdiction as to the substance of the matter may, if they consider that a court of another Member State, with which the child has a particular connection, would be better placed to hear the case, or a specific part thereof, and where this is in the best interests of the child:

(a) stay the case or the part thereof in question and invite the parties to introduce a request before the court of that other Member State in accordance with paragraph 4; or

(b) request a court of another Member State to assume jurisdiction in accordance with paragraph 5.

2. Paragraph 1 shall apply:

(a) upon application from a party; or

(b) of the court's own motion; or

(c) upon application from a court of another Member State with which the child has a particular connection, in accordance with paragraph 3.

A transfer made of the court's own motion or by application of a court of another Member State must be accepted by at least one of the parties.

3. The child shall be considered to have a particular connection to a Member State as mentioned in paragraph 1, if that Member State:

(a) has become the habitual residence of the child after the court referred to in paragraph 1 was seised; or

(b) is the former habitual residence of the child; or

(c) is the place of the child's nationality; or

(d) is the habitual residence of a holder of parental responsibility; or

(e) is the place where property of the child is located and the case concerns measures for the protection of the child relating to the administration, conservation or disposal of this property.

4. The court of the Member State having jurisdiction as to the substance of the matter shall set a time limit by which the courts of that other Member State shall be seised in accordance with paragraph 1.

If the courts are not seised by that time, the court which has been seised shall continue to exercise jurisdiction in accordance with Articles 8 to 14.

5. The courts of that other Member State may, where due to the specific circumstances of the case, this is in the best interests of the child, accept jurisdiction within six weeks of their seisure in accordance with paragraph 1(a) or 1(b). In this case, the court first seised shall decline jurisdiction. Otherwise, the court first seised shall continue to exercise jurisdiction in accordance with Articles 8 to 14.

6. The courts shall cooperate for the purposes of this Article, either directly or through the central authorities designated pursuant to Article 53.

Section 3

Common provisions

Article 16. Seising of a Court
1. A court shall be deemed to be seised:

(a) at the time when the document instituting the proceedings or an equivalent document is lodged with the court, provided that the applicant has not subsequently failed to take the steps he was required to take to have service effected on the respondent; or

(b) if the document has to be served before being lodged with the court, at the time when it is received by the authority responsible for service, provided that the applicant has not subsequently failed to take the steps he was required to take to have the document lodged with the court.

Article 17. Examination as to jurisdiction
Where a court of a Member State is seised of a case over which it has no jurisdiction under this Regulation and over which a court of another Member State has jurisdiction by virtue of this Regulation, it shall declare of its own motion that it has no jurisdiction.

Article 18. Examination as to admissibility
1.   Where a respondent habitually resident in a State other than the Member State where the action was brought does not enter an appearance, the court with jurisdiction shall stay the proceedings so long as it is not shown that the respondent has been able to receive the document instituting the proceedings or an equivalent document in sufficient time to enable him to arrange for his defence, or that all necessary steps have been taken to this end.

2.   Article 19 of Regulation (EC) No 1348/2000 shall apply instead of the provisions of paragraph 1 of this Article if the document instituting the proceedings or an equivalent document had to be transmitted from one Member State to another pursuant to that Regulation.

3.   Where the provisions of Regulation (EC) No 1348/2000 are not applicable, Article 15 of the Hague Convention of 15 November 1965 on the service abroad of judicial and extrajudicial documents in civil or commercial matters shall apply if the document instituting the proceedings or an equivalent document had to be transmitted abroad pursuant to that Convention.

Article 19. Lis pendens and dependent actions
1.   Where proceedings relating to divorce, legal separation or marriage annulment between the same parties are brought before courts of different Member States, the court second seised shall of its own motion stay its proceedings until such time as the jurisdiction of the court first seised is established.

2.   Where proceedings relating to parental responsibility relating to the same child and involving the same cause of action are brought before courts of different Member States, the court second seised shall of its own motion stay its proceedings until such time as the jurisdiction of the court first seised is established.

3.   Where the jurisdiction of the court first seised is established, the court second seised shall decline jurisdiction in favour of that court.

In that case, the party who brought the relevant action before the court second seised may bring that action before the court first seised.

Article 20. Provisional, including protective, measures
1.   In urgent cases, the provisions of this Regulation shall not prevent the courts of a Member State from taking such provisional, including protective, measures in respect of persons or assets in that State as may be available under the law of that Member State, even if, under this Regulation, the court of another Member State has jurisdiction as to the substance of the matter.

2.   The measures referred to in paragraph 1 shall cease to apply when the court of the Member State having jurisdiction under this Regulation as to the substance of the matter has taken the measures it considers appropriate.

CHAPTER III
RECOGNITION AND ENFORCEMENT

Section 1
Recognition

Article 21. Recognition of a judgment

1.   A judgment given in a Member State shall be recognised in the other Member States without any special procedure being required.

2.   In particular, and without prejudice to paragraph 3, no special procedure shall be required for updating the civil-status records of a Member State on the basis of a judgment relating to divorce, legal separation or marriage annulment given in another Member State, and against which no further appeal lies under the law of that Member State.

3.   Without prejudice to Section 4 of this Chapter, any interested party may, in accordance with the procedures provided for in Section 2 of this Chapter, apply for a decision that the judgment be or not be recognised.

The local jurisdiction of the court appearing in the list notified by each Member State to the Commission pursuant to Article 68 shall be determined by the internal law of the Member State in which proceedings for recognition or non-recognition are brought.

4.   Where the recognition of a judgment is raised as an incidental question in a court of a Member State, that court may determine that issue.

Article 22. Grounds of non-recognition for judgments relating to divorce, legal separation or marriage annulment

A judgment relating to a divorce, legal separation or marriage annulment shall not be recognised:

(a)   if such recognition is manifestly contrary to the public policy of the Member State in which recognition is sought;

(b)   where it was given in default of appearance, if the respondent was not served with the document which instituted the proceedings or with an equivalent document in sufficient time and in such a way as to enable the respondent to arrange for his or her defence unless it is determined that the respondent has accepted the judgment unequivocally;

(c)   if it is irreconcilable with a judgment given in proceedings between the same parties in the Member State in which recognition is sought; or

(d)   if it is irreconcilable with an earlier judgment given in another Member State or in a non-Member State between the same parties, provided that the earlier judgment fulfils the conditions necessary for its recognition in the Member State in which recognition is sought.

Article 23. Grounds of non-recognition for judgments relating to parental responsibility

A judgment relating to parental responsibility shall not be recognised:

(a)   if such recognition is manifestly contrary to the public policy of the Member State in which recognition is sought taking into account the best interests of the child;

(b)   if it was given, except in case of urgency, without the child having been given an opportunity to be heard, in violation of fundamental principles of procedure of the Member State in which recognition is sought;

(c)   where it was given in default of appearance if the person in default was not served with the document which instituted the proceedings or with an equivalent document in sufficient time and in such a way as to enable that person to arrange for his or her defence unless it is determined that such person has accepted the judgment unequivocally;

(d)   on the request of any person claiming that the judgment infringes his or her parental responsibility, if it was given without such person having been given an opportunity to be heard;

(e) if it is irreconcilable with a later judgment relating to parental responsibility given in the Member State in which recognition is sought;

(f) if it is irreconcilable with a later judgment relating to parental responsibility given in another Member State or in the non-Member State of the habitual residence of the child provided that the later judgment fulfils the conditions necessary for its recognition in the Member State in which recognition is sought. or

(g) if the procedure laid down in Article 56 has not been complied with.

Article 24. Prohibition of review of jurisdiction of the court of origin
The jurisdiction of the court of the Member State of origin may not be reviewed. The test of public policy referred to in Articles 22(a) and 23(a) may not be applied to the rules relating to jurisdiction set out in Articles 3 to 14.

Article 25. Differences in applicable law
The recognition of a judgment may not be refused because the law of the Member State in which such recognition is sought would not allow divorce, legal separation or marriage annulment on the same facts.

Article 26. Non-review as to substance
Under no circumstances may a judgment be reviewed as to its substance.

Article 27. Stay of proceedings
1. A court of a Member State in which recognition is sought of a judgment given in another Member State may stay the proceedings if an ordinary appeal against the judgment has been lodged.

2. A court of a Member State in which recognition is sought of a judgment given in Ireland or the United Kingdom may stay the proceedings if enforcement is suspended in the Member State of origin by reason of an appeal.

Section 2
Application for a declaration of enforceability

Article 28. Enforceable judgments
1. A judgment on the exercise of parental responsibility in respect of a child given in a Member State which is enforceable in that Member State and has been served shall be enforced in another Member State when, on the application of any interested party, it has been declared enforceable there.

2. However, in the United Kingdom, such a judgment shall be enforced in England and Wales, in Scotland or in Northern Ireland only when, on the application of any interested party, it has been registered for enforcement in that part of the United Kingdom.

Article 29. Jurisdiction of local courts
1. An application for a declaration of enforceability shall be submitted to the court appearing in the list notified by each Member State to the Commission pursuant to Article 68.

2. The local jurisdiction shall be determined by reference to the place of habitual residence of the person against whom enforcement is sought or by reference to the habitual residence of any child to whom the application relates.

Where neither of the places referred to in the first subparagraph can be found in the Member State of enforcement, the local jurisdiction shall be determined by reference to the place of enforcement.

Article 30. Procedure
1. The procedure for making the application shall be governed by the law of the Member State of enforcement.

2. The applicant must give an address for service within the area of jurisdiction of the court applied to. However, if the law of the Member State of enforcement does not provide for the furnishing of such an address, the applicant shall appoint a representative ad litem.

3. The documents referred to in Articles 37 and 39 shall be attached to the application.

Article 31. Decision of the court

1. The court applied to shall give its decision without delay. Neither the person against whom enforcement is sought, nor the child shall, at this stage of the proceedings, be entitled to make any submissions on the application.

2. The application may be refused only for one of the reasons specified in Articles 22, 23 and 24.

3. Under no circumstances may a judgment be reviewed as to its substance.

Article 32. Notice of the decision

The appropriate officer of the court shall without delay bring to the notice of the applicant the decision given on the application in accordance with the procedure laid down by the law of the Member State of enforcement.

Article 33. Appeal against the decision

1. The decision on the application for a declaration of enforceability may be appealed against by either party.

2. The appeal shall be lodged with the court appearing in the list notified by each Member State to the Commission pursuant to Article 68.

3. The appeal shall be dealt with in accordance with the rules governing procedure in contradictory matters.

4. If the appeal is brought by the applicant for a declaration of enforceability, the party against whom enforcement is sought shall be summoned to appear before the appellate court. If such person fails to appear, the provisions of Article 18 shall apply.

5. An appeal against a declaration of enforceability must be lodged within one month of service thereof. If the party against whom enforcement is sought is habitually resident in a Member State other than that in which the declaration of enforceability was given, the time for appealing shall be two months and shall run from the date of service, either on him or at his residence. No extension of time may be granted on account of distance.

Article 34. Courts of appeal and means of contest

The judgment given on appeal may be contested only by the proceedings referred to in the list notified by each Member State to the Commission pursuant to Article 68.

Article 35. Stay of proceedings

1. The court with which the appeal is lodged under Articles 33 or 34 may, on the application of the party against whom enforcement is sought, stay the proceedings if an ordinary appeal has been lodged in the Member State of origin, or if the time for such appeal has not yet expired. In the latter case, the court may specify the time within which an appeal is to be lodged.

2. Where the judgment was given in Ireland or the United Kingdom, any form of appeal available in the Member State of origin shall be treated as an ordinary appeal for the purposes of paragraph 1.

Article 36. Partial enforcement

1. Where a judgment has been given in respect of several matters and enforcement cannot be authorised for all of them, the court shall authorise enforcement for one or more of them.

2. An applicant may request partial enforcement of a judgment.

Section 3
Provisions common to Sections 1 and 2

Article 37. Documents

1. A party seeking or contesting recognition or applying for a declaration of enforceability shall produce:

(a) a copy of the judgment which satisfies the conditions necessary to establish its authenticity; and

(b) the certificate referred to in Article 39.

2. In addition, in the case of a judgment given in default, the party seeking recognition or applying for a declaration of enforceability shall produce:

(a) the original or certified true copy of the document which establishes that the defaulting party was served with the document instituting the proceedings or with an equivalent document; or

(b) any document indicating that the defendant has accepted the judgment unequivocally.

Article 38. Absence of documents

1. If the documents specified in Article 37(1)(b) or (2) are not produced, the court may specify a time for their production, accept equivalent documents or, if it considers that it has sufficient information before it, dispense with their production.

2. If the court so requires, a translation of such documents shall be furnished. The translation shall be certified by a person qualified to do so in one of the Member States.

Article 39. Certificate concerning judgments in matrimonial matters and certificate concerning judgments on parental responsibility

The competent court or authority of a Member State of origin shall, at the request of any interested party, issue a certificate using the standard form set out in Annex I (judgments in matrimonial matters) or in Annex II (judgments on parental responsibility).

Section 4
Enforceability of certain judgments concerning rights of access and of certain judgments which require the return of the child

Article 40. Scope

1. This Section shall apply to:

(a) rights of access; and

(b) the return of a child entailed by a judgment given pursuant to Article 11(8).

2. The provisions of this Section shall not prevent a holder of parental responsibility from seeking recognition and enforcement of a judgment in accordance with the provisions in Sections 1 and 2 of this Chapter.

Article 41. Rights of access

1. The rights of access referred to in Article 40(1)(a) granted in an enforceable judgment given in a Member State shall be recognised and enforceable in another Member State without the need for a declaration of enforceability and without any possibility of opposing its recognition if the judgment has been certified in the Member State of origin in accordance with paragraph 2.

Even if national law does not provide for enforceability by operation of law of a judgment granting access rights, the court of origin may declare that the judgment shall be enforceable, notwithstanding any appeal.

2. The judge of origin shall issue the certificate referred to in paragraph 1 using the standard form in Annex III (certificate concerning rights of access) only if:

(a) where the judgment was given in default, the person defaulting was served with the document which instituted the proceedings or with an equivalent document in sufficient time and in such a way as to enable that person to arrange for his or her defence, or, the person has been served with the document but not in compliance with these conditions, it is nevertheless established that he or she accepted the decision unequivocally;

(b)   all parties concerned were given an opportunity to be heard; and

(c)   the child was given an opportunity to be heard, unless a hearing was considered inappropriate having regard to his or her age or degree of maturity.

The certificate shall be completed in the language of the judgment.

3.   Where the rights of access involve a cross-border situation at the time of the delivery of the judgment, the certificate shall be issued ex officio when the judgment becomes enforceable, even if only provisionally. If the situation subsequently acquires a cross-border character, the certificate shall be issued at the request of one of the parties.

Article 42. Return of the child

1.   The return of a child referred to in Article 40(1)(b) entailed by an enforceable judgment given in a Member State shall be recognised and enforceable in another Member State without the need for a declaration of enforceability and without any possibility of opposing its recognition if the judgment has been certified in the Member State of origin in accordance with paragraph 2.

Even if national law does not provide for enforceability by operation of law, notwithstanding any appeal, of a judgment requiring the return of the child mentioned in Article 11(b)(8), the court of origin may declare the judgment enforceable.

2.   The judge of origin who delivered the judgment referred to in Article 40(1)(b) shall issue the certificate referred to in paragraph 1 only if:

(a)   the child was given an opportunity to be heard, unless a hearing was considered inappropriate having regard to his or her age or degree of maturity;

(b)   the parties were given an opportunity to be heard; and

(c)   the court has taken into account in issuing its judgment the reasons for and evidence underlying the order issued pursuant to Article 13 of the 1980 Hague Convention.

In the event that the court or any other authority takes measures to ensure the protection of the child after its return to the State of habitual residence, the certificate shall contain details of such measures.

The judge of origin shall of his or her own motion issue that certificate using the standard form in Annex IV (certificate concerning return of the child(ren)).

The certificate shall be completed in the language of the judgment.

Article 43. Rectification of the certificate

1.   The law of the Member State of origin shall be applicable to any rectification of the certificate.

2.   No appeal shall lie against the issuing of a certificate pursuant to Articles 41(1) or 42(1).

Article 44. Effects of the certificate

The certificate shall take effect only within the limits of the enforceability of the judgment.

Article 45. Documents

1.   A party seeking enforcement of a judgment shall produce:

(a)   a copy of the judgment which satisfies the conditions necessary to establish its authenticity; and

(b)   the certificate referred to in Article 41(1) or Article 42(1).

2.   For the purposes of this Article,

– the certificate referred to in Article 41(1) shall be accompanied by a translation of point 12 relating to the arrangements for exercising right of access,

– the certificate referred to in Article 42(1) shall be accompanied by a translation of its point 14 relating to the arrangements for implementing the measures taken to ensure the child's return.

The translation shall be into the official language or one of the official languages of the Member State of enforcement or any other language that the Member State of enforcement expressly accepts. The translation shall be certified by a person qualified to do so in one of the Member States.

Section 5
Authentic instruments and agreements

Article 46
Documents which have been formally drawn up or registered as authentic instruments and are enforceable in one Member State and also agreements between the parties that are enforceable in the Member State in which they were concluded shall be recognised and declared enforceable under the same conditions as judgments.

Section 6
Other provisions

Article 47. Enforcement procedure
1. The enforcement procedure is governed by the law of the Member State of enforcement.

2. Any judgment delivered by a court of another Member State and declared to be enforceable in accordance with Section 2 or certified in accordance with Article 41(1) or Article 42(1) shall be enforced in the Member State of enforcement in the same conditions as if it had been delivered in that Member State.

In particular, a judgment which has been certified according to Article 41(1) or Article 42(1) cannot be enforced if it is irreconcilable with a subsequent enforceable judgment.

Article 48. Practical arrangements for the exercise of rights of access
1. The courts of the Member State of enforcement may make practical arrangements for organising the exercise of rights of access, if the necessary arrangements have not or have not sufficiently been made in the judgment delivered by the courts of the Member State having jurisdiction as to the substance of the matter and provided the essential elements of this judgment are respected.

2. The practical arrangements made pursuant to paragraph 1 shall cease to apply pursuant to a later judgment by the courts of the Member State having jurisdiction as to the substance of the matter.

...

CHAPTER IV
COOPERATION BETWEEN CENTRAL AUTHORITIES IN MATTERS OF PARENTAL RESPONSIBILITY

...

Article 55. Cooperation on cases specific to parental responsibility
The central authorities shall, upon request from a central authority of another Member State or from a holder of parental responsibility, cooperate on specific cases to achieve the purposes of this Regulation. To this end, they shall, acting directly or through public authorities or other bodies, take all appropriate steps in accordance with the law of that Member State in matters of personal data protection to:
    (a)   collect and exchange information:
        (i)   on the situation of the child;
        (ii)   on any procedures under way; or
        (iii)   on decisions taken concerning the child;

(b)   provide information and assistance to holders of parental responsibility seeking the recognition and enforcement of decisions on their territory, in particular concerning rights of access and the return of the child;

(c)   facilitate communications between courts, in particular for the application of Article 11(6) and (7) and Article 15;

(d)   provide such information and assistance as is needed by courts to apply Article 56; and

(e)   facilitate agreement between holders of parental responsibility through mediation or other means, and facilitate cross-border cooperation to this end.

Article 56. Placement of a child in another Member State

1.   Where a court having jurisdiction under Articles 8 to 15 contemplates the placement of a child in institutional care or with a foster family and where such placement is to take place in another Member State, it shall first consult the central authority or other authority having jurisdiction in the latter State where public authority intervention in that Member State is required for domestic cases of child placement.

2.   The judgment on placement referred to in paragraph 1 may be made in the requesting State only if the competent authority of the requested State has consented to the placement.

3.   The procedures for consultation or consent referred to in paragraphs 1 and 2 shall be governed by the national law of the requested State.

4.   Where the authority having jurisdiction under Articles 8 to 15 decides to place the child in a foster family, and where such placement is to take place in another Member State and where no public authority intervention is required in the latter Member State for domestic cases of child placement, it shall so inform the central authority or other authority having jurisdiction in the latter State.

Article 57. Working method

1.   Any holder of parental responsibility may submit, to the central authority of the Member State of his or her habitual residence or to the central authority of the Member State where the child is habitually resident or present, a request for assistance as mentioned in Article 55. In general, the request shall include all available information of relevance to its enforcement. Where the request for assistance concerns the recognition or enforcement of a judgment on parental responsibility that falls within the scope of this Regulation, the holder of parental responsibility shall attach the relevant certificates provided for in Articles 39, 41(1) or 42(1).

2.   Member States shall communicate to the Commission the official language or languages of the Community institutions other than their own in which communications to the central authorities can be accepted.

3.   The assistance provided by the central authorities pursuant to Article 55 shall be free of charge.

4.   Each central authority shall bear its own costs.

...

CHAPTER V
RELATIONS WITH OTHER INSTRUMENTS

Article 59. Relation with other instruments

1.   Subject to the provisions of Articles 60, 63, 64 and paragraph 2 of this Article, this Regulation shall, for the Member States, supersede conventions existing at the time of entry into force of this Regulation which have been concluded between two or more Member States and relate to matters governed by this Regulation.

2.   (a) Finland and Sweden shall have the option of declaring that the Convention of 6 February 1931 between Denmark, Finland, Iceland, Norway and Sweden comprising international private law provisions on marriage, adoption and guar-

dianship, together with the Final Protocol thereto, will apply, in whole or in part, in their mutual relations, in place of the rules of this Regulation. Such declarations shall be annexed to this Regulation and published in the Official Journal of the European Union. They may be withdrawn, in whole or in part, at any moment by the said Member States.

(b)　The principle of non-discrimination on the grounds of nationality between citizens of the Union shall be respected.

(c)　The rules of jurisdiction in any future agreement to be concluded between the Member States referred to in subparagraph (a) which relate to matters governed by this Regulation shall be in line with those laid down in this Regulation.

(d)　Judgments handed down in any of the Nordic States which have made the declaration provided for in subparagraph (a) under a forum of jurisdiction corresponding to one of those laid down in Chapter II of this Regulation, shall be recognised and enforced in the other Member States under the rules laid down in Chapter III of this Regulation.

3.　Member States shall send to the Commission:

(a)　a copy of the agreements and uniform laws implementing these agreements referred to in paragraph 2(a) and (c);

(b)　any denunciations of, or amendments to, those agreements or uniform laws.

Article 60. Relations with certain multilateral conventions

In relations between Member States, this Regulation shall take precedence over the following Conventions in so far as they concern matters governed by this Regulation:

(a)　the Hague Convention of 5 October 1961 concerning the Powers of Authorities and the Law Applicable in respect of the Protection of Minors;

(b)　the Luxembourg Convention of 8 September 1967 on the Recognition of Decisions Relating to the Validity of Marriages;

(c)　the Hague Convention of 1 June 1970 on the Recognition of Divorces and Legal Separations;

(d)　the European Convention of 20 May 1980 on Recognition and Enforcement of Decisions concerning Custody of Children and on Restoration of Custody of Children; and

(e)　the Hague Convention of 25 October 1980 on the Civil Aspects of International Child Abduction.

Article 61. Relation with the Hague Convention of 19 October 1996 on Jurisdiction, Applicable law, Recognition, Enforcement and Cooperation in Respect of Parental Responsibility and Measures for the Protection of Children

As concerns the relation with the Hague Convention of 19 October 1996 on Jurisdiction, Applicable law, Recognition, Enforcement and Cooperation in Respect of Parental Responsibility and Measures for the Protection of Children, this Regulation shall apply:

(a)　where the child concerned has his or her habitual residence on the territory of a Member State;

(b)　as concerns the recognition and enforcement of a judgment given in a court of a Member State on the territory of another Member State, even if the child concerned has his or her habitual residence on the territory of a third State which is a contracting Party to the said Convention.

Article 62. Scope of effects

1.　The agreements and conventions referred to in Articles 59(1), 60 and 61 shall continue to have effect in relation to matters not governed by this Regulation.

2.　The conventions mentioned in Article 60, in particular the 1980 Hague Convention, continue to produce effects between the Member States which are party thereto, in compliance with Article 60.

...

CHAPTER VI
TRANSITIONAL PROVISIONS

Article 64

1.   The provisions of this Regulation shall apply only to legal proceedings instituted, to documents formally drawn up or registered as authentic instruments and to agreements concluded between the parties after its date of application in accordance with Article 72.

2.   Judgments given after the date of application of this Regulation in proceedings instituted before that date but after the date of entry into force of Regulation (EC) No 1347/2000 shall be recognised and enforced in accordance with the provisions of Chapter III of this Regulation if jurisdiction was founded on rules which accorded with those provided for either in Chapter II or in Regulation (EC) No 1347/2000 or in a convention concluded between the Member State of origin and the Member State addressed which was in force when the proceedings were instituted.

3.   Judgments given before the date of application of this Regulation in proceedings instituted after the entry into force of Regulation (EC) No 1347/2000 shall be recognised and enforced in accordance with the provisions of Chapter III of this Regulation provided they relate to divorce, legal separation or marriage annulment or parental responsibility for the children of both spouses on the occasion of these matrimonial proceedings.

4.   Judgments given before the date of application of this Regulation but after the date of entry into force of Regulation (EC) No 1347/2000 in proceedings instituted before the date of entry into force of Regulation (EC) No 1347/2000 shall be recognised and enforced in accordance with the provisions of Chapter III of this Regulation provided they relate to divorce, legal separation or marriage annulment or parental responsibility for the children of both spouses on the occasion of these matrimonial proceedings and that jurisdiction was founded on rules which accorded with those provided for either in Chapter II of this Regulation or in Regulation (EC) No 1347/2000 or in a convention concluded between the Member State of origin and the Member State addressed which was in force when the proceedings were instituted.

CHAPTER VII
FINAL PROVISIONS

Article 65. Review

No later than 1 January 2012, and every five years thereafter, the Commission shall present to the European Parliament, to the Council and to the European Economic and Social Committee a report on the application of this Regulation on the basis of information supplied by the Member States. The report shall be accompanied if need be by proposals for adaptations.

Article 66. Member States with two or more legal systems

With regard to a Member State in which two or more systems of law or sets of rules concerning matters governed by this Regulation apply in different territorial units:

(a)   any reference to habitual residence in that Member State shall refer to habitual residence in a territorial unit;

(b)   any reference to nationality, or in the case of the United Kingdom 'domicile', shall refer to the territorial unit designated by the law of that State;

(c)   any reference to the authority of a Member State shall refer to the authority of a territorial unit within that State which is concerned;

(d)   any reference to the rules of the requested Member State shall refer to the rules of the territorial unit in which jurisdiction, recognition or enforcement is invoked.

...

Article 71. Repeal of Regulation (EC) No 1347/2000

1.   Regulation (EC) No 1347/2000 shall be repealed as from the date of application of this Regulation.

2.   Any reference to Regulation (EC) No 1347/2000 shall be construed as a reference to this Regulation according to the comparative table in Annex V.

Article 72. Entry into force

This Regulation shall enter into force on 1 August 2004.

The Regulation shall apply from 1 March 2005, with the exception of Articles 67, 68, 69 and 70, which shall apply from 1 August 2004.

This Regulation shall be binding in its entirety and directly applicable in the Member States in accordance with the Treaty establishing the European Community.

Done at Brussels, 27 November 2003.

REGULATION (EC) NO 805/2004 OF THE EUROPEAN PARLIAMENT AND OF THE COUNCIL OF 21 APRIL 2004 CREATING A EUROPEAN ENFORCEMENT ORDER FOR UNCONTESTED CLAIMS

Official Journal L 143, 30/04/2004 p 15

THE EUROPEAN PARLIAMENT AND THE COUNCIL OF THE EUROPEAN UNION,

Having regard to the Treaty establishing the European Community, and in particular Articles 61(c) and the second indent of Article 67(5) thereof,

Having regard to the proposal from the Commission,

Having regard to the Opinion of the European Economic and Social Committee,

Acting in accordance with the procedure laid down in Article 251 of the Treaty,

Whereas:

(1)   The Community has set itself the objective of maintaining and developing an area of freedom, security and justice, in which the free movement of persons is ensured. To this end, the Community is to adopt, inter alia, measures in the field of judicial cooperation in civil matters that are necessary for the proper functioning of the internal market.

(2)   On 3 December 1998, the Council adopted an Action Plan of the Council and the Commission on how best to implement the provisions of the Treaty of Amsterdam on an area of freedom, security and justice (the Vienna Action Plan).

(3)   The European Council meeting in Tampere on 15 and 16 October 1999 endorsed the principle of mutual recognition of judicial decisions as the cornerstone for the creation of a genuine judicial area.

(4)   On 30 November 2000, the Council adopted a programme of measures for implementation of the principle of mutual recognition of decisions in civil and commercial matters. This programme includes in its first stage the abolition of exequatur, that is to say, the creation of a European Enforcement Order for uncontested claims.

(5)   The concept of 'uncontested claims' should cover all situations in which a creditor, given the verified absence of any dispute by the debtor as to the nature or extent of a pecuniary claim, has obtained either a court decision against that debtor or an enforceable document that requires the debtor's express consent, be it a court settlement or an authentic instrument.

(6)   The absence of objections from the debtor as stipulated in Article 3(1)(b) can take the shape of default of appearance at a court hearing or of failure to comply with an invitation by the court to give written notice of an intention to defend the case.

(7)   This Regulation should apply to judgments, court settlements and authentic instruments on uncontested claims and to decisions delivered following challenges to judgments, court settlements and authentic instruments certified as European Enforcement Orders.

(8)   In its Tampere conclusions, the European Council considered that access to enforcement in a Member State other than that in which the judgment has been given should be accelerated and simplified by dispensing with any intermediate measures to be taken prior to enforcement in the Member State in which enforcement is sought. A judgment that has been certified as a European Enforcement Order by the court of origin should, for enforcement purposes, be treated as if it had been delivered in the Member State in which enforcement is sought. In the United Kingdom, for example, the registration of a certified foreign judgment will therefore follow the same rules as the registration of a judgment from another part of the United Kingdom and is not to imply a review as to the substance of the foreign judgment. Arrangements for the enforcement of judgments should continue to be governed by national law.

(9)   Such a procedure should offer significant advantages as compared with the exequatur procedure provided for in Council Regulation (EC) No 44/2001 of 22 December 2000 on jurisdiction and the recognition and enforcement of judgments in civil and commercial matters, in that there is no need for approval by the judiciary in a second Member State with the delays and expenses that this entails.

(10)   Where a court in a Member State has given judgment on an uncontested claim in the absence of participation of the debtor in the proceedings, the abolition of any checks in the Member State of enforcement is inextricably linked to and dependent upon the existence of a sufficient guarantee of observance of the rights of the defence.

(11)   This Regulation seeks to promote the fundamental rights and takes into account the principles recognised in particular by the Charter of Fundamental Rights of the European Union. In particular, it seeks to ensure full respect for the right to a fair trial as recognised in Article 47 of the Charter.

(12)   Minimum standards should be established for the proceedings leading to the judgment in order to ensure that the debtor is informed about the court action against him, the requirements for his active participation in the proceedings to contest the claim and the consequences of his non-participation in sufficient time and in such a way as to enable him to arrange for his defence.

(13)   Due to differences between the Member States as regards the rules of civil procedure and especially those governing the service of documents, it is necessary to lay down a specific and detailed definition of those minimum standards. In particular, any method of service that is based on a legal fiction as regards the fulfilment of those minimum standards cannot be considered sufficient for the certification of a judgment as a European Enforcement Order.

(14)   All the methods of service listed in Articles 13 and 14 are characterised by either full certainty (Article 13) or a very high degree of likelihood (Article 14) that the document served has reached its addressee. In the second category, a judgment should only be certified as a European Enforcement Order if the Member State of origin has an appropriate mechanism in place enabling the debtor to apply for a full review of the judgment under the conditions set out in Article 19 in those

exceptional cases where, in spite of compliance with Article 14, the document has not reached the addressee.

(15)   Personal service on certain persons other than the debtor himself pursuant to Article 14(1)(a) and (b) should be understood to meet the requirements of those provisions only if those persons actually accepted/received the document in question.

(16)   Article 15 should apply to situations where the debtor cannot represent himself in court, as in the case of a legal person, and where a person to represent him is determined by law as well as situations where the debtor has authorised another person, in particular a lawyer, to represent him in the specific court proceedings at issue.

(17)   The courts competent for scrutinising full compliance with the minimum procedural standards should, if satisfied, issue a standardised European Enforcement Order certificate that makes that scrutiny and its result transparent.

(18)   Mutual trust in the administration of justice in the Member States justifies the assessment by the court of one Member State that all conditions for certification as a European Enforcement Order are fulfilled to enable a judgment to be enforced in all other Member States without judicial review of the proper application of the minimum procedural standards in the Member State where the judgment is to be enforced.

(19)   This Regulation does not imply an obligation for the Member States to adapt their national legislation to the minimum procedural standards set out herein. It provides an incentive to that end by making available a more efficient and rapid enforceability of judgments in other Member States only if those minimum standards are met.

(20)   Application for certification as a European Enforcement Order for uncontested claims should be optional for the creditor, who may instead choose the system of recognition and enforcement under Regulation (EC) No 44/2001 or other Community instruments.

(21)   When a document has to be sent from one Member State to another for service there, this Regulation and in particular the rules on service set out herein should apply together with Council Regulation (EC) No 1348/2000 of 29 May 2000 on the service in the Member States of judicial and extrajudicial documents in civil or commercial matters, and in particular Article 14 thereof in conjunction with Member States declarations made under Article 23 thereof.

(22)   Since the objectives of the proposed action cannot be sufficiently achieved by the Member States and can therefore, by reason of the scale or effects of the action, be better achieved at Community level, the Community may adopt measures, in accordance with the principle of subsidiarity as set out in Article 5 of the Treaty. In accordance with the principle of proportionality, as set out in that Article, this Regulation does not go beyond what is necessary in order to achieve those objectives.

(23)   The measures necessary for the implementation of this Regulation should be adopted in accordance with Council Decision 1999/468/EC of 28 June 1999 laying down the procedures for the exercise of implementing powers conferred on the Commission (8).

(24)   In accordance with Article 3 of the Protocol on the position of the United Kingdom and Ireland annexed to the Treaty on European Union and the Treaty establishing the European Community, the United Kingdom and Ireland have notified their wish to take part in the adoption and application of this Regulation.

(25)   In accordance with Articles 1 and 2 of the Protocol on the position of Denmark annexed to the Treaty on European Union and the Treaty establishing the European Community, Denmark does not take part in the adoption of this Regulation, and is therefore not bound by it or subject to its application.

(26)   Pursuant to the second indent of Article 67(5) of the Treaty, the codecision

procedure is applicable from 1 February 2003 for the measures laid down in this Regulation,

HAVE ADOPTED THIS REGULATION:

CHAPTER I
SUBJECT MATTER, SCOPE AND DEFINITIONS

Article 1. Subject matter

The purpose of this Regulation is to create a European Enforcement Order for uncontested claims to permit, by laying down minimum standards, the free circulation of judgments, court settlements and authentic instruments throughout all Member States without any intermediate proceedings needing to be brought in the Member State of enforcement prior to recognition and enforcement.

Article 2. Scope

1. This Regulation shall apply in civil and commercial matters, whatever the nature of the court or tribunal. It shall not extend, in particular, to revenue, customs or administrative matters or the liability of the State for acts and omissions in the exercise of State authority ('acta iure imperii').

2. This Regulation shall not apply to:

(a)   the status or legal capacity of natural persons, rights in property arising out of a matrimonial relationship, wills and succession;

(b)   bankruptcy, proceedings relating to the winding-up of insolvent companies or other legal persons, judicial arrangements, compositions and analogous proceedings;

(c)   social security;

(d)   arbitration.

3. In this Regulation, the term 'Member State' shall mean Member States with the exception of Denmark.

Article 3. Enforcement titles to be certified as a European Enforcement Order

1. This Regulation shall apply to judgments, court settlements and authentic instruments on uncontested claims.

A claim shall be regarded as uncontested if:

(a)   the debtor has expressly agreed to it by admission or by means of a settlement which has been approved by a court or concluded before a court in the course of proceedings; or

(b)   the debtor has never objected to it, in compliance with the relevant procedural requirements under the law of the Member State of origin, in the course of the court proceedings; or

(c)   the debtor has not appeared or been represented at a court hearing regarding that claim after having initially objected to the claim in the course of the court proceedings, provided that such conduct amounts to a tacit admission of the claim or of the facts alleged by the creditor under the law of the Member State of origin; or

(d)   the debtor has expressly agreed to it in an authentic instrument.

2. This Regulation shall also apply to decisions delivered following challenges to judgments, court settlements or authentic instruments certified as European Enforcement Orders.

Article 4. Definitions

For the purposes of this Regulation, the following definitions shall apply:

1. 'judgment': any judgment given by a court or tribunal of a Member State, whatever the judgment may be called, including a decree, order, decision or writ of execution, as well as the determination of costs or expenses by an officer of the court;

2. 'claim': a claim for payment of a specific sum of money that has fallen due or for which the due date is indicated in the judgment, court settlement or authentic instrument;

3. 'authentic instrument':

(a) a document which has been formally drawn up or registered as an authentic instrument, and the authenticity of which:

(i) relates to the signature and the content of the instrument; and

(ii) has been established by a public authority or other authority empowered for that purpose by the Member State in which it originates; or

(b) an arrangement relating to maintenance obligations concluded with administrative authorities or authenticated by them;

4. 'Member State of origin': the Member State in which the judgment has been given, the court settlement has been approved or concluded or the authentic instrument has been drawn up or registered, and is to be certified as a European Enforcement Order;

5. 'Member State of enforcement': the Member State in which enforcement of the judgment, court settlement or authentic instrument certified as a European Enforcement Order is sought;

6. 'court of origin': the court or tribunal seised of the proceedings at the time of fulfilment of the conditions set out in Article 3(1)(a), (b) or (c);

7. in Sweden, in summary proceedings concerning orders to pay (betalningsforelaggande), the expression 'court' includes the Swedish enforcement service (kronofogdemyndighet).

CHAPTER II
EUROPEAN ENFORCEMENT ORDER

Article 5. Abolition of exequatur
A judgment which has been certified as a European Enforcement Order in the Member State of origin shall be recognised and enforced in the other Member States without the need for a declaration of enforceability and without any possibility of opposing its recognition.

Article 6. Requirements for certification as a European Enforcement Order
1. A judgment on an uncontested claim delivered in a Member State shall, upon application at any time to the court of origin, be certified as a European Enforcement Order if:

(a) the judgment is enforceable in the Member State of origin; and

(b) the judgment does not conflict with the rules on jurisdiction as laid down in sections 3 and 6 of Chapter II of Regulation (EC) No 44/2001; and

(c) the court proceedings in the Member State of origin met the requirements as set out in Chapter III where a claim is uncontested within the meaning of Article 3(1)(b) or (c); and

(d) the judgment was given in the Member State of the debtor's domicile within the meaning of Article 59 of Regulation (EC) No 44/2001, in cases where

– a claim is uncontested within the meaning of Article 3(1)(b) or (c); and

– it relates to a contract concluded by a person, the consumer, for a purpose which can be regarded as being outside his trade or profession; and

– the debtor is the consumer.

2. Where a judgment certified as a European Enforcement Order has ceased to be enforceable or its enforceability has been suspended or limited, a certificate indicating the lack or limitation of enforceability shall, upon application at any time to the court of origin, be issued, using the standard form in Annex IV.

3. Without prejudice to Article 12(2), where a decision has been delivered following a challenge to a judgment certified as a European Enforcement Order in accordance with paragraph 1 of this Article, a replacement certificate shall, upon

application at any time, be issued, using the standard form in Annex V, if that decision on the challenge is enforceable in the Member State of origin.

Article 7. Costs related to court proceedings
Where a judgment includes an enforceable decision on the amount of costs related to the court proceedings, including the interest rates, it shall be certified as a European Enforcement Order also with regard to the costs unless the debtor has specifically objected to his obligation to bear such costs in the course of the court proceedings, in accordance with the law of the Member State of origin.

Article 8. Partial European Enforcement Order certificate
If only parts of the judgment meet the requirements of this Regulation, a partial European Enforcement Order certificate shall be issued for those parts.

Article 9. Issue of the European Enforcement Order certificate
1. The European Enforcement Order certificate shall be issued using the standard form in Annex I.
2. The European Enforcement Order certificate shall be issued in the language of the judgment.

Article 10. Rectification or withdrawal of the European Enforcement Order certificate
1. The European Enforcement Order certificate shall, upon application to the court of origin, be
(a) rectified where, due to a material error, there is a discrepancy between the judgment and the certificate;
(b) withdrawn where it was clearly wrongly granted, having regard to the requirements laid down in this Regulation.
2. The law of the Member State of origin shall apply to the rectification or withdrawal of the European Enforcement Order certificate.
3. An application for the rectification or withdrawal of a European Enforcement Order certificate may be made using the standard form in Annex VI.
4. No appeal shall lie against the issuing of a European Enforcement Order certificate.

Article 11. Effect of the European Enforcement Order certificate
The European Enforcement Order certificate shall take effect only within the limits of the enforceability of the judgment.

CHAPTER III
MINIMUM STANDARDS FOR UNCONTESTED CLAIMS PROCEDURES

Article 12. Scope of application of minimum standards
1. A judgment on a claim that is uncontested within the meaning of Article 3(1)(b) or (c) can be certified as a European Enforcement Order only if the court proceedings in the Member State of origin met the procedural requirements as set out in this Chapter.
2. The same requirements shall apply to the issuing of a European Enforcement Order certificate or a replacement certificate within the meaning of Article 6(3) for a decision following a challenge to a judgment where, at the time of that decision, the conditions of Article 3(1)(b) or (c) are fulfilled.

Article 13. Service with proof of receipt by the debtor
1. The document instituting the proceedings or an equivalent document may have been served on the debtor by one of the following methods:
(a) personal service attested by an acknowledgement of receipt, including the date of receipt, which is signed by the debtor;
(b) personal service attested by a document signed by the competent person

who effected the service stating that the debtor has received the document or refused to receive it without any legal justification, and the date of the service;

(c)   postal service attested by an acknowledgement of receipt including the date of receipt, which is signed and returned by the debtor;

(d)   service by electronic means such as fax or e-mail, attested by an acknowledgement of receipt including the date of receipt, which is signed and returned by the debtor.

2.   Any summons to a court hearing may have been served on the debtor in compliance with paragraph 1 or orally in a previous court hearing on the same claim and stated in the minutes of that previous court hearing.

Article 14. Service without proof of receipt by the debtor

1.   Service of the document instituting the proceedings or an equivalent document and any summons to a court hearing on the debtor may also have been effected by one of the following methods:

(a)   personal service at the debtor's personal address on persons who are living in the same household as the debtor or are employed there;

(b)   in the case of a self-employed debtor or a legal person, personal service at the debtor's business premises on persons who are employed by the debtor;

(c)   deposit of the document in the debtor's mailbox;

(d)   deposit of the document at a post office or with competent public authorities and the placing in the debtor's mailbox of written notification of that deposit, provided that the written notification clearly states the character of the document as a court document or the legal effect of the notification as effecting service and setting in motion the running of time for the purposes of time limits;

(e)   postal service without proof pursuant to paragraph 3 where the debtor has his address in the Member State of origin;

(f)   electronic means attested by an automatic confirmation of delivery, provided that the debtor has expressly accepted this method of service in advance.

2.   For the purposes of this Regulation, service under paragraph 1 is not admissible if the debtor's address is not known with certainty.

3.   Service pursuant to paragraph 1, (a) to (d), shall be attested by:

(a)   a document signed by the competent person who effected the service, indicating:

(i)   the method of service used; and

(ii)   the date of service; and

(iii)   where the document has been served on a person other than the debtor, the name of that person and his relation to the debtor, or

(b)   an acknowledgement of receipt by the person served, for the purposes of paragraphs 1(a) and (b).

Article 15. Service on the debtor's representatives

Service pursuant to Articles 13 or 14 may also have been effected on a debtor's representative.

Article 16. Provision to the debtor of due information about the claim

In order to ensure that the debtor was provided with due information about the claim, the document instituting the proceedings or the equivalent document must have contained the following:

(a)   the names and the addresses of the parties;

(b)   the amount of the claim;

(c)   if interest on the claim is sought, the interest rate and the period for which interest is sought unless statutory interest is automatically added to the principal under the law of the Member State of origin;

(d)   a statement of the reason for the claim.

Article 17. Provision to the debtor of due information about the procedural steps necessary to contest the claim

The following must have been clearly stated in or together with the document instituting the proceedings, the equivalent document or any summons to a court hearing:

(a)   the procedural requirements for contesting the claim, including the time limit for contesting the claim in writing or the time for the court hearing, as applicable, the name and the address of the institution to which to respond or before which to appear, as applicable, and whether it is mandatory to be represented by a lawyer;

(b)   the consequences of an absence of objection or default of appearance, in particular, where applicable, the possibility that a judgment may be given or enforced against the debtor and the liability for costs related to the court proceedings.

Article 18. Cure of non-compliance with minimum standards

1.   If the proceedings in the Member State of origin did not meet the procedural requirements as set out in Articles 13 to 17, such non-compliance shall be cured and a judgment may be certified as a European Enforcement Order if:

(a)   the judgment has been served on the debtor in compliance with the requirements pursuant to Article 13 or Article 14; and

(b)   it was possible for the debtor to challenge the judgment by means of a full review and the debtor has been duly informed in or together with the judgment about the procedural requirements for such a challenge, including the name and address of the institution with which it must be lodged and, where applicable, the time limit for so doing; and

(c)   the debtor has failed to challenge the judgment in compliance with the relevant procedural requirements.

2.   If the proceedings in the Member State of origin did not comply with the procedural requirements as set out in Article 13 or Article 14, such non-compliance shall be cured if it is proved by the conduct of the debtor in the court proceedings that he has personally received the document to be served in sufficient time to arrange for his defence.

Article 19. Minimum standards for review in exceptional cases

1.   Further to Articles 13 to 18, a judgment can only be certified as a European Enforcement Order if the debtor is entitled, under the law of the Member State of origin, to apply for a review of the judgment where:

(a)   (i) the document instituting the proceedings or an equivalent document or, where applicable, the summons to a court hearing, was served by one of the methods provided for in Article 14; and

(ii)   service was not effected in sufficient time to enable him to arrange for his defence, without any fault on his part; or

(b)   the debtor was prevented from objecting to the claim by reason of force majeure, or due to extraordinary circumstances without any fault on his part, provided in either case that he acts promptly.

2.   This Article is without prejudice to the possibility for Member States to grant access to a review of the judgment under more generous conditions than those mentioned in paragraph 1.

CHAPTER IV

ENFORCEMENT

Article 20. Enforcement procedure

1.   Without prejudice to the provisions of this Chapter, the enforcement procedures shall be governed by the law of the Member State of enforcement.

A judgment certified as a European Enforcement Order shall be enforced under the same conditions as a judgment handed down in the Member State of enforcement.

2. The creditor shall be required to provide the competent enforcement authorities of the Member State of enforcement with:

(a)   a copy of the judgment which satisfies the conditions necessary to establish its authenticity; and

(b)   a copy of the European Enforcement Order certificate which satisfies the conditions necessary to establish its authenticity; and

(c)   where necessary, a transcription of the European Enforcement Order certificate or a translation thereof into the official language of the Member State of enforcement or, if there are several official languages in that Member State, the official language or one of the official languages of court proceedings of the place where enforcement is sought, in conformity with the law of that Member State, or into another language that the Member State of enforcement has indicated it can accept. Each Member State may indicate the official language or languages of the institutions of the European Community other than its own which it can accept for the completion of the certificate. The translation shall be certified by a person qualified to do so in one of the Member States.

3. No security, bond or deposit, however described, shall be required of a party who in one Member State applies for enforcement of a judgment certified as a European Enforcement Order in another Member State on the ground that he is a foreign national or that he is not domiciled or resident in the Member State of enforcement.

Article 21. Refusal of enforcement

1. Enforcement shall, upon application by the debtor, be refused by the competent court in the Member State of enforcement if the judgment certified as a European Enforcement Order is irreconcilable with an earlier judgment given in any Member State or in a third country, provided that:

(a)   the earlier judgment involved the same cause of action and was between the same parties; and

(b)   the earlier judgment was given in the Member State of enforcement or fulfils the conditions necessary for its recognition in the Member State of enforcement; and

(c)   the irreconcilability was not and could not have been raised as an objection in the court proceedings in the Member State of origin.

2. Under no circumstances may the judgment or its certification as a European Enforcement Order be reviewed as to their substance in the Member State of enforcement.

Article 22. Agreements with third countries

This Regulation shall not affect agreements by which Member States undertook, prior to the entry into force of Regulation (EC) No 44/2001, pursuant to Article 59 of the Brussels Convention on jurisdiction and the enforcement of judgments in civil and commercial matters, not to recognise judgments given, in particular in other Contracting States to that Convention, against defendants domiciled or habitually resident in a third country where, in cases provided for in Article 4 of that Convention, the judgment could only be founded on a ground of jurisdiction specified in the second paragraph of Article 3 of that Convention.

Article 23. Stay or limitation of enforcement

Where the debtor has

– challenged a judgment certified as a European Enforcement Order, including an application for review within the meaning of Article 19, or

– applied for the rectification or withdrawal of a European Enforcement Order certificate in accordance with Article 10,

the competent court or authority in the Member State of enforcement may, upon application by the debtor:
(a)   limit the enforcement proceedings to protective measures; or
(b)   make enforcement conditional on the provision of such security as it shall determine; or
(c)   under exceptional circumstances, stay the enforcement proceedings.

CHAPTER V
COURT SETTLEMENTS AND AUTHENTIC INSTRUMENTS

Article 24. Court settlements
1.   A settlement concerning a claim within the meaning of Article 4(2) which has been approved by a court or concluded before a court in the course of proceedings and is enforceable in the Member State in which it was approved or concluded shall, upon application to the court that approved it or before which it was concluded, be certified as a European Enforcement Order using the standard form in Annex II.
2.   A settlement which has been certified as a European Enforcement Order in the Member State of origin shall be enforced in the other Member States without the need for a declaration of enforceability and without any possibility of opposing its enforceability.
3.   The provisions of Chapter II, with the exception of Articles 5, 6(1) and 9(1), and of Chapter IV, with the exception of Articles 21(1) and 22, shall apply as appropriate.

Article 25. Authentic instruments
1.   An authentic instrument concerning a claim within the meaning of Article 4(2) which is enforceable in one Member State shall, upon application to the authority designated by the Member State of origin, be certified as a European Enforcement Order, using the standard form in Annex III.
2.   An authentic instrument which has been certified as a European Enforcement Order in the Member State of origin shall be enforced in the other Member States without the need for a declaration of enforceability and without any possibility of opposing its enforceability.
3.   The provisions of Chapter II, with the exception of Articles 5, 6(1) and 9(1), and of Chapter IV, with the exception of Articles 21(1) and 22, shall apply as appropriate.

CHAPTER VI
TRANSITIONAL PROVISION

Article 26. Transitional provision
This Regulation shall apply only to judgments given, to court settlements approved or concluded and to documents formally drawn up or registered as authentic instruments after the entry into force of this Regulation.

CHAPTER VII
RELATIONSHIP WITH OTHER COMMUNITY INSTRUMENTS

Article 27. Relationship with Regulation (EC) No 44/2001
This Regulation shall not affect the possibility of seeking recognition and enforcement, in accordance with Regulation (EC) No 44/2001, of a judgment, a court settlement or an authentic instrument on an uncontested claim.

Article 28. Relationship with Regulation (EC) No 1348/2000
This Regulation shall not affect the application of Regulation (EC) No 1348/2000.

CHAPTER VIII
GENERAL AND FINAL PROVISIONS

Article 33. Entry into force

This Regulation shall enter into force on 21 January 2004.

It shall apply from 21 October 2005, with the exception of Articles 30, 31 and 32, which shall apply from 21 January 2005.

This Regulation shall be binding in its entirety and directly applicable in the Member States in accordance with the Treaty establishing the European Community.

Done at Strasbourg, 21 April 2004.

AGREEMENT MADE 19TH OCTOBER 2005 BETWEEN THE EUROPEAN COMMUNITY AND THE KINGDOM OF DENMARK ON JURISDICTION AND THE RECOGNITION AND ENFORCEMENT OF JUDGMENTS IN CIVIL AND COMMERCIAL MATTERS (RE IMPLEMENTATION OF BRUSSELS I REGULATION)

Official Journal L 299, 16/11/2005 p 62

THE EUROPEAN COMMUNITY, hereinafter referred to as 'the Community', of the one part, and

THE KINGDOM OF DENMARK, hereinafter referred to as 'Denmark', of the other part,

DESIRING to unify the rules of conflict of jurisdiction in civil and commercial matters and to simplify the formalities with a view to rapid and simple recognition and enforcement of judgments within the Community,

WHEREAS on 27 September 1968 the Member States, acting under Article 293, fourth indent, of the Treaty establishing the European Community, concluded the Brussels Convention on Jurisdiction and the Enforcement of Judgments in Civil and Commercial Matters (the Brussels Convention), as amended by Conventions on the Accession of the new Member States to that Convention. On 16 September 1988 the Member States and the EFTA States concluded the Convention on Jurisdiction and the Enforcement of Judgments in Civil and Commercial Matters (the Lugano Convention), which is a parallel Convention to the Brussels Convention,

WHEREAS the main content of the Brussels Convention has been taken over in Council Regulation (EC) No 44/2001 of 22 December 2000 on jurisdiction and the recognition and enforcement of judgments in civil and commercial matters (the Brussels I Regulation),

REFERRING to the Protocol on the position of Denmark annexed to the Treaty on European Union and to the Treaty establishing the European Community (the Protocol on the position of Denmark) pursuant to which the Brussels I Regulation shall not be binding upon or applicable in Denmark,

STRESSING that a solution to the unsatisfactory legal situation arising from differences in applicable rules on jurisdiction, recognition and enforcement of judgments within the Community must be found,

DESIRING that the provisions of the Brussels I Regulation, future amendments thereto and the implementing measures relating to it should under international law apply to the relations between the Community and Denmark being a Member State with a special position with respect to Title IV of the Treaty establishing the European Community,

STRESSING that continuity between the Brussels Convention and this Agreement should be ensured, and that transitional provisions as in the Brussels I Regulation should be applied to this Agreement as well. The same need for continuity applies as regards the interpretation of the Brussels Convention by the Court of Justice of the European Communities and the 1971 Protocol should remain applicable also to cases already pending when this Agreement enters into force,

STRESSING that the Brussels Convention also continues to apply to the territories of the Member States which fall within the territorial scope of that Convention and which are excluded from this Agreement,

STRESSING the importance of proper coordination between the Community and Denmark with regard to the negotiation and conclusion of international agreements that may affect or alter the scope of the Brussels I Regulation,

STRESSING that Denmark should seek to join international agreements entered into by the Community where Danish participation in such agreements is relevant for the coherent application of the Brussels I Regulation and this Agreement,

STATING that the Court of Justice of the European Communities should have jurisdiction in order to secure the uniform application and interpretation of this Agreement including the provisions of the Brussels I Regulation and any implementing Community measures forming part of this Agreement,

REFERRING to the jurisdiction conferred to the Court of Justice of the European Communities pursuant to Article 68(1) of the Treaty establishing the European Community to give rulings on preliminary questions relating to the validity and interpretation of acts of the institutions of the Community based on Title IV of the Treaty, including the validity and interpretation of this Agreement, and to the circumstance that this provision shall not be binding upon or applicable in Denmark, as results from the Protocol on the position of Denmark,

CONSIDERING that the Court of Justice of the European Communities should have jurisdiction under the same conditions to give preliminary rulings on questions concerning the validity and interpretation of this Agreement which are raised by a Danish court or tribunal, and that Danish courts and tribunals should therefore request preliminary rulings under the same conditions as courts and tribunals of other Member States in respect of the interpretation of the Brussels I Regulation and its implementing measures,

REFERRING to the provision that, pursuant to Article 68(3) of the Treaty establishing the European Community, the Council of the European Union, the European Commission and the Member States may request the Court of Justice of the European Communities to give a ruling on the interpretation of acts of the institutions of the Community based on Title IV of the Treaty, including the interpretation of this Agreement, and the circumstance that this provision shall not be binding upon or applicable in Denmark, as results from the Protocol on the position of Denmark,

CONSIDERING that Denmark should, under the same conditions as other Member States in respect of the Brussels I Regulation and its implementing measures, be accorded the possibility to request the Court of Justice of the European Communities to give rulings on questions relating to the interpretation of this Agreement,

STRESSING that under Danish law the courts in Denmark should, when interpreting this Agreement including the provisions of the Brussels I Regulation and any implementing Community measures forming part of this Agreement, take due account of the rulings contained in the case law of the Court of Justice of the European Communities and of the courts of the Member States of the European Communities in respect of provisions of the Brussels Convention, the Brussels I Regulation and any implementing Community measures,

CONSIDERING that it should be possible to request the Court of Justice of the European Communities to rule on questions relating to compliance with obligations under this Agreement pursuant to the provisions of the Treaty establishing the European Community governing proceedings before the Court,

WHEREAS, by virtue of Article 300(7) of the Treaty establishing the European Community, this Agreement binds Member States; it is therefore appropriate that

Denmark, in the case of non-compliance by a Member State, should be able to seize the Commission as guardian of the Treaty,

HAVE AGREED AS FOLLOWS:

Article 1. Aim

1.   The aim of this Agreement is to apply the provisions of the Brussels I Regulation and its implementing measures to the relations between the Community and Denmark, in accordance with Article 2(1) of this Agreement.

2.   It is the objective of the Contracting Parties to arrive at a uniform application and interpretation of the provisions of the Brussels I Regulation and its implementing measures in all Member States.

3.   The provisions of Articles 3(1), 4(1) and 5(1) of this Agreement result from the Protocol on the position of Denmark.

Article 2. Jurisdiction and the recognition and enforcement of judgments in civil and commercial matters

1.   The provisions of the Brussels I Regulation, which is annexed to this Agreement and forms part thereof, together with its implementing measures adopted pursuant to Article 74(2) of the Regulation and, in respect of implementing measures adopted after the entry into force of this Agreement, implemented by Denmark as referred to in Article 4 of this Agreement, and the measures adopted pursuant to Article 74(1) of the Regulation, shall under international law apply to the relations between the Community and Denmark.

2.   However, for the purposes of this Agreement, the application of the provisions of that Regulation shall be modified as follows:

(a)   Article 1(3) shall not apply.

(b)   Article 50 shall be supplemented by the following paragraph (as paragraph 2):

'2.   However, an applicant who requests the enforcement of a decision given by an administrative authority in Denmark in respect of a maintenance order may, in the Member State addressed, claim the benefits referred to in the first paragraph if he presents a statement from the Danish Ministry of Justice to the effect that he fulfils the financial requirements to qualify for the grant of complete or partial legal aid or exemption from costs or expenses.'

(c)   Article 62 shall be supplemented by the following paragraph (as paragraph 2):

'2.   In matters relating to maintenance, the expression "court" includes the Danish administrative authorities.'

(d)   Article 64 shall apply to seagoing ships registered in Denmark as well as in Greece and Portugal.

(e)   The date of entry into force of this Agreement shall apply instead of the date of entry into force of the Regulation as referred to in Articles 70(2), 72 and 76 thereof.

(f)   The transitional provisions of this Agreement shall apply instead of Article 66 of the Regulation.

Article 3. Amendments to the Brussels I Regulation

1.   Denmark shall not take part in the adoption of amendments to the Brussels I Regulation and no such amendments shall be binding upon or applicable in Denmark.

2.   Whenever amendments to the Regulation are adopted Denmark shall notify the Commission of its decision whether or not to implement the content of such amendments. Notification shall be given at the time of the adoption of the amendments or within 30 days thereafter.

3.   If Denmark decides that it will implement the content of the amendments the notification shall indicate whether implementation can take place administratively or requires parliamentary approval.

4. If the notification indicates that implementation can take place administratively the notification shall, moreover, state that all necessary administrative measures enter into force on the date of entry into force of the amendments to the Regulation or have entered into force on the date of the notification, whichever date is the latest.

5. If the notification indicates that implementation requires parliamentary approval in Denmark, the following rules shall apply:

(a) Legislative measures in Denmark shall enter into force on the date of entry into force of the amendments to the Regulation or within 6 months after the notification, whichever date is the latest;

(b) Denmark shall notify the Commission of the date upon which the implementing legislative measures enter into force.

6. A Danish notification that the content of the amendments has been implemented in Denmark, in accordance with paragraphs 4 and 5, creates mutual obligations under international law between Denmark and the Community. The amendments to the Regulation shall then constitute amendments to this Agreement and shall be considered annexed hereto.

7. In cases where:

(a) Denmark notifies its decision not to implement the content of the amendments; or

(b) Denmark does not make a notification within the 30-day time-limit set out in paragraph 2; or

(c) Legislative measures in Denmark do not enter into force within the time-limits set out in paragraph 5,

this Agreement shall be considered terminated unless the parties decide otherwise within 90 days or, in the situation referred to under (c), legislative measures in Denmark enter into force within the same period. Termination shall take effect three months after the expiry of the 90-day period.

8. Legal proceedings instituted and documents formally drawn up or registered as authentic instruments before the date of termination of the Agreement as set out in paragraph 7 are not affected hereby.

Article 4. Implementing measures

1. Denmark shall not take part in the adoption of opinions by the Committee referred to in Article 75 of the Brussels I Regulation. Implementing measures adopted pursuant to Article 74(2) of that Regulation shall not be binding upon and shall not be applicable in Denmark.

2. Whenever implementing measures are adopted pursuant to Article 74(2) of the Regulation, the implementing measures shall be communicated to Denmark. Denmark shall notify the Commission of its decision whether or not to implement the content of the implementing measures. Notification shall be given upon receipt of the implementing measures or within 30 days thereafter.

3. The notification shall state that all necessary administrative measures in Denmark enter into force on the date of entry into force of the implementing measures or have entered into force on the date of the notification, whichever date is the latest.

4. A Danish notification that the content of the implementing measures has been implemented in Denmark creates mutual obligations under international law between Denmark and the Community. The implementing measures will then form part of this Agreement.

5. In cases where:

(a) Denmark notifies its decision not to implement the content of the implementing measures; or

(b) Denmark does not make a notification within the 30-day time-limit set out in paragraph 2,

this Agreement shall be considered terminated unless the parties decide otherwise within 90 days. Termination shall take effect three months after the expiry of the 90-day period.

6. Legal proceedings instituted and documents formally drawn up or registered as authentic instruments before the date of termination of the Agreement as set out in paragraph 5 are not affected hereby.

7. If in exceptional cases the implementation requires parliamentary approval in Denmark, the Danish notification under paragraph 2 shall indicate this and the provisions of Article 3(5) to (8) shall apply.

8. Denmark shall notify the Commission of texts amending the items set out in Article 2(2)(g) to (j) of this Agreement. The Commission shall adapt Article 2(2)(g) to (j) accordingly.

Article 5. International agreements which affect the Brussels I Regulation

1. International agreements entered into by the Community based on the rules of the Brussels I Regulation shall not be binding upon and shall not be applicable in Denmark.

2. Denmark will abstain from entering into international agreements which may affect or alter the scope of the Brussels I Regulation as annexed to this Agreement unless it is done in agreement with the Community and satisfactory arrangements have been made with regard to the relationship between this Agreement and the international agreement in question.

3. When negotiating international agreements that may affect or alter the scope of the Brussels I Regulation as annexed to this Agreement, Denmark will coordinate its position with the Community and will abstain from any actions that would jeopardise the objectives of a Community position within its sphere of competence in such negotiations.

Article 6. Jurisdiction of the Court of Justice of the European Communities in relation to the interpretation of the Agreement

1. Where a question on the validity or interpretation of this Agreement is raised in a case pending before a Danish court or tribunal, that court or tribunal shall request the Court of Justice to give a ruling thereon whenever under the same circumstances a court or tribunal of another Member State of the European Union would be required to do so in respect of the Brussels I Regulation and its implementing measures referred to in Article 2(1) of this Agreement.

2. Under Danish law, the courts in Denmark shall, when interpreting this Agreement, take due account of the rulings contained in the case law of the Court of Justice in respect of provisions of the Brussels Convention, the Brussels I Regulation and any implementing Community measures.

3. Denmark may, like the Council, the Commission and any Member State, request the Court of Justice to give a ruling on a question of interpretation of this Agreement. The ruling given by the Court of Justice in response to such a request shall not apply to judgments of courts or tribunals of the Member States which have become res judicata.

4. Denmark shall be entitled to submit observations to the Court of Justice in cases where a question has been referred to it by a court or tribunal of a Member State for a preliminary ruling concerning the interpretation of any provision referred to in Article 2(1).

5. The Protocol on the Statute of the Court of Justice of the European Communities and its Rules of Procedure shall apply.

6. If the provisions of the Treaty establishing the European Community regarding rulings by the Court of Justice are amended with consequences for rulings in respect of the Brussels I Regulation, Denmark may notify the Commission of its decision not to apply the amendments in respect of this Agreement. Notification shall be given at the time of the entry into force of the amendments or within 60 days thereafter.

In such a case this Agreement shall be considered terminated. Termination shall take effect three months after the notification.

7. Legal proceedings instituted and documents formally drawn up or registered as authentic instruments before the date of termination of the Agreement as set out in paragraph 6 are not affected hereby.

Article 7. Jurisdiction of the Court of Justice of the European Communities in relation to compliance with the Agreement

1. The Commission may bring before the Court of Justice cases against Denmark concerning non-compliance with any obligation under this Agreement.

2. Denmark may bring a complaint before the Commission as to the non-compliance by a Member State of its obligations under this Agreement.

3. The relevant provisions of the Treaty establishing the European Community governing proceedings before the Court of Justice as well as the Protocol on the Statute of the Court of Justice of the European Communities and its Rules of Procedure shall apply.

Article 8. Territorial application

1. This Agreement shall apply to the territories referred to in Article 299 of the Treaty establishing the European Community.

2. If the Community decides to extend the application of the Brussels I Regulation to territories currently governed by the Brussels Convention, the Community and Denmark shall cooperate in order to ensure that such an application also extends to Denmark.

Article 9. Transitional provisions

1. This Agreement shall apply only to legal proceedings instituted and to documents formally drawn up or registered as authentic instruments after the entry into force thereof.

2. However, if the proceedings in the Member State of origin were instituted before the entry into force of this Agreement, judgments given after that date shall be recognised and enforced in accordance with this Agreement,

(a) if the proceedings in the Member State of origin were instituted after the entry into force of the Brussels or the Lugano Convention both in the Member State of origin and in the Member State addressed;

(b) in all other cases, if jurisdiction was founded upon rules which accorded with those provided for either in this Agreement or in a convention concluded between the Member State of origin and the Member State addressed which was in force when the proceedings were instituted.

Article 10. Relationship to the Brussels I Regulation

1. This Agreement shall not prejudice the application by the Member States of the Community other than Denmark of the Brussels I Regulation.

2. However, this Agreement shall in any event be applied:

(a) in matters of jurisdiction, where the defendant is domiciled in Denmark, or where Article 22 or 23 of the Regulation, applicable to the relations between the Community and Denmark by virtue of Article 2 of this Agreement, confer jurisdiction on the courts of Denmark;

(b) in relation to a lis pendens or to related actions as provided for in Articles 27 and 28 of the Brussels I Regulation, applicable to the relations between the Community and Denmark by virtue of Article 2 of this Agreement, when proceedings are instituted in a Member State other than Denmark and in Denmark;

(c) in matters of recognition and enforcement, where Denmark is either the State of origin or the State addressed.

Article 11. Termination of the agreement

1. This Agreement shall terminate if Denmark informs the other Member States

that it no longer wishes to avail itself of the provisions of Part I of the Protocol on the position of Denmark, in accordance with Article 7 of that Protocol.

2.   This Agreement may be terminated by either Contracting Party giving notice to the other Contracting Party. Termination shall be effective six months after the date of such notice.

3.   Legal proceedings instituted and documents formally drawn up or registered as authentic instruments before the date of termination of the Agreement as set out in paragraph 1 or 2 are not affected hereby.

Article 12. Entry into force

1.   The Agreement shall be adopted by the Contracting Parties in accordance with their respective procedures.

2.   The Agreement shall enter into force on the first day of the sixth month following the notification by the Contracting Parties of the completion of their respective procedures required for this purpose.

REGULATION (EC) NO 864/2007 OF THE EUROPEAN PARLIAMENT AND OF THE COUNCIL OF 11 JULY 2007 ON THE LAW APPLICABLE TO NON-CONTRACTUAL OBLIGATIONS ('ROME II')

THE EUROPEAN PARLIAMENT AND THE COUNCIL OF THE EUROPEAN UNION,

Having regard to the Treaty establishing the European Community, and in particular Articles 61(c) and 67 thereof,

Having regard to the proposal from the Commission,

Having regard to the opinion of the European Economic and Social Committee,

Acting in accordance with the procedure laid down in Article 251 of the Treaty in the light of the joint text approved by the Conciliation Committee on 25 June 2007.

Whereas:

(1)   The Community has set itself the objective of maintaining and developing an area of freedom, security and justice. For the progressive establishment of such an area, the Community is to adopt measures relating to judicial cooperation in civil matters with a cross-border impact to the extent necessary for the proper functioning of the internal market.

(2)   According to Article 65(b) of the Treaty, these measures are to include those promoting the compatibility of the rules applicable in the Member States concerning the conflict of laws and of jurisdiction.

(3)   The European Council meeting in Tampere on 15 and 16 October 1999 endorsed the principle of mutual recognition of judgments and other decisions of judicial authorities as the cornerstone of judicial cooperation in civil matters and invited the Council and the Commission to adopt a programme of measures to implement the principle of mutual recognition.

(4)   On 30 November 2000, the Council adopted a joint Commission and Council programme of measures for implementation of the principle of mutual recognition of decisions in civil and commercial matters. The programme identifies measures relating to the harmonisation of conflict-of-law rules as those facilitating the mutual recognition of judgments.

(5)   The Hague Programme, adopted by the European Council on 5 November 2004, called for work to be pursued actively on the rules of conflict of laws regarding non-contractual obligations ('Rome II').

(6)   The proper functioning of the internal market creates a need, in order to improve the predictability of the outcome of litigation, certainty as to the law applicable and the free movement of judgments, for the conflict-of-law rules in the

Member States to designate the same national law irrespective of the country of the court in which an action is brought.

(7)   The substantive scope and the provisions of this Regulation should be consistent with Council Regulation (EC) No 44/2001 of 22 December 2000 on jurisdiction and the recognition and enforcement of judgments in civil and commercial matters ('Brussels I') and the instruments dealing with the law applicable to contractual obligations.

(8)   This Regulation should apply irrespective of the nature of the court or tribunal seised.

(9)   Claims arising out of *acta iure imperii* should include claims against officials who act on behalf of the State and liability for acts of public authorities, including liability of publicly appointed office-holders. Therefore, these matters should be excluded from the scope of this Regulation.

(10)   Family relationships should cover parentage, marriage, affinity and collateral relatives. The reference in Article 1(2) to relationships having comparable effects to marriage and other family relationships should be interpreted in accordance with the law of the Member State in which the court is seised.

(11)   The concept of a non-contractual obligation varies from one Member State to another. Therefore for the purposes of this Regulation non-contractual obligation should be understood as an autonomous concept. The conflict-of-law rules set out in this Regulation should also cover non-contractual obligations arising out of strict liability.

(12)   The law applicable should also govern the question of the capacity to incur liability in tort/delict.

(13)   Uniform rules applied irrespective of the law they designate may avert the risk of distortions of competition between Community litigants.

(14)   The requirement of legal certainty and the need to do justice in individual cases are essential elements of an area of justice. This Regulation provides for the connecting factors which are the most appropriate to achieve these objectives. Therefore, this Regulation provides for a general rule but also for specific rules and, in certain provisions, for an 'escape clause' which allows a departure from these rules where it is clear from all the circumstances of the case that the tort/delict is manifestly more closely connected with another country. This set of rules thus creates a flexible framework of conflict-of-law rules. Equally, it enables the court seised to treat individual cases in an appropriate manner.

(15)   The principle of the *lex loci delicti commissi* is the basic solution for non-contractual obligations in virtually all the Member States, but the practical application of the principle where the component factors of the case are spread over several countries varies. This situation engenders uncertainty as to the law applicable.

(16)   Uniform rules should enhance the foreseeability of court decisions and ensure a reasonable balance between the interests of the person claimed to be liable and the person who has sustained damage. A connection with the country where the direct damage occurred (*lex loci damni*) strikes a fair balance between the interests of the person claimed to be liable and the person sustaining the damage, and also reflects the modern approach to civil liability and the development of systems of strict liability.

(17)   The law applicable should be determined on the basis of where the damage occurs, regardless of the country or countries in which the indirect consequences could occur. Accordingly, in cases of personal injury or damage to property, the country in which the damage occurs should be the country where the injury was sustained or the property was damaged respectively.

(18)   The general rule in this Regulation should be the '*lex loci damni*' provided for in Article 4(1). Article 4(2) should be seen as an exception to this general principle, creating a special connection where the parties have their habitual residence in the same country. Article 4(3) should be understood as an 'escape

clause' from Article 4(1) and (2), where it is clear from all the circumstances of the case that the tort/delict is manifestly more closely connected with another country.

(19)   Specific rules should be laid down for special torts/delicts where the general rule does not allow a reasonable balance to be struck between the interests at stake.

(20)   The conflict-of-law rule in matters of product liability should meet the objectives of fairly spreading the risks inherent in a modern high-technology society, protecting consumers' health, stimulating innovation, securing undistorted competition and facilitating trade. Creation of a cascade system of connecting factors, together with a foreseeability clause, is a balanced solution in regard to these objectives. The first element to be taken into account is the law of the country in which the person sustaining the damage had his or her habitual residence when the damage occurred, if the product was marketed in that country. The other elements of the cascade are triggered if the product was not marketed in that country, without prejudice to Article 4(2) and to the possibility of a manifestly closer connection to another country.

(21)   The special rule in Article 6 is not an exception to the general rule in Article 4(1) but rather a clarification of it. In matters of unfair competition, the conflict-of-law rule should protect competitors, consumers and the general public and ensure that the market economy functions properly. The connection to the law of the country where competitive relations or the collective interests of consumers are, or are likely to be, affected generally satisfies these objectives.

(22)   The non-contractual obligations arising out of restrictions of competition in Article 6(3) should cover infringements of both national and Community competition law. The law applicable to such non-contractual obligations should be the law of the country where the market is, or is likely to be, affected. In cases where the market is, or is likely to be, affected in more than one country, the claimant should be able in certain circumstances to choose to base his or her claim on the law of the court seised.

(23)   For the purposes of this Regulation, the concept of restriction of competition should cover prohibitions on agreements between undertakings, decisions by associations of undertakings and concerted practices which have as their object or effect the prevention, restriction or distortion of competition within a Member State or within the internal market, as well as prohibitions on the abuse of a dominant position within a Member State or within the internal market, where such agreements, decisions, concerted practices or abuses are prohibited by Articles 81 and 82 of the Treaty or by the law of a Member State.

(24)   'Environmental damage' should be understood as meaning adverse change in a natural resource, such as water, land or air, impairment of a function performed by that resource for the benefit of another natural resource or the public, or impairment of the variability among living organisms.

(25)   Regarding environmental damage, Article 174 of the Treaty, which provides that there should be a high level of protection based on the precautionary principle and the principle that preventive action should be taken, the principle of priority for corrective action at source and the principle that the polluter pays, fully justifies the use of the principle of discriminating in favour of the person sustaining the damage. The question of when the person seeking compensation can make the choice of the law applicable should be determined in accordance with the law of the Member State in which the court is seised.

(26)   Regarding infringements of intellectual property rights, the universally acknowledged principle of the *lex loci protectionis* should be preserved. For the purposes of this Regulation, the term 'intellectual property rights' should be interpreted as meaning, for instance, copyright, related rights, the *sui generis* right for the protection of databases and industrial property rights.

(27)   The exact concept of industrial action, such as strike action or lock-out,

varies from one Member State to another and is governed by each Member State's internal rules. Therefore, this Regulation assumes as a general principle that the law of the country where the industrial action was taken should apply, with the aim of protecting the rights and obligations of workers and employers.

(28)   The special rule on industrial action in Article 9 is without prejudice to the conditions relating to the exercise of such action in accordance with national law and without prejudice to the legal status of trade unions or of the representative organisations of workers as provided for in the law of the Member States.

(29)   Provision should be made for special rules where damage is caused by an act other than a tort/delict, such as unjust enrichment, *negotiorum gestio* and *culpa in contrahendo*.

(30)   Culpa in contrahendo for the purposes of this Regulation is an autonomous concept and should not necessarily be interpreted within the meaning of national law. It should include the violation of the duty of disclosure and the breakdown of contractual negotiations. Article 12 covers only non-contractual obligations presenting a direct link with the dealings prior to the conclusion of a contract. This means that if, while a contract is being negotiated, a person suffers personal injury, Article 4 or other relevant provisions of this Regulation should apply.

(31)   To respect the principle of party autonomy and to enhance legal certainty, the parties should be allowed to make a choice as to the law applicable to a non-contractual obligation. This choice should be expressed or demonstrated with reasonable certainty by the circumstances of the case. Where establishing the existence of the agreement, the court has to respect the intentions of the parties. Protection should be given to weaker parties by imposing certain conditions on the choice.

(32)   Considerations of public interest justify giving the courts of the Member States the possibility, in exceptional circumstances, of applying exceptions based on public policy and overriding mandatory provisions. In particular, the application of a provision of the law designated by this Regulation which would have the effect of causing non-compensatory exemplary or punitive damages of an excessive nature to be awarded may, depending on the circumstances of the case and the legal order of the Member State of the court seised, be regarded as being contrary to the public policy (*ordre public*) of the forum.

(33)   According to the current national rules on compensation awarded to victims of road traffic accidents, when quantifying damages for personal injury in cases in which the accident takes place in a State other than that of the habitual residence of the victim, the court seised should take into account all the relevant actual circumstances of the specific victim, including in particular the actual losses and costs of after-care and medical attention.

(34)   In order to strike a reasonable balance between the parties, account must be taken, in so far as appropriate, of the rules of safety and conduct in operation in the country in which the harmful act was committed, even where the non-contractual obligation is governed by the law of another country. The term 'rules of safety and conduct' should be interpreted as referring to all regulations having any relation to safety and conduct, including, for example, road safety rules in the case of an accident.

(35)   A situation where conflict-of-law rules are dispersed among several instruments and where there are differences between those rules should be avoided. This Regulation, however, does not exclude the possibility of inclusion of conflict-of-law rules relating to non-contractual obligations in provisions of Community law with regard to particular matters.

This Regulation should not prejudice the application of other instruments laying down provisions designed to contribute to the proper functioning of the internal market in so far as they cannot be applied in conjunction with the law designated by the rules of this Regulation. The application of provisions of the applicable law designated by the rules of this Regulation should not restrict the free movement of goods and services as regulated by Community instruments, such as Directive 2000/31/EC of the European Parliament and of the Council of 8 June 2000 on certain legal aspects of information society services, in particular electronic commerce, in the Internal Market ('Directive on electronic commerce').

(36)   Respect for international commitments entered into by the Member States means that this Regulation should not affect international conventions to which one or more Member States are parties at the time this Regulation is adopted. To make the rules more accessible, the Commission should publish the list of the relevant conventions in the *Official Journal of the European Union* on the basis of information supplied by the Member States.

(37)   The Commission will make a proposal to the European Parliament and the Council concerning the procedures and conditions according to which Member States would be entitled to negotiate and conclude on their own behalf agreements with third countries in individual and exceptional cases, concerning sectoral matters, containing provisions on the law applicable to non-contractual obligations.

(38)   Since the objective of this Regulation cannot be sufficiently achieved by the Member States, and can therefore, by reason of the scale and effects of this Regulation, be better achieved at Community level, the Community may adopt measures, in accordance with the principle of subsidiarity set out in Article 5 of the Treaty. In accordance with the principle of proportionality set out in that Article, this Regulation does not go beyond what is necessary to attain that objective.

(39)   In accordance with Article 3 of the Protocol on the position of the United Kingdom and Ireland annexed to the Treaty on European Union and to the Treaty establishing the European Community, the United Kingdom and Ireland are taking part in the adoption and application of this Regulation.

(40)   In accordance with Articles 1 and 2 of the Protocol on the position of Denmark, annexed to the Treaty on European Union and to the Treaty establishing the European Community, Denmark does not take part in the adoption of this Regulation, and is not bound by it or subject to its application,

HAVE ADOPTED THIS REGULATION:

CHAPTER I
SCOPE

Article 1. Scope
1.   This Regulation shall apply, in situations involving a conflict of laws, to non-contractual obligations in civil and commercial matters. It shall not apply, in particular, to revenue, customs or administrative matters or to the liability of the State for acts and omissions in the exercise of State authority (*acta iure imperii*).

2.   The following shall be excluded from the scope of this Regulation:

(a)   non-contractual obligations arising out of family relationships and relationships deemed by the law applicable to such relationships to have comparable effects including maintenance obligations;

(b)   non-contractual obligations arising out of matrimonial property regimes, property regimes of relationships deemed by the law applicable to such relationships to have comparable effects to marriage, and wills and succession;

(c)   non-contractual obligations arising under bills of exchange, cheques and promissory notes and other negotiable instruments to the extent that the obligations under such other negotiable instruments arise out of their negotiable character;

(d)   non-contractual obligations arising out of the law of companies and other bodies corporate or unincorporated regarding matters such as the creation, by registration or otherwise, legal capacity, internal organisation or winding up of companies and other bodies corporate or unincorporated, the personal liability of officers and members as such for the obligations of the company or body and the personal liability of auditors to a company or to its members in the statutory audits of accounting documents;

(e)   non-contractual obligations arising out of the relations between the settlors, trustees and beneficiaries of a trust created voluntarily;

(f)   non-contractual obligations arising out of nuclear damage;

(g)   non-contractual obligations arising out of violations of privacy and rights relating to personality, including defamation.

3.   This Regulation shall not apply to evidence and procedure, without prejudice to Articles 21 and 22.

4.   For the purposes of this Regulation, 'Member State' shall mean any Member State other than Denmark.

Article 2. Non-contractual obligations

1.   For the purposes of this Regulation, damage shall cover any consequence arising out of tort/delict, unjust enrichment, *negotiorum gestio* or *culpa in contrahendo*.

2.   This Regulation shall apply also to non-contractual obligations that are likely to arise.

3.   Any reference in this Regulation to:

(a)   an event giving rise to damage shall include events giving rise to damage that are likely to occur; and

(b)   damage shall include damage that is likely to occur.

Article 3. Universal application

Any law specified by this Regulation shall be applied whether or not it is the law of a Member State.

CHAPTER II
TORTS/DELICTS

Article 4. General rule

1.   Unless otherwise provided for in this Regulation, the law applicable to a non-contractual obligation arising out of a tort/delict shall be the law of the country in which the damage occurs irrespective of the country in which the event giving rise to the damage occurred and irrespective of the country or countries in which the indirect consequences of that event occur.

2.   However, where the person claimed to be liable and the person sustaining damage both have their habitual residence in the same country at the time when the damage occurs, the law of that country shall apply.

3.   Where it is clear from all the circumstances of the case that the tort/delict is manifestly more closely connected with a country other than that indicated in paragraphs 1 or 2, the law of that other country shall apply. A manifestly closer connection with another country might be based in particular on a pre-existing relationship between the parties, such as a contract, that is closely connected with the tort/delict in question.

Article 5. Product liability

1.   Without prejudice to Article 4(2), the law applicable to a non-contractual obligation arising out of damage caused by a product shall be:

(a)   the law of the country in which the person sustaining the damage had his or her habitual residence when the damage occurred, if the product was marketed in that country; or, failing that,

(b)   the law of the country in which the product was acquired, if the product was marketed in that country; or, failing that,

(c)   the law of the country in which the damage occurred, if the product was marketed in that country.

However, the law applicable shall be the law of the country in which the person claimed to be liable is habitually resident if he or she could not reasonably foresee the marketing of the product, or a product of the same type, in the country the law of which is applicable under (a), (b) or (c).

2.   Where it is clear from all the circumstances of the case that the tort/delict is manifestly more closely connected with a country other than that indicated in paragraph 1, the law of that other country shall apply. A manifestly closer connection with another country might be based in particular on a pre-existing relationship between the parties, such as a contract, that is closely connected with the tort/delict in question.

Article 6. Unfair competition and acts restricting free competition

1.   The law applicable to a non-contractual obligation arising out of an act of unfair competition shall be the law of the country where competitive relations or the collective interests of consumers are, or are likely to be, affected.

2.   Where an act of unfair competition affects exclusively the interests of a specific competitor, Article 4 shall apply.

3.   (a) The law applicable to a non-contractual obligation arising out of a restriction of competition shall be the law of the country where the market is, or is likely to be, affected.

(b)   When the market is, or is likely to be, affected in more than one country, the person seeking compensation for damage who sues in the court of the domicile of the defendant, may instead choose to base his or her claim on the law of the court seised, provided that the market in that Member State is amongst those directly and substantially affected by the restriction of competition out of which the non-contractual obligation on which the claim is based arises; where the claimant sues, in accordance with the applicable rules on jurisdiction, more than one defendant in that court, he or she can only choose to base his or her claim on the law of that court if the restriction of competition on which the claim against each of these defendants relies directly and substantially affects also the market in the Member State of that court.

4.   The law applicable under this Article may not be derogated from by an agreement pursuant to Article 14.

Article 7. Environmental damage

The law applicable to a non-contractual obligation arising out of environmental damage or damage sustained by persons or property as a result of such damage shall be the law determined pursuant to Article 4(1), unless the person seeking compensation for damage chooses to base his or her claim on the law of the country in which the event giving rise to the damage occurred.

Article 8. Infringement of intellectual property rights

1.   The law applicable to a non-contractual obligation arising from an infringement of an intellectual property right shall be the law of the country for which protection is claimed.

2.   In the case of a non-contractual obligation arising from an infringement of a unitary Community intellectual property right, the law applicable shall, for any question that is not governed by the relevant Community instrument, be the law of the country in which the act of infringement was committed.

3.   The law applicable under this Article may not be derogated from by an agreement pursuant to Article 14.

Article 9. Industrial action

Without prejudice to Article 4(2), the law applicable to a non-contractual obligation in respect of the liability of a person in the capacity of a worker or an employer or the organisations representing their professional interests for damages caused by an industrial action, pending or carried out, shall be the law of the country where the action is to be, or has been, taken.

CHAPTER III
UNJUST ENRICHMENT, NEGOTIORUM GESTIO AND CULPA IN CONTRAHENDO

Article 10. Unjust enrichment
1.   If a non-contractual obligation arising out of unjust enrichment, including payment of amounts wrongly received, concerns a relationship existing between the parties, such as one arising out of a contract or a tort/delict, that is closely connected with that unjust enrichment, it shall be governed by the law that governs that relationship.
2.   Where the law applicable cannot be determined on the basis of paragraph 1 and the parties have their habitual residence in the same country when the event giving rise to unjust enrichment occurs, the law of that country shall apply.
3.   Where the law applicable cannot be determined on the basis of paragraphs 1 or 2, it shall be the law of the country in which the unjust enrichment took place.
4.   Where it is clear from all the circumstances of the case that the non-contractual obligation arising out of unjust enrichment is manifestly more closely connected with a country other than that indicated in paragraphs 1, 2 and 3, the law of that other country shall apply.

Article 11. Negotiorum gestio
1.   If a non-contractual obligation arising out of an act performed without due authority in connection with the affairs of another person concerns a relationship existing between the parties, such as one arising out of a contract or a tort/delict, that is closely connected with that non-contractual obligation, it shall be governed by the law that governs that relationship.
2.   Where the law applicable cannot be determined on the basis of paragraph 1, and the parties have their habitual residence in the same country when the event giving rise to the damage occurs, the law of that country shall apply.
3.   Where the law applicable cannot be determined on the basis of paragraphs 1 or 2, it shall be the law of the country in which the act was performed.
4.   Where it is clear from all the circumstances of the case that the non-contractual obligation arising out of an act performed without due authority in connection with the affairs of another person is manifestly more closely connected with a country other than that indicated in paragraphs 1, 2 and 3, the law of that other country shall apply.

Article 12. Culpa in contrahendo
1.   The law applicable to a non-contractual obligation arising out of dealings prior to the conclusion of a contract, regardless of whether the contract was actually concluded or not, shall be the law that applies to the contract or that would have been applicable to it had it been entered into.
2.   Where the law applicable cannot be determined on the basis of paragraph 1, it shall be:
    (a)   the law of the country in which the damage occurs, irrespective of the country in which the event giving rise to the damage occurred and irrespective of the country or countries in which the indirect consequences of that event occurred; or
    (b)   where the parties have their habitual residence in the same country at the time when the event giving rise to the damage occurs, the law of that country; or
    (c)   where it is clear from all the circumstances of the case that the non-contractual obligation arising out of dealings prior to the conclusion of a contract

is manifestly more closely connected with a country other than that indicated in points (a) and (b),the law of that other country.

Article 13. Applicability of Article 8
For the purposes of this Chapter, Article 8 shall apply to non-contractual obligations arising from an infringement of an intellectual property right.

CHAPTER IV
FREEDOM OF CHOICE

Article 14. Freedom of choice
1. The parties may agree to submit non-contractual obligations to the law of their choice:

(a) by an agreement entered into after the event giving rise to the damage occurred; or

(b) where all the parties are pursuing a commercial activity, also by an agreement freely negotiated before the event giving rise to the damage occurred.

The choice shall be expressed or demonstrated with reasonable certainty by the circumstances of the case and shall not prejudice the rights of third parties.

2. Where all the elements relevant to the situation at the time when the event giving rise to the damage occurs are located in a country other than the country whose law has been chosen, the choice of the parties shall not prejudice the application of provisions of the law of that other country which cannot be derogated from by agreement.

3. Where all the elements relevant to the situation at the time when the event giving rise to the damage occurs are located in one or more of the Member States, the parties' choice of the law applicable other than that of a Member State shall not prejudice the application of provisions of Community law, where appropriate as implemented in the Member State of the forum, which cannot be derogated from by agreement.

CHAPTER V
COMMON RULES

Article 15. Scope of the law applicable
The law applicable to non-contractual obligations under this Regulation shall govern in particular:

(a) the basis and extent of liability, including the determination of persons who may be held liable for acts performed by them;

(b) the grounds for exemption from liability, any limitation of liability and any division of liability;

(c) the existence, the nature and the assessment of damage or the remedy claimed;

(d) within the limits of powers conferred on the court by its procedural law, the measures which a court may take to prevent or terminate injury or damage or to ensure the provision of compensation;

(e) the question whether a right to claim damages or a remedy may be transferred, including by inheritance;

(f) persons entitled to compensation for damage sustained personally;

(g) liability for the acts of another person;

(h) the manner in which an obligation may be extinguished and rules of prescription and limitation, including rules relating to the commencement, interruption and suspension of a period of prescription or limitation.

Article 16. Overriding mandatory provisions
Nothing in this Regulation shall restrict the application of the provisions of the law of the forum in a situation where they are mandatory irrespective of the law otherwise applicable to the non-contractual obligation.

Article 17. Rules of safety and conduct
In assessing the conduct of the person claimed to be liable, account shall be taken, as a matter of fact and in so far as is appropriate, of the rules of safety and conduct which were in force at the place and time of the event giving rise to the liability.

Article 18. Direct action against the insurer of the person liable
The person having suffered damage may bring his or her claim directly against the insurer of the person liable to provide compensation if the law applicable to the non-contractual obligation or the law applicable to the insurance contract so provides.

Article 19. Subrogation
Where a person ('the creditor') has a non-contractual claim upon another ('the debtor'), and a third person has a duty to satisfy the creditor, or has in fact satisfied the creditor in discharge of that duty, the law which governs the third person's duty to satisfy the creditor shall determine whether, and the extent to which, the third person is entitled to exercise against the debtor the rights which the creditor had against the debtor under the law governing their relationship.

Article 20. Multiple liability
If a creditor has a claim against several debtors who are liable for the same claim, and one of the debtors has already satisfied the claim in whole or in part, the question of that debtor's right to demand compensation from the other debtors shall be governed by the law applicable to that debtor's non-contractual obligation towards the creditor.

Article 21. Formal validity
A unilateral act intended to have legal effect and relating to a non-contractual obligation shall be formally valid if it satisfies the formal requirements of the law governing the non-contractual obligation in question or the law of the country in which the act is performed.

Article 22. Burden of proof
1.   The law governing a non-contractual obligation under this Regulation shall apply to the extent that, in matters of non-contractual obligations, it contains rules which raise presumptions of law or determine the burden of proof.

2.   Acts intended to have legal effect may be proved by any mode of proof recognised by the law of the forum or by any of the laws referred to in Article 21 under which that act is formally valid, provided that such mode of proof can be administered by the forum.

CHAPTER VI
OTHER PROVISIONS

Article 23. Habitual residence
1.   For the purposes of this Regulation, the habitual residence of companies and other bodies, corporate or unincorporated, shall be the place of central administration.

Where the event giving rise to the damage occurs, or the damage arises, in the course of operation of a branch, agency or any other establishment, the place where the branch, agency or any other establishment is located shall be treated as the place of habitual residence.

2.   For the purposes of this Regulation, the habitual residence of a natural person acting in the course of his or her business activity shall be his or her principal place of business.

Article 24. Exclusion of renvoi
The application of the law of any country specified by this Regulation means the

application of the rules of law in force in that country other than its rules of private international law.

Article 25. States with more than one legal system*
1. Where a State comprises several territorial units, each of which has its own rules of law in respect of non-contractual obligations, each territorial unit shall be considered as a country for the purposes of identifying the law applicable under this Regulation.

2. A Member State within which different territorial units have their own rules of law in respect of non-contractual obligations shall not be required to apply this Regulation to conflicts solely between the laws of such units.

Article 26. Public policy of the forum
The application of a provision of the law of any country specified by this Regulation may be refused only if such application is manifestly incompatible with the public policy (*ordre public*) of the forum.

Article 27. Relationship with other provisions of Community law
This Regulation shall not prejudice the application of provisions of Community law which, in relation to particular matters, lay down conflict-of-law rules relating to non-contractual obligations.

Article 28. Relationship with existing international conventions
1. This Regulation shall not prejudice the application of international conventions to which one or more Member States are parties at the time when this Regulation is adopted and which lay down conflict-of-law rules relating to non-contractual obligations.

2. However, this Regulation shall, as between Member States, take precedence over conventions concluded exclusively between two or more of them in so far as such conventions concern matters governed by this Regulation.

CHAPTER VII
FINAL PROVISIONS

Article 29. List of conventions
1. By 11 July 2008, Member States shall notify the Commission of the conventions referred to in Article 28(1). After that date, Member States shall notify the Commission of all denunciations of such conventions.

2. The Commission shall publish in the *Official Journal of the European Union* within six months of receipt:
    (i) a list of the conventions referred to in paragraph 1;
    (ii) the denunciations referred to in paragraph 1.

Article 30. Review clause
1. Not later than 20 August 2011, the Commission shall submit to the European Parliament, the Council and the European Economic and Social Committee a report on the application of this Regulation. If necessary, the report shall be accompanied by proposals to adapt this Regulation. The report shall include:
    (i) a study on the effects of the way in which foreign law is treated in the different jurisdictions and on the extent to which courts in the Member States apply foreign law in practice pursuant to this Regulation;

---

*Reg 4 of The Law Applicable to Non-Contractual Obligations (Scotland) Regulations 2008 (SSI 2008/404) provides that, notwithstanding Art 25(2), the Regulation applies in the case of conflicts between (a) the laws of different parts of the UK; or (b) between the laws of one or more parts of the UK and Gibraltar.

(ii)   a study on the effects of Article 28 of this Regulation with respect to the Hague Convention of 4 May 1971 on the law applicable to traffic accidents.

2.   Not later than 31 December 2008, the Commission shall submit to the European Parliament, the Council and the European Economic and Social Committee a study on the situation in the field of the law applicable to non-contractual obligations arising out of violations of privacy and rights relating to personality, taking into account rules relating to freedom of the press and freedom of expression in the media, and conflict-of-law issues related to Directive 95/46/EC of the European Parliament and of the Council of 24 October 1995 on the protection of individuals with regard to the processing of personal data and on the free movement of such data.

Article 31. Application in time

This Regulation shall apply to events giving rise to damage which occur after its entry into force.

Article 32. Date of application

This Regulation shall apply from 11 January 2009, except for Article 29, which shall apply from 11 July 2007. This Regulation shall be binding in its entirety and directly applicable in the Member States in accordance with the Treaty establishing the European Community.

Done at Strasbourg, 11 July 2007

REGULATION (EC) NO 1393/2007 OF THE EUROPEAN PARLIAMENTAND OF THE COUNCIL OF 13 NOVEMBER 2007 ON THE SERVICE IN THE MEMBER STATES OF JUDICIAL AND EXTRAJUDICIAL DOCUMENTS IN CIVIL OR COMMERCIAL MATTERS (SERVICE OF DOCUMENTS), AND REPEALING COUNCIL REGULATION (EC) NO 1348/2000

Official Journal L 324, 10/12/2007 pp 79-120

THE EUROPEAN PARLIAMENT AND THE COUNCIL OF THE EUROPEAN UNION,

Having regard to the Treaty establishing the European Community, and in particular Article 61(c) and Article 67(5), second indent, thereof,

Having regard to the proposal from the Commission,

Having regard to the opinion of the European Economic and Social Committee,

Acting in accordance with the procedure laid down in Article 251 of the Treaty,

Whereas:

(1)   The Union has set itself the objective of maintaining and developing the Union as an area of freedom, security and justice, in which the free movement of persons is assured. To establish such an area, the Community is to adopt, among others, the measures relating to judicial cooperation in civil matters needed for the proper functioning of the internal market.

(2)   The proper functioning of the internal market entails the need to improve and expedite the transmission of judicial and extrajudicial documents in civil or commercial matters for service between the Member States.

(3)   The Council, by an Act dated 26 May 1997, drew up a Convention on the service in the Member States of the European Union of judicial and extrajudicial

documents in civil or commercial matters and recommended it for adoption by the Member States in accordance with their respective constitutional rules. That Convention has not entered into force. Continuity in the results of the negotiations for conclusion of the Convention should be ensured.

(4)   On 29 May 2000 the Council adopted Regulation (EC) No 1348/2000 on the service in the Member States of judicial and extrajudicial documents in civil or commercial matters. The main content of that Regulation is based on the Convention.

(5)   On 1 October 2004 the Commission adopted a report on the application of Regulation (EC) No 1348/2000. The report concludes that the application of Regulation (EC) No 1348/2000 has generally improved and expedited the transmission and the service of documents between Member States since its entry into force in 2001, but that nevertheless the application of certain provisions is not fully satisfactory.

(6)   Efficiency and speed in judicial procedures in civil matters require that judicial and extrajudicial documents be transmitted directly and by rapid means between local bodies designated by the Member States. Member States may indicate their intention to designate only one transmitting or receiving agency or one agency to perform both functions, for a period of five years. This designation may, however, be renewed every five years.

(7)   Speed in transmission warrants the use of all appropriate means, provided that certain conditions as to the legibility and reliability of the document received are observed. Security in transmission requires that the document to be transmitted be accompanied by a standard form, to be completed in the official language or one of the official languages of the place where service is to be effected, or in another language accepted by the Member State in question.

(8)   This Regulation should not apply to service of a document on the party's authorised representative in the Member State where the proceedings are taking place regardless of the place of residence of that party.

(9)   The service of a document should be effected as soon as possible, and in any event within one month of receipt by the receiving agency.

(10)   To secure the effectiveness of this Regulation, the possibility of refusing service of documents should be confined to exceptional situations.

(11)   In order to facilitate the transmission and service of documents between Member States, the standard forms set out in the Annexes to this Regulation should be used.

(12)   The receiving agency should inform the addressee in writing using the standard form that he may refuse to accept the document to be served at the time of service or by returning the document to the receiving agency within one week if it is not either in a language which he understands or in the official language or one of the official languages of the place of service. This rule should also apply to the subsequent service once the addressee has exercised his right of refusal. These rules on refusal should also apply to service by diplomatic or consular agents, service by postal services and direct service. It should be established that the service of the refused document can be remedied through the service on the addressee of a translation of the document.

(13)   Speed in transmission warrants documents being served within days of receipt of the document. However, if service has not been effected after one month has elapsed, the receiving agency should inform the transmitting agency. The expiry of this period should not imply that the request be returned to the transmitting agency where it is clear that service is feasible within a reasonable period.

(14)   The receiving agency should continue to take all necessary steps to effect the service of the document also in cases where it has not been possible to effect service within the month, for example, because the defendant has been away from his home on holiday or away from his office on business. However, in order to avoid an open-ended obligation for the receiving agency to take steps to effect the

service of a document, the transmitting agency should be able to specify a time limit in the standard form after which service is no longer required.

(15) Given the differences between the Member States as regards their rules of procedure, the material date for the purposes of service varies from one Member State to another. Having regard to such situations and the possible difficulties that may arise, this Regulation should provide for a system where it is the law of the Member State addressed which determines the date of service. However, where according to the law of a Member State a document has to be served within a particular period, the date to be taken into account with respect to the applicant should be that determined by the law of that Member State. This double date system exists only in a limited number of Member States. Those Member States which apply this system should communicate this to the Commission, which should publish the information in the Official Journal of the European Union and make it available through the European Judicial Network in Civil and Commercial Matters established by Council Decision 2001/470/EC.

(16) In order to facilitate access to justice, costs occasioned by recourse to a judicial officer or a person competent under the law of the Member State addressed should correspond to a single fixed fee laid down by that Member State in advance which respects the principles of proportionality and non-discrimination. The requirement of a single fixed fee should not preclude the possibility for Member States to set different fees for different types of service as long as they respect these principles.

(17) Each Member State should be free to effect service of documents directly by postal services on persons residing in another Member State by registered letter with acknowledgement of receipt or equivalent.

(18) It should be possible for any person interested in a judicial proceeding to effect service of documents directly through the judicial officers, officials or other competent persons of the Member State addressed, where such direct service is permitted under the law of that Member State.

(19) The Commission should draw up a manual containing information relevant for the proper application of this Regulation, which should be made available through the European Judicial Network in Civil and Commercial Matters. The Commission and the Member States should do their utmost to ensure that this information is up to date and complete especially as regards contact details of receiving and transmitting agencies.

(20) In calculating the periods and time limits provided for in this Regulation, Regulation (EEC, Euratom) No 1182/71 of the Council of 3 June 1971 determining the rules applicable to periods, dates and time limits should apply.

(21) The measures necessary for the implementation of this Regulation should be adopted in accordance with Council Decision 1999/468/EC of 28 June 1999 laying down the procedures for the exercise of implementing powers conferred on the Commission.

(22) In particular, power should be conferred on the Commission to update or make technical amendments to the standard forms set out in the Annexes. Since those measures are of general scope and are designed to amend/delete nonessential elements of this Regulation, they must be adopted in accordance with the regulatory procedure with scrutiny provided for in Article 5a of Decision 1999/468/EC.

(23) This Regulation prevails over the provisions contained in bilateral or multilateral agreements or arrangements having the same scope, concluded by the Member States, and in particular the Protocol annexed to the Brussels Convention of 27 September 1968 and the Hague Convention of 15 November 1965 in relations between the Member States party thereto. This Regulation does not preclude Member States from maintaining or concluding agreements or arrangements to expedite or simplify the transmission of documents, provided that they are compatible with this Regulation.

(24)   The information transmitted pursuant to this Regulation should enjoy suitable protection. This matter falls within the scope of Directive 95/46/EC of the European Parliament and of the Council of 24 October 1995 on the protection of individuals with regard to the processing of personal data and on the free movement of such data, and of Directive 2002/58/EC of the European Parliament and of the Council of 12 July 2002 concerning the processing of personal data and the protection of privacy in the electronic communications sector (Directive on privacy and electronic communications).

(25)   No later than 1 June 2011 and every five years thereafter, the Commission should review the application of this Regulation and propose such amendments as may appear necessary.

(26)   Since the objectives of this Regulation cannot be sufficiently achieved by the Member States and can therefore, by reason of the scale or effects of the action, be better achieved at Community level, the Community may adopt measures, in accordance with the principle of subsidiarity as set out in Article 5 of the Treaty. In accordance with the principle of proportionality, as set out in that Article, this Regulation does not go beyond what is necessary in order to achieve those objectives.

(27)   In order to make the provisions more easily accessible and readable, Regulation (EC) No 1348/2000 should be repealed and replaced by this Regulation.

(28)   In accordance with Article 3 of the Protocol on the position of the United Kingdom and Ireland, annexed to the Treaty on European Union and to the Treaty establishing the European Community, the United Kingdom and Ireland are taking part in the adoption and application of this Regulation.

(29)   In accordance with Articles 1 and 2 of the Protocol on the position of Denmark, annexed to the Treaty on European Union and to the Treaty establishing the European Community, Denmark does not take part in the adoption of this Regulation and is not bound by it or subject to its application,

HAVE ADOPTED THIS REGULATION:

CHAPTER I
GENERAL PROVISIONS

Article 1. Scope

1.   This Regulation shall apply in civil and commercial matters where a judicial or extrajudicial document has to be transmitted from one Member State to another for service there. It shall not extend in particular to revenue, customs or administrative matters or to liability of the State for actions or omissions in the exercise of state authority (acta iure imperii).

2.   This Regulation shall not apply where the address of the person to be served with the document is not known.

3.   In this Regulation, the term 'Member State' shall mean the Member States with the exception of Denmark.

Article 2. Transmitting and receiving agencies

1.   Each Member State shall designate the public officers, authorities or other persons, hereinafter referred to as 'transmitting agencies', competent for the transmission of judicial or extrajudicial documents to be served in another Member State.

2.   Each Member State shall designate the public officers, authorities or other persons, hereinafter referred to as 'receiving agencies', competent for the receipt of judicial or extrajudicial documents from another Member State.

3.   A Member State may designate one transmitting agency and one receiving agency, or one agency to perform both functions. A federal State, a State in which several legal systems apply or a State with autonomous territorial units shall be

free to designate more than one such agency. The designation shall have effect for a period of five years and may be renewed at five-year intervals.

4.   Each Member State shall provide the Commission with the following information:

(a)   the names and addresses of the receiving agencies referred to in paragraphs 2 and 3;

(b)   the geographical areas in which they have jurisdiction;

(c)   the means of receipt of documents available to them; and

(d)   the languages that may be used for the completion of the standard form set out in Annex I.

Member States shall notify the Commission of any subsequent modification of such information.

Article 3. Central body

Each Member State shall designate a central body responsible for:

(a)   supplying information to the transmitting agencies;

(b)   seeking solutions to any difficulties which may arise during transmission of documents for service;

(c)   forwarding, in exceptional cases, at the request of a transmitting agency, a request for service to the competent receiving agency.

A federal State, a State in which several legal systems apply or a State with autonomous territorial units shall be free to designate more than one central body.

CHAPTER II
JUDICIAL DOCUMENTS

Section 1
Transmission and service of judicial documents

Article 4. Transmission of documents

1.   Judicial documents shall be transmitted directly and as soon as possible between the agencies designated pursuant to Article 2.

2.   The transmission of documents, requests, confirmations, receipts, certificates and any other papers between transmitting agencies and receiving agencies may be carried out by any appropriate means, provided that the content of the document received is true and faithful to that of the document forwarded and that all information in it is easily legible.

3.   The document to be transmitted shall be accompanied by a request drawn up using the standard form set out in Annex I. The form shall be completed in the official language of the Member State addressed or, if there are several official languages in that Member State, the official language or one of the official languages of the place where service is to be effected, or in another language which that Member State has indicated it can accept. Each Member State shall indicate the official language or languages of the institutions of the European Union other than its own which is or are acceptable to it for completion of the form.

4.   The documents and all papers that are transmitted shall be exempted from legalisation or any equivalent formality.

5.   When the transmitting agency wishes a copy of the document to be returned together with the certificate referred to in Article 10, it shall send the document in duplicate.

Article 5. Translation of documents

1.   The applicant shall be advised by the transmitting agency to which he forwards the document for transmission that the addressee may refuse to accept it if it is not in one of the languages provided for in Article 8.

2.   The applicant shall bear any costs of translation prior to the transmission of

the document, without prejudice to any possible subsequent decision by the court or competent authority on liability for such costs.

Article 6. Receipt of documents by receiving agency

1.   On receipt of a document, a receiving agency shall, as soon as possible and in any event within seven days of receipt, send a receipt to the transmitting agency by the swiftest possible means of transmission using the standard form set out in Annex I.

2.   Where the request for service cannot be fulfilled on the basis of the information or documents transmitted, the receiving agency shall contact the transmitting agency by the swiftest possible means in order to secure the missing information or documents.

3.   If the request for service is manifestly outside the scope of this Regulation or if non-compliance with the formal conditions required makes service impossible, the request and the documents transmitted shall be returned, on receipt, to the transmitting agency, together with the notice of return using the standard form set out in Annex I.

4.   A receiving agency receiving a document for service but not having territorial jurisdiction to serve it shall forward it, as well as the request, to the receiving agency having territorial jurisdiction in the same Member State if the request complies with the conditions laid down in Article 4(3) and shall inform the transmitting agency accordingly using the standard form set out in Annex I. That receiving agency shall inform the transmitting agency when it receives the document, in the manner provided for in paragraph 1.

Article 7. Service of documents

1.   The receiving agency shall itself serve the document or have it served, either in accordance with the law of the Member State addressed or by a particular method requested by the transmitting agency, unless that method is incompatible with the law of that Member State.

2.   The receiving agency shall take all necessary steps to effect the service of the document as soon as possible, and in any event within one month of receipt. If it has not been possible to effect service within one month of receipt, the receiving agency shall:

(a)   immediately inform the transmitting agency by means of the certificate in the standard form set out in Annex I, which shall be drawn up under the conditions referred to in Article 10(2); and

(b)   continue to take all necessary steps to effect the service of the document, unless indicated otherwise by the transmitting agency, where service seems to be possible within a reasonable period of time.

Article 8. Refusal to accept a document

1.   The receiving agency shall inform the addressee, using the standard form set out in Annex II, that he may refuse to accept the document to be served at the time of service or by returning the document to the receiving agency within one week if it is not written in, or accompanied by a translation into, either of the following languages:

(a)   a language which the addressee understands; or

(b)   the official language of the Member State addressed or, if there are several official languages in that Member State, the official language or one of the official languages of the place where service is to be effected.

2.   Where the receiving agency is informed that the addressee refuses to accept the document in accordance with paragraph 1, it shall immediately inform the transmitting agency by means of the certificate provided for in Article 10 and return the request and the documents of which a translation is requested.

3.   If the addressee has refused to accept the document pursuant to paragraph 1, the service of the document can be remedied through the service on the

addressee in accordance with the provisions of this Regulation of the document accompanied by a translation into a language provided for in paragraph 1. In that case, the date of service of the document shall be the date on which the document accompanied by the translation is served in accordance with the law of the Member State addressed. However, where according to the law of a Member State, a document has to be served within a particular period, the date to be taken into account with respect to the applicant shall be the date of the service of the initial document determined pursuant to Article 9(2).

4.   Paragraphs 1, 2 and 3 shall also apply to the means of transmission and service of judicial documents provided for in Section 2.

5.   For the purposes of paragraph 1, the diplomatic or consular agents, where service is effected in accordance with Article 13, or the authority or person, where service is effected in accordance with Article 14, shall inform the addressee that he may refuse to accept the document and that any document refused must be sent to those agents or to that authority or person respectively.

Article 9. Date of service

1.   Without prejudice to Article 8, the date of service of a document pursuant to Article 7 shall be the date on which it is served in accordance with the law of the Member State addressed.

2.   However, where according to the law of a Member State a document has to be served within a particular period, the date to be taken into account with respect to the applicant shall be that determined by the law of that Member State.

3.   Paragraphs 1 and 2 shall also apply to the means of transmission and service of judicial documents provided for in Section 2.

Article 10. Certificate of service and copy of the document served

1.   When the formalities concerning the service of the document have been completed, a certificate of completion of those formalities shall be drawn up in the standard form set out in Annex I and addressed to the transmitting agency, together with, where Article 4(5) applies, a copy of the document served.

2.   The certificate shall be completed in the official language or one of the official languages of the Member State of origin or in another language which the Member State of origin has indicated that it can accept. Each Member State shall indicate the official language or languages of the institutions of the European Union other than its own which is or are acceptable to it for completion of the form.

Article 11. Costs of service

1.   The service of judicial documents coming from a Member State shall not give rise to any payment or reimbursement of taxes or costs for services rendered by the Member State addressed.

2.   However, the applicant shall pay or reimburse the costs occasioned by:

(a)   recourse to a judicial officer or to a person competent under the law of the Member State addressed;

(b)   the use of a particular method of service.

Costs occasioned by recourse to a judicial officer or to a person competent under the law of the Member State addressed shall correspond to a single fixed fee laid down by that Member State in advance which respects the principles of proportionality and non-discrimination. Member States shall communicate such fixed fees to the Commission.

Section 2
Other means of transmission and service of judicial documents

Article 12. Transmission by consular or diplomatic channels

Each Member State shall be free, in exceptional circumstances, to use consular or diplomatic channels to forward judicial documents, for the purpose of service, to those agencies of another Member State which are designated pursuant to Articles 2 or 3.

Article 13. Service by diplomatic or consular agents

1.   Each Member State shall be free to effect service of judicial documents on persons residing in another Member State, without application of any compulsion, directly through its diplomatic or consular agents.

2.   Any Member State may make it known, in accordance with Article 23(1), that it is opposed to such service within its territory, unless the documents are to be served on nationals of the Member State in which the documents originate.

Article 14. Service by postal services

Each Member State shall be free to effect service of judicial documents directly by postal services on persons residing in another Member State by registered letter with acknowledgement of receipt or equivalent.

Article 15. Direct service

Any person interested in a judicial proceeding may effect service of judicial documents directly through the judicial officers, officials or other competent persons of the Member State addressed, where such direct service is permitted under the law of that Member State.

CHAPTER III
EXTRAJUDICIAL DOCUMENTS

Article 16. Transmission

Extrajudicial documents may be transmitted for service in another Member State in accordance with the provisions of this Regulation.

CHAPTER IV
FINAL PROVISIONS

Article 17. Implementing rules

Measures designed to amend non-essential elements of this Regulation relating to the updating or to the making of technical amendments to the standard forms set out in Annexes I and II shall be adopted in accordance with the regulatory procedure with scrutiny referred to in Article 18(2).

Article 18. Committee

1.   The Commission shall be assisted by a committee.

2.   Where reference is made to this paragraph, Article 5a(1) to (4), and Article 7 of Decision 1999/468/EC shall apply, having regard to the provisions of Article 8 thereof.

Article 19. Defendant not entering an appearance

1.   Where a writ of summons or an equivalent document has had to be transmitted to another Member State for the purpose of service under the provisions of this Regulation and the defendant has not appeared, judgment shall not be given until it is established that:

   (a)   the document was served by a method prescribed by the internal law of the Member State addressed for the service of documents in domestic actions upon persons who are within its territory; or

   (b)   the document was actually delivered to the defendant or to his residence by another method provided for by this Regulation;

and that in either of these cases the service or the delivery was effected in sufficient time to enable the defendant to defend.

2.   Each Member State may make it known, in accordance with Article 23(1), that the judge, notwithstanding the provisions of paragraph 1, may give judgment

even if no certificate of service or delivery has been received, if all the following conditions are fulfilled:

(a)   the document was transmitted by one of the methods provided for in this Regulation;

(b)   a period of time of not less than six months, considered adequate by the judge in the particular case, has elapsed since the date of the transmission of the document;

(c)   no certificate of any kind has been received, even though every reasonable effort has been made to obtain it through the competent authorities or bodies of the Member State addressed.

3.   Notwithstanding paragraphs 1 and 2, the judge may order, in case of urgency, any provisional or protective measures.

4.   When a writ of summons or an equivalent document has had to be transmitted to another Member State for the purpose of service under the provisions of this Regulation and a judgment has been entered against a defendant who has not appeared, the judge shall have the power to relieve the defendant from the effects of the expiry of the time for appeal from the judgment if the following conditions are fulfilled:

(a)   the defendant, without any fault on his part, did not have knowledge of the document in sufficient time to defend, or knowledge of the judgment in sufficient time to appeal; and

(b)   the defendant has disclosed a prima facie defence to the action on the merits.

An application for relief may be filed only within a reasonable time after the defendant has knowledge of the judgment.

Each Member State may make it known, in accordance with Article 23(1), that such application will not be entertained if it is filed after the expiry of a time to be stated by it in that communication, but which shall in no case be less than one year following the date of the judgment.

5.   Paragraph 4 shall not apply to judgments concerning the status or capacity of persons.

Article 20. Relationship with agreements or arrangements to which Member States are party

1.   This Regulation shall, in relation to matters to which it applies, prevail over other provisions contained in bilateral or multilateral agreements or arrangements concluded by the Member States, and in particular Article IV of the Protocol to the Brussels Convention of 1968 and the Hague Convention of 15 November 1965.

2.   This Regulation shall not preclude individual Member States from maintaining or concluding agreements or arrangements to expedite further or simplify the transmission of documents, provided that they are compatible with this Regulation.

3.   Member States shall send to the Commission:

(a)   a copy of the agreements or arrangements referred to in paragraph 2 concluded between the Member States as well as drafts of such agreements or arrangements which they intend to adopt; and

(b)   any denunciation of, or amendments to, these agreements or arrangements.

Article 21. Legal aid

This Regulation shall not affect the application of Article 23 of the Convention on civil procedure of 17 July 1905, Article 24 of the Convention on civil procedure of 1 March 1954 or Article 13 of the Convention on international access to justice of 25 October 1980 between the Member States party to those Conventions.

Article 22. Protection of information transmitted

1.   Information, including in particular personal data, transmitted under this Regulation shall be used by the receiving agency only for the purpose for which it was transmitted.

2. Receiving agencies shall ensure the confidentiality of such information, in accordance with their national law.

3. Paragraphs 1 and 2 shall not affect national laws enabling data subjects to be informed of the use made of information transmitted under this Regulation.

4. This Regulation shall be without prejudice to Directives 95/46/EC and 2002/58/EC.

Article 23. Communication and publication

1. Member States shall communicate to the Commission the information referred to in Articles 2, 3, 4, 10, 11, 13, 15 and 19. Member States shall communicate to the Commission if, according to their law, a document has to be served within a particular period as referred to in Articles 8(3) and 9(2).

2. The Commission shall publish the information communicated in accordance with paragraph 1 in the Official Journal of the European Union with the exception of the addresses and other contact details of the agencies and of the central bodies and the geographical areas in which they have jurisdiction.

3. The Commission shall draw up and update regularly a manual containing the information referred to in paragraph 1, which shall be available electronically, in particular through the European Judicial Network in Civil and Commercial Matters.

Article 24. Review

No later than 1 June 2011, and every five years thereafter, the Commission shall present to the European Parliament, the Council and the European Economic and Social Committee a report on the application of this Regulation, paying special attention to the effectiveness of the agencies designated pursuant to Article 2 and to the practical application of Article 3(c) and Article 9. The report shall be accompanied if need be by proposals for adaptations of this Regulation in line with the evolution of notification systems.

Article 25. Repeal

1. Regulation (EC) No 1348/2000 shall be repealed as from the date of application of this Regulation.

2. References made to the repealed Regulation shall be construed as being made to this Regulation and should be read in accordance with the correlation table in Annex III.

Article 26. Entry into force

This Regulation shall enter into force on the 20th day following its publication in the Official Journal of the European Union.

It shall apply from 13 November 2008 with the exception of Article 23 which shall apply from 13 August 2008.

This Regulation shall be binding in its entirety and directly applicable in the Member States in accordance with the Treaty establishing the European Community.

Done at Strasbourg, 13 November 2007.

**REGULATION (EC) NO 593/2008 OF THE EUROPEAN PARLIAMENT AND
OF THE COUNCIL OF 17 JUNE 2008 ON THE LAW APPLICABLE TO
CONTRACTUAL OBLIGATIONS (ROME I)**

Official Journal L 177, 04/07/2008 pp 6-16

THE EUROPEAN PARLIAMENT AND THE COUNCIL OF THE EUROPEAN
UNION,

Having regard to the Treaty establishing the European Community, and in particular Article 61(c) and the second indent of Article 67(5) thereof,
    Having regard to the proposal from the Commission,
    Having regard to the opinion of the European Economic and Social Committee,
    Acting in accordance with the procedure laid down in Article 251 of the Treaty,

Whereas:
    (1)   The Community has set itself the objective of maintaining and developing
an area of freedom, security and justice. For the progressive establishment of such
an area, the Community is to adopt measures relating to judicial cooperation in
civil matters with a cross-border impact to the extent necessary for the proper
functioning of the internal market.
    (2)   According to Article 65, point (b) of the Treaty, these measures are to
include those promoting the compatibility of the rules applicable in the Member
States concerning the conflict of laws and of jurisdiction.
    (3)   The European Council meeting in Tampere on 15 and 16 October 1999
endorsed the principle of mutual recognition of judgments and other decisions of
judicial authorities as the cornerstone of judicial cooperation in civil matters and
invited the Council and the Commission to adopt a programme of measures to
implement that principle.
    (4)   On 30 November 2000 the Council adopted a joint Commission and Council
programme of measures for implementation of the principle of mutual recognition
of decisions in civil and commercial matters. The programme identifies measures
relating to the harmonisation of conflict-of-law rules as those facilitating the
mutual recognition of judgments.
    (5)   The Hague Programme, adopted by the European Council on 5 November
2004, called for work to be pursued actively on the conflict-of-law rules regarding
contractual obligations (Rome I).
    (6)   The proper functioning of the internal market creates a need, in order to
improve the predictability of the outcome of litigation, certainty as to the law
applicable and the free movement of judgments, for the conflict-of-law rules in the
Member States to designate the same national law irrespective of the country of
the court in which an action is brought.
    (7)   The substantive scope and the provisions of this Regulation should be con-
sistent with Council Regulation (EC) No 44/2001 of 22 December 2000 on jurisdiction and the recognition and enforcement of judgments in civil and commercial
matters (Brussels I) and Regulation (EC) No 864/2007 of the European Parliament
and of the Council of 11 July 2007 on the law applicable to non-contractual obligations (Rome II).
    (8)   Family relationships should cover parentage, marriage, affinity and col-
lateral relatives. The reference in Article 1(2) to relationships having comparable
effects to marriage and other family relationships should be interpreted in accordance with the law of the Member State in which the court is seised.
    (9)   Obligations under bills of exchange, cheques and promissory notes and
other negotiable instruments should also cover bills of lading to the extent that the
obligations under the bill of lading arise out of its negotiable character.
    (10)   Obligations arising out of dealings prior to the conclusion of the contract

are covered by Article 12 of Regulation (EC) No 864/2007. Such obligations should therefore be excluded from the scope of this Regulation.

(11)   The parties' freedom to choose the applicable law should be one of the cornerstones of the system of conflict-of-law rules in matters of contractual obligations.

(12)   An agreement between the parties to confer on one or more courts or tribunals of a Member State exclusive jurisdiction to determine disputes under the contract should be one of the factors to be taken into account in determining whether a choice of law has been clearly demonstrated.

(13)   This Regulation does not preclude parties from incorporating by reference into their contract a non-State body of law or an international convention.

(14)   Should the Community adopt, in an appropriate legal instrument, rules of substantive contract law, including standard terms and conditions, such instrument may provide that the parties may choose to apply those rules.

(15)   Where a choice of law is made and all other elements relevant to the situation are located in a country other than the country whose law has been chosen, the choice of law should not prejudice the application of provisions of the law of that country which cannot be derogated from by agreement. This rule should apply whether or not the choice of law was accompanied by a choice of court or tribunal. Whereas no substantial change is intended as compared with Article 3(3) of the 1980 Convention on the Law Applicable to Contractual Obligations (the Rome Convention), the wording of this Regulation is aligned as far as possible with Article 14 of Regulation (EC) No 864/2007.

(16)   To contribute to the general objective of this Regulation, legal certainty in the European judicial area, the conflict-of-law rules should be highly foreseeable. The courts should, however, retain a degree of discretion to determine the law that is most closely connected to the situation.

(17)   As far as the applicable law in the absence of choice is concerned, the concept of 'provision of services' and 'sale of goods' should be interpreted in the same way as when applying Article 5 of Regulation (EC) No 44/2001 in so far as sale of goods and provision of services are covered by that Regulation. Although franchise and distribution contracts are contracts for services, they are the subject of specific rules.

(18)   As far as the applicable law in the absence of choice is concerned, multilateral systems should be those in which trading is conducted, such as regulated markets and multilateral trading facilities as referred to in Article 4 of Directive 2004/39/EC of the European Parliament and of the Council of 21 April 2004 on markets in financial instruments, regardless of whether or not they rely on a central counterparty.

(19)   Where there has been no choice of law, the applicable law should be determined in accordance with the rule specified for the particular type of contract. Where the contract cannot be categorised as being one of the specified types or where its elements fall within more than one of the specified types, it should be governed by the law of the country where the party required to effect the characteristic performance of the contract has his habitual residence. In the case of a contract consisting of a bundle of rights and obligations capable of being categorised as falling within more than one of the specified types of contract, the characteristic performance of the contract should be determined having regard to its centre of gravity.

(20)   Where the contract is manifestly more closely connected with a country other than that indicated in Article 4(1) or (2), an escape clause should provide that the law of that other country is to apply. In order to determine that country, account should be taken, inter alia, of whether the contract in question has a very close relationship with another contract or contracts.

(21)   In the absence of choice, where the applicable law cannot be determined either on the basis of the fact that the contract can be categorised as one of the

specified types or as being the law of the country of habitual residence of the party required to effect the characteristic performance of the contract, the contract should be governed by the law of the country with which it is most closely connected. In order to determine that country, account should be taken, inter alia, of whether the contract in question has a very close relationship with another contract or contracts.

(22)   As regards the interpretation of contracts for the carriage of goods, no change in substance is intended with respect to Article 4(4), third sentence, of the Rome Convention. Consequently, single-voyage charter parties and other contracts the main purpose of which is the carriage of goods should be treated as contracts for the carriage of goods. For the purposes of this Regulation, the term 'consignor' should refer to any person who enters into a contract of carriage with the carrier and the term 'the carrier' should refer to the party to the contract who undertakes to carry the goods, whether or not he performs the carriage himself.

(23)   As regards contracts concluded with parties regarded as being weaker, those parties should be protected by conflict-of-law rules that are more favourable to their interests than the general rules.

(24)   With more specific reference to consumer contracts, the conflict-of-law rule should make it possible to cut the cost of settling disputes concerning what are commonly relatively small claims and to take account of the development of distance-selling techniques. Consistency with Regulation (EC) No 44/2001 requires both that there be a reference to the concept of directed activity as a condition for applying the consumer protection rule and that the concept be interpreted harmoniously in Regulation (EC) No 44/2001 and this Regulation, bearing in mind that a joint declaration by the Council and the Commission on Article 15 of Regulation (EC) No 44/2001 states that 'for Article 15(1)(c) to be applicable it is not sufficient for an undertaking to target its activities at the Member State of the consumer's residence, or at a number of Member States including that Member State; a contract must also be concluded within the framework of its activities'. The declaration also states that 'the mere fact that an Internet site is accessible is not sufficient for Article 15 to be applicable, although a factor will be that this Internet site solicits the conclusion of distance contracts and that a contract has actually been concluded at a distance, by whatever means. In this respect, the language or currency which a website uses does not constitute a relevant factor.'

(25)   Consumers should be protected by such rules of the country of their habitual residence that cannot be derogated from by agreement, provided that the consumer contract has been concluded as a result of the professional pursuing his commercial or professional activities in that particular country. The same protection should be guaranteed if the professional, while not pursuing his commercial or professional activities in the country where the consumer has his habitual residence, directs his activities by any means to that country or to several countries, including that country, and the contract is concluded as a result of such activities.

(26)   For the purposes of this Regulation, financial services such as investment services and activities and ancillary services provided by a professional to a consumer, as referred to in sections A and B of Annex I to Directive 2004/39/EC, and contracts for the sale of units in collective investment undertakings, whether or not covered by Council Directive 85/611/EEC of 20 December 1985 on the coordination of laws, regulations and administrative provisions relating to undertakings for collective investment in transferable securities (UCITS) should be subject to Article 6 of this Regulation. Consequently, when a reference is made to terms and conditions governing the issuance or offer to the public of transferable securities or to the subscription and redemption of units in collective investment undertakings, that reference should include all aspects binding the issuer or the offeror to the consumer, but should not include those aspects involving the provision of financial services.

(27)   Various exceptions should be made to the general conflict-of-law rule for

consumer contracts. Under one such exception the general rule should not apply to contracts relating to rights in rem in immovable property or tenancies of such property unless the contract relates to the right to use immovable property on a timeshare basis within the meaning of Directive 94/47/EC of the European Parliament and of the Council of 26 October 1994 on the protection of purchasers in respect of certain aspects of contracts relating to the purchase of the right to use immovable properties on a timeshare basis.

(28) It is important to ensure that rights and obligations which constitute a financial instrument are not covered by the general rule applicable to consumer contracts, as that could lead to different laws being applicable to each of the instruments issued, therefore changing their nature and preventing their fungible trading and offering. Likewise, whenever such instruments are issued or offered, the contractual relationship established between the issuer or the offeror and the consumer should not necessarily be subject to the mandatory application of the law of the country of habitual residence of the consumer, as there is a need to ensure uniformity in the terms and conditions of an issuance or an offer. The same rationale should apply with regard to the multilateral systems covered by Article 4(1)(h), in respect of which it should be ensured that the law of the country of habitual residence of the consumer will not interfere with the rules applicable to contracts concluded within those systems or with the operator of such systems.

(29) For the purposes of this Regulation, references to rights and obligations constituting the terms and conditions governing the issuance, offers to the public or public take-over bids of transferable securities and references to the subscription and redemption of units in collective investment undertakings should include the terms governing, inter alia, the allocation of securities or units, rights in the event of over-subscription, withdrawal rights and similar matters in the context of the offer as well as those matters referred to in Articles 10, 11, 12 and 13, thus ensuring that all relevant contractual aspects of an offer binding the issuer or the offeror to the consumer are governed by a single law.

(30) For the purposes of this Regulation, financial instruments and transferable securities are those instruments referred to in Article 4 of Directive 2004/39/EC.

(31) Nothing in this Regulation should prejudice the operation of a formal arrangement designated as a system under Article 2(a) of Directive 98/26/EC of the European Parliament and of the Council of 19 May 1998 on settlement finality in payment and securities settlement systems.

(32) Owing to the particular nature of contracts of carriage and insurance contracts, specific provisions should ensure an adequate level of protection of passengers and policy holders. Therefore, Article 6 should not apply in the context of those particular contracts.

(33) Where an insurance contract not covering a large risk covers more than one risk, at least one of which is situated in a Member State and at least one of which is situated in a third country, the special rules on insurance contracts in this Regulation should apply only to the risk or risks situated in the relevant Member State or Member States.

(34) The rule on individual employment contracts should not prejudice the application of the overriding mandatory provisions of the country to which a worker is posted in accordance with Directive 96/71/EC of the European Parliament and of the Council of 16 December 1996 concerning the posting of workers in the framework of the provision of services.

(35) Employees should not be deprived of the protection afforded to them by provisions which cannot be derogated from by agreement or which can only be derogated from to their benefit.

(36) As regards individual employment contracts, work carried out in another country should be regarded as temporary if the employee is expected to resume working in the country of origin after carrying out his tasks abroad. The conclusion of a new contract of employment with the original employer or an employer

belonging to the same group of companies as the original employer should not preclude the employee from being regarded as carrying out his work in another country temporarily.

(37)   Considerations of public interest justify giving the courts of the Member States the possibility, in exceptional circumstances, of applying exceptions based on public policy and overriding mandatory provisions. The concept of 'overriding mandatory provisions' should be distinguished from the expression 'provisions which cannot be derogated from by agreement' and should be construed more restrictively.

(38)   In the context of voluntary assignment, the term 'relationship' should make it clear that Article 14(1) also applies to the property aspects of an assignment, as between assignor and assignee, in legal orders where such aspects are treated separately from the aspects under the law of obligations. However, the term 'relationship' should not be understood as relating to any relationship that may exist between assignor and assignee. In particular, it should not cover preliminary questions as regards a voluntary assignment or a contractual subrogation. The term should be strictly limited to the aspects which are directly relevant to the voluntary assignment or contractual subrogation in question.

(39)   For the sake of legal certainty there should be a clear definition of habitual residence, in particular for companies and other bodies, corporate or unincorporated. Unlike Article 60(1) of Regulation (EC) No 44/2001, which establishes three criteria, the conflict-of-law rule should proceed on the basis of a single criterion; otherwise, the parties would be unable to foresee the law applicable to their situation.

(40)   A situation where conflict-of-law rules are dispersed among several instruments and where there are differences between those rules should be avoided. This Regulation, however, should not exclude the possibility of inclusion of conflict-of-law rules relating to contractual obligations in provisions of Community law with regard to particular matters.

This Regulation should not prejudice the application of other instruments laying down provisions designed to contribute to the proper functioning of the internal market in so far as they cannot be applied in conjunction with the law designated by the rules of this Regulation. The application of provisions of the applicable law designated by the rules of this Regulation should not restrict the free movement of goods and services as regulated by Community instruments, such as Directive 2000/31/EC of the European Parliament and of the Council of 8 June 2000 on certain legal aspects of information society services, in particular electronic commerce, in the Internal Market (Directive on electronic commerce).

(41)   Respect for international commitments entered into by the Member States means that this Regulation should not affect international conventions to which one or more Member States are parties at the time when this Regulation is adopted. To make the rules more accessible, the Commission should publish the list of the relevant conventions in the Official Journal of the European Union on the basis of information supplied by the Member States.

(42)   The Commission will make a proposal to the European Parliament and to the Council concerning the procedures and conditions according to which Member States would be entitled to negotiate and conclude, on their own behalf, agreements with third countries in individual and exceptional cases, concerning sectoral matters and containing provisions on the law applicable to contractual obligations.

(43)   Since the objective of this Regulation cannot be sufficiently achieved by the Member States and can therefore, by reason of the scale and effects of this Regulation, be better achieved at Community level, the Community may adopt measures, in accordance with the principle of subsidiarity as set out in Article 5 of the Treaty. In accordance with the principle of proportionality, as set out in that Article, this Regulation does not go beyond what is necessary to attain its objective.

(44)   In accordance with Article 3 of the Protocol on the position of the United Kingdom and Ireland, annexed to the Treaty on European Union and to the Treaty establishing the European Community, Ireland has notified its wish to take part in the adoption and application of the present Regulation.

(45)   In accordance with Articles 1 and 2 of the Protocol on the position of the United Kingdom and Ireland, annexed to the Treaty on European Union and to the Treaty establishing the European Community, and without prejudice to Article 4 of the said Protocol, the United Kingdom is not taking part in the adoption of this Regulation and is not bound by it or subject to its application.

(46)   In accordance with Articles 1 and 2 of the Protocol on the position of Denmark, annexed to the Treaty on European Union and to the Treaty establishing the European Community, Denmark is not taking part in the adoption of this Regulation and is not bound by it or subject to its application,

HAVE ADOPTED THIS REGULATION:

CHAPTER I
SCOPE

Article 1. Material scope

1.   This Regulation shall apply, in situations involving a conflict of laws, to contractual obligations in civil and commercial matters.

It shall not apply, in particular, to revenue, customs or administrative matters.

2.   The following shall be excluded from the scope of this Regulation:

(a)   questions involving the status or legal capacity of natural persons, without prejudice to Article 13;

(b)   obligations arising out of family relationships and relationships deemed by the law applicable to such relationships to have comparable effects, including maintenance obligations;

(c)   obligations arising out of matrimonial property regimes, property regimes of relationships deemed by the law applicable to such relationships to have comparable effects to marriage, and wills and succession;

(d)   obligations arising under bills of exchange, cheques and promissory notes and other negotiable instruments to the extent that the obligations under such other negotiable instruments arise out of their negotiable character;

(e)   arbitration agreements and agreements on the choice of court;

(f)   questions governed by the law of companies and other bodies, corporate or unincorporated, such as the creation, by registration or otherwise, legal capacity, internal organisation or winding-up of companies and other bodies, corporate or unincorporated, and the personal liability of officers and members as such for the obligations of the company or body;

(g)   the question whether an agent is able to bind a principal, or an organ to bind a company or other body corporate or unincorporated, in relation to a third party;

(h)   the constitution of trusts and the relationship between settlors, trustees and beneficiaries;

(i)   obligations arising out of dealings prior to the conclusion of a contract;

(j)   insurance contracts arising out of operations carried out by organisations other than undertakings referred to in Article 2 of Directive 2002/83/EC of the European Parliament and of the Council of 5 November 2002 concerning life assurance the object of which is to provide benefits for employed or self-employed persons belonging to an undertaking or group of undertakings, or to a trade or group of trades, in the event of death or survival or of discontinuance or curtailment of activity, or of sickness related to work or accidents at work.

3.   This Regulation shall not apply to evidence and procedure, without prejudice to Article 18.

4.   In this Regulation, the term 'Member State' shall mean Member States to which this Regulation applies. However, in Article 3(4) and Article 7 the term shall mean all the Member States.

Article 2. Universal application

Any law specified by this Regulation shall be applied whether or not it is the law of a Member State.

CHAPTER II
UNIFORM RULES

Article 3. Freedom of choice

1.   A contract shall be governed by the law chosen by the parties. The choice shall be made expressly or clearly demonstrated by the terms of the contract or the circumstances of the case. By their choice the parties can select the law applicable to the whole or to part only of the contract.

2.   The parties may at any time agree to subject the contract to a law other than that which previously governed it, whether as a result of an earlier choice made under this Article or of other provisions of this Regulation. Any change in the law to be applied that is made after the conclusion of the contract shall not prejudice its formal validity under Article 11 or adversely affect the rights of third parties.

3.   Where all other elements relevant to the situation at the time of the choice are located in a country other than the country whose law has been chosen, the choice of the parties shall not prejudice the application of provisions of the law of that other country which cannot be derogated from by agreement.

4.   Where all other elements relevant to the situation at the time of the choice are located in one or more Member States, the parties' choice of applicable law other than that of a Member State shall not prejudice the application of provisions of Community law, where appropriate as implemented in the Member State of the forum, which cannot be derogated from by agreement.

5.   The existence and validity of the consent of the parties as to the choice of the applicable law shall be determined in accordance with the provisions of Articles 10, 11 and 13.

Article 4. Applicable law in the absence of choice

1.   To the extent that the law applicable to the contract has not been chosen in accordance with Article 3 and without prejudice to Articles 5 to 8, the law governing the contract shall be determined as follows:

   (a)   a contract for the sale of goods shall be governed by the law of the country where the seller has his habitual residence;

   (b)   a contract for the provision of services shall be governed by the law of the country where the service provider has his habitual residence;

   (c)   a contract relating to a right in rem in immovable property or to a tenancy of immovable property shall be governed by the law of the country where the property is situated;

   (d)   notwithstanding point (c), a tenancy of immovable property concluded for temporary private use for a period of no more than six consecutive months shall be governed by the law of the country where the landlord has his habitual residence, provided that the tenant is a natural person and has his habitual residence in the same country;

   (e)   a franchise contract shall be governed by the law of the country where the franchisee has his habitual residence;

   (f)   a distribution contract shall be governed by the law of the country where the distributor has his habitual residence;

   (g)   a contract for the sale of goods by auction shall be governed by the law of the country where the auction takes place, if such a place can be determined;

(h) a contract concluded within a multilateral system which brings together or facilitates the bringing together of multiple third-party buying and selling interests in financial instruments, as defined by Article 4(1), point (17) of Directive 2004/39/EC, in accordance with non-discretionary rules and governed by a single law, shall be governed by that law.

2. Where the contract is not covered by paragraph 1 or where the elements of the contract would be covered by more than one of points (a) to (h) of paragraph 1, the contract shall be governed by the law of the country where the party required to effect the characteristic performance of the contract has his habitual residence.

3. Where it is clear from all the circumstances of the case that the contract is manifestly more closely connected with a country other than that indicated in paragraphs 1 or 2, the law of that other country shall apply.

4. Where the law applicable cannot be determined pursuant to paragraphs 1 or 2, the contract shall be governed by the law of the country with which it is most closely connected.

Article 5. Contracts of carriage

1. To the extent that the law applicable to a contract for the carriage of goods has not been chosen in accordance with Article 3, the law applicable shall be the law of the country of habitual residence of the carrier, provided that the place of receipt or the place of delivery or the habitual residence of the consignor is also situated in that country. If those requirements are not met, the law of the country where the place of delivery as agreed by the parties is situated shall apply.

2. To the extent that the law applicable to a contract for the carriage of passengers has not been chosen by the parties in accordance with the second subparagraph, the law applicable shall be the law of the country where the passenger has his habitual residence, provided that either the place of departure or the place of destination is situated in that country. If these requirements are not met, the law of the country where the carrier has his habitual residence shall apply.

The parties may choose as the law applicable to a contract for the carriage of passengers in accordance with Article 3 only the law of the country where:

(a) the passenger has his habitual residence; or
(b) the carrier has his habitual residence; or
(c) the carrier has his place of central administration; or
(d) the place of departure is situated; or
(e) the place of destination is situated.

3. Where it is clear from all the circumstances of the case that the contract, in the absence of a choice of law, is manifestly more closely connected with a country other than that indicated in paragraphs 1 or 2, the law of that other country shall apply.

Article 6. Consumer contracts

1. Without prejudice to Articles 5 and 7, a contract concluded by a natural person for a purpose which can be regarded as being outside his trade or profession (the consumer) with another person acting in the exercise of his trade or profession (the professional) shall be governed by the law of the country where the consumer has his habitual residence, provided that the professional:

(a) pursues his commercial or professional activities in the country where the consumer has his habitual residence, or
(b) by any means, directs such activities to that country or to several countries including that country,

and the contract falls within the scope of such activities.

2. Notwithstanding paragraph 1, the parties may choose the law applicable to a contract which fulfils the requirements of paragraph 1, in accordance with Article 3. Such a choice may not, however, have the result of depriving the consumer of the protection afforded to him by provisions that cannot be derogated

from by agreement by virtue of the law which, in the absence of choice, would have been applicable on the basis of paragraph 1.

3.   If the requirements in points (a) or (b) of paragraph 1 are not fulfilled, the law applicable to a contract between a consumer and a professional shall be determined pursuant to Articles 3 and 4.

4.   Paragraphs 1 and 2 shall not apply to:

(a)   a contract for the supply of services where the services are to be supplied to the consumer exclusively in a country other than that in which he has his habitual residence;

(b)   a contract of carriage other than a contract relating to package travel within the meaning of Council Directive 90/314/EEC of 13 June 1990 on package travel, package holidays and package tours;

(c)   a contract relating to a right in rem in immovable property or a tenancy of immovable property other than a contract relating to the right to use immovable properties on a timeshare basis within the meaning of Directive 94/47/EC;

(d)   rights and obligations which constitute a financial instrument and rights and obligations constituting the terms and conditions governing the issuance or offer to the public and public take-over bids of transferable securities, and the subscription and redemption of units in collective investment undertakings in so far as these activities do not constitute provision of a financial service;

(e)   a contract concluded within the type of system falling within the scope of Article 4(1)(h)

Article 7. Insurance contracts

1.   This Article shall apply to contracts referred to in paragraph 2, whether or not the risk covered is situated in a Member State, and to all other insurance contracts covering risks situated inside the territory of the Member States. It shall not apply to reinsurance contracts.

2.   An insurance contract covering a large risk as defined in Article 5(d) of the First Council Directive 73/239/EEC of 24 July 1973 on the coordination of laws, regulations and administrative provisions relating to the taking-up and pursuit of the business of direct insurance other than life assurance shall be governed by the law chosen by the parties in accordance with Article 3 of this Regulation.

To the extent that the applicable law has not been chosen by the parties, the insurance contract shall be governed by the law of the country where the insurer has his habitual residence. Where it is clear from all the circumstances of the case that the contract is manifestly more closely connected with another country, the law of that other country shall apply.

3.   In the case of an insurance contract other than a contract falling within paragraph 2, only the following laws may be chosen by the parties in accordance with Article 3:

(a)   the law of any Member State where the risk is situated at the time of conclusion of the contract;

(b)   the law of the country where the policy holder has his habitual residence;

(c)   in the case of life assurance, the law of the Member State of which the policy holder is a national;

(d)   for insurance contracts covering risks limited to events occurring in one Member State other than the Member State where the risk is situated, the law of that Member State;

(e)   where the policy holder of a contract falling under this paragraph pursues a commercial or industrial activity or a liberal profession and the insurance contract covers two or more risks which relate to those activities and are situated in different Member States, the law of any of the Member States concerned or the law of the country of habitual residence of the policy holder.

Where, in the cases set out in points (a), (b) or (e), the Member States referred to grant greater freedom of choice of the law applicable to the insurance contract, the parties may take advantage of that freedom.

To the extent that the law applicable has not been chosen by the parties in accordance with this paragraph, such a contract shall be governed by the law of the Member State in which the risk is situated at the time of conclusion of the contract.

4.   The following additional rules shall apply to insurance contracts covering risks for which a Member State imposes an obligation to take out insurance:

(a)   the insurance contract shall not satisfy the obligation to take out insurance unless it complies with the specific provisions relating to that insurance laid down by the Member State that imposes the obligation. Where the law of the Member State in which the risk is situated and the law of the Member State imposing the obligation to take out insurance contradict each other, the latter shall prevail;

(b)   by way of derogation from paragraphs 2 and 3, a Member State may lay down that the insurance contract shall be governed by the law of the Member State that imposes the obligation to take out insurance.

5.   For the purposes of paragraph 3, third subparagraph, and paragraph 4, where the contract covers risks situated in more than one Member State, the contract shall be considered as constituting several contracts each relating to only one Member State.

6.   For the purposes of this Article, the country in which the risk is situated shall be determined in accordance with Article 2(d) of the Second Council Directive 88/357/EEC of 22 June 1988 on the coordination of laws, regulations and administrative provisions relating to direct insurance other than life assurance and laying down provisions to facilitate the effective exercise of freedom to provide services and, in the case of life assurance, the country in which the risk is situated shall be the country of the commitment within the meaning of Article 1(1)(g) of Directive 2002/83/EC.

Article 8. Individual employment contracts

1.   An individual employment contract shall be governed by the law chosen by the parties in accordance with Article 3. Such a choice of law may not, however, have the result of depriving the employee of the protection afforded to him by provisions that cannot be derogated from by agreement under the law that, in the absence of choice, would have been applicable pursuant to paragraphs 2, 3 and 4 of this Article.

2.   To the extent that the law applicable to the individual employment contract has not been chosen by the parties, the contract shall be governed by the law of the country in which or, failing that, from which the employee habitually carries out his work in performance of the contract. The country where the work is habitually carried out shall not be deemed to have changed if he is temporarily employed in another country.

3.   Where the law applicable cannot be determined pursuant to paragraph 2, the contract shall be governed by the law of the country where the place of business through which the employee was engaged is situated.

4.   Where it appears from the circumstances as a whole that the contract is more closely connected with a country other than that indicated in paragraphs 2 or 3, the law of that other country shall apply.

Article 9. Overriding mandatory provisions

1.   Overriding mandatory provisions are provisions the respect for which is regarded as crucial by a country for safeguarding its public interests, such as its political, social or economic organisation, to such an extent that they are applicable to any situation falling within their scope, irrespective of the law otherwise applicable to the contract under this Regulation.

2.   Nothing in this Regulation shall restrict the application of the overriding mandatory provisions of the law of the forum.

3.   Effect may be given to the overriding mandatory provisions of the law of the country where the obligations arising out of the contract have to be or have been performed, in so far as those overriding mandatory provisions render the performance of the contract unlawful. In considering whether to give effect to those provisions, regard shall be had to their nature and purpose and to the consequences of their application or non-application.

Article 10. Consent and material validity

1.   The existence and validity of a contract, or of any term of a contract, shall be determined by the law which would govern it under this Regulation if the contract or term were valid.

2.   Nevertheless, a party, in order to establish that he did not consent, may rely upon the law of the country in which he has his habitual residence if it appears from the circumstances that it would not be reasonable to determine the effect of his conduct in accordance with the law specified in paragraph 1.

Article 11. Formal validity

1.   A contract concluded between persons who, or whose agents, are in the same country at the time of its conclusion is formally valid if it satisfies the formal requirements of the law which governs it in substance under this Regulation or of the law of the country where it is concluded.

2.   A contract concluded between persons who, or whose agents, are in different countries at the time of its conclusion is formally valid if it satisfies the formal requirements of the law which governs it in substance under this Regulation, or of the law of either of the countries where either of the parties or their agent is present at the time of conclusion, or of the law of the country where either of the parties had his habitual residence at that time.

3.   A unilateral act intended to have legal effect relating to an existing or contemplated contract is formally valid if it satisfies the formal requirements of the law which governs or would govern the contract in substance under this Regulation, or of the law of the country where the act was done, or of the law of the country where the person by whom it was done had his habitual residence at that time.

4.   Paragraphs 1, 2 and 3 of this Article shall not apply to contracts that fall within the scope of Article 6. The form of such contracts shall be governed by the law of the country where the consumer has his habitual residence.

5.   Notwithstanding paragraphs 1 to 4, a contract the subject matter of which is a right in rem in immovable property or a tenancy of immovable property shall be subject to the requirements of form of the law of the country where the property is situated if by that law:

    (a)   those requirements are imposed irrespective of the country where the contract is concluded and irrespective of the law governing the contract; and

    (b)   those requirements cannot be derogated from by agreement.

Article 12. Scope of the law applicable

1.   The law applicable to a contract by virtue of this Regulation shall govern in particular:

    (a)   interpretation;

    (b)   performance;

    (c)   within the limits of the powers conferred on the court by its procedural law, the consequences of a total or partial breach of obligations, including the assessment of damages in so far as it is governed by rules of law;

    (d)   the various ways of extinguishing obligations, and prescription and limitation of actions;

    (e)   the consequences of nullity of the contract.

2.   In relation to the manner of performance and the steps to be taken in the event of defective performance, regard shall be had to the law of the country in which performance takes place.

Article 13. Incapacity
In a contract concluded between persons who are in the same country, a natural person who would have capacity under the law of that country may invoke his incapacity resulting from the law of another country, only if the other party to the contract was aware of that incapacity at the time of the conclusion of the contract or was not aware thereof as a result of negligence.

Article 14. Voluntary assignment and contractual subrogation
1.   The relationship between assignor and assignee under a voluntary assignment or contractual subrogation of a claim against another person (the debtor) shall be governed by the law that applies to the contract between the assignor and assignee under this Regulation.
2.   The law governing the assigned or subrogated claim shall determine its assignability, the relationship between the assignee and the debtor, the conditions under which the assignment or subrogation can be invoked against the debtor and whether the debtor's obligations have been discharged.
3.   The concept of assignment in this Article includes outright transfers of claims, transfers of claims by way of security and pledges or other security rights over claims.

Article 15. Legal subrogation
Where a person (the creditor) has a contractual claim against another (the debtor) and a third person has a duty to satisfy the creditor, or has in fact satisfied the creditor in discharge of that duty, the law which governs the third person's duty to satisfy the creditor shall determine whether and to what extent the third person is entitled to exercise against the debtor the rights which the creditor had against the debtor under the law governing their relationship.

Article 16. Multiple liability
If a creditor has a claim against several debtors who are liable for the same claim, and one of the debtors has already satisfied the claim in whole or in part, the law governing the debtor's obligation towards the creditor also governs the debtor's right to claim recourse from the other debtors. The other debtors may rely on the defences they had against the creditor to the extent allowed by the law governing their obligations towards the creditor.

Article 17. Set-off
Where the right to set-off is not agreed by the parties, set-off shall be governed by the law applicable to the claim against which the right to set-off is asserted.

Article 18. Burden of proof
1.   The law governing a contractual obligation under this Regulation shall apply to the extent that, in matters of contractual obligations, it contains rules which raise presumptions of law or determine the burden of proof.
2.   A contract or an act intended to have legal effect may be proved by any mode of proof recognised by the law of the forum or by any of the laws referred to in Article 11 under which that contract or act is formally valid, provided that such mode of proof can be administered by the forum.

CHAPTER III
OTHER PROVISIONS

Article 19. Habitual residence

1. For the purposes of this Regulation, the habitual residence of companies and other bodies, corporate or unincorporated, shall be the place of central administration.

The habitual residence of a natural person acting in the course of his business activity shall be his principal place of business.

2. Where the contract is concluded in the course of the operations of a branch, agency or any other establishment, or if, under the contract, performance is the responsibility of such a branch, agency or establishment, the place where the branch, agency or any other establishment is located shall be treated as the place of habitual residence.

3. For the purposes of determining the habitual residence, the relevant point in time shall be the time of the conclusion of the contract.

Article 20. Exclusion of renvoi

The application of the law of any country specified by this Regulation means the application of the rules of law in force in that country other than its rules of private international law, unless provided otherwise in this Regulation.

Article 21. Public policy of the forum

The application of a provision of the law of any country specified by this Regulation may be refused only if such application is manifestly incompatible with the public policy (ordre public) of the forum.

Article 22. States with more than one legal system*

1. Where a State comprises several territorial units, each of which has its own rules of law in respect of contractual obligations, each territorial unit shall be considered as a country for the purposes of identifying the law applicable under this Regulation.

2. A Member State where different territorial units have their own rules of law in respect of contractual obligations shall not be required to apply this Regulation to conflicts solely between the laws of such units.

Article 23. Relationship with other provisions of Community law

With the exception of Article 7, this Regulation shall not prejudice the application of provisions of Community law which, in relation to particular matters, lay down conflict-of-law rules relating to contractual obligations.

Article 24. Relationship with the Rome Convention

1. This Regulation shall replace the Rome Convention in the Member States, except as regards the territories of the Member States which fall within the territorial scope of that Convention and to which this Regulation does not apply pursuant to Article 299 of the Treaty.

2. In so far as this Regulation replaces the provisions of the Rome Convention, any reference to that Convention shall be understood as a reference to this Regulation.

Article 25. Relationship with existing international conventions

1. This Regulation shall not prejudice the application of international conventions to which one or more Member States are parties at the time when this Regu-

---

*Reg 4 of The Law Applicable to Contractual Obligations (Scotland) Regulations 2009 (SSI 2009/410) provides that, notwithstanding Art 22(2), the Regulation with the exception of Art 7 applies in the case of conflicts between (a) the laws of different parts of the UK; or (b) between the laws of one or more parts of the UK and Gibraltar.

lation is adopted and which lay down conflict-of-law rules relating to contractual obligations.

2.   However, this Regulation shall, as between Member States, take precedence over conventions concluded exclusively between two or more of them in so far as such conventions concern matters governed by this Regulation.

Article 26. List of Conventions

1.   By 17 June 2009, Member States shall notify the Commission of the conventions referred to in Article 25(1). After that date, Member States shall notify the Commission of all denunciations of such conventions.

2.   Within six months of receipt of the notifications referred to in paragraph 1, the Commission shall publish in the Official Journal of the European Union:

   (a)   a list of the conventions referred to in paragraph 1;
   (b)   the denunciations referred to in paragraph 1.

Article 27. Review clause

1.   By 17 June 2013, the Commission shall submit to the European Parliament, the Council and the European Economic and Social Committee a report on the application of this Regulation. If appropriate, the report shall be accompanied by proposals to amend this Regulation. The report shall include:

   (a)   a study on the law applicable to insurance contracts and an assessment of the impact of the provisions to be introduced, if any; and
   (b)   an evaluation on the application of Article 6, in particular as regards the coherence of Community law in the field of consumer protection.

2.   By 17 June 2010, the Commission shall submit to the European Parliament, the Council and the European Economic and Social Committee a report on the question of the effectiveness of an assignment or subrogation of a claim against third parties and the priority of the assigned or subrogated claim over a right of another person. The report shall be accompanied, if appropriate, by a proposal to amend this Regulation and an assessment of the impact of the provisions to be introduced.

Article 28. Application in time

This Regulation shall apply to contracts concluded as from* 17 December 2009.

CHAPTER IV
FINAL PROVISIONS

Article 29. Entry into force and application

This Regulation shall enter into force on the 20th day following its publication in the Official Journal of the European Union.

It shall apply from 17 December 2009 except for Article 26 which shall apply from 17 June 2009.

This Regulation shall be binding in its entirety and directly applicable in the Member States in accordance with the Treaty establishing the European Community.

Done at Strasbourg, 17 June 2008.

---

* *Per* Corrigendum to the Rome I Regulation 13497/1/09, REV 1, JUR 369 [2008 OJ L177].

COUNCIL REGULATION (EC) NO 4/2009 OF 18 DECEMBER 2008 ON
JURISDICTION, APPLICABLE LAW, RECOGNITION AND ENFORCEMENT
OF DECISIONS AND COOPERATION IN MATTERS RELATING TO
MAINTENANCE OBLIGATIONS

Official Journal L 007, 10/01/2009 pp 1-79

THE COUNCIL OF THE EUROPEAN UNION,

Having regard to the Treaty establishing the European Community, and in particular Article 61(c) and Article 67(2) thereof,
   Having regard to the proposal from the Commission,
   Having regard to the opinion of the European Parliament,
   Having regard to the opinion of the European Economic and Social Committee,

Whereas:
   (1)   The Community has set itself the objective of maintaining and developing an area of freedom, security and justice, in which the free movement of persons is ensured. For the gradual establishment of such an area, the Community is to adopt, among others, measures relating to judicial cooperation in civil matters having cross-border implications, in so far as necessary for the proper functioning of the internal market.
   (2)   In accordance with Article 65(b) of the Treaty, these measures must aim, inter alia, to promote the compatibility of the rules applicable in the Member States concerning the conflict of laws and of jurisdiction.
   (3)   In this respect, the Community has among other measures already adopted Council Regulation (EC) No 44/2001 of 22 December 2000 on jurisdiction and the recognition and enforcement of judgments in civil and commercial matters, Council Decision 2001/470/EC of 28 May 2001 establishing a European Judicial Network in civil and commercial matters, Council Regulation (EC) No 1206/2001 of 28 May 2001 on cooperation between the courts of the Member States in the taking of evidence in civil or commercial matters, Council Directive 2003/8/EC of 27 January 2003 to improve access to justice in cross-border disputes by establishing minimum common rules relating to legal aid for such disputes, Council Regulation (EC) No 2201/2003 of 27 November 2003 on jurisdiction and the recognition and enforcement of judgments in matrimonial matters and in matters of parental responsibility, Regulation (EC) No 805/2004 of the European Parliament and of the Council of 21 April 2004 creating a European Enforcement Order for uncontested claims, and Regulation (EC) No 1393/2007 of the European Parliament and of the Council of 13 November 2007 on the service in the Member States of judicial and extrajudicial documents in civil or commercial matters (service of documents).
   (4)   The European Council in Tampere on 15 and 16 October 1999 invited the Council and the Commission to establish special common procedural rules to simplify and accelerate the settlement of cross-border disputes concerning, inter alia, maintenance claims. It also called for the abolition of intermediate measures required for the recognition and enforcement in the requested State of a decision given in another Member State, particularly a decision relating to a maintenance claim.
   (5)   A programme of measures for the enforcement of the principle of mutual recognition of decisions in civil and commercial matters, common to the Commission and to the Council, was adopted on 30 November 2000. That programme provides for the abolition of the exequatur procedure for maintenance claims in order to boost the effectiveness of the means by which maintenance creditors safeguard their rights.

(6) The European Council meeting in Brussels on 4 and 5 November 2004 adopted a new programme called 'The Hague Programme: strengthening freedom, security and justice in the European Union' (hereinafter referred to as The Hague Programme).

(7) At its meeting on 2 and 3 June 2005, the Council adopted a Council and Commission Action Plan which implements The Hague Programme in concrete actions and which mentions the necessity of adopting proposals on maintenance obligations.

(8) In the framework of The Hague Conference on Private International Law, the Community and its Member States took part in negotiations which led to the adoption on 23 November 2007 of the Convention on the International Recovery of Child Support and other Forms of Family Maintenance (hereinafter referred to as the 2007 Hague Convention) and the Protocol on the Law Applicable to Maintenance Obligations (hereinafter referred to as the 2007 Hague Protocol). Both those instruments should therefore be taken into account in this Regulation.

(9) A maintenance creditor should be able to obtain easily, in a Member State, a decision which will be automatically enforceable in another Member State without further formalities.

(10) In order to achieve this goal, it is advisable to create a Community instrument in matters relating to maintenance obligations bringing together provisions on jurisdiction, conflict of laws, recognition and enforceability, enforcement, legal aid and cooperation between Central Authorities.

(11) The scope of this Regulation should cover all maintenance obligations arising from a family relationship, parentage, marriage or affinity, in order to guarantee equal treatment of all maintenance creditors. For the purposes of this Regulation, the term 'maintenance obligation' should be interpreted autonomously.

(12) In order to take account of the various ways of resolving maintenance obligation issues in the Member States, this Regulation should apply both to court decisions and to decisions given by administrative authorities, provided that the latter offer guarantees with regard to, in particular, their impartiality and the right of all parties to be heard. Those authorities should therefore apply all the rules of this Regulation.

(13) For the reasons set out above, this Regulation should also ensure the recognition and enforcement of court settlements and authentic instruments without affecting the right of either party to such a settlement or instrument to challenge the settlement or instrument before the courts of the Member State of origin.

(14) It should be provided in this Regulation that for the purposes of an application for the recognition and enforcement of a decision relating to maintenance obligations the term 'creditor' includes public bodies which are entitled to act in place of a person to whom maintenance is owed or to claim reimbursement of benefits provided to the creditor in place of maintenance. Where a public body acts in this capacity, it should be entitled to the same services and the same legal aid as a creditor.

(15) In order to preserve the interests of maintenance creditors and to promote the proper administration of justice within the European Union, the rules on jurisdiction as they result from Regulation (EC) No 44/2001 should be adapted. The circumstance that the defendant is habitually resident in a third State should no longer entail the non-application of Community rules on jurisdiction, and there should no longer be any referral to national law. This Regulation should therefore determine the cases in which a court in a Member State may exercise subsidiary jurisdiction.

(16) In order to remedy, in particular, situations of denial of justice this Regulation should provide a forum necessitatis allowing a court of a Member State, on an exceptional basis, to hear a case which is closely connected with a third State. Such an exceptional basis may be deemed to exist when proceedings prove impos-

sible in the third State in question, for example because of civil war, or when an applicant cannot reasonably be expected to initiate or conduct proceedings in that State. Jurisdiction based on the forum necessitatis should, however, be exercised only if the dispute has a sufficient connection with the Member State of the court seised, for instance the nationality of one of the parties.

(17)   An additional rule of jurisdiction should provide that, except under specific conditions, proceedings to modify an existing maintenance decision or to have a new decision given can be brought by the debtor only in the State in which the creditor was habitually resident at the time the decision was given and in which he remains habitually resident. To ensure proper symmetry between the 2007 Hague Convention and this Regulation, this rule should also apply as regards decisions given in a third State which is party to the said Convention in so far as that Convention is in force between that State and the Community and covers the same maintenance obligations in that State and in the Community.

(18)   For the purposes of this Regulation, it should be provided that in Ireland the concept of 'domicile' replaces the concept of 'nationality' which is also the case in the United Kingdom, subject to this Regulation being applicable in the latter Member State in accordance with Article 4 of the Protocol on the position of the United Kingdom and Ireland annexed to the Treaty on European Union and the Treaty establishing the European Community.

(19)   In order to increase legal certainty, predictability and the autonomy of the parties, this Regulation should enable the parties to choose the competent court by agreement on the basis of specific connecting factors. To protect the weaker party, such a choice of court should not be allowed in the case of maintenance obligations towards a child under the age of 18.

(20)   It should be provided in this Regulation that, for Member States bound by the 2007 Hague Protocol, the rules on conflict of laws in respect of maintenance obligations will be those set out in that Protocol. To that end, a provision referring to the said Protocol should be inserted. The 2007 Hague Protocol will be concluded by the Community in time to enable this Regulation to apply. To take account of a scenario in which the 2007 Hague Protocol does not apply to all the Member States a distinction for the purposes of recognition, enforceability and enforcement of decisions needs to be made in this Regulation between the Member States bound by the 2007 Hague Protocol and those not bound by it.

(21)   It needs to be made clear in this Regulation that these rules on conflict of laws determine only the law applicable to maintenance obligations and do not determine the law applicable to the establishment of the family relationships on which the maintenance obligations are based. The establishment of family relationships continues to be covered by the national law of the Member States, including their rules of private international law.

(22)   In order to ensure swift and efficient recovery of a maintenance obligation and to prevent delaying actions, decisions in matters relating to maintenance obligations given in a Member State should in principle be provisionally enforceable. This Regulation should therefore provide that the court of origin should be able to declare the decision provisionally enforceable even if the national law does not provide for enforceability by operation of law and even if an appeal has been or could still be lodged against the decision under national law.

(23)   To limit the costs of proceedings subject to this Regulation, the greatest possible use of modern communications technologies, particularly for hearing parties, would be helpful.

(24)   The guarantees provided by the application of rules on conflict of laws should provide the justification for having decisions relating to maintenance obligations given in a Member State bound by the 2007 Hague Protocol recognised and regarded as enforceable in all the other Member States without any procedure being necessary and without any form of control on the substance in the Member State of enforcement.

(25)   Recognition in a Member State of a decision relating to maintenance obligations has as its only object to allow the recovery of the maintenance claim determined in the decision. It does not imply the recognition by that Member State of the family relationship, parentage, marriage or affinity underlying the maintenance obligations which gave rise to the decision.

(26)   For decisions on maintenance obligations given in a Member State not bound by the 2007 Hague Protocol, there should be provision in this Regulation for a procedure for recognition and declaration of enforceability. That procedure should be modelled on the procedure and the grounds for refusing recognition set out in Regulation (EC) No 44/2001. To accelerate proceedings and enable the creditor to recover his claim quickly, the court seised should be required to give its decision within a set time, unless there are exceptional circumstances.

(27)   It would also be appropriate to limit as far as possible the formal enforcement requirements likely to increase the costs to be borne by the maintenance creditor. To that end, this Regulation should provide that a maintenance creditor ought not to be required to have a postal address or an authorised representative in the Member State of enforcement, without this otherwise affecting the internal organisation of the Member States in matters relating to enforcement proceedings.

(28)   In order to limit the costs of enforcement proceedings, no translation should be required unless enforcement is contested, and without prejudice to the rules applicable to service of documents.

(29)   In order to guarantee compliance with the requirements of a fair trial, this Regulation should provide for the right of a defendant who did not enter an appearance in the court of origin of a Member State bound by the 2007 Hague Protocol to apply for a review of the decision given against him at the stage of enforcement. However, the defendant must apply for this review within a set period which should start no later than the day on which, in the enforcement proceedings, his property was first made non-disposable in whole or in part. That right to apply for a review should be an extraordinary remedy granted to the defendant in default and not affecting the application of any extraordinary remedies laid down in the law of the Member State of origin provided that those remedies are not incompatible with the right to a review under this Regulation.

(30)   In order to speed up the enforcement in another Member State of a decision given in a Member State bound by the 2007 Hague Protocol it is necessary to limit the grounds of refusal or of suspension of enforcement which may be invoked by the debtor on account of the cross-border nature of the maintenance claim. This limitation should not affect the grounds of refusal or of suspension laid down in national law which are not incompatible with those listed in this Regulation, such as the debtor's discharge of his debt at the time of enforcement or the unattachable nature of certain assets.

(31)   To facilitate cross-border recovery of maintenance claims, provision should be made for a system of cooperation between Central Authorities designated by the Member States. These Authorities should assist maintenance creditors and debtors in asserting their rights in another Member State by submitting applications for recognition, enforceability and enforcement of existing decisions, for the modification of such decisions or for the establishment of a decision. They should also exchange information in order to locate debtors and creditors, and identify their income and assets, as necessary. Lastly, they should cooperate with each other by exchanging general information and promoting cooperation amongst the competent authorities in their Member States.

(32)   A Central Authority designated under this Regulation should bear its own costs, except in specifically determined cases, and should provide assistance for all applicants residing in its Member State. The criterion for determining a person's right to request assistance from a Central Authority should be less strict than the connecting factor of 'habitual residence' used elsewhere in this Regulation. However, the 'residence' criterion should exclude mere presence.

(33)   In order to provide full assistance to maintenance creditors and debtors and to facilitate as much as possible cross-border recovery of maintenance, the Central Authorities should be able to obtain a certain amount of personal information. This Regulation should therefore oblige the Member States to ensure that their Central Authorities have access to such information through the public authorities or administrations which hold the information concerned in the course of their ordinary activities. It should however be left to each Member State to decide on the arrangements for such access. Accordingly, a Member State should be able to designate the public authorities or administrations which will be required to supply the information to the Central Authority in accordance with this Regulation, including, if appropriate, public authorities or administrations already designated in the context of other systems for access to information. Where a Member State designates public authorities or administrations, it should ensure that its Central Authority is able to access the requisite information held by those bodies as provided for in this Regulation. A Member State should also be able to allow its Central Authority to access requisite information from any other legal person which holds it and controls its processing.

(34)   In the context of access to personal data and the use and transmission thereof, the requirements of Directive 95/46/EC of the European Parliament and of the Council of 24 October 1995 on the protection of individuals with regard to the processing of personal data and on the free movement of such data, as transposed into the national law of the Member States, should be complied with.

(35)   For the purposes of the application of this Regulation it is however necessary to define the specific conditions of access to personal data and of the use and transmission of such data. In this context, the opinion of the European Data Protection Supervisor has been taken into consideration. Notification of the data subject should take place in accordance with national law. It should however be possible to defer the notification to prevent the debtor from transferring his assets and thus jeopardising the recovery of the maintenance claim.

(36)   On account of the costs of proceedings it is appropriate to provide for a very favourable legal aid scheme, that is, full coverage of the costs relating to proceedings concerning maintenance obligations in respect of children under the age of 21 initiated via the Central authorities. Specific rules should therefore be added to the current rules on legal aid in the European Union which exist by virtue of Directive 2003/8/EC thus setting up a special legal aid scheme for maintenance obligations. In this context, the competent authority of the requested Member State should be able, exceptionally, to recover costs from an applicant having received free legal aid and lost the case, provided that the person's financial situation so permits. This would apply, in particular, where someone well-off had acted in bad faith.

(37)   In addition, for maintenance obligations other than those referred to in the preceding recital, all parties should be guaranteed the same treatment in terms of legal aid at the time of enforcement of a decision in another Member State. Accordingly, the provisions of this Regulation on continuity of legal aid should be understood as also granting such aid to a party who, while not having received legal aid in the proceedings to obtain or amend a decision in the Member State of origin, did then benefit from such aid in that State in the context of an application for enforcement of the decision. Similarly, a party who benefited from free proceedings before an administrative authority listed in Annex X should, in the Member State of enforcement, benefit from the most favourable legal aid or the most extensive exemption from costs or expenses, provided that he shows that he would have so benefited in the Member State of origin.

(38)   In order to minimise the costs of translating supporting documents the court seised should only require a translation of such documents when this is necessary, without prejudice to the rights of the defence and the rules applicable concerning service of documents.

(39)   To facilitate the application of this Regulation, Member States should be obliged to provide the Commission with the names and contact details of their Central Authorities and with other information. That information should be made available to practitioners and to the public through publication in the Official Journal of the European Union or through electronic access to the European Judicial Network in civil and commercial matters established by Decision 2001/470/EC. Furthermore, the use of forms provided for in this Regulation should facilitate and speed up communication between the Central Authorities and make it possible to submit applications electronically.

(40)   The relationship between this Regulation and the bilateral or multilateral conventions and agreements on maintenance obligations to which the Member States are party should be specified. In this context it should be stipulated that Member States which are party to the Convention of 23 March 1962 between Sweden, Denmark, Finland, Iceland and Norway on the recovery of maintenance by the Member States may continue to apply that Convention since it contains more favourable rules on recognition and enforcement than those in this Regulation. As regards the conclusion of future bilateral agreements on maintenance obligations with third States, the procedures and conditions under which Member States would be authorised to negotiate and conclude such agreements on their own behalf should be determined in the course of discussions relating to a Commission proposal on the subject.

(41)   In calculating the periods and time limits provided for in this Regulation, Regulation (EEC, Euratom) No 1182/71 of the Council of 3 June 1971 determining the rules applicable to periods, dates and time limits should apply.

(42)   The measures necessary for the implementation of this Regulation should be adopted in accordance with Council Decision 1999/468/EC of 28 June 1999 laying down the procedures for the exercise of implementing powers conferred on the Commission.

(43)   In particular, the Commission should be empowered to adopt any amendments to the forms provided for in this Regulation in accordance with the advisory procedure provided for in Article 3 of Decision 1999/468/EC. For the establishment of the list of the administrative authorities falling within the scope of this Regulation, and the list of authorities competent to certify the right to legal aid, the Commission should be empowered to act in accordance with the management procedure provided for in Article 4 of that Decision.

(44)   This Regulation should amend Regulation (EC) No 44/2001 by replacing the provisions of that Regulation applicable to maintenance obligations. Subject to the transitional provisions of this Regulation, Member States should, in matters relating to maintenance obligations, apply the provisions of this Regulation on jurisdiction, recognition, enforceability and enforcement of decisions and on legal aid instead of those of Regulation (EC) No 44/2001 as from the date on which this Regulation becomes applicable.

(45)   Since the objectives of this Regulation, namely the introduction of a series of measures to ensure the effective recovery of maintenance claims in cross-border situations and thus to facilitate the free movement of persons within the European Union, cannot be sufficiently achieved by the Member States and can therefore, by reason of the scale and effects of this Regulation, be better achieved at Community level, the Community may adopt measures in accordance with the principle of subsidiarity as set out in Article 5 of the Treaty. In accordance with the principle of proportionality as set out in that Article this Regulation does not go beyond what is necessary to achieve those objectives.

(46)   In accordance with Article 3 of the Protocol on the position of the United Kingdom and Ireland, annexed to the Treaty on European Union and to the Treaty establishing the European Community, Ireland has given notice of its wish to take part in the adoption and application of this Regulation.

(47)   In accordance with Articles 1 and 2 of the Protocol on the position of the

United Kingdom and Ireland, annexed to the Treaty on European Union and to the Treaty establishing the European Community, the United Kingdom is not taking part in the adoption of this Regulation and is not bound by it or subject to its application. This is, however, without prejudice to the possibility for the United Kingdom of notifying its intention of accepting this Regulation after its adoption in accordance with Article 4 of the said Protocol.

(48)   In accordance with Articles 1 and 2 of the Protocol on the position of Denmark annexed to the Treaty on European Union and the Treaty establishing the European Community, Denmark is not taking part in the adoption of this Regulation and is not bound by it or subject to its application, without prejudice to the possibility for Denmark of applying the amendments made here to Regulation (EC) No 44/2001 pursuant to Article 3 of the Agreement of 19 October 2005 between the European Community and the Kingdom of Denmark on jurisdiction and the recognition and enforcement of judgments in civil and commercial matters,

HAS ADOPTED THIS REGULATION:

CHAPTER I
SCOPE AND DEFINITIONS

Article 1. Scope of application
1.   This Regulation shall apply to maintenance obligations arising from a family relationship, parentage, marriage or affinity.

2.   In this Regulation, the term 'Member State' shall mean Member States to which this Regulation applies.

Article 2. Definitions
1.   For the purposes of this Regulation:

1.   the term 'decision' shall mean a decision in matters relating to maintenance obligations given by a court of a Member State, whatever the decision may be called, including a decree, order, judgment or writ of execution, as well as a decision by an officer of the court determining the costs or expenses. For the purposes of Chapters VII and VIII, the term 'decision' shall also mean a decision in matters relating to maintenance obligations given in a third State;

2.   the term 'court settlement' shall mean a settlement in matters relating to maintenance obligations which has been approved by a court or concluded before a court in the course of proceedings;

3.   the term 'authentic instrument' shall mean:

(a)   a document in matters relating to maintenance obligations which has been formally drawn up or registered as an authentic instrument in the Member State of origin and the authenticity of which:

(i)   relates to the signature and the content of the instrument, and

(ii)   has been established by a public authority or other authority empowered for that purpose; or,

(b)   an arrangement relating to maintenance obligations concluded with administrative authorities of the Member State of origin or authenticated by them;

4.   the term 'Member State of origin' shall mean the Member State in which, as the case may be, the decision has been given, the court settlement has been approved or concluded, or the authentic instrument has been established;

5.   the term 'Member State of enforcement' shall mean the Member State in which the enforcement of the decision, the court settlement or the authentic instrument is sought;

6.   the term 'requesting Member State' shall mean the Member State whose Central Authority transmits an application pursuant to Chapter VII;

7.   the term 'requested Member State' shall mean the Member State whose Central Authority receives an application pursuant to Chapter VII;

8.   the term '2007 Hague Convention Contracting State' shall mean a State which is a contracting party to the Hague Convention of 23 November 2007 on the International Recovery of Child Support and other Forms of Family Maintenance (hereinafter referred to as the 2007 Hague Convention) to the extent that the said Convention applies between the Community and that State;

9.   the term 'court of origin' shall mean the court which has given the decision to be enforced;

10.   the term 'creditor' shall mean any individual to whom maintenance is owed or is alleged to be owed;

11.   the term 'debtor' shall mean any individual who owes or who is alleged to owe maintenance.

2.   For the purposes of this Regulation, the term 'court' shall include administrative authorities of the Member States with competence in matters relating to maintenance obligations provided that such authorities offer guarantees with regard to impartiality and the right of all parties to be heard and provided that their decisions under the law of the Member State where they are established:

(i)   may be made the subject of an appeal to or review by a judicial authority; and

(ii)   have a similar force and effect as a decision of a judicial authority on the same matter.

These administrative authorities shall be listed in Annex X. That Annex shall be established and amended in accordance with the management procedure referred to in Article 73(2) at the request of the Member State in which the administrative authority concerned is established.

3.   For the purposes of Articles 3, 4 and 6, the concept of 'domicile' shall replace that of 'nationality' in those Member States which use this concept as a connecting factor in family matters.

For the purposes of Article 6, parties which have their 'domicile' in different territorial units of the same Member State shall be deemed to have their common 'domicile' in that Member State.

CHAPTER II
JURISDICTION

Article 3. General provisions
In matters relating to maintenance obligations in Member States, jurisdiction shall lie with:

(a)   the court for the place where the defendant is habitually resident, or

(b)   the court for the place where the creditor is habitually resident, or

(c)   the court which, according to its own law, has jurisdiction to entertain proceedings concerning the status of a person if the matter relating to maintenance is ancillary to those proceedings, unless that jurisdiction is based solely on the nationality of one of the parties, or

(d)   the court which, according to its own law, has jurisdiction to entertain proceedings concerning parental responsibility if the matter relating to maintenance is ancillary to those proceedings, unless that jurisdiction is based solely on the nationality of one of the parties.

Article 4. Choice of court
1.   The parties may agree that the following court or courts of a Member State shall have jurisdiction to settle any disputes in matters relating to a maintenance obligation which have arisen or may arise between them:

(a)   a court or the courts of a Member State in which one of the parties is habitually resident;

(b)   a court or the courts of a Member State of which one of the parties has the nationality;

(c)   in the case of maintenance obligations between spouses or former spouses:

(i)   the court which has jurisdiction to settle their dispute in matrimonial matters; or

(ii)   a court or the courts of the Member State which was the Member State of the spouses' last common habitual residence for a period of at least one year.

The conditions referred to in points (a), (b) or (c) have to be met at the time the choice of court agreement is concluded or at the time the court is seised.

The jurisdiction conferred by agreement shall be exclusive unless the parties have agreed otherwise.

2.   A choice of court agreement shall be in writing. Any communication by electronic means which provides a durable record of the agreement shall be equivalent to 'writing'.

3.   This Article shall not apply to a dispute relating to a maintenance obligation towards a child under the age of 18.

4.   If the parties have agreed to attribute exclusive jurisdiction to a court or courts of a State party to the Convention on jurisdiction and the recognition and enforcement of judgments in civil and commercial matters, signed on 30 October 2007 in Lugano (hereinafter referred to as the Lugano Convention), where that State is not a Member State, the said Convention shall apply except in the case of the disputes referred to in paragraph 3.

Article 5. Jurisdiction based on the appearance of the defendant
Apart from jurisdiction derived from other provisions of this Regulation, a court of a Member State before which a defendant enters an appearance shall have jurisdiction. This rule shall not apply where appearance was entered to contest the jurisdiction.

Article 6. Subsidiary jurisdiction
Where no court of a Member State has jurisdiction pursuant to Articles 3, 4 and 5 and no court of a State party to the Lugano Convention which is not a Member State has jurisdiction pursuant to the provisions of that Convention, the courts of the Member State of the common nationality of the parties shall have jurisdiction.

Article 7. Forum necessitatis
Where no court of a Member State has jurisdiction pursuant to Articles 3, 4, 5 and 6, the courts of a Member State may, on an exceptional basis, hear the case if proceedings cannot reasonably be brought or conducted or would be impossible in a third State with which the dispute is closely connected.

The dispute must have a sufficient connection with the Member State of the court seised.

Article 8. Limit on proceedings
1.   Where a decision is given in a Member State or a 2007 Hague Convention Contracting State where the creditor is habitually resident, proceedings to modify the decision or to have a new decision given cannot be brought by the debtor in any other Member State as long as the creditor remains habitually resident in the State in which the decision was given.

2.   Paragraph 1 shall not apply:

(a)   where the parties have agreed in accordance with Article 4 to the jurisdiction of the courts of that other Member State;

(b)   where the creditor submits to the jurisdiction of the courts of that other Member State pursuant to Article 5;

(c)   where the competent authority in the 2007 Hague Convention Contracting State of origin cannot, or refuses to, exercise jurisdiction to modify the decision or give a new decision; or

(d) where the decision given in the 2007 Hague Convention Contracting State of origin cannot be recognised or declared enforceable in the Member State where proceedings to modify the decision or to have a new decision given are contemplated.

Article 9. Seising of a court
For the purposes of this Chapter, a court shall be deemed to be seised:

(a) at the time when the document instituting the proceedings or an equivalent document is lodged with the court, provided that the claimant has not subsequently failed to take the steps he was required to take to have service effected on the defendant; or

(b) if the document has to be served before being lodged with the court, at the time when it is received by the authority responsible for service, provided that the claimant has not subsequently failed to take the steps he was required to take to have the document lodged with the court.

Article 10. Examination as to jurisdiction
Where a court of a Member State is seised of a case over which it has no jurisdiction under this Regulation it shall declare of its own motion that it has no jurisdiction.

Article 11. Examination as to admissibility
1. Where a defendant habitually resident in a State other than the Member State where the action was brought does not enter an appearance, the court with jurisdiction shall stay the proceedings so long as it is not shown that the defendant has been able to receive the document instituting the proceedings or an equivalent document in sufficient time to enable him to arrange for his defence, or that all necessary steps have been taken to this end.

2. Article 19 of Regulation (EC) No 1393/2007 shall apply instead of the provisions of paragraph 1 of this Article if the document instituting the proceedings or an equivalent document had to be transmitted from one Member State to another pursuant to that Regulation.

3. Where the provisions of Regulation (EC) No 1393/2007 are not applicable, Article 15 of the Hague Convention of 15 November 1965 on the service abroad of judicial and extrajudicial documents in civil or commercial matters shall apply if the document instituting the proceedings or an equivalent document had to be transmitted abroad pursuant to that Convention.

Article 12. Lis pendens
1. Where proceedings involving the same cause of action and between the same parties are brought in the courts of different Member States, any court other than the court first seised shall of its own motion stay its proceedings until such time as the jurisdiction of the court first seised is established.

2. Where the jurisdiction of the court first seised is established, any court other than the court first seised shall decline jurisdiction in favour of that court.

Article 13. Related actions
1. Where related actions are pending in the courts of different Member States, any court other than the court first seised may stay its proceedings.

2. Where these actions are pending at first instance, any court other than the court first seised may also, on the application of one of the parties, decline jurisdiction if the court first seised has jurisdiction over the actions in question and its law permits the consolidation thereof.

3. For the purposes of this Article, actions are deemed to be related where they are so closely connected that it is expedient to hear and determine them together to avoid the risk of irreconcilable judgments resulting from separate proceedings.

Article 14. Provisional, including protective, measures
Application may be made to the courts of a Member State for such provisional, including protective, measures as may be available under the law of that State, even if, under this Regulation, the courts of another Member State have jurisdiction as to the substance of the matter.

CHAPTER III
APPLICABLE LAW

Article 15. Determination of the applicable law
The law applicable to maintenance obligations shall be determined in accordance with the Hague Protocol of 23 November 2007 on the law applicable to maintenance obligations (hereinafter referred to as the 2007 Hague Protocol) in the Member States bound by that instrument.

CHAPTER IV
RECOGNITION, ENFORCEABILITY AND ENFORCEMENT OF DECISIONS

Article 16. Scope of application of this Chapter
    1.   This Chapter shall govern the recognition, enforceability and enforcement of decisions falling within the scope of this Regulation.
    2.   Section 1 shall apply to decisions given in a Member State bound by the 2007 Hague Protocol.
    3.   Section 2 shall apply to decisions given in a Member State not bound by the 2007 Hague Protocol.
    4.   Section 3 shall apply to all decisions.

Section 1
Decisions given in a Member State bound by the 2007 Hague Protocol

Article 17. Abolition of exequatur
    1.   A decision given in a Member State bound by the 2007 Hague Protocol shall be recognised in another Member State without any special procedure being required and without any possibility of opposing its recognition.
    2.   A decision given in a Member State bound by the 2007 Hague Protocol which is enforceable in that State shall be enforceable in another Member State without the need for a declaration of enforceability.

Article 18. Protective measures
An enforceable decision shall carry with it by operation of law the power to proceed to any protective measures which exist under the law of the Member State of enforcement.

Article 19. Right to apply for a review
    1.   A defendant who did not enter an appearance in the Member State of origin shall have the right to apply for a review of the decision before the competent court of that Member State where:
        (a)   he was not served with the document instituting the proceedings or an equivalent document in sufficient time and in such a way as to enable him to arrange for his defence; or
        (b)   he was prevented from contesting the maintenance claim by reason of force majeure or due to extraordinary circumstances without any fault on his part;
unless he failed to challenge the decision when it was possible for him to do so.
    2.   The time limit for applying for a review shall run from the day the defendant was effectively acquainted with the contents of the decision and was able to react, at the latest from the date of the first enforcement measure having the effect

of making his property non-disposable in whole or in part. The defendant shall react promptly, in any event within 45 days. No extension may be granted on account of distance.

3.   If the court rejects the application for a review referred to in paragraph 1 on the basis that none of the grounds for a review set out in that paragraph apply, the decision shall remain in force.

If the court decides that a review is justified for one of the reasons laid down in paragraph 1, the decision shall be null and void. However, the creditor shall not lose the benefits of the interruption of prescription or limitation periods, or the right to claim retroactive maintenance acquired in the initial proceedings.

Article 20. Documents for the purposes of enforcement

1.   For the purposes of enforcement of a decision in another Member State, the claimant shall provide the competent enforcement authorities with:

(a)   a copy of the decision which satisfies the conditions necessary to establish its authenticity;

(b)   the extract from the decision issued by the court of origin using the form set out in Annex I;

(c)   where appropriate, a document showing the amount of any arrears and the date such amount was calculated;

(d)   where necessary, a transliteration or a translation of the content of the form referred to in point (b) into the official language of the Member State of enforcement or, where there are several official languages in that Member State, into the official language or one of the official languages of court proceedings of the place where the application is made, in accordance with the law of that Member State, or into another language that the Member State concerned has indicated it can accept. Each Member State may indicate the official language or languages of the institutions of the European Union other than its own which it can accept for the completion of the form.

2.   The competent authorities of the Member State of enforcement may not require the claimant to provide a translation of the decision. However, a translation may be required if the enforcement of the decision is challenged.

3.   Any translation under this Article must be done by a person qualified to do translations in one of the Member States.

Article 21. Refusal or suspension of enforcement

1.   The grounds of refusal or suspension of enforcement under the law of the Member State of enforcement shall apply in so far as they are not incompatible with the application of paragraphs 2 and 3.

2.   The competent authority in the Member State of enforcement shall, on application by the debtor, refuse, either wholly or in part, the enforcement of the decision of the court of origin if the right to enforce the decision of the court of origin is extinguished by the effect of prescription or the limitation of action, either under the law of the Member State of origin or under the law of the Member State of enforcement, whichever provides for the longer limitation period.

Furthermore, the competent authority in the Member State of enforcement may, on application by the debtor, refuse, either wholly or in part, the enforcement of the decision of the court of origin if it is irreconcilable with a decision given in the Member State of enforcement or with a decision given in another Member State or in a third State which fulfils the conditions necessary for its recognition in the Member State of enforcement.

A decision which has the effect of modifying an earlier decision on maintenance on the basis of changed circumstances shall not be considered an irreconcilable decision within the meaning of the second subparagraph.

3.   The competent authority in the Member State of enforcement may, on application by the debtor, suspend, either wholly or in part, the enforcement of the

decision of the court of origin if the competent court of the Member State of origin has been seised of an application for a review of the decision of the court of origin pursuant to Article 19.

Furthermore, the competent authority of the Member State of enforcement shall, on application by the debtor, suspend the enforcement of the decision of the court of origin where the enforceability of that decision is suspended in the Member State of origin.

Article 22. No effect on the existence of family relationships
The recognition and enforcement of a decision on maintenance under this Regulation shall not in any way imply the recognition of the family relationship, parentage, marriage or affinity underlying the maintenance obligation which gave rise to the decision.

Section 2
Decisions given in a Member State not bound by the 2007 Hague Protocol

Article 23. Recognition
1.   A decision given in a Member State not bound by the 2007 Hague Protocol shall be recognised in the other Member States without any special procedure being required.

2.   Any interested party who raises the recognition of a decision as the principal issue in a dispute may, in accordance with the procedures provided for in this Section, apply for a decision that the decision be recognised.

3.   If the outcome of proceedings in a court of a Member State depends on the determination of an incidental question of recognition, that court shall have jurisdiction over that question.

Article 24. Grounds of refusal of recognition
A decision shall not be recognised:

(a)   if such recognition is manifestly contrary to public policy in the Member State in which recognition is sought. The test of public policy may not be applied to the rules relating to jurisdiction;

(b)   where it was given in default of appearance, if the defendant was not served with the document which instituted the proceedings or with an equivalent document in sufficient time and in such a way as to enable him to arrange for his defence, unless the defendant failed to commence proceedings to challenge the decision when it was possible for him to do so;

(c)   if it is irreconcilable with a decision given in a dispute between the same parties in the Member State in which recognition is sought;

(d)   if it is irreconcilable with an earlier decision given in another Member State or in a third State in a dispute involving the same cause of action and between the same parties, provided that the earlier decision fulfils the conditions necessary for its recognition in the Member State in which recognition is sought.

A decision which has the effect of modifying an earlier decision on maintenance on the basis of changed circumstances shall not be considered an irreconcilable decision within the meaning of points (c) or (d).

Article 25. Staying of recognition proceedings
A court of a Member State in which recognition is sought of a decision given in a Member State not bound by the 2007 Hague Protocol shall stay the proceedings if the enforceability of the decision is suspended in the Member State of origin by reason of an appeal.

Article 26. Enforceability
A decision given in a Member State not bound by the 2007 Hague Protocol and enforceable in that State shall be enforceable in another Member State when, on the application of any interested party, it has been declared enforceable there.

Article 27. Jurisdiction of local courts

1.   The application for a declaration of enforceability shall be submitted to the court or competent authority of the Member State of enforcement notified by that Member State to the Commission in accordance with Article 71.

2.   The local jurisdiction shall be determined by reference to the place of habitual residence of the party against whom enforcement is sought, or to the place of enforcement.

Article 28. Procedure

1.   The application for a declaration of enforceability shall be accompanied by the following documents:

(a)   a copy of the decision which satisfies the conditions necessary to establish its authenticity;

(b)   an extract from the decision issued by the court of origin using the form set out in Annex II, without prejudice to Article 29;

(c)   where necessary, a transliteration or a translation of the content of the form referred to in point (b) into the official language of the Member State of enforcement or, where there are several official languages in that Member State, into the official language or one of the official languages of court proceedings of the place where the application is made, in accordance with the law of that Member State, or into another language that the Member State concerned has indicated it can accept. Each Member State may indicate the official language or languages of the institutions of the European Union other than its own which it can accept for the completion of the form.

2.   The court or competent authority seised of the application may not require the claimant to provide a translation of the decision. However, a translation may be required in connection with an appeal under Articles 32 or 33.

3.   Any translation under this Article must be done by a person qualified to do translations in one of the Member States.

Article 29. Non-production of the extract

1.   If the extract referred to in Article 28(1)(b) is not produced, the competent court or authority may specify a time for its production or accept an equivalent document or, if it considers that it has sufficient information before it, dispense with its production.

2.   In the situation referred to in paragraph 1, if the competent court or authority so requires, a translation of the documents shall be produced. The translation shall be done by a person qualified to do translations in one of the Member States.

Article 30. Declaration of enforceability

The decision shall be declared enforceable without any review under Article 24 immediately on completion of the formalities in Article 28 and at the latest within 30 days of the completion of those formalities, except where exceptional circumstances make this impossible. The party against whom enforcement is sought shall not at this stage of the proceedings be entitled to make any submissions on the application.

Article 31. Notice of the decision on the application for a declaration

1.   The decision on the application for a declaration of enforceability shall forthwith be brought to the notice of the applicant in accordance with the procedure laid down by the law of the Member State of enforcement.

2.   The declaration of enforceability shall be served on the party against whom enforcement is sought, accompanied by the decision, if not already served on that party.

Article 32. Appeal against the decision on the application for a declaration

1.   The decision on the application for a declaration of enforceability may be appealed against by either party.

2. The appeal shall be lodged with the court notified by the Member State concerned to the Commission in accordance with Article 71.

3. The appeal shall be dealt with in accordance with the rules governing procedure in contradictory matters.

4. If the party against whom enforcement is sought fails to appear before the appellate court in proceedings concerning an appeal brought by the applicant, Article 11 shall apply even where the party against whom enforcement is sought is not habitually resident in any of the Member States.

5. An appeal against the declaration of enforceability shall be lodged within 30 days of service thereof. If the party against whom enforcement is sought has his habitual residence in a Member State other than that in which the declaration of enforceability was given, the time for appealing shall be 45 days and shall run from the date of service, either on him in person or at his residence. No extension may be granted on account of distance.

Article 33. Proceedings to contest the decision given on appeal
The decision given on appeal may be contested only by the procedure notified by the Member State concerned to the Commission in accordance with Article 71.

Article 34. Refusal or revocation of a declaration of enforceability
1. The court with which an appeal is lodged under Articles 32 or 33 shall refuse or revoke a declaration of enforceability only on one of the grounds specified in Article 24.

2. Subject to Article 32(4), the court seised of an appeal under Article 32 shall give its decision within 90 days from the date it was seised, except where exceptional circumstances make this impossible.

3. The court seised of an appeal under Article 33 shall give its decision without delay.

Article 35. Staying of proceedings
The court with which an appeal is lodged under Articles 32 or 33 shall, on the application of the party against whom enforcement is sought, stay the proceedings if the enforceability of the decision is suspended in the Member State of origin by reason of an appeal.

Article 36. Provisional, including protective measures
1. When a decision must be recognised in accordance with this Section, nothing shall prevent the applicant from availing himself of provisional, including protective, measures in accordance with the law of the Member State of enforcement without a declaration of enforceability under Article 30 being required.

2. The declaration of enforceability shall carry with it by operation of law the power to proceed to any protective measures.

3. During the time specified for an appeal pursuant to Article 32(5) against the declaration of enforceability and until any such appeal has been determined, no measures of enforcement may be taken other than protective measures against the property of the party against whom enforcement is sought.

Article 37. Partial enforceability
1. Where a decision has been given in respect of several matters and the declaration of enforceability cannot be given for all of them, the competent court or authority shall give it for one or more of them.

2. An applicant may request a declaration of enforceability limited to parts of a decision.

Article 38. No charge, duty or fee
In proceedings for the issue of a declaration of enforceability, no charge, duty or fee calculated by reference to the value of the matter at issue may be levied in the Member State of enforcement.

Section 3
Common provisions

Article 39. Provisional enforceability

The court of origin may declare the decision provisionally enforceable, notwithstanding any appeal, even if national law does not provide for enforceability by operation of law.

Article 40. Invoking a recognised decision

1. A party who wishes to invoke in another Member State a decision recognised within the meaning of Article 17(1) or recognised pursuant to Section 2 shall produce a copy of the decision which satisfies the conditions necessary to establish its authenticity.

2. If necessary, the court before which the recognised decision is invoked may ask the party invoking the recognised decision to produce an extract issued by the court of origin using the form set out in Annex I or in Annex II, as the case may be.

The court of origin shall also issue such an extract at the request of any interested party.

3. Where necessary, the party invoking the recognised decision shall provide a transliteration or a translation of the content of the form referred to in paragraph 2 into the official language of the Member State concerned or, where there are several official languages in that Member State, into the official language or one of the official languages of court proceedings of the place where the recognized decision is invoked, in accordance with the law of that Member State, or into another language that the Member State concerned has indicated it can accept. Each Member State may indicate the official language or languages of the institutions of the European Union other than its own which it can accept for the completion of the form.

4. Any translation under this Article must be done by a person qualified to do translations in one of the Member States.

Article 41. Proceedings and conditions for enforcement

1. Subject to the provisions of this Regulation, the procedure for the enforcement of decisions given in another Member State shall be governed by the law of the Member State of enforcement. A decision given in a Member State which is enforceable in the Member State of enforcement shall be enforced there under the same conditions as a decision given in that Member State of enforcement.

2. The party seeking the enforcement of a decision given in another Member State shall not be required to have a postal address or an authorised representative in the Member State of enforcement, without prejudice to persons with competence in matters relating to enforcement proceedings.

Article 42. No review as to substance

Under no circumstances may a decision given in a Member State be reviewed as to its substance in the Member State in which recognition, enforceability or enforcement is sought.

Article 43. No precedence for the recovery of costs

Recovery of any costs incurred in the application of this Regulation shall not take precedence over the recovery of maintenance.

CHAPTER V
ACCESS TO JUSTICE

Article 44. Right to legal aid

1. Parties who are involved in a dispute covered by this Regulation shall have effective access to justice in another Member State, including enforcement and appeal or review procedures, in accordance with the conditions laid down in this Chapter.

In cases covered by Chapter VII, effective access to justice shall be provided by the requested Member State to any applicant who is resident in the requesting Member State.

2. To ensure such effective access, Member States shall provide legal aid in accordance with this Chapter, unless paragraph 3 applies.

3. In cases covered by Chapter VII, a Member State shall not be obliged to provide legal aid if and to the extent that the procedures of that Member State enable the parties to make the case without the need for legal aid, and the Central Authority provides such services as are necessary free of charge.

4. Entitlements to legal aid shall not be less than those available in equivalent domestic cases.

5. No security, bond or deposit, however described, shall be required to guarantee the payment of costs and expenses in proceedings concerning maintenance obligations.

Article 45. Content of legal aid

Legal aid granted under this Chapter shall mean the assistance necessary to enable parties to know and assert their rights and to ensure that their applications, lodged through the Central Authorities or directly with the competent authorities, are fully and effectively dealt with. It shall cover as necessary the following:

(a) pre-litigation advice with a view to reaching a settlement prior to bringing judicial proceedings;

(b) legal assistance in bringing a case before an authority or a court and representation in court;

(c) exemption from or assistance with the costs of proceedings and the fees to persons mandated to perform acts during the proceedings;

(d) in Member States in which an unsuccessful party is liable for the costs of the opposing party, if the recipient of legal aid loses the case, the costs incurred by the opposing party, if such costs would have been covered had the recipient been habitually resident in the Member State of the court seised;

(e) interpretation;

(f) translation of the documents required by the court or by the competent authority and presented by the recipient of legal aid which are necessary for the resolution of the case;

(g) travel costs to be borne by the recipient of legal aid where the physical presence of the persons concerned with the presentation of the recipient's case is required in court by the law or by the court of the Member State concerned and the court decides that the persons concerned cannot be heard to the satisfaction of the court by any other means.

Article 46. Free legal aid for applications through Central Authorities concerning maintenance to children

1. The requested Member State shall provide free legal aid in respect of all applications by a creditor under Article 56 concerning maintenance obligations arising from a parent-child relationship towards a person under the age of 21.

2. Notwithstanding paragraph 1, the competent authority of the requested Member State may, in relation to applications other than those under Article 56(1)(a) and (b), refuse free legal aid if it considers that, on the merits, the application or any appeal or review is manifestly unfounded.

Article 47. Cases not covered by Article 46

1. Subject to Articles 44 and 45, in cases not covered by Article 46, legal aid may be granted in accordance with national law, particularly as regards the conditions for the means test or the merits test.

2. Notwithstanding paragraph 1, a party who, in the Member State of origin, has benefited from complete or partial legal aid or exemption from costs or expenses, shall be entitled, in any proceedings for recognition, enforceability or enforce-

ment, to benefit from the most favourable legal aid or the most extensive exemption from costs or expenses provided for by the law of the Member State of enforcement.

3.   Notwithstanding paragraph 1, a party who, in the Member State of origin, has benefited from free proceedings before an administrative authority listed in Annex X, shall be entitled, in any proceedings for recognition, enforceability or enforcement, to benefit from legal aid in accordance with paragraph 2. To that end, he shall present a statement from the competent authority in the Member State of origin to the effect that he fulfils the financial requirements to qualify for the grant of complete or partial legal aid or exemption from costs or expenses.

Competent authorities for the purposes of this paragraph shall be listed in Annex XI. That Annex shall be established and amended in accordance with the management procedure referred to in Article 73(2).

CHAPTER VI
COURT SETTLEMENTS AND AUTHENTIC INSTRUMENTS

Article 48. Application of this Regulation to court settlements and authentic instruments

1.   Court settlements and authentic instruments which are enforceable in the Member State of origin shall be recognised in another Member State and be enforceable there in the same way as decisions, in accordance with Chapter IV.

2.   The provisions of this Regulation shall apply as necessary to court settlements and authentic instruments.

3.   The competent authority of the Member State of origin shall issue, at the request of any interested party, an extract from the court settlement or the authentic instrument using the forms set out in Annexes I and II or in Annexes III and IV as the case may be.

CHAPTER VII
COOPERATION BETWEEN CENTRAL AUTHORITIES

Article 49. Designation of Central Authorities

1.   Each Member State shall designate a Central Authority to discharge the duties which are imposed by this Regulation on such an authority.

2.   Federal Member States, Member States with more than one system of law or Member States having autonomous territorial units shall be free to appoint more than one Central Authority and shall specify the territorial or personal extent of their functions. Where a Member State has appointed more than one Central Authority, it shall designate the Central Authority to which any communication may be addressed for transmission to the appropriate Central Authority within that Member State. If a communication is sent to a Central Authority which is not competent, the latter shall be responsible for forwarding it to the competent Central Authority and for informing the sender accordingly.

3.   The designation of the Central Authority or Central Authorities, their contact details, and where appropriate the extent of their functions as specified in paragraph 2, shall be communicated by each Member State to the Commission in accordance with Article 71.

Article 50. General functions of Central Authorities

1.   Central Authorities shall:

(a)   cooperate with each other, including by exchanging information, and promote cooperation amongst the competent authorities in their Member States to achieve the purposes of this Regulation;

(b)   seek as far as possible solutions to difficulties which arise in the application of this Regulation.

2.   Central Authorities shall take measures to facilitate the application of this Regulation and to strengthen their cooperation. For this purpose the European Judicial Network in civil and commercial matters established by Decision 2001/470/EC shall be used.

Article 51. Specific functions of Central Authorities

1.   Central Authorities shall provide assistance in relation to applications under Article 56 and shall in particular:

(a)   transmit and receive such applications;

(b)   initiate or facilitate the institution of proceedings in respect of such applications.

2.   In relation to such applications Central Authorities shall take all appropriate measures:

(a)   where the circumstances require, to provide or facilitate the provision of legal aid;

(b)   to help locate the debtor or the creditor, in particular pursuant to Articles 61, 62 and 63;

(c)   to help obtain relevant information concerning the income and, if necessary, other financial circumstances of the debtor or creditor, including the location of assets, in particular pursuant to Articles 61, 62 and 63;

(d)   to encourage amicable solutions with a view to obtaining voluntary payment of maintenance, where suitable by use of mediation, conciliation or similar processes;

(e)   to facilitate the ongoing enforcement of maintenance decisions, including any arrears;

(f)   to facilitate the collection and expeditious transfer of maintenance payments;

(g)   to facilitate the obtaining of documentary or other evidence, without prejudice to Regulation (EC) No 1206/2001;

(h)   to provide assistance in establishing parentage where necessary for the recovery of maintenance;

(i)   to initiate or facilitate the institution of proceedings to obtain any necessary provisional measures which are territorial in nature and the purpose of which is to secure the outcome of a pending maintenance application;

(j)   to facilitate the service of documents, without prejudice to Regulation (EC) No 1393/2007.

3.   The functions of the Central Authority under this Article may, to the extent permitted under the law of the Member State concerned, be performed by public bodies, or other bodies subject to the supervision of the competent authorities of that Member State. The designation of any such public bodies or other bodies, as well as their contact details and the extent of their functions, shall be communicated by each Member State to the Commission in accordance with Article 71.

4.   Nothing in this Article or in Article 53 shall impose an obligation on a Central Authority to exercise powers that can be exercised only by judicial authorities under the law of the requested Member State.

Article 52. Power of attorney

The Central Authority of the requested Member State may require a power of attorney from the applicant only if it acts on his behalf in judicial proceedings or before other authorities, or in order to designate a representative so to act.

Article 53. Requests for specific measures

1.   A Central Authority may make a request, supported by reasons, to another Central Authority to take appropriate specific measures under points (b), (c), (g), (h), (i) and (j) of Article 51(2) when no application under Article 56 is pending. The requested Central Authority shall take such measures as are appropriate if satisfied that they are necessary to assist a potential applicant in making an application

under Article 56 or in determining whether such an application should be initiated.

2.   Where a request for measures under Article 51(2)(b) and (c) is made, the requested Central Authority shall seek the information requested, if necessary pursuant to Article 61. However, the information referred to in points (b), (c) and (d) of Article 61(2) may be sought only when the creditor produces a copy of the decision, court settlement or authentic instrument to be enforced, accompanied by the extract provided for in Articles 20, 28 or 48, as appropriate.

The requested Central Authority shall communicate the information obtained to the requesting Central Authority. Where that information was obtained pursuant to Article 61, this communication shall specify only the address of the potential defendant in the requested Member State. In the case of a request with a view to recognition, declaration of enforceability or enforcement, the communication shall, in addition, specify merely whether the debtor has income or assets in that State.

If the requested Central Authority is not able to provide the information requested it shall inform the requesting Central Authority without delay and specify the grounds for this impossibility.

3.   A Central Authority may also take specific measures at the request of another Central Authority in relation to a case having an international element concerning the recovery of maintenance pending in the requesting Member State.

4.   For requests under this Article, the Central Authorities shall use the form set out in Annex V.

Article 54. Central Authority costs
1.   Each Central Authority shall bear its own costs in applying this Regulation.

2.   Central Authorities may not impose any charge on an applicant for the provision of their services under this Regulation save for exceptional costs arising from a request for a specific measure under Article 53.

For the purposes of this paragraph, costs relating to locating the debtor shall not be regarded as exceptional.

3.   The requested Central Authority may not recover the costs of the services referred to in paragraph 2 without the prior consent of the applicant to the provision of those services at such cost.

Article 55. Application through Central Authorities
An application under this Chapter shall be made through the Central Authority of the Member State in which the applicant resides to the Central Authority of the requested Member State.

Article 56. Available applications
1.   A creditor seeking to recover maintenance under this Regulation may make applications for the following:

(a)   recognition or recognition and declaration of enforceability of a decision;

(b)   enforcement of a decision given or recognised in the requested Member State;

(c)   establishment of a decision in the requested Member State where there is no existing decision, including where necessary the establishment of parentage;

(d)   establishment of a decision in the requested Member State where the recognition and declaration of enforceability of a decision given in a State other than the requested Member State is not possible;

(e)   modification of a decision given in the requested Member State;

(f)   modification of a decision given in a State other than the requested Member State.

2.   A debtor against whom there is an existing maintenance decision may make applications for the following:

(a)   recognition of a decision leading to the suspension, or limiting the enforcement, of a previous decision in the requested Member State;

(b)   modification of a decision given in the requested Member State;

(c)   modification of a decision given in a State other than the requested Member State.

3.   For applications under this Article, the assistance and representation referred to in Article 45(b) shall be provided by the Central Authority of the requested Member State directly or through public authorities or other bodies or persons.

4.   Save as otherwise provided in this Regulation, the applications referred to in paragraphs 1 and 2 shall be determined under the law of the requested Member State and shall be subject to the rules of jurisdiction applicable in that Member State.

Article 57. Application contents

1.   An application under Article 56 shall be made using the form set out in Annex VI or in Annex VII.

2.   An application under Article 56 shall as a minimum include:

(a)   a statement of the nature of the application or applications;

(b)   the name and contact details, including the address, and date of birth of the applicant;

(c)   the name and, if known, address and date of birth of the defendant;

(d)   the name and the date of birth of any person for whom maintenance is sought;

(e)   the grounds upon which the application is based;

(f)   in an application by a creditor, information concerning where the maintenance payment should be sent or electronically transmitted;

(g)   the name and contact details of the person or unit from the Central Authority of the requesting Member State responsible for processing the application.

3.   For the purposes of paragraph 2(b), the applicant's personal address may be replaced by another address in cases of family violence, if the national law of the requested Member State does not require the applicant to supply his or her personal address for the purposes of proceedings to be brought.

4.   As appropriate, and to the extent known, the application shall in addition in particular include:

(a)   the financial circumstances of the creditor;

(b)   the financial circumstances of the debtor, including the name and address of the employer of the debtor and the nature and location of the assets of the debtor;

(c)   any other information that may assist with the location of the defendant.

5.   The application shall be accompanied by any necessary supporting information or documentation including, where appropriate, documentation concerning the entitlement of the applicant to legal aid. Applications under Article 56(1)(a) and (b) and under Article 56(2)(a) shall be accompanied, as appropriate, only by the documents listed in Articles 20, 28 and 48, or in Article 25 of the 2007 Hague Convention.

Article 58. Transmission, receipt and processing of applications and cases through Central Authorities

1.   The Central Authority of the requesting Member State shall assist the applicant in ensuring that the application is accompanied by all the information and documents known by it to be necessary for consideration of the application.

2.   The Central Authority of the requesting Member State shall, when satisfied that the application complies with the requirements of this Regulation, transmit the application to the Central Authority of the requested Member State.

3.   The requested Central Authority shall, within 30 days from the date of receipt of the application, acknowledge receipt using the form set out in Annex VIII, and inform the Central Authority of the requesting Member State what initial steps have been or will be taken to deal with the application, and may request any

further necessary documents and information. Within the same 30-day period, the requested Central Authority shall provide to the requesting Central Authority the name and contact details of the person or unit responsible for responding to inquiries regarding the progress of the application.

4. Within 60 days from the date of acknowledgement, the requested Central Authority shall inform the requesting Central Authority of the status of the application.

5. Requesting and requested Central Authorities shall keep each other informed of:

(a) the person or unit responsible for a particular case;

(b) the progress of the case;

and shall provide timely responses to enquiries.

6. Central Authorities shall process a case as quickly as a proper consideration of the issues will allow.

7. Central Authorities shall employ the most rapid and efficient means of communication at their disposal.

8. A requested Central Authority may refuse to process an application only if it is manifest that the requirements of this Regulation are not fulfilled. In such a case, that Central Authority shall promptly inform the requesting Central Authority of its reasons for refusal using the form set out in Annex IX.

9. The requested Central Authority may not reject an application solely on the basis that additional documents or information are needed. However, the requested Central Authority may ask the requesting Central Authority to provide these additional documents or this information. If the requesting Central Authority does not do so within 90 days or a longer period specified by the requested Central Authority, the requested Central Authority may decide that it will no longer process the application. In this case, it shall promptly notify the requesting Central Authority using the form set out in Annex IX.

Article 59. Languages

1. The request or application form shall be completed in the official language of the requested Member State or, if there are several official languages in that Member State, in the official language or one of the official languages of the place of the Central Authority concerned, or in any other official language of the institutions of the European Union which that Member State has indicated it can accept, unless the Central Authority of that Member State dispenses with translation.

2. The documents accompanying the request or application form shall not be translated into the language determined in accordance with paragraph 1 unless a translation is necessary in order to provide the assistance requested, without prejudice to Articles 20, 28, 40 and 66.

3. Any other communication between Central Authorities shall be in the language determined in accordance with paragraph 1 unless the Central Authorities agree otherwise.

Article 60. Meetings

1. In order to facilitate the application of this Regulation, Central Authorities shall meet regularly.

2. These meetings shall be convened in compliance with Decision 2001/470/EC.

Article 61. Access to information for Central Authorities

1. Under the conditions laid down in this Chapter and by way of exception to Article 51(4), the requested Central Authority shall use all appropriate and reasonable means to obtain the information referred to in paragraph 2 necessary to facilitate, in a given case, the establishment, the modification, the recognition, the declaration of enforceability or the enforcement of a decision.

The public authorities or administrations which, in the course of their ordinary activities, hold, within the requested State, the information referred to in paragraph 2 and which control the processing thereof within the meaning of Directive 95/46/EC shall, subject to limitations justified on grounds of national security or public safety, provide the information to the requested Central Authority at its request in cases where the requested Central Authority does not have direct access to it.

Member States may designate the public authorities or administrations able to provide the requested Central Authority with the information referred to in paragraph 2. Where a Member State makes such a designation, it shall ensure that its choice of authorities and administrations permits its Central Authority to have access, in accordance with this Article, to the information requested.

Any other legal person which holds within the requested Member State the information referred to in paragraph 2 and controls the processing thereof within the meaning of Directive 95/46/EC shall provide the information to the requested Central Authority at the latter's request if it is authorised to do so by the law of the requested Member State.

The requested Central Authority shall, as necessary, transmit the information thus obtained to the requesting Central Authority.

2.   The information referred to in this Article shall be the information already held by the authorities, administrations or persons referred to in paragraph 1. It shall be adequate, relevant and not excessive and shall relate to:

    (a)   the address of the debtor or of the creditor;

    (b)   the debtor's income;

    (c)   the identification of the debtor's employer and/or of the debtor's bank account(s);

    (d)   the debtor's assets.

For the purpose of obtaining or modifying a decision, only the information listed in point (a) may be requested by the requested Central Authority.

For the purpose of having a decision recognised, declared enforceable or enforced, all the information listed in the first subparagraph may be requested by the requested Central Authority. However, the information listed in point (d) may be requested only if the information listed in points (b) and (c) is insufficient to allow enforcement of the decision.

Article 62. Transmission and use of information

1.   The Central Authorities shall, within their Member State, transmit the information referred to in Article 61(2) to the competent courts, the competent authorities responsible for service of documents and the competent authorities responsible for enforcement of a decision, as the case may be.

2.   Any authority or court to which information has been transmitted pursuant to Article 61 may use this only to facilitate the recovery of maintenance claims.

Except for information merely indicating the existence of an address, income or assets in the requested Member State, the information referred to in Article 61(2) may not be disclosed to the person having applied to the requesting Central Authority, subject to the application of procedural rules before a court.

3.   Any authority processing information transmitted to it pursuant to Article 61 may not store such information beyond the period necessary for the purposes for which it was transmitted.

4.   Any authority processing information communicated to it pursuant to Article 61 shall ensure the confidentiality of such information, in accordance with its national law.

Article 63. Notification of the data subject

1.   Notification of the data subject of the communication of all or part of the information collected on him shall take place in accordance with the national law of the requested Member State.

2.   Where there is a risk that it may prejudice the effective recovery of the main-

tenance claim, such notification may be deferred for a period which shall not exceed 90 days from the date on which the information was provided to the requested Central Authority.

CHAPTER VIII
PUBLIC BODIES

Article 64. Public bodies as applicants

1. For the purposes of an application for recognition and declaration of enforceability of decisions or for the purposes of enforcement of decisions, the term 'creditor' shall include a public body acting in place of an individual to whom maintenance is owed or one to which reimbursement is owed for benefits provided in place of maintenance.

2. The right of a public body to act in place of an individual to whom maintenance is owed or to seek reimbursement of benefits provided to the creditor in place of maintenance shall be governed by the law to which the body is subject.

3. A public body may seek recognition and a declaration of enforceability or claim enforcement of:

(a) a decision given against a debtor on the application of a public body which claims payment of benefits provided in place of maintenance;

(b) a decision given between a creditor and a debtor to the extent of the benefits provided to the creditor in place of maintenance.

4. The public body seeking recognition and a declaration of enforceability or claiming enforcement of a decision shall upon request provide any document necessary to establish its right under paragraph 2 and to establish that benefits have been provided to the creditor.

CHAPTER IX
GENERAL AND FINAL PROVISIONS

Article 65. Legalisation or other similar formality

No legalisation or other similar formality shall be required in the context of this Regulation.

Article 66. Translation of supporting documents

Without prejudice to Articles 20, 28 and 40, the court seised may require the parties to provide a translation of supporting documents which are not in the language of proceedings only if it deems a translation necessary in order to give a decision or to respect the rights of the defence.

Article 67. Recovery of costs

Without prejudice to Article 54, the competent authority of the requested Member State may recover costs from an unsuccessful party having received free legal aid pursuant to Article 46, on an exceptional basis and if his financial circumstances so allow.

Article 68. Relations with other Community instruments

1. Subject to Article 75(2), this Regulation shall modify Regulation (EC) No 44/2001 by replacing the provisions of that Regulation applicable to matters relating to maintenance obligations.

2. This Regulation shall replace, in matters relating to maintenance obligations, Regulation (EC) No 805/2004, except with regard to European Enforcement Orders on maintenance obligations issued in a Member State not bound by the 2007 Hague Protocol.

3. In matters relating to maintenance obligations, this Regulation shall be without prejudice to the application of Directive 2003/8/EC, subject to Chapter V.

4. This Regulation shall be without prejudice to the application of Directive 95/46/EC.

Article 69. Relations with existing international conventions and agreements

1.   This Regulation shall not affect the application of bilateral or multilateral conventions and agreements to which one or more Member States are party at the time of adoption of this Regulation and which concern matters governed by this Regulation, without prejudice to the obligations of Member States under Article 307 of the Treaty.

2.   Notwithstanding paragraph 1, and without prejudice to paragraph 3, this Regulation shall, in relations between Member States, take precedence over the conventions and agreements which concern matters governed by this Regulation and to which Member States are party.

3.   This Regulation shall not preclude the application of the Convention of 23 March 1962 between Sweden, Denmark, Finland, Iceland and Norway on the recovery of maintenance by the Member States which are party thereto, since, with regard to the recognition, enforceability and enforcement of decisions, that Convention provides for:

(a)   simplified and more expeditious procedures for the enforcement of decisions relating to maintenance obligations, and

(b)   legal aid which is more favourable than that provided for in Chapter V of this Regulation.

However, the application of the said Convention may not have the effect of depriving the defendant of his protection under Articles 19 and 21 of this Regulation.

Article 70. Information made available to the public

The Member States shall provide within the framework of the European Judicial Network in civil and commercial matters established by Decision 2001/470/EC the following information with a view to making it available to the public:

(a)   a description of the national laws and procedures concerning maintenance obligations;

(b)   a description of the measures taken to meet the obligations under Article 51;

(c)   a description of how effective access to justice is guaranteed, as required under Article 44, and

(d)   a description of national enforcement rules and procedures, including information on any limitations on enforcement, in particular debtor protection rules and limitation or prescription periods.

Member States shall keep this information permanently updated.

Article 71. Information on contact details and languages (modelled on Article 25 of Regulation (EC) No 861/2007)

1.   By 18 September 2010, the Member States shall communicate to the Commission:

(a)   the names and contact details of the courts or authorities with competence to deal with applications for a declaration of enforceability in accordance with Article 27(1) and with appeals against decisions on such applications in accordance with Article 32(2);

(b)   the redress procedures referred to in Article 33;

(c)   the review procedure for the purposes of Article 19 and the names and contact details of the courts having jurisdiction;

(d)   the names and contact details of their Central Authorities and, where appropriate, the extent of their functions, in accordance with Article 49(3);

(e)   the names and contact details of the public bodies or other bodies and, where appropriate, the extent of their functions, in accordance with Article 51(3);

(f)   the names and contact details of the authorities with competence in matters of enforcement for the purposes of Article 21;

(g)   the languages accepted for translations of the documents referred to in Articles 20, 28 and 40;

(h)   the languages accepted by their Central Authorities for communication with other Central Authorities referred to in Article 59.

The Member States shall apprise the Commission of any subsequent changes to this information.

2.   The Commission shall publish the information communicated in accordance with paragraph 1 in the Official Journal of the European Union, with the exception of the addresses and other contact details of the courts and authorities referred to in points (a), (c) and (f).

3.   The Commission shall make all information communicated in accordance with paragraph 1 publicly available through any other appropriate means, in particular through the European Judicial Network in civil and commercial matters established by Decision 2001/470/EC.

Article 72. Amendments to the forms
Any amendment to the forms provided for in this Regulation shall be adopted in accordance with the advisory procedure referred to in Article 73(3).

Article 73. Committee
1.   The Commission shall be assisted by the committee established by Article 70 of Regulation (EC) No 2201/2003.

2.   Where reference is made to this paragraph, Articles 4 and 7 of Decision 1999/468/EC shall apply.

The period laid down in Article 4(3) of Decision 1999/468/EC shall be set at three months.

3.   Where reference is made to this paragraph, Articles 3 and 7 of Decision 1999/468/EC shall apply.

Article 74. Review clause
By five years from the date of application determined in the third subparagraph of Article 76 at the latest, the Commission shall submit to the European Parliament, the Council and the European Economic and Social Committee a report on the application of this Regulation, including an evaluation of the practical experiences relating to the cooperation between Central Authorities, in particular regarding those Authorities' access to the information held by public authorities and administrations, and an evaluation of the functioning of the procedure for recognition, declaration of enforceability and enforcement applicable to decisions given in a Member State not bound by the 2007 Hague Protocol. If necessary the report shall be accompanied by proposals for adaptation.

Article 75. Transitional provisions
1.   This Regulation shall apply only to proceedings instituted, to court settlements approved or concluded, and to authentic instruments established after its date of application, subject to paragraphs 2 and 3.

2.   Sections 2 and 3 of Chapter IV shall apply:
   (a)   to decisions given in the Member States before the date of application of this Regulation for which recognition and the declaration of enforceability are requested after that date;
   (b)   to decisions given after the date of application of this Regulation following proceedings begun before that date, in so far as those decisions fall within the scope of Regulation (EC) No 44/2001 for the purposes of recognition and enforcement.

Regulation (EC) No 44/2001 shall continue to apply to procedures for recognition and enforcement under way on the date of application of this Regulation.

The first and second subparagraphs shall apply mutatis mutandis to court settlements approved or concluded and to authentic instruments established in the Member States.

3.   Chapter VII on cooperation between Central Authorities shall apply to

requests and applications received by the Central Authority as from the date of application of this Regulation.

Article 76. Entry into force
This Regulation shall enter into force on the 20th day following its publication in the Official Journal of the European Union.

Articles 2(2), 47(3), 71, 72 and 73 shall apply from 18 September 2010.

Except for the provisions referred to in the second paragraph, this Regulation shall apply from 18 June 2011, subject to the 2007 Hague Protocol being applicable in the Community by that date. Failing that, this Regulation shall apply from the date of application of that Protocol in the Community.

This Regulation shall be binding in its entirety and directly applicable in the Member States in accordance with the Treaty establishing the European Community.

Done at Brussels, 18 December 2008.

COUNCIL REGULATION (EU) NO 1259/2010 OF 20 DECEMBER 2010 IMPLEMENTING ENHANCED COOPERATION IN THE AREA OF THE LAW APPLICABLE TO DIVORCE AND LEGAL SEPARATION ('ROME III')

Official Journal L 343, 29/12/2010 pp 10–16

THE COUNCIL OF THE EUROPEAN UNION,

Having regard to the Treaty on the Functioning of the European Union, and in particular Article 81(3) thereof,

Having regard to Council Decision 2010/405/EU of 12 July 2010 authorising enhanced cooperation in the area of the law applicable to divorce and legal separation,

Having regard to the proposal from the European Commission,

After transmission of the draft legislative act to the national parliaments,

Having regard to the opinion of the European Parliament,

Having regard to the opinion of the European Economic and Social Committee,

Acting in accordance with a special legislative procedure,

Whereas:

(1)   The Union has set itself the objective of maintaining and developing an area of freedom, security and justice, in which the free movement of persons is assured. For the gradual establishment of such an area, the Union must adopt measures relating to judicial cooperation in civil matters having cross-border implications, particularly when necessary for the proper functioning of the internal market.

(2)   Pursuant to Article 81 of the Treaty on the Functioning of the European Union, those measures are to include measures aimed at ensuring the compatibility of the rules applicable in the Member States concerning conflict of laws.

(3)   On 14 March 2005 the Commission adopted a Green Paper on applicable law and jurisdiction in divorce matters. The Green Paper launched a wide-ranging public consultation on possible solutions to the problems that may arise under the current situation.

(4)   On 17 July 2006 the Commission proposed a Regulation amending Council Regulation (EC) No 2201/2003 as regards jurisdiction and introducing rules concerning applicable law in matrimonial matters.

(5)   At its meeting in Luxembourg on 5 and 6 June 2008, the Council concluded that there was a lack of unanimity on the proposal and that there were insurmountable difficulties that made unanimity impossible both then and in the near future.

It established that the proposal's objectives could not be attained within a reasonable period by applying the relevant provisions of the Treaties.

(6)   Belgium, Bulgaria, Germany, Greece, Spain, France, Italy, Latvia, Luxembourg, Hungary, Malta, Austria, Portugal, Romania and Slovenia subsequently addressed a request to the Commission indicating that they intended to establish enhanced cooperation between themselves in the area of applicable law in matrimonial matters. On 3 March 2010, Greece withdrew its request.

(7)   On 12 July 2010 the Council adopted Decision 2010/405/EU authorising enhanced cooperation in the area of the law applicable to divorce and legal separation.

(8)   According to Article 328(1) of the Treaty on the Functioning of the European Union, when enhanced cooperation is being established, it is to be open to all Member States, subject to compliance with any conditions of participation laid down by the authorising decision. It is also to be open to them at any other time, subject to compliance with the acts already adopted within that framework, in addition to those conditions. The Commission and the Member States participating in enhanced cooperation shall ensure that they promote participation by as many Member States as possible. This Regulation should be binding in its entirety and directly applicable only in the participating Member States in accordance with the Treaties.

(9)   This Regulation should create a clear, comprehensive legal framework in the area of the law applicable to divorce and legal separation in the participating Member States, provide citizens with appropriate outcomes in terms of legal certainty, predictability and flexibility, and prevent a situation from arising where one of the spouses applies for divorce before the other one does in order to ensure that the proceeding is governed by a given law which he or she considers more favourable to his or her own interests.

(10)   The substantive scope and enacting terms of this Regulation should be consistent with Regulation (EC) No 2201/2003. However, it should not apply to marriage annulment.

This Regulation should apply only to the dissolution or loosening of marriage ties. The law determined by the conflict-of-laws rules of this Regulation should apply to the grounds for divorce and legal separation.

Preliminary questions such as legal capacity and the validity of the marriage, and matters such as the effects of divorce or legal separation on property, name, parental responsibility, maintenance obligations or any other ancillary measures should be determined by the conflict-of-laws rules applicable in the participating Member State concerned.

(11)   In order to clearly delimit the territorial scope of this Regulation, the Member States participating in the enhanced cooperation should be specified.

(12)   This Regulation should be universal, i.e. it should be possible for its uniform conflict-of-laws rules to designate the law of a participating Member State, the law of a non-participating Member State or the law of a State which is not a member of the European Union.

(13)   This Regulation should apply irrespective of the nature of the court or tribunal seized. Where applicable, a court should be deemed to be seized in accordance with Regulation (EC) No 2201/2003.

(14)   In order to allow the spouses to choose an applicable law with which they have a close connection or, in the absence of such choice, in order that that law might apply to their divorce or legal separation, the law in question should apply even if it is not that of a participating Member State. Where the law of another Member State is designated, the network created by Council Decision 2001/470/EC of 28 May 2001 establishing a European Judicial Network in civil and commercial matters, could play a part in assisting the courts with regard to the content of foreign law.

(15)   Increasing the mobility of citizens calls for more flexibility and greater

legal certainty. In order to achieve that objective, this Regulation should enhance the parties' autonomy in the areas of divorce and legal separation by giving them a limited possibility to choose the law applicable to their divorce or legal separation.

(16)   Spouses should be able to choose the law of a country with which they have a special connection or the law of the forum as the law applicable to divorce and legal separation. The law chosen by the spouses must be consonant with the fundamental rights recognised by the Treaties and the Charter of Fundamental Rights of the European Union.

(17)   Before designating the applicable law, it is important for spouses to have access to up-to-date information concerning the essential aspects of national and Union law and of the procedures governing divorce and legal separation. To guarantee such access to appropriate, good-quality information, the Commission regularly updates it in the Internet-based public information system set up by Council Decision 2001/470/EC.

(18)   The informed choice of both spouses is a basic principle of this Regulation. Each spouse should know exactly what are the legal and social implications of the choice of applicable law. The possibility of choosing the applicable law by common agreement should be without prejudice to the rights of, and equal opportunities for, the two spouses. Hence judges in the participating Member States should be aware of the importance of an informed choice on the part of the two spouses concerning the legal implications of the choice-of-law agreement concluded.

(19)   Rules on material and formal validity should be defined so that the informed choice of the spouses is facilitated and that their consent is respected with a view to ensuring legal certainty as well as better access to justice. As far as formal validity is concerned, certain safeguards should be introduced to ensure that spouses are aware of the implications of their choice. The agreement on the choice of applicable law should at least be expressed in writing, dated and signed by both parties. However, if the law of the participating Member State in which the two spouses have their habitual residence at the time the agreement is concluded lays down additional formal rules, those rules should be complied with. For example, such additional formal rules may exist in a participating Member State where the agreement is inserted in a marriage contract. If, at the time the agreement is concluded, the spouses are habitually resident in different participating Member States which lay down different formal rules, compliance with the formal rules of one of these States would suffice. If, at the time the agreement is concluded, only one of the spouses is habitually resident in a participating Member State which lays down additional formal rules, these rules should be complied with.

(20)   An agreement designating the applicable law should be able to be concluded and modified at the latest at the time the court is seized, and even during the course of the proceeding if the law of the forum so provides. In that event, it should be sufficient for such designation to be recorded in court in accordance with the law of the forum.

(21)   Where no applicable law is chosen, and with a view to guaranteeing legal certainty and predictability and preventing a situation from arising in which one of the spouses applies for divorce before the other one does in order to ensure that the proceeding is governed by a given law which he considers more favourable to his own interests, this Regulation should introduce harmonised conflict-of-laws rules on the basis of a scale of successive connecting factors based on the existence of a close connection between the spouses and the law concerned. Such connecting factors should be chosen so as to ensure that proceedings relating to divorce or legal separation are governed by a law with which the spouses have a close connection.

(22)   Where this Regulation refers to nationality as a connecting factor for the application of the law of a State, the question of how to deal with cases of multiple

nationality should be left to national law, in full observance of the general principles of the European Union.

(23) If the court is seized in order to convert a legal separation into divorce, and where the parties have not made any choice as to the law applicable, the law which applied to the legal separation should also apply to the divorce. Such continuity would promote predictability for the parties and increase legal certainty. If the law applied to the legal separation does not provide for the conversion of legal separation into divorce, the divorce should be governed by the conflict-of-laws rules which apply in the absence of a choice by the parties. This should not prevent the spouses from seeking divorce on the basis of other rules in this Regulation.

(24) In certain situations, such as where the applicable law makes no provision for divorce or where it does not grant one of the spouses equal access to divorce or legal separation on grounds of their sex, the law of the court seized should nevertheless apply. This, however, should be without prejudice to the public policy clause.

(25) Considerations of public interest should allow courts in the Member States the opportunity in exceptional circumstances to disregard the application of a provision of foreign law in a given case where it would be manifestly contrary to the public policy of the forum. However, the courts should not be able to apply the public policy exception in order to disregard a provision of the law of another State when to do so would be contrary to the Charter of Fundamental Rights of the European Union, and in particular Article 21 thereof, which prohibits all forms of discrimination.

(26) Where this Regulation refers to the fact that the law of the participating Member State whose court is seized does not provide for divorce, this should be interpreted to mean that the law of this Member State does not have the institute of divorce. In such a case, the court should not be obliged to pronounce a divorce by virtue of this Regulation.

Where this Regulation refers to the fact that the law of the participating Member State whose court is seized does not deem the marriage in question valid for the purposes of divorce proceedings, this should be interpreted to mean, inter alia, that such a marriage does not exist in the law of that Member State. In such a case, the court should not be obliged to pronounce a divorce or a legal separation by virtue of this Regulation.

(27) Since there are States and participating Member States in which two or more systems of law or sets of rules concerning matters governed by this Regulation coexist, there should be a provision governing the extent to which this Regulation applies in the different territorial units of those States and participating Member States or to different categories of persons of those States and participating Member States.

(28) In the absence of rules designating the applicable law, parties choosing the law of the State of the nationality of one of them should at the same time indicate which territorial unit's law they have agreed upon in case the State whose law is chosen comprises several territorial units each of which has its own system of law or a set of rules in respect of divorce.

(29) Since the objectives of this Regulation, namely the enhancement of legal certainty, predictability and flexibility in international matrimonial proceedings and hence the facilitation of the free movement of persons within the Union, cannot be sufficiently achieved by the Member States and can therefore, by reasons of the scale and effects of this Regulation be better achieved at Union level, the Union may adopt measures, by means of enhanced cooperation where appropriate, in accordance with the principle of subsidiarity as set out in Article 5 of the Treaty on European Union. In accordance with the principle of proportionality, as set out in that Article, this Regulation does not go beyond what is necessary in order to achieve those objectives.

(30) This Regulation respects fundamental rights and observes the principles recognised by the Charter of Fundamental Rights of the European Union, and in particular by Article 21 thereof, which states that any discrimination based on any ground such as sex, race, colour, ethnic or social origin, genetic features, language, religion or belief, political or any other opinion, membership of a national minority, property, birth, disability, age or sexual orientation shall be prohibited. This Regulation should be applied by the courts of the participating Member States in observance of those rights and principles,

HAS ADOPTED THIS REGULATION:

CHAPTER I
SCOPE, RELATION WITH REGULATION (EC) NO 2201/2003, DEFINITIONS AND UNIVERSAL APPLICATION

Article 1. Scope
1. This Regulation shall apply, in situations involving a conflict of laws, to divorce and legal separation.
2. This Regulation shall not apply to the following matters, even if they arise merely as a preliminary question within the context of divorce or legal separation proceedings:
   (a)   the legal capacity of natural persons;
   (b)   the existence, validity or recognition of a marriage;
   (c)   the annulment of a marriage;
   (d)   the name of the spouses;
   (e)   the property consequences of the marriage;
   (f)   parental responsibility;
   (g)   maintenance obligations;
   (h)   trusts or successions.

Article 2. Relation with Regulation (EC) No 2201/2003
This Regulation shall not affect the application of Regulation (EC) No 2201/2003.

Article 3. Definitions
For the purposes of this Regulation:
1. 'participating Member State' means a Member State which participates in enhanced cooperation on the law applicable to divorce and legal separation by virtue of Decision 2010/405/EU, or by virtue of a decision adopted in accordance with the second or third subparagraph of Article 331(1) of the Treaty on the Functioning of the European Union;
2. the term 'court' shall cover all the authorities in the participating Member States with jurisdiction in the matters falling within the scope of this Regulation.

Article 4. Universal application
The law designated by this Regulation shall apply whether or not it is the law of a participating Member State.

CHAPTER II
UNIFORM RULES ON THE LAW APPLICABLE TO DIVORCE AND LEGAL SEPARATION

Article 5. Choice of applicable law by the parties
1. The spouses may agree to designate the law applicable to divorce and legal separation provided that it is one of the following laws:
   (a)   the law of the State where the spouses are habitually resident at the time the agreement is concluded; or
   (b)   the law of the State where the spouses were last habitually resident, in so far as one of them still resides there at the time the agreement is concluded; or

(c) the law of the State of nationality of either spouse at the time the agreement is concluded; or

(d) the law of the forum.

2. Without prejudice to paragraph 3, an agreement designating the applicable law may be concluded and modified at any time, but at the latest at the time the court is seized.

3. If the law of the forum so provides, the spouses may also designate the law applicable before the court during the course of the proceeding. In that event, such designation shall be recorded in court in accordance with the law of the forum.

Article 6. Consent and material validity

1. The existence and validity of an agreement on choice of law or of any term thereof, shall be determined by the law which would govern it under this Regulation if the agreement or term were valid.

2. Nevertheless, a spouse, in order to establish that he did not consent, may rely upon the law of the country in which he has his habitual residence at the time the court is seized if it appears from the circumstances that it would not be reasonable to determine the effect of his conduct in accordance with the law specified in paragraph 1.

Article 7. Formal validity

1. The agreement referred to in Article 5(1) and (2), shall be expressed in writing, dated and signed by both spouses. Any communication by electronic means which provides a durable record of the agreement shall be deemed equivalent to writing.

2. However, if the law of the participating Member State in which the two spouses have their habitual residence at the time the agreement is concluded lays down additional formal requirements for this type of agreement, those requirements shall apply.

3. If the spouses are habitually resident in different participating Member States at the time the agreement is concluded and the laws of those States provide for different formal requirements, the agreement shall be formally valid if it satisfies the requirements of either of those laws.

4. If only one of the spouses is habitually resident in a participating Member State at the time the agreement is concluded and that State lays down additional formal requirements for this type of agreement, those requirements shall apply.

Article 8. Applicable law in the absence of a choice by the parties

In the absence of a choice pursuant to Article 5, divorce and legal separation shall be subject to the law of the State:

(a) where the spouses are habitually resident at the time the court is seized; or, failing that

(b) where the spouses were last habitually resident, provided that the period of residence did not end more than 1 year before the court was seized, in so far as one of the spouses still resides in that State at the time the court is seized; or, failing that

(c) of which both spouses are nationals at the time the court is seized; or, failing that

(d) where the court is seized.

Article 9. Conversion of legal separation into divorce

1. Where legal separation is converted into divorce, the law applicable to divorce shall be the law applied to the legal separation, unless the parties have agreed otherwise in accordance with Article 5.

2. However, if the law applied to the legal separation does not provide for the conversion of legal separation into divorce, Article 8 shall apply, unless the parties have agreed otherwise in accordance with Article 5.

Article 10. Application of the law of the forum
Where the law applicable pursuant to Article 5 or Article 8 makes no provision for divorce or does not grant one of the spouses equal access to divorce or legal separation on grounds of their sex, the law of the forum shall apply.

Article 11. Exclusion of renvoi
Where this Regulation provides for the application of the law of a State, it refers to the rules of law in force in that State other than its rules of private international law.

Article 12. Public policy
Application of a provision of the law designated by virtue of this Regulation may be refused only if such application is manifestly incompatible with the public policy of the forum.

Article 13. Differences in national law
Nothing in this Regulation shall oblige the courts of a participating Member State whose law does not provide for divorce or does not deem the marriage in question valid for the purposes of divorce proceedings to pronounce a divorce by virtue of the application of this Regulation.

Article 14. States with two or more legal systems — territorial conflicts of laws
Where a State comprises several territorial units each of which has its own system of law or a set of rules concerning matters governed by this Regulation:
  (a) any reference to the law of such State shall be construed, for the purposes of determining the law applicable under this Regulation, as referring to the law in force in the relevant territorial unit;
  (b) any reference to habitual residence in that State shall be construed as referring to habitual residence in a territorial unit;
  (c) any reference to nationality shall refer to the territorial unit designated by the law of that State, or, in the absence of relevant rules, to the territorial unit chosen by the parties or, in absence of choice, to the territorial unit with which the spouse or spouses has or have the closest connection.

Article 15. States with two or more legal systems — inter-personal conflicts of laws
In relation to a State which has two or more systems of law or sets of rules applicable to different categories of persons concerning matters governed by this Regulation, any reference to the law of such a State shall be construed as referring to the legal system determined by the rules in force in that State. In the absence of such rules, the system of law or the set of rules with which the spouse or spouses has or have the closest connection applies.

Article 16. Non-application of this Regulation to internal conflicts of laws
A participating Member State in which different systems of law or sets of rules apply to matters governed by this Regulation shall not be required to apply this Regulation to conflicts of laws arising solely between such different systems of law or sets of rules.

CHAPTER III
OTHER PROVISIONS

Article 17. Information to be provided by participating Member States
  1. By 21 September 2011 the participating Member States shall communicate to the Commission their national provisions, if any, concerning:
  (a) the formal requirements applicable to agreements on the choice of applicable law pursuant to Article 7(2) to (4); and
  (b) the possibility of designating the applicable law in accordance with Article 5(3).

The participating Member States shall inform the Commission of any subsequent changes to these provisions.

2. The Commission shall make all information communicated in accordance with paragraph 1 publicly available through appropriate means, in particular through the website of the European Judicial Network in civil and commercial matters.

Article 18. Transitional provisions

1. This Regulation shall apply only to legal proceedings instituted and to agreements of the kind referred to in Article 5 concluded as from 21 June 2012.

However, effect shall also be given to an agreement on the choice of the applicable law concluded before 21 June 2012, provided that it complies with Articles 6 and 7.

2. This Regulation shall be without prejudice to agreements on the choice of applicable law concluded in accordance with the law of a participating Member State whose court is seized before 21 June 2012.

Article 19. Relationship with existing international conventions

1. Without prejudice to the obligations of the participating Member States pursuant to Article 351 of the Treaty on the Functioning of the European Union, this Regulation shall not affect the application of international conventions to which one or more participating Member States are party at the time when this Regulation is adopted or when the decision pursuant to the second or third subparagraph of Article 331(1) of the Treaty on the Functioning of the European Union is adopted and which lay down conflict-of-laws rules relating to divorce or separation.

2. However, this Regulation shall, as between participating Member States, take precedence over conventions concluded exclusively between two or more of them in so far as such conventions concern matters governed by this Regulation.

Article 20. Review clause

1. By 31 December 2015, and every 5 years thereafter, the Commission shall present to the European Parliament, the Council and the European Economic and Social Committee a report on the application of this Regulation. The report shall be accompanied, where appropriate, by proposals to adapt this Regulation.

2. To that end, the participating Member States shall communicate to the Commission the relevant information on the application of this Regulation by their courts.

CHAPTER IV
FINAL PROVISIONS

Article 21. Entry into force and date of application

This Regulation shall enter into force on the day following its publication in the Official Journal of the European Union.

It shall apply from 21 June 2012, with the exception of Article 17, which shall apply from 21 June 2011.

For those participating Member States which participate in enhanced cooperation by virtue of a decision adopted in accordance with the second or third subparagraph of Article 331(1) of the Treaty on the Functioning of the European Union, this Regulation shall apply as from the date indicated in the decision concerned.

This Regulation shall be binding in its entirety and directly applicable in the participating Member States in accordance with the Treaties.

Done at Brussels, 20 December 2010.

REGULATION (EU) NO 650/2012 OF THE EUROPEAN PARLIAMENT AND OF THE COUNCIL OF 4 JULY 2012 ON JURISDICTION, APPLICABLE LAW, RECOGNITION AND ENFORCEMENT OF DECISIONS AND ACCEPTANCE AND ENFORCEMENT OF AUTHENTIC INSTRUMENTS IN MATTERS OF SUCCESSION AND ON THE CREATION OF A EUROPEAN CERTIFICATE OF SUCCESSION

Official Journal L 201, 27/07/2012 pp 107–134

THE EUROPEAN PARLIAMENT AND THE COUNCIL OF THE EUROPEAN UNION,

Having regard to the Treaty on the Functioning of the European Union, and in particular Article 81(2) thereof,

Having regard to the proposal from the European Commission,

Having regard to the opinion of the European Economic and Social Committee,

Acting in accordance with the ordinary legislative procedure,

Whereas:

(1) The Union has set itself the objective of maintaining and developing an area of freedom, security and justice in which the free movement of persons is ensured. For the gradual establishment of such an area, the Union is to adopt measures relating to judicial cooperation in civil matters having cross-border implications, particularly when necessary for the proper functioning of the internal market.

(2) In accordance with point (c) of Article 81(2) of the Treaty on the Functioning of the European Union, such measures may include measures aimed at ensuring the compatibility of the rules applicable in the Member States concerning conflict of laws and of jurisdiction.

(3) The European Council meeting in Tampere on 15 and 16 October 1999 endorsed the principle of mutual recognition of judgments and other decisions of judicial authorities as the cornerstone of judicial cooperation in civil matters and invited the Council and the Commission to adopt a programme of measures to implement that principle.

(4) A programme of measures for implementation of the principle of mutual recognition of decisions in civil and commercial matters, common to the Commission and to the Council, was adopted on 30 November 2000. That programme identifies measures relating to the harmonisation of conflict-of-laws rules as measures facilitating the mutual recognition of decisions, and provides for the drawing-up of an instrument relating to wills and succession.

(5) The European Council meeting in Brussels on 4 and 5 November 2004 adopted a new programme called 'The Hague Programme: strengthening freedom, security and justice in the European Union'. That programme underlines the need to adopt an instrument in matters of succession dealing, in particular, with the questions of conflict of laws, jurisdiction, mutual recognition and enforcement of decisions in the area of succession and a European Certificate of Succession.

(6) At its meeting in Brussels on 10 and 11 December 2009 the European Council adopted a new multiannual programme called 'The Stockholm Programme – An open and secure Europe serving and protecting citizens'. In that programme the European Council considered that mutual recognition should be extended to fields that are not yet covered but are essential to everyday life, for example succession and wills, while taking into consideration Member States' legal systems, including public policy (ordre public), and national traditions in this area.

(7) The proper functioning of the internal market should be facilitated by removing the obstacles to the free movement of persons who currently face difficulties in asserting their rights in the context of a succession having cross-border implications. In the European area of justice, citizens must be able to organise their

succession in advance. The rights of heirs and legatees, of other persons close to the deceased and of creditors of the succession must be effectively guaranteed.

(8)   In order to achieve those objectives, this Regulation should bring together provisions on jurisdiction, on applicable law, on recognition or, as the case may be, acceptance, enforceability and enforcement of decisions, authentic instruments and court settlements and on the creation of a European Certificate of Succession.

(9)   The scope of this Regulation should include all civil-law aspects of succession to the estate of a deceased person, namely all forms of transfer of assets, rights and obligations by reason of death, whether by way of a voluntary transfer under a disposition of property upon death or a transfer through intestate succession.

(10)   This Regulation should not apply to revenue matters or to administrative matters of a public-law nature. It should therefore be for national law to determine, for instance, how taxes and other liabilities of a public-law nature are calculated and paid, whether these be taxes payable by the deceased at the time of death or any type of succession-related tax to be paid by the estate or the beneficiaries. It should also be for national law to determine whether the release of succession property to beneficiaries under this Regulation or the recording of succession property in a register may be made subject to the payment of taxes.

(11)   This Regulation should not apply to areas of civil law other than succession. For reasons of clarity, a number of questions which could be seen as having a link with matters of succession should be explicitly excluded from the scope of this Regulation.

(12)   Accordingly, this Regulation should not apply to questions relating to matrimonial property regimes, including marriage settlements as known in some legal systems to the extent that such settlements do not deal with succession matters, and property regimes of relationships deemed to have comparable effects to marriage. The authorities dealing with a given succession under this Regulation should nevertheless, depending on the situation, take into account the winding-up of the matrimonial property regime or similar property regime of the deceased when determining the estate of the deceased and the respective shares of the beneficiaries.

(13)   Questions relating to the creation, administration and dissolution of trusts should also be excluded from the scope of this Regulation. This should not be understood as a general exclusion of trusts. Where a trust is created under a will or under statute in connection with intestate succession the law applicable to the succession under this Regulation should apply with respect to the devolution of the assets and the determination of the beneficiaries.

(14)   Property rights, interests and assets created or transferred otherwise than by succession, for instance by way of gifts, should also be excluded from the scope of this Regulation. However, it should be the law specified by this Regulation as the law applicable to the succession which determines whether gifts or other forms of dispositions inter vivos giving rise to a right in rem prior to death should be restored or accounted for for the purposes of determining the shares of the beneficiaries in accordance with the law applicable to the succession.

(15)   This Regulation should allow for the creation or the transfer by succession of a right in immovable or movable property as provided for in the law applicable to the succession. It should, however, not affect the limited number ('numerus clausus') of rights in rem known in the national law of some Member States. A Member State should not be required to recognise a right in rem relating to property located in that Member State if the right in rem in question is not known in its law.

(16)   However, in order to allow the beneficiaries to enjoy in another Member State the rights which have been created or transferred to them by succession, this Regulation should provide for the adaptation of an unknown right in rem to the closest equivalent right in rem under the law of that other Member State. In the

context of such an adaptation, account should be taken of the aims and the interests pursued by the specific right in rem and the effects attached to it. For the purposes of determining the closest equivalent national right in rem, the authorities or competent persons of the State whose law applied to the succession may be contacted for further information on the nature and the effects of the right. To that end, the existing networks in the area of judicial cooperation in civil and commercial matters could be used, as well as any other available means facilitating the understanding of foreign law.

(17)   The adaptation of unknown rights in rem as explicitly provided for by this Regulation should not preclude other forms of adaptation in the context of the application of this Regulation.

(18)   The requirements for the recording in a register of a right in immovable or movable property should be excluded from the scope of this Regulation. It should therefore be the law of the Member State in which the register is kept (for immovable property, the lex rei sitae) which determines under what legal conditions and how the recording must be carried out and which authorities, such as land registers or notaries, are in charge of checking that all requirements are met and that the documentation presented or established is sufficient or contains the necessary information. In particular, the authorities may check that the right of the deceased to the succession property mentioned in the document presented for registration is a right which is recorded as such in the register or which is otherwise demonstrated in accordance with the law of the Member State in which the register is kept. In order to avoid duplication of documents, the registration authorities should accept such documents drawn up in another Member State by the competent authorities whose circulation is provided for by this Regulation. In particular, the European Certificate of Succession issued under this Regulation should constitute a valid document for the recording of succession property in a register of a Member State. This should not preclude the authorities involved in the registration from asking the person applying for registration to provide such additional information, or to present such additional documents, as are required under the law of the Member State in which the register is kept, for instance information or documents relating to the payment of revenue. The competent authority may indicate to the person applying for registration how the missing information or documents can be provided.

(19)   The effects of the recording of a right in a register should also be excluded from the scope of this Regulation. It should therefore be the law of the Member State in which the register is kept which determines whether the recording is, for instance, declaratory or constitutive in effect. Thus, where, for example, the acquisition of a right in immovable property requires a recording in a register under the law of the Member State in which the register is kept in order to ensure the erga omnes effect of registers or to protect legal transactions, the moment of such acquisition should be governed by the law of that Member State.

(20)   This Regulation should respect the different systems for dealing with matters of succession applied in the Member States. For the purposes of this Regulation, the term 'court' should therefore be given a broad meaning so as to cover not only courts in the true sense of the word, exercising judicial functions, but also the notaries or registry offices in some Member States who or which, in certain matters of succession, exercise judicial functions like courts, and the notaries and legal professionals who, in some Member States, exercise judicial functions in a given succession by delegation of power by a court. All courts as defined in this Regulation should be bound by the rules of jurisdiction set out in this Regulation. Conversely, the term 'court' should not cover non-judicial authorities of a Member State empowered under national law to deal with matters of succession, such as the notaries in most Member States where, as is usually the case, they are not exercising judicial functions.

(21)   This Regulation should allow all notaries who have competence in matters

of succession in the Member States to exercise such competence. Whether or not the notaries in a given Member State are bound by the rules of jurisdiction set out in this Regulation should depend on whether or not they are covered by the term 'court' for the purposes of this Regulation.

(22)   Acts issued by notaries in matters of succession in the Member States should circulate under this Regulation. When notaries exercise judicial functions they are bound by the rules of jurisdiction, and the decisions they give should circulate in accordance with the provisions on recognition, enforceability and enforcement of decisions. When notaries do not exercise judicial functions they are not bound by the rules of jurisdiction, and the authentic instruments they issue should circulate in accordance with the provisions on authentic instruments.

(23)   In view of the increasing mobility of citizens and in order to ensure the proper administration of justice within the Union and to ensure that a genuine connecting factor exists between the succession and the Member State in which jurisdiction is exercised, this Regulation should provide that the general connecting factor for the purposes of determining both jurisdiction and the applicable law should be the habitual residence of the deceased at the time of death. In order to determine the habitual residence, the authority dealing with the succession should make an overall assessment of the circumstances of the life of the deceased during the years preceding his death and at the time of his death, taking account of all relevant factual elements, in particular the duration and regularity of the deceased's presence in the State concerned and the conditions and reasons for that presence. The habitual residence thus determined should reveal a close and stable connection with the State concerned taking into account the specific aims of this Regulation.

(24)   In certain cases, determining the deceased's habitual residence may prove complex. Such a case may arise, in particular, where the deceased for professional or economic reasons had gone to live abroad to work there, sometimes for a long time, but had maintained a close and stable connection with his State of origin. In such a case, the deceased could, depending on the circumstances of the case, be considered still to have his habitual residence in his State of origin in which the centre of interests of his family and his social life was located. Other complex cases may arise where the deceased lived in several States alternately or travelled from one State to another without settling permanently in any of them. If the deceased was a national of one of those States or had all his main assets in one of those States, his nationality or the location of those assets could be a special factor in the overall assessment of all the factual circumstances.

(25)   With regard to the determination of the law applicable to the succession the authority dealing with the succession may in exceptional cases – where, for instance, the deceased had moved to the State of his habitual residence fairly recently before his death and all the circumstances of the case indicate that he was manifestly more closely connected with another State – arrive at the conclusion that the law applicable to the succession should not be the law of the State of the habitual residence of the deceased but rather the law of the State with which the deceased was manifestly more closely connected. That manifestly closest connection should, however, not be resorted to as a subsidiary connecting factor whenever the determination of the habitual residence of the deceased at the time of death proves complex.

(26)   Nothing in this Regulation should prevent a court from applying mechanisms designed to tackle the evasion of the law, such as fraude à la loi in the context of private international law.

(27)   The rules of this Regulation are devised so as to ensure that the authority dealing with the succession will, in most situations, be applying its own law. This Regulation therefore provides for a series of mechanisms which would come into play where the deceased had chosen as the law to govern his succession the law of a Member State of which he was a national.

(28)   One such mechanism should be to allow the parties concerned to conclude a choice-of-court agreement in favour of the courts of the Member State of the chosen law. It would have to be determined on a case-by-case basis, depending in particular on the issue covered by the choice-of-court agreement, whether the agreement would have to be concluded between all parties concerned by the succession or whether some of them could agree to bring a specific issue before the chosen court in a situation where the decision by that court on that issue would not affect the rights of the other parties to the succession.

(29)   If succession proceedings are opened by a court of its own motion, as is the case in certain Member States, that court should close the proceedings if the parties agree to settle the succession amicably out of court in the Member State of the chosen law. Where succession proceedings are not opened by a court of its own motion, this Regulation should not prevent the parties from settling the succession amicably out of court, for instance before a notary, in a Member State of their choice where this is possible under the law of that Member State. This should be the case even if the law applicable to the succession is not the law of that Member State.

(30)   In order to ensure that the courts of all Member States may, on the same grounds, exercise jurisdiction in relation to the succession of persons not habitually resident in a Member State at the time of death, this Regulation should list exhaustively, in a hierarchical order, the grounds on which such subsidiary jurisdiction may be exercised.

(31)   In order to remedy, in particular, situations of denial of justice, this Regulation should provide a forum necessitatis allowing a court of a Member State, on an exceptional basis, to rule on a succession which is closely connected with a third State. Such an exceptional basis may be deemed to exist when proceedings prove impossible in the third State in question, for example because of civil war, or when a beneficiary cannot reasonably be expected to initiate or conduct proceedings in that State. Jurisdiction based on forum necessitatis should, however, be exercised only if the case has a sufficient connection with the Member State of the court seised.

(32)   In order to simplify the lives of heirs and legatees habitually resident in a Member State other than that in which the succession is being or will be dealt with, this Regulation should allow any person entitled under the law applicable to the succession to make declarations concerning the acceptance or waiver of the succession, of a legacy or of a reserved share, or concerning the limitation of his liability for the debts under the succession, to make such declarations in the form provided for by the law of the Member State of his habitual residence before the courts of that Member State. This should not preclude such declarations being made before other authorities in that Member State which are competent to receive declarations under national law. Persons choosing to avail themselves of the possibility to make declarations in the Member State of their habitual residence should themselves inform the court or authority which is or will be dealing with the succession of the existence of such declarations within any time limit set by the law applicable to the succession.

(33)   It should not be possible for a person who wishes to limit his liability for the debts under the succession to do so by a mere declaration to that effect before the courts or other competent authorities of the Member State of his habitual residence where the law applicable to the succession requires him to initiate specific legal proceedings, for instance inventory proceedings, before the competent court. A declaration made in such circumstances by a person in the Member State of his habitual residence in the form provided for by the law of that Member State should therefore not be formally valid for the purposes of this Regulation. Nor should the documents instituting the legal proceedings be regarded as declarations for the purposes of this Regulation.

(34)   In the interests of the harmonious functioning of justice, the giving of irre-

concilable decisions in different Member States should be avoided. To that end, this Regulation should provide for general procedural rules similar to those of other Union instruments in the area of judicial cooperation in civil matters.

(35)   One such procedural rule is a lis pendens rule which will come into play if the same succession case is brought before different courts in different Member States. That rule will then determine which court should proceed to deal with the succession case.

(36)   Given that succession matters in some Member States may be dealt with by non-judicial authorities, such as notaries, who are not bound by the rules of jurisdiction under this Regulation, it cannot be excluded that an amicable out-of-court settlement and court proceedings relating to the same succession, or two amicable out-of-court settlements relating to the same succession, may be initiated in parallel in different Member States. In such a situation, it should be for the parties involved, once they become aware of the parallel proceedings, to agree among themselves how to proceed. If they cannot agree, the succession would have to be dealt with and decided upon by the courts having jurisdiction under this Regulation.

(37)   In order to allow citizens to avail themselves, with all legal certainty, of the benefits offered by the internal market, this Regulation should enable them to know in advance which law will apply to their succession. Harmonised conflict-of-laws rules should be introduced in order to avoid contradictory results. The main rule should ensure that the succession is governed by a predictable law with which it is closely connected. For reasons of legal certainty and in order to avoid the fragmentation of the succession, that law should govern the succession as a whole, that is to say, all of the property forming part of the estate, irrespective of the nature of the assets and regardless of whether the assets are located in another Member State or in a third State.

(38)   This Regulation should enable citizens to organise their succession in advance by choosing the law applicable to their succession. That choice should be limited to the law of a State of their nationality in order to ensure a connection between the deceased and the law chosen and to avoid a law being chosen with the intention of frustrating the legitimate expectations of persons entitled to a reserved share.

(39)   A choice of law should be made expressly in a declaration in the form of a disposition of property upon death or be demonstrated by the terms of such a disposition. A choice of law could be regarded as demonstrated by a disposition of property upon death where, for instance, the deceased had referred in his disposition to specific provisions of the law of the State of his nationality or where he had otherwise mentioned that law.

(40)   A choice of law under this Regulation should be valid even if the chosen law does not provide for a choice of law in matters of succession. It should however be for the chosen law to determine the substantive validity of the act of making the choice, that is to say, whether the person making the choice may be considered to have understood and consented to what he was doing. The same should apply to the act of modifying or revoking a choice of law.

(41)   For the purposes of the application of this Regulation, the determination of the nationality or the multiple nationalities of a person should be resolved as a preliminary question. The issue of considering a person as a national of a State falls outside the scope of this Regulation and is subject to national law, including, where applicable, international Conventions, in full observance of the general principles of the European Union.

(42)   The law determined as the law applicable to the succession should govern the succession from the opening of the succession to the transfer of ownership of the assets forming part of the estate to the beneficiaries as determined by that law. It should include questions relating to the administration of the estate and to liability for the debts under the succession. The payment of the debts under the

succession may, depending, in particular, on the law applicable to the succession, include the taking into account of a specific ranking of the creditors.

(43) The rules of jurisdiction laid down by this Regulation may, in certain cases, lead to a situation where the court having jurisdiction to rule on the succession will not be applying its own law. When that situation occurs in a Member State whose law provides for the mandatory appointment of an administrator of the estate, this Regulation should allow the courts of that Member State, when seised, to appoint one or more such administrators under their own law. This should be without prejudice to any choice made by the parties to settle the succession amicably out of court in another Member State where this is possible under the law of that Member State. In order to ensure a smooth coordination between the law applicable to the succession and the law of the Member State of the appointing court, the court should appoint the person(s) who would be entitled to administer the estate under the law applicable to the succession, such as for instance the executor of the will of the deceased or the heirs themselves or, if the law applicable to the succession so requires, a third-party administrator. The courts may, however, in specific cases where their law so requires, appoint a third party as administrator even if this is not provided for in the law applicable to the succession. If the deceased had appointed an executor of the will, that person may not be deprived of his powers unless the law applicable to the succession allows for the termination of his mandate.

(44) The powers exercised by the administrators appointed in the Member State of the court seised should be the powers of administration which they may exercise under the law applicable to the succession. Thus, if, for instance, the heir is appointed as administrator he should have the powers to administer the estate which an heir would have under that law. Where the powers of administration which may be exercised under the law applicable to the succession are not sufficient to preserve the assets of the estate or to protect the rights of the creditors or of other persons having guaranteed the debts of the deceased, the administrator(s) appointed in the Member State of the court seised may, on a residual basis, exercise powers of administration to that end provided for by the law of that Member State. Such residual powers could include, for instance, establishing a list of the assets of the estate and the debts under the succession, informing creditors of the opening of the succession and inviting them to make their claims known, and taking any provisional, including protective, measures intended to preserve the assets of the estate. The acts performed by an administrator in exercise of the residual powers should respect the law applicable to the succession as regards the transfer of ownership of succession property, including any transaction entered into by the beneficiaries prior to the appointment of the administrator, liability for the debts under the succession and the rights of the beneficiaries, including, where applicable, the right to accept or to waive the succession. Such acts could, for instance, only entail the alienation of assets or the payment of debts where this would be allowed under the law applicable to the succession. Where under the law applicable to the succession the appointment of a third-party administrator changes the liability of the heirs, such a change of liability should be respected.

(45) This Regulation should not preclude creditors, for instance through a representative, from taking such further steps as may be available under national law, where applicable, in accordance with the relevant Union instruments, in order to safeguard their rights.

(46) This Regulation should allow for potential creditors in other Member States where assets are located to be informed of the opening of the succession. In the context of the application of this Regulation, consideration should therefore be given to the possibility of establishing a mechanism, if appropriate by way of the e-Justice portal, to enable potential creditors in other Member States to access the relevant information so that they can make their claims known.

(47) The law applicable to the succession should determine who the bene-

ficiaries are in any given succession. Under most laws, the term 'beneficiaries' would cover heirs and legatees and persons entitled to a reserved share although, for instance, the legal position of legatees is not the same under all laws. Under some laws, the legatee may receive a direct share in the estate whereas under other laws the legatee may acquire only a claim against the heirs.

(48) In order to ensure legal certainty for persons wishing to plan their succession in advance, this Regulation should lay down a specific conflict-of-laws rule concerning the admissibility and substantive validity of dispositions of property upon death. To ensure the uniform application of that rule, this Regulation should list which elements should be considered as elements pertaining to substantive validity. The examination of the substantive validity of a disposition of property upon death may lead to the conclusion that that disposition is without legal existence.

(49) An agreement as to succession is a type of disposition of property upon death the admissibility and acceptance of which vary among the Member States. In order to make it easier for succession rights acquired as a result of an agreement as to succession to be accepted in the Member States, this Regulation should determine which law is to govern the admissibility of such agreements, their substantive validity and their binding effects between the parties, including the conditions for their dissolution.

(50) The law which, under this Regulation, will govern the admissibility and substantive validity of a disposition of property upon death and, as regards agreements as to succession, the binding effects of such an agreement as between the parties, should be without prejudice to the rights of any person who, under the law applicable to the succession, has a right to a reserved share or another right of which he cannot be deprived by the person whose estate is involved.

(51) Where reference is made in this Regulation to the law which would have been applicable to the succession of the person making a disposition of property upon death if he had died on the day on which the disposition was, as the case may be, made, modified or revoked, such reference should be understood as a reference to either the law of the State of the habitual residence of the person concerned on that day or, if he had made a choice of law under this Regulation, the law of the State of his nationality on that day.

(52) This Regulation should regulate the validity as to form of all dispositions of property upon death made in writing by way of rules which are consistent with those of the Hague Convention of 5 October 1961 on the Conflicts of Laws Relating to the Form of Testamentary Dispositions. When determining whether a given disposition of property upon death is formally valid under this Regulation, the competent authority should disregard the fraudulent creation of an international element to circumvent the rules on formal validity.

(53) For the purposes of this Regulation, any provision of law limiting the permitted forms of dispositions of property upon death by reference to certain personal qualifications of the person making the disposition, such as, for instance, his age, should be deemed to pertain to matters of form. This should not be interpreted as meaning that the law applicable to the formal validity of a disposition of property upon death under this Regulation should determine whether or not a minor has the capacity to make a disposition of property upon death. That law should only determine whether a personal qualification such as, for instance, minority should bar a person from making a disposition of property upon death in a certain form.

(54) For economic, family or social considerations, certain immovable property, certain enterprises and other special categories of assets are subject to special rules in the Member State in which they are located imposing restrictions concerning or affecting the succession in respect of those assets. This Regulation should ensure the application of such special rules. However, this exception to the application of the law applicable to the succession requires a strict interpretation in order to

remain compatible with the general objective of this Regulation. Therefore, neither conflict-of-laws rules subjecting immovable property to a law different from that applicable to movable property nor provisions providing for a reserved share of the estate greater than that provided for in the law applicable to the succession under this Regulation may be regarded as constituting special rules imposing restrictions concerning or affecting the succession in respect of certain assets.

(55)   To ensure uniform handling of a situation in which it is uncertain in what order two or more persons whose succession would be governed by different laws died, this Regulation should lay down a rule providing that none of the deceased persons is to have any rights in the succession of the other or others.

(56)   In some situations an estate may be left without a claimant. Different laws provide differently for such situations. Under some laws, the State will be able to claim the vacant estate as an heir irrespective of where the assets are located. Under some other laws, the State will be able to appropriate only the assets located on its territory. This Regulation should therefore lay down a rule providing that the application of the law applicable to the succession should not preclude a Member State from appropriating under its own law the assets located on its territory. However, to ensure that this rule is not detrimental to the creditors of the estate, a proviso should be added enabling the creditors to seek satisfaction of their claims out of all the assets of the estate, irrespective of their location.

(57)   The conflict-of-laws rules laid down in this Regulation may lead to the application of the law of a third State. In such cases regard should be had to the private international law rules of that State. If those rules provide for renvoi either to the law of a Member State or to the law of a third State which would apply its own law to the succession, such renvoi should be accepted in order to ensure international consistency. Renvoi should, however, be excluded in situations where the deceased had made a choice of law in favour of the law of a third State.

(58)   Considerations of public interest should allow courts and other competent authorities dealing with matters of succession in the Member States to disregard, in exceptional circumstances, certain provisions of a foreign law where, in a given case, applying such provisions would be manifestly incompatible with the public policy (ordre public) of the Member State concerned. However, the courts or other competent authorities should not be able to apply the public-policy exception in order to set aside the law of another State or to refuse to recognise or, as the case may be, accept or enforce a decision, an authentic instrument or a court settlement from another Member State when doing so would be contrary to the Charter of Fundamental Rights of the European Union, and in particular Article 21 thereof, which prohibits all forms of discrimination.

(59)   In the light of its general objective, which is the mutual recognition of decisions given in the Member States in matters of succession, irrespective of whether such decisions were given in contentious or non-contentious proceedings, this Regulation should lay down rules relating to the recognition, enforceability and enforcement of decisions similar to those of other Union instruments in the area of judicial cooperation in civil matters.

(60)   In order to take into account the different systems for dealing with matters of succession in the Member States, this Regulation should guarantee the acceptance and enforceability in all Member States of authentic instruments in matters of succession.

(61)   Authentic instruments should have the same evidentiary effects in another Member State as they have in the Member State of origin, or the most comparable effects. When determining the evidentiary effects of a given authentic instrument in another Member State or the most comparable effects, reference should be made to the nature and the scope of the evidentiary effects of the authentic instrument in the Member State of origin. The evidentiary effects which a given authentic instrument should have in another Member State will therefore depend on the law of the Member State of origin.

(62)   The 'authenticity' of an authentic instrument should be an autonomous concept covering elements such as the genuineness of the instrument, the formal prerequisites of the instrument, the powers of the authority drawing up the instrument and the procedure under which the instrument is drawn up. It should also cover the factual elements recorded in the authentic instrument by the authority concerned, such as the fact that the parties indicated appeared before that authority on the date indicated and that they made the declarations indicated. A party wishing to challenge the authenticity of an authentic instrument should do so before the competent court in the Member State of origin of the authentic instrument under the law of that Member State.

(63)   The term 'the legal acts or legal relationships recorded in an authentic instrument' should be interpreted as referring to the contents as to substance recorded in the authentic instrument. The legal acts recorded in an authentic instrument could be, for instance, the agreement between the parties on the sharing-out or the distribution of the estate, or a will or an agreement as to succession, or another declaration of intent. The legal relationships could be, for instance, the determination of the heirs and other beneficiaries as established under the law applicable to the succession, their respective shares and the existence of a reserved share, or any other element established under the law applicable to the succession. A party wishing to challenge the legal acts or legal relationships recorded in an authentic instrument should do so before the courts having jurisdiction under this Regulation, which should decide on the challenge in accordance with the law applicable to the succession.

(64)   If a question relating to the legal acts or legal relationships recorded in an authentic instrument is raised as an incidental question in proceedings before a court of a Member State, that court should have jurisdiction over that question.

(65)   An authentic instrument which is being challenged should not produce any evidentiary effects in a Member State other than the Member State of origin as long as the challenge is pending. If the challenge concerns only a specific matter relating to the legal acts or legal relationships recorded in the authentic instrument, the authentic instrument in question should not produce any evidentiary effects in a Member State other than the Member State of origin with regard to the matter being challenged as long as the challenge is pending. An authentic instrument which has been declared invalid as a result of a challenge should cease to produce any evidentiary effects.

(66)   Should an authority, in the application of this Regulation, be presented with two incompatible authentic instruments, it should assess the question as to which authentic instrument, if any, should be given priority, taking into account the circumstances of the particular case. Where it is not clear from those circumstances which authentic instrument, if any, should be given priority, the question should be determined by the courts having jurisdiction under this Regulation, or, where the question is raised as an incidental question in the course of proceedings, by the court seised of those proceedings. In the event of incompatibility between an authentic instrument and a decision, regard should be had to the grounds of non-recognition of decisions under this Regulation.

(67)   In order for a succession with cross-border implications within the Union to be settled speedily, smoothly and efficiently, the heirs, legatees, executors of the will or administrators of the estate should be able to demonstrate easily their status and/or rights and powers in another Member State, for instance in a Member State in which succession property is located. To enable them to do so, this Regulation should provide for the creation of a uniform certificate, the European Certificate of Succession (hereinafter referred to as 'the Certificate'), to be issued for use in another Member State. In order to respect the principle of subsidiarity, the Certificate should not take the place of internal documents which may exist for similar purposes in the Member States.

(68)   The authority which issues the Certificate should have regard to the

formalities required for the registration of immovable property in the Member State in which the register is kept. For that purpose, this Regulation should provide for an exchange of information on such formalities between the Member States.

(69)   The use of the Certificate should not be mandatory. This means that persons entitled to apply for a Certificate should be under no obligation to do so but should be free to use the other instruments available under this Regulation (decisions, authentic instruments and court settlements). However, no authority or person presented with a Certificate issued in another Member State should be entitled to request that a decision, authentic instrument or court settlement be presented instead of the Certificate.

(70)   The Certificate should be issued in the Member State whose courts have jurisdiction under this Regulation. It should be for each Member State to determine in its internal legislation which authorities are to have competence to issue the Certificate, whether they be courts as defined for the purposes of this Regulation or other authorities with competence in matters of succession, such as, for instance, notaries. It should also be for each Member State to determine in its internal legislation whether the issuing authority may involve other competent bodies in the issuing process, for instance bodies competent to receive statutory declarations in lieu of an oath. The Member States should communicate to the Commission the relevant information concerning their issuing authorities in order for that information to be made publicly available.

(71)   The Certificate should produce the same effects in all Member States. It should not be an enforceable title in its own right but should have an evidentiary effect and should be presumed to demonstrate accurately elements which have been established under the law applicable to the succession or under any other law applicable to specific elements, such as the substantive validity of dispositions of property upon death. The evidentiary effect of the Certificate should not extend to elements which are not governed by this Regulation, such as questions of affiliation or the question whether or not a particular asset belonged to the deceased. Any person who makes payments or passes on succession property to a person indicated in the Certificate as being entitled to accept such payment or property as an heir or legatee should be afforded appropriate protection if he acted in good faith relying on the accuracy of the information certified in the Certificate. The same protection should be afforded to any person who, relying on the accuracy of the information certified in the Certificate, buys or receives succession property from a person indicated in the Certificate as being entitled to dispose of such property. The protection should be ensured if certified copies which are still valid are presented. Whether or not such an acquisition of property by a third person is effective should not be determined by this Regulation.

(72)   The competent authority should issue the Certificate upon request. The original of the Certificate should remain with the issuing authority, which should issue one or more certified copies of the Certificate to the applicant and to any other person demonstrating a legitimate interest. This should not preclude a Member State, in accordance with its national rules on public access to documents, from allowing copies of the Certificate to be disclosed to members of the public. This Regulation should provide for redress against decisions of the issuing authority, including decisions to refuse the issue of a Certificate. Where the Certificate is rectified, modified or withdrawn, the issuing authority should inform the persons to whom certified copies have been issued so as to avoid wrongful use of such copies.

(73)   Respect for international commitments entered into by the Member States means that this Regulation should not affect the application of international conventions to which one or more Member States are party at the time when this Regulation is adopted. In particular, the Member States which are Contracting Parties to the Hague Convention of 5 October 1961 on the Conflicts of Laws

Relating to the Form of Testamentary Dispositions should be able to continue to apply the provisions of that Convention instead of the provisions of this Regulation with regard to the formal validity of wills and joint wills. Consistency with the general objectives of this Regulation requires, however, that this Regulation take precedence, as between Member States, over conventions concluded exclusively between two or more Member States in so far as such conventions concern matters governed by this Regulation.

(74) This Regulation should not preclude Member States which are parties to the Convention of 19 November 1934 between Denmark, Finland, Iceland, Norway and Sweden comprising private international law provisions on succession, wills and estate administration from continuing to apply certain provisions of that Convention, as revised by the intergovernmental agreement between the States parties thereto.

(75) In order to facilitate the application of this Regulation, provision should be made for an obligation requiring the Member States to communicate certain information regarding their legislation and procedures relating to succession within the framework of the European Judicial Network in civil and commercial matters established by Council Decision 2001/470/EC. In order to allow for the timely publication in the Official Journal of the European Union of all information of relevance for the practical application of this Regulation, the Member States should also communicate such information to the Commission before this Regulation starts to apply.

(76) Equally, to facilitate the application of this Regulation and to allow for the use of modern communication technologies, standard forms should be prescribed for the attestations to be provided in connection with the application for a declaration of enforceability of a decision, authentic instrument or court settlement and for the application for a European Certificate of Succession, as well as for the Certificate itself.

(77) In calculating the periods and time limits provided for in this Regulation, Regulation (EEC, Euratom) No 1182/71 of the Council of 3 June 1971 determining the rules applicable to periods, dates and time limits should apply.

(78) In order to ensure uniform conditions for the implementation of this Regulation, implementing powers should be conferred on the Commission with regard to the establishment and subsequent amendment of the attestations and forms pertaining to the declaration of enforceability of decisions, court settlements and authentic instruments and to the European Certificate of Succession. Those powers should be exercised in accordance with Regulation (EU) No 182/2011 of the European Parliament and of the Council of 16 February 2011 laying down the rules and general principles concerning mechanisms for control by Member States of the Commission's exercise of implementing powers.

(79) The advisory procedure should be used for the adoption of implementing acts establishing and subsequently amending the attestations and forms provided for in this Regulation in accordance with the procedure laid down in Article 4 of Regulation (EU) No 182/2011.

(80) Since the objectives of this Regulation, namely the free movement of persons, the organisation in advance by citizens of their succession in a Union context and the protection of the rights of heirs and legatees and of persons close to the deceased, as well as of the creditors of the succession, cannot be sufficiently achieved by the Member States and can therefore, by reason of the scale and effects of this Regulation, be better achieved at Union level, the Union may adopt measures in accordance with the principle of subsidiarity as set out in Article 5 of the Treaty on European Union. In accordance with the principle of proportionality, as set out in that Article, this Regulation does not go beyond what is necessary in order to achieve those objectives.

(81) This Regulation respects the fundamental rights and observes the principles recognised in the Charter of Fundamental Rights of the European Union.

This Regulation must be applied by the courts and other competent authorities of the Member States in observance of those rights and principles.

(82)   In accordance with Articles 1 and 2 of Protocol No 21 on the position of the United Kingdom and Ireland in respect of the area of freedom, security and justice, annexed to the Treaty on European Union and to the Treaty on the Functioning of the European Union, those Member States are not taking part in the adoption of this Regulation and are not bound by it or subject to its application. This is, however, without prejudice to the possibility for the United Kingdom and Ireland of notifying their intention of accepting this Regulation after its adoption in accordance with Article 4 of the said Protocol.

(83)   In accordance with Articles 1 and 2 of Protocol No 22 on the position of Denmark, annexed to the Treaty on European Union and to the Treaty on the Functioning of the European Union, Denmark is not taking part in the adoption of this Regulation and is not bound by it or subject to its application,

HAVE ADOPTED THIS REGULATION:

CHAPTER I
SCOPE AND DEFINITIONS

Article 1. Scope
1.   This Regulation shall apply to succession to the estates of deceased persons. It shall not apply to revenue, customs or administrative matters.

2.   The following shall be excluded from the scope of this Regulation:

(a)   the status of natural persons, as well as family relationships and relationships deemed by the law applicable to such relationships to have comparable effects;

(b)   the legal capacity of natural persons, without prejudice to point (c) of Article 23(2) and to Article 26;

(c)   questions relating to the disappearance, absence or presumed death of a natural person;

(d)   questions relating to matrimonial property regimes and property regimes of relationships deemed by the law applicable to such relationships to have comparable effects to marriage;

(e)   maintenance obligations other than those arising by reason of death;

(f)   the formal validity of dispositions of property upon death made orally;

(g)   property rights, interests and assets created or transferred otherwise than by succession, for instance by way of gifts, joint ownership with a right of survivorship, pension plans, insurance contracts and arrangements of a similar nature, without prejudice to point (i) of Article 23(2);

(h)   questions governed by the law of companies and other bodies, corporate or unincorporated, such as clauses in the memoranda of association and articles of association of companies and other bodies, corporate or unincorporated, which determine what will happen to the shares upon the death of the members;

(i)   the dissolution, extinction and merger of companies and other bodies, corporate or unincorporated;

(j)   the creation, administration and dissolution of trusts;

(k)   the nature of rights in rem; and

(l)   any recording in a register of rights in immovable or movable property, including the legal requirements for such recording, and the effects of recording or failing to record such rights in a register.

Article 2. Competence in matters of succession within the Member States
This Regulation shall not affect the competence of the authorities of the Member States to deal with matters of succession.

Article 3. Definitions
1.   For the purposes of this Regulation:
(a)   'succession' means succession to the estate of a deceased person and covers all forms of transfer of assets, rights and obligations by reason of death, whether by way of a voluntary transfer under a disposition of property upon death or a transfer through intestate succession;
(b)   'agreement as to succession' means an agreement, including an agreement resulting from mutual wills, which, with or without consideration, creates, modifies or terminates rights to the future estate or estates of one or more persons party to the agreement;
(c)   'joint will' means a will drawn up in one instrument by two or more persons;
(d)   'disposition of property upon death' means a will, a joint will or an agreement as to succession;
(e)   'Member State of origin' means the Member State in which the decision has been given, the court settlement approved or concluded, the authentic instrument established or the European Certificate of Succession issued;
(f)   'Member State of enforcement' means the Member State in which the declaration of enforceability or the enforcement of the decision, court settlement or authentic instrument is sought;
(g)   'decision' means any decision in a matter of succession given by a court of a Member State, whatever the decision may be called, including a decision on the determination of costs or expenses by an officer of the court;
(h)   'court settlement' means a settlement in a matter of succession which has been approved by a court or concluded before a court in the course of proceedings;
(i)   'authentic instrument' means a document in a matter of succession which has been formally drawn up or registered as an authentic instrument in a Member State and the authenticity of which:
(i)   relates to the signature and the content of the authentic instrument; and
(ii)   has been established by a public authority or other authority empowered for that purpose by the Member State of origin.
2.   For the purposes of this Regulation, the term 'court' means any judicial authority and all other authorities and legal professionals with competence in matters of succession which exercise judicial functions or act pursuant to a delegation of power by a judicial authority or act under the control of a judicial authority, provided that such other authorities and legal professionals offer guarantees with regard to impartiality and the right of all parties to be heard and provided that their decisions under the law of the Member State in which they operate:
(a)   may be made the subject of an appeal to or review by a judicial authority; and
(b)   have a similar force and effect as a decision of a judicial authority on the same matter.
The Member States shall notify the Commission of the other authorities and legal professionals referred to in the first subparagraph in accordance with Article 79.

CHAPTER II
JURISDICTION

Article 4. General jurisdiction
The courts of the Member State in which the deceased had his habitual residence at the time of death shall have jurisdiction to rule on the succession as a whole.

Article 5. Choice-of-court agreement
1.   Where the law chosen by the deceased to govern his succession pursuant to

Article 22 is the law of a Member State, the parties concerned may agree that a court or the courts of that Member State are to have exclusive jurisdiction to rule on any succession matter.

2. Such a choice-of-court agreement shall be expressed in writing, dated and signed by the parties concerned. Any communication by electronic means which provides a durable record of the agreement shall be deemed equivalent to writing.

Article 6. Declining of jurisdiction in the event of a choice of law

Where the law chosen by the deceased to govern his succession pursuant to Article 22 is the law of a Member State, the court seised pursuant to Article 4 or Article 10:

(a) may, at the request of one of the parties to the proceedings, decline jurisdiction if it considers that the courts of the Member State of the chosen law are better placed to rule on the succession, taking into account the practical circumstances of the succession, such as the habitual residence of the parties and the location of the assets; or

(b) shall decline jurisdiction if the parties to the proceedings have agreed, in accordance with Article 5, to confer jurisdiction on a court or the courts of the Member State of the chosen law.

Article 7. Jurisdiction in the event of a choice of law

The courts of a Member State whose law had been chosen by the deceased pursuant to Article 22 shall have jurisdiction to rule on the succession if:

(a) a court previously seised has declined jurisdiction in the same case pursuant to Article 6;

(b) the parties to the proceedings have agreed, in accordance with Article 5, to confer jurisdiction on a court or the courts of that Member State; or

(c) the parties to the proceedings have expressly accepted the jurisdiction of the court seised.

Article 8. Closing of own-motion proceedings in the event of a choice of law

A court which has opened succession proceedings of its own motion under Article 4 or Article 10 shall close the proceedings if the parties to the proceedings have agreed to settle the succession amicably out of court in the Member State whose law had been chosen by the deceased pursuant to Article 22.

Article 9. Jurisdiction based on appearance

1. Where, in the course of proceedings before a court of a Member State exercising jurisdiction pursuant to Article 7, it appears that not all the parties to those proceedings were party to the choice-of-court agreement, the court shall continue to exercise jurisdiction if the parties to the proceedings who were not party to the agreement enter an appearance without contesting the jurisdiction of the court.

2. If the jurisdiction of the court referred to in paragraph 1 is contested by parties to the proceedings who were not party to the agreement, the court shall decline jurisdiction.

In that event, jurisdiction to rule on the succession shall lie with the courts having jurisdiction pursuant to Article 4 or Article 10.

Article 10. Subsidiary jurisdiction

1. Where the habitual residence of the deceased at the time of death is not located in a Member State, the courts of a Member State in which assets of the estate are located shall nevertheless have jurisdiction to rule on the succession as a whole in so far as:

(a) the deceased had the nationality of that Member State at the time of death; or, failing that,

(b) the deceased had his previous habitual residence in that Member State, provided that, at the time the court is seised, a period of not more than five years has elapsed since that habitual residence changed.

2. Where no court in a Member State has jurisdiction pursuant to paragraph 1, the courts of the Member State in which assets of the estate are located shall nevertheless have jurisdiction to rule on those assets.

Article 11. Forum necessitatis

Where no court of a Member State has jurisdiction pursuant to other provisions of this Regulation, the courts of a Member State may, on an exceptional basis, rule on the succession if proceedings cannot reasonably be brought or conducted or would be impossible in a third State with which the case is closely connected.

The case must have a sufficient connection with the Member State of the court seised.

Article 12. Limitation of proceedings

1. Where the estate of the deceased comprises assets located in a third State, the court seised to rule on the succession may, at the request of one of the parties, decide not to rule on one or more of such assets if it may be expected that its decision in respect of those assets will not be recognised and, where applicable, declared enforceable in that third State.

2. Paragraph 1 shall not affect the right of the parties to limit the scope of the proceedings under the law of the Member State of the court seised.

Article 13. Acceptance or waiver of the succession, of a legacy or of a reserved share

In addition to the court having jurisdiction to rule on the succession pursuant to this Regulation, the courts of the Member State of the habitual residence of any person who, under the law applicable to the succession, may make, before a court, a declaration concerning the acceptance or waiver of the succession, of a legacy or of a reserved share, or a declaration designed to limit the liability of the person concerned in respect of the liabilities under the succession, shall have jurisdiction to receive such declarations where, under the law of that Member State, such declarations may be made before a court.

Article 14. Seising of a court

For the purposes of this Chapter, a court shall be deemed to be seised:

(a) at the time when the document instituting the proceedings or an equivalent document is lodged with the court, provided that the applicant has not subsequently failed to take the steps he was required to take to have service effected on the defendant;

(b) if the document has to be served before being lodged with the court, at the time when it is received by the authority responsible for service, provided that the applicant has not subsequently failed to take the steps he was required to take to have the document lodged with the court; or

(c) if the proceedings are opened of the court's own motion, at the time when the decision to open the proceedings is taken by the court, or, where such a decision is not required, at the time when the case is registered by the court.

Article 15. Examination as to jurisdiction

Where a court of a Member State is seised of a succession matter over which it has no jurisdiction under this Regulation, it shall declare of its own motion that it has no jurisdiction.

Article 16. Examination as to admissibility

1. Where a defendant habitually resident in a State other than the Member State where the action was brought does not enter an appearance, the court having jurisdiction shall stay the proceedings so long as it is not shown that the defendant has been able to receive the document instituting the proceedings or an equivalent document in time to arrange for his defence, or that all necessary steps have been taken to that end.

2. Article 19 of Regulation (EC) No 1393/2007 of the European Parliament and

of the Council of 13 November 2007 on the service in the Member States of judicial and extrajudicial documents in civil or commercial matters (service of documents) shall apply instead of paragraph 1 of this Article if the document instituting the proceedings or an equivalent document had to be transmitted from one Member State to another pursuant to that Regulation.

3.   Where Regulation (EC) No 1393/2007 is not applicable, Article 15 of the Hague Convention of 15 November 1965 on the Service Abroad of Judicial and Extrajudicial Documents in Civil or Commercial Matters shall apply if the document instituting the proceedings or an equivalent document had to be transmitted abroad pursuant to that Convention.

Article 17. Lis pendens

1.   Where proceedings involving the same cause of action and between the same parties are brought in the courts of different Member States, any court other than the court first seised shall of its own motion stay its proceedings until such time as the jurisdiction of the court first seised is established.

2.   Where the jurisdiction of the court first seised is established, any court other than the court first seised shall decline jurisdiction in favour of that court.

Article 18. Related actions

1.   Where related actions are pending in the courts of different Member States, any court other than the court first seised may stay its proceedings.

2.   Where those actions are pending at first instance, any court other than the court first seised may also, on the application of one of the parties, decline jurisdiction if the court first seised has jurisdiction over the actions in question and its law permits the consolidation thereof.

3.   For the purposes of this Article, actions are deemed to be related where they are so closely connected that it is expedient to hear and determine them together to avoid the risk of irreconcilable decisions resulting from separate proceedings.

Article 19. Provisional, including protective, measures

Application may be made to the courts of a Member State for such provisional, including protective, measures as may be available under the law of that State, even if, under this Regulation, the courts of another Member State have jurisdiction as to the substance of the matter.

CHAPTER III
APPLICABLE LAW

Article 20. Universal application

Any law specified by this Regulation shall be applied whether or not it is the law of a Member State.

Article 21. General rule

1.   Unless otherwise provided for in this Regulation, the law applicable to the succession as a whole shall be the law of the State in which the deceased had his habitual residence at the time of death.

2.   Where, by way of exception, it is clear from all the circumstances of the case that, at the time of death, the deceased was manifestly more closely connected with a State other than the State whose law would be applicable under paragraph 1, the law applicable to the succession shall be the law of that other State.

Article 22. Choice of law

1.   A person may choose as the law to govern his succession as a whole the law of the State whose nationality he possesses at the time of making the choice or at the time of death.

A person possessing multiple nationalities may choose the law of any of the

States whose nationality he possesses at the time of making the choice or at the time of death.

2. The choice shall be made expressly in a declaration in the form of a disposition of property upon death or shall be demonstrated by the terms of such a disposition.

3. The substantive validity of the act whereby the choice of law was made shall be governed by the chosen law.

4. Any modification or revocation of the choice of law shall meet the requirements as to form for the modification or revocation of a disposition of property upon death.

Article 23. The scope of the applicable law

1. The law determined pursuant to Article 21 or Article 22 shall govern the succession as a whole.

2. That law shall govern in particular:

(a) the causes, time and place of the opening of the succession;

(b) the determination of the beneficiaries, of their respective shares and of the obligations which may be imposed on them by the deceased, and the determination of other succession rights, including the succession rights of the surviving spouse or partner;

(c) the capacity to inherit;

(d) disinheritance and disqualification by conduct;

(e) the transfer to the heirs and, as the case may be, to the legatees of the assets, rights and obligations forming part of the estate, including the conditions and effects of the acceptance or waiver of the succession or of a legacy;

(f) the powers of the heirs, the executors of the wills and other administrators of the estate, in particular as regards the sale of property and the payment of creditors, without prejudice to the powers referred to in Article 29(2) and (3);

(g) liability for the debts under the succession;

(h) the disposable part of the estate, the reserved shares and other restrictions on the disposal of property upon death as well as claims which persons close to the deceased may have against the estate or the heirs;

(i) any obligation to restore or account for gifts, advancements or legacies when determining the shares of the different beneficiaries; and

(j) the sharing-out of the estate.

Article 24. Dispositions of property upon death other than agreements as to succession

1. A disposition of property upon death other than an agreement as to succession shall be governed, as regards its admissibility and substantive validity, by the law which, under this Regulation, would have been applicable to the succession of the person who made the disposition if he had died on the day on which the disposition was made.

2. Notwithstanding paragraph 1, a person may choose as the law to govern his disposition of property upon death, as regards its admissibility and substantive validity, the law which that person could have chosen in accordance with Article 22 on the conditions set out therein.

3. Paragraph 1 shall apply, as appropriate, to the modification or revocation of a disposition of property upon death other than an agreement as to succession. In the event of a choice of law in accordance with paragraph 2, the modification or revocation shall be governed by the chosen law.

Article 25. Agreements as to succession

1. An agreement as to succession regarding the succession of one person shall be governed, as regards its admissibility, its substantive validity and its binding effects between the parties, including the conditions for its dissolution, by the law

which, under this Regulation, would have been applicable to the succession of that person if he had died on the day on which the agreement was concluded.

2.   An agreement as to succession regarding the succession of several persons shall be admissible only if it is admissible under all the laws which, under this Regulation, would have governed the succession of all the persons involved if they had died on the day on which the agreement was concluded.

An agreement as to succession which is admissible pursuant to the first sub-paragraph shall be governed, as regards its substantive validity and its binding effects between the parties, including the conditions for its dissolution, by the law, from among those referred to in the first subparagraph, with which it has the closest connection.

3.   Notwithstanding paragraphs 1 and 2, the parties may choose as the law to govern their agreement as to succession, as regards its admissibility, its substantive validity and its binding effects between the parties, including the conditions for its dissolution, the law which the person or one of the persons whose estate is involved could have chosen in accordance with Article 22 on the conditions set out therein.

Article 26. Substantive validity of dispositions of property upon death

1.   For the purposes of Articles 24 and 25 the following elements shall pertain to substantive validity:

(a)   the capacity of the person making the disposition of property upon death to make such a disposition;

(b)   the particular causes which bar the person making the disposition from disposing in favour of certain persons or which bar a person from receiving succession property from the person making the disposition;

(c)   the admissibility of representation for the purposes of making a disposition of property upon death;

(d)   the interpretation of the disposition;

(e)   fraud, duress, mistake and any other questions relating to the consent or intention of the person making the disposition.

2.   Where a person has the capacity to make a disposition of property upon death under the law applicable pursuant to Article 24 or Article 25, a subsequent change of the law applicable shall not affect his capacity to modify or revoke such a disposition.

Article 27. Formal validity of dispositions of property upon death made in writing

1.   A disposition of property upon death made in writing shall be valid as regards form if its form complies with the law:

(a)   of the State in which the disposition was made or the agreement as to succession concluded;

(b)   of a State whose nationality the testator or at least one of the persons whose succession is concerned by an agreement as to succession possessed, either at the time when the disposition was made or the agreement concluded, or at the time of death;

(c)   of a State in which the testator or at least one of the persons whose succession is concerned by an agreement as to succession had his domicile, either at the time when the disposition was made or the agreement concluded, or at the time of death;

(d)   of the State in which the testator or at least one of the persons whose succession is concerned by an agreement as to succession had his habitual residence, either at the time when the disposition was made or the agreement concluded, or at the time of death; or

(e)   in so far as immovable property is concerned, of the State in which that property is located.

The determination of the question whether or not the testator or any person whose succession is concerned by the agreement as to succession had his domicile in a particular State shall be governed by the law of that State.

2. Paragraph 1 shall also apply to dispositions of property upon death modifying or revoking an earlier disposition. The modification or revocation shall also be valid as regards form if it complies with any one of the laws according to the terms of which, under paragraph 1, the disposition of property upon death which has been modified or revoked was valid.

3. For the purposes of this Article, any provision of law which limits the permitted forms of dispositions of property upon death by reference to the age, nationality or other personal conditions of the testator or of the persons whose succession is concerned by an agreement as to succession shall be deemed to pertain to matters of form. The same rule shall apply to the qualifications to be possessed by any witnesses required for the validity of a disposition of property upon death.

Article 28. Validity as to form of a declaration concerning acceptance or waiver

A declaration concerning the acceptance or waiver of the succession, of a legacy or of a reserved share, or a declaration designed to limit the liability of the person making the declaration, shall be valid as to form where it meets the requirements of:

(a) the law applicable to the succession pursuant to Article 21 or Article 22; or

(b) the law of the State in which the person making the declaration has his habitual residence.

Article 29. Special rules on the appointment and powers of an administrator of the estate in certain situations

1. Where the appointment of an administrator is mandatory or mandatory upon request under the law of the Member State whose courts have jurisdiction to rule on the succession pursuant to this Regulation and the law applicable to the succession is a foreign law, the courts of that Member State may, when seised, appoint one or more administrators of the estate under their own law, subject to the conditions laid down in this Article.

The administrator(s) appointed pursuant to this paragraph shall be the person(s) entitled to execute the will of the deceased and/or to administer the estate under the law applicable to the succession. Where that law does not provide for the administration of the estate by a person who is not a beneficiary, the courts of the Member State in which the administrator is to be appointed may appoint a third-party administrator under their own law if that law so requires and there is a serious conflict of interests between the beneficiaries or between the beneficiaries and the creditors or other persons having guaranteed the debts of the deceased, a disagreement amongst the beneficiaries on the administration of the estate or a complex estate to administer due to the nature of the assets.

The administrator(s) appointed pursuant to this paragraph shall be the only person(s) entitled to exercise the powers referred to in paragraph 2 or 3.

2. The person(s) appointed as administrator(s) pursuant to paragraph 1 shall exercise the powers to administer the estate which he or they may exercise under the law applicable to the succession. The appointing court may, in its decision, lay down specific conditions for the exercise of such powers in accordance with the law applicable to the succession.

Where the law applicable to the succession does not provide for sufficient powers to preserve the assets of the estate or to protect the rights of the creditors or of other persons having guaranteed the debts of the deceased, the appointing court may decide to allow the administrator(s) to exercise, on a residual basis, the powers provided for to that end by its own law and may, in its decision, lay down specific conditions for the exercise of such powers in accordance with that law.

When exercising such residual powers, however, the administrator(s) shall respect the law applicable to the succession as regards the transfer of ownership of succession property, liability for the debts under the succession, the rights of the beneficiaries, including, where applicable, the right to accept or to waive the succession, and, where applicable, the powers of the executor of the will of the deceased.

3. Notwithstanding paragraph 2, the court appointing one or more administrators pursuant to paragraph 1 may, by way of exception, where the law applicable to the succession is the law of a third State, decide to vest in those administrators all the powers of administration provided for by the law of the Member State in which they are appointed.

When exercising such powers, however, the administrators shall respect, in particular, the determination of the beneficiaries and their succession rights, including their rights to a reserved share or claim against the estate or the heirs under the law applicable to the succession.

Article 30. Special rules imposing restrictions concerning or affecting the succession in respect of certain assets

Where the law of the State in which certain immovable property, certain enterprises or other special categories of assets are located contains special rules which, for economic, family or social considerations, impose restrictions concerning or affecting the succession in respect of those assets, those special rules shall apply to the succession in so far as, under the law of that State, they are applicable irrespective of the law applicable to the succession.

Article 31. Adaptation of rights in rem

Where a person invokes a right in rem to which he is entitled under the law applicable to the succession and the law of the Member State in which the right is invoked does not know the right in rem in question, that right shall, if necessary and to the extent possible, be adapted to the closest equivalent right in rem under the law of that State, taking into account the aims and the interests pursued by the specific right in rem and the effects attached to it.

Article 32. Commorientes

Where two or more persons whose successions are governed by different laws die in circumstances in which it is uncertain in what order their deaths occurred, and where those laws provide differently for that situation or make no provision for it at all, none of the deceased persons shall have any rights to the succession of the other or others.

Article 33. Estate without a claimant

To the extent that, under the law applicable to the succession pursuant to this Regulation, there is no heir or legatee for any assets under a disposition of property upon death and no natural person is an heir by operation of law, the application of the law so determined shall not preclude the right of a Member State or of an entity appointed for that purpose by that Member State to appropriate under its own law the assets of the estate located on its territory, provided that the creditors are entitled to seek satisfaction of their claims out of the assets of the estate as a whole.

Article 34. Renvoi

1. The application of the law of any third State specified by this Regulation shall mean the application of the rules of law in force in that State, including its rules of private international law in so far as those rules make a renvoi:

(a)   to the law of a Member State; or

(b)   to the law of another third State which would apply its own law.

2. No renvoi shall apply with respect to the laws referred to in Article 21(2), Article 22, Article 27, point (b) of Article 28 and Article 30.

Article 35. Public policy (ordre public)

The application of a provision of the law of any State specified by this Regulation may be refused only if such application is manifestly incompatible with the public policy (ordre public) of the forum.

Article 36. States with more than one legal system – territorial conflicts of laws

1.   Where the law specified by this Regulation is that of a State which comprises several territorial units each of which has its own rules of law in respect of succession, the internal conflict-of-laws rules of that State shall determine the relevant territorial unit whose rules of law are to apply.

2.   In the absence of such internal conflict-of-laws rules:

(a)   any reference to the law of the State referred to in paragraph 1 shall, for the purposes of determining the law applicable pursuant to provisions referring to the habitual residence of the deceased, be construed as referring to the law of the territorial unit in which the deceased had his habitual residence at the time of death;

(b)   any reference to the law of the State referred to in paragraph 1 shall, for the purposes of determining the law applicable pursuant to provisions referring to the nationality of the deceased, be construed as referring to the law of the territorial unit with which the deceased had the closest connection;

(c)   any reference to the law of the State referred to in paragraph 1 shall, for the purposes of determining the law applicable pursuant to any other provisions referring to other elements as connecting factors, be construed as referring to the law of the territorial unit in which the relevant element is located.

3.   Notwithstanding paragraph 2, any reference to the law of the State referred to in paragraph 1 shall, for the purposes of determining the relevant law pursuant to Article 27, in the absence of internal conflict-of-laws rules in that State, be construed as referring to the law of the territorial unit with which the testator or the persons whose succession is concerned by the agreement as to succession had the closest connection.

Article 37. States with more than one legal system – inter-personal conflicts of laws

In relation to a State which has two or more systems of law or sets of rules applicable to different categories of persons in respect of succession, any reference to the law of that State shall be construed as referring to the system of law or set of rules determined by the rules in force in that State. In the absence of such rules, the system of law or the set of rules with which the deceased had the closest connection shall apply.

Article 38. Non-application of this Regulation to internal conflicts of laws

A Member State which comprises several territorial units each of which has its own rules of law in respect of succession shall not be required to apply this Regulation to conflicts of laws arising between such units only.

CHAPTER IV
RECOGNITION, ENFORCEABILITY AND ENFORCEMENT OF DECISIONS

Article 39. Recognition

1.   A decision given in a Member State shall be recognised in the other Member States without any special procedure being required.

2.   Any interested party who raises the recognition of a decision as the principal issue in a dispute may, in accordance with the procedure provided for in Articles 45 to 58, apply for that decision to be recognised.

3.   If the outcome of the proceedings in a court of a Member State depends on the determination of an incidental question of recognition, that court shall have jurisdiction over that question.

Article 40. Grounds of non-recognition
A decision shall not be recognised:

(a)   if such recognition is manifestly contrary to public policy (ordre public) in the Member State in which recognition is sought;

(b)   where it was given in default of appearance, if the defendant was not served with the document which instituted the proceedings or with an equivalent document in sufficient time and in such a way as to enable him to arrange for his defence, unless the defendant failed to commence proceedings to challenge the decision when it was possible for him to do so;

(c)   if it is irreconcilable with a decision given in proceedings between the same parties in the Member State in which recognition is sought;

(d)   if it is irreconcilable with an earlier decision given in another Member State or in a third State in proceedings involving the same cause of action and between the same parties, provided that the earlier decision fulfils the conditions necessary for its recognition in the Member State in which recognition is sought.

Article 41. No review as to the substance
Under no circumstances may a decision given in a Member State be reviewed as to its substance.

Article 42. Staying of recognition proceedings
A court of a Member State in which recognition is sought of a decision given in another Member State may stay the proceedings if an ordinary appeal against the decision has been lodged in the Member State of origin.

Article 43. Enforceability
Decisions given in a Member State and enforceable in that State shall be enforceable in another Member State when, on the application of any interested party, they have been declared enforceable there in accordance with the procedure provided for in Articles 45 to 58.

Article 44. Determination of domicile
To determine whether, for the purposes of the procedure provided for in Articles 45 to 58, a party is domiciled in the Member State of enforcement, the court seised shall apply the internal law of that Member State.

Article 45. Jurisdiction of local courts
1.   The application for a declaration of enforceability shall be submitted to the court or competent authority of the Member State of enforcement communicated by that Member State to the Commission in accordance with Article 78.

2.   The local jurisdiction shall be determined by reference to the place of domicile of the party against whom enforcement is sought, or to the place of enforcement.

Article 46. Procedure
1.   The application procedure shall be governed by the law of the Member State of enforcement.

2.   The applicant shall not be required to have a postal address or an authorised representative in the Member State of enforcement.

3.   The application shall be accompanied by the following documents:

(a)   a copy of the decision which satisfies the conditions necessary to establish its authenticity;

(b)   the attestation issued by the court or competent authority of the Member State of origin using the form established in accordance with the advisory procedure referred to in Article 81(2), without prejudice to Article 47.

Article 47. Non-production of the attestation
1.   If the attestation referred to in point (b) of Article 46(3) is not produced, the court or competent authority may specify a time for its production or accept an

equivalent document or, if it considers that it has sufficient information before it, dispense with its production.

2.   If the court or competent authority so requires, a translation of the documents shall be produced. The translation shall be done by a person qualified to do translations in one of the Member States.

Article 48. Declaration of enforceability

The decision shall be declared enforceable immediately on completion of the formalities in Article 46 without any review under Article 40. The party against whom enforcement is sought shall not at this stage of the proceedings be entitled to make any submissions on the application.

Article 49. Notice of the decision on the application for a declaration of enforceability

1.   The decision on the application for a declaration of enforceability shall forthwith be brought to the notice of the applicant in accordance with the procedure laid down by the law of the Member State of enforcement.

2.   The declaration of enforceability shall be served on the party against whom enforcement is sought, accompanied by the decision, if not already served on that party.

Article 50. Appeal against the decision on the application for a declaration of enforceability

1.   The decision on the application for a declaration of enforceability may be appealed against by either party.

2.   The appeal shall be lodged with the court communicated by the Member State concerned to the Commission in accordance with Article 78.

3.   The appeal shall be dealt with in accordance with the rules governing procedure in contradictory matters.

4.   If the party against whom enforcement is sought fails to appear before the appellate court in proceedings concerning an appeal brought by the applicant, Article 16 shall apply even where the party against whom enforcement is sought is not domiciled in any of the Member States.

5.   An appeal against the declaration of enforceability shall be lodged within 30 days of service thereof. If the party against whom enforcement is sought is domiciled in a Member State other than that in which the declaration of enforceability was given, the time for appealing shall be 60 days and shall run from the date of service, either on him in person or at his residence. No extension may be granted on account of distance.

Article 51. Procedure to contest the decision given on appeal

The decision given on the appeal may be contested only by the procedure communicated by the Member State concerned to the Commission in accordance with Article 78.

Article 52. Refusal or revocation of a declaration of enforceability

The court with which an appeal is lodged under Article 50 or Article 51 shall refuse or revoke a declaration of enforceability only on one of the grounds specified in Article 40. It shall give its decision without delay.

Article 53. Staying of proceedings

The court with which an appeal is lodged under Article 50 or Article 51 shall, on the application of the party against whom enforcement is sought, stay the proceedings if the enforceability of the decision is suspended in the Member State of origin by reason of an appeal.

Article 54. Provisional, including protective, measures

1.   When a decision must be recognised in accordance with this Chapter, nothing shall prevent the applicant from availing himself of provisional, including

protective, measures in accordance with the law of the Member State of enforcement without a declaration of enforceability under Article 48 being required.

2.   The declaration of enforceability shall carry with it by operation of law the power to proceed to any protective measures.

3.   During the time specified for an appeal pursuant to Article 50(5) against the declaration of enforceability and until any such appeal has been determined, no measures of enforcement may be taken other than protective measures against the property of the party against whom enforcement is sought.

Article 55. Partial enforceability

1.   Where a decision has been given in respect of several matters and the declaration of enforceability cannot be given for all of them, the court or competent authority shall give it for one or more of them.

2.   An applicant may request a declaration of enforceability limited to parts of a decision.

Article 56. Legal aid

An applicant who, in the Member State of origin, has benefited from complete or partial legal aid or exemption from costs or expenses shall be entitled, in any proceedings for a declaration of enforceability, to benefit from the most favourable legal aid or the most extensive exemption from costs or expenses provided for by the law of the Member State of enforcement.

Article 57. No security, bond or deposit

No security, bond or deposit, however described, shall be required of a party who in one Member State applies for recognition, enforceability or enforcement of a decision given in another Member State on the ground that he is a foreign national or that he is not domiciled or resident in the Member State of enforcement.

Article 58. No charge, duty or fee

In proceedings for the issue of a declaration of enforceability, no charge, duty or fee calculated by reference to the value of the matter at issue may be levied in the Member State of enforcement.

CHAPTER V
AUTHENTIC INSTRUMENTS AND COURT SETTLEMENTS

Article 59. Acceptance of authentic instruments

1.   An authentic instrument established in a Member State shall have the same evidentiary effects in another Member State as it has in the Member State of origin, or the most comparable effects, provided that this is not manifestly contrary to public policy (ordre public) in the Member State concerned.

A person wishing to use an authentic instrument in another Member State may ask the authority establishing the authentic instrument in the Member State of origin to fill in the form established in accordance with the advisory procedure referred to in Article 81(2) describing the evidentiary effects which the authentic instrument produces in the Member State of origin.

2.   Any challenge relating to the authenticity of an authentic instrument shall be made before the courts of the Member State of origin and shall be decided upon under the law of that State. The authentic instrument challenged shall not produce any evidentiary effect in another Member State as long as the challenge is pending before the competent court.

3.   Any challenge relating to the legal acts or legal relationships recorded in an authentic instrument shall be made before the courts having jurisdiction under this Regulation and shall be decided upon under the law applicable pursuant to Chapter III. The authentic instrument challenged shall not produce any evidentiary effect in a Member State other than the Member State of origin as regards the

matter being challenged as long as the challenge is pending before the competent court.

4. If the outcome of proceedings in a court of a Member State depends on the determination of an incidental question relating to the legal acts or legal relationships recorded in an authentic instrument in matters of succession, that court shall have jurisdiction over that question.

Article 60. Enforceability of authentic instruments

1. An authentic instrument which is enforceable in the Member State of origin shall be declared enforceable in another Member State on the application of any interested party in accordance with the procedure provided for in Articles 45 to 58.

2. For the purposes of point (b) of Article 46(3), the authority which established the authentic instrument shall, on the application of any interested party, issue an attestation using the form established in accordance with the advisory procedure referred to in Article 81(2).

3. The court with which an appeal is lodged under Article 50 or Article 51 shall refuse or revoke a declaration of enforceability only if enforcement of the authentic instrument is manifestly contrary to public policy (ordre public) in the Member State of enforcement.

Article 61. Enforceability of court settlements

1. Court settlements which are enforceable in the Member State of origin shall be declared enforceable in another Member State on the application of any interested party in accordance with the procedure provided for in Articles 45 to 58.

2. For the purposes of point (b) of Article 46(3), the court which approved the settlement or before which it was concluded shall, on the application of any interested party, issue an attestation using the form established in accordance with the advisory procedure referred to in Article 81(2).

3. The court with which an appeal is lodged under Article 50 or Article 51 shall refuse or revoke a declaration of enforceability only if enforcement of the court settlement is manifestly contrary to public policy (ordre public) in the Member State of enforcement.

CHAPTER VI
EUROPEAN CERTIFICATE OF SUCCESSION

Article 62. Creation of a European Certificate of Succession

1. This Regulation creates a European Certificate of Succession (hereinafter referred to as 'the Certificate') which shall be issued for use in another Member State and shall produce the effects listed in Article 69.

2. The use of the Certificate shall not be mandatory.

3. The Certificate shall not take the place of internal documents used for similar purposes in the Member States. However, once issued for use in another Member State, the Certificate shall also produce the effects listed in Article 69 in the Member State whose authorities issued it in accordance with this Chapter.

Article 63. Purpose of the Certificate

1. The Certificate is for use by heirs, legatees having direct rights in the succession and executors of wills or administrators of the estate who, in another Member State, need to invoke their status or to exercise respectively their rights as heirs or legatees and/or their powers as executors of wills or administrators of the estate.

2. The Certificate may be used, in particular, to demonstrate one or more of the following:

(a) the status and/or the rights of each heir or, as the case may be, each legatee mentioned in the Certificate and their respective shares of the estate;

(b) the attribution of a specific asset or specific assets forming part of the estate to the heir(s) or, as the case may be, the legatee(s) mentioned in the Certificate;

(c)   the powers of the person mentioned in the Certificate to execute the will or administer the estate.

Article 64. Competence to issue the Certificate

The Certificate shall be issued in the Member State whose courts have jurisdiction under Article 4, Article 7, Article 10 or Article 11. The issuing authority shall be:

(a)   a court as defined in Article 3(2); or

(b)   another authority which, under national law, has competence to deal with matters of succession.

Article 65. Application for a Certificate

1.   The Certificate shall be issued upon application by any person referred to in Article 63(1) (hereinafter referred to as 'the applicant').

2.   For the purposes of submitting an application, the applicant may use the form established in accordance with the advisory procedure referred to in Article 81(2).

3.   The application shall contain the information listed below, to the extent that such information is within the applicant's knowledge and is necessary in order to enable the issuing authority to certify the elements which the applicant wants certified, and shall be accompanied by all relevant documents either in the original or by way of copies which satisfy the conditions necessary to establish their authenticity, without prejudice to Article 66(2):

(a)   details concerning the deceased: surname (if applicable, surname at birth), given name(s), sex, date and place of birth, civil status, nationality, identification number (if applicable), address at the time of death, date and place of death;

(b)   details concerning the applicant: surname (if applicable, surname at birth), given name(s), sex, date and place of birth, civil status, nationality, identification number (if applicable), address and relationship to the deceased, if any;

(c)   details concerning the representative of the applicant, if any: surname (if applicable, surname at birth), given name(s), address and representative capacity;

(d)   details of the spouse or partner of the deceased and, if applicable, ex-spouse(s) or ex-partner(s): surname (if applicable, surname at birth), given name(s), sex, date and place of birth, civil status, nationality, identification number (if applicable) and address;

(e)   details of other possible beneficiaries under a disposition of property upon death and/or by operation of law: surname and given name(s) or organisation name, identification number (if applicable) and address;

(f)   the intended purpose of the Certificate in accordance with Article 63;

(g)   the contact details of the court or other competent authority which is dealing with or has dealt with the succession as such, if applicable;

(h)   the elements on which the applicant founds, as appropriate, his claimed right to succession property as a beneficiary and/or his right to execute the will of the deceased and/or to administer the estate of the deceased;

(i)   an indication of whether the deceased had made a disposition of property upon death; if neither the original nor a copy is appended, an indication regarding the location of the original;

(j)   an indication of whether the deceased had entered into a marriage contract or into a contract regarding a relationship which may have comparable effects to marriage; if neither the original nor a copy of the contract is appended, an indication regarding the location of the original;

(k)   an indication of whether any of the beneficiaries has made a declaration concerning acceptance or waiver of the succession;

(l)   a declaration stating that, to the applicant's best knowledge, no dispute is pending relating to the elements to be certified;

(m) any other information which the applicant deems useful for the purposes of the issue of the Certificate.

Article 66. Examination of the application

1. Upon receipt of the application the issuing authority shall verify the information and declarations and the documents and other evidence provided by the applicant. It shall carry out the enquiries necessary for that verification of its own motion where this is provided for or authorised by its own law, or shall invite the applicant to provide any further evidence which it deems necessary.

2. Where the applicant has been unable to produce copies of the relevant documents which satisfy the conditions necessary to establish their authenticity, the issuing authority may decide to accept other forms of evidence.

3. Where this is provided for by its own law and subject to the conditions laid down therein, the issuing authority may require that declarations be made on oath or by a statutory declaration in lieu of an oath.

4. The issuing authority shall take all necessary steps to inform the beneficiaries of the application for a Certificate. It shall, if necessary for the establishment of the elements to be certified, hear any person involved and any executor or administrator and make public announcements aimed at giving other possible beneficiaries the opportunity to invoke their rights.

5. For the purposes of this Article, the competent authority of a Member State shall, upon request, provide the issuing authority of another Member State with information held, in particular, in the land registers, the civil status registers and registers recording documents and facts of relevance for the succession or for the matrimonial property regime or an equivalent property regime of the deceased, where that competent authority would be authorised, under national law, to provide another national authority with such information.

Article 67. Issue of the Certificate

1. The issuing authority shall issue the Certificate without delay in accordance with the procedure laid down in this Chapter when the elements to be certified have been established under the law applicable to the succession or under any other law applicable to specific elements. It shall use the form established in accordance with the advisory procedure referred to in Article 81(2).

The issuing authority shall not issue the Certificate in particular if:

(a) the elements to be certified are being challenged; or

(b) the Certificate would not be in conformity with a decision covering the same elements.

2. The issuing authority shall take all necessary steps to inform the beneficiaries of the issue of the Certificate.

Article 68. Contents of the Certificate

The Certificate shall contain the following information, to the extent required for the purpose for which it is issued:

(a) the name and address of the issuing authority;

(b) the reference number of the file;

(c) the elements on the basis of which the issuing authority considers itself competent to issue the Certificate;

(d) the date of issue;

(e) details concerning the applicant: surname (if applicable, surname at birth), given name(s), sex, date and place of birth, civil status, nationality, identification number (if applicable), address and relationship to the deceased, if any;

(f) details concerning the deceased: surname (if applicable, surname at birth), given name(s), sex, date and place of birth, civil status, nationality, identification number (if applicable), address at the time of death, date and place of death;

(g)   details concerning the beneficiaries: surname (if applicable, surname at birth), given name(s) and identification number (if applicable);

(h)   information concerning a marriage contract entered into by the deceased or, if applicable, a contract entered into by the deceased in the context of a relationship deemed by the law applicable to such a relationship to have comparable effects to marriage, and information concerning the matrimonial property regime or equivalent property regime;

(i)   the law applicable to the succession and the elements on the basis of which that law has been determined;

(j)   information as to whether the succession is testate or intestate, including information concerning the elements giving rise to the rights and/or powers of the heirs, legatees, executors of wills or administrators of the estate;

(k)   if applicable, information in respect of each beneficiary concerning the nature of the acceptance or waiver of the succession;

(l)   the share for each heir and, if applicable, the list of rights and/or assets for any given heir;

(m)   the list of rights and/or assets for any given legatee;

(n)   the restrictions on the rights of the heir(s) and, as appropriate, legatee(s) under the law applicable to the succession and/or under the disposition of property upon death;

(o)   the powers of the executor of the will and/or the administrator of the estate and the restrictions on those powers under the law applicable to the succession and/or under the disposition of property upon death.

Article 69. Effects of the Certificate

1.   The Certificate shall produce its effects in all Member States, without any special procedure being required.

2.   The Certificate shall be presumed to accurately demonstrate elements which have been established under the law applicable to the succession or under any other law applicable to specific elements. The person mentioned in the Certificate as the heir, legatee, executor of the will or administrator of the estate shall be presumed to have the status mentioned in the Certificate and/or to hold the rights or the powers stated in the Certificate, with no conditions and/or restrictions being attached to those rights or powers other than those stated in the Certificate.

3.   Any person who, acting on the basis of the information certified in a Certificate, makes payments or passes on property to a person mentioned in the Certificate as authorised to accept payment or property shall be considered to have transacted with a person with authority to accept payment or property, unless he knows that the contents of the Certificate are not accurate or is unaware of such inaccuracy due to gross negligence.

4.   Where a person mentioned in the Certificate as authorised to dispose of succession property disposes of such property in favour of another person, that other person shall, if acting on the basis of the information certified in the Certificate, be considered to have transacted with a person with authority to dispose of the property concerned, unless he knows that the contents of the Certificate are not accurate or is unaware of such inaccuracy due to gross negligence.

5.   The Certificate shall constitute a valid document for the recording of succession property in the relevant register of a Member State, without prejudice to points (k) and (l) of Article 1(2).

Article 70. Certified copies of the Certificate

1.   The issuing authority shall keep the original of the Certificate and shall issue one or more certified copies to the applicant and to any person demonstrating a legitimate interest.

2.   The issuing authority shall, for the purposes of Articles 71(3) and 73(2), keep a list of persons to whom certified copies have been issued pursuant to paragraph 1.

3. The certified copies issued shall be valid for a limited period of six months, to be indicated in the certified copy by way of an expiry date. In exceptional, duly justified cases, the issuing authority may, by way of derogation, decide that the period of validity is to be longer. Once this period has elapsed, any person in possession of a certified copy must, in order to be able to use the Certificate for the purposes indicated in Article 63, apply for an extension of the period of validity of the certified copy or request a new certified copy from the issuing authority.

Article 71. Rectification, modification or withdrawal of the Certificate
1. The issuing authority shall, at the request of any person demonstrating a legitimate interest or of its own motion, rectify the Certificate in the event of a clerical error.
2. The issuing authority shall, at the request of any person demonstrating a legitimate interest or, where this is possible under national law, of its own motion, modify or withdraw the Certificate where it has been established that the Certificate or individual elements thereof are not accurate.
3. The issuing authority shall without delay inform all persons to whom certified copies of the Certificate have been issued pursuant to Article 70(1) of any rectification, modification or withdrawal thereof.

Article 72. Redress procedures
1. Decisions taken by the issuing authority pursuant to Article 67 may be challenged by any person entitled to apply for a Certificate.

Decisions taken by the issuing authority pursuant to Article 71 and point (a) of Article 73(1) may be challenged by any person demonstrating a legitimate interest.

The challenge shall be lodged before a judicial authority in the Member State of the issuing authority in accordance with the law of that State.
2. If, as a result of a challenge as referred to in paragraph 1, it is established that the Certificate issued is not accurate, the competent judicial authority shall rectify, modify or withdraw the Certificate or ensure that it is rectified, modified or withdrawn by the issuing authority.

If, as a result of a challenge as referred to in paragraph 1, it is established that the refusal to issue the Certificate was unjustified, the competent judicial authority shall issue the Certificate or ensure that the issuing authority re-assesses the case and makes a fresh decision.

Article 73. Suspension of the effects of the Certificate
1. The effects of the Certificate may be suspended by:
    (a) the issuing authority, at the request of any person demonstrating a legitimate interest, pending a modification or withdrawal of the Certificate pursuant to Article 71; or
    (b) the judicial authority, at the request of any person entitled to challenge a decision taken by the issuing authority pursuant to Article 72, pending such a challenge.
2. The issuing authority or, as the case may be, the judicial authority shall without delay inform all persons to whom certified copies of the Certificate have been issued pursuant to Article 70(1) of any suspension of the effects of the Certificate.

During the suspension of the effects of the Certificate no further certified copies of the Certificate may be issued.

CHAPTER VII
GENERAL AND FINAL PROVISIONS

Article 74. Legalisation and other similar formalities
No legalisation or other similar formality shall be required in respect of documents issued in a Member State in the context of this Regulation.

Article 75. Relationship with existing international conventions
1.   This Regulation shall not affect the application of international conventions to which one or more Member States are party at the time of adoption of this Regulation and which concern matters covered by this Regulation.

In particular, Member States which are Contracting Parties to the Hague Convention of 5 October 1961 on the Conflicts of Laws Relating to the Form of Testamentary Dispositions shall continue to apply the provisions of that Convention instead of Article 27 of this Regulation with regard to the formal validity of wills and joint wills.

2.   Notwithstanding paragraph 1, this Regulation shall, as between Member States, take precedence over conventions concluded exclusively between two or more of them in so far as such conventions concern matters governed by this Regulation.

3.   This Regulation shall not preclude the application of the Convention of 19 November 1934 between Denmark, Finland, Iceland, Norway and Sweden comprising private international law provisions on succession, wills and estate administration, as revised by the intergovernmental agreement between those States of 1 June 2012, by the Member States which are parties thereto, in so far as it provides for:

(a)   rules on the procedural aspects of estate administration as defined by the Convention and assistance in that regard by the authorities of the States Contracting Parties to the Convention; and

(b)   simplified and more expeditious procedures for the recognition and enforcement of decisions in matters of succession.

Article 76. Relationship with Council Regulation (EC) No 1346/2000
This Regulation shall not affect the application of Council Regulation (EC) No 1346/2000 of 29 May 2000 on insolvency proceedings.

Article 77. Information made available to the public
The Member States shall, with a view to making the information available to the public within the framework of the European Judicial Network in civil and commercial matters, provide the Commission with a short summary of their national legislation and procedures relating to succession, including information on the type of authority which has competence in matters of succession and information on the type of authority competent to receive declarations of acceptance or waiver of the succession, of a legacy or of a reserved share.

The Member States shall also provide fact sheets listing all the documents and/ or information usually required for the purposes of registration of immovable property located on their territory.

The Member States shall keep the information permanently updated.

Article 78. Information on contact details and procedures
1.   By 16 January 2014, the Member States shall communicate to the Commission:

(a)   the names and contact details of the courts or authorities with competence to deal with applications for a declaration of enforceability in accordance with Article 45(1) and with appeals against decisions on such applications in accordance with Article 50(2);

(b)   the procedures to contest the decision given on appeal referred to in Article 51;

(c)   the relevant information regarding the authorities competent to issue the Certificate pursuant to Article 64; and

(d)   the redress procedures referred to in Article 72.
The Member States shall apprise the Commission of any subsequent changes to that information.

2.   The Commission shall publish the information communicated in accordance

with paragraph 1 in the Official Journal of the European Union, with the exception of the addresses and other contact details of the courts and authorities referred to in point (a) of paragraph 1.

3. The Commission shall make all information communicated in accordance with paragraph 1 publicly available through any other appropriate means, in particular through the European Judicial Network in civil and commercial matters.

Article 79. Establishment and subsequent amendment of the list containing the information referred to in Article 3(2)

1. The Commission shall, on the basis of the notifications by the Member States, establish the list of the other authorities and legal professionals referred to in Article 3(2).

2. The Member States shall notify the Commission of any subsequent changes to the information contained in that list. The Commission shall amend the list accordingly.

3. The Commission shall publish the list and any subsequent amendments in the Official Journal of the European Union.

4. The Commission shall make all information notified in accordance with paragraphs 1 and 2 publicly available through any other appropriate means, in particular through the European Judicial Network in civil and commercial matters.

Article 80. Establishment and subsequent amendment of the attestations and forms referred to in Articles 46, 59, 60, 61, 65 and 67

The Commission shall adopt implementing acts establishing and subsequently amending the attestations and forms referred to in Articles 46, 59, 60, 61, 65 and 67. Those implementing acts shall be adopted in accordance with the advisory procedure referred to in Article 81(2).

Article 81. Committee procedure

1. The Commission shall be assisted by a committee. That committee shall be a committee within the meaning of Regulation (EU) No 182/2011.

2. Where reference is made to this paragraph, Article 4 of Regulation (EU) No 182/2011 shall apply.

Article 82. Review

By 18 August 2025 the Commission shall submit to the European Parliament, the Council and the European Economic and Social Committee a report on the application of this Regulation, including an evaluation of any practical problems encountered in relation to parallel out-of-court settlements of succession cases in different Member States or an out-of-court settlement in one Member State effected in parallel with a settlement before a court in another Member State. The report shall be accompanied, where appropriate, by proposals for amendments.

Article 83. Transitional provisions

1. This Regulation shall apply to the succession of persons who die on or after 17 August 2015.

2. Where the deceased had chosen the law applicable to his succession prior to 17 August 2015, that choice shall be valid if it meets the conditions laid down in Chapter III or if it is valid in application of the rules of private international law which were in force, at the time the choice was made, in the State in which the deceased had his habitual residence or in any of the States whose nationality he possessed.

3. A disposition of property upon death made prior to 17 August 2015 shall be admissible and valid in substantive terms and as regards form if it meets the conditions laid down in Chapter III or if it is admissible and valid in substantive terms and as regards form in application of the rules of private international law which were in force, at the time the disposition was made, in the State in which

the deceased had his habitual residence or in any of the States whose nationality he possessed or in the Member State of the authority dealing with the succession.

4.   If a disposition of property upon death was made prior to 17 August 2015 in accordance with the law which the deceased could have chosen in accordance with this Regulation, that law shall be deemed to have been chosen as the law applicable to the succession.

Article 84. Entry into force
This Regulation shall enter into force on the twentieth day following that of its publication in the Official Journal of the European Union.

It shall apply from 17 August 2015, except for Articles 77 and 78, which shall apply from 16 January 2014, and Articles 79, 80 and 81, which shall apply from 5 July 2012.

This Regulation shall be binding in its entirety and directly applicable in the Member States in accordance with the Treaties.

Done at Strasbourg, 4 July 2012.

REGULATION (EU) NO 1215/2012 OF THE EUROPEAN PARLIAMENT AND OF THE COUNCIL OF 12 DECEMBER 2012 ON JURISDICTION AND THE RECOGNITION AND ENFORCEMENT OF JUDGMENTS IN CIVIL AND COMMERCIAL MATTERS (RECAST)

Official Journal L 351, 20/12/2012 pp 1–32

THE EUROPEAN PARLIAMENT AND THE COUNCIL OF THE EUROPEAN UNION,

Having regard to the Treaty on the Functioning of the European Union, and in particular Article 67(4) and points (a), (c) and (e) of Article 81(2) thereof,
    Having regard to the proposal from the European Commission,
    After transmission of the draft legislative act to the national parliaments,
    Having regard to the opinion of the European Economic and Social Committee,
    Acting in accordance with the ordinary legislative procedure,

Whereas:

(1)   On 21 April 2009, the Commission adopted a report on the application of Council Regulation (EC) No 44/2001 of 22 December 2000 on jurisdiction and the recognition and enforcement of judgments in civil and commercial matters. The report concluded that, in general, the operation of that Regulation is satisfactory, but that it is desirable to improve the application of certain of its provisions, to further facilitate the free circulation of judgments and to further enhance access to justice. Since a number of amendments are to be made to that Regulation it should, in the interests of clarity, be recast.

(2)   At its meeting in Brussels on 10 and 11 December 2009, the European Council adopted a new multiannual programme entitled 'The Stockholm Programme – an open and secure Europe serving and protecting citizens'. In the Stockholm Programme the European Council considered that the process of abolishing all intermediate measures (the exequatur) should be continued during the period covered by that Programme. At the same time the abolition of the exequatur should also be accompanied by a series of safeguards.

(3)   The Union has set itself the objective of maintaining and developing an area of freedom, security and justice, inter alia, by facilitating access to justice, in parti-

cular through the principle of mutual recognition of judicial and extra-judicial decisions in civil matters. For the gradual establishment of such an area, the Union is to adopt measures relating to judicial cooperation in civil matters having cross-border implications, particularly when necessary for the proper functioning of the internal market.

(4)   Certain differences between national rules governing jurisdiction and recognition of judgments hamper the sound operation of the internal market. Provisions to unify the rules of conflict of jurisdiction in civil and commercial matters, and to ensure rapid and simple recognition and enforcement of judgments given in a Member State, are essential.

(5)   Such provisions fall within the area of judicial cooperation in civil matters within the meaning of Article 81 of the Treaty on the Functioning of the European Union (TFEU).

(6)   In order to attain the objective of free circulation of judgments in civil and commercial matters, it is necessary and appropriate that the rules governing jurisdiction and the recognition and enforcement of judgments be governed by a legal instrument of the Union which is binding and directly applicable.

(7)   On 27 September 1968, the then Member States of the European Communities, acting under Article 220, fourth indent, of the Treaty establishing the European Economic Community, concluded the Brussels Convention on Jurisdiction and the Enforcement of Judgments in Civil and Commercial Matters, subsequently amended by conventions on the accession to that Convention of new Member States ('the 1968 Brussels Convention'). On 16 September 1988, the then Member States of the European Communities and certain EFTA States concluded the Lugano Convention on Jurisdiction and the Enforcement of Judgments in Civil and Commercial Matters ('the 1988 Lugano Convention'), which is a parallel convention to the 1968 Brussels Convention. The 1988 Lugano Convention became applicable to Poland on 1 February 2000.

(8)   On 22 December 2000, the Council adopted Regulation (EC) No 44/2001, which replaces the 1968 Brussels Convention with regard to the territories of the Member States covered by the TFEU, as between the Member States except Denmark. By Council Decision 2006/325/EC, the Community concluded an agreement with Denmark ensuring the application of the provisions of Regulation (EC) No 44/2001 in Denmark. The 1988 Lugano Convention was revised by the Convention on Jurisdiction and the Recognition and Enforcement of Judgments in Civil and Commercial Matters, signed at Lugano on 30 October 2007 by the Community, Denmark, Iceland, Norway and Switzerland ('the 2007 Lugano Convention').

(9)   The 1968 Brussels Convention continues to apply to the territories of the Member States which fall within the territorial scope of that Convention and which are excluded from this Regulation pursuant to Article 355 of the TFEU.

(10)   The scope of this Regulation should cover all the main civil and commercial matters apart from certain well-defined matters, in particular maintenance obligations, which should be excluded from the scope of this Regulation following the adoption of Council Regulation (EC) No 4/2009 of 18 December 2008 on jurisdiction, applicable law, recognition and enforcement of decisions and cooperation in matters relating to maintenance obligations.

(11)   For the purposes of this Regulation, courts or tribunals of the Member States should include courts or tribunals common to several Member States, such as the Benelux Court of Justice when it exercises jurisdiction on matters falling within the scope of this Regulation. Therefore, judgments given by such courts should be recognised and enforced in accordance with this Regulation.

(12)   This Regulation should not apply to arbitration. Nothing in this Regulation should prevent the courts of a Member State, when seised of an action in a matter in respect of which the parties have entered into an arbitration agreement, from

referring the parties to arbitration, from staying or dismissing the proceedings, or from examining whether the arbitration agreement is null and void, inoperative or incapable of being performed, in accordance with their national law.

A ruling given by a court of a Member State as to whether or not an arbitration agreement is null and void, inoperative or incapable of being performed should not be subject to the rules of recognition and enforcement laid down in this Regulation, regardless of whether the court decided on this as a principal issue or as an incidental question.

On the other hand, where a court of a Member State, exercising jurisdiction under this Regulation or under national law, has determined that an arbitration agreement is null and void, inoperative or incapable of being performed, this should not preclude that court's judgment on the substance of the matter from being recognised or, as the case may be, enforced in accordance with this Regulation. This should be without prejudice to the competence of the courts of the Member States to decide on the recognition and enforcement of arbitral awards in accordance with the Convention on the Recognition and Enforcement of Foreign Arbitral Awards, done at New York on 10 June 1958 ('the 1958 New York Convention'), which takes precedence over this Regulation.

This Regulation should not apply to any action or ancillary proceedings relating to, in particular, the establishment of an arbitral tribunal, the powers of arbitrators, the conduct of an arbitration procedure or any other aspects of such a procedure, nor to any action or judgment concerning the annulment, review, appeal, recognition or enforcement of an arbitral award.

(13)   There must be a connection between proceedings to which this Regulation applies and the territory of the Member States. Accordingly, common rules of jurisdiction should, in principle, apply when the defendant is domiciled in a Member State.

(14)   A defendant not domiciled in a Member State should in general be subject to the national rules of jurisdiction applicable in the territory of the Member State of the court seised.

However, in order to ensure the protection of consumers and employees, to safeguard the jurisdiction of the courts of the Member States in situations where they have exclusive jurisdiction and to respect the autonomy of the parties, certain rules of jurisdiction in this Regulation should apply regardless of the defendant's domicile.

(15)   The rules of jurisdiction should be highly predictable and founded on the principle that jurisdiction is generally based on the defendant's domicile. Jurisdiction should always be available on this ground save in a few well-defined situations in which the subject-matter of the dispute or the autonomy of the parties warrants a different connecting factor. The domicile of a legal person must be defined autonomously so as to make the common rules more transparent and avoid conflicts of jurisdiction.

(16)   In addition to the defendant's domicile, there should be alternative grounds of jurisdiction based on a close connection between the court and the action or in order to facilitate the sound administration of justice. The existence of a close connection should ensure legal certainty and avoid the possibility of the defendant being sued in a court of a Member State which he could not reasonably have foreseen. This is important, particularly in disputes concerning non-contractual obligations arising out of violations of privacy and rights relating to personality, including defamation.

(17)   The owner of a cultural object as defined in Article 1(1) of Council Directive 93/7/EEC of 15 March 1993 on the return of cultural objects unlawfully removed from the territory of a Member State should be able under this Regulation to initiate proceedings as regards a civil claim for the recovery, based on ownership, of such a cultural object in the courts for the place where the cultural object is situated at the time the court is seised. Such proceedings

should be without prejudice to proceedings initiated under Directive 93/7/EEC.

(18) In relation to insurance, consumer and employment contracts, the weaker party should be protected by rules of jurisdiction more favourable to his interests than the general rules.

(19) The autonomy of the parties to a contract, other than an insurance, consumer or employment contract, where only limited autonomy to determine the courts having jurisdiction is allowed, should be respected subject to the exclusive grounds of jurisdiction laid down in this Regulation.

(20) Where a question arises as to whether a choice-of-court agreement in favour of a court or the courts of a Member State is null and void as to its substantive validity, that question should be decided in accordance with the law of the Member State of the court or courts designated in the agreement, including the conflict-of-laws rules of that Member State.

(21) In the interests of the harmonious administration of justice it is necessary to minimise the possibility of concurrent proceedings and to ensure that irreconcilable judgments will not be given in different Member States. There should be a clear and effective mechanism for resolving cases of lis pendens and related actions, and for obviating problems flowing from national differences as to the determination of the time when a case is regarded as pending. For the purposes of this Regulation, that time should be defined autonomously.

(22) However, in order to enhance the effectiveness of exclusive choice-of-court agreements and to avoid abusive litigation tactics, it is necessary to provide for an exception to the general lis pendens rule in order to deal satisfactorily with a particular situation in which concurrent proceedings may arise. This is the situation where a court not designated in an exclusive choice-of-court agreement has been seised of proceedings and the designated court is seised subsequently of proceedings involving the same cause of action and between the same parties. In such a case, the court first seised should be required to stay its proceedings as soon as the designated court has been seised and until such time as the latter court declares that it has no jurisdiction under the exclusive choice-of-court agreement. This is to ensure that, in such a situation, the designated court has priority to decide on the validity of the agreement and on the extent to which the agreement applies to the dispute pending before it. The designated court should be able to proceed irrespective of whether the non-designated court has already decided on the stay of proceedings.

This exception should not cover situations where the parties have entered into conflicting exclusive choice-of-court agreements or where a court designated in an exclusive choice-of-court agreement has been seised first. In such cases, the general lis pendens rule of this Regulation should apply.

(23) This Regulation should provide for a flexible mechanism allowing the courts of the Member States to take into account proceedings pending before the courts of third States, considering in particular whether a judgment of a third State will be capable of recognition and enforcement in the Member State concerned under the law of that Member State and the proper administration of justice.

(24) When taking into account the proper administration of justice, the court of the Member State concerned should assess all the circumstances of the case before it. Such circumstances may include connections between the facts of the case and the parties and the third State concerned, the stage to which the proceedings in the third State have progressed by the time proceedings are initiated in the court of the Member State and whether or not the court of the third State can be expected to give a judgment within a reasonable time.

That assessment may also include consideration of the question whether the court of the third State has exclusive jurisdiction in the particular case in circumstances where a court of a Member State would have exclusive jurisdiction.

(25) The notion of provisional, including protective, measures should include,

for example, protective orders aimed at obtaining information or preserving evidence as referred to in Articles 6 and 7 of Directive 2004/48/EC of the European Parliament and of the Council of 29 April 2004 on the enforcement of intellectual property rights. It should not include measures which are not of a protective nature, such as measures ordering the hearing of a witness. This should be without prejudice to the application of Council Regulation (EC) No 1206/2001 of 28 May 2001 on cooperation between the courts of the Member States in the taking of evidence in civil or commercial matters.

(26)   Mutual trust in the administration of justice in the Union justifies the principle that judgments given in a Member State should be recognised in all Member States without the need for any special procedure. In addition, the aim of making cross-border litigation less time-consuming and costly justifies the abolition of the declaration of enforceability prior to enforcement in the Member State addressed. As a result, a judgment given by the courts of a Member State should be treated as if it had been given in the Member State addressed.

(27)   For the purposes of the free circulation of judgments, a judgment given in a Member State should be recognised and enforced in another Member State even if it is given against a person not domiciled in a Member State.

(28)   Where a judgment contains a measure or order which is not known in the law of the Member State addressed, that measure or order, including any right indicated therein, should, to the extent possible, be adapted to one which, under the law of that Member State, has equivalent effects attached to it and pursues similar aims. How, and by whom, the adaptation is to be carried out should be determined by each Member State.

(29)   The direct enforcement in the Member State addressed of a judgment given in another Member State without a declaration of enforceability should not jeopardise respect for the rights of the defence. Therefore, the person against whom enforcement is sought should be able to apply for refusal of the recognition or enforcement of a judgment if he considers one of the grounds for refusal of recognition to be present. This should include the ground that he had not had the opportunity to arrange for his defence where the judgment was given in default of appearance in a civil action linked to criminal proceedings. It should also include the grounds which could be invoked on the basis of an agreement between the Member State addressed and a third State concluded pursuant to Article 59 of the 1968 Brussels Convention.

(30)   A party challenging the enforcement of a judgment given in another Member State should, to the extent possible and in accordance with the legal system of the Member State addressed, be able to invoke, in the same procedure, in addition to the grounds for refusal provided for in this Regulation, the grounds for refusal available under national law and within the time-limits laid down in that law.

The recognition of a judgment should, however, be refused only if one or more of the grounds for refusal provided for in this Regulation are present.

(31)   Pending a challenge to the enforcement of a judgment, it should be possible for the courts in the Member State addressed, during the entire proceedings relating to such a challenge, including any appeal, to allow the enforcement to proceed subject to a limitation of the enforcement or to the provision of security.

(32)   In order to inform the person against whom enforcement is sought of the enforcement of a judgment given in another Member State, the certificate established under this Regulation, if necessary accompanied by the judgment, should be served on that person in reasonable time before the first enforcement measure. In this context, the first enforcement measure should mean the first enforcement measure after such service.

(33)   Where provisional, including protective, measures are ordered by a court having jurisdiction as to the substance of the matter, their free circulation should

be ensured under this Regulation. However, provisional, including protective, measures which were ordered by such a court without the defendant being summoned to appear should not be recognised and enforced under this Regulation unless the judgment containing the measure is served on the defendant prior to enforcement. This should not preclude the recognition and enforcement of such measures under national law. Where provisional, including protective, measures are ordered by a court of a Member State not having jurisdiction as to the substance of the matter, the effect of such measures should be confined, under this Regulation, to the territory of that Member State.

(34)   Continuity between the 1968 Brussels Convention, Regulation (EC) No 44/2001 and this Regulation should be ensured, and transitional provisions should be laid down to that end. The same need for continuity applies as regards the interpretation by the Court of Justice of the European Union of the 1968 Brussels Convention and of the Regulations replacing it.

(35)   Respect for international commitments entered into by the Member States means that this Regulation should not affect conventions relating to specific matters to which the Member States are parties.

(36)   Without prejudice to the obligations of the Member States under the Treaties, this Regulation should not affect the application of bilateral conventions and agreements between a third State and a Member State concluded before the date of entry into force of Regulation (EC) No 44/2001 which concern matters governed by this Regulation.

(37)   In order to ensure that the certificates to be used in connection with the recognition or enforcement of judgments, authentic instruments and court settlements under this Regulation are kept up-to-date, the power to adopt acts in accordance with Article 290 of the TFEU should be delegated to the Commission in respect of amendments to Annexes I and II to this Regulation. It is of particular importance that the Commission carry out appropriate consultations during its preparatory work, including at expert level. The Commission, when preparing and drawing up delegated acts, should ensure a simultaneous, timely and appropriate transmission of relevant documents to the European Parliament and to the Council.

(38)   This Regulation respects fundamental rights and observes the principles recognised in the Charter of Fundamental Rights of the European Union, in particular the right to an effective remedy and to a fair trial guaranteed in Article 47 of the Charter.

(39)   Since the objective of this Regulation cannot be sufficiently achieved by the Member States and can be better achieved at Union level, the Union may adopt measures in accordance with the principle of subsidiarity as set out in Article 5 of the Treaty on European Union (TEU). In accordance with the principle of proportionality, as set out in that Article, this Regulation does not go beyond what is necessary in order to achieve that objective.

(40)   The United Kingdom and Ireland, in accordance with Article 3 of the Protocol on the position of the United Kingdom and Ireland, annexed to the TEU and to the then Treaty establishing the European Community, took part in the adoption and application of Regulation (EC) No 44/2001. In accordance with Article 3 of Protocol No 21 on the position of the United Kingdom and Ireland in respect of the area of freedom, security and justice, annexed to the TEU and to the TFEU, the United Kingdom and Ireland have notified their wish to take part in the adoption and application of this Regulation.

(41)   In accordance with Articles 1 and 2 of Protocol No 22 on the position of Denmark annexed to the TEU and to the TFEU, Denmark is not taking part in the adoption of this Regulation and is not bound by it or subject to its application, without prejudice to the possibility for Denmark of applying the amendments to Regulation (EC) No 44/2001 pursuant to Article 3 of the Agreement of 19 October 2005 between the European Community and the Kingdom of Denmark on juris-

diction and the recognition and enforcement of judgments in civil and commercial matters,*

HAVE ADOPTED THIS REGULATION:

CHAPTER I
SCOPE AND DEFINITIONS

Article 1

1. This Regulation shall apply in civil and commercial matters whatever the nature of the court or tribunal. It shall not extend, in particular, to revenue, customs or administrative matters or to the liability of the State for acts and omissions in the exercise of State authority (acta iure imperii).

2. This Regulation shall not apply to:

(a)   the status or legal capacity of natural persons, rights in property arising out of a matrimonial relationship or out of a relationship deemed by the law applicable to such relationship to have comparable effects to marriage;

(b)   bankruptcy, proceedings relating to the winding-up of insolvent companies or other legal persons, judicial arrangements, compositions and analogous proceedings;

(c)   social security;

(d)   arbitration;

(e)   maintenance obligations arising from a family relationship, parentage, marriage or affinity;

(f)   wills and succession, including maintenance obligations arising by reason of death.

Article 2

For the purposes of this Regulation:

(a)   judgment' means any judgment given by a court or tribunal of a Member State, whatever the judgment may be called, including a decree, order, decision or writ of execution, as well as a decision on the determination of costs or expenses by an officer of the court.

For the purposes of Chapter III, 'judgment' includes provisional, including protective, measures ordered by a court or tribunal which by virtue of this Regulation has jurisdiction as to the substance of the matter. It does not include a provisional, including protective, measure which is ordered by such a court or tribunal without the defendant being summoned to appear, unless the judgment containing the measure is served on the defendant prior to enforcement;

(b)   'court settlement' means a settlement which has been approved by a court of a Member State or concluded before a court of a Member State in the course of proceedings;

(c)   'authentic instrument' means a document which has been formally drawn up or registered as an authentic instrument in the Member State of origin and the authenticity of which:

(i)   relates to the signature and the content of the instrument; and

(ii)   has been established by a public authority or other authority empowered for that purpose;

(d)   'Member State of origin' means the Member State in which, as the case may be, the judgment has been given, the court settlement has been approved or concluded, or the authentic instrument has been formally drawn up or registered;

---

*But see Agreement between the European Community and the Kingdom of Denmark on jurisdiction and the recognition and enforcement of judgments in civil and commercial matters (implementing Regulation (EU) No 1215/2012): p 434 below.

(e) 'Member State addressed' means the Member State in which the recognition of the judgment is invoked or in which the enforcement of the judgment, the court settlement or the authentic instrument is sought;

(f) 'court of origin' means the court which has given the judgment the recognition of which is invoked or the enforcement of which is sought.

Article 3
For the purposes of this Regulation, 'court' includes the following authorities to the extent that they have jurisdiction in matters falling within the scope of this Regulation:

(a) in Hungary, in summary proceedings concerning orders to pay (fizetési meghagyásos eljárás), the notary (közjegyző);

(b) in Sweden, in summary proceedings concerning orders to pay (betalningsföreläggande) and assistance (handräckning), the Enforcement Authority (Kronofogdemyndigheten).

CHAPTER II
JURISDICTION

Section 1
General provisions

Article 4
1. Subject to this Regulation, persons domiciled in a Member State shall, whatever their nationality, be sued in the courts of that Member State.

2. Persons who are not nationals of the Member State in which they are domiciled shall be governed by the rules of jurisdiction applicable to nationals of that Member State.

Article 5
1. Persons domiciled in a Member State may be sued in the courts of another Member State only by virtue of the rules set out in Sections 2 to 7 of this Chapter.

2. In particular, the rules of national jurisdiction of which the Member States are to notify the Commission pursuant to point (a) of Article 76(1) shall not be applicable as against the persons referred to in paragraph 1.

Article 6
1. If the defendant is not domiciled in a Member State, the jurisdiction of the courts of each Member State shall, subject to Article 18(1), Article 21(2) and Articles 24 and 25, be determined by the law of that Member State.

2. As against such a defendant, any person domiciled in a Member State may, whatever his nationality, avail himself in that Member State of the rules of jurisdiction there in force, and in particular those of which the Member States are to notify the Commission pursuant to point (a) of Article 76(1), in the same way as nationals of that Member State.

Section 2
Special jurisdiction

Article 7
A person domiciled in a Member State may be sued in another Member State:

(1) (a) in matters relating to a contract, in the courts for the place of performance of the obligation in question;

(b) for the purpose of this provision and unless otherwise agreed, the place of performance of the obligation in question shall be:
—in the case of the sale of goods, the place in a Member State where, under the contract, the goods were delivered or should have been delivered,
—in the case of the provision of services, the place in a Member State

where, under the contract, the services were provided or should have been provided;

(c)   if point (b) does not apply then point (a) applies;

(2)   in matters relating to tort, delict or quasi-delict, in the courts for the place where the harmful event occurred or may occur;

(3)   as regards a civil claim for damages or restitution which is based on an act giving rise to criminal proceedings, in the court seised of those proceedings, to the extent that that court has jurisdiction under its own law to entertain civil proceedings;

(4)   as regards a civil claim for the recovery, based on ownership, of a cultural object as defined in point 1 of Article 1 of Directive 93/7/EEC initiated by the person claiming the right to recover such an object, in the courts for the place where the cultural object is situated at the time when the court is seised;

(5)   as regards a dispute arising out of the operations of a branch, agency or other establishment, in the courts for the place where the branch, agency or other establishment is situated;

(6)   as regards a dispute brought against a settlor, trustee or beneficiary of a trust created by the operation of a statute, or by a written instrument, or created orally and evidenced in writing, in the courts of the Member State in which the trust is domiciled;

(7)   as regards a dispute concerning the payment of remuneration claimed in respect of the salvage of a cargo or freight, in the court under the authority of which the cargo or freight in question:

(a)   has been arrested to secure such payment; or

(b)   could have been so arrested, but bail or other security has been given; provided that this provision shall apply only if it is claimed that the defendant has an interest in the cargo or freight or had such an interest at the time of salvage.

Article 8
A person domiciled in a Member State may also be sued:

(1)   where he is one of a number of defendants, in the courts for the place where any one of them is domiciled, provided the claims are so closely connected that it is expedient to hear and determine them together to avoid the risk of irreconcilable judgments resulting from separate proceedings;

(2)   as a third party in an action on a warranty or guarantee or in any other third-party proceedings, in the court seised of the original proceedings, unless these were instituted solely with the object of removing him from the jurisdiction of the court which would be competent in his case;

(3)   on a counter-claim arising from the same contract or facts on which the original claim was based, in the court in which the original claim is pending;

(4)   in matters relating to a contract, if the action may be combined with an action against the same defendant in matters relating to rights in rem in immovable property, in the court of the Member State in which the property is situated.

Article 9
Where by virtue of this Regulation a court of a Member State has jurisdiction in actions relating to liability from the use or operation of a ship, that court, or any other court substituted for this purpose by the internal law of that Member State, shall also have jurisdiction over claims for limitation of such liability.

Section 3

Jurisdiction in matters relating to insurance

Article 10
In matters relating to insurance, jurisdiction shall be determined by this Section, without prejudice to Article 6 and point 5 of Article 7.

Article 11

1.   An insurer domiciled in a Member State may be sued:

(a)   in the courts of the Member State in which he is domiciled;

(b)   in another Member State, in the case of actions brought by the policy-holder, the insured or a beneficiary, in the courts for the place where the claimant is domiciled; or

(c)   if he is a co-insurer, in the courts of a Member State in which proceedings are brought against the leading insurer.

2.   An insurer who is not domiciled in a Member State but has a branch, agency or other establishment in one of the Member States shall, in disputes arising out of the operations of the branch, agency or establishment, be deemed to be domiciled in that Member State.

Article 12

In respect of liability insurance or insurance of immovable property, the insurer may in addition be sued in the courts for the place where the harmful event occurred. The same applies if movable and immovable property are covered by the same insurance policy and both are adversely affected by the same contingency.

Article 13

1.   In respect of liability insurance, the insurer may also, if the law of the court permits it, be joined in proceedings which the injured party has brought against the insured.

2.   Articles 10, 11 and 12 shall apply to actions brought by the injured party directly against the insurer, where such direct actions are permitted.

3.   If the law governing such direct actions provides that the policyholder or the insured may be joined as a party to the action, the same court shall have jurisdiction over them.

Article 14

1.   Without prejudice to Article 13(3), an insurer may bring proceedings only in the courts of the Member State in which the defendant is domiciled, irrespective of whether he is the policyholder, the insured or a beneficiary.

2.   The provisions of this Section shall not affect the right to bring a counter-claim in the court in which, in accordance with this Section, the original claim is pending.

Article 15

The provisions of this Section may be departed from only by an agreement:

(1)   which is entered into after the dispute has arisen;

(2)   which allows the policyholder, the insured or a beneficiary to bring proceedings in courts other than those indicated in this Section;

(3)   which is concluded between a policyholder and an insurer, both of whom are at the time of conclusion of the contract domiciled or habitually resident in the same Member State, and which has the effect of conferring jurisdiction on the courts of that Member State even if the harmful event were to occur abroad, provided that such an agreement is not contrary to the law of that Member State;

(4)   which is concluded with a policyholder who is not domiciled in a Member State, except in so far as the insurance is compulsory or relates to immovable property in a Member State; or

(5)   which relates to a contract of insurance in so far as it covers one or more of the risks set out in Article 16.

Article 16

The following are the risks referred to in point 5 of Article 15:

(1)   any loss of or damage to:

(a)   seagoing ships, installations situated offshore or on the high seas, or air-craft, arising from perils which relate to their use for commercial purposes;

(b)   goods in transit other than passengers' baggage where the transit con-sists of or includes carriage by such ships or aircraft;

(2)   any liability, other than for bodily injury to passengers or loss of or damage to their baggage:

(a)   arising out of the use or operation of ships, installations or aircraft as referred to in point 1(a) in so far as, in respect of the latter, the law of the Member State in which such aircraft are registered does not prohibit agreements on jurisdiction regarding insurance of such risks;

(b)   for loss or damage caused by goods in transit as described in point 1(b);

(3)   any financial loss connected with the use or operation of ships, installations or aircraft as referred to in point 1(a), in particular loss of freight or charter-hire;

(4)   any risk or interest connected with any of those referred to in points 1 to 3;

(5)   notwithstanding points 1 to 4, all 'large risks' as defined in Directive 2009/138/EC of the European Parliament and of the Council of 25 November 2009 on the taking-up and pursuit of the business of Insurance and Reinsurance (Solvency II).

Section 4
Jurisdiction over consumer contracts

Article 17

1.   In matters relating to a contract concluded by a person, the consumer, for a purpose which can be regarded as being outside his trade or profession, juris-diction shall be determined by this Section, without prejudice to Article 6 and point 5 of Article 7, if:

(a)   it is a contract for the sale of goods on instalment credit terms;

(b)   it is a contract for a loan repayable by instalments, or for any other form of credit, made to finance the sale of goods; or

(c)   in all other cases, the contract has been concluded with a person who pursues commercial or professional activities in the Member State of the con-sumer's domicile or, by any means, directs such activities to that Member State or to several States including that Member State, and the contract falls within the scope of such activities.

2.   Where a consumer enters into a contract with a party who is not domiciled in a Member State but has a branch, agency or other establishment in one of the Member States, that party shall, in disputes arising out of the operations of the branch, agency or establishment, be deemed to be domiciled in that Member State.

3.   This Section shall not apply to a contract of transport other than a contract which, for an inclusive price, provides for a combination of travel and accom-modation.

Article 18

1.   A consumer may bring proceedings against the other party to a contract either in the courts of the Member State in which that party is domiciled or, regardless of the domicile of the other party, in the courts for the place where the consumer is domiciled.

2.   Proceedings may be brought against a consumer by the other party to the contract only in the courts of the Member State in which the consumer is domiciled.

3.   This Article shall not affect the right to bring a counter-claim in the court in which, in accordance with this Section, the original claim is pending.

Article 19

The provisions of this Section may be departed from only by an agreement:

(1)   which is entered into after the dispute has arisen;

(2)   which allows the consumer to bring proceedings in courts other than those indicated in this Section; or

(3)   which is entered into by the consumer and the other party to the contract, both of whom are at the time of conclusion of the contract domiciled or habitually resident in the same Member State, and which confers jurisdiction on the courts of that Member State, provided that such an agreement is not contrary to the law of that Member State.

Section 5
Jurisdiction over individual contracts of employment

Article 20

1.   In matters relating to individual contracts of employment, jurisdiction shall be determined by this Section, without prejudice to Article 6, point 5 of Article 7 and, in the case of proceedings brought against an employer, point 1 of Article 8.

2.   Where an employee enters into an individual contract of employment with an employer who is not domiciled in a Member State but has a branch, agency or other establishment in one of the Member States, the employer shall, in disputes arising out of the operations of the branch, agency or establishment, be deemed to be domiciled in that Member State.

Article 21

1.   An employer domiciled in a Member State may be sued:

(a)   in the courts of the Member State in which he is domiciled; or

(b)   in another Member State:

(i)   in the courts for the place where or from where the employee habitually carries out his work or in the courts for the last place where he did so; or

(ii)   if the employee does not or did not habitually carry out his work in any one country, in the courts for the place where the business which engaged the employee is or was situated.

2.   An employer not domiciled in a Member State may be sued in a court of a Member State in accordance with point (b) of paragraph 1.

Article 22

1.   An employer may bring proceedings only in the courts of the Member State in which the employee is domiciled.

2.   The provisions of this Section shall not affect the right to bring a counterclaim in the court in which, in accordance with this Section, the original claim is pending.

Article 23

The provisions of this Section may be departed from only by an agreement:

(1)   which is entered into after the dispute has arisen; or

(2)   which allows the employee to bring proceedings in courts other than those indicated in this Section.

Section 6
Exclusive jurisdiction

Article 24

The following courts of a Member State shall have exclusive jurisdiction, regardless of the domicile of the parties:

(1)   in proceedings which have as their object rights in rem in immovable property or tenancies of immovable property, the courts of the Member State in which the property is situated.

However, in proceedings which have as their object tenancies of immovable property concluded for temporary private use for a maximum period of six consecutive months, the courts of the Member State in which the defendant is domiciled shall also have jurisdiction, provided that the tenant is a natural person and that the landlord and the tenant are domiciled in the same Member State;

(2)   in proceedings which have as their object the validity of the constitution, the nullity or the dissolution of companies or other legal persons or associations of natural or legal persons, or the validity of the decisions of their organs, the courts of the Member State in which the company, legal person or association has its seat. In order to determine that seat, the court shall apply its rules of private international law;

(3)   in proceedings which have as their object the validity of entries in public registers, the courts of the Member State in which the register is kept;

(4)   in proceedings concerned with the registration or validity of patents, trade marks, designs, or other similar rights required to be deposited or registered, irrespective of whether the issue is raised by way of an action or as a defence, the courts of the Member State in which the deposit or registration has been applied for, has taken place or is under the terms of an instrument of the Union or an international convention deemed to have taken place.

Without prejudice to the jurisdiction of the European Patent Office under the Convention on the Grant of European Patents, signed at Munich on 5 October 1973, the courts of each Member State shall have exclusive jurisdiction in proceedings concerned with the registration or validity of any European patent granted for that Member State;

(5)   in proceedings concerned with the enforcement of judgments, the courts of the Member State in which the judgment has been or is to be enforced.

Section 7
Prorogation of jurisdiction

Article 25

1.   If the parties, regardless of their domicile, have agreed that a court or the courts of a Member State are to have jurisdiction to settle any disputes which have arisen or which may arise in connection with a particular legal relationship, that court or those courts shall have jurisdiction, unless the agreement is null and void as to its substantive validity under the law of that Member State. Such jurisdiction shall be exclusive unless the parties have agreed otherwise. The agreement conferring jurisdiction shall be either:

(a)   in writing or evidenced in writing;

(b)   in a form which accords with practices which the parties have established between themselves; or

(c)   in international trade or commerce, in a form which accords with a usage of which the parties are or ought to have been aware and which in such trade or commerce is widely known to, and regularly observed by, parties to contracts of the type involved in the particular trade or commerce concerned.

2.   Any communication by electronic means which provides a durable record of the agreement shall be equivalent to 'writing'.

3.   The court or courts of a Member State on which a trust instrument has conferred jurisdiction shall have exclusive jurisdiction in any proceedings brought against a settlor, trustee or beneficiary, if relations between those persons or their rights or obligations under the trust are involved.

4.   Agreements or provisions of a trust instrument conferring jurisdiction shall have no legal force if they are contrary to Articles 15, 19 or 23, or if the courts whose jurisdiction they purport to exclude have exclusive jurisdiction by virtue of Article 24.

5.   An agreement conferring jurisdiction which forms part of a contract shall be treated as an agreement independent of the other terms of the contract.

The validity of the agreement conferring jurisdiction cannot be contested solely on the ground that the contract is not valid.

Article 26

1. Apart from jurisdiction derived from other provisions of this Regulation, a court of a Member State before which a defendant enters an appearance shall have jurisdiction. This rule shall not apply where appearance was entered to contest the jurisdiction, or where another court has exclusive jurisdiction by virtue of Article 24.

2. In matters referred to in Sections 3, 4 or 5 where the policyholder, the insured, a beneficiary of the insurance contract, the injured party, the consumer or the employee is the defendant, the court shall, before assuming jurisdiction under paragraph 1, ensure that the defendant is informed of his right to contest the jurisdiction of the court and of the consequences of entering or not entering an appearance.

Section 8
Examination as to jurisdiction and admissibility

Article 27

Where a court of a Member State is seised of a claim which is principally concerned with a matter over which the courts of another Member State have exclusive jurisdiction by virtue of Article 24, it shall declare of its own motion that it has no jurisdiction.

Article 28

1. Where a defendant domiciled in one Member State is sued in a court of another Member State and does not enter an appearance, the court shall declare of its own motion that it has no jurisdiction unless its jurisdiction is derived from the provisions of this Regulation.

2. The court shall stay the proceedings so long as it is not shown that the defendant has been able to receive the document instituting the proceedings or an equivalent document in sufficient time to enable him to arrange for his defence, or that all necessary steps have been taken to this end.

3. Article 19 of Regulation (EC) No 1393/2007 of the European Parliament and of the Council of 13 November 2007 on the service in the Member States of judicial and extrajudicial documents in civil or commercial matters (service of documents) shall apply instead of paragraph 2 of this Article if the document instituting the proceedings or an equivalent document had to be transmitted from one Member State to another pursuant to that Regulation.

4. Where Regulation (EC) No 1393/2007 is not applicable, Article 15 of the Hague Convention of 15 November 1965 on the Service Abroad of Judicial and Extrajudicial Documents in Civil or Commercial Matters shall apply if the document instituting the proceedings or an equivalent document had to be transmitted abroad pursuant to that Convention.

Section 9
Lis pendens — related actions

Article 29

1. Without prejudice to Article 31(2), where proceedings involving the same cause of action and between the same parties are brought in the courts of different Member States, any court other than the court first seised shall of its own motion stay its proceedings until such time as the jurisdiction of the court first seised is established.

2. In cases referred to in paragraph 1, upon request by a court seised of the dispute, any other court seised shall without delay inform the former court of the date when it was seised in accordance with Article 32.

3.   Where the jurisdiction of the court first seised is established, any court other than the court first seised shall decline jurisdiction in favour of that court.

Article 30
1.   Where related actions are pending in the courts of different Member States, any court other than the court first seised may stay its proceedings.
2.   Where the action in the court first seised is pending at first instance, any other court may also, on the application of one of the parties, decline jurisdiction if the court first seised has jurisdiction over the actions in question and its law permits the consolidation thereof.
3.   For the purposes of this Article, actions are deemed to be related where they are so closely connected that it is expedient to hear and determine them together to avoid the risk of irreconcilable judgments resulting from separate proceedings.

Article 31
1.   Where actions come within the exclusive jurisdiction of several courts, any court other than the court first seised shall decline jurisdiction in favour of that court.
2.   Without prejudice to Article 26, where a court of a Member State on which an agreement as referred to in Article 25 confers exclusive jurisdiction is seised, any court of another Member State shall stay the proceedings until such time as the court seised on the basis of the agreement declares that it has no jurisdiction under the agreement.
3.   Where the court designated in the agreement has established jurisdiction in accordance with the agreement, any court of another Member State shall decline jurisdiction in favour of that court.
4.   Paragraphs 2 and 3 shall not apply to matters referred to in Sections 3, 4 or 5 where the policyholder, the insured, a beneficiary of the insurance contract, the injured party, the consumer or the employee is the claimant and the agreement is not valid under a provision contained within those Sections.

Article 32
1.   For the purposes of this Section, a court shall be deemed to be seised:
    (a)   at the time when the document instituting the proceedings or an equivalent document is lodged with the court, provided that the claimant has not subsequently failed to take the steps he was required to take to have service effected on the defendant; or
    (b)   if the document has to be served before being lodged with the court, at the time when it is received by the authority responsible for service, provided that the claimant has not subsequently failed to take the steps he was required to take to have the document lodged with the court.
The authority responsible for service referred to in point (b) shall be the first authority receiving the documents to be served.
2.   The court, or the authority responsible for service, referred to in paragraph 1, shall note, respectively, the date of the lodging of the document instituting the proceedings or the equivalent document, or the date of receipt of the documents to be served.

Article 33
1.   Where jurisdiction is based on Article 4 or on Articles 7, 8 or 9 and proceedings are pending before a court of a third State at the time when a court in a Member State is seised of an action involving the same cause of action and between the same parties as the proceedings in the court of the third State, the court of the Member State may stay the proceedings if:
    (a)   it is expected that the court of the third State will give a judgment capable of recognition and, where applicable, of enforcement in that Member State; and

(b)   the court of the Member State is satisfied that a stay is necessary for the proper administration of justice.

2.   The court of the Member State may continue the proceedings at any time if:

(a)   the proceedings in the court of the third State are themselves stayed or discontinued;

(b)   it appears to the court of the Member State that the proceedings in the court of the third State are unlikely to be concluded within a reasonable time; or

(c)   the continuation of the proceedings is required for the proper administration of justice.

3.   The court of the Member State shall dismiss the proceedings if the proceedings in the court of the third State are concluded and have resulted in a judgment capable of recognition and, where applicable, of enforcement in that Member State.

4.   The court of the Member State shall apply this Article on the application of one of the parties or, where possible under national law, of its own motion.

Article 34

1.   Where jurisdiction is based on Article 4 or on Articles 7, 8 or 9 and an action is pending before a court of a third State at the time when a court in a Member State is seised of an action which is related to the action in the court of the third State, the court of the Member State may stay the proceedings if:

(a)   it is expedient to hear and determine the related actions together to avoid the risk of irreconcilable judgments resulting from separate proceedings;

(b)   it is expected that the court of the third State will give a judgment capable of recognition and, where applicable, of enforcement in that Member State; and

(c)   the court of the Member State is satisfied that a stay is necessary for the proper administration of justice.

2.   The court of the Member State may continue the proceedings at any time if:

(a)   it appears to the court of the Member State that there is no longer a risk of irreconcilable judgments;

(b)   the proceedings in the court of the third State are themselves stayed or discontinued;

(c)   it appears to the court of the Member State that the proceedings in the court of the third State are unlikely to be concluded within a reasonable time; or

(d)   the continuation of the proceedings is required for the proper administration of justice.

3.   The court of the Member State may dismiss the proceedings if the proceedings in the court of the third State are concluded and have resulted in a judgment capable of recognition and, where applicable, of enforcement in that Member State.

4.   The court of the Member State shall apply this Article on the application of one of the parties or, where possible under national law, of its own motion.

Section 10
Provisional, including protective, measures

Article 35

Application may be made to the courts of a Member State for such provisional, including protective, measures as may be available under the law of that Member State, even if the courts of another Member State have jurisdiction as to the substance of the matter.

CHAPTER III
RECOGNITION AND ENFORCEMENT

Section 1
Recognition

Article 36

1. A judgment given in a Member State shall be recognised in the other Member States without any special procedure being required.

2. Any interested party may, in accordance with the procedure provided for in Subsection 2 of Section 3, apply for a decision that there are no grounds for refusal of recognition as referred to in Article 45.

3. If the outcome of proceedings in a court of a Member State depends on the determination of an incidental question of refusal of recognition, that court shall have jurisdiction over that question.

Article 37

1. A party who wishes to invoke in a Member State a judgment given in another Member State shall produce:

  (a)   a copy of the judgment which satisfies the conditions necessary to establish its authenticity; and

  (b)   the certificate issued pursuant to Article 53.

2. The court or authority before which a judgment given in another Member State is invoked may, where necessary, require the party invoking it to provide, in accordance with Article 57, a translation or a transliteration of the contents of the certificate referred to in point (b) of paragraph 1. The court or authority may require the party to provide a translation of the judgment instead of a translation of the contents of the certificate if it is unable to proceed without such a translation.

Article 38

The court or authority before which a judgment given in another Member State is invoked may suspend the proceedings, in whole or in part, if:

  (a)   the judgment is challenged in the Member State of origin; or

  (b)   an application has been submitted for a decision that there are no grounds for refusal of recognition as referred to in Article 45 or for a decision that the recognition is to be refused on the basis of one of those grounds.

Section 2
Enforcement

Article 39

A judgment given in a Member State which is enforceable in that Member State shall be enforceable in the other Member States without any declaration of enforceability being required.

Article 40

An enforceable judgment shall carry with it by operation of law the power to proceed to any protective measures which exist under the law of the Member State addressed.

Article 41

1. Subject to the provisions of this Section, the procedure for the enforcement of judgments given in another Member State shall be governed by the law of the Member State addressed. A judgment given in a Member State which is enforceable in the Member State addressed shall be enforced there under the same conditions as a judgment given in the Member State addressed.

2. Notwithstanding paragraph 1, the grounds for refusal or of suspension of

enforcement under the law of the Member State addressed shall apply in so far as they are not incompatible with the grounds referred to in Article 45.

3. The party seeking the enforcement of a judgment given in another Member State shall not be required to have a postal address in the Member State addressed. Nor shall that party be required to have an authorised representative in the Member State addressed unless such a representative is mandatory irrespective of the nationality or the domicile of the parties.

Article 42

1. For the purposes of enforcement in a Member State of a judgment given in another Member State, the applicant shall provide the competent enforcement authority with:

    (a) a copy of the judgment which satisfies the conditions necessary to establish its authenticity; and

    (b) the certificate issued pursuant to Article 53, certifying that the judgment is enforceable and containing an extract of the judgment as well as, where appropriate, relevant information on the recoverable costs of the proceedings and the calculation of interest.

2. For the purposes of enforcement in a Member State of a judgment given in another Member State ordering a provisional, including a protective, measure, the applicant shall provide the competent enforcement authority with:

    (a) a copy of the judgment which satisfies the conditions necessary to establish its authenticity;

    (b) the certificate issued pursuant to Article 53, containing a description of the measure and certifying that:

        (i) the court has jurisdiction as to the substance of the matter;

        (ii) the judgment is enforceable in the Member State of origin; and

    (c) where the measure was ordered without the defendant being summoned to appear, proof of service of the judgment.

3. The competent enforcement authority may, where necessary, require the applicant to provide, in accordance with Article 57, a translation or a transliteration of the contents of the certificate.

4. The competent enforcement authority may require the applicant to provide a translation of the judgment only if it is unable to proceed without such a translation.

Article 43

1. Where enforcement is sought of a judgment given in another Member State, the certificate issued pursuant to Article 53 shall be served on the person against whom the enforcement is sought prior to the first enforcement measure. The certificate shall be accompanied by the judgment, if not already served on that person.

2. Where the person against whom enforcement is sought is domiciled in a Member State other than the Member State of origin, he may request a translation of the judgment in order to contest the enforcement if the judgment is not written in or accompanied by a translation into either of the following languages:

    (a) a language which he understands; or

    (b) the official language of the Member State in which he is domiciled or, where there are several official languages in that Member State, the official language or one of the official languages of the place where he is domiciled.

Where a translation of the judgment is requested under the first subparagraph, no measures of enforcement may be taken other than protective measures until that translation has been provided to the person against whom enforcement is sought.

This paragraph shall not apply if the judgment has already been served on the person against whom enforcement is sought in one of the languages referred to in the first subparagraph or is accompanied by a translation into one of those languages.

3.   This Article shall not apply to the enforcement of a protective measure in a judgment or where the person seeking enforcement proceeds to protective measures in accordance with Article 40.

Article 44
1.   In the event of an application for refusal of enforcement of a judgment pursuant to Subsection 2 of Section 3, the court in the Member State addressed may, on the application of the person against whom enforcement is sought:
  (a)   limit the enforcement proceedings to protective measures;
  (b)   make enforcement conditional on the provision of such security as it shall determine; or
  (c)   suspend, either wholly or in part, the enforcement proceedings.
2.   The competent authority in the Member State addressed shall, on the application of the person against whom enforcement is sought, suspend the enforcement proceedings where the enforceability of the judgment is suspended in the Member State of origin.

Section 3
Refusal of recognition and enforcement

Subsection 1
Refusal of recognition

Article 45
1.   On the application of any interested party, the recognition of a judgment shall be refused:
  (a)   if such recognition is manifestly contrary to public policy (ordre public) in the Member State addressed;
  (b)   where the judgment was given in default of appearance, if the defendant was not served with the document which instituted the proceedings or with an equivalent document in sufficient time and in such a way as to enable him to arrange for his defence, unless the defendant failed to commence proceedings to challenge the judgment when it was possible for him to do so;
  (c)   if the judgment is irreconcilable with a judgment given between the same parties in the Member State addressed;
  (d)   if the judgment is irreconcilable with an earlier judgment given in another Member State or in a third State involving the same cause of action and between the same parties, provided that the earlier judgment fulfils the conditions necessary for its recognition in the Member State addressed; or
  (e)   if the judgment conflicts with:
      (i)   Sections 3, 4 or 5 of Chapter II where the policyholder, the insured, a beneficiary of the insurance contract, the injured party, the consumer or the employee was the defendant; or
      (ii)   Section 6 of Chapter II.
2.   In its examination of the grounds of jurisdiction referred to in point (e) of paragraph 1, the court to which the application was submitted shall be bound by the findings of fact on which the court of origin based its jurisdiction.
3.   Without prejudice to point (e) of paragraph 1, the jurisdiction of the court of origin may not be reviewed. The test of public policy referred to in point (a) of paragraph 1 may not be applied to the rules relating to jurisdiction.
4.   The application for refusal of recognition shall be made in accordance with the procedures provided for in Subsection 2 and, where appropriate, Section 4.

Subsection 2
Refusal of enforcement

Article 46
On the application of the person against whom enforcement is sought, the enforcement of a judgment shall be refused where one of the grounds referred to in Article 45 is found to exist.

Article 47
1. The application for refusal of enforcement shall be submitted to the court which the Member State concerned has communicated to the Commission pursuant to point (a) of Article 75 as the court to which the application is to be submitted.
2. The procedure for refusal of enforcement shall, in so far as it is not covered by this Regulation, be governed by the law of the Member State addressed.
3. The applicant shall provide the court with a copy of the judgment and, where necessary, a translation or transliteration of it.
The court may dispense with the production of the documents referred to in the first subparagraph if it already possesses them or if it considers it unreasonable to require the applicant to provide them. In the latter case, the court may require the other party to provide those documents.
4. The party seeking the refusal of enforcement of a judgment given in another Member State shall not be required to have a postal address in the Member State addressed. Nor shall that party be required to have an authorised representative in the Member State addressed unless such a representative is mandatory irrespective of the nationality or the domicile of the parties.

Article 48
The court shall decide on the application for refusal of enforcement without delay.

Article 49
1. The decision on the application for refusal of enforcement may be appealed against by either party.
2. The appeal is to be lodged with the court which the Member State concerned has communicated to the Commission pursuant to point (b) of Article 75 as the court with which such an appeal is to be lodged.

Article 50
The decision given on the appeal may only be contested by an appeal where the courts with which any further appeal is to be lodged have been communicated by the Member State concerned to the Commission pursuant to point (c) of Article 75.

Article 51
1. The court to which an application for refusal of enforcement is submitted or the court which hears an appeal lodged under Article 49 or Article 50 may stay the proceedings if an ordinary appeal has been lodged against the judgment in the Member State of origin or if the time for such an appeal has not yet expired. In the latter case, the court may specify the time within which such an appeal is to be lodged.
2. Where the judgment was given in Ireland, Cyprus or the United Kingdom, any form of appeal available in the Member State of origin shall be treated as an ordinary appeal for the purposes of paragraph 1.

Section 4
Common provisions

Article 52
Under no circumstances may a judgment given in a Member State be reviewed as to its substance in the Member State addressed.

Article 53

The court of origin shall, at the request of any interested party, issue the certificate using the form set out in Annex I.

Article 54

1.   If a judgment contains a measure or an order which is not known in the law of the Member State addressed, that measure or order shall, to the extent possible, be adapted to a measure or an order known in the law of that Member State which has equivalent effects attached to it and which pursues similar aims and interests.

Such adaptation shall not result in effects going beyond those provided for in the law of the Member State of origin.

2.   Any party may challenge the adaptation of the measure or order before a court.

3.   If necessary, the party invoking the judgment or seeking its enforcement may be required to provide a translation or a transliteration of the judgment.

Article 55

A judgment given in a Member State which orders a payment by way of a penalty shall be enforceable in the Member State addressed only if the amount of the payment has been finally determined by the court of origin.

Article 56

No security, bond or deposit, however described, shall be required of a party who in one Member State applies for the enforcement of a judgment given in another Member State on the ground that he is a foreign national or that he is not domiciled or resident in the Member State addressed.

Article 57

1.   When a translation or a transliteration is required under this Regulation, such translation or transliteration shall be into the official language of the Member State concerned or, where there are several official languages in that Member State, into the official language or one of the official languages of court proceedings of the place where a judgment given in another Member State is invoked or an application is made, in accordance with the law of that Member State.

2.   For the purposes of the forms referred to in Articles 53 and 60, translations or transliterations may also be into any other official language or languages of the institutions of the Union that the Member State concerned has indicated it can accept.

3.   Any translation made under this Regulation shall be done by a person qualified to do translations in one of the Member States.

CHAPTER IV

AUTHENTIC INSTRUMENTS AND COURT SETTLEMENTS

Article 58

1.   An authentic instrument which is enforceable in the Member State of origin shall be enforceable in the other Member States without any declaration of enforceability being required. Enforcement of the authentic instrument may be refused only if such enforcement is manifestly contrary to public policy (ordre public) in the Member State addressed.

The provisions of Section 2, Subsection 2 of Section 3, and Section 4 of Chapter III shall apply as appropriate to authentic instruments.

2.   The authentic instrument produced must satisfy the conditions necessary to establish its authenticity in the Member State of origin.

Article 59

A court settlement which is enforceable in the Member State of origin shall be enforced in the other Member States under the same conditions as authentic instruments.

Article 60

The competent authority or court of the Member State of origin shall, at the request of any interested party, issue the certificate using the form set out in Annex II containing a summary of the enforceable obligation recorded in the authentic instrument or of the agreement between the parties recorded in the court settlement.

CHAPTER V
GENERAL PROVISIONS

Article 61

No legalisation or other similar formality shall be required for documents issued in a Member State in the context of this Regulation.

Article 62

1. In order to determine whether a party is domiciled in the Member State whose courts are seised of a matter, the court shall apply its internal law.

2. If a party is not domiciled in the Member State whose courts are seised of the matter, then, in order to determine whether the party is domiciled in another Member State, the court shall apply the law of that Member State.

Article 63

1. For the purposes of this Regulation, a company or other legal person or association of natural or legal persons is domiciled at the place where it has its:
   (a)   statutory seat;
   (b)   central administration; or
   (c)   principal place of business.

2. For the purposes of Ireland, Cyprus and the United Kingdom, 'statutory seat' means the registered office or, where there is no such office anywhere, the place of incorporation or, where there is no such place anywhere, the place under the law of which the formation took place.

3. In order to determine whether a trust is domiciled in the Member State whose courts are seised of the matter, the court shall apply its rules of private international law.

Article 64

Without prejudice to any more favourable provisions of national laws, persons domiciled in a Member State who are being prosecuted in the criminal courts of another Member State of which they are not nationals for an offence which was not intentionally committed may be defended by persons qualified to do so, even if they do not appear in person. However, the court seised of the matter may order appearance in person; in the case of failure to appear, a judgment given in the civil action without the person concerned having had the opportunity to arrange for his defence need not be recognised or enforced in the other Member States.

Article 65

1. The jurisdiction specified in point 2 of Article 8 and Article 13 in actions on a warranty or guarantee or in any other third-party proceedings may be resorted to in the Member States included in the list established by the Commission pursuant to point (b) of Article 76(1) and Article 76(2) only in so far as permitted under national law. A person domiciled in another Member State may be invited to join the proceedings before the courts of those Member States pursuant to the rules on third-party notice referred to in that list.

2. Judgments given in a Member State by virtue of point 2 of Article 8 or Article 13 shall be recognised and enforced in accordance with Chapter III in any other Member State. Any effects which judgments given in the Member States included in the list referred to in paragraph 1 may have, in accordance with the

law of those Member States, on third parties by application of paragraph 1 shall be recognised in all Member States.

3.   The Member States included in the list referred to in paragraph 1 shall, within the framework of the European Judicial Network in civil and commercial matters established by Council Decision 2001/470/EC ('the European Judicial Network') provide information on how to determine, in accordance with their national law, the effects of the judgments referred to in the second sentence of paragraph 2.

CHAPTER VI
TRANSITIONAL PROVISIONS

Article 66

1.   This Regulation shall apply only to legal proceedings instituted, to authentic instruments formally drawn up or registered and to court settlements approved or concluded on or after 10 January 2015.

2.   Notwithstanding Article 80, Regulation (EC) No 44/2001 shall continue to apply to judgments given in legal proceedings instituted, to authentic instruments formally drawn up or registered and to court settlements approved or concluded before 10 January 2015 which fall within the scope of that Regulation.

CHAPTER VII
RELATIONSHIP WITH OTHER INSTRUMENTS

Article 67

This Regulation shall not prejudice the application of provisions governing jurisdiction and the recognition and enforcement of judgments in specific matters which are contained in instruments of the Union or in national legislation harmonised pursuant to such instruments.

Article 68

1.   This Regulation shall, as between the Member States, supersede the 1968 Brussels Convention, except as regards the territories of the Member States which fall within the territorial scope of that Convention and which are excluded from this Regulation pursuant to Article 355 of the TFEU.

2.   In so far as this Regulation replaces the provisions of the 1968 Brussels Convention between the Member States, any reference to that Convention shall be understood as a reference to this Regulation.

Article 69

Subject to Articles 70 and 71, this Regulation shall, as between the Member States, supersede the conventions that cover the same matters as those to which this Regulation applies. In particular, the conventions included in the list established by the Commission pursuant to point (c) of Article 76(1) and Article 76(2) shall be superseded.

Article 70

1.   The conventions referred to in Article 69 shall continue to have effect in relation to matters to which this Regulation does not apply.

2.   They shall continue to have effect in respect of judgments given, authentic instruments formally drawn up or registered and court settlements approved or concluded before the date of entry into force of Regulation (EC) No 44/2001.

Article 71

1.   This Regulation shall not affect any conventions to which the Member States are parties and which, in relation to particular matters, govern jurisdiction or the recognition or enforcement of judgments.

2.   With a view to its uniform interpretation, paragraph 1 shall be applied in the following manner:

(a)   this Regulation shall not prevent a court of a Member State which is party to a convention on a particular matter from assuming jurisdiction in accordance with that convention, even where the defendant is domiciled in another Member State which is not party to that convention. The court hearing the action shall, in any event, apply Article 28 of this Regulation;

(b)   judgments given in a Member State by a court in the exercise of jurisdiction provided for in a convention on a particular matter shall be recognised and enforced in the other Member States in accordance with this Regulation.

Where a convention on a particular matter to which both the Member State of origin and the Member State addressed are parties lays down conditions for the recognition or enforcement of judgments, those conditions shall apply. In any event, the provisions of this Regulation on recognition and enforcement of judgments may be applied.

Article 72

This Regulation shall not affect agreements by which Member States, prior to the entry into force of Regulation (EC) No 44/2001, undertook pursuant to Article 59 of the 1968 Brussels Convention not to recognise judgments given, in particular in other Contracting States to that Convention, against defendants domiciled or habitually resident in a third State where, in cases provided for in Article 4 of that Convention, the judgment could only be founded on a ground of jurisdiction specified in the second paragraph of Article 3 of that Convention.

Article 73

1.   This Regulation shall not affect the application of the 2007 Lugano Convention.

2.   This Regulation shall not affect the application of the 1958 New York Convention.

3.   This Regulation shall not affect the application of bilateral conventions and agreements between a third State and a Member State concluded before the date of entry into force of Regulation (EC) No 44/2001 which concern matters governed by this Regulation.

CHAPTER VIII
FINAL PROVISIONS

Article 74

The Member States shall provide, within the framework of the European Judicial Network and with a view to making the information available to the public, a description of national rules and procedures concerning enforcement, including authorities competent for enforcement, and information on any limitations on enforcement, in particular debtor protection rules and limitation or prescription periods.

The Member States shall keep this information permanently updated.

Article 75

By 10 January 2014, the Member States shall communicate to the Commission:

(a)   the courts to which the application for refusal of enforcement is to be submitted pursuant to Article 47(1);

(b)   the courts with which an appeal against the decision on the application for refusal of enforcement is to be lodged pursuant to Article 49(2);

(c)   the courts with which any further appeal is to be lodged pursuant to Article 50; and

(d)   the languages accepted for translations of the forms as referred to in Article 57(2).

The Commission shall make the information publicly available through any appropriate means, in particular through the European Judicial Network.

Article 76
 1.   The Member States shall notify the Commission of:
   (a)   the rules of jurisdiction referred to in Articles 5(2) and 6(2);
   (b)   the rules on third-party notice referred to in Article 65; and
   (c)   the conventions referred to in Article 69.
 2.   The Commission shall, on the basis of the notifications by the Member States referred to in paragraph 1, establish the corresponding lists.
 3.   The Member States shall notify the Commission of any subsequent amendments required to be made to those lists. The Commission shall amend those lists accordingly.
 4.   The Commission shall publish the lists and any subsequent amendments made to them in the Official Journal of the European Union.
 5.   The Commission shall make all information notified pursuant to paragraphs 1 and 3 publicly available through any other appropriate means, in particular through the European Judicial Network.

Article 77
The Commission shall be empowered to adopt delegated acts in accordance with Article 78 concerning the amendment of Annexes I and II.

Article 78
 1.   The power to adopt delegated acts is conferred on the Commission subject to the conditions laid down in this Article.
 2.   The power to adopt delegated acts referred to in Article 77 shall be conferred on the Commission for an indeterminate period of time from 9 January 2013.
 3.   The delegation of power referred to in Article 77 may be revoked at any time by the European Parliament or by the Council. A decision to revoke shall put an end to the delegation of the power specified in that decision. It shall take effect the day following the publication of the decision in the Official Journal of the European Union or at a later date specified therein. It shall not affect the validity of any delegated acts already in force.
 4.   As soon as it adopts a delegated act, the Commission shall notify it simultaneously to the European Parliament and to the Council.
 5.   A delegated act adopted pursuant to Article 77 shall enter into force only if no objection has been expressed either by the European Parliament or the Council within a period of two months of notification of that act to the European Parliament and the Council or if, before the expiry of that period, the European Parliament and the Council have both informed the Commission that they will not object. That period shall be extended by two months at the initiative of the European Parliament or of the Council.

Article 79
By 11 January 2022 the Commission shall present a report to the European Parliament, to the Council and to the European Economic and Social Committee on the application of this Regulation. That report shall include an evaluation of the possible need for a further extension of the rules on jurisdiction to defendants not domiciled in a Member State, taking into account the operation of this Regulation and possible developments at international level. Where appropriate, the report shall be accompanied by a proposal for amendment of this Regulation.

Article 80
This Regulation shall repeal Regulation (EC) No 44/2001. References to the repealed Regulation shall be construed as references to this Regulation and shall be read in accordance with the correlation table set out in Annex III.

Article 81

This Regulation shall enter into force on the twentieth day following that of its publication in the Official Journal of the European Union.

It shall apply from 10 January 2015, with the exception of Articles 75 and 76, which shall apply from 10 January 2014.

This Regulation shall be binding in its entirety and directly applicable in the Member States in accordance with the Treaties.

Done at Strasbourg, 12 December 2012.

ANNEX III

CORRELATION TABLE

Regulation (EC) No 44/2001	This Regulation
Article 1(1)	Article 1(1)
Article 1(2), introductory words	Article 1(2), introductory words
Article 1(2) point (a)	Article 1(2), points (a) and (f)
Article 1(2), points (b) to (d)	Article 1(2), points (b) to (d)
—	Article 1(2), point (e)
Article 1(3)	—
—	Article 2
Article 2	Article 4
Article 3	Article 5
Article 4	Article 6
Article 5, introductory words	Article 7, introductory words
Article 5, point (1)	Article 7, point (1)
Article 5, point (2)	—
Article 5, points (3) and (4)	Article 7, points (2) and (3)
—	Article 7, point (4)
Article 5, points (5) to (7)	Article 7, points (5) to (7)
Article 6	Article 8
Article 7	Article 9
Article 8	Article 10
Article 9	Article 11
Article 10	Article 12
Article 11	Article 13
Article 12	Article 14
Article 13	Article 15
Article 14	Article 16
Article 15	Article 17
Article 16	Article 18
Article 17	Article 19
Article 18	Article 20
Article 19, points (1) and (2)	Article 21(1)
—	Article 21(2)
Article 20	Article 22
Article 21	Article 23
Article 22	Article 24
Article 23(1) and (2)	Article 25(1) and (2)
Article 23(3)	—
Article 23(4) and (5)	Article 25(3) and (4)
—	Article 25(5)

Regulation (EC) No 44/2001	This Regulation
Article 24	Article 26(1)
—	Article 26(2)
Article 25	Article 27
Article 26	Article 28
Article 27(1)	Article 29(1)
—	Article 29(2)
Article 27(2)	Article 29(3)
Article 28	Article 30
Article 29	Article 31(1)
—	Article 31(2)
—	Article 31(3)
—	Article 31(4)
Article 30	Article 32(1), points (a) and (b)
—	Article 32(1), second subparagraph
—	Article 32(2)
—	Article 33
—	Article 34
Article 31	Article 35
Article 32	Article 2, point (a)
Article 33	Article 36
—	Article 37
—	Article 39
—	Article 40
—	Article 41
—	Article 42
—	Article 43
—	Article 44
Article 34	Article 45(1), points (a) to (d)
Article 35(1)	Article 45(1), point (e)
Article 35(2)	Article 45(2)
Article 35(3)	Article 45(3)
—	Article 45(4)
Article 36	Article 52
Article 37(1)	Article 38, point (a)
Article 38	—
Article 39	—
Article 40	—
Article 41	—
Article 42	—
Article 43	—
Article 44	—
Article 45	—
Article 46	—
Article 47	—
Article 48	—
—	Article 46
—	Article 47
—	Article 48
—	Article 49
—	Article 50
—	Article 51
—	Article 54
Article 49	Article 55

Regulation (EC) No 44/2001	This Regulation
Article 50	—
Article 51	Article 56
Article 52	—
Article 53	—
Article 54	Article 53
Article 55(1)	—
Article 55(2)	Article 37(2), Article 47(3) and Article 57
Article 56	Article 61
Article 57(1)	Article 58(1)
Article 57(2)	—
Article 57(3)	Article 58(2)
Article 57(4)	Article 60
Article 58	Article 59 and Article 60
Article 59	Article 62
Article 60	Article 63
Article 61	Article 64
Article 62	Article 3
Article 63	—
Article 64	—
Article 65	Article 65(1) and (2)
—	Article 65(3)
Article 66	Article 66
Article 67	Article 67
Article 68	Article 68
Article 69	Article 69
Article 70	Article 70
Article 71	Article 71
Article 72	Article 72
—	Article 73
Article 73	Article 79
Article 74(1)	Article 75, first paragraph, points (a), (b) and (c), and Article 76(1), point (a)
Article 74(2)	Article 77
—	Article 78
—	Article 80
Article 75	—
Article 76	Article 81
Annex I	Article 76(1), point (a)
Annex II	Article 75, point (a)
Annex III	Article 75, point (b)
Annex IV	Article 75, point (c)
Annex V	Annex I and Annex II
Annex VI	Annex II
—	Annex III

AGREEMENT BETWEEN THE EUROPEAN COMMUNITY AND THE KINGDOM OF DENMARK ON JURISDICTION AND THE RECOGNITION AND ENFORCEMENT OF JUDGMENTS IN CIVIL AND COMMERCIAL MATTERS (IMPLEMENTING REGULATION (EU) NO 1215/2012)

Official Journal L 79, 21/3/2013 p 4

According to Article 3(2) of the Agreement of 19 October 2005 between the European Community and the Kingdom of Denmark on jurisdiction and the recognition and enforcement of judgments in civil and commercial matters (hereafter the Agreement), concluded by Council Decision 2006/325/EC, whenever amendments to Council Regulation (EC) No 44/2001 of 22 December 2000 on jurisdiction and the recognition and enforcement of judgments in civil and commercial matters are adopted, Denmark shall notify the Commission of its decision whether or not to implement the content of such amendments.

Regulation (EU) No 1215/2012 of the European Parliament and of the Council of 12 December 2012 on jurisdiction and the recognition and enforcement of judgments in civil and commercial matters was adopted on 12 December 2012.

In accordance with Article 3(2) of the Agreement, Denmark has by letter of 20 December 2012 notified the Commission of its decision to implement the contents of Regulation (EU) No 1215/2012. This means that the provisions of Regulation (EU) No 1215/2012 will be applied to relations between the Union and Denmark.

In accordance with Article 3(6) of the Agreement, the Danish notification creates mutual obligations between Denmark and the Community. Thus, Regulation (EU) No 1215/2012 constitutes an amendment to the Agreement and is considered annexed thereto.

With reference to Article 3(3) and (4) of the Agreement, implementation of Regulation (EU) No 1215/2012 in Denmark can take place by amending existing legislation by the decision of Danish Parliament. In accordance with Article 3(5)(b) of the Agreement, Denmark shall notify the Commission of the date upon which such implementing legislative measures enter into force.

REGULATION (EU) NO 655/2014 OF THE EUROPEAN PARLIAMENT AND OF THE COUNCIL OF 15 MAY 2014 ESTABLISHING A EUROPEAN ACCOUNT PRESERVATION ORDER PROCEDURE TO FACILITATE CROSS-BORDER DEBT RECOVERY IN CIVIL AND COMMERCIAL MATTERS

Official Journal L 189/59

THE EUROPEAN PARLIAMENT AND THE COUNCIL OF THE EUROPEAN UNION,

Having regard to the Treaty on the Functioning of the European Union, and in particular points (a), (e) and (f) of Article 81(2) thereof,

Having regard to the proposal from the European Commission,

After transmission of the draft legislative act to the national parliaments,

Having regard to the opinion of the European Economic and Social Committee,

Acting in accordance with the ordinary legislative procedure,

Whereas:

(1)   The Union has set itself the objective of maintaining and developing an area of freedom, security and justice in which the free movement of persons is ensured. For the gradual establishment of such an area, the Union is to adopt measures

relating to judicial cooperation in civil matters having cross-border implications, particularly when necessary for the proper functioning of the internal market.

(2) In accordance with Article 81(2) of the Treaty on the Functioning of the European Union (TFEU), such measures may include measures aimed at ensuring, inter alia, the mutual recognition and enforcement of judgments between Member States, effective access to justice and the elimination of obstacles to the proper functioning of civil proceedings, if necessary by promoting the compatibility of the rules on civil procedure applicable in the Member States.

(3) On 24 October 2006, by way of the 'Green Paper on improving the efficiency of the enforcement of judgments in the European Union: the attachment of bank accounts', the Commission launched a consultation on the need for a uniform European procedure for the preservation of bank accounts and the possible features of such a procedure.

(4) In the Stockholm Programme of December 2009, which sets freedom, security and justice priorities for 2010 to 2014, the European Council invited the Commission to assess the need for, and the feasibility of, providing for certain provisional, including protective, measures at Union level, to prevent for example the disappearance of assets before the enforcement of a claim, and to put forward appropriate proposals for improving the efficiency of enforcement of judgments in the Union regarding bank accounts and debtors' assets.

(5) National procedures for obtaining protective measures such as account preservation orders exist in all Member States, but the conditions for the grant of such measures and the efficiency of their implementation vary considerably. Moreover, recourse to national protective measures may prove cumbersome in cases having cross-border implications, in particular when the creditor seeks to preserve several accounts located in different Member States. It therefore seems necessary and appropriate to adopt a binding and directly applicable legal instrument of the Union which establishes a new Union procedure allowing, in cross-border cases, for the preservation, in an efficient and speedy way, of funds held in bank accounts.

(6) The procedure established by this Regulation should serve as an additional and optional means for the creditor, who remains free to make use of any other procedure for obtaining an equivalent measure under national law.

(7) A creditor should be able to obtain a protective measure in the form of a European Account Preservation Order ('Preservation Order' or 'Order') preventing the transfer or withdrawal of funds held by his debtor in a bank account maintained in a Member State if there is a risk that, without such a measure, the subsequent enforcement of his claim against the debtor will be impeded or made substantially more difficult. The preservation of funds held in the debtor's account should have the effect of preventing not only the debtor himself, but also persons authorised by him to make payments through that account, for example by way of a standing order or through direct debit or the use of a credit card, from using the funds.

(8) The scope of this Regulation should cover all civil and commercial matters apart from certain well-defined matters. In particular, this Regulation should not apply to claims against a debtor in insolvency proceedings. This should mean that no Preservation Order can be issued against the debtor once insolvency proceedings as defined in Council Regulation (EC) No 1346/2000 have been opened in relation to him. On the other hand, the exclusion should allow the Preservation Order to be used to secure the recovery of detrimental payments made by such a debtor to third parties.

(9) This Regulation should apply to accounts held with credit institutions whose business is to take deposits or other repayable funds from the public and to grant credits for their own account.

It should thus not apply to financial institutions which do not take such deposits, for instance institutions providing financing for export and investment projects or projects in developing countries or institutions providing financial market services. Furthermore, this Regulation should not apply to accounts held by or with central banks when acting in their capacity as monetary authorities, nor to accounts that cannot be preserved by national orders equivalent to a Preservation Order or which are otherwise immune from seizure under the law of the Member State where the account in question is maintained.

(10)   This Regulation should apply to cross-border cases only and should define what constitutes a cross-border case in this particular context. For the purposes of this Regulation, a cross-border case should be considered to exist when the court dealing with the application for the Preservation Order is located in one Member State and the bank account concerned by the Order is maintained in another Member State. A cross-border case should also be considered to exist when the creditor is domiciled in one Member State and the court and the bank account to be preserved are located in another Member State.

This Regulation should not apply to the preservation of accounts maintained in the Member State of the court seized of the application for the Preservation Order if the creditor's domicile is also in that Member State, even if the creditor applies at the same time for a Preservation Order which concerns an account or accounts maintained in another Member State. In such a case, the creditor should make two separate applications, one for a Preservation Order and one for a national measure.

(11)   The procedure for a Preservation Order should be available to a creditor wishing to secure the enforcement of a later judgment on the substance of the matter prior to initiating proceedings on the substance of the matter and at any stage during such proceedings. It should also be available to a creditor who has already obtained a judgment, court settlement or authentic instrument requiring the debtor to pay the creditor's claim.

(12)   The Preservation Order should be available for the purpose of securing claims that have already fallen due. It should also be available for claims that are not yet due as long as such claims arise from a transaction or an event that has already occurred and their amount can be determined, including claims relating to tort, delict or quasi-delict and civil claims for damages or restitution which are based on an act giving rise to criminal proceedings.

A creditor should be able to request that the Preservation Order be issued in the amount of the principal claim or in a lower amount. The latter may be in his interest, for instance, where he has already obtained some other security for part of his claim.

(13)   In order to ensure a close link between the proceedings for the Preservation Order and the proceedings on the substance of the matter, international jurisdiction to issue the Order should lie with the courts of the Member State whose courts have jurisdiction to rule on the substance of the matter. For the purposes of this Regulation, the notion of proceedings on the substance of the matter should cover any proceedings aimed at obtaining an enforceable title on the underlying claim including, for instance, summary proceedings concerning orders to pay and proceedings such as the French 'procédure de référé'. If the debtor is a consumer domiciled in a Member State, jurisdiction to issue the Order should lie only with the courts of that Member State.

(14)   The conditions for issuing the Preservation Order should strike an appropriate balance between the interest of the creditor in obtaining an Order and the interest of the debtor in preventing abuse of the Order.

Consequently, when the creditor applies for a Preservation Order prior to obtaining a judgment, the court with which the application is lodged should have to be satisfied on the basis of the evidence submitted by the creditor that the creditor is likely to succeed on the substance of his claim against the debtor.

Furthermore, the creditor should be required in all situations, including when he has already obtained a judgment, to demonstrate to the satisfaction of the court that his claim is in urgent need of judicial protection and that, without the Order, the enforcement of the existing or a future judgment may be impeded or made substantially more difficult because there is a real risk that, by the time the creditor is able to have the existing or a future judgment enforced, the debtor may have dissipated, concealed or destroyed his assets or have disposed of them under value, to an unusual extent or through unusual action.

The court should assess the evidence submitted by the creditor to support the existence of such a risk. This could relate, for instance, to the debtor's conduct in respect of the creditor's claim or in a previous dispute between the parties, to the debtor's credit history, to the nature of the debtor's assets and to any recent action taken by the debtor with regard to his assets. In assessing the evidence, the court may consider that withdrawals from accounts and instances of expenditure by the debtor to sustain the normal course of his business or recurrent family expenses are not, in themselves, unusual. The mere non-payment or contesting of the claim or the mere fact that the debtor has more than one creditor should not, in themselves, be considered sufficient evidence to justify the issuing of an Order. Nor should the mere fact that the financial circumstances of the debtor are poor or deteriorating, in itself, constitute a sufficient ground for the issuing of an Order. However, the court may take these factors into account in the overall assessment of the existence of the risk.

(15) In order to ensure the surprise effect of the Preservation Order, and to ensure that it will be a useful tool for a creditor trying to recover debts from a debtor in cross-border cases, the debtor should not be informed about the creditor's application nor be heard prior to the issue of the Order or notified of the Order prior to its implementation. Where, on the basis of the evidence and information provided by the creditor or, if applicable, by his witness(es), the court is not satisfied that the preservation of the account or accounts in question is justified, it should not issue the Order.

(16) In situations where the creditor applies for a Preservation Order before initiating proceedings on the substance of the matter before a court, this Regulation should oblige him to initiate such proceedings within a specified period of time and should also oblige him to provide proof of such initiation to the court with which he lodged his application for an Order. Should the creditor fail to comply with this obligation, the Order should be revoked by the court of its own motion or should terminate automatically.

(17) In view of the absence of a prior hearing of the debtor, this Regulation should provide for specific safeguards in order to prevent abuse of the Order and to protect the debtor's rights.

(18) One such important safeguard should be the possibility of requiring the creditor to provide security so as to ensure that the debtor can be compensated at a later stage for any damage caused to him by the Preservation Order. Depending on national law, such security could be provided in the form of a security deposit or an alternative assurance, such as a bank guarantee or a mortgage. The court should have discretion in determining the amount of security sufficient to prevent abuse of the Order and to ensure compensation to the debtor and it should be open to the court, in the absence of specific evidence as to the amount of the potential damage, to consider the amount in which the Order is to be issued as a guideline for determining the amount of the security.

In cases where the creditor has not yet obtained a judgment, court settlement or authentic instrument requiring the debtor to pay the creditor's claim, the provision of security should be the rule and the court should dispense with this requirement, or require the provision of security in a lower amount, only exceptionally if it considers that such security is inappropriate, superfluous or disproportionate in the circumstances of the case. Such circumstances could be, for instance, that the creditor has a particularly strong case but does not have sufficient means to provide security, that the claim relates to maintenance or to the payment of wages or that the size of the claim is such that the Order is unlikely to cause any damage to the debtor, for instance a small business debt.

In cases where the creditor has already obtained a judgment, court settlement or authentic instrument, the provision of security should be left to the discretion of the court. The provision of security may, for instance, be appropriate, except in the abovementioned exceptional circumstances, where the judgment the enforcement of which the Preservation Order intends to secure is not yet enforceable or only provisionally enforceable due to a pending appeal.

(19) Another important element for striking an appropriate balance between the creditor's and the debtor's interests should be a rule on the creditor's liability for any damage caused to the debtor by the Preservation Order. This Regulation should therefore, as a minimum standard, provide for the liability of the creditor where the damage caused to the debtor by the Preservation Order is due to fault on the creditor's part. In this context, the burden of proof should lie with the debtor. As regards the grounds for liability specified in this Regulation, provision should be made for a harmonised rule establishing a rebuttable presumption of fault on the part of the creditor.

Furthermore, the Member States should be able to maintain or introduce in their national law grounds for liability other than those specified in this Regulation. For such other grounds of liability, the Member States should also be able to maintain or introduce other types of liability, such as strict liability.

This Regulation should also lay down a conflict-of-laws rule specifying that the law applicable to the creditor's liability should be the law of the Member State of enforcement. Where there are several Member States of enforcement, the law applicable should be the law of the Member State of enforcement in which the debtor is habitually resident. In a case in which the debtor is not habitually resident in any of the Member States of enforcement, the law applicable should be the law of the Member State of enforcement with which the case has the closest connection. In determining the closest connection, the size of the amount preserved in the different Member States of enforcement could be one of the factors to be taken into account by the court.

(20) In order to overcome existing practical difficulties in obtaining information about the whereabouts of the debtor's bank account in a cross-border context, this Regulation should set out a mechanism allowing the creditor to request that the information needed to identify the debtor's account be obtained by the court, before a Preservation Order is issued, from the designated information authority of the Member State in which the creditor believes that the debtor holds an account. Given the particular nature of such an intervention by public authorities and of such access to private data, access to account information should, as a rule, be given only in cases where the creditor has already obtained an enforceable judgment, court settlement or authentic instrument. However, by way of exception, it should be possible for the creditor to make a request for account information even though his judgment, court settlement or authentic instrument is not yet enforceable. Such a request should be possible where the amount to be preserved is substantial taking into account the relevant circumstances and the court is satisfied, on the basis of the evidence submitted by the creditor, that there is an urgent need for such account information because there is a risk that, without it, the subsequent enforcement of the creditor's claim against the debtor is likely to be jeopardised and that this could consequently lead to a substantial deterioration of the creditor's financial situation.

To allow that mechanism to work, the Member States should make available in their national law one or more methods for obtaining such information which are effective and efficient and which are not disproportionately costly or time-consuming. The mechanism should apply only if all the conditions and requirements for issuing the Preservation Order are met and the creditor has duly substantiated in his request why there are reasons to believe that the debtor holds one or more accounts in a specific Member State, for instance because the debtor works or exercises a professional activity in that Member State or has property there.

(21) In order to ensure protection of the personal data of the debtor, the information obtained regarding the identification of the debtor's bank account or accounts should not be provided to the creditor. It should be provided only to the requesting court and, exceptionally, to the debtor's bank if the bank or other entity responsible for enforcing the Order in the Member State of enforcement is not able to identify an account of the debtor on the basis of the information provided in the Order, for instance where there are accounts held with the same bank by several persons having the same name and the same address. Where, in such a case, it is indicated in the Order that the number or numbers of the account(s) to be preserved was or were obtained through a request for information, the bank should request that information from the information authority of the Member State of enforcement and should be able to make such a request in an informal and simple manner.

(22) This Regulation should grant the creditor the right to appeal against a refusal to issue the Preservation Order. That right should be without prejudice to the possibility for the creditor to make a new application for a Preservation Order on the basis of new facts or new evidence.

(23) Enforcement structures for preserving bank accounts vary considerably in the Member States. In order to avoid duplication of those structures in the Member States and to respect national procedures to the extent possible, this Regulation should, as regards the enforcement and actual implementation of the Preservation Order, build on the methods and structures in place for the enforcement and implementation of equivalent national orders in the Member State in which the Order is to be enforced.

(24) In order to ensure swift enforcement, this Regulation should provide for transmission of the Order from the Member State of origin to the competent authority of the Member State of enforcement by any appropriate means which ensure that the content of the documents transmitted is true and faithful and easily legible.

(25) Upon receiving the Preservation Order, the competent authority of the Member State of enforcement should take the necessary steps to have the Order enforced in accordance with its national law, either by transmitting the Order received to the bank or other entity responsible for enforcing such orders in that Member State or, where national law so provides, by otherwise instructing the bank to implement the Order.

(26) Depending on the method available under the law of the Member State of enforcement for equivalent national orders, the Preservation Order should be implemented by blocking the preserved amount in the debtor's account or, where national law so provides, by transferring that amount to an account dedicated for preservation purposes, which could be an account held by either the competent enforcement authority, the court, the bank with which the debtor holds his account or a bank designated as coordinating entity for the preservation in a given case.

(27) This Regulation should not prevent the payment of fees for the enforcement of the Preservation Order from being requested in advance. This issue should be left to the national law of the Member State in which the Order is to be enforced.

(28) A Preservation Order should have the same rank, if any, as an equivalent national order in the Member State of enforcement. If, under national law, certain enforcement measures have priority over preservation measures, the same priority should be given to them in relation to Preservation Orders under this Regulation. For the purposes of this Regulation, the in personam orders which exist in some national legal systems should be considered to be equivalent national orders.

(29) This Regulation should provide for the imposition on the bank or other

entity responsible for enforcing the Preservation Order in the Member State of enforcement of an obligation to declare whether and, if so, to what extent the Order has led to the preservation of any funds of the debtor, and of an obligation on the creditor to ensure the release of any funds preserved that exceed the amount specified in the Order.

(30) This Regulation should safeguard the debtor's right to a fair trial and his right to an effective remedy and should therefore, having regard to the ex parte nature of the proceedings for the issue of the Preservation Order, enable him to contest the Order or its enforcement on the grounds provided for in this Regulation immediately after the implementation of the Order.

(31) In this context, this Regulation should require that the Preservation Order, all documents submitted by the creditor to the court in the Member State of origin and the necessary translations be served on the debtor promptly after the implementation of the Order. The court should have discretionary powers to append any further documents on which it based its decision and which the debtor might need for his remedy action, such as verbatim transcripts of any oral hearing.

(32) The debtor should be able to request a review of the Preservation Order, in particular if the conditions or requirements set out in this Regulation were not met or if the circumstances that led to the issuing of the Order have changed in such a way that the issuing of the Order would no longer be founded. For instance, a remedy should be available to the debtor if the case did not constitute a cross-border case as defined in this Regulation, if the jurisdiction rules set out in this Regulation were not respected, if the creditor did not initiate proceedings on the substance of the matter within the period of time provided for in this Regulation and the court did not, as a consequence, revoke the Order of its own motion or the Order did not terminate automatically, if the creditor's claim was not in need of urgent protection in the form of a Preservation Order because there was no risk that the subsequent enforcement of that claim would be impeded or made substantially more difficult, or if the provision of security was not in conformity with the requirements set out in this Regulation.

A remedy should also be available to the debtor if the Order and the declaration on the preservation have not been served on him as provided for in this Regulation or if the documents served on him did not meet the language requirements provided for in this Regulation. However, such a remedy should not be granted if the lack of service or translation is cured within a given period of time. In order to cure the lack of service, the creditor should make a request to the body responsible for service in the Member State of origin to have the relevant documents served by registered post on the debtor or, where the debtor has agreed to collect the documents at the court, should provide the necessary translations of the documents to the court. Such a request should not be required if the lack of service has already been cured by other means, for instance if, in accordance with national law, the court initiated the service of its own motion.

(33) The question as to who has to provide any translations required under this Regulation and who has to bear the costs for such translations is left to national law.

(34) Jurisdiction to grant the remedies against the issue of the Preservation Order should lie with the courts of the Member State in which the Order was issued. Jurisdiction to grant the remedies against the enforcement of the Order should lie with the courts or, where applicable, with the competent enforcement authorities in the Member State of enforcement.

(35) The debtor should have the right to apply for the release of the preserved funds if he provides appropriate alternative security. Such alternative security could be provided in the form of a security deposit or an alternative assurance, such as a bank guarantee or a mortgage.

(36) This Regulation should ensure that the preservation of the debtor's account does not affect amounts which are exempt from seizure under the law of

the Member State of enforcement, for example amounts necessary to ensure the livelihood of the debtor and his family. Depending on the procedural system applicable in that Member State, the relevant amount should either be exempted ex officio by the body responsible, which could be the court, the bank or the competent enforcement authority, before the Order is implemented, or be exempted at the request of the debtor after the implementation of the Order. Where accounts in several Member States are preserved and the exemption has been applied more than once, the creditor should be able to apply to the competent court of any of the Member States of enforcement or, where the national law of the Member State of enforcement concerned so provides, to the competent enforcement authority in that Member State, for an adjustment of the exemption applied in that Member State.

(37) In order to ensure that the Preservation Order is issued and enforced swiftly and without delay, this Regulation should establish time-limits by which the different steps in the procedure must be completed. Courts or authorities involved in the procedure should only be allowed to derogate from those time-limits in exceptional circumstances, for instance in cases which are legally or factually complex.

(38) For the purposes of calculating the periods and time-limits provided for in this Regulation, Regulation (EEC, Euratom) No 1182/71 of the Council should apply.

(39) In order to facilitate the application of this Regulation, provision should be made for an obligation on the Member States to communicate certain information regarding their legislation and procedures relating to Preservation Orders and equivalent national orders to the Commission.

(40) In order to facilitate the application of this Regulation in practice, standard forms should be established, in particular, for the application for an Order, for the Order itself, for the declaration concerning the preservation of funds and for the application for a remedy or appeal under this Regulation.

(41) To increase the efficiency of proceedings, this Regulation should allow for the greatest possible use of modern communication technologies accepted under the procedural rules of the Member States concerned, particularly for the purposes of filling in the standard forms provided for in this Regulation and of communication between the authorities involved in the proceedings. Furthermore, the methods for signing the Preservation Order and other documents under this Regulation should be technologically neutral in order to allow for the application of existing methods, such as digital certification or secure authentication, and for future technical developments in this field.

(42) In order to ensure uniform conditions for the implementation of this Regulation, implementing powers should be conferred on the Commission with regard to the establishment and subsequent amendment of the standard forms provided for in this Regulation. Those powers should be exercised in accordance with Regulation (EU) No 182/2011 of the European Parliament and of the Council.

(43) The advisory procedure should be used for the adoption of implementing acts establishing and subsequently amending the standard forms provided for in this Regulation in accordance with Article 4 of Regulation (EU) No 182/2011.

(44) This Regulation respects the fundamental rights and observes the principles recognised in the Charter of Fundamental Rights of the European Union. In particular, it seeks to ensure respect for private and family life, the protection of personal data, the right to property, and the right to an effective remedy and to a fair trial as established in Articles 7, 8, 17 and 47 thereof respectively.

(45) In the context of access to personal data and the use and transmission of such data under this Regulation, the requirements of Directive 95/46/EC of the European Parliament and of the Council, as transposed into the national law of the Member States, should be complied with.

(46) For the purposes of the application of this Regulation, it is however neces-

sary to lay down certain specific conditions for access to personal data and for the use and transmission of such data. In this context, the opinion of the European Data Protection Supervisor has been taken into account. Notification of the data subject should take place in accordance with national law. However, the notification of the debtor about the disclosure of information relating to his account or accounts should be deferred for 30 days, in order to prevent an early notification from jeopardising the effect of the Preservation Order.

(47) Since the objective of this Regulation, namely to establish a Union procedure for a protective measure which enables a creditor to obtain a Preservation Order preventing the subsequent enforcement of the creditor's claim from being jeopardised through the transfer or withdrawal of funds held by the debtor in a bank account within the Union, cannot be sufficiently achieved by the Member States but can rather, by reason of its scale and effects, be better achieved at Union level, the Union may adopt measures, in accordance with the principle of subsidiarity as set out in Article 5 of the Treaty on European Union (TEU). In accordance with the principle of proportionality, as set out in that Article, this Regulation does not go beyond what is necessary in order to achieve that objective.

(48) This Regulation should apply only to those Member States which are bound by it in accordance with the Treaties. The procedure for obtaining a Preservation Order provided for in this Regulation should therefore be available only to creditors who are domiciled in a Member State bound by this Regulation and Orders issued under this Regulation should relate only to the preservation of bank accounts which are maintained in such a Member State.

(49) In accordance with Article 3 of Protocol No 21 on the position of the United Kingdom and Ireland in respect of the area of freedom, security and justice, annexed to the TEU and to the TFEU, Ireland has notified its wish to take part in the adoption and application of this Regulation.

(50) In accordance with Articles 1 and 2 of Protocol No 21 on the position of the United Kingdom and Ireland in respect of the area of freedom, security and justice, annexed to the TEU and to the TFEU, and without prejudice to Article 4 of that Protocol, the United Kingdom is not taking part in the adoption of this Regulation and is not bound by it or subject to its application.

(51) In accordance with Articles 1 and 2 of Protocol No 22 on the position of Denmark, annexed to the TEU and to the TFEU, Denmark is not taking part in the adoption of this Regulation and is not bound by it or subject to its application,

HAVE ADOPTED THIS REGULATION:

CHAPTER 1
SUBJECT MATTER, SCOPE AND DEFINITIONS

Article 1. Subject matter

1 This Regulation establishes a Union procedure enabling a creditor to obtain a European Account Preservation Order ('Preservation Order' or 'Order') which prevents the subsequent enforcement of the creditor's claim from being jeopardised through the transfer or withdrawal of funds up to the amount specified in the Order which are held by the debtor or on his behalf in a bank account maintained in a Member State.

2. The Preservation Order shall be available to the creditor as an alternative to preservation measures under national law.

Article 2. Scope

1. This Regulation applies to pecuniary claims in civil and commercial matters in cross-border cases as defined in Article 3, whatever the nature of the court or tribunal concerned (the 'court'). It does not extend, in particular, to revenue, customs or administrative matters or to the liability of the State for acts and omissions in the exercise of State authority ('acta iure imperii').

2. This Regulation does not apply to:

(a)   rights in property arising out of a matrimonial relationship or out of a relationship deemed by the law applicable to such relationship to have comparable effects to marriage;

(b)   wills and succession, including maintenance obligations arising by reason of death;

(c)   claims against a debtor in relation to whom bankruptcy proceedings, proceedings for the winding-up of insolvent companies or other legal persons, judicial arrangements, compositions, or analogous proceedings have been opened;

(d)   social security;

(e)   arbitration.

3. This Regulation does not apply to bank accounts which are immune from seizure under the law of the Member State in which the account is maintained nor to accounts maintained in connection with the operation of any system as defined in point (a) of Article 2 of Directive 98/26/EC of the European Parliament and of the Council.

4. This Regulation does not apply to bank accounts held by or with central banks when acting in their capacity as monetary authorities.

Article 3. Cross-border cases

1. For the purposes of this Regulation, a cross-border case is one in which the bank account or accounts to be preserved by the Preservation Order are maintained in a Member State other than:

(a)   the Member State of the court seised of the application for the Preservation Order pursuant to Article 6; or

(b)   the Member State in which the creditor is domiciled.

2. The relevant moment for determining whether a case is a cross-border case is the date on which the application for the Preservation Order is lodged with the court having jurisdiction to issue the Preservation Order.

Article 4. Definitions

For the purposes of this Regulation:

(1)   'bank account' or 'account' means any account containing funds which is held with a bank in the name of the debtor or in the name of a third party on behalf of the debtor;

(2)   'bank' means a credit institution as defined in point (1) of Article 4(1) of Regulation (EU) No 575/2013 of the European Parliament and of the Council, including branches, within the meaning of point (17) of Article 4(1) of that Regulation, of credit institutions having their head offices inside or, in accordance with Article 47 of Directive 2013/36/EU of the European Parliament and of the Council, outside the Union where such branches are located in the Union;

(3)   'funds' means money credited to an account in any currency, or similar claims for the repayment of money, such as money market deposits;

(4)   'Member State in which the bank account is maintained' means:

(a)   the Member State indicated in the account's IBAN (International Bank Account Number); or

(b)   for a bank account which does not have an IBAN, the Member State in which the bank with which the account is held has its head office or, where the account is held with a branch, the Member State in which the branch is located;

(5)   'claim' means a claim for payment of a specific amount of money that has fallen due or a claim for payment of a determinable amount of money arising from a transaction or an event that has already occurred, provided that such a claim can be brought before a court;

(6)   'creditor' means a natural person domiciled in a Member State or a legal person domiciled in a Member State or any other entity domiciled in a Member State having legal capacity to sue or be sued under the law of a Member State,

who or which applies for, or has already obtained, a Preservation Order relating to a claim;

(7) 'debtor' means a natural person or a legal person or any other entity having legal capacity to sue or be sued under the law of a Member State, against whom or which the creditor seeks to obtain, or has already obtained, a Preservation Order relating to a claim;

(8) 'judgment' means any judgment given by a court of a Member State, whatever the judgment may be called, including a decision on the determination of costs or expenses by an officer of the court;

(9) 'court settlement' means a settlement which has been approved by a court of a Member State or concluded before a court of a Member State in the course of proceedings;

(10) 'authentic instrument' means a document which has been formally drawn up or registered as an authentic instrument in a Member State and the authenticity of which:

(a)   relates to the signature and the content of the instrument; and

(b)   has been established by a public authority or other authority empowered for that purpose;

(11) 'Member State of origin' means the Member State in which the Preservation Order was issued;

(12) 'Member State of enforcement' means the Member State in which the bank account to be preserved is maintained;

(13) 'information authority' means the authority which a Member State has designated as competent for the purposes of obtaining the necessary information on the debtor's account or accounts pursuant to Article 14;

(14) 'competent authority' means the authority or authorities which a Member State has designated as competent for receipt, transmission or service pursuant to Article 10(2), Article 23(3), (5) and (6), Articles 25(3), 27(2) and 28(3) and the second subparagraph of Article 36(5);

(15) 'domicile' means domicile as determined in accordance with Articles 62 and 63 of Regulation (EU) No 1215/2012 of the European Parliament and of the Council.

CHAPTER 2
PROCEDURE FOR OBTAINING A PRESERVATION ORDER

Article 5. Availability
The Preservation Order shall be available to the creditor in the following situations:

(a)   before the creditor initiates proceedings in a Member State against the debtor on the substance of the matter, or at any stage during such proceedings up until the issuing of the judgment or the approval or conclusion of a court settlement;

(b)   after the creditor has obtained in a Member State a judgment, court settlement or authentic instrument which requires the debtor to pay the creditor's claim.

Article 6. Jurisdiction
1. Where the creditor has not yet obtained a judgment, court settlement or authentic instrument, jurisdiction to issue a Preservation Order shall lie with the courts of the Member State which have jurisdiction to rule on the substance of the matter in accordance with the relevant rules of jurisdiction applicable.

2. Notwithstanding paragraph 1, where the debtor is a consumer who has concluded a contract with the creditor for a purpose which can be regarded as being outside the debtor's trade or profession, jurisdiction to issue a Preservation Order intended to secure a claim relating to that contract shall lie only with the courts of the Member State in which the debtor is domiciled.

3. Where the creditor has already obtained a judgment or court settlement, jurisdiction to issue a Preservation Order for the claim specified in the judgment or court settlement shall lie with the courts of the Member State in which the judgment was issued or the court settlement was approved or concluded.

4. Where the creditor has obtained an authentic instrument, jurisdiction to issue a Preservation Order for the claim specified in that instrument shall lie with the courts designated for that purpose in the Member State in which that instrument was drawn up.

Article 7. Conditions for issuing a Preservation Order

1. The court shall issue the Preservation Order when the creditor has submitted sufficient evidence to satisfy the court that there is an urgent need for a protective measure in the form of a Preservation Order because there is a real risk that, without such a measure, the subsequent enforcement of the creditor's claim against the debtor will be impeded or made substantially more difficult.

2. Where the creditor has not yet obtained in a Member State a judgment, court settlement or authentic instrument requiring the debtor to pay the creditor's claim, the creditor shall also submit sufficient evidence to satisfy the court that he is likely to succeed on the substance of his claim against the debtor.

Article 8. Application for a Preservation Order

1. Applications for a Preservation Order shall be lodged using the form established in accordance with the advisory procedure referred to in Article 52(2).

2. The application shall include the following information:

(a)   the name and address of the court with which the application is lodged;

(b)   details concerning the creditor: name and contact details and, where applicable, name and contact details of the creditor's representative, and:

(i)   where the creditor is a natural person, his date of birth and, if applicable and available, his identification or passport number; or

(ii)   where the creditor is a legal person or any other entity having legal capacity to sue or be sued under the law of a Member State, the State of its incorporation, formation or registration and its identification or registration number or, where no such number exists, the date and place of its incorporation, formation or registration;

(c)   details concerning the debtor: name and contact details and, where applicable, name and contact details of the debtor's representative and, if available:

(i)   where the debtor is a natural person, his date of birth and identification or passport number; or

(ii)   where the debtor is a legal person or any other entity having legal capacity to sue or be sued under the law of a Member State, the State of its incorporation, formation or registration and its identification or registration number or, where no such number exists, the date and place of its incorporation, formation or registration;

(d)   a number enabling the identification of the bank, such as the IBAN or BIC and/or the name and address of the bank, with which the debtor holds one or more accounts to be preserved;

(e)   if available, the number of the account or accounts to be preserved and, in such a case, an indication as to whether any other accounts held by the debtor with the same bank should be preserved;

(f)   where none of the information required under point (d) can be provided, a statement that a request is made for the obtaining of account information pursuant to Article 14, where such a request is possible, and a substantiation as to why the creditor believes that the debtor holds one or more accounts with a bank in a specific Member State;

(g)   the amount for which the Preservation Order is sought:

(i)   where the creditor has not yet obtained a judgment, court settlement or authentic instrument, the amount of the principal claim or part thereof and of any interest recoverable pursuant to Article 15;

(ii) where the creditor has already obtained a judgment, court settlement or authentic instrument, the amount of the principal claim as specified in the judgment, court settlement or authentic instrument or part thereof and of any interest and costs recoverable pursuant to Article 15;

(h) where the creditor has not yet obtained a judgment, court settlement or authentic instrument:

(i) a description of all relevant elements supporting the jurisdiction of the court with which the application for the Preservation Order is lodged;

(ii) a description of all relevant circumstances invoked as the basis of the claim, and, where applicable, of the interest claimed;

(iii) a statement indicating whether the creditor has already initiated proceedings against the debtor on the substance of the matter;

(i) where the creditor has already obtained a judgment, court settlement or authentic instrument, a declaration that the judgment, court settlement or authentic instrument has not yet been complied with or, where it has been complied with in part, an indication of the extent of non-compliance;

(j) a description of all relevant circumstances justifying the issuing of the Preservation Order as required by Article 7(1);

(k) where applicable, an indication of the reasons why the creditor believes he should be exempted from providing security pursuant to Article 12;

(l) a list of the evidence provided by the creditor;

(m) a declaration as provided for in Article 16 as to whether the creditor has lodged with other courts or authorities an application for an equivalent national order or whether such an order has already been obtained or refused and, if obtained, the extent to which it has been implemented;

(n) an optional indication of the creditor's bank account to be used for any voluntary payment of the claim by the debtor;

(o) a declaration that the information provided by the creditor in the application is true and complete to the best of his knowledge and that the creditor is aware that any deliberately false or incomplete statements may lead to legal consequences under the law of the Member State in which the application is lodged or to liability pursuant to Article 13.

3. The application shall be accompanied by all relevant supporting documents and, where the creditor has already obtained a judgment, court settlement or authentic instrument, by a copy of the judgment, court settlement or authentic instrument which satisfies the conditions necessary to establish its authenticity.

4. The application and supporting documents may be submitted by any means of communication, including electronic, which are accepted under the procedural rules of the Member State in which the application is lodged.

Article 9. Taking of evidence

1. The court shall take its decision by means of a written procedure on the basis of the information and evidence provided by the creditor in or with his application. If the court considers that the evidence provided is insufficient, it may, where national law so allows, request the creditor to provide additional documentary evidence.

2. Notwithstanding paragraph 1 and subject to Article 11, the court may, provided that this does not delay the proceedings unduly, also use any other appropriate method of taking evidence available under its national law, such as an oral hearing of the creditor or of his witness(es) including through videoconference or other communication technology.

Article 10. Initiation of proceedings on the substance of the matter

1. Where the creditor has applied for a Preservation Order before initiating proceedings on the substance of the matter, he shall initiate such proceedings

and provide proof of such initiation to the court with which the application for the Preservation Order was lodged within 30 days of the date on which he lodged the application or within 14 days of the date of the issue of the Order, whichever date is the later. The court may also, at the request of the debtor, extend that time period, for example in order to allow the parties to settle the claim, and shall inform the two parties accordingly.

2. If the court has not received proof of the initiation of proceedings within the time period referred to in paragraph 1, the Preservation Order shall be revoked or shall terminate and the parties shall be informed accordingly.

Where the court that issued the Order is located in the Member State of enforcement, the revocation or termination of the Order in that Member State shall be done in accordance with the law of that Member State.

Where the revocation or termination needs to be implemented in a Member State other than the Member State of origin, the court shall revoke the Preservation Order by using the revocation form established by means of implementing acts adopted in accordance with the advisory procedure referred to in Article 52(2), and shall transmit the revocation form in accordance with Article 29 to the competent authority of the Member State of enforcement. That authority shall take the necessary steps by applying Article 23 as appropriate to have the revocation or termination implemented.

3. For the purposes of paragraph 1, proceedings on the substance of the matter shall be deemed to have been initiated:

(a)   at the time when the document instituting the proceedings or an equivalent document is lodged with the court, provided that the creditor has not subsequently failed to take the steps he was required to take to have service effected on the debtor; or

(b)   if the document has to be served before being lodged with the court, at the time when it is received by the authority responsible for service, provided that the creditor has not subsequently failed to take the steps he was required to take to have the document lodged with the court.

The authority responsible for service referred to in point (b) of the first subparagraph shall be the first authority receiving the documents to be served.

Article 11. Ex parte procedure
The debtor shall not be notified of the application for a Preservation Order or be heard prior to the issuing of the Order.

Article 12. Security to be provided by the creditor
1. Before issuing a Preservation Order in a case where the creditor has not yet obtained a judgment, court settlement or authentic instrument, the court shall require the creditor to provide security for an amount sufficient to prevent abuse of the procedure provided for by this Regulation and to ensure compensation for any damage suffered by the debtor as a result of the Order to the extent that the creditor is liable for such damage pursuant to Article 13.

By way of exception, the court may dispense with the requirement set out in the first subparagraph if it considers that the provision of security referred to in that subparagraph is inappropriate in the circumstances of the case.

2. Where the creditor has already obtained a judgment, court settlement or authentic instrument, the court may, before issuing the Order, require the creditor to provide security as referred to in the first subparagraph of paragraph 1 if it considers this necessary and appropriate in the circumstances of the case.

3. If the court requires security to be provided pursuant to this Article, it shall inform the creditor of the amount required and of the forms of security acceptable under the law of the Member State in which the court is located. It shall indicate to the creditor that it will issue the Preservation Order once security in accordance with those requirements has been provided.

Article 13. Liability of the creditor

1. The creditor shall be liable for any damage caused to the debtor by the Preservation Order due to fault on the creditor's part. The burden of proof shall lie with the debtor.

2. In the following cases, the fault of the creditor shall be presumed unless he proves otherwise:

(a) if the Order is revoked because the creditor has failed to initiate proceedings on the substance of the matter, unless that omission was a consequence of the debtor's payment of the claim or another form for settlement between the parties;

(b) if the creditor has failed to request the release of over-preserved amounts as provided for in Article 27;

(c) if it is subsequently found that the issue of the Order was not appropriate or appropriate only in a lower amount due to a failure on the part of the creditor to comply with his obligations under Article 16; or

(d) if the Order is revoked or its enforcement terminated because the creditor has failed to comply with his obligations under this Regulation with regard to service or translation of documents or with regard to curing the lack of service or the lack of translation.

3. Notwithstanding paragraph 1, Member States may maintain or introduce in their national law other grounds or types of liability or rules on the burden of proof. All other aspects relating to the creditor's liability towards the debtor not specifically addressed in paragraph 1 or 2 shall be governed by national law.

4. The law applicable to the liability of the creditor shall be the law of the Member State of enforcement.

If accounts are preserved in more than one Member State, the law applicable to the liability of the creditor shall be the law of the Member State of enforcement:

(a) in which the debtor has his habitual residence as defined in Article 23 of Regulation (EC) No 864/2007 of the European Parliament and of the Council, or, failing that,

(b) which has the closest connection with the case.

5. This Article does not deal with the question of possible liability of the creditor towards the bank or any third party.

Article 14. Request for the obtaining of account information

1. Where the creditor has obtained in a Member State an enforceable judgment, court settlement or authentic instrument which requires the debtor to pay the creditor's claim and the creditor has reasons to believe that the debtor holds one or more accounts with a bank in a specific Member State, but knows neither the name and/or address of the bank nor the IBAN, BIC or another bank number allowing the bank to be identified, he may request the court with which the application for the Preservation Order is lodged to request that the information authority of the Member State of enforcement obtain the information necessary to allow the bank or banks and the debtor's account or accounts to be identified.

Notwithstanding the first subparagraph, the creditor may make the request referred to in that subparagraph where the judgment, court settlement or authentic instrument obtained by the creditor is not yet enforceable and the amount to be preserved is substantial taking into account the relevant circumstances, and the creditor has submitted sufficient evidence to satisfy the court that there is an urgent need for account information because there is a risk that, without such information, the subsequent enforcement of the creditor's claim against the debtor is likely to be jeopardised and that this could consequently lead to a substantial deterioration of the creditor's financial situation.

2. The creditor shall make the request referred to in paragraph 1 in the application for the Preservation Order. The creditor shall substantiate why he believes that the debtor holds one or more accounts with a bank in the specific Member

State and shall provide all relevant information available to him about the debtor and the account or accounts to be preserved. If the court with which the application for a Preservation Order is lodged considers that the creditor's request is not sufficiently substantiated, it shall reject it.

3. When the court is satisfied that the creditor's request is well substantiated and that all the conditions and requirements for issuing the Preservation Order are met, except for the information requirement set out in point (d) of Article 8(2) and, where applicable, the security requirement pursuant to Article 12, the court shall transmit the request for information to the information authority of the Member State of enforcement in accordance with Article 29.

4. To obtain the information referred to in paragraph 1, the information authority in the Member State of enforcement shall use one of the methods available in that Member State pursuant to paragraph 5.

5. Each Member State shall make available in its national law at least one of the following methods of obtaining the information referred to in paragraph 1:

(a) an obligation on all banks in its territory to disclose, upon request by the information authority, whether the debtor holds an account with them;

(b) access for the information authority to the relevant information where that information is held by public authorities or administrations in registers or otherwise;

(c) the possibility for its courts to oblige the debtor to disclose with which bank or banks in its territory he holds one or more accounts where such an obligation is accompanied by an in personam order by the court prohibiting the withdrawal or transfer by him of funds held in his account or accounts up to the amount to be preserved by the Preservation Order; or

(d) any other methods which are effective and efficient for the purposes of obtaining the relevant information, provided that they are not disproportionately costly or time-consuming.

Irrespective of the method or methods made available by a Member State, all authorities involved in obtaining the information shall act expeditiously.

6. As soon as the information authority of the Member State of enforcement has obtained the account information, it shall transmit it to the requesting court in accordance with Article 29.

7. If the information authority is unable to obtain the information referred to in paragraph 1, it shall inform the requesting court accordingly. Where, as a result of the unavailability of account information, the application for a Preservation Order is rejected in full, the requesting court shall without delay release any security that the creditor may have provided pursuant to Article 12.

8. Where under this Article the information authority is provided with information by a bank or is granted access to account information held by public authorities or administrations in registers, the notification of the debtor of the disclosure of his personal data shall be deferred for 30 days, in order to prevent an early notification from jeopardising the effect of the Preservation Order.

Article 15. Interest and costs

1. At the request of the creditor, the Preservation Order shall include any interest accrued under the law applicable to the claim up to the date when the Order is issued, provided that the amount or type of interest is not such that its inclusion constitutes a violation of overriding mandatory provisions in the law of the Member State of origin.

2. Where the creditor has already obtained a judgment, court settlement or authentic instrument, the Preservation Order shall, at the request of the creditor, also include the costs of obtaining such judgment, settlement or instrument, to the extent that a determination has been made that those costs must be borne by the debtor.

Article 16. Parallel applications

1. The creditor may not submit to several courts at the same time parallel applications for a Preservation Order against the same debtor aimed at securing the same claim.

2. In his application for a Preservation Order, the creditor shall declare whether he has lodged with any other court or authority an application for an equivalent national order against the same debtor and aimed at securing the same claim or has already obtained such an order. He shall also indicate any applications for such an order which have been rejected as inadmissible or unfounded.

3. If the creditor obtains an equivalent national order against the same debtor and aimed at securing the same claim during the proceedings for the issuing of a Preservation Order, he shall without delay inform the court thereof and of any subsequent implementation of the national order granted. He shall also inform the court of any applications for an equivalent national order which have been rejected as inadmissible or unfounded.

4. Where the court is informed that the creditor has already obtained an equivalent national order, it shall consider, having regard to all the circumstances of the case, whether it is still appropriate to issue the Preservation Order, in full or in part.

Article 17. Decision on the application for the Preservation Order

1. The court seised of an application for a Preservation Order shall examine whether the conditions and requirements set out in this Regulation are met.

2. The court shall decide on the application without delay, but no later than by the expiry of the time-limits set out in Article 18.

3. Where the creditor has not provided all the information required by Article 8, the court may, unless the application is clearly inadmissible or unfounded, give the creditor the opportunity to complete or rectify the application within a period of time to be specified by the court. If the creditor fails to complete or rectify the application within that period, the application shall be rejected.

4. The Preservation Order shall be issued in the amount justified by the evidence referred to in Article 9 and as determined by the law applicable to the underlying claim, and shall include, where appropriate, interest and/or costs pursuant to Article 15.

The Order may not under any circumstances be issued in an amount exceeding the amount indicated by the creditor in his application.

5. The decision on the application shall be brought to the notice of the creditor in accordance with the procedure provided for by the law of the Member State of origin for equivalent national orders.

Article 18. Time-limits for the decision on the application for a Preservation Order

1. Where the creditor has not yet obtained a judgment, court settlement or authentic instrument, the court shall issue its decision by the end of the tenth working day after the creditor lodged or, where applicable, completed his application.

2. Where the creditor has already obtained a judgment, court settlement or authentic instrument, the court shall issue its decision by the end of the fifth working day after the creditor lodged or, where applicable, completed his application.

3. Where the court determines pursuant to Article 9(2) that an oral hearing of the creditor and, as the case may be, his witness(es) is necessary, the court shall hold the hearing without delay and shall issue its decision by the end of the fifth working day after the hearing has taken place.

4. In the situations referred to in Article 12, the time-limits set out in paragraphs 1, 2 and 3 of this Article shall apply to the decision requiring the creditor to provide security. The court shall issue its decision on the application for a

Preservation Order without delay once the creditor has provided the security required.

5. Notwithstanding paragraphs 1, 2 and 3 of this Article, in situations referred to in Article 14, the court shall issue its decision without delay once it has received the information referred to in Article 14(6) or (7), provided that any security required has been provided by the creditor by that time.

Article 19. Form and content of the Preservation Order

1. The Preservation Order shall be issued using the form established by means of implementing acts adopted in accordance with the advisory procedure referred to in Article 52(2) and shall bear a stamp, a signature and/or any other authentication of the court. The form shall consist of two parts:

(a) part A, containing the information set out in paragraph 2 to be provided to the bank, the creditor and the debtor; and

(b) part B, containing the information set out in paragraph 3 to be provided to the creditor and the debtor in addition to the information pursuant to paragraph 2.

2. Part A shall include the following information:

(a) the name and address of the court and the file number of the case;

(b) details of the creditor as indicated in point (b) of Article 8(2);

(c) details of the debtor as indicated in point (c) of Article 8(2);

(d) the name and address of the bank concerned by the Order;

(e) if the creditor has provided the account number of the debtor in the application, the number of the account or accounts to be preserved, and, where applicable, an indication as to whether any other accounts held by the debtor with the same bank also have to be preserved;

(f) where applicable, an indication that the number of any account to be preserved was obtained by means of a request pursuant to Article 14 and that the bank, where necessary pursuant to the second subparagraph of Article 24(4), is to obtain the number or numbers concerned from the information authority of the Member State of enforcement;

(g) the amount to be preserved by the Order;

(h) an instruction to the bank to implement the Order in accordance with Article 24;

(i) the date of issue of the Order;

(j) if the creditor has indicated an account in his application pursuant to point (n) of Article 8(2), an authorisation to the bank pursuant to Article 24(3) to release and transfer, if so requested by the debtor and if allowed by the law of the Member State of enforcement, funds up to the amount specified in the Order from the preserved account to the account that the creditor has indicated in his application;

(k) information on where to find the electronic version of the form to be used for the declaration pursuant to Article 25.

3. Part B shall include the following information:

(a) a description of the subject matter of the case and the court's reasoning for issuing the Order;

(b) the amount of the security provided by the creditor, if any;

(c) where applicable, the time-limit for initiating the proceedings on the substance of the matter and for proving such initiation to the issuing court;

(d) where applicable, an indication as to which documents must be translated pursuant to the second sentence of Article 49(1);

(e) where applicable, an indication that the creditor is responsible for initiating the enforcement of the Order and consequently, where applicable, an indication that the creditor is responsible for transmitting it to the competent authority of the Member State of enforcement pursuant to Article 23(3) and for initiating service on the debtor pursuant to Article 28(2), (3) and (4); and

(f)   information about the remedies available to the debtor.

4. Where the Preservation Order concerns accounts in different banks, a separate form (part A pursuant to paragraph 2) shall be filled in for each bank. In such a case, the form provided to the creditor and the debtor (parts A and B pursuant to paragraphs 2 and 3 respectively) shall contain a list of all banks concerned.

Article 20. Duration of the preservation

The funds preserved by the Preservation Order shall remain preserved as provided for in the Order or in any subsequent modification or limitation of that Order pursuant to Chapter 4:

(a)   until the Order is revoked;

(b)   until the enforcement of the Order is terminated; or

(c)   until a measure to enforce a judgment, court settlement or authentic instrument obtained by the creditor relating to the claim which the Preservation Order was aimed at securing has taken effect with respect to the funds preserved by the Order.

Article 21. Appeal against a refusal to issue the Preservation Order

1. The creditor shall have the right to appeal against any decision of the court rejecting, wholly or in part, his application for a Preservation Order.

2. Such an appeal shall be lodged within 30 days of the date on which the decision referred to in paragraph 1 was brought to the notice of the creditor. It shall be lodged with the court which the Member State concerned has communicated to the Commission pursuant to point (d) of Article 50(1).

3. Where the application for the Preservation Order was rejected in whole, the appeal shall be dealt with in ex parte proceedings as provided for in Article 11.

CHAPTER 3
RECOGNITION, ENFORCEABILITY AND ENFORCEMENT OF THE
PRESERVATION ORDER

Article 22. Recognition and enforceability

A Preservation Order issued in a Member State in accordance with this Regulation shall be recognised in the other Member States without any special procedure being required and shall be enforceable in the other Member States without the need for a declaration of enforceability.

Article 23. Enforcement of the Preservation Order

1. Subject to the provisions of this Chapter, the Preservation Order shall be enforced in accordance with the procedures applicable to the enforcement of equivalent national orders in the Member State of enforcement.

2. All authorities involved in the enforcement of the Order shall act without delay.

3. Where the Preservation Order was issued in a Member State other than the Member State of enforcement, part A of the Order as indicated in Article 19(2) and a blank standard form for the declaration pursuant to Article 25 shall, for the purposes of paragraph 1 of this Article, be transmitted in accordance with Article 29 to the competent authority of the Member State of enforcement.

The transmission shall be done by the issuing court or the creditor, depending on who is responsible under the law of the Member State of origin for initiating the enforcement procedure.

4. The Order shall be accompanied, where necessary, by a translation or transliteration into the official language of the Member State of enforcement or, where there are several official languages in that Member State, the official language or one of the official languages of the place where the Order is to be implemented. Such translation or transliteration shall be provided by the issuing court by making use of the appropriate language version of the standard form referred to in Article 19.

5. The competent authority of the Member State of enforcement shall take the necessary steps to have the Order enforced in accordance with its national law.

6. Where the Preservation Order concerns more than one bank in the same Member State or in different Member States, a separate form for each bank as indicated in Article 19(4) shall be transmitted to the competent authority in the relevant Member State of enforcement.

Article 24. Implementation of the Preservation Order

1. A bank to which a Preservation Order is addressed shall implement it without delay following receipt of the Order or, where the law of the Member State of enforcement so provides, of a corresponding instruction to implement the Order.

2. To implement the Preservation Order, the bank shall, subject to the provisions of Article 31, preserve the amount specified in the Order either:

(a)   by ensuring that that amount is not transferred or withdrawn from the account or accounts indicated in the Order or identified pursuant to paragraph 4; or

(b)   where national law so provides, by transferring that amount to an account dedicated for preservation purposes.

The final amount preserved may be subject to the settlement of transactions which are already pending at the moment when the Order or a corresponding instruction is received by the bank. However, such pending transactions may only be taken into account when they are settled before the bank issues the declaration pursuant to Article 25 by the time-limits set out in Article 25(1).

3. Notwithstanding point (a) of paragraph 2, the bank shall be authorised, at the request of the debtor, to release funds preserved and to transfer those funds to the account of the creditor indicated in the Order for the purposes of paying the creditor's claim, if all the following conditions are met:

(a)   such authorisation of the bank is specifically indicated in the Order in accordance with point (j) of Article 19(2);

(b)   the law of the Member State of enforcement allows for such release and transfer; and

(c)   there are no competing Orders with regard to the account concerned.

4. Where the Preservation Order does not specify the number or numbers of the account or accounts of the debtor but provides only the name and other details regarding the debtor, the bank or other entity responsible for enforcing the Order shall identify the account or accounts held by the debtor with the bank indicated in the Order.

If, on the basis of the information provided in the Order, it is not possible for the bank or other entity to identify with certainty an account of the debtor, the bank shall:

(a)   where, in accordance with point (f) of Article 19(2), it is indicated in the Order that the number or numbers of the account or accounts to be preserved was or were obtained by means of a request pursuant to Article 14, obtain that number or those numbers from the information authority of the Member State of enforcement; and

(b)   in all other cases, not implement the Order.

5. Any funds held in the account or accounts referred to in point (a) of paragraph 2 which exceed the amount specified in the Preservation Order shall remain unaffected by the implementation of the Order.

6. Where, at the time of the implementation of the Preservation Order, the funds held in the account or accounts referred to in point (a) of paragraph 2 are insufficient to preserve the full amount specified in the Order, the Order shall be implemented only in the amount available in the account or accounts.

7. Where the Preservation Order covers several accounts held by the debtor with the same bank and those accounts contain funds that exceed the amount specified in the Order, the Order shall be implemented in the following order of priority:

(a)   savings accounts in the sole name of the debtor;
(b)   current accounts in the sole name of the debtor;
(c)   savings accounts in joint names, subject to Article 30;
(d)   current accounts in joint names, subject to Article 30.

8. Where the currency of the funds held in the account or accounts referred to in point (a) of paragraph 2 is not the same as that in which the Preservation Order was issued, the bank shall convert the amount specified in the Order into the currency of the funds by reference to the foreign exchange reference rate of the European Central Bank or the exchange rate of the central bank of the Member State of enforcement for sale of that currency on the day and at the time of the implementation of the Order, and shall preserve the corresponding amount in the currency of the funds.

Article 25. Declaration concerning the preservation of funds

1. By the end of the third working day following the implementation of the Preservation Order, the bank or other entity responsible for enforcing the Order in the Member State of enforcement shall issue a declaration using the declaration form established by means of implementing acts adopted in accordance with the advisory procedure referred to in Article 52(2), indicating whether and to what extent funds in the debtor's account or accounts have been preserved and, if so, on which date the Order was implemented. If, in exceptional circumstances, it is not possible for the bank or other entity to issue the declaration within three working days, it shall issue it as soon as possible but by no later than the end of the eighth working day following the implementation of the Order.

The declaration shall be transmitted, without delay, in accordance with paragraphs 2 and 3.

2. Where the Order was issued in the Member State of enforcement, the bank or other entity responsible for enforcing the Order shall transmit the declaration in accordance with Article 29 to the issuing court and by registered post attested by an acknowledgment of receipt, or by equivalent electronic means, to the creditor.

3. Where the Order was issued in a Member State other than the Member State of enforcement, the declaration shall be transmitted in accordance with Article 29 to the competent authority of the Member State of enforcement, unless it was issued by that same authority.

By the end of the first working day following the receipt or issue of the declaration, that authority shall transmit the declaration in accordance with Article 29 to the issuing court and by registered post attested by an acknowledgment of receipt, or by equivalent electronic means, to the creditor.

4. The bank or other entity responsible for enforcing the Preservation Order shall, upon request by the debtor, disclose to the debtor the details of the Order. The bank or entity may also do so in the absence of such a request.

Article 26. Liability of the bank

Any liability of the bank for failure to comply with its obligations under this Regulation shall be governed by the law of the Member State of enforcement.

Article 27. Duty of the creditor to request the release of over-preserved amounts

1. The creditor shall be under a duty to take the necessary steps to ensure the release of any amount which, following the implementation of the Preservation Order, exceeds the amount specified in the Preservation Order:

(a)   where the Order covers several accounts in the same Member State or in different Member States; or

(b)   where the Order was issued after the implementation of one or more equivalent national orders against the same debtor and aimed at securing the same claim.

2. By the end of the third working day following receipt of any declaration

pursuant to Article 25 showing such over-preservation, the creditor shall, by the swiftest possible means and using the form for requesting the release of over-preserved amounts, established by means of implementing acts adopted in accordance with the advisory procedure referred to in Article 52(2), submit a request for the release to the competent authority of the Member State of enforcement in which the over-preservation has occurred.

That authority shall, upon receipt of the request, promptly instruct the bank concerned to effect the release of the over-preserved amounts. Article 24(7) shall apply, as appropriate, in the reverse order of priority.

3. This Article shall not preclude a Member State from providing in its national law that the release of over-preserved funds from any account maintained in its territory is to be initiated by the competent enforcement authority of that Member State of its own motion.

Article 28. Service on the debtor

1. The Preservation Order, the other documents referred to in paragraph 5 of this Article and the declaration pursuant to Article 25 shall be served on the debtor in accordance with this Article.

2. Where the debtor is domiciled in the Member State of origin, service shall be effected in accordance with the law of that Member State. Service shall be initiated by the issuing court or the creditor, depending on who is responsible for initiating service in the Member State of origin, by the end of the third working day following the day of receipt of the declaration pursuant to Article 25 showing that amounts have been preserved.

3. Where the debtor is domiciled in a Member State other than the Member State of origin, the issuing court or the creditor, depending on who is responsible for initiating service in the Member State of origin, shall, by the end of the third working day following the day of receipt of the declaration pursuant to Article 25 showing that amounts have been preserved, transmit the documents referred to in paragraph 1 of this Article in accordance with Article 29 to the competent authority of the Member State in which the debtor is domiciled. That authority shall, without delay, take the necessary steps to have service effected on the debtor in accordance with the law of the Member State in which the debtor is domiciled.

Where the Member State in which the debtor is domiciled is the only Member State of enforcement, the documents referred to in paragraph 5 of this Article shall be transmitted to the competent authority of that Member State at the time of transmission of the Order in accordance with Article 23(3). In such a case, that competent authority shall initiate the service of all documents referred to in paragraph 1 of this Article by the end of the third working day following the day of receipt or issue of the declaration pursuant to Article 25 showing that amounts have been preserved.

The competent authority shall inform the issuing court or the creditor, depending on who transmitted the documents to be served, of the result of the service on the debtor.

4. Where the debtor is domiciled in a third State, service shall be effected in accordance with the rules on international service applicable in the Member State of origin.

5. The following documents shall be served on the debtor and shall, where necessary, be accompanied by a translation or transliteration as provided for in Article 49(1):

(a) the Preservation Order using parts A and B of the form referred to in Article 19(2) and (3);

(b) the application for the Preservation Order submitted by the creditor to the court;

(c) copies of all documents submitted by the creditor to the court in order to obtain the Order.

6. Where the Preservation Order concerns more than one bank, only the first declaration pursuant to Article 25 showing that amounts have been preserved shall be served on the debtor in accordance with this Article. Any subsequent declarations pursuant to Article 25 shall be brought to the notice of the debtor without delay.

Article 29. Transmission of documents

1. Where this Regulation provides for transmission of documents in accordance with this Article, such transmission may be carried out by any appropriate means, provided that the content of the document received is true and faithful to that of the document transmitted and that all information contained in it is easily legible.

2. The court or authority that received documents in accordance with paragraph 1 of this Article shall, by the end of the working day following the day of receipt, send to the authority, creditor or bank that transmitted the documents an acknowledgment of receipt, employing the swiftest possible means of transmission and using the standard form established by means of implementing acts adopted in accordance with the advisory procedure referred to in Article 52(2).

Article 30. Preservation of joint and nominee accounts

Funds held in accounts which, according to the bank's records, are not exclusively held by the debtor or are held by a third party on behalf of the debtor or by the debtor on behalf of a third party, may be preserved under this Regulation only to the extent to which they may be subject to preservation under the law of the Member State of enforcement.

Article 31. Amounts exempt from preservation

1. Amounts that are exempt from seizure under the law of the Member State of enforcement shall be exempt from preservation under this Regulation.

2. Where, under the law of the Member State of enforcement, the amounts referred to in paragraph 1 are exempted from seizure without any request from the debtor, the body responsible for exempting such amounts in that Member State shall, of its own motion, exempt the relevant amounts from preservation.

3. Where, under the law of the Member State of enforcement, the amounts referred to in paragraph 1 of this Article are exempted from seizure at the request of the debtor, such amounts shall be exempted from preservation upon application by the debtor as provided for by point (a) of Article 34(1).

Article 32. Ranking of the Preservation Order

The Preservation Order shall have the same rank, if any, as an equivalent national order in the Member State of enforcement.

CHAPTER 4
REMEDIES

Article 33. Remedies of the debtor against the Preservation Order

1. Upon application by the debtor to the competent court of the Member State of origin, the Preservation Order shall be revoked or, where applicable, modified on the ground that:

(a)   the conditions or requirements set out in this Regulation were not met;

(b)   the Order, the declaration pursuant to Article 25 and/or the other documents referred to in Article 28(5) were not served on the debtor within 14 days of the preservation of his account or accounts;

(c)   the documents served on the debtor in accordance with Article 28 did not meet the language requirements set out in Article 49(1);

(d)   preserved amounts exceeding the amount of the Order were not released in accordance with Article 27;

(e)   the claim the enforcement of which the creditor was seeking to secure by means of the Order has been paid in full or in part;

(f)   a judgment on the substance of the matter has dismissed the claim the enforcement of which the creditor was seeking to secure by means of the Order; or

(g)   the judgment on the substance of the matter, or the court settlement or authentic instrument, the enforcement of which the creditor was seeking to secure by means of the Order has been set aside or, as the case may be, annulled.

2. Upon application by the debtor to the competent court of the Member State of origin, the decision concerning the security pursuant to Article 12 shall be reviewed on the ground that the conditions or requirements of that Article were not met.

Where, on the basis of such a remedy, the court requires the creditor to provide security or additional security, the first sentence of Article 12(3) shall apply as appropriate and the court shall indicate that the Preservation Order will be revoked or modified if the (additional) security required is not provided by the time-limit specified by the court.

3. The remedy applied for under point (b) of paragraph 1 shall be granted unless the lack of service is cured within 14 days of the creditor being informed of the debtor's application for a remedy pursuant to point (b) of paragraph 1.

Unless the lack of service was already cured by other means, the lack of service shall, for the purposes of assessing whether or not the remedy pursuant to point (b) of paragraph 1 is to be granted, be deemed to be cured:

(a)   if the creditor requests the body responsible for service under the law of the Member State of origin to serve the documents on the debtor; or

(b)   where the debtor has indicated in his application for a remedy that he agrees to collect the documents at the court of the Member State of origin and where the creditor was responsible for providing translations, if the creditor transmits to that court any translations required pursuant to Article 49(1).

The body responsible for service under the law of the Member State of origin shall, at the request of the creditor pursuant to point (a) of the second sub-paragraph of this paragraph, without delay serve the documents on the debtor by registered post attested by an acknowledgment of receipt at the address indicated by the debtor in accordance with paragraph 5 of this Article.

Where the creditor was responsible for initiating the service of the documents referred to in Article 28, a lack of service may only be cured if the creditor demonstrates that he had taken all the steps he was required to take to have the initial service of the documents effected.

4. The remedy applied for under point (c) of paragraph 1 shall be granted unless the creditor provides to the debtor the translations required pursuant to this Regulation within 14 days of the creditor being informed of the application by the debtor for a remedy pursuant to point (c) of paragraph 1.

The second and third subparagraphs of paragraph 3 shall apply as appropriate.

5. In his application for a remedy under points (b) and (c) of paragraph 1, the debtor shall indicate an address to which the documents and the translations referred to in Article 28 can be sent in accordance with paragraphs 3 and 4 of this Article or, alternatively, shall indicate that he agrees to collect those documents at the court of the Member State of origin.

Article 34. Remedies of the debtor against enforcement of the Preservation Order

1. Notwithstanding Articles 33 and 35, upon application by the debtor to the competent court or, where national law so provides, to the competent enforcement authority in the Member State of enforcement, the enforcement of the Preservation Order in that Member State shall be:

(a)   limited on the ground that certain amounts held in the account should be exempt from seizure in accordance with Article 31(3), or that amounts exempt from seizure have not or not correctly been taken into account in the implementation of the Order in accordance with Article 31(2); or

(b) terminated on the ground that:

(i) the account preserved is excluded from the scope of this Regulation pursuant to Article 2(3) and (4);

(ii) enforcement of the judgment, court settlement or authentic instrument which the creditor was seeking to secure by means of the Order has been refused in the Member State of enforcement;

(iii) the enforceability of the judgment the enforcement of which the creditor was seeking to secure by means of the Order has been suspended in the Member State of origin; or

(iv) point (b), (c), (d), (e), (f) or (g) of Article 33(1) applies. Article 33(3), (4) and (5) shall apply as appropriate.

2. Upon application by the debtor to the competent court in the Member State of enforcement, the enforcement of the Preservation Order in that Member State shall be terminated if it is manifestly contrary to the public policy (ordre public) of the Member State of enforcement.

Article 35. Other remedies available to the debtor and the creditor

1. The debtor or the creditor may apply to the court that issued the Preservation Order for a modification or a revocation of the Order on the ground that the circumstances on the basis of which the Order was issued have changed.

2. The court that issued the Preservation Order may also, where the law of the Member State of origin so permits, of its own motion modify or revoke the Order due to changed circumstances.

3. The debtor and the creditor may, on the ground that they have agreed to settle the claim, apply jointly to the court that issued the Preservation Order for revocation or modification of the Order or to the competent court of the Member State of enforcement or, where national law so provides, to the competent enforcement authority in that Member State, for termination or limitation of the enforcement of the Order.

4. The creditor may apply to the competent court of the Member State of enforcement or, where national law so provides, to the competent enforcement authority in that Member State, for modification of the enforcement of the Preservation Order, consisting of an adjustment to the exemption applied in that Member State pursuant to Article 31, on the ground that other exemptions have already been applied in a sufficiently high amount in relation to one or several accounts maintained in one or more other Member States and that an adjustment is therefore appropriate.

Article 36. Procedure for the remedies pursuant to Articles 33, 34 and 35

1. The application for a remedy pursuant to Article 33, 34 or 35 shall be made using the remedy form established by means of implementing acts adopted in accordance with the advisory procedure referred to in Article 52(2). The application may be made at any time and may be submitted by any means of communication, including electronic means, which are accepted under the procedural rules of the Member State in which the application is lodged.

2. The application shall be brought to the notice of the other party.

3. Except where the application was submitted by the debtor pursuant to point (a) of Article 34(1) or pursuant to Article 35(3), the decision on the application shall be issued after both parties have been given the opportunity to present their case, including by such appropriate means of communication technology as are available and accepted under the national law of each of the Member States involved.

4. The decision shall be issued without delay, but no later than 21 days after the court or, where national law so provides, the competent enforcement authority has received all the information necessary for its decision. The decision shall be brought to the notice of the parties.

5. The decision revoking or modifying the Preservation Order and the decision limiting or terminating the enforcement of the Preservation Order shall be enforceable immediately.

Where the remedy was applied for in the Member State of origin, the court shall, in accordance with Article 29, transmit the decision on the remedy without delay to the competent authority of the Member State of enforcement, using the form established by means of implementing acts adopted in accordance with the advisory procedure referred to in Article 52(2). That authority shall, immediately upon receipt, ensure that the decision on the remedy is implemented.

Where the decision on the remedy relates to a bank account maintained in the Member State of origin, it shall be implemented with respect to that bank account in accordance with the law of the Member State of origin.

Where the remedy was applied for in the Member State of enforcement, the decision on the remedy shall be implemented in accordance with the law of the Member State of enforcement.

Article 37. Right to appeal

Either party shall have the right to appeal against a decision issued pursuant to Article 33, 34 or 35. Such an appeal shall be submitted using the appeal form established by means of implementing acts adopted in accordance with the advisory procedure referred to in Article 52(2).

Article 38. Right to provide security in lieu of preservation

1 Upon application by the debtor:

(a)   the court that issued the Preservation Order may order the release of the funds preserved if the debtor provides to that court security in the amount of the Order, or an alternative assurance in a form acceptable under the law of the Member State in which the court is located and of a value at least equivalent to that amount;

(b)   the competent court or, where national law so provides, the competent enforcement authority of the Member State of enforcement may terminate the enforcement of the Preservation Order in the Member State of enforcement if the debtor provides to that court or authority security in the amount preserved in that Member State, or an alternative assurance in a form acceptable under the law of the Member State in which the court is located and of a value at least equivalent to that amount.

2. Articles 23 and 24 shall apply as appropriate to the release of the funds preserved. The provision of the security in lieu of preservation shall be brought to the notice of the creditor in accordance with national law.

Article 39. Right of third parties

1. The right of a third party to contest a Preservation Order shall be governed by the law of the Member State of origin.

2. The right of a third party to contest the enforcement of a Preservation Order shall be governed by the law of the Member State of enforcement.

3. Without prejudice to other rules of jurisdiction laid down in Union law or national law, jurisdiction in respect of any action brought by a third party:

(a)   to contest a Preservation Order shall lie with the courts of the Member State of origin, and

(b)   to contest the enforcement of the Preservation Order in the Member State of enforcement shall lie with the courts of the Member State of enforcement or, where the national law of that Member State so provides, with the competent enforcement authority.

CHAPTER 5
GENERAL PROVISIONS

Article 40. Legalisation or other similar formality

No legalisation or other similar formality shall be required in the context of this Regulation.

Article 41. Legal representation

Representation by a lawyer or other legal professional shall not be mandatory in proceedings to obtain a Preservation Order. In proceedings pursuant to Chapter 4, representation by a lawyer or another legal professional shall not be mandatory unless, under the law of the Member State of the court or authority with which the application for a remedy is lodged, such representation is mandatory irrespective of the nationality or domicile of the parties.

Article 42. Court fees

The court fees in proceedings to obtain a Preservation Order or a remedy against an Order shall not be higher than the fees for obtaining an equivalent national order or a remedy against such a national order.

Article 43. Costs incurred by the banks

1. A bank shall be entitled to seek payment or reimbursement from the creditor or the debtor of the costs incurred in implementing a Preservation Order only where, under the law of the Member State of enforcement, the bank is entitled to such payment or reimbursement in relation to equivalent national orders.

2. Fees charged by a bank to cover the costs referred to in paragraph 1 shall be determined taking into account the complexity of the implementation of the Preservation Order, and may not be higher than the fees charged for the implementation of equivalent national orders.

3. Fees charged by a bank to cover the costs of providing account information pursuant to Article 14 may not be higher than the costs actually incurred and, where applicable, not higher than the fees charged for the provision of account information in the context of equivalent national orders.

Article 44. Fees charged by authorities

Fees charged by any authority or other body in the Member State of enforcement which is involved in the processing or enforcement of a Preservation Order, or in providing account information pursuant to Article 14, shall be determined on the basis of a scale of fees or other set of rules established in advance by each Member State and transparently setting out the applicable fees. In establishing that scale or other set of rules, a Member State may take into account the amount of the Order and the complexity involved in processing it. Where applicable, the fees may not be higher than the fees charged in connection with equivalent national orders.

Article 45. Time frames

Where, in exceptional circumstances, it is not possible for the court or the authority involved to respect the time frames provided for in Article 14(7), Article 18, Article 23(2), the second subparagraph of Article 25(3), Article 28(2), (3) and (6), Article 33(3) and Article 36(4) and (5), the court or authority shall take the steps required by those provisions as soon as possible.

Article 46. Relationship with national procedural law

1. All procedural issues not specifically dealt with in this Regulation shall be governed by the law of the Member State in which the procedure takes place.

2. The effects of the opening of insolvency proceedings on individual enforcement actions, such as the enforcement of a Preservation Order, shall be governed by the law of the Member State in which the insolvency proceedings have been opened.

Article 47. Data protection
1. Personal data which are obtained, processed or transmitted under this Regulation shall be adequate, relevant and not excessive in relation to the purpose for which they were obtained, processed or transmitted, and shall be used only for that purpose.
2. The competent authority, the information authority and any other entity responsible for enforcing the Preservation Order may not store the data referred to in paragraph 1 beyond the period necessary for the purpose for which they were obtained, processed or transmitted, which in any event shall not be longer than six months after the proceedings have ended, and shall, during that period, ensure the appropriate protection of those data. This paragraph does not apply to data processed or stored by courts in the exercise of their judicial functions.

Article 48. Relationship with other instruments
This Regulation is without prejudice to:
(a) Regulation (EC) No 1393/2007 of the European Parliament and of the Council, except as provided for in Article 10(2), Article 14(3) and (6), Article 17(5), Article 23(3) and (6), Article 25(2) and (3), Article 28(1), (3), (5) and (6), Article 29, Article 33(3), Article 36(2) and (4), and Article 49(1) of this Regulation;
(b) Regulation (EU) No 1215/2012;
(c) Regulation (EC) No 1346/2000;
(d) Directive 95/46/EC, except as provided for in Articles 14(8) and 47 of this Regulation;
(e) Regulation (EC) No 1206/2001 of the European Parliament and of the Council;
(f) Regulation (EC) No 864/2007, except as provided for in Article 13(4) of this Regulation.

Article 49. Languages
1. Any documents listed in points (a) and (b) of Article 28(5) to be served on the debtor which are not in the official language of the Member State in which the debtor is domiciled or, where there are several official languages in that Member State, the official language or one of the official languages of the place where the debtor is domiciled or another language which he understands, shall be accompanied by a translation or transliteration into one of those languages. Documents listed in point (c) of Article 28(5) shall not be translated unless the court decides, exceptionally, that specific documents need to be translated or transliterated in order to enable the debtor to assert his rights.
2. Any documents to be addressed under this Regulation to a court or competent authority may also be in any other official language of the institutions of the Union, if the Member State concerned has indicated that it can accept such other language.
3. Any translation made under this Regulation shall be done by a person qualified to do translations in one of the Member States.

Article 50. Information to be provided by Member States
1. By 18 July 2016, the Member States shall communicate the following information to the Commission:
(a) the courts designated as competent to issue a Preservation Order (Article 6(4));
(b) the authority designated as competent to obtain account information (Article 14);
(c) the methods of obtaining account information available under their national law (Article 14(5));
(d) the courts with which an appeal is to be lodged (Article 21);
(e) the authority or authorities designated as competent to receive, transmit

and serve the Preservation Order and other documents under this Regulation (point (14) of Article 4);

(f)   the authority competent to enforce the Preservation Order in accordance with Chapter 3;

(g)   the extent to which joint and nominee accounts can be preserved under their national law (Article 30);

(h)   the rules applicable to amounts exempt from seizure under national law (Article 31);

(i)   whether, under their national law, banks are entitled to charge fees for the implementation of equivalent national orders or for providing account information and, if so, which party is liable, provisionally and finally, to pay those fees (Article 43);

(j)   the scale of fees or other set of rules setting out the applicable fees charged by any authority or other body involved in the processing or enforcement of the Preservation Order (Article 44);

(k)   whether any ranking is conferred on equivalent national orders under national law (Article 32);

(l)   the courts or, where applicable, the enforcement authority, competent to grant a remedy (Article 33(1), Article 34(1) or (2));

(m)   the courts with which an appeal is to be lodged, the period of time, if prescribed, within which such an appeal must be lodged under national law and the event marking the start of that period (Article 37);

(n)   an indication of court fees (Article 42); and

(o)   the languages accepted for translations of the documents (Article 49(2)).

The Member States shall apprise the Commission of any subsequent changes to that information.

2. The Commission shall make the information publicly available through any appropriate means, in particular through the European Judicial Network in civil and commercial matters.

Article 51. Establishment and subsequent amendment of the forms

The Commission shall adopt implementing acts establishing and subsequently amending the forms referred to in Articles 8(1), 10(2), 19(1), 25(1), 27(2), 29(2) and 36(1), the second subparagraph of Article 36(5) and Article 37. Those implementing acts shall be adopted in accordance with the advisory procedure referred to in Article 52(2).

Article 52. Committee procedure

1. The Commission shall be assisted by a committee. That committee shall be a committee within the meaning of Regulation (EU) No 182/2011.

2. Where reference is made to this paragraph, Article 4 of Regulation (EU) No 182/2011 shall apply.

Article 53. Monitoring and review

1. By 18 January 2022, the Commission shall submit to the European Parliament, to the Council and to the European Economic and Social Committee a report on the application of this Regulation, including an evaluation as to whether:

(a)   financial instruments should be included in the scope of this Regulation, and

(b)   amounts credited to the debtor's account after the implementation of the Preservation Order could be made subject to preservation under the Order.

The report shall be accompanied, if appropriate, by a proposal to amend this Regulation and an assessment of the impact of the amendments to be introduced.

2. For the purposes of paragraph 1, the Member States shall collect and make available to the Commission upon request information on:

(a)   the number of applications for a Preservation Order and the number of cases in which the Order was issued;

(b)   the number of applications for a remedy pursuant to Articles 33 and 34 and, if possible, the number of cases in which the remedy was granted; and

(c)   the number of appeals lodged pursuant to Article 37 and, if possible, the number of cases in which such an appeal was successful.

CHAPTER 6
FINAL PROVISIONS

Article 54. Entry into force

This Regulation shall enter into force on the twentieth day following that of its publication in the Official Journal of the European Union.

It shall apply from 18 January 2017, with the exception of Article 50, which shall apply from 18 July 2016.

This Regulation shall be binding in its entirety and directly applicable in the Member States in accordance with the Treaties.

Done at Brussels, 15 May 2014.

REGULATION (EU) 2015/848 OF THE EUROPEAN PARLIAMENT AND OF THE COUNCIL OF 20 MAY 2015 ON INSOLVENCY PROCEEDINGS (RECAST)

THE EUROPEAN PARLIAMENT AND THE COUNCIL OF THE EUROPEAN UNION,

Having regard to the Treaty on the Functioning of the European Union, and in particular Article 81 thereof,

Having regard to the proposal from the European Commission,

After transmission of the draft legislative act to the national parliaments,

Having regard to the opinion of the European Economic and Social Committee,

Acting in accordance with the ordinary legislative procedure,

Whereas:

(1)   On 12 December 2012, the Commission adopted a report on the application of Council Regulation (EC) No 1346/2000. The report concluded that the Regulation is functioning well in general but that it would be desirable to improve the application of certain of its provisions in order to enhance the effective administration of cross-border insolvency proceedings. Since that Regulation has been amended several times and further amendments are to be made, it should be recast in the interest of clarity.

(2)   The Union has set the objective of establishing an area of freedom, security and justice.

(3)   The proper functioning of the internal market requires that cross-border insolvency proceedings should operate efficiently and effectively. This Regulation needs to be adopted in order to achieve that objective, which falls within the scope of judicial cooperation in civil matters within the meaning of Article 81 of the Treaty.

(4)   The activities of undertakings have more and more cross-border effects and are therefore increasingly being regulated by Union law. The insolvency of such undertakings also affects the proper functioning of the internal market, and there is a need for a Union act requiring coordination of the measures to be taken regarding an insolvent debtor's assets.

(5)   It is necessary for the proper functioning of the internal market to avoid incentives for parties to transfer assets or judicial proceedings from one Member

State to another, seeking to obtain a more favourable legal position to the detriment of the general body of creditors (forum shopping).

(6)   This Regulation should include provisions governing jurisdiction for opening insolvency proceedings and actions which are directly derived from insolvency proceedings and are closely linked with them. This Regulation should also contain provisions regarding the recognition and enforcement of judgments issued in such proceedings, and provisions regarding the law applicable to insolvency proceedings. In addition, this Regulation should lay down rules on the coordination of insolvency proceedings which relate to the same debtor or to several members of the same group of companies.

(7)   Bankruptcy, proceedings relating to the winding-up of insolvent companies or other legal persons, judicial arrangements, compositions and analogous proceedings and actions related to such proceedings are excluded from the scope of Regulation (EU) No 1215/2012 of the European Parliament and of the Council. Those proceedings should be covered by this Regulation. The interpretation of this Regulation should as much as possible avoid regulatory loopholes between the two instruments. However, the mere fact that a national procedure is not listed in Annex A to this Regulation should not imply that it is covered by Regulation (EU) No 1215/2012.

(8)   In order to achieve the aim of improving the efficiency and effectiveness of insolvency proceedings having cross-border effects, it is necessary, and appropriate, that the provisions on jurisdiction, recognition and applicable law in this area should be contained in a Union measure which is binding and directly applicable in Member States.

(9)   This Regulation should apply to insolvency proceedings which meet the conditions set out in it, irrespective of whether the debtor is a natural person or a legal person, a trader or an individual. Those insolvency proceedings are listed exhaustively in Annex A. In respect of the national procedures contained in Annex A, this Regulation should apply without any further examination by the courts of another Member State as to whether the conditions set out in this Regulation are met. National insolvency procedures not listed in Annex A should not be covered by this Regulation.

(10)   The scope of this Regulation should extend to proceedings which promote the rescue of economically viable but distressed businesses and which give a second chance to entrepreneurs. It should, in particular, extend to proceedings which provide for restructuring of a debtor at a stage where there is only a likelihood of insolvency, and to proceedings which leave the debtor fully or partially in control of its assets and affairs. It should also extend to proceedings providing for a debt discharge or a debt adjustment in relation to consumers and self-employed persons, for example by reducing the amount to be paid by the debtor or by extending the payment period granted to the debtor. Since such proceedings do not necessarily entail the appointment of an insolvency practitioner, they should be covered by this Regulation if they take place under the control or supervision of a court. In this context, the term 'control' should include situations where the court only intervenes on appeal by a creditor or other interested parties.

(11)   This Regulation should also apply to procedures which grant a temporary stay on enforcement actions brought by individual creditors where such actions could adversely affect negotiations and hamper the prospects of a restructuring of the debtor's business. Such procedures should not be detrimental to the general body of creditors and, if no agreement on a restructuring plan can be reached, should be preliminary to other procedures covered by this Regulation.

(12)   This Regulation should apply to proceedings the opening of which is subject to publicity in order to allow creditors to become aware of the proceedings and to lodge their claims, thereby ensuring the collective nature of the proceedings, and in order to give creditors the opportunity to challenge the jurisdiction of the court which has opened the proceedings.

(13) Accordingly, insolvency proceedings which are confidential should be excluded from the scope of this Regulation. While such proceedings may play an important role in some Member States, their confidential nature makes it impossible for a creditor or a court located in another Member State to know that such proceedings have been opened, thereby making it difficult to provide for the recognition of their effects throughout the Union.

(14) The collective proceedings which are covered by this Regulation should include all or a significant part of the creditors to whom a debtor owes all or a substantial proportion of the debtor's outstanding debts provided that the claims of those creditors who are not involved in such proceedings remain unaffected. Proceedings which involve only the financial creditors of a debtor should also be covered. Proceedings which do not include all the creditors of a debtor should be proceedings aimed at rescuing the debtor. Proceedings that lead to a definitive cessation of the debtor's activities or the liquidation of the debtor's assets should include all the debtor's creditors. Moreover, the fact that some insolvency proceedings for natural persons exclude specific categories of claims, such as maintenance claims, from the possibility of a debt-discharge should not mean that such proceedings are not collective.

(15) This Regulation should also apply to proceedings that, under the law of some Member States, are opened and conducted for a certain period of time on an interim or provisional basis before a court issues an order confirming the continuation of the proceedings on a non-interim basis. Although labelled as 'interim', such proceedings should meet all other requirements of this Regulation.

(16) This Regulation should apply to proceedings which are based on laws relating to insolvency. However, proceedings that are based on general company law not designed exclusively for insolvency situations should not be considered to be based on laws relating to insolvency. Similarly, the purpose of adjustment of debt should not include specific proceedings in which debts of a natural person of very low income and very low asset value are written off, provided that this type of proceedings never makes provision for payment to creditors.

(17) This Regulation's scope should extend to proceedings which are triggered by situations in which the debtor faces non-financial difficulties, provided that such difficulties give rise to a real and serious threat to the debtor's actual or future ability to pay its debts as they fall due. The time frame relevant for the determination of such threat may extend to a period of several months or even longer in order to account for cases in which the debtor is faced with non-financial difficulties threatening the status of its business as a going concern and, in the medium term, its liquidity. This may be the case, for example, where the debtor has lost a contract which is of key importance to it.

(18) This Regulation should be without prejudice to the rules on the recovery of State aid from insolvent companies as interpreted by the case-law of the Court of Justice of the European Union.

(19) Insolvency proceedings concerning insurance undertakings, credit institutions, investment firms and other firms, institutions or undertakings covered by Directive 2001/24/EC of the European Parliament and of the Council and collective investment undertakings should be excluded from the scope of this Regulation, as they are all subject to special arrangements and the national supervisory authorities have wide-ranging powers of intervention.

(20) Insolvency proceedings do not necessarily involve the intervention of a judicial authority. Therefore, the term 'court' in this Regulation should, in certain provisions, be given a broad meaning and include a person or body empowered by national law to open insolvency proceedings. In order for this Regulation to apply, proceedings (comprising acts and formalities set down in law) should not only have to comply with the provisions of this Regulation, but they should also be officially recognised and legally effective in the Member State in which the insolvency proceedings are opened.

(21)   Insolvency practitioners are defined in this Regulation and listed in Annex B. Insolvency practitioners who are appointed without the involvement of a judicial body should, under national law, be appropriately regulated and authorised to act in insolvency proceedings. The national regulatory framework should provide for proper arrangements to deal with potential conflicts of interest.

(22)   This Regulation acknowledges the fact that as a result of widely differing substantive laws it is not practical to introduce insolvency proceedings with universal scope throughout the Union. The application without exception of the law of the State of the opening of proceedings would, against this background, frequently lead to difficulties. This applies, for example, to the widely differing national laws on security interests to be found in the Member States. Furthermore, the preferential rights enjoyed by some creditors in insolvency proceedings are, in some cases, completely different. At the next review of this Regulation, it will be necessary to identify further measures in order to improve the preferential rights of employees at European level. This Regulation should take account of such differing national laws in two different ways. On the one hand, provision should be made for special rules on the applicable law in the case of particularly significant rights and legal relationships (e.g. rights in rem and contracts of employment). On the other hand, national proceedings covering only assets situated in the State of the opening of proceedings should also be allowed alongside main insolvency proceedings with universal scope.

(23)   This Regulation enables the main insolvency proceedings to be opened in the Member State where the debtor has the centre of its main interests. Those proceedings have universal scope and are aimed at encompassing all the debtor's assets. To protect the diversity of interests, this Regulation permits secondary insolvency proceedings to be opened to run in parallel with the main insolvency proceedings. Secondary insolvency proceedings may be opened in the Member State where the debtor has an establishment. The effects of secondary insolvency proceedings are limited to the assets located in that State. Mandatory rules of coordination with the main insolvency proceedings satisfy the need for unity in the Union.

(24)   Where main insolvency proceedings concerning a legal person or company have been opened in a Member State other than that of its registered office, it should be possible to open secondary insolvency proceedings in the Member State of the registered office, provided that the debtor is carrying out an economic activity with human means and assets in that State, in accordance with the case-law of the Court of Justice of the European Union.

(25)   This Regulation applies only to proceedings in respect of a debtor whose centre of main interests is located in the Union.

(26)   The rules of jurisdiction set out in this Regulation establish only international jurisdiction, that is to say, they designate the Member State the courts of which may open insolvency proceedings. Territorial jurisdiction within that Member State should be established by the national law of the Member State concerned.

(27)   Before opening insolvency proceedings, the competent court should examine of its own motion whether the centre of the debtor's main interests or the debtor's establishment is actually located within its jurisdiction.

(28)   When determining whether the centre of the debtor's main interests is ascertainable by third parties, special consideration should be given to the creditors and to their perception as to where a debtor conducts the administration of its interests. This may require, in the event of a shift of centre of main interests, informing creditors of the new location from which the debtor is carrying out its activities in due course, for example by drawing attention to the change of address in commercial correspondence, or by making the new location public through other appropriate means.

(29)   This Regulation should contain a number of safeguards aimed at preventing fraudulent or abusive forum shopping.

(30) Accordingly, the presumptions that the registered office, the principal place of business and the habitual residence are the centre of main interests should be rebuttable, and the relevant court of a Member State should carefully assess whether the centre of the debtor's main interests is genuinely located in that Member State. In the case of a company, it should be possible to rebut this presumption where the company's central administration is located in a Member State other than that of its registered office, and where a comprehensive assessment of all the relevant factors establishes, in a manner that is ascertainable by third parties, that the company's actual centre of management and supervision and of the management of its interests is located in that other Member State. In the case of an individual not exercising an independent business or professional activity, it should be possible to rebut this presumption, for example where the major part of the debtor's assets is located outside the Member State of the debtor's habitual residence, or where it can be established that the principal reason for moving was to file for insolvency proceedings in the new jurisdiction and where such filing would materially impair the interests of creditors whose dealings with the debtor took place prior to the relocation.

(31) With the same objective of preventing fraudulent or abusive forum shopping, the presumption that the centre of main interests is at the place of the registered office, at the individual's principal place of business or at the individual's habitual residence should not apply where, respectively, in the case of a company, legal person or individual exercising an independent business or professional activity, the debtor has relocated its registered office or principal place of business to another Member State within the 3-month period prior to the request for opening insolvency proceedings, or, in the case of an individual not exercising an independent business or professional activity, the debtor has relocated his habitual residence to another Member State within the 6-month period prior to the request for opening insolvency proceedings.

(32) In all cases, where the circumstances of the matter give rise to doubts about the court's jurisdiction, the court should require the debtor to submit additional evidence to support its assertions and, where the law applicable to the insolvency proceedings so allows, give the debtor's creditors the opportunity to present their views on the question of jurisdiction.

(33) In the event that the court seised of the request to open insolvency proceedings finds that the centre of main interests is not located on its territory, it should not open main insolvency proceedings.

(34) In addition, any creditor of the debtor should have an effective remedy against the decision to open insolvency proceedings. The consequences of any challenge to the decision to open insolvency proceedings should be governed by national law.

(35) The courts of the Member State within the territory of which insolvency proceedings have been opened should also have jurisdiction for actions which derive directly from the insolvency proceedings and are closely linked with them. Such actions should include avoidance actions against defendants in other Member States and actions concerning obligations that arise in the course of the insolvency proceedings, such as advance payment for costs of the proceedings. In contrast, actions for the performance of the obligations under a contract concluded by the debtor prior to the opening of proceedings do not derive directly from the proceedings. Where such an action is related to another action based on general civil and commercial law, the insolvency practitioner should be able to bring both actions in the courts of the defendant's domicile if he considers it more efficient to bring the action in that forum. This could, for example, be the case where the insolvency practitioner wishes to combine an action for director's liability on the basis of insolvency law with an action based on company law or general tort law.

(36) The court having jurisdiction to open the main insolvency proceedings should be able to order provisional and protective measures as from the time of

the request to open proceedings. Preservation measures both prior to and after the commencement of the insolvency proceedings are important to guarantee the effectiveness of the insolvency proceedings. In that connection, this Regulation should provide for various possibilities. On the one hand, the court competent for the main insolvency proceedings should also be able to order provisional and protective measures covering assets situated in the territory of other Member States. On the other hand, an insolvency practitioner temporarily appointed prior to the opening of the main insolvency proceedings should be able, in the Member States in which an establishment belonging to the debtor is to be found, to apply for the preservation measures which are possible under the law of those Member States.

(37) Prior to the opening of the main insolvency proceedings, the right to request the opening of insolvency proceedings in the Member State where the debtor has an establishment should be limited to local creditors and public authorities, or to cases in which main insolvency proceedings cannot be opened under the law of the Member State where the debtor has the centre of its main interests. The reason for this restriction is that cases in which territorial insolvency proceedings are requested before the main insolvency proceedings are intended to be limited to what is absolutely necessary.

(38) Following the opening of the main insolvency proceedings, this Regulation does not restrict the right to request the opening of insolvency proceedings in a Member State where the debtor has an establishment. The insolvency practitioner in the main insolvency proceedings or any other person empowered under the national law of that Member State may request the opening of secondary insolvency proceedings.

(39) This Regulation should provide for rules to determine the location of the debtor's assets, which should apply when determining which assets belong to the main or secondary insolvency proceedings, or to situations involving third parties' rights in rem. In particular, this Regulation should provide that European patents with unitary effect, a Community trade mark or any other similar rights, such as Community plant variety rights or Community designs, should only be included in the main insolvency proceedings.

(40) Secondary insolvency proceedings can serve different purposes, besides the protection of local interests. Cases may arise in which the insolvency estate of the debtor is too complex to administer as a unit, or the differences in the legal systems concerned are so great that difficulties may arise from the extension of effects deriving from the law of the State of the opening of proceedings to the other Member States where the assets are located. For that reason, the insolvency practitioner in the main insolvency proceedings may request the opening of secondary insolvency proceedings where the efficient administration of the insolvency estate so requires.

(41) Secondary insolvency proceedings may also hamper the efficient administration of the insolvency estate. Therefore, this Regulation sets out two specific situations in which the court seised of a request to open secondary insolvency proceedings should be able, at the request of the insolvency practitioner in the main insolvency proceedings, to postpone or refuse the opening of such proceedings.

(42) First, this Regulation confers on the insolvency practitioner in main insolvency proceedings the possibility of giving an undertaking to local creditors that they will be treated as if secondary insolvency proceedings had been opened. That undertaking has to meet a number of conditions set out in this Regulation, in particular that it be approved by a qualified majority of local creditors. Where such an undertaking has been given, the court seised of a request to open secondary insolvency proceedings should be able to refuse that request if it is satisfied that the undertaking adequately protects the general interests of local creditors. When assessing those interests, the court should take into account the fact that the undertaking has been approved by a qualified majority of local creditors.

(43) For the purposes of giving an undertaking to local creditors, the assets and

rights located in the Member State where the debtor has an establishment should form a sub-category of the insolvency estate, and, when distributing them or the proceeds resulting from their realisation, the insolvency practitioner in the main insolvency proceedings should respect the priority rights that creditors would have had if secondary insolvency proceedings had been opened in that Member State.

(44) National law should be applicable, as appropriate, in relation to the approval of an undertaking. In particular, where under national law the voting rules for adopting a restructuring plan require the prior approval of creditors' claims, those claims should be deemed to be approved for the purpose of voting on the undertaking. Where there are different procedures for the adoption of restructuring plans under national law, Member States should designate the specific procedure which should be relevant in this context.

(45) Second, this Regulation should provide for the possibility that the court temporarily stays the opening of secondary insolvency proceedings, when a temporary stay of individual enforcement proceedings has been granted in the main insolvency proceedings, in order to preserve the efficiency of the stay granted in the main insolvency proceedings. The court should be able to grant the temporary stay if it is satisfied that suitable measures are in place to protect the general interest of local creditors. In such a case, all creditors that could be affected by the outcome of the negotiations on a restructuring plan should be informed of the negotiations and be allowed to participate in them.

(46) In order to ensure effective protection of local interests, the insolvency practitioner in the main insolvency proceedings should not be able to realise or relocate, in an abusive manner, assets situated in the Member State where an establishment is located, in particular, with the purpose of frustrating the possibility that such interests can be effectively satisfied if secondary insolvency proceedings are opened subsequently.

(47) This Regulation should not prevent the courts of a Member State in which secondary insolvency proceedings have been opened from sanctioning a debtor's directors for violation of their duties, provided that those courts have jurisdiction to address such disputes under their national law.

(48) Main insolvency proceedings and secondary insolvency proceedings can contribute to the efficient administration of the debtor's insolvency estate or to the effective realisation of the total assets if there is proper cooperation between the actors involved in all the concurrent proceedings. Proper cooperation implies the various insolvency practitioners and the courts involved cooperating closely, in particular by exchanging a sufficient amount of information. In order to ensure the dominant role of the main insolvency proceedings, the insolvency practitioner in such proceedings should be given several possibilities for intervening in secondary insolvency proceedings which are pending at the same time. In particular, the insolvency practitioner should be able to propose a restructuring plan or composition or apply for a suspension of the realisation of the assets in the secondary insolvency proceedings. When cooperating, insolvency practitioners and courts should take into account best practices for cooperation in cross-border insolvency cases, as set out in principles and guidelines on communication and cooperation adopted by European and international organisations active in the area of insolvency law, and in particular the relevant guidelines prepared by the United Nations Commission on International Trade Law (Uncitral).

(49) In light of such cooperation, insolvency practitioners and courts should be able to enter into agreements and protocols for the purpose of facilitating cross-border cooperation of multiple insolvency proceedings in different Member States concerning the same debtor or members of the same group of companies, where this is compatible with the rules applicable to each of the proceedings. Such agreements and protocols may vary in form, in that they may be written or oral, and in scope, in that they may range from generic to specific, and may be entered into by

different parties. Simple generic agreements may emphasise the need for close cooperation between the parties, without addressing specific issues, while more detailed, specific agreements may establish a framework of principles to govern multiple insolvency proceedings and may be approved by the courts involved, where the national law so requires. They may reflect an agreement between the parties to take, or to refrain from taking, certain steps or actions.

(50)   Similarly, the courts of different Member States may cooperate by coordinating the appointment of insolvency practitioners. In that context, they may appoint a single insolvency practitioner for several insolvency proceedings concerning the same debtor or for different members of a group of companies, provided that this is compatible with the rules applicable to each of the proceedings, in particular with any requirements concerning the qualification and licensing of the insolvency practitioner.

(51)   This Regulation should ensure the efficient administration of insolvency proceedings relating to different companies forming part of a group of companies.

(52)   Where insolvency proceedings have been opened for several companies of the same group, there should be proper cooperation between the actors involved in those proceedings.

The various insolvency practitioners and the courts involved should therefore be under a similar obligation to cooperate and communicate with each other as those involved in main and secondary insolvency proceedings relating to the same debtor. Cooperation between the insolvency practitioners should not run counter to the interests of the creditors in each of the proceedings, and such cooperation should be aimed at finding a solution that would leverage synergies across the group.

(53)   The introduction of rules on the insolvency proceedings of groups of companies should not limit the possibility for a court to open insolvency proceedings for several companies belonging to the same group in a single jurisdiction if the court finds that the centre of main interests of those companies is located in a single Member State. In such cases, the court should also be able to appoint, if appropriate, the same insolvency practitioner in all proceedings concerned, provided that this is not incompatible with the rules applicable to them.

(54)   With a view to further improving the coordination of the insolvency proceedings of members of a group of companies, and to allow for a coordinated restructuring of the group, this Regulation should introduce procedural rules on the coordination of the insolvency proceedings of members of a group of companies. Such coordination should strive to ensure the efficiency of the coordination, whilst at the same time respecting each group member's separate legal personality.

(55)   An insolvency practitioner appointed in insolvency proceedings opened in relation to a member of a group of companies should be able to request the opening of group coordination proceedings. However, where the law applicable to the insolvency so requires, that insolvency practitioner should obtain the necessary authorisation before making such a request. The request should specify the essential elements of the coordination, in particular an outline of the coordination plan, a proposal as to whom should be appointed as coordinator and an outline of the estimated costs of the coordination.

(56)   In order to ensure the voluntary nature of group coordination proceedings, the insolvency practitioners involved should be able to object to their participation in the proceedings within a specified time period. In order to allow the insolvency practitioners involved to take an informed decision on participation in the group coordination proceedings, they should be informed at an early stage of the essential elements of the coordination. However, any insolvency practitioner who initially objects to inclusion in the group coordination proceedings should be able to subsequently request to participate in them. In such a case, the coordinator should take a decision on the admissibility of the request. All insolvency practi-

tioners, including the requesting insolvency practitioner, should be informed of the coordinator's decision and should have the opportunity of challenging that decision before the court which has opened the group coordination proceedings.

(57) Group coordination proceedings should always strive to facilitate the effective administration of the insolvency proceedings of the group members, and to have a generally positive impact for the creditors. This Regulation should therefore ensure that the court with which a request for group coordination proceedings has been filed makes an assessment of those criteria prior to opening group coordination proceedings.

(58) The advantages of group coordination proceedings should not be outweighed by the costs of those proceedings. Therefore, it is necessary to ensure that the costs of the coordination, and the share of those costs that each group member will bear, are adequate, proportionate and reasonable, and are determined in accordance with the national law of the Member State in which group coordination proceedings have been opened. The insolvency practitioners involved should also have the possibility of controlling those costs from an early stage of the proceedings. Where the national law so requires, controlling costs from an early stage of proceedings could involve the insolvency practitioner seeking the approval of a court or creditors' committee.

(59) Where the coordinator considers that the fulfilment of his or her tasks requires a significant increase in costs compared to the initially estimated costs and, in any case, where the costs exceed 10 % of the estimated costs, the coordinator should be authorised by the court which has opened the group coordination proceedings to exceed such costs. Before taking its decision, the court which has opened the group coordination proceedings should give the possibility to the participating insolvency practitioners to be heard before it in order to allow them to communicate their observations on the appropriateness of the coordinator's request.

(60) For members of a group of companies which are not participating in group coordination proceedings, this Regulation should also provide for an alternative mechanism to achieve a coordinated restructuring of the group. An insolvency practitioner appointed in proceedings relating to a member of a group of companies should have standing to request a stay of any measure related to the realisation of the assets in the proceedings opened with respect to other members of the group which are not subject to group coordination proceedings. It should only be possible to request such a stay if a restructuring plan is presented for the members of the group concerned, if the plan is to the benefit of the creditors in the proceedings in respect of which the stay is requested, and if the stay is necessary to ensure that the plan can be properly implemented.

(61) This Regulation should not prevent Member States from establishing national rules which would supplement the rules on cooperation, communication and coordination with regard to the insolvency of members of groups of companies set out in this Regulation, provided that the scope of application of those national rules is limited to the national jurisdiction and that their application would not impair the efficiency of the rules laid down by this Regulation.

(62) The rules on cooperation, communication and coordination in the framework of the insolvency of members of a group of companies provided for in this Regulation should only apply to the extent that proceedings relating to different members of the same group of companies have been opened in more than one Member State.

(63) Any creditor which has its habitual residence, domicile or registered office in the Union should have the right to lodge its claims in each of the insolvency proceedings pending in the Union relating to the debtor's assets. This should also apply to tax authorities and social insurance institutions. This Regulation should not prevent the insolvency practitioner from lodging claims on behalf of certain groups of creditors, for example employees, where the national law so provides.

However, in order to ensure the equal treatment of creditors, the distribution of proceeds should be coordinated. Every creditor should be able to keep what it has received in the course of insolvency proceedings, but should be entitled only to participate in the distribution of total assets in other proceedings if creditors with the same standing have obtained the same proportion of their claims.

(64) It is essential that creditors which have their habitual residence, domicile or registered office in the Union be informed about the opening of insolvency proceedings relating to their debtor's assets. In order to ensure a swift transmission of information to creditors, Regulation (EC) No 1393/2007 of the European Parliament and of the Council should not apply where this Regulation refers to the obligation to inform creditors. The use of standard forms available in all official languages of the institutions of the Union should facilitate the task of creditors when lodging claims in proceedings opened in another Member State. The consequences of the incomplete filing of the standard forms should be a matter for national law.

(65) This Regulation should provide for the immediate recognition of judgments concerning the opening, conduct and closure of insolvency proceedings which fall within its scope, and of judgments handed down in direct connection with such insolvency proceedings. Automatic recognition should therefore mean that the effects attributed to the proceedings by the law of the Member State in which the proceedings were opened extend to all other Member States. The recognition of judgments delivered by the courts of the Member States should be based on the principle of mutual trust. To that end, grounds for non-recognition should be reduced to the minimum necessary. This is also the basis on which any dispute should be resolved where the courts of two Member States both claim competence to open the main insolvency proceedings. The decision of the first court to open proceedings should be recognised in the other Member States without those Member States having the power to scrutinise that court's decision.

(66) This Regulation should set out, for the matters covered by it, uniform rules on conflict of laws which replace, within their scope of application, national rules of private international law. Unless otherwise stated, the law of the Member State of the opening of proceedings should be applicable (lex concursus). This rule on conflict of laws should be valid both for the main insolvency proceedings and for local proceedings. The lex concursus determines all the effects of the insolvency proceedings, both procedural and substantive, on the persons and legal relations concerned. It governs all the conditions for the opening, conduct and closure of the insolvency proceedings.

(67) Automatic recognition of insolvency proceedings to which the law of the State of the opening of proceedings normally applies may interfere with the rules under which transactions are carried out in other Member States. To protect legitimate expectations and the certainty of transactions in Member States other than that in which proceedings are opened, provision should be made for a number of exceptions to the general rule.

(68) There is a particular need for a special reference diverging from the law of the opening State in the case of rights in rem, since such rights are of considerable importance for the granting of credit. The basis, validity and extent of rights in rem should therefore normally be determined according to the lex situs and not be affected by the opening of insolvency proceedings. The proprietor of a right in rem should therefore be able to continue to assert its right to segregation or separate settlement of the collateral security. Where assets are subject to rights in rem under the lex situs in one Member State but the main insolvency proceedings are being carried out in another Member State, the insolvency practitioner in the main insolvency proceedings should be able to request the opening of secondary insolvency proceedings in the jurisdiction where the rights in rem arise if the debtor has an establishment there. If secondary insolvency proceedings are not opened, any surplus on the sale of an asset covered by rights in rem should be paid to the insolvency practitioner in the main insolvency proceedings.

(69) This Regulation lays down several provisions for a court to order a stay of opening proceedings or a stay of enforcement proceedings. Any such stay should not affect the rights in rem of creditors or third parties.

(70) If a set-off of claims is not permitted under the law of the State of the opening of proceedings, a creditor should nevertheless be entitled to the set-off if it is possible under the law applicable to the claim of the insolvent debtor. In this way, set-off would acquire a kind of guarantee function based on legal provisions on which the creditor concerned can rely at the time when the claim arises.

(71) There is also a need for special protection in the case of payment systems and financial markets, for example in relation to the position-closing agreements and netting agreements to be found in such systems, as well as the sale of securities and the guarantees provided for such transactions as governed in particular by Directive 98/26/EC of the European Parliament and of the Council. For such transactions, the only law which is relevant should be that applicable to the system or market concerned. That law is intended to prevent the possibility of mechanisms for the payment and settlement of transactions, and provided for in payment and set-off systems or on the regulated financial markets of the Member States, being altered in the case of insolvency of a business partner. Directive 98/26/EC contains special provisions which should take precedence over the general rules laid down in this Regulation.

(72) In order to protect employees and jobs, the effects of insolvency proceedings on the continuation or termination of employment and on the rights and obligations of all parties to such employment should be determined by the law applicable to the relevant employment agreement, in accordance with the general rules on conflict of laws. Moreover, in cases where the termination of employment contracts requires approval by a court or administrative authority, the Member State in which an establishment of the debtor is located should retain jurisdiction to grant such approval even if no insolvency proceedings have been opened in that Member State. Any other questions relating to the law of insolvency, such as whether the employees' claims are protected by preferential rights and the status such preferential rights may have, should be determined by the law of the Member State in which the insolvency proceedings (main or secondary) have been opened, except in cases where an undertaking to avoid secondary insolvency proceedings has been given in accordance with this Regulation.

(73) The law applicable to the effects of insolvency proceedings on any pending lawsuit or pending arbitral proceedings concerning an asset or right which forms part of the debtor's insolvency estate should be the law of the Member State where the lawsuit is pending or where the arbitration has its seat. However, this rule should not affect national rules on recognition and enforcement of arbitral awards.

(74) In order to take account of the specific procedural rules of court systems in certain Member States flexibility should be provided with regard to certain rules of this Regulation. Accordingly, references in this Regulation to notice being given by a judicial body of a Member State should include, where a Member State's procedural rules so require, an order by that judicial body directing that notice be given.

(75) For business considerations, the main content of the decision opening the proceedings should be published, at the request of the insolvency practitioner, in a Member State other than that of the court which delivered that decision. If there is an establishment in the Member State concerned, such publication should be mandatory. In neither case, however, should publication be a prior condition for recognition of the foreign proceedings.

(76) In order to improve the provision of information to relevant creditors and courts and to prevent the opening of parallel insolvency proceedings, Member States should be required to publish relevant information in cross-border insolvency cases in a publicly accessible electronic register. In order to facilitate access

to that information for creditors and courts domiciled or located in other Member States, this Regulation should provide for the interconnection of such insolvency registers via the European e-Justice Portal. Member States should be free to publish relevant information in several registers and it should be possible to inter-connect more than one register per Member State.

(77)   This Regulation should determine the minimum amount of information to be published in the insolvency registers. Member States should not be precluded from including additional information. Where the debtor is an individual, the insolvency registers should only have to indicate a registration number if the debtor is exercising an independent business or professional activity. That regis-tration number should be understood to be the unique registration number of the debtor's independent business or professional activity published in the trade register, if any.

(78)   Information on certain aspects of insolvency proceedings is essential for creditors, such as time limits for lodging claims or for challenging decisions. This Regulation should, however, not require Member States to calculate those time-limits on a case-by-case basis. Member States should be able to fulfil their obliga-tions by adding hyperlinks to the European e-Justice Portal, where self-explanatory information on the criteria for calculating those time-limits is to be provided.

(79)   In order to grant sufficient protection to information relating to indivi-duals not exercising an independent business or professional activity, Member States should be able to make access to that information subject to supplementary search criteria such as the debtor's personal identification number, address, date of birth or the district of the competent court, or to make access conditional upon a request to a competent authority or upon the verification of a legitimate interest.

(80)   Member States should also be able not to include in their insolvency registers information on individuals not exercising an independent business or professional activity. In such cases, Member States should ensure that the relevant information is given to the creditors by individual notice, and that claims of credi-tors who have not received the information are not affected by the proceedings.

(81)   It may be the case that some of the persons concerned are not aware that insolvency proceedings have been opened, and act in good faith in a way that con-flicts with the new circumstances. In order to protect such persons who, unaware that foreign proceedings have been opened, make a payment to the debtor instead of to the foreign insolvency practitioner, provision should be made for such a pay-ment to have a debt-discharging effect.

(82)   In order to ensure uniform conditions for the implementation of this Regulation, implementing powers should be conferred on the Commission. Those powers should be exercised in accordance with Regulation (EU) No 182/2011 of the European Parliament and of the Council. (83) This Regulation respects the fundamental rights and observes the principles recognised in the Charter of Fundamental Rights of the European Union. In particular, this Regulation seeks to promote the application of Articles 8, 17 and 47 concerning, respectively, the pro-tection of personal data, the right to property and the right to an effective remedy and to a fair trial.

(84)   Directive 95/46/EC of the European Parliament and of the Council and Regulation (EC) No 45/2001 of the European Parliament and of the Council apply to the processing of personal data within the framework of this Regulation.

(85)   This Regulation is without prejudice to Regulation (EEC, Euratom) No 1182/71 of the Council.

(86)   Since the objective of this Regulation cannot be sufficiently achieved by the Member States but can rather, by reason of the creation of a legal framework for the proper administration of cross-border insolvency proceedings, be better achieved at Union level, the Union may adopt measures in accordance with the principle of subsidiarity as set out in Article 5 of the Treaty on European Union. In accordance with the principle of proportionality, as set out in that

Article, this Regulation does not go beyond what is necessary in order to achieve that objective.

(87)   In accordance with Article 3 and Article 4a(1) of Protocol No 21 on the position of the United Kingdom and Ireland in respect of the area of freedom, security and justice, annexed to the Treaty on European Union and the Treaty on the Functioning of the European Union, the United Kingdom and Ireland have notified their wish to take part in the adoption and application of this Regulation.

(88)   In accordance with Articles 1 and 2 of Protocol No 22 on the position of Denmark annexed to the Treaty on European Union and the Treaty on the Functioning of the European Union, Denmark is not taking part in the adoption of this Regulation and is not bound by it or subject to its application.

(89)   The European Data Protection Supervisor was consulted and delivered an opinion on 27 March 2013,

HAVE ADOPTED THIS REGULATION:

CHAPTER I
GENERAL PROVISIONS

Article 1. Scope

1. This Regulation shall apply to public collective proceedings, including interim proceedings, which are based on laws relating to insolvency and in which, for the purpose of rescue, adjustment of debt, reorganisation or liquidation:

(a)   a debtor is totally or partially divested of its assets and an insolvency practitioner is appointed;

(b)   the assets and affairs of a debtor are subject to control or supervision by a court; or

(c)   a temporary stay of individual enforcement proceedings is granted by a court or by operation of law, in order to allow for negotiations between the debtor and its creditors, provided that the proceedings in which the stay is granted provide for suitable measures to protect the general body of creditors, and, where no agreement is reached, are preliminary to one of the proceedings referred to in point (a) or (b).

Where the proceedings referred to in this paragraph may be commenced in situations where there is only a likelihood of insolvency, their purpose shall be to avoid the debtor's insolvency or the cessation of the debtor's business activities.

The proceedings referred to in this paragraph are listed in Annex A.

2. This Regulation shall not apply to proceedings referred to in paragraph 1 that concern:

(a)   insurance undertakings;

(b)   credit institutions;

(c)   investment firms and other firms, institutions and undertakings to the extent that they are covered by Directive 2001/24/EC; or

(d)   collective investment undertakings.

Article 2. Definitions

For the purposes of this Regulation:

(1)   'collective proceedings' means proceedings which include all or a significant part of a debtor's creditors, provided that, in the latter case, the proceedings do not affect the claims of creditors which are not involved in them;

(2)   'collective investment undertakings' means undertakings for collective investment in transferable securities (UCITS) as defined in Directive 2009/65/EC of the European Parliament and of the Council and alternative investment funds (AIFs) as defined in Directive 2011/61/EU of the European Parliament and of the Council;

(3)   'debtor in possession' means a debtor in respect of which insolvency proceedings have been opened which do not necessarily involve the appointment of

an insolvency practitioner or the complete transfer of the rights and duties to administer the debtor's assets to an insolvency practitioner and where, therefore, the debtor remains totally or at least partially in control of its assets and affairs;

(4) 'insolvency proceedings' means the proceedings listed in Annex A;

(5) 'insolvency practitioner' means any person or body whose function, including on an interim basis, is to:

(i) verify and admit claims submitted in insolvency proceedings;

(ii) represent the collective interest of the creditors;

(iii) administer, either in full or in part, assets of which the debtor has been divested;

(iv) liquidate the assets referred to in point (iii); or

(v) supervise the administration of the debtor's affairs.

The persons and bodies referred to in the first subparagraph are listed in Annex B;

(6) 'court' means:

(i) in points (b) and (c) of Article 1(1), Article 4(2), Articles 5 and 6, Article 21(3), point (j) of Article 24(2), Articles 36 and 39, and Articles 61 to 77, the judicial body of a Member State;

(ii) in all other articles, the judicial body or any other competent body of a Member State empowered to open insolvency proceedings, to confirm such opening or to take decisions in the course of such proceedings;

(7) 'judgment opening insolvency proceedings' includes:

(i) the decision of any court to open insolvency proceedings or to confirm the opening of such proceedings; and

(ii) the decision of a court to appoint an insolvency practitioner;

(8) 'the time of the opening of proceedings' means the time at which the judgment opening insolvency proceedings becomes effective, regardless of whether the judgment is final or not;

(9) 'the Member State in which assets are situated' means, in the case of:

(i) registered shares in companies other than those referred to in point (ii), the Member State within the territory of which the company having issued the shares has its registered office;

(ii) financial instruments, the title to which is evidenced by entries in a register or account maintained by or on behalf of an intermediary ('book entry securities'), the Member State in which the register or account in which the entries are made is maintained;

(iii) cash held in accounts with a credit institution, the Member State indicated in the account's IBAN, or, for cash held in accounts with a credit institution which does not have an IBAN, the Member State in which the credit institution holding the account has its central administration or, where the account is held with a branch, agency or other establishment, the Member State in which the branch, agency or other establishment is located;

(iv) property and rights, ownership of or entitlement to which is entered in a public register other than those referred to in point (i), the Member State under the authority of which the register is kept;

(v) European patents, the Member State for which the European patent is granted;

(vi) copyright and related rights, the Member State within the territory of which the owner of such rights has its habitual residence or registered office;

(vii) tangible property, other than that referred to in points (i) to (iv), the Member State within the territory of which the property is situated;

(viii) claims against third parties, other than those relating to assets referred to in point (iii), the Member State within the territory of which the third party required to meet the claims has the centre of its main interests, as determined in accordance with Article 3(1);

(10) 'establishment' means any place of operations where a debtor carries out

or has carried out in the 3-month period prior to the request to open main insolvency proceedings a non-transitory economic activity with human means and assets;

(11) 'local creditor' means a creditor whose claims against a debtor arose from or in connection with the operation of an establishment situated in a Member State other than the Member State in which the centre of the debtor's main interests is located;

(12) 'foreign creditor' means a creditor which has its habitual residence, domicile or registered office in a Member State other than the State of the opening of proceedings, including the tax authorities and social security authorities of Member States;

(13) 'group of companies' means a parent undertaking and all its subsidiary undertakings;

(14) 'parent undertaking' means an undertaking which controls, either directly or indirectly, one or more subsidiary undertakings. An undertaking which prepares consolidated financial statements in accordance with Directive 2013/34/EU of the European Parliament and of the Council shall be deemed to be a parent undertaking.

Article 3. International jurisdiction

1. The courts of the Member State within the territory of which the centre of the debtor's main interests is situated shall have jurisdiction to open insolvency proceedings ('main insolvency proceedings'). The centre of main interests shall be the place where the debtor conducts the administration of its interests on a regular basis and which is ascertainable by third parties.

In the case of a company or legal person, the place of the registered office shall be presumed to be the centre of its main interests in the absence of proof to the contrary. That presumption shall only apply if the registered office has not been moved to another Member State within the 3-month period prior to the request for the opening of insolvency proceedings.

In the case of an individual exercising an independent business or professional activity, the centre of main interests shall be presumed to be that individual's principal place of business in the absence of proof to the contrary. That presumption shall only apply if the individual's principal place of business has not been moved to another Member State within the 3-month period prior to the request for the opening of insolvency proceedings.

In the case of any other individual, the centre of main interests shall be presumed to be the place of the individual's habitual residence in the absence of proof to the contrary. This presumption shall only apply if the habitual residence has not been moved to another Member State within the 6-month period prior to the request for the opening of insolvency proceedings.

2. Where the centre of the debtor's main interests is situated within the territory of a Member State, the courts of another Member State shall have jurisdiction to open insolvency proceedings against that debtor only if it possesses an establishment within the territory of that other Member State. The effects of those proceedings shall be restricted to the assets of the debtor situated in the territory of the latter Member State.

3. Where insolvency proceedings have been opened in accordance with paragraph 1, any proceedings opened subsequently in accordance with paragraph 2 shall be secondary insolvency proceedings.

4. The territorial insolvency proceedings referred to in paragraph 2 may only be opened prior to the opening of main insolvency proceedings in accordance with paragraph 1 where

(a) insolvency proceedings under paragraph 1 cannot be opened because of the conditions laid down by the law of the Member State within the territory of which the centre of the debtor's main interests is situated; or

(b)   the opening of territorial insolvency proceedings is requested by:
(i) a creditor whose claim arises from or is in connection with the operation of an establishment situated within the territory of the Member State where the opening of territorial proceedings is requested; or
(ii) a public authority which, under the law of the Member State within the territory of which the establishment is situated, has the right to request the opening of insolvency proceedings.
When main insolvency proceedings are opened, the territorial insolvency proceedings shall become secondary insolvency proceedings.

Article 4. Examination as to jurisdiction
1. A court seised of a request to open insolvency proceedings shall of its own motion examine whether it has jurisdiction pursuant to Article 3. The judgment opening insolvency proceedings shall specify the grounds on which the jurisdiction of the court is based, and, in particular, whether jurisdiction is based on Article 3(1) or (2).
2. Notwithstanding paragraph 1, where insolvency proceedings are opened in accordance with national law without a decision by a court, Member States may entrust the insolvency practitioner appointed in such proceedings to examine whether the Member State in which a request for the opening of proceedings is pending has jurisdiction pursuant to Article 3. Where this is the case, the insolvency practitioner shall specify in the decision opening the proceedings the grounds on which jurisdiction is based and, in particular, whether jurisdiction is based on Article 3(1) or (2).

Article 5. Judicial review of the decision to open main insolvency proceedings
1. The debtor or any creditor may challenge before a court the decision opening main insolvency proceedings on grounds of international jurisdiction.
2. The decision opening main insolvency proceedings may be challenged by parties other than those referred to in paragraph 1 or on grounds other than a lack of international jurisdiction where national law so provides.

Article 6. Jurisdiction for actions deriving directly from insolvency proceedings and closely linked with them
1. The courts of the Member State within the territory of which insolvency proceedings have been opened in accordance with Article 3 shall have jurisdiction for any action which derives directly from the insolvency proceedings and is closely linked with them, such as avoidance actions.
2. Where an action referred to in paragraph 1 is related to an action in civil and commercial matters against the same defendant, the insolvency practitioner may bring both actions before the courts of the Member State within the territory of which the defendant is domiciled, or, where the action is brought against several defendants, before the courts of the Member State within the territory of which any of them is domiciled, provided that those courts have jurisdiction pursuant to Regulation (EU) No 1215/2012.
The first subparagraph shall apply to the debtor in possession, provided that national law allows the debtor in possession to bring actions on behalf of the insolvency estate.
3. For the purpose of paragraph 2, actions are deemed to be related where they are so closely connected that it is expedient to hear and determine them together to avoid the risk of irreconcilable judgments resulting from separate proceedings.

Article 7. Applicable law
1. Save as otherwise provided in this Regulation, the law applicable to insolvency proceedings and their effects shall be that of the Member State within the territory of which such proceedings are opened (the 'State of the opening of proceedings').
2. The law of the State of the opening of proceedings shall determine the con-

ditions for the opening of those proceedings, their conduct and their closure. In particular, it shall determine the following:

(a)   the debtors against which insolvency proceedings may be brought on account of their capacity;

(b)   the assets which form part of the insolvency estate and the treatment of assets acquired by or devolving on the debtor after the opening of the insolvency proceedings;

(c)   the respective powers of the debtor and the insolvency practitioner;

(d)   the conditions under which set-offs may be invoked;

(e)   the effects of insolvency proceedings on current contracts to which the debtor is party;

(f)   the effects of the insolvency proceedings on proceedings brought by individual creditors, with the exception of pending lawsuits;

(g)   the claims which are to be lodged against the debtor's insolvency estate and the treatment of claims arising after the opening of insolvency proceedings;

(h)   the rules governing the lodging, verification and admission of claims;

(i)   the rules governing the distribution of proceeds from the realisation of assets, the ranking of claims and the rights of creditors who have obtained partial satisfaction after the opening of insolvency proceedings by virtue of a right in rem or through a set-off;

(j)   the conditions for, and the effects of closure of, insolvency proceedings, in particular by composition;

(k)   creditors' rights after the closure of insolvency proceedings;

(l)   who is to bear the costs and expenses incurred in the insolvency proceedings;

(m)   the rules relating to the voidness, voidability or unenforceability of legal acts detrimental to the general body of creditors.

Article 8. Third parties' rights in rem

1. The opening of insolvency proceedings shall not affect the rights in rem of creditors or third parties in respect of tangible or intangible, moveable or immoveable assets, both specific assets and collections of indefinite assets as a whole which change from time to time, belonging to the debtor which are situated within the territory of another Member State at the time of the opening of proceedings.

2. The rights referred to in paragraph 1 shall, in particular, mean:

(a)   the right to dispose of assets or have them disposed of and to obtain satisfaction from the proceeds of or income from those assets, in particular by virtue of a lien or a mortgage;

(b)   the exclusive right to have a claim met, in particular a right guaranteed by a lien in respect of the claim or by assignment of the claim by way of a guarantee;

(c)   the right to demand assets from, and/or to require restitution by, anyone having possession or use of them contrary to the wishes of the party so entitled;

(d)   a right in rem to the beneficial use of assets.

3. The right, recorded in a public register and enforceable against third parties, based on which a right in rem within the meaning of paragraph 1 may be obtained shall be considered to be a right in rem.

4. Paragraph 1 shall not preclude actions for voidness, voidability or unenforceability as referred to in point (m) of Article 7(2).

Article 9. Set-off

1. The opening of insolvency proceedings shall not affect the right of creditors to demand the set-off of their claims against the claims of a debtor, where such a set-off is permitted by the law applicable to the insolvent debtor's claim.

2. Paragraph 1 shall not preclude actions for voidness, voidability or unenforceability as referred to in point (m) of Article 7(2).

Article 10. Reservation of title

1. The opening of insolvency proceedings against the purchaser of an asset shall not affect sellers' rights that are based on a reservation of title where at the time of the opening of proceedings the asset is situated within the territory of a Member State other than the State of the opening of proceedings.

2. The opening of insolvency proceedings against the seller of an asset, after delivery of the asset, shall not constitute grounds for rescinding or terminating the sale and shall not prevent the purchaser from acquiring title where at the time of the opening of proceedings the asset sold is situated within the territory of a Member State other than the State of the opening of proceedings.

3. Paragraphs 1 and 2 shall not preclude actions for voidness, voidability or unenforceability as referred to in point (m) of Article 7(2).

Article 11. Contracts relating to immoveable property

1. The effects of insolvency proceedings on a contract conferring the right to acquire or make use of immoveable property shall be governed solely by the law of the Member State within the territory of which the immoveable property is situated.

2. The court which opened main insolvency proceedings shall have jurisdiction to approve the termination or modification of the contracts referred to in this Article where:

    (a)   the law of the Member State applicable to those contracts requires that such a contract may only be terminated or modified with the approval of the court opening insolvency proceedings; and

    (b)   no insolvency proceedings have been opened in that Member State.

Article 12. Payment systems and financial markets

1. Without prejudice to Article 8, the effects of insolvency proceedings on the rights and obligations of the parties to a payment or settlement system or to a financial market shall be governed solely by the law of the Member State applicable to that system or market.

2. Paragraph 1 shall not preclude any action for voidness, voidability or unenforceability which may be taken to set aside payments or transactions under the law applicable to the relevant payment system or financial market.

Article 13. Contracts of employment

1. The effects of insolvency proceedings on employment contracts and relationships shall be governed solely by the law of the Member State applicable to the contract of employment.

2. The courts of the Member State in which secondary insolvency proceedings may be opened shall retain jurisdiction to approve the termination or modification of the contracts referred to in this Article even if no insolvency proceedings have been opened in that Member State.

The first subparagraph shall also apply to an authority competent under national law to approve the termination or modification of the contracts referred to in this Article.

Article 14. Effects on rights subject to registration

The effects of insolvency proceedings on the rights of a debtor in immoveable property, a ship or an aircraft subject to registration in a public register shall be determined by the law of the Member State under the authority of which the register is kept.

Article 15. European patents with unitary effect and Community trade marks

For the purposes of this Regulation, a European patent with unitary effect, a Community trade mark or any other similar right established by Union law may be included only in the proceedings referred to in Article 3(1).

Article 16. Detrimental acts
Point (m) of Article 7(2) shall not apply where the person who benefited from an act detrimental to all the creditors provides proof that:

(a)   the act is subject to the law of a Member State other than that of the State of the opening of proceedings; and

(b)   the law of that Member State does not allow any means of challenging that act in the relevant case.

Article 17. Protection of third-party purchasers
Where, by an act concluded after the opening of insolvency proceedings, a debtor disposes, for consideration, of:

(a)   an immoveable asset;

(b)   a ship or an aircraft subject to registration in a public register; or

(c)   securities the existence of which requires registration in a register laid down by law;

the validity of that act shall be governed by the law of the State within the territory of which the immoveable asset is situated or under the authority of which the register is kept.

Article 18. Effects of insolvency proceedings on pending lawsuits or arbitral proceedings
The effects of insolvency proceedings on a pending lawsuit or pending arbitral proceedings concerning an asset or a right which forms part of a debtor's insolvency estate shall be governed solely by the law of the Member State in which that lawsuit is pending or in which the arbitral tribunal has its seat.

CHAPTER II
RECOGNITION OF INSOLVENCY PROCEEDINGS

Article 19. Principle
1. Any judgment opening insolvency proceedings handed down by a court of a Member State which has jurisdiction pursuant to Article 3 shall be recognised in all other Member States from the moment that it becomes effective in the State of the opening of proceedings.

The rule laid down in the first subparagraph shall also apply where, on account of a debtor's capacity, insolvency proceedings cannot be brought against that debtor in other Member States.

2. Recognition of the proceedings referred to in Article 3(1) shall not preclude the opening of the proceedings referred to in Article 3(2) by a court in another Member State. The latter proceedings shall be secondary insolvency proceedings within the meaning of Chapter III.

Article 20. Effects of recognition
1. The judgment opening insolvency proceedings as referred to in Article 3(1) shall, with no further formalities, produce the same effects in any other Member State as under the law of the State of the opening of proceedings, unless this Regulation provides otherwise and as long as no proceedings referred to in Article 3(2) are opened in that other Member State.

2. The effects of the proceedings referred to in Article 3(2) may not be challenged in other Member States. Any restriction of creditors' rights, in particular a stay or discharge, shall produce effects vis-à-vis assets situated within the territory of another Member State only in the case of those creditors who have given their consent.

Article 21. Powers of the insolvency practitioner
1. The insolvency practitioner appointed by a court which has jurisdiction pursuant to Article 3(1) may exercise all the powers conferred on it, by the law of the State of the opening of proceedings, in another Member State, as long as no other

insolvency proceedings have been opened there and no preservation measure to the contrary has been taken there further to a request for the opening of insolvency proceedings in that State. Subject to Articles 8 and 10, the insolvency practitioner may, in particular, remove the debtor's assets from the territory of the Member State in which they are situated.

2. The insolvency practitioner appointed by a court which has jurisdiction pursuant to Article 3(2) may in any other Member State claim through the courts or out of court that moveable property was removed from the territory of the State of the opening of proceedings to the territory of that other Member State after the opening of the insolvency proceedings. The insolvency practitioner may also bring any action to set aside which is in the interests of the creditors.

3. In exercising its powers, the insolvency practitioner shall comply with the law of the Member State within the territory of which it intends to take action, in particular with regard to procedures for the realisation of assets. Those powers may not include coercive measures, unless ordered by a court of that Member State, or the right to rule on legal proceedings or disputes.

Article 22. Proof of the insolvency practitioner's appointment

The insolvency practitioner's appointment shall be evidenced by a certified copy of the original decision appointing it or by any other certificate issued by the court which has jurisdiction.

A translation into the official language or one of the official languages of the Member State within the territory of which it intends to act may be required. No legalisation or other similar formality shall be required.

Article 23. Return and imputation

1. A creditor which, after the opening of the proceedings referred to in Article 3(1), obtains by any means, in particular through enforcement, total or partial satisfaction of its claim on the assets belonging to a debtor situated within the territory of another Member State, shall return what it has obtained to the insolvency practitioner, subject to Articles 8 and 10.

2. In order to ensure the equal treatment of creditors, a creditor which has, in the course of insolvency proceedings, obtained a dividend on its claim shall share in distributions made in other proceedings only where creditors of the same ranking or category have, in those other proceedings, obtained an equivalent dividend.

Article 24. Establishment of insolvency registers

1. Member States shall establish and maintain in their territory one or several registers in which information concerning insolvency proceedings is published ('insolvency registers'). That information shall be published as soon as possible after the opening of such proceedings.

2. The information referred to in paragraph 1 shall be made publicly available, subject to the conditions laid down in Article 27, and shall include the following ('mandatory information'):

(a)   the date of the opening of insolvency proceedings;

(b)   the court opening insolvency proceedings and the case reference number, if any;

(c)   the type of insolvency proceedings referred to in Annex A that were opened and, where applicable, any relevant subtype of such proceedings opened in accordance with national law;

(d)   whether jurisdiction for opening proceedings is based on Article 3(1), 3(2) or 3(4);

(e)   if the debtor is a company or a legal person, the debtor's name, registration number, registered office or, if different, postal address;

(f)   if the debtor is an individual whether or not exercising an independent business or professional activity, the debtor's name, registration number, if any, and postal address or, where the address is protected, the debtor's place and date of birth;

(g)   the name, postal address or e-mail address of the insolvency practitioner, if any, appointed in the proceedings;

(h)   the time limit for lodging claims, if any, or a reference to the criteria for calculating that time limit;

(i)   the date of closing main insolvency proceedings, if any;

(j)   the court before which and, where applicable, the time limit within which a challenge of the decision opening insolvency proceedings is to be lodged in accordance with Article 5, or a reference to the criteria for calculating that time limit.

3. Paragraph 2 shall not preclude Member States from including documents or additional information in their national insolvency registers, such as directors' disqualifications related to insolvency.

4. Member States shall not be obliged to include in the insolvency registers the information referred to in paragraph 1 of this Article in relation to individuals not exercising an independent business or professional activity, or to make such information publicly available through the system of interconnection of those registers, provided that known foreign creditors are informed, pursuant to Article 54, of the elements referred to under point (j) of paragraph 2 of this Article.

Where a Member State makes use of the possibility referred to in the first subparagraph, the insolvency proceedings shall not affect the claims of foreign creditors who have not received the information referred to in the first subparagraph.

5. The publication of information in the registers under this Regulation shall not have any legal effects other than those set out in national law and in Article 55(6).

Article 25. Interconnection of insolvency registers

1. The Commission shall establish a decentralised system for the interconnection of insolvency registers by means of implementing acts. That system shall be composed of the insolvency registers and the European e-Justice Portal, which shall serve as a central public electronic access point to information in the system. The system shall provide a search service in all the official languages of the institutions of the Union in order to make available the mandatory information and any other documents or information included in the insolvency registers which the Member States choose to make available through the European e-Justice Portal.

2. By means of implementing acts in accordance with the procedure referred to in Article 87, the Commission shall adopt the following by 26 June 2019:

(a)   the technical specification defining the methods of communication and information exchange by electronic means on the basis of the established interface specification for the system of interconnection of insolvency registers;

(b)   the technical measures ensuring the minimum information technology security standards for communication and distribution of information within the system of interconnection of insolvency registers;

(c)   minimum criteria for the search service provided by the European e-Justice Portal based on the information set out in Article 24;

(d)   minimum criteria for the presentation of the results of such searches based on the information set out in Article 24;

(e)   the means and the technical conditions of availability of services provided by the system of interconnection; and

(f)   a glossary containing a basic explanation of the national insolvency proceedings listed in Annex A.

Article 26. Costs of establishing and interconnecting insolvency registers

1. The establishment, maintenance and future development of the system of interconnection of insolvency registers shall be financed from the general budget of the Union.

2. Each Member State shall bear the costs of establishing and adjusting its national insolvency registers to make them interoperable with the European e-Justice Portal, as well as the costs of administering, operating and maintaining those registers. This shall be without prejudice to the possibility to apply for grants to support such activities under the Union's financial programmes.

Article 27. Conditions of access to information via the system of interconnection

1. Member States shall ensure that the mandatory information referred to in points (a) to (j) of Article 24(2) is available free of charge via the system of interconnection of insolvency registers.

2. This Regulation shall not preclude Member States from charging a reasonable fee for access to the documents or additional information referred to in Article 24(3) via the system of interconnection of insolvency registers.

3. Member States may make access to mandatory information concerning individuals who are not exercising an independent business or professional activity, and concerning individuals exercising an independent business or professional activity when the insolvency proceedings are not related to that activity, subject to supplementary search criteria relating to the debtor in addition to the minimum criteria referred to in point (c) of Article 25(2).

4. Member States may require that access to the information referred to in paragraph 3 be made conditional upon a request to the competent authority. Member States may make access conditional upon the verification of the existence of a legitimate interest for accessing such information. The requesting person shall be able to submit the request for information electronically by means of a standard form via the European e-Justice Portal. Where a legitimate interest is required, it shall be permissible for the requesting person to justify his request by electronic copies of relevant documents. The requesting person shall be provided with an answer by the competent authority within 3 working days.

The requesting person shall not be obliged to provide translations of the documents justifying his request, or to bear any costs of translation which the competent authority may incur.

Article 28. Publication in another Member State

1. The insolvency practitioner or the debtor in possession shall request that notice of the judgment opening insolvency proceedings and, where appropriate, the decision appointing the insolvency practitioner be published in any other Member State where an establishment of the debtor is located in accordance with the publication procedures provided for in that Member State. Such publication shall specify, where appropriate, the insolvency practitioner appointed and whether the jurisdiction rule applied is that pursuant to Article 3(1) or (2).

2. The insolvency practitioner or the debtor in possession may request that the information referred to in paragraph 1 be published in any other Member State where the insolvency practitioner or the debtor in possession deems it necessary in accordance with the publication procedures provided for in that Member State.

Article 29. Registration in public registers of another Member State

1. Where the law of a Member State in which an establishment of the debtor is located and this establishment has been entered into a public register of that Member State, or the law of a Member State in which immovable property belonging to the debtor is located, requires information on the opening of insolvency proceedings referred to in Article 28 to be published in the land register, company register or any other public register, the insolvency practitioner or the debtor in possession shall take all the necessary measures to ensure such a registration.

2. The insolvency practitioner or the debtor in possession may request such registration in any other Member State, provided that the law of the Member State where the register is kept allows such registration.

Article 30. Costs
The costs of the publication and registration provided for in Articles 28 and 29 shall be regarded as costs and expenses incurred in the proceedings.

Article 31. Honouring of an obligation to a debtor
1. Where an obligation has been honoured in a Member State for the benefit of a debtor who is subject to insolvency proceedings opened in another Member State, when it should have been honoured for the benefit of the insolvency practitioner in those proceedings, the person honouring the obligation shall be deemed to have discharged it if he was unaware of the opening of the proceedings.

2. Where such an obligation is honoured before the publication provided for in Article 28 has been effected, the person honouring the obligation shall be presumed, in the absence of proof to the contrary, to have been unaware of the opening of insolvency proceedings. Where the obligation is honoured after such publication has been effected, the person honouring the obligation shall be presumed, in the absence of proof to the contrary, to have been aware of the opening of proceedings.

Article 32. Recognition and enforceability of other judgments
1. Judgments handed down by a court whose judgment concerning the opening of proceedings is recognised in accordance with Article 19 and which concern the course and closure of insolvency proceedings, and compositions approved by that court, shall also be recognised with no further formalities. Such judgments shall be enforced in accordance with Articles 39 to 44 and 47 to 57 of Regulation (EU) No 1215/2012.

The first subparagraph shall also apply to judgments deriving directly from the insolvency proceedings and which are closely linked with them, even if they were handed down by another court.

The first subparagraph shall also apply to judgments relating to preservation measures taken after the request for the opening of insolvency proceedings or in connection with it.

2. The recognition and enforcement of judgments other than those referred to in paragraph 1 of this Article shall be governed by Regulation (EU) No 1215/2012 provided that that Regulation is applicable.

Article 33. Public policy
Any Member State may refuse to recognise insolvency proceedings opened in another Member State or to enforce a judgment handed down in the context of such proceedings where the effects of such recognition or enforcement would be manifestly contrary to that State's public policy, in particular its fundamental principles or the constitutional rights and liberties of the individual.

CHAPTER III
SECONDARY INSOLVENCY PROCEEDINGS

Article 34. Opening of proceedings
Where main insolvency proceedings have been opened by a court of a Member State and recognised in another Member State, a court of that other Member State which has jurisdiction pursuant to Article 3(2) may open secondary insolvency proceedings in accordance with the provisions set out in this Chapter. Where the main insolvency proceedings required that the debtor be insolvent, the debtor's insolvency shall not be re-examined in the Member State in which secondary insolvency proceedings may be opened. The effects of secondary insolvency proceedings shall be restricted to the assets of the debtor situated within the territory of the Member State in which those proceedings have been opened.

Article 35. Applicable law
Save as otherwise provided for in this Regulation, the law applicable to secondary

insolvency proceedings shall be that of the Member State within the territory of which the secondary insolvency proceedings are opened.

Article 36. Right to give an undertaking in order to avoid secondary insolvency proceedings

1. In order to avoid the opening of secondary insolvency proceedings, the insolvency practitioner in the main insolvency proceedings may give a unilateral undertaking (the 'undertaking') in respect of the assets located in the Member State in which secondary insolvency proceedings could be opened, that when distributing those assets or the proceeds received as a result of their realisation, it will comply with the distribution and priority rights under national law that creditors would have if secondary insolvency proceedings were opened in that Member State. The undertaking shall specify the factual assumptions on which it is based, in particular in respect of the value of the assets located in the Member State concerned and the options available to realise such assets.

2. Where an undertaking has been given in accordance with this Article, the law applicable to the distribution of proceeds from the realisation of assets referred to in paragraph 1, to the ranking of creditors' claims, and to the rights of creditors in relation to the assets referred to in paragraph 1 shall be the law of the Member State in which secondary insolvency proceedings could have been opened. The relevant point in time for determining the assets referred to in paragraph 1 shall be the moment at which the undertaking is given.

3. The undertaking shall be made in the official language or one of the official languages of the Member State where secondary insolvency proceedings could have been opened, or, where there are several official languages in that Member State, the official language or one of the official languages of the place in which secondary insolvency proceedings could have been opened.

4. The undertaking shall be made in writing. It shall be subject to any other requirements relating to form and approval requirements as to distributions, if any, of the State of the opening of the main insolvency proceedings.

5. The undertaking shall be approved by the known local creditors. The rules on qualified majority and voting that apply to the adoption of restructuring plans under the law of the Member State where secondary insolvency proceedings could have been opened shall also apply to the approval of the undertaking. Creditors shall be able to participate in the vote by distance means of communication, where national law so permits. The insolvency practitioner shall inform the known local creditors of the undertaking, of the rules and procedures for its approval, and of the approval or rejection of the undertaking.

6. An undertaking given and approved in accordance with this Article shall be binding on the estate. If secondary insolvency proceedings are opened in accordance with Articles 37 and 38, the insolvency practitioner in the main insolvency proceedings shall transfer any assets which it removed from the territory of that Member State after the undertaking was given or, where those assets have already been realised, their proceeds, to the insolvency practitioner in the secondary insolvency proceedings.

7. Where the insolvency practitioner has given an undertaking, it shall inform local creditors about the intended distributions prior to distributing the assets and proceeds referred to in paragraph 1. If that information does not comply with the terms of the undertaking or the applicable law, any local creditor may challenge such distribution before the courts of the Member State in which main insolvency proceedings have been opened in order to obtain a distribution in accordance with the terms of the undertaking and the applicable law. In such cases, no distribution shall take place until the court has taken a decision on the challenge.

8. Local creditors may apply to the courts of the Member State in which main insolvency proceedings have been opened, in order to require the insolvency practitioner in the main insolvency proceedings to take any suitable measures neces-

sary to ensure compliance with the terms of the undertaking available under the law of the State of the opening of main insolvency proceedings.

9. Local creditors may also apply to the courts of the Member State in which secondary insolvency proceedings could have been opened in order to require the court to take provisional or protective measures to ensure compliance by the insolvency practitioner with the terms of the undertaking.

10. The insolvency practitioner shall be liable for any damage caused to local creditors as a result of its non-compliance with the obligations and requirements set out in this Article.

11. For the purpose of this Article, an authority which is established in the Member State where secondary insolvency proceedings could have been opened and which is obliged under Directive 2008/94/EC of the European Parliament and of the Council to guarantee the payment of employees' outstanding claims resulting from contracts of employment or employment relationships shall be considered to be a local creditor, where the national law so provides.

Article 37. Right to request the opening of secondary insolvency proceedings

1. The opening of secondary insolvency proceedings may be requested by:
   (a) the insolvency practitioner in the main insolvency proceedings;
   (b) any other person or authority empowered to request the opening of insolvency proceedings under the law of the Member State within the territory of which the opening of secondary insolvency proceedings is requested.

2. Where an undertaking has become binding in accordance with Article 36, the request for opening secondary insolvency proceedings shall be lodged within 30 days of having received notice of the approval of the undertaking.

Article 38. Decision to open secondary insolvency proceedings

1. A court seised of a request to open secondary insolvency proceedings shall immediately give notice to the insolvency practitioner or the debtor in possession in the main insolvency proceedings and give it an opportunity to be heard on the request.

2. Where the insolvency practitioner in the main insolvency proceedings has given an undertaking in accordance with Article 36, the court referred to in paragraph 1 of this Article shall, at the request of the insolvency practitioner, not open secondary insolvency proceedings if it is satisfied that the undertaking adequately protects the general interests of local creditors.

3. Where a temporary stay of individual enforcement proceedings has been granted in order to allow for negotiations between the debtor and its creditors, the court, at the request of the insolvency practitioner or the debtor in possession, may stay the opening of secondary insolvency proceedings for a period not exceeding 3 months, provided that suitable measures are in place to protect the interests of local creditors.

The court referred to in paragraph 1 may order protective measures to protect the interests of local creditors by requiring the insolvency practitioner or the debtor in possession not to remove or dispose of any assets which are located in the Member State where its establishment is located unless this is done in the ordinary course of business. The court may also order other measures to protect the interest of local creditors during a stay, unless this is incompatible with the national rules on civil procedure.

The stay of the opening of secondary insolvency proceedings shall be lifted by the court of its own motion or at the request of any creditor if, during the stay, an agreement in the negotiations referred to in the first subparagraph has been concluded.

The stay may be lifted by the court of its own motion or at the request of any creditor if the continuation of the stay is detrimental to the creditor's rights, in particular if the negotiations have been disrupted or it has become evident that they are unlikely to be concluded, or if the insolvency practitioner or the debtor in possession has infringed the prohibition on disposal of its assets or on removal of them from the territory of the Member State where the establishment is located.

4. At the request of the insolvency practitioner in the main insolvency proceedings, the court referred to in paragraph 1 may open a type of insolvency proceedings as listed in Annex A other than the type initially requested, provided that the conditions for opening that type of proceedings under national law are fulfilled and that that type of proceedings is the most appropriate as regards the interests of the local creditors and coherence between the main and secondary insolvency proceedings. The second sentence of Article 34 shall apply.

Article 39. Judicial review of the decision to open secondary insolvency proceedings

The insolvency practitioner in the main insolvency proceedings may challenge the decision to open secondary insolvency proceedings before the courts of the Member State in which secondary insolvency proceedings have been opened on the ground that the court did not comply with the conditions and requirements of Article 38.

Article 40. Advance payment of costs and expenses

Where the law of the Member State in which the opening of secondary insolvency proceedings is requested requires that the debtor's assets be sufficient to cover in whole or in part the costs and expenses of the proceedings, the court may, when it receives such a request, require the applicant to make an advance payment of costs or to provide appropriate security.

Article 41. Cooperation and communication between insolvency practitioners

1. The insolvency practitioner in the main insolvency proceedings and the insolvency practitioner or practitioners in secondary insolvency proceedings concerning the same debtor shall cooperate with each other to the extent such cooperation is not incompatible with the rules applicable to the respective proceedings. Such cooperation may take any form, including the conclusion of agreements or protocols.

2. In implementing the cooperation set out in paragraph 1, the insolvency practitioners shall:

(a)   as soon as possible communicate to each other any information which may be relevant to the other proceedings, in particular any progress made in lodging and verifying claims and all measures aimed at rescuing or restructuring the debtor, or at terminating the proceedings, provided appropriate arrangements are made to protect confidential information;

(b)   explore the possibility of restructuring the debtor and, where such a possibility exists, coordinate the elaboration and implementation of a restructuring plan;

(c)   coordinate the administration of the realisation or use of the debtor's assets and affairs; the insolvency practitioner in the secondary insolvency proceedings shall give the insolvency practitioner in the main insolvency proceedings an early opportunity to submit proposals on the realisation or use of the assets in the secondary insolvency proceedings.

3. Paragraphs 1 and 2 shall apply mutatis mutandis to situations where, in the main or in the secondary insolvency proceedings or in any territorial insolvency proceedings concerning the same debtor and open at the same time, the debtor remains in possession of its assets.

Article 42. Cooperation and communication between courts

1. In order to facilitate the coordination of main, territorial and secondary insolvency proceedings concerning the same debtor, a court before which a request to open insolvency proceedings is pending, or which has opened such proceedings, shall cooperate with any other court before which a request to open insolvency proceedings is pending, or which has opened such proceedings, to the extent that

such cooperation is not incompatible with the rules applicable to each of the proceedings. For that purpose, the courts may, where appropriate, appoint an independent person or body acting on its instructions, provided that it is not incompatible with the rules applicable to them.

2. In implementing the cooperation set out in paragraph 1, the courts, or any appointed person or body acting on their behalf, as referred to in paragraph 1, may communicate directly with, or request information or assistance directly from, each other provided that such communication respects the procedural rights of the parties to the proceedings and the confidentiality of information.

3. The cooperation referred to in paragraph 1 may be implemented by any means that the court considers appropriate. It may, in particular, concern:

(a)   coordination in the appointment of the insolvency practitioners;

(b)   communication of information by any means considered appropriate by the court;

(c)   coordination of the administration and supervision of the debtor's assets and affairs;

(d)   coordination of the conduct of hearings;

(e)   coordination in the approval of protocols, where necessary.

Article 43. Cooperation and communication between insolvency practitioners and courts

1. In order to facilitate the coordination of main, territorial and secondary insolvency proceedings opened in respect of the same debtor:

(a)   an insolvency practitioner in main insolvency proceedings shall cooperate and communicate with any court before which a request to open secondary insolvency proceedings is pending or which has opened such proceedings;

(b)   an insolvency practitioner in territorial or secondary insolvency proceedings shall cooperate and communicate with the court before which a request to open main insolvency proceedings is pending or which has opened such proceedings; and

(c)   an insolvency practitioner in territorial or secondary insolvency proceedings shall cooperate and communicate with the court before which a request to open other territorial or secondary insolvency proceedings is pending or which has opened such proceedings;

to the extent that such cooperation and communication are not incompatible with the rules applicable to each of the proceedings and do not entail any conflict of interest.

2. The cooperation referred to in paragraph 1 may be implemented by any appropriate means, such as those set out in Article 42(3).

Article 44. Costs of cooperation and communication

The requirements laid down in Articles 42 and 43 shall not result in courts charging costs to each other for cooperation and communication.

Article 45. Exercise of creditors' rights

1. Any creditor may lodge its claim in the main insolvency proceedings and in any secondary insolvency proceedings.

2. The insolvency practitioners in the main and any secondary insolvency proceedings shall lodge in other proceedings claims which have already been lodged in the proceedings for which they were appointed, provided that the interests of creditors in the latter proceedings are served by doing so, subject to the right of creditors to oppose such lodgement or to withdraw the lodgement of their claims where the law applicable so provides.

3. The insolvency practitioner in the main or secondary insolvency proceedings shall be entitled to participate in other proceedings on the same basis as a creditor, in particular by attending creditors' meetings.

Article 46. Stay of the process of realisation of assets
1. The court which opened the secondary insolvency proceedings shall stay the process of realisation of assets in whole or in part on receipt of a request from the insolvency practitioner in the main insolvency proceedings. In such a case, it may require the insolvency practitioner in the main insolvency proceedings to take any suitable measure to guarantee the interests of the creditors in the secondary insolvency proceedings and of individual classes of creditors. Such a request from the insolvency practitioner may be rejected only if it is manifestly of no interest to the creditors in the main insolvency proceedings. Such a stay of the process of realisation of assets may be ordered for up to 3 months. It may be continued or renewed for similar periods.
2. The court referred to in paragraph 1 shall terminate the stay of the process of realisation of assets:
    (a)   at the request of the insolvency practitioner in the main insolvency proceedings;
    (b)   of its own motion, at the request of a creditor or at the request of the insolvency practitioner in the secondary insolvency proceedings if that measure no longer appears justified, in particular, by the interests of creditors in the main insolvency proceedings or in the secondary insolvency proceedings.

Article 47. Power of the insolvency practitioner to propose restructuring plans
1. Where the law of the Member State where secondary insolvency proceedings have been opened allows for such proceedings to be closed without liquidation by a restructuring plan, a composition or a comparable measure, the insolvency practitioner in the main insolvency proceedings shall be empowered to propose such a measure in accordance with the procedure of that Member State.
2. Any restriction of creditors' rights arising from a measure referred to in paragraph 1 which is proposed in secondary insolvency proceedings, such as a stay of payment or discharge of debt, shall have no effect in respect of assets of a debtor that are not covered by those proceedings, without the consent of all the creditors having an interest.

Article 48. Impact of closure of insolvency proceedings
1. Without prejudice to Article 49, the closure of insolvency proceedings shall not prevent the continuation of other insolvency proceedings concerning the same debtor which are still open at that point in time.
2. Where insolvency proceedings concerning a legal person or a company in the Member State of that person's or company's registered office would entail the dissolution of the legal person or of the company, that legal person or company shall not cease to exist until any other insolvency proceedings concerning the same debtor have been closed, or the insolvency practitioner or practitioners in such proceedings have given consent to the dissolution.

Article 49. Assets remaining in the secondary insolvency proceedings
If, by the liquidation of assets in the secondary insolvency proceedings, it is possible to meet all claims allowed under those proceedings, the insolvency practitioner appointed in those proceedings shall immediately transfer any assets remaining to the insolvency practitioner in the main insolvency proceedings.

Article 50. Subsequent opening of the main insolvency proceedings
Where the proceedings referred to in Article 3(1) are opened following the opening of the proceedings referred to in Article 3(2) in another Member State, Articles 41, 45, 46, 47 and 49 shall apply to those opened first, in so far as the progress of those proceedings so permits.

Article 51. Conversion of secondary insolvency proceedings
1. At the request of the insolvency practitioner in the main insolvency proceedings, the court of the Member State in which secondary insolvency proceedings

have been opened may order the conversion of the secondary insolvency proceedings into another type of insolvency proceedings listed in Annex A, provided that the conditions for opening that type of proceedings under national law are fulfilled and that that type of proceedings is the most appropriate as regards the interests of the local creditors and coherence between the main and secondary insolvency proceedings.

2. When considering the request referred to in paragraph 1, the court may seek information from the insolvency practitioners involved in both proceedings.

Article 52. Preservation measures
Where the court of a Member State which has jurisdiction pursuant to Article 3(1) appoints a temporary administrator in order to ensure the preservation of a debtor's assets, that temporary administrator shall be empowered to request any measures to secure and preserve any of the debtor's assets situated in another Member State, provided for under the law of that Member State, for the period between the request for the opening of insolvency proceedings and the judgment opening the proceedings.

CHAPTER IV
PROVISION OF INFORMATION FOR CREDITORS AND LODGEMENT OF THEIR CLAIMS

Article 53. Right to lodge claims
Any foreign creditor may lodge claims in insolvency proceedings by any means of communication, which are accepted by the law of the State of the opening of proceedings. Representation by a lawyer or another legal professional shall not be mandatory for the sole purpose of lodging of claims.

Article 54. Duty to inform creditors
1. As soon as insolvency proceedings are opened in a Member State, the court of that State having jurisdiction or the insolvency practitioner appointed by that court shall immediately inform the known foreign creditors.

2. The information referred to in paragraph 1, provided by an individual notice, shall in particular include time limits, the penalties laid down with regard to those time limits, the body or authority empowered to accept the lodgement of claims and any other measures laid down. Such notice shall also indicate whether creditors whose claims are preferential or secured in rem need to lodge their claims. The notice shall also include a copy of the standard form for lodging of claims referred to in Article 55 or information on where that form is available.

3. The information referred to in paragraphs 1 and 2 of this Article shall be provided using the standard notice form to be established in accordance with Article 88. The form shall be published in the European e-Justice Portal and shall bear the heading 'Notice of insolvency proceedings' in all the official languages of the institutions of the Union. It shall be transmitted in the official language of the State of the opening of proceedings or, if there are several official languages in that Member State, in the official language or one of the official languages of the place where insolvency proceedings have been opened, or in another language which that State has indicated it can accept, in accordance with Article 55(5), if it can be assumed that that language is easier to understand for the foreign creditors.

4. In insolvency proceedings relating to an individual not exercising a business or professional activity, the use of the standard form referred to in this Article shall not be obligatory if creditors are not required to lodge their claims in order to have their claims taken into account in the proceedings.

Article 55. Procedure for lodging claims
1. Any foreign creditor may lodge its claim using the standard claims form to be established in accordance with Article 88. The form shall bear the heading 'Lodgement of claims' in all the official languages of the institutions of the Union.

2. The standard claims form referred to in paragraph 1 shall include the following information:

(a)   the name, postal address, e-mail address, if any, personal identification number, if any, and bank details of the foreign creditor referred to in paragraph 1;

(b)   the amount of the claim, specifying the principal and, where applicable, interest and the date on which it arose and the date on which it became due, if different;

(c)   if interest is claimed, the interest rate, whether the interest is of a legal or contractual nature, the period of time for which the interest is claimed and the capitalised amount of interest;

(d)   if costs incurred in asserting the claim prior to the opening of proceedings are claimed, the amount and the details of those costs;

(e)   the nature of the claim;

(f)   whether any preferential creditor status is claimed and the basis of such a claim;

(g)   whether security in rem or a reservation of title is alleged in respect of the claim and if so, what assets are covered by the security interest being invoked, the date on which the security was granted and, where the security has been registered, the registration number; and

(h)   whether any set-off is claimed and, if so, the amounts of the mutual claims existing on the date when insolvency proceedings were opened, the date on which they arose and the amount net of set-off claimed.

The standard claims form shall be accompanied by copies of any supporting documents.

3. The standard claims form shall indicate that the provision of information concerning the bank details and the personal identification number of the creditor referred to in point (a) of paragraph 2 is not compulsory.

4. When a creditor lodges its claim by means other than the standard form referred to in paragraph 1, the claim shall contain the information referred to in paragraph 2.

5. Claims may be lodged in any official language of the institutions of the Union. The court, the insolvency practitioner or the debtor in possession may require the creditor to provide a translation in the official language of the State of the opening of proceedings or, if there are several official languages in that Member State, in the official language or one of the official languages of the place where insolvency proceedings have been opened, or in another language which that Member State has indicated it can accept. Each Member State shall indicate whether it accepts any official language of the institutions of the Union other than its own for the purpose of the lodging of claims.

6. Claims shall be lodged within the period stipulated by the law of the State of the opening of proceedings. In the case of a foreign creditor, that period shall not be less than 30 days following the publication of the opening of insolvency proceedings in the insolvency register of the State of the opening of proceedings. Where a Member State relies on Article 24(4), that period shall not be less than 30 days following a creditor having been informed pursuant to Article 54.

7. Where the court, the insolvency practitioner or the debtor in possession has doubts in relation to a claim lodged in accordance with this Article, it shall give the creditor the opportunity to provide additional evidence on the existence and the amount of the claim.

CHAPTER V
INSOLVENCY PROCEEDINGS OF MEMBERS OF A GROUP OF COMPANIES

Section 1
Cooperation and communication

Article 56. Cooperation and communication between insolvency practitioners

1. Where insolvency proceedings relate to two or more members of a group of companies, an insolvency practitioner appointed in proceedings concerning a member of the group shall cooperate with any insolvency practitioner appointed in proceedings concerning another member of the same group to the extent that such cooperation is appropriate to facilitate the effective administration of those proceedings, is not incompatible with the rules applicable to such proceedings and does not entail any conflict of interest. That cooperation may take any form, including the conclusion of agreements or protocols.

2. In implementing the cooperation set out in paragraph 1, insolvency practitioners shall:

(a)   as soon as possible communicate to each other any information which may be relevant to the other proceedings, provided appropriate arrangements are made to protect confidential information;

(b)   consider whether possibilities exist for coordinating the administration and supervision of the affairs of the group members which are subject to insolvency proceedings, and if so, coordinate such administration and supervision;

(c)   consider whether possibilities exist for restructuring group members which are subject to insolvency proceedings and, if so, coordinate with regard to the proposal and negotiation of a coordinated restructuring plan.

For the purposes of points (b) and (c), all or some of the insolvency practitioners referred to in paragraph 1 may agree to grant additional powers to an insolvency practitioner appointed in one of the proceedings where such an agreement is permitted by the rules applicable to each of the proceedings. They may also agree on the allocation of certain tasks amongst them, where such allocation of tasks is permitted by the rules applicable to each of the proceedings.

Article 57. Cooperation and communication between courts

1. Where insolvency proceedings relate to two or more members of a group of companies, a court which has opened such proceedings shall cooperate with any other court before which a request to open proceedings concerning another member of the same group is pending or which has opened such proceedings to the extent that such cooperation is appropriate to facilitate the effective administration of the proceedings, is not incompatible with the rules applicable to them and does not entail any conflict of interest. For that purpose, the courts may, where appropriate, appoint an independent person or body to act on its instructions, provided that this is not incompatible with the rules applicable to them.

2. In implementing the cooperation set out in paragraph 1, courts, or any appointed person or body acting on their behalf, as referred to in paragraph 1, may communicate directly with each other, or request information or assistance directly from each other, provided that such communication respects the procedural rights of the parties to the proceedings and the confidentiality of information.

3. The cooperation referred to in paragraph 1 may be implemented by any means that the court considers appropriate. It may, in particular, concern:

(a)   coordination in the appointment of insolvency practitioners;

(b)   communication of information by any means considered appropriate by the court;

(c)   coordination of the administration and supervision of the assets and affairs of the members of the group;

(d)   coordination of the conduct of hearings;

(e)   coordination in the approval of protocols where necessary.

Article 58. Cooperation and communication between insolvency practitioners and courts

An insolvency practitioner appointed in insolvency proceedings concerning a member of a group of companies:

(a)   shall cooperate and communicate with any court before which a request for the opening of proceedings in respect of another member of the same group of companies is pending or which has opened such proceedings; and

(b)   may request information from that court concerning the proceedings regarding the other member of the group or request assistance concerning the proceedings in which he has been appointed;

to the extent that such cooperation and communication are appropriate to facilitate the effective administration of the proceedings, do not entail any conflict of interest and are not incompatible with the rules applicable to them.

Article 59. Costs of cooperation and communication in proceedings concerning members of a group of companies

The costs of the cooperation and communication provided for in Articles 56 to 60 incurred by an insolvency practitioner or a court shall be regarded as costs and expenses incurred in the respective proceedings.

Article 60. Powers of the insolvency practitioner in proceedings concerning members of a group of companies

1. An insolvency practitioner appointed in insolvency proceedings opened in respect of a member of a group of companies may, to the extent appropriate to facilitate the effective administration of the proceedings:

(a)   be heard in any of the proceedings opened in respect of any other member of the same group;

(b)   request a stay of any measure related to the realisation of the assets in the proceedings opened with respect to any other member of the same group, provided that:

(i)   a restructuring plan for all or some members of the group for which insolvency proceedings have been opened has been proposed under point (c) of Article 56(2) and presents a reasonable chance of success;

(ii)   such a stay is necessary in order to ensure the proper implementation of the restructuring plan;

(iii)   the restructuring plan would be to the benefit of the creditors in the proceedings for which the stay is requested; and

(iv)   neither the insolvency proceedings in which the insolvency practitioner referred to in paragraph 1 of this Article has been appointed nor the proceedings in respect of which the stay is requested are subject to co-ordination under Section 2 of this Chapter;

(c)   apply for the opening of group coordination proceedings in accordance with Article 61.2. The court having opened proceedings referred to in point (b) of paragraph 1 shall stay any measure related to the realisation of the assets in the proceedings in whole or in part if it is satisfied that the conditions referred to in point (b) of paragraph 1 are fulfilled.

Before ordering the stay, the court shall hear the insolvency practitioner appointed in the proceedings for which the stay is requested. Such a stay may be ordered for any period, not exceeding 3 months, which the court considers appropriate and which is compatible with the rules applicable to the proceedings.

The court ordering the stay may require the insolvency practitioner referred to in paragraph 1 to take any suitable measure available under national law to guarantee the interests of the creditors in the proceedings.

The court may extend the duration of the stay by such further period or periods as it considers appropriate and which are compatible with the rules applicable to the proceedings, provided that the conditions referred to in points (b)(ii) to (iv) of paragraph 1 continue to be fulfilled and that the total duration of the stay (the initial period together with any such extensions) does not exceed 6 months.

Section 2
Coordination

Subsection 1
Procedure

Article 61. Request to open group coordination proceedings
1. Group coordination proceedings may be requested before any court having jurisdiction over the insolvency proceedings of a member of the group, by an insolvency practitioner appointed in insolvency proceedings opened in relation to a member of the group.

2. The request referred to in paragraph 1 shall be made in accordance with the conditions provided for by the law applicable to the proceedings in which the insolvency practitioner has been appointed.

3. The request referred to in paragraph 1 shall be accompanied by:

(a)   a proposal as to the person to be nominated as the group coordinator ('the coordinator'), details of his or her eligibility pursuant to Article 71, details of his or her qualifications and his or her written agreement to act as coordinator;

(b)   an outline of the proposed group coordination, and in particular the reasons why the conditions set out in Article 63(1) are fulfilled;

(c)   a list of the insolvency practitioners appointed in relation to the members of the group and, where relevant, the courts and competent authorities involved in the insolvency proceedings of the members of the group;

(d)   an outline of the estimated costs of the proposed group coordination and the estimation of the share of those costs to be paid by each member of the group.

Article 62. Priority rule
Without prejudice to Article 66, where the opening of group coordination proceedings is requested before courts of different Member States, any court other than the court first seised shall decline jurisdiction in favour of that court.

Article 63. Notice by the court seised
1. The court seised of a request to open group coordination proceedings shall give notice as soon as possible of the request for the opening of group coordination proceedings and of the proposed coordinator to the insolvency practitioners appointed in relation to the members of the group as indicated in the request referred to in point (c) of Article 61(3), if it is satisfied that:

(a)   the opening of such proceedings is appropriate to facilitate the effective administration of the insolvency proceedings relating to the different group members;

(b)   no creditor of any group member expected to participate in the proceedings is likely to be financially disadvantaged by the inclusion of that member in such proceedings; and

(c)   the proposed coordinator fulfils the requirements laid down in Article 71.

2. The notice referred to in paragraph 1 of this Article shall list the elements referred to in points (a) to (d) of Article 61(3).

3. The notice referred to in paragraph 1 shall be sent by registered letter, attested by an acknowledgment of receipt.

4. The court seised shall give the insolvency practitioners involved the opportunity to be heard.

Article 64. Objections by insolvency practitioners

1. An insolvency practitioner appointed in respect of any group member may object to:

   (a) the inclusion within group coordination proceedings of the insolvency proceedings in respect of which it has been appointed; or

   (b) the person proposed as a coordinator.

2. Objections pursuant to paragraph 1 of this Article shall be lodged with the court referred to in Article 63 within 30 days of receipt of notice of the request for the opening of group coordination proceedings by the insolvency practitioner referred to in paragraph 1 of this Article.

The objection may be made by means of the standard form established in accordance with Article 88.

3. Prior to taking the decision to participate or not to participate in the coordination in accordance with point (a) of paragraph 1, an insolvency practitioner shall obtain any approval which may be required under the law of the State of the opening of proceedings for which it has been appointed.

Article 65. Consequences of objection to the inclusion in group coordination

1. Where an insolvency practitioner has objected to the inclusion of the proceedings in respect of which it has been appointed in group coordination proceedings, those proceedings shall not be included in the group coordination proceedings.

2. The powers of the court referred to in Article 68 or of the coordinator arising from those proceedings shall have no effect as regards that member, and shall entail no costs for that member.

Article 66. Choice of court for group coordination proceedings

1. Where at least two-thirds of all insolvency practitioners appointed in insolvency proceedings of the members of the group have agreed that a court of another Member State having jurisdiction is the most appropriate court for the opening of group coordination proceedings, that court shall have exclusive jurisdiction.

2. The choice of court shall be made by joint agreement in writing or evidenced in writing. It may be made until such time as group coordination proceedings have been opened in accordance with Article 68.

3. Any court other than the court seised under paragraph 1 shall decline jurisdiction in favour of that court.

4. The request for the opening of group coordination proceedings shall be submitted to the court agreed in accordance with Article 61.

Article 67. Consequences of objections to the proposed coordinator

Where objections to the person proposed as coordinator have been received from an insolvency practitioner which does not also object to the inclusion in the group coordination proceedings of the member in respect of which it has been appointed, the court may refrain from appointing that person and invite the objecting insolvency practitioner to submit a new request in accordance with Article 61(3).

Article 68. Decision to open group coordination proceedings

1. After the period referred to in Article 64(2) has elapsed, the court may open group coordination proceedings where it is satisfied that the conditions of Article 63(1) are met. In such a case, the court shall:

   (a) appoint a coordinator;

   (b) decide on the outline of the coordination; and

   (c) decide on the estimation of costs and the share to be paid by the group members.

2. The decision opening group coordination proceedings shall be brought to the notice of the participating insolvency practitioners and of the coordinator.

Article 69. Subsequent opt-in by insolvency practitioners

1. In accordance with its national law, any insolvency practitioner may request, after the court decision referred to in Article 68, the inclusion of the proceedings in respect of which it has been appointed, where:

(a)   there has been an objection to the inclusion of the insolvency proceedings within the group coordination proceedings; or

(b)   insolvency proceedings with respect to a member of the group have been opened after the court has opened group coordination proceedings.

2. Without prejudice to paragraph 4, the coordinator may accede to such a request, after consulting the insolvency practitioners involved, where

(a)   he or she is satisfied that, taking into account the stage that the group coordination proceedings has reached at the time of the request, the criteria set out in points (a) and (b) of Article 63(1) are met; or

(b)   all insolvency practitioners involved agree, subject to the conditions in their national law.

3. The coordinator shall inform the court and the participating insolvency practitioners of his or her decision pursuant to paragraph 2 and of the reasons on which it is based.

4. Any participating insolvency practitioner or any insolvency practitioner whose request for inclusion in the group coordination proceedings has been rejected may challenge the decision referred to in paragraph 2 in accordance with the procedure set out under the law of the Member State in which the group coordination proceedings have been opened.

Article 70. Recommendations and group coordination plan

1. When conducting their insolvency proceedings, insolvency practitioners shall consider the recommendations of the coordinator and the content of the group coordination plan referred to in Article 72(1).

2. An insolvency practitioner shall not be obliged to follow in whole or in part the coordinator's recommendations or the group coordination plan.

If it does not follow the coordinator's recommendations or the group coordination plan, it shall give reasons for not doing so to the persons or bodies that it is to report to under its national law, and to the coordinator.

Subsection 2
General provisions

Article 71. The coordinator

1. The coordinator shall be a person eligible under the law of a Member State to act as an insolvency practitioner.

2. The coordinator shall not be one of the insolvency practitioners appointed to act in respect of any of the group members, and shall have no conflict of interest in respect of the group members, their creditors and the insolvency practitioners appointed in respect of any of the group members.

Article 72. Tasks and rights of the coordinator

1. The coordinator shall:

(a)   identify and outline recommendations for the coordinated conduct of the insolvency proceedings;

(b)   propose a group coordination plan that identifies, describes and recommends a comprehensive set of measures appropriate to an integrated approach to the resolution of the group members' insolvencies. In particular, the plan may contain proposals for:

(i)   the measures to be taken in order to re-establish the economic performance and the financial soundness of the group or any part of it;

(ii)   the settlement of intra-group disputes as regards intra-group transactions and avoidance actions;

(iii) agreements between the insolvency practitioners of the insolvent group members.

2. The coordinator may also:

(a)   be heard and participate, in particular by attending creditors' meetings, in any of the proceedings opened in respect of any member of the group;

(b)   mediate any dispute arising between two or more insolvency practitioners of group members;

(c)   present and explain his or her group coordination plan to the persons or bodies that he or she is to report to under his or her national law;

(d)   request information from any insolvency practitioner in respect of any member of the group where that information is or might be of use when identifying and outlining strategies and measures in order to coordinate the proceedings; and

(e)   request a stay for a period of up to 6 months of the proceedings opened in respect of any member of the group, provided that such a stay is necessary in order to ensure the proper implementation of the plan and would be to the benefit of the creditors in the proceedings for which the stay is requested; or request the lifting of any existing stay. Such a request shall be made to the court that opened the proceedings for which a stay is requested.

3. The plan referred to in point (b) of paragraph 1 shall not include recommendations as to any consolidation of proceedings or insolvency estates.

4. The coordinator's tasks and rights as defined under this Article shall not extend to any member of the group not participating in group coordination proceedings.

5. The coordinator shall perform his or her duties impartially and with due care.

6. Where the coordinator considers that the fulfilment of his or her tasks requires a significant increase in the costs compared to the cost estimate referred to in point (d) of Article 61(3), and in any case, where the costs exceed 10 % of the estimated costs, the coordinator shall:

(a)   inform without delay the participating insolvency practitioners; and

(b)   seek the prior approval of the court opening group coordination proceedings.

Article 73. Languages

1. The coordinator shall communicate with the insolvency practitioner of a participating group member in the language agreed with the insolvency practitioner or, in the absence of an agreement, in the official language or one of the official languages of the institutions of the Union, and of the court which opened the proceedings in respect of that group member.

2. The coordinator shall communicate with a court in the official language applicable to that court.

Article 74. Cooperation between insolvency practitioners and the coordinator

1. Insolvency practitioners appointed in relation to members of a group and the coordinator shall cooperate with each other to the extent that such cooperation is not incompatible with the rules applicable to the respective proceedings.

2. In particular, insolvency practitioners shall communicate any information that is relevant for the coordinator to perform his or her tasks.

Article 75. Revocation of the appointment of the coordinator

The court shall revoke the appointment of the coordinator of its own motion or at the request of the insolvency practitioner of a participating group member where:

(a)   the coordinator acts to the detriment of the creditors of a participating group member; or

(b)   the coordinator fails to comply with his or her obligations under this Chapter.

Article 76. Debtor in possession
The provisions applicable, under this Chapter, to the insolvency practitioner shall also apply, where appropriate, to the debtor in possession.

Article 77. Costs and distribution
1. The remuneration for the coordinator shall be adequate, proportionate to the tasks fulfilled and reflect reasonable expenses.

2. On having completed his or her tasks, the coordinator shall establish the final statement of costs and the share to be paid by each member, and submit this statement to each participating insolvency practitioner and to the court opening coordination proceedings.

3. In the absence of objections by the insolvency practitioners within 30 days of receipt of the statement referred to in paragraph 2, the costs and the share to be paid by each member shall be deemed to be agreed. The statement shall be submitted to the court opening coordination proceedings for confirmation.

4. In the event of an objection, the court that opened the group coordination proceedings shall, upon the application of the coordinator or any participating insolvency practitioner, decide on the costs and the share to be paid by each member in accordance with the criteria set out in paragraph 1 of this Article, and taking into account the estimation of costs referred to in Article 68(1) and, where applicable, Article 72(6).

5. Any participating insolvency practitioner may challenge the decision referred to in paragraph 4 in accordance with the procedure set out under the law of the Member State where group coordination proceedings have been opened.

CHAPTER VI
DATA PROTECTION

Article 78. Data protection
1. National rules implementing Directive 95/46/EC shall apply to the processing of personal data carried out in the Member States pursuant to this Regulation, provided that processing operations referred to in Article 3(2) of Directive 95/46/EC are not concerned.

2. Regulation (EC) No 45/2001 shall apply to the processing of personal data carried out by the Commission pursuant to this Regulation.

Article 79. Responsibilities of Member States regarding the processing of personal data in national insolvency registers
1. Each Member State shall communicate to the Commission the name of the natural or legal person, public authority, agency or any other body designated by national law to exercise the functions of controller in accordance with point (d) of Article 2 of Directive 95/46/EC, with a view to its publication on the European e-Justice Portal.

2. Member States shall ensure that the technical measures for ensuring the security of personal data processed in their national insolvency registers referred to in Article 24 are implemented.

3. Member States shall be responsible for verifying that the controller, designated by national law in accordance with point (d) of Article 2 of Directive 95/46/EC, ensures compliance with the principles of data quality, in particular the accuracy and the updating of data stored in national insolvency registers.

4. Member States shall be responsible, in accordance with Directive 95/46/EC, for the collection and storage of data in national databases and for decisions taken to make such data available in the interconnected register that can be consulted via the European e-Justice Portal.

5. As part of the information that should be provided to data subjects to enable them to exercise their rights, and in particular the right to the erasure of data,

Member States shall inform data subjects of the accessibility period set for personal data stored in insolvency registers.

Article 80. Responsibilities of the Commission in connection with the processing of personal data

1. The Commission shall exercise the responsibilities of controller pursuant to Article 2(d) of Regulation (EC) No 45/2001 in accordance with its respective responsibilities defined in this Article.

2. The Commission shall define the necessary policies and apply the necessary technical solutions to fulfil its responsibilities within the scope of the function of controller.

3. The Commission shall implement the technical measures required to ensure the security of personal data while in transit, in particular the confidentiality and integrity of any transmission to and from the European e-Justice Portal.

4. The obligations of the Commission shall not affect the responsibilities of the Member States and other bodies for the content and operation of the inter-connected national databases run by them.

Article 81. Information obligations

Without prejudice to the information to be given to data subjects in accordance with Articles 11 and 12 of Regulation (EC) No 45/2001, the Commission shall inform data subjects, by means of publication through the European e-Justice Portal, about its role in the processing of data and the purposes for which those data will be processed.

Article 82. Storage of personal data

As regards information from interconnected national databases, no personal data relating to data subjects shall be stored in the European e-Justice Portal. All such data shall be stored in the national databases operated by the Member States or other bodies.

Article 83. Access to personal data via the European e-Justice Portal

Personal data stored in the national insolvency registers referred to in Article 24 shall be accessible via the European e-Justice Portal for as long as they remain accessible under national law.

CHAPTER VII
TRANSITIONAL AND FINAL PROVISIONS

Article 84. Applicability in time

1. The provisions of this Regulation shall apply only to insolvency proceedings opened after 26 June 2017. Acts committed by a debtor before that date shall continue to be governed by the law which was applicable to them at the time they were committed.

2. Notwithstanding Article 91 of this Regulation, Regulation (EC) No 1346/2000 shall continue to apply to insolvency proceedings which fall within the scope of that Regulation and which have been opened before 26 June 2017.

Article 85. Relationship to Conventions

1. This Regulation replaces, in respect of the matters referred to therein, and as regards relations between Member States, the Conventions concluded between two or more Member States, in particular:

    (a)   the Convention between Belgium and France on Jurisdiction and the Validity and Enforcement of Judgments, Arbitration Awards and Authentic Instruments, signed at Paris on 8 July 1899;

    (b)   the Convention between Belgium and Austria on Bankruptcy, Winding-up, Arrangements, Compositions and Suspension of Payments (with Additional Protocol of 13 June 1973), signed at Brussels on 16 July 1969;

    (c)   the Convention between Belgium and the Netherlands on Territorial

Jurisdiction, Bankruptcy and the Validity and Enforcement of Judgments, Arbitration Awards and Authentic Instruments, signed at Brussels on 28 March 1925;

(d)   the Treaty between Germany and Austria on Bankruptcy, Winding-up, Arrangements and Compositions, signed at Vienna on 25 May 1979;

(e)   the Convention between France and Austria on Jurisdiction, Recognition and Enforcement of Judgments on Bankruptcy, signed at Vienna on 27 February 1979;

(f)   the Convention between France and Italy on the Enforcement of Judgments in Civil and Commercial Matters, signed at Rome on 3 June 1930;

(g)   the Convention between Italy and Austria on Bankruptcy, Winding-up, Arrangements and Compositions, signed at Rome on 12 July 1977;

(h)   the Convention between the Kingdom of the Netherlands and the Federal Republic of Germany on the Mutual Recognition and Enforcement of Judgments and other Enforceable Instruments in Civil and Commercial Matters, signed at The Hague on 30 August 1962;

(i)   the Convention between the United Kingdom and the Kingdom of Belgium providing for the Reciprocal Enforcement of Judgments in Civil and Commercial Matters, with Protocol, signed at Brussels on 2 May 1934;

(j)   the Convention between Denmark, Finland, Norway, Sweden and Iceland on Bankruptcy, signed at Copenhagen on 7 November 1933;

(k)   the European Convention on Certain International Aspects of Bankruptcy, signed at Istanbul on 5 June 1990;

(l)   the Convention between the Federative People's Republic of Yugoslavia and the Kingdom of Greece on the Mutual Recognition and Enforcement of Judgments, signed at Athens on 18 June 1959;

(m)   the Agreement between the Federative People's Republic of Yugoslavia and the Republic of Austria on the Mutual Recognition and Enforcement of Arbitral Awards and Arbitral Settlements in Commercial Matters, signed at Belgrade on 18 March 1960;

(n)   the Convention between the Federative People's Republic of Yugoslavia and the Italian Republic on Mutual Judicial Cooperation in Civil and Administrative Matters, signed at Rome on 3 December 1960;

(o)   the Agreement between the Socialist Federative Republic of Yugoslavia and the Kingdom of Belgium on Judicial Cooperation in Civil and Commercial Matters, signed at Belgrade on 24 September 1971;

(p)   the Convention between the Governments of Yugoslavia and France on the Recognition and Enforcement of Judgments in Civil and Commercial Matters, signed at Paris on 18 May 1971;

(q)   the Agreement between the Czechoslovak Socialist Republic and the Hellenic Republic on Legal Aid in Civil and Criminal Matters, signed at Athens on 22 October 1980, still in force between the Czech Republic and Greece;

(r)   the Agreement between the Czechoslovak Socialist Republic and the Republic of Cyprus on Legal Aid in Civil and Criminal Matters, signed at Nicosia on 23 April 1982, still in force between the Czech Republic and Cyprus;

(s)   the Treaty between the Government of the Czechoslovak Socialist Republic and the Government of the Republic of France on Legal Aid and the Recognition and Enforcement of Judgments in Civil, Family and Commercial Matters, signed at Paris on 10 May 1984, still in force between the Czech Republic and France;

(t)   the Treaty between the Czechoslovak Socialist Republic and the Italian Republic on Legal Aid in Civil and Criminal Matters, signed at Prague on 6 December 1985, still in force between the Czech Republic and Italy;

(u)   the Agreement between the Republic of Latvia, the Republic of Estonia and the Republic of Lithuania on Legal Assistance and Legal Relationships, signed at Tallinn on 11 November 1992;

(v)   the Agreement between Estonia and Poland on Granting Legal Aid and Legal Relations on Civil, Labour and Criminal Matters, signed at Tallinn on 27 November 1998;

(w)   the Agreement between the Republic of Lithuania and the Republic of Poland on Legal Assistance and Legal Relations in Civil, Family, Labour and Criminal Matters, signed at Warsaw on 26 January 1993;

(x)   the Convention between the Socialist Republic of Romania and the Hellenic Republic on legal assistance in civil and criminal matters and its Protocol, signed at Bucharest on 19 October 1972;

(y)   the Convention between the Socialist Republic of Romania and the French Republic on legal assistance in civil and commercial matters, signed at Paris on 5 November 1974;

(z)   the Agreement between the People's Republic of Bulgaria and the Hellenic Republic on Legal Assistance in Civil and Criminal Matters, signed at Athens on 10 April 1976;

(aa)   the Agreement between the People's Republic of Bulgaria and the Republic of Cyprus on Legal Assistance in Civil and Criminal Matters, signed at Nicosia on 29 April 1983;

(ab)   the Agreement between the Government of the People's Republic of Bulgaria and the Government of the French Republic on Mutual Legal Assistance in Civil Matters, signed at Sofia on 18 January 1989;

(ac)   the Treaty between Romania and the Czech Republic on judicial assistance in civil matters, signed at Bucharest on 11 July 1994;

(ad)   the Treaty between Romania and the Republic of Poland on legal assistance and legal relations in civil cases, signed at Bucharest on 15 May 1999.

2. The Conventions referred to in paragraph 1 shall continue to have effect with regard to proceedings opened before the entry into force of Regulation (EC) No 1346/2000.

3. This Regulation shall not apply:

(a)   in any Member State, to the extent that it is irreconcilable with the obligations arising in relation to bankruptcy from a convention concluded by that Member State with one or more third countries before the entry into force of Regulation (EC) No 1346/2000;

(b)   in the United Kingdom of Great Britain and Northern Ireland, to the extent that is irreconcilable with the obligations arising in relation to bankruptcy and the winding-up of insolvent companies from any arrangements with the Commonwealth existing at the time Regulation (EC) No 1346/2000 entered into force.

Article 86. Information on national and Union insolvency law

1. The Member States shall provide, within the framework of the European Judicial Network in civil and commercial matters established by Council Decision 2001/470/EC, and with a view to making the information available to the public, a short description of their national legislation and procedures relating to insolvency, in particular relating to the matters listed in Article 7(2).

2. The Member States shall update the information referred to in paragraph 1 regularly.

3. The Commission shall make information concerning this Regulation available to the public.

Article 87. Establishment of the interconnection of registers

The Commission shall adopt implementing acts establishing the interconnection of insolvency registers as referred to in Article 25. Those implementing acts shall be adopted in accordance with the examination procedure referred to in Article 89(3).

Article 88. Establishment and subsequent amendment of standard forms

The Commission shall adopt implementing acts establishing and, where necessary, amending the forms referred to in Article 27(4), Articles 54 and 55 and Article 64(2). Those implementing acts shall be adopted in accordance with the advisory procedure referred to in Article 89(2).

Article 89. Committee procedure

1. The Commission shall be assisted by a committee. That committee shall be a committee within the meaning of Regulation (EU) No 182/2011.

2. Where reference is made to this paragraph, Article 4 of Regulation (EU) No 182/2011 shall apply.

3. Where reference is made to this paragraph, Article 5 of Regulation (EU) No 182/2011 shall apply.

Article 90. Review clause

1. No later than 27 June 2027, and every 5 years thereafter, the Commission shall present to the European Parliament, the Council and the European Economic and Social Committee a report on the application of this Regulation. The report shall be accompanied where necessary by a proposal for adaptation of this Regulation.

2. No later than 27 June 2022, the Commission shall present to the European Parliament, the Council and the European Economic and Social Committee a report on the application of the group coordination proceedings. The report shall be accompanied where necessary by a proposal for adaptation of this Regulation.

3. No later than 1 January 2016, the Commission shall submit to the European Parliament, the Council and the European Economic and Social Committee a study on the cross-border issues in the area of directors' liability and disqualifications.

4. No later than 27 June 2020, the Commission shall submit to the European Parliament, the Council and the European Economic and Social Committee a study on the issue of abusive forum shopping.

Article 91. Repeal

Regulation (EC) No 1346/2000 is repealed.

References to the repealed Regulation shall be construed as references to this Regulation and shall be read in accordance with the correlation table set out in Annex D to this Regulation.

Article 92. Entry into force

This Regulation shall enter into force on the twentieth day following that of its publication in the Official Journal of the European Union.

It shall apply from 26 June 2017, with the exception of:

    (a)   Article 86, which shall apply from 26 June 2016;

    (b)   Article 24(1), which shall apply from 26 June 2018; and

    (c)   Article 25, which shall apply from 26 June 2019.

This Regulation shall be binding in its entirety and directly applicable in the Member States in accordance with the Treaties.

Done at Strasbourg, 20 May 2015.

ANNEX A
INSOLVENCY PROCEEDINGS REFERRED TO IN POINT (4) OF
ARTICLE 2

...

UNITED KINGDOM

    — Winding-up by or subject to the supervision of the court,

    — Creditors' voluntary winding-up (with confirmation by the court),

    — Administration, including appointments made by filing prescribed documents with the court,

    — Voluntary arrangements under insolvency legislation,

    — Bankruptcy or sequestration.

ANNEX B
INSOLVENCY PRACTITIONERS REFERRED TO IN POINT (5) OF ARTICLE 2

...

UNITED KINGDOM
— Liquidator,
— Supervisor of a voluntary arrangement,
— Administrator,
— Official Receiver,
— Trustee,
— Provisional Liquidator,
— Interim Receiver,
— Judicial factor.

ANNEX D
CORRELATION TABLE

Regulation (EC) No 1346/2000	This Regulation
Article 1	Article 1
Article 2,introductory words	Article 2, introductory words
Article 2, point (a)	Article 2, point (4)
Article 2, point (b)	Article 2, point (5)
Article 2, point (c)	—
Article 2, point (d)	Article 2, point (6)
Article 2, point (e)	Article 2, point (7)
Article 2, point (f)	Article 2, point (8)
Article 2, point (g), introductory words	Article 2, point (9), introductory words
Article 2, point (g), first indent	Article 2, point (9)(vii)
Article 2, point (g), second indent	Article 2, point (9)(iv)
Article 2, point (g), third indent	Article 2, point (9)(viii)
Article 2, point (h)	Article 2, point 10
—	Article 2, points (1) to (3) and (11) to (13)
—	Article 2, point (9)(i) to (iii), (v), (vi)
Article 3	Article 3
—	Article 4
—	Article 5
—	Article 6
Article 4	Article 7
Article 5	Article 8
Article 6	Article 9
Article 7	Article 10
Article 8	Article 11(1)
—	Article 11(2)
Article 9	Article 12
Article 10	Article 13(1)
—	Article 13(2)
Article 11	Article 14
Article 12	Article 15
Article 13, first indent	Article 16, point (a)
Article 13, second indent	Article 16, point (b)
Article 14, first indent	Article 17, point (a)
Article 14, second indent	Article 17, point (b)
Article 14, third indent	Article 17, point (c)
Article 15	Article 18
Article 16	Article 19

ANNEX D (continued)

Regulation (EC) No 1346/2000	This Regulation
Article 17	Article 20
Article 18	Article 21
Article 19	Article 22
Article 20	Article 23
—	Article 24
—	Article 25
—	Article 26
—	Article 27
Article 21(1)	Article 28(2)
Article 21(2)	Article 28(1)
Article 22	Article 29
Article 23	Article 30
Article 24	Article 31
Article 25	Article 32
Article 26	Article 33
Article 27	Article 34
Article 28	Article 35
—	Article 36
Article 29	Article 37(1)
—	Article 37(2)
—	Article 38
—	Article 39
Article 30	Article 40
Article 31	Article 41
—	Article 42
—	Article 43
—	Article 44
Article 32	Article 45
Article 33	Article 46
Article 34(1)	Article 47(1)
Article 34(2)	Article 47(2)
Article 34(3)	—
—	Article 48
Article 35	Article 49
Article 36	Article 50
Article 37	Article 51
Article 38	Article 52
Article 39	Article 53
Article 40	Article 54
Article 41	Article 55
Article 42	—
—	Article 56
—	Article 57
—	Article 58
—	Article 59
—	Article 60
—	Article 61
—	Article 62
—	Article 63
—	Article 64
—	Article 65
—	Article 66
—	Article 67
—	Article 68
—	Article 69
—	Article 70
—	Article 71

ANNEX D (continued)

Regulation (EC) No 1346/2000	This Regulation
—	Article 72
—	Article 73
—	Article 74
—	Article 75
—	Article 76
—	Article 77
—	Article 78
—	Article 79
—	Article 80
—	Article 81
—	Article 82
—	Article 83
Article 43	Article 84(1)
—	Article 84(2)
Article 44	Article 85
—	Article 86
Article 45	—
—	Article 87
—	Article 88
—	Article 89
Article 46	Article 90(1)
—	Article 90(2) to (4)
—	Article 91
Article 47	Article 92
Annex A	Annex A
Annex B	—
Annex C	Annex B
—	Annex C
—	Annex D

PART V

INTERNATIONAL CONVENTIONS

HAGUE CONVENTION ON THE CIVIL ASPECTS OF INTERNATIONAL CHILD ABDUCTION 1980

See Child Abduction and Custody Act 1985, Schedule 1, p 93 above.

HAGUE CONVENTION ON THE LAW APPLICABLE TO TRUSTS AND ON THEIR RECOGNITION 1986

See Recognition of Trusts Act 1987, Schedule, p 113 above.

ROME CONVENTION ON THE LAW APPLICABLE TO CONTRACTUAL OBLIGATIONS (Arts 3, 4, 5, 6, 7)

See Contracts (Applicable Law) Act 1990, Schedule 1, p 116 above.

CONVENTION ON JURISDICTION, APPLICABLE LAW, RECOGNITION, ENFORCEMENT AND CO-OPERATION IN RESPECT OF PARENTAL RESPONSIBILITY AND MEASURES FOR THE PROTECTION OF CHILDREN*

Concluded 19 October 1996

The States signatory to the present Convention,

Considering the need to improve the protection of children in international situations,

Wishing to avoid conflicts between their legal systems in respect of jurisdiction, applicable law, recognition and enforcement of measures for the protection of children,

Recalling the importance of international co-operation for the protection of children,

Confirming that the best interests of the child are to be a primary consideration,

Noting that the Convention of 5 October 1961 concerning the powers of authorities and the law applicable in respect of the protection of minors is in need of revision,

Desiring to establish common provisions to this effect, taking into account the United Nations Convention on the Rights of the Child of 20 November 1989,

Have agreed on the following provisions

CHAPTER I
SCOPE OF THE CONVENTION

Article 1

(1) The objects of the present Convention are—

(a) to determine the State whose authorities have jurisdiction to take measures directed to the protection of the person or property of the child;

* © Hague Conference on Private International Law.

(b)   to determine which law is to be applied by such authorities in exercising their jurisdiction;

(c)   to determine the law applicable to parental responsibility;

(d)   to provide for the recognition and enforcement of such measures of protection in all Contracting States;

(e)   to establish such co-operation between the authorities of the Contracting States as may be necessary in order to achieve the purposes of this Convention.

(2)   For the purposes of this Convention, the term 'parental responsibility' includes parental authority, or any analogous relationship of authority determining the rights, powers and responsibilities of parents, guardians or other legal representatives in relation to the person or the property of the child.

Article 2

The Convention applies to children from the moment of their birth until they reach the age of 18 years.

Article 3

The measures referred to in Article 1 may deal in particular with—

(a)   the attribution, exercise, termination or restriction of parental responsibility, as well as its delegation;

(b)   rights of custody, including rights relating to the care of the person of the child and, in particular, the right to determine the child's place of residence, as well as rights of access including the right to take a child for a limited period of time to a place other than the child's habitual residence;

(c)   guardianship, curatorship and analogous institutions;

(d)   the designation and functions of any person or body having charge of the child's person or property, representing or assisting the child;

(e)   the placement of the child in a foster family or in institutional care, or the provision of care by kafala or an analogous institution;

(f)   the supervision by a public authority of the care of a child by any person having charge of the child;

(g)   the administration, conservation or disposal of the child's property.

Article 4

The Convention does not apply to—

(a)   the establishment or contesting of a parent-child relationship;

(b)   decisions on adoption, measures preparatory to adoption, or the annulment or revocation of adoption;

(c)   the name and forenames of the child;

(d)   emancipation;

(e)   maintenance obligations;

(f)   trusts or succession;

(g)   social security;

(h)   public measures of a general nature in matters of education or health;

(i)   measures taken as a result of penal offences committed by children;

(j)   decisions on the right of asylum and on immigration.

CHAPTER II
JURISDICTION

Article 5

(1)   The judicial or administrative authorities of the Contracting State of the habitual residence of the child have jurisdiction to take measures directed to the protection of the child's person or property.

(2)   Subject to Article 7, in case of a change of the child's habitual residence to another Contracting State, the authorities of the State of the new habitual residence have jurisdiction.

Article 6

(1) For refugee children and children who, due to disturbances occurring in their country, are internationally displaced, the authorities of the Contracting State on the territory of which these children are present as a result of their displacement have the jurisdiction provided for in paragraph 1 of Article 5.

(2) The provisions of the preceding paragraph also apply to children whose habitual residence cannot be established.

Article 7

(1) In case of wrongful removal or retention of the child, the authorities of the Contracting State in which the child was habitually resident immediately before the removal or retention keep their jurisdiction until the child has acquired a habitual residence in another State, and

(a) each person, institution or other body having rights of custody has acquiesced in the removal or retention; or

(b) the child has resided in that other State for a period of at least one year after the person, institution or other body having rights of custody has or should have had knowledge of the whereabouts of the child, no request for return lodged within that period is still pending, and the child is settled in his or her new environment.

(2) The removal or the retention of a child is to be considered wrongful where—

(a) it is in breach of rights of custody attributed to a person, an institution or any other body, either jointly or alone, under the law of the State in which the child was habitually resident immediately before the removal or retention; and

(b) at the time of removal or retention those rights were actually exercised, either jointly or alone, or would have been so exercised but for the removal or retention.

The rights of custody mentioned in sub-paragraph (a) above, may arise in particular by operation of law or by reason of a judicial or administrative decision, or by reason of an agreement having legal effect under the law of that State.

(3) So long as the authorities first mentioned in paragraph 1 keep their jurisdiction, the authorities of the Contracting State to which the child has been removed or in which he or she has been retained can take only such urgent measures under Article 11 as are necessary for the protection of the person or property of the child.

Article 8

(1) By way of exception, the authority of a Contracting State having jurisdiction under Article 5 or 6, if it considers that the authority of another Contracting State would be better placed in the particular case to assess the best interests of the child, may either

– request that other authority, directly or with the assistance of the Central Authority of its State, to assume jurisdiction to take such measures of protection as it considers to be necessary, or

– suspend consideration of the case and invite the parties to introduce such a request before the authority of that other State.

(2) The Contracting States whose authorities may be addressed as provided in the preceding paragraph are

(a) a State of which the child is a national,

(b) a State in which property of the child is located,

(c) a State whose authorities are seised of an application for divorce or legal separation of the child's parents, or for annulment of their marriage,

(d) a State with which the child has a substantial connection

(3) The authorities concerned may proceed to an exchange of views.

(4) The authority addressed as provided in paragraph 1 may assume juris-

diction, in place of the authority having jurisdiction under Article 5 or 6, if it considers that this is in the child's best interests.

Article 9

(1) If the authorities of a Contracting State referred to in Article 8, paragraph 2, consider that they are better placed in the particular case to assess the child's best interests, they may either

– request the competent authority of the Contracting State of the habitual residence of the child, directly or with the assistance of the Central Authority of that State, that they be authorised to exercise jurisdiction to take the measures of protection which they consider to be necessary, or

– invite the parties to introduce such a request before the authority of the Contracting State of the habitual residence of the child.

(2) The authorities concerned may proceed to an exchange of views.

(3) The authority initiating the request may exercise jurisdiction in place of the authority of the Contracting State of the habitual residence of the child only if the latter authority has accepted the request.

Article 10

(1) Without prejudice to Articles 5 to 9, the authorities of a Contracting State exercising jurisdiction to decide upon an application for divorce or legal separation of the parents of a child habitually resident in another Contracting State, or for annulment of their marriage, may, if the law of their State so provides, take measures directed to the protection of the person or property of such child if

(a) at the time of commencement of the proceedings, one of his or her parents habitually resides in that State and one of them has parental responsibility in relation to the child, and

(b) the jurisdiction of these authorities to take such measures has been accepted by the parents, as well as by any other person who has parental responsibility in relation to the child, and is in the best interests of the child.

(2) The jurisdiction provided for by paragraph 1 to take measures for the protection of the child ceases as soon as the decision allowing or refusing the application for divorce, legal separation or annulment of the marriage has become final, or the proceedings have come to an end for another reason.

Article 11

(1) In all cases of urgency, the authorities of any Contracting State in whose territory the child or property belonging to the child is present have jurisdiction to take any necessary measures of protection.

(2) The measures taken under the preceding paragraph with regard to a child habitually resident in a Contracting State shall lapse as soon as the authorities which have jurisdiction under Articles 5 to 10 have taken the measures required by the situation.

(3) The measures taken under paragraph 1 with regard to a child who is habitually resident in a non-Contracting State shall lapse in each Contracting State as soon as measures required by the situation and taken by the authorities of another State are recognised in the Contracting State in question.

Article 12

(1) Subject to Article 7, the authorities of a Contracting State in whose territory the child or property belonging to the child is present have jurisdiction to take measures of a provisional character for the protection of the person or property of the child which have a territorial effect limited to the State in question, in so far as such measures are not incompatible with measures already taken by authorities which have jurisdiction under Articles 5 to 10.

(2) The measures taken under the preceding paragraph with regard to a child habitually resident in a Contracting State shall lapse as soon as the authorities

which have jurisdiction under Articles 5 to 10 have taken a decision in respect of the measures of protection which may be required by the situation.

(3)   The measures taken under paragraph 1 with regard to a child who is habitually resident in a non-Contracting State shall lapse in the Contracting State where the measures were taken as soon as measures required by the situation and taken by the authorities of another State are recognised in the Contracting State in question.

Article 13

(1)   The authorities of a Contracting State which have jurisdiction under Articles 5 to 10 to take measures for the protection of the person or property of the child must abstain from exercising this jurisdiction if, at the time of the commencement of the proceedings, corresponding measures have been requested from the authorities of another Contracting State having jurisdiction under Articles 5 to 10 at the time of the request and are still under consideration.

(2)   The provisions of the preceding paragraph shall not apply if the authorities before whom the request for measures was initially introduced have declined jurisdiction.

Article 14

The measures taken in application of Articles 5 to 10 remain in force according to their terms, even if a change of circumstances has eliminated the basis upon which jurisdiction was founded, so long as the authorities which have jurisdiction under the Convention have not modified, replaced or terminated such measures.

CHAPTER III
APPLICABLE LAW

Article 15

(1)   In exercising their jurisdiction under the provisions of Chapter II, the authorities of the Contracting States shall apply their own law.

(2)   However, in so far as the protection of the person or the property of the child requires, they may exceptionally apply or take into consideration the law of another State with which the situation has a substantial connection.

(3)   If the child's habitual residence changes to another Contracting State, the law of that other State governs, from the time of the change, the conditions of application of the measures taken in the State of the former habitual residence.

Article 16

(1)   The attribution or extinction of parental responsibility by operation of law, without the intervention of a judicial or administrative authority, is governed by the law of the State of the habitual residence of the child.

(2)   The attribution or extinction of parental responsibility by an agreement or a unilateral act, without intervention of a judicial or administrative authority, is governed by the law of the State of the child's habitual residence at the time when the agreement or unilateral act takes effect.

(3)   Parental responsibility which exists under the law of the State of the child's habitual residence subsists after a change of that habitual residence to another State.

(4)   If the child's habitual residence changes, the attribution of parental responsibility by operation of law to a person who does not already have such responsibility is governed by the law of the State of the new habitual residence.

Article 17

The exercise of parental responsibility is governed by the law of the State of the child's habitual residence. If the child's habitual residence changes, it is governed by the law of the State of the new habitual residence.

Article 18

The parental responsibility referred to in Article 16 may be terminated, or the conditions of its exercise modified, by measures taken under this Convention.

Article 19

(1)   The validity of a transaction entered into between a third party and another person who would be entitled to act as the child's legal representative under the law of the State where the transaction was concluded cannot be contested, and the third party cannot be held liable, on the sole ground that the other person was not entitled to act as the child's legal representative under the law designated by the provisions of this Chapter, unless the third party knew or should have known that the parental responsibility was governed by the latter law.

(2)   The preceding paragraph applies only if the transaction was entered into between persons present on the territory of the same State.

Article 20

The provisions of this Chapter apply even if the law designated by them is the law of a non-Contracting State.

Article 21

(1)   In this Chapter the term 'law' means the law in force in a State other than its choice of law rules.

(2)   However,if the law applicable according to Article 16 is that of a non-Contracting State and if the choice of law rules of that State designate the law of another non-Contracting State which would apply its own law, the law of the latter State applies. If that other non-Contracting State would not apply its own law, the applicable law is that designated by Article 16.

Article 22

The application of the law designated by the provisions of this Chapter can be refused only if this application would be manifestly contrary to public policy, taking into account the best interests of the child.

CHAPTER IV
RECOGNITION AND ENFORCEMENT

Article 23

(1)   The measures taken by the authorities of a Contracting State shall be recognised by operation of law in all other Contracting States.

(2)   Recognition may however be refused—

(a)   if the measure was taken by an authority whose jurisdiction was not based on one of the grounds provided for in Chapter II;

(b)   if the measure was taken, except in a case of urgency, in the context of a judicial or administrative proceeding, without the child having been provided the opportunity to be heard, in violation of fundamental principles of procedure of the requested State;

(c)   on the request of any person claiming that the measure infringes his or her parental responsibility, if such measure was taken, except in a case of urgency, without such person having been given an opportunity to be heard;

(d)   if such recognition is manifestly contrary to public policy of the requested State, taking into account the best interests of the child;

(e)   if the measure is incompatible with a later measure taken in the non-Contracting State of the habitual residence of the child, where this later measure fulfils the requirements for recognition in the requested State;

(f)   if the procedure provided in Article 33 has not been complied with.

Article 24

Without prejudice to Article 23, paragraph 1, any interested person may request from the competent authorities of a Contracting State that they decide on the recognition or non-recognition of a measure taken in another Contracting State. The procedure is governed by the law of the requested State.

Article 25
The authority of the requested State is bound by the findings of fact on which the authority of the State where the measure was taken based its jurisdiction.

Article 26
(1) If measures taken in one Contracting State and enforceable there require enforcement in another Contracting State, they shall, upon request by an interested party, be declared enforceable or registered for the purpose of enforcement in that other State according to the procedure provided in the law of the latter State.

(2) Each Contracting State shall apply to the declaration of enforceability or registration a simple and rapid procedure.

(3) The declaration of enforceability or registration may be refused only for one of the reasons set out in Article 23, paragraph 2.

Article 27
Without prejudice to such review as is necessary in the application of the preceding Articles, there shall be no review of the merits of the measure taken.

Article 28
Measures taken in one Contracting State and declared enforceable, or registered for the purpose of enforcement, in another Contracting State shall be enforced in the latter State as if they had been taken by the authorities of that State. Enforcement takes place in accordance with the law of the requested State to the extent provided by such law, taking into consideration the best interests of the child.

CHAPTER V
CO-OPERATION

Article 29
(1) A Contracting State shall designate a Central Authority to discharge the duties which are imposed by the Convention on such authorities.

(2) Federal States, States with more than one system of law or States having autonomous territorial units shall be free to appoint more than one Central Authority and to specify the territorial or personal extent of their functions. Where a State has appointed more than one Central Authority, it shall designate the Central Authority to which any communication may be addressed for transmission to the appropriate Central Authority within that State.

Article 30
(1) Central Authorities shall co-operate with each other and promote co-operation amongst the competent authorities in their States to achieve the purposes of the Convention.

(2) They shall, in connection with the application of the Convention, take appropriate steps to provide information as to the laws of, and services available in, their States relating to the protection of children.

Article 31
The Central Authority of a Contracting State, either directly or through public authorities or other bodies, shall take all appropriate steps to—
(a) facilitate the communications and offer the assistance provided for in Articles 8 and 9 and in this Chapter;
(b) facilitate, by mediation, conciliation or similar means, agreed solutions for the protection of the person or property of the child in situations to which the Convention applies;
(c) provide, on the request of a competent authority of another Contracting State, assistance in discovering the whereabouts of a child where it appears that

the child may be present and in need of protection within the territory of the requested State.

Article 32

On a request made with supporting reasons by the Central Authority or other competent authority of any Contracting State with which the child has a substantial connection, the Central Authority of the Contracting State in which the child is habitually resident and present may, directly or through public authorities or other bodies,

(a)   provide a report on the situation of the child;

(b)   request the competent authority of its State to consider the need to take measures for the protection of the person or property of the child.

Article 33

(1)   If an authority having jurisdiction under Articles 5 to 10 contemplates the placement of the child in a foster family or institutional care, or the provision of care by kafala or an analogous institution, and if such placement or such provision of care is to take place in another Contracting State, it shall first consult with the Central Authority or other competent authority of the latter State. To that effect it shall transmit a report on the child together with the reasons for the proposed placement or provision of care.

(2)   The decision on the placement or provision of care may be made in the requesting State only if the Central Authority or other competent authority of the requested State has consented to the placement or provision of care, taking into account the child's best interests.

Article 34

(1)   Where a measure of protection is contemplated, the competent authorities under the Convention, if the situation of the child so requires, may request any authority of another Contracting State which has information relevant to the protection of the child to communicate such information.

(2)   A Contracting State may declare that requests under paragraph 1 shall be communicated to its authorities only through its Central Authority.

Article 35

(1)   The competent authorities of a Contracting State may request the authorities of another Contracting State to assist in the implementation of measures of protection taken under this Convention, especially in securing the effective exercise of rights of access as well as of the right to maintain direct contacts on a regular basis.

(2)   The authorities of a Contracting State in which the child does not habitually reside may, on the request of a parent residing in that State who is seeking to obtain or to maintain access to the child, gather information or evidence and may make a finding on the suitability of that parent to exercise access and on the conditions under which access is to be exercised. An authority exercising jurisdiction under Articles 5 to 10 to determine an application concerning access to the child, shall admit and consider such information, evidence and finding before reaching its decision.

(3)   An authority having jurisdiction under Articles 5 to 10 to decide on access may adjourn a proceeding pending the outcome of a request made under paragraph 2, in particular, when it is considering an application to restrict or terminate access rights granted in the State of the child's former habitual residence.

(4)   Nothing in this Article shall prevent an authority having jurisdiction under Articles 5 to 10 from taking provisional measures pending the outcome of the request made under paragraph 2.

Article 36

In any case where the child is exposed to a serious danger, the competent authorities of the Contracting State where measures for the protection of the child have been taken or are under consideration, if they are informed that the child's residence has changed to, or that the child is present in another State, shall inform the authorities of that other State about the danger involved and the measures taken or under consideration.

Article 37
An authority shall not request or transmit any information under this Chapter if to do so would, in its opinion, be likely to place the child's person or property in danger, or constitute a serious threat to the liberty or life of a member of the child's family.

Article 38
(1) Without prejudice to the possibility of imposing reasonable charges for the provision of services, Central Authorities and other public authorities of Contracting States shall bear their own costs in applying the provisions of this Chapter.

(2) Any Contracting State may enter into agreements with one or more other Contracting States concerning the allocation of charges.

Article 39
Any Contracting State may enter into agreements with one or more other Contracting States with a view to improving the application of this Chapter in their mutual relations. The States which have concluded such an agreement shall transmit a copy to the depositary of the Convention.

CHAPTER VI
GENERAL PROVISIONS

Article 40
(1) The authorities of the Contracting State of the child's habitual residence, or of the Contracting State where a measure of protection has been taken, may deliver to the person having parental responsibility or to the person entrusted with protection of the child's person or property, at his or her request, a certificate indicating the capacity in which that person is entitled to act and the powers conferred upon him or her.

(2) The capacity and powers indicated in the certificate are presumed to be vested in that person, in the absence of proof to the contrary.

(3) Each Contracting State shall designate the authorities competent to draw up the certificate.

Article 41
Personal data gathered or transmitted under the Convention shall be used only for the purposes for which they were gathered or transmitted.

Article 42
The authorities to whom information is transmitted shall ensure its confidentiality, in accordance with the law of their State.

Article 43
All documents forwarded or delivered under this Convention shall be exempt from legalisation or any analogous formality.

Article 44
Each Contracting State may designate the authorities to which requests under Articles 8, 9 and 33 are to be addressed.

Article 45
(1) The designations referred to in Articles 29 and 44 shall be communicated to the Permanent Bureau of the Hague Conference on Private International Law.

(2)   The declaration referred to in Article 34, paragraph 2, shall be made to the depositary of the Convention.

Article 46
A Contracting State in which different systems of law or sets of rules of law apply to the protection of the child and his or her property shall not be bound to apply the rules of the Convention to conflicts solely between such different systems or sets of rules of law.

Article 47
In relation to a State in which two or more systems of law or sets of rules of law with regard to any matter dealt with in this Convention apply in different territorial units—

(1)   any reference to habitual residence in that State shall be construed as referring to habitual residence in a territorial unit;

(2)   any reference to the presence of the child in that State shall be construed as referring to presence in a territorial unit;

(3)   any reference to the location of property of the child in that State shall be construed as referring to location of property of the child in a territorial unit;

(4)   any reference to the State of which the child is a national shall be construed as referring to the territorial unit designated by the law of that State or, in the absence of relevant rules, to the territorial unit with which the child has the closest connection;

(5)   any reference to the State whose authorities are seised of an application for divorce or legal separation of the child's parents, or for annulment of their marriage, shall be construed as referring to the territorial unit whose authorities are seised of such application;

(6)   ny reference to the State with which the child has a substantial connection shall be construed as referring to the territorial unit with which the child has such connection;

(7)   any reference to the State to which the child has been removed or in which he or she has been retained shall be construed as referring to the relevant territorial unit to which the child has been removed or in which he or she has been retained;

(8)   any reference to bodies or authorities of that State, other than Central Authorities, shall be construed as referring to those authorised to act in the relevant territorial unit;

(9)   any reference to the law or procedure or authority of the State in which a measure has been taken shall be construed as referring to the law or procedure or authority of the territorial unit in which such measure was taken;

(10)   any reference to the law or procedure or authority of the requested State shall be construed as referring to the law or procedure or authority of the territorial unit in which recognition or enforcement is sought.

Article 48
For the purpose of identifying the applicable law under Chapter III, in relation to a State which comprises two or more territorial units each of which has its own system of law or set of rules of law in respect of matters covered by this Convention, the following rules apply—

(a)   if there are rules in force in such a State identifying which territorial unit's law is applicable, the law of that unit applies;

(b)   in the absence of such rules, the law of the relevant territorial unit as defined in Article 47 applies.

Article 49
For the purpose of identifying the applicable law under Chapter III, in relation to a State which has two or more systems of law or sets of rules of law applicable to

different categories of persons in respect of matters covered by this Convention, the following rules apply—

    (a) if there are rules in force in such a State identifying which among such laws applies, that law applies;

    (b) in the absence of such rules, the law of the system or the set of rules of law with which the child has the closest connection applies.

Article 50

This Convention shall not affect the application of the Convention of 25 October 1980 on the Civil Aspects of International Child Abduction, as between Parties to both Conventions. Nothing, however, precludes provisions of this Convention from being invoked for the purposes of obtaining the return of a child who has been wrongfully removed or retained or of organising access rights.

Article 51

In relations between the Contracting States this Convention replaces the Convention of 5 October 1961 concerning the powers of authorities and the law applicable in respect of the protection of minors, and the Convention governing the guardianship of minors, signed at The Hague 12 June 1902, without prejudice to the recognition of measures taken under the Convention of 5 October 1961 mentioned above.

Article 52

(1) This Convention does not affect any international instrument to which Contracting States are Parties and which contains provisions on matters governed by the Convention, unless a contrary declaration is made by the States Parties to such instrument.

(2) This Convention does not affect the possibility for one or more Contracting States to conclude agreements which contain, in respect of children habitually resident in any of the States Parties to such agreements, provisions on matters governed by this Convention.

(3) Agreements to be concluded by one or more Contracting States on matters within the scope of this Convention do not affect, in the relationship of such States with other Contracting States, the application of the provisions of this Convention.

(4) The preceding paragraphs also apply to uniform laws based on special ties of a regional or other nature between the States concerned.

Article 53

(1) The Convention shall apply to measures only if they are taken in a State after the Convention has entered into force for that State.

(2) The Convention shall apply to the recognition and enforcement of measures taken after its entry into force as between the State where the measures have been taken and the requested State.

Article 54

(1) Any communication sent to the Central Authority or to another authority of a Contracting State shall be in the original language, and shall be accompanied by a translation into the official language or one of the official languages of the other State or, where that is not feasible, a translation into French or English.

(2) However, a Contracting State may, by making a reservation in accordance with Article 60, object to the use of either French or English, but not both.

Article 55

(1) A Contracting State may, in accordance with Article 60,

    (a) reserve the jurisdiction of its authorities to take measures directed to the protection of property of a child situated on its territory;

    (b) reserve the right not to recognise any parental responsibility or measure in so far as it is incompatible with any measure taken by its authorities in relation to that property.

(2)   The reservation may be restricted to certain categories of property.

Article 56

The Secretary General of the Hague Conference on Private International Law shall at regular intervals convoke a Special Commission in order to review the practical operation of the Convention.

CHAPTER VII
FINAL CLAUSES

Article 57

(1)   The Convention shall be open for signature by the States which were Members of the Hague Conference on Private International Law at the time of its Eighteenth Session.

(2)   It shall be ratified, accepted or approved and the instruments of ratification, acceptance or approval shall be deposited with the Ministry of Foreign Affairs of the Kingdom of the Netherlands, depositary of the Convention.

Article 58

(1)   Any other State may accede to the Convention after it has entered into force in accordance with Article 61, paragraph 1.

(2)   Theinstrument of accession shall be deposited with the depositary.

(3)   Such accession shall have effect only as regards the relations between the acceding State and those Contracting States which have not raised an objection to its accession in the six months after the receipt of the notification referred to in sub-paragraph b of Article 63. Such an objection may also be raised by States at the time when they ratify, accept or approve the Convention after an accession. Any such objection shall be notified to the depositary.

Article 59

(1)   If a State has two or more territorial units in which different systems of law are applicable in relation to matters dealt with in this Convention, it may at the time of signature, ratification, acceptance, approval or accession declare that the Convention shall extend to all its territorial units or only to one or more of them and may modify this declaration by submitting another declaration at any time.

(2)   Any such declaration shall be notified to the depositary and shall state expressly the territorial units to which the Convention applies.

(3)   If a State makes no declaration under this Article, the Convention is to extend to all territorial units of that State.

Article 60

(1)   Any State may, not later than the time of ratification, acceptance, approval or accession, or at the time of making a declaration in terms of Article 59, make one or both of the reservations provided for in Articles 54, paragraph 2, and 55. No other reservation shall be permitted.

(2)   Any State may at any time withdraw a reservation it has made. The withdrawal shall be notified to the depositary.

(3)   The reservation shall cease to have effect on the first day of the third calendar month after the notification referred to in the preceding paragraph.

Article 61

(1)   The Convention shall enter into force on the first day of the month following the expiration of three months after the deposit of the third instrument of ratification, acceptance or approval referred to in Article 57.

(2)   Thereafter theConvention shall enter into force—

(a)   for each State ratifying, accepting or approving it subsequently, on the first day of the month following the expiration of three months after the deposit of its instrument of ratification, acceptance, approval or accession;

(b)   for each State acceding, on the first day of the month following the expiration of three months after the expiration of the period of six months provided in Article 58, paragraph 3;

(c) for a territorial unit to which the Convention has been extended in conformity with Article 59, on the first day of the month following the expiration of three months after the notification referred to in that Article.

Article 62

(1) A State Party to the Convention may denounce it by a notification in writing addressed to the depositary. The denunciation may be limited to certain territorial units to which the Convention applies.

(2) The denunciation takes effect on the first day of the month following the expiration of twelve months after the notification is received by the depositary. Where a longer period for the denunciation to take effect is specified in the notification, the denunciation takes effect upon the expiration of such longer period.

Article 63

The depositary shall notify the States Members of the Hague Conference on Private International Law and the States which have acceded in accordance with Article 58 of the following—

(a) the signatures, ratifications, acceptances and approvals referred to in Article 57;

(b) the accessions and objections raised to accessions referred to in Article 58;

(c) the date on which the Convention enters into force in accordance with Article 61;

(d) the declarations referred to in Articles 34, paragraph 2, and 59;

(e) the agreements referred to in Article 39;

(f) the reservations referred to in Articles 54, paragraph 2, and 55 and the withdrawals referred to in Article 60, paragraph 2;

(g) the denunciations referred to in Article 62.

In witness whereof the undersigned, being duly authorised thereto, have signed this Convention.

Done at The Hague, on the 19th day of October 1996, in the English and French languages, both texts being equally authentic, in a single copy which shall be deposited in the archives of the Government of the Kingdom of the Netherlands, and of which a certified copy shall be sent, through diplomatic channels, to each of the States Members of the Hague Conference on Private International Law at the date of its Eighteenth Session.

HAGUE CONVENTION ON CHOICE OF COURT AGREEMENTS*

(Concluded 30 June 2005)

CHAPTER I – SCOPE AND DEFINITIONS

Article 1. Scope

1. This Convention shall apply in international cases to exclusive choice of court agreements concluded in civil or commercial matters.

2. For the purposes of Chapter II, a case is international unless the parties are resident in the same Contracting State and the relationship of the parties and all other elements relevant to the dispute, regardless of the location of the chosen court, are connected only with that State.

3. For the purposes of Chapter III, a case is international where recognition or enforcement of a foreign judgment is sought.

* © Hague Conference on Private International Law.

Article 2. Exclusions from scope
1.   This Convention shall not apply to exclusive choice of court agreements—
    (a)   to which a natural person acting primarily for personal, family or household purposes (a consumer) is a party;
    (b)   relating to contracts of employment, including collective agreements.
2.   This Convention shall not apply to the following matters—
    (a)   the status and legal capacity of natural persons;
    (b)   maintenance obligations;
    (c)   other family law matters, including matrimonial property regimes and other rights or obligations arising out of marriage or similar relationships;
    (d)   wills and succession;
    (e)   insolvency, composition and analogous matters;
    (f)   the carriage of passengers and goods;
    (g)   marine pollution, limitation of liability for maritime claims, general average, and emergency towage and salvage;
    (h)   anti-trust (competition) matters;
    (i)   liability for nuclear damage;
    (j)   claims for personal injury brought by or on behalf of natural persons;
    (k)   tort or delict claims for damage to tangible property that do not arise from a contractual relationship;
    (l)   rights *in rem* in immovable property, and tenancies of immovable property;
    (m)   the validity, nullity, or dissolution of legal persons, and the validity of decisions of their organs;
    (n)   the validity of intellectual property rights other than copyright and related rights;
    (o)   infringement of intellectual property rights other than copyright and related rights, except where infringement proceedings are brought for breach of a contract between the parties relating to such rights, or could have been brought for breach of that contract;
    (p)   the validity of entries in public registers.
3.   Notwithstanding paragraph 2, proceedings are not excluded from the scope of this Convention where a matter excluded under that paragraph arises merely as a preliminary question and not as an object of the proceedings. In particular, the mere fact that a matter excluded under paragraph 2 arises by way of defence does not exclude proceedings from the Convention, if that matter is not an object of the proceedings.
4.   This Convention shall not apply to arbitration and related proceedings.
5.   Proceedings are not excluded from the scope of this Convention by the mere fact that a State, including a government, a governmental agency or any person acting for a State, is a party thereto.
6.   Nothing in this Convention shall affect privileges and immunities of States or of international organisations, in respect of themselves and of their property.

Article 3. Exclusive choice of court agreements
For the purposes of this Convention—
    (a)   "exclusive choice of court agreement" means an agreement concluded by two or more parties that meets the requirements of paragraph *c)* and designates, for the purpose of deciding disputes which have arisen or may arise in connection with a particular legal relationship, the courts of one Contracting State or one or more specific courts of one Contracting State to the exclusion of the jurisdiction of any other courts;
    (b)   a choice of court agreement which designates the courts of one Contracting State or one or more specific courts of one Contracting State shall be deemed to be exclusive unless the parties have expressly provided otherwise;

(c)   an exclusive choice of court agreement must be concluded or documented—

    (i)   in writing; or

    (ii)   by any other means of communication which renders information accessible so as to be usable for subsequent reference;

(d)   an exclusive choice of court agreement that forms part of a contract shall be treated as an agreement independent of the other terms of the contract. The validity of the exclusive choice of court agreement cannot be contested solely on the ground that the contract is not valid.

Article 4. Other definitions

1.   In this Convention, "judgment" means any decision on the merits given by a court, whatever it may be called, including a decree or order, and a determination of costs or expenses by the court (including an officer of the court), provided that the determination relates to a decision on the merits which may be recognised or enforced under this Convention. An interim measure of protection is not a judgment.

2.   For the purposes of this Convention, an entity or person other than a natural person shall be considered to be resident in the State—

(a)   where it has its statutory seat;

(b)   under whose law it was incorporated or formed;

(c)   where it has its central administration; or

(d)   where it has its principal place of business.

CHAPTER II – JURISDICTION

Article 5 Jurisdiction of the chosen court

1.   The court or courts of a Contracting State designated in an exclusive choice of court agreement shall have jurisdiction to decide a dispute to which the agreement applies, unless the agreement is null and void under the law of that State.

2.   A court that has jurisdiction under paragraph 1 shall not decline to exercise jurisdiction on the ground that the dispute should be decided in a court of another State.

3.   The preceding paragraphs shall not affect rules—

(a)   on jurisdiction related to subject matter or to the value of the claim;

(b)   on the internal allocation of jurisdiction among the courts of a Contracting State.

However, where the chosen court has discretion as to whether to transfer a case, due consideration should be given to the choice of the parties.

Article 6. Obligations of a court not chosen

A court of a Contracting State other than that of the chosen court shall suspend or dismiss proceedings to which an exclusive choice of court agreement applies unless—

(a)   the agreement is null and void under the law of the State of the chosen court;

(b)   a party lacked the capacity to conclude the agreement under the law of the State of the court seised;

(c)   giving effect to the agreement would lead to a manifest injustice or would be manifestly contrary to the public policy of the State of the court seised;

(d)   for exceptional reasons beyond the control of the parties, the agreement cannot reasonably be performed; or

(e)   the chosen court has decided not to hear the case.

Article 7. Interim measures of protection

Interim measures of protection are not governed by this Convention. This Convention neither requires nor precludes the grant, refusal or termination of interim measures of protection by a court of a Contracting State and does not affect whether or not a party may request or a court should grant, refuse or terminate such measures.

CHAPTER III – RECOGNITION AND ENFORCEMENT

Article 8 Recognition and enforcement

1. A judgment given by a court of a Contracting State designated in an exclusive choice of court agreement shall be recognised and enforced in other Contracting States in accordance with this Chapter. Recognition or enforcement may be refused only on the grounds specified in this Convention.

2. Without prejudice to such review as is necessary for the application of the provisions of this Chapter, there shall be no review of the merits of the judgment given by the court of origin. The court addressed shall be bound by the findings of fact on which the court of origin based its jurisdiction, unless the judgment was given by default.

3. A judgment shall be recognised only if it has effect in the State of origin, and shall be enforced only if it is enforceable in the State of origin.

4. Recognition or enforcement may be postponed or refused if the judgment is the subject of review in the State of origin or if the time limit for seeking ordinary review has not expired. A refusal does not prevent a subsequent application for recognition or enforcement of the judgment.

5. This Article shall also apply to a judgment given by a court of a Contracting State pursuant to a transfer of the case from the chosen court in that Contracting State as permitted by Article 5, paragraph 3. However, where the chosen court had discretion as to whether to transfer the case to another court, recognition or enforcement of the judgment may be refused against a party who objected to the transfer in a timely manner in the State of origin.

Article 9. Refusal of recognition or enforcement

Recognition or enforcement may be refused if—

(a) the agreement was null and void under the law of the State of the chosen court, unless the chosen court has determined that the agreement is valid;

(b) a party lacked the capacity to conclude the agreement under the law of the requested State;

(c) the document which instituted the proceedings or an equivalent document, including the essential elements of the claim,

(i) was not notified to the defendant in sufficient time and in such a way as to enable him to arrange for his defence, unless the defendant entered an appearance and presented his case without contesting notification in the court of origin, provided that the law of the State of origin permitted notification to be contested; or

(ii) was notified to the defendant in the requested State in a manner that is incompatible with fundamental principles of the requested State concerning service of documents;

(d) the judgment was obtained by fraud in connection with a matter of procedure;

(e) recognition or enforcement would be manifestly incompatible with the public policy of the requested State, including situations where the specific proceedings leading to the judgment were incompatible with fundamental principles of procedural fairness of that State;

(f) the judgment is inconsistent with a judgment given in the requested State in a dispute between the same parties; or

(g) the judgment is inconsistent with an earlier judgment given in another State between the same parties on the same cause of action, provided that the earlier judgment fulfils the conditions necessary for its recognition in the requested State.

Article 10. Preliminary questions
1. Where a matter excluded under Article 2, paragraph 2, or under Article 21, arose as a preliminary question, the ruling on that question shall not be recognised or enforced under this Convention.
2. Recognition or enforcement of a judgment may be refused if, and to the extent that, the judgment was based on a ruling on a matter excluded under Article 2, paragraph 2.
3. However, in the case of a ruling on the validity of an intellectual property right other than copyright or a related right, recognition or enforcement of a judgment may be refused or postponed under the preceding paragraph only where—
    (a) that ruling is inconsistent with a judgment or a decision of a competent authority on that matter given in the State under the law of which the intellectual property right arose; or
    (b) proceedings concerning the validity of the intellectual property right are pending in that State.
4. Recognition or enforcement of a judgment may be refused if, and to the extent that, the judgment was based on a ruling on a matter excluded pursuant to a declaration made by the requested State under Article 21.

Article 11. Damages
1. Recognition or enforcement of a judgment may be refused if, and to the extent that, the judgment awards damages, including exemplary or punitive damages, that do not compensate a party for actual loss or harm suffered.
2. The court addressed shall take into account whether and to what extent the damages awarded by the court of origin serve to cover costs and expenses relating to the proceedings.

Article 12. Judicial settlements (transactions judiciaires)
Judicial settlements (*transactions judiciaires*) which a court of a Contracting State designated in an exclusive choice of court agreement has approved, or which have been concluded before that court in the course of proceedings, and which are enforceable in the same manner as a judgment in the State of origin, shall be enforced under this Convention in the same manner as a judgment.

Article 13. Documents to be produced
1. The party seeking recognition or applying for enforcement shall produce—
    (a) a complete and certified copy of the judgment;
    (b) the exclusive choice of court agreement, a certified copy thereof, or other evidence of its existence;
    (c) if the judgment was given by default, the original or a certified copy of a document establishing that the document which instituted the proceedings or an equivalent document was notified to the defaulting party;
    (d) any documents necessary to establish that the judgment has effect or, where applicable, is enforceable in the State of origin;
    (e) in the case referred to in Article 12, a certificate of a court of the State of origin that the judicial settlement or a part of it is enforceable in the same manner as a judgment in the State of origin.
2. If the terms of the judgment do not permit the court addressed to verify whether the conditions of this Chapter have been complied with, that court may require any necessary documents.
3. An application for recognition or enforcement may be accompanied by a document, issued by a court (including an officer of the court) of the State of origin, in the form recommended and published by the Hague Conference on Private International Law.
4. If the documents referred to in this Article are not in an official language of the requested State, they shall be accompanied by a certified translation into an official language, unless the law of the requested State provides otherwise.

Article 14. Procedure

The procedure for recognition, declaration of enforceability or registration for enforcement, and the enforcement of the judgment, are governed by the law of the requested State unless this Convention provides otherwise. The court addressed shall act expeditiously.

Article 15. Severability

Recognition or enforcement of a severable part of a judgment shall be granted where recognition or enforcement of that part is applied for, or only part of the judgment is capable of being recognised or enforced under this Convention.

CHAPTER IV – GENERAL CLAUSES

Article 16. Transitional provisions

1. This Convention shall apply to exclusive choice of court agreements concluded after its entry into force for the State of the chosen court.

2. This Convention shall not apply to proceedings instituted before its entry into force for the State of the court seised.

Article 17. Contracts of insurance and reinsurance

1. Proceedings under a contract of insurance or reinsurance are not excluded from the scope of this Convention on the ground that the contract of insurance or reinsurance relates to a matter to which this Convention does not apply.

2. Recognition and enforcement of a judgment in respect of liability under the terms of a contract of insurance or reinsurance may not be limited or refused on the ground that the liability under that contract includes liability to indemnify the insured or reinsured in respect of—

    (a)   a matter to which this Convention does not apply; or

    (b)   an award of damages to which Article 11 might apply.

...

Article 19. Declarations limiting jurisdiction

A State may declare that its courts may refuse to determine disputes to which an exclusive choice of court agreement applies if, except for the location of the chosen court, there is no connection between that State and the parties or the dispute.

Article 20. Declarations limiting recognition and enforcement

A State may declare that its courts may refuse to recognise or enforce a judgment given by a court of another Contracting State if the parties were resident in the requested State, and the relationship of the parties and all other elements relevant to the dispute, other than the location of the chosen court, were connected only with the requested State.

Article 21. Declarations with respect to specific matters

1. Where a State has a strong interest in not applying this Convention to a specific matter, that State may declare that it will not apply the Convention to that matter. The State making such a declaration shall ensure that the declaration is no broader than necessary and that the specific matter excluded is clearly and precisely defined.

2. With regard to that matter, the Convention shall not apply—

    (a)   in the Contracting State that made the declaration;

    (b)   in other Contracting States, where an exclusive choice of court agreement designates the courts, or one or more specific courts, of the State that made the declaration.

Article 22. Reciprocal declarations on non-exclusive choice of court agreements

1. A Contracting State may declare that its courts will recognise and enforce judgments given by courts of other Contracting States designated in a choice of court agreement concluded by two or more parties that meets the requirements of

Article 3, paragraph c), and designates, for the purpose of deciding disputes which have arisen or may arise in connection with a particular legal relationship, a court or courts of one or more Contracting States (a non-exclusive choice of court agreement).

2. Where recognition or enforcement of a judgment given in a Contracting State that has made such a declaration is sought in another Contracting State that has made such a declaration, the judgment shall be recognised and enforced under this Convention, if—

(a) the court of origin was designated in a non-exclusive choice of court agreement;

(b) there exists neither a judgment given by any other court before which proceedings could be brought in accordance with the non-exclusive choice of court agreement, nor a proceeding pending between the same parties in any other such court on the same cause of action; and

(c) the court of origin was the court first seised.

Article 23. Uniform interpretation
In the interpretation of this Convention, regard shall be had to its international character and to the need to promote uniformity in its application.

Article 24. Review of operation of the Convention
The Secretary General of the Hague Conference on Private International Law shall at regular intervals make arrangements for—

(a) review of the operation of this Convention, including any declarations; and

(b) consideration of whether any amendments to this Convention are desirable.

Article 25. Non-unified legal systems
1. In relation to a Contracting State in which two or more systems of law apply in different territorial units with regard to any matter dealt with in this Convention—

(a) any reference to the law or procedure of a State shall be construed as referring, where appropriate, to the law or procedure in force in the relevant territorial unit;

(b) any reference to residence in a State shall be construed as referring, where appropriate, to residence in the relevant territorial unit;

(c) any reference to the court or courts of a State shall be construed as referring, where appropriate, to the court or courts in the relevant territorial unit;

(d) any reference to a connection with a State shall be construed as referring, where appropriate, to a connection with the relevant territorial unit.

2. Notwithstanding the preceding paragraph, a Contracting State with two or more territorial units in which different systems of law apply shall not be bound to apply this Convention to situations which involve solely such different territorial units.

3. A court in a territorial unit of a Contracting State with two or more territorial units in which different systems of law apply shall not be bound to recognise or enforce a judgment from another Contracting State solely because the judgment has been recognised or enforced in another territorial unit of the same Contracting State under this Convention.

4. This Article shall not apply to a Regional Economic Integration Organisation.

Article 26. Relationship with other international instruments
1. This Convention shall be interpreted so far as possible to be compatible with other treaties in force for Contracting States, whether concluded before or after this Convention.

2. This Convention shall not affect the application by a Contracting State of a

treaty, whether concluded before or after this Convention, in cases where none of the parties is resident in a Contracting State that is not a Party to the treaty.

3. This Convention shall not affect the application by a Contracting State of a treaty that was concluded before this Convention entered into force for that Contracting State, if applying this Convention would be inconsistent with the obligations of that Contracting State to any non-Contracting State. This paragraph shall also apply to treaties that revise or replace a treaty concluded before this Convention entered into force for that Contracting State, except to the extent that the revision or replacement creates new inconsistencies with this Convention.

4. This Convention shall not affect the application by a Contracting State of a treaty, whether concluded before or after this Convention, for the purposes of obtaining recognition or enforcement of a judgment given by a court of a Contracting State that is also a Party to that treaty. However, the judgment shall not be recognised or enforced to a lesser extent than under this Convention.

5. This Convention shall not affect the application by a Contracting State of a treaty which, in relation to a specific matter, governs jurisdiction or the recognition or enforcement of judgments, even if concluded after this Convention and even if all States concerned are Parties to this Convention. This paragraph shall apply only if the Contracting State has made a declaration in respect of the treaty under this paragraph. In the case of such a declaration, other Contracting States shall not be obliged to apply this Convention to that specific matter to the extent of any inconsistency, where an exclusive choice of court agreement designates the courts, or one or more specific courts, of the Contracting State that made the declaration.

6. This Convention shall not affect the application of the rules of a Regional Economic Integration Organisation that is a Party to this Convention, whether adopted before or after this Convention—

   (a)   where none of the parties is resident in a Contracting State that is not a Member State of the Regional Economic Integration Organisation;

   (b)   as concerns the recognition or enforcement of judgments as between Member States of the Regional Economic Integration Organisation.

CHAPTER V – FINAL CLAUSES

Article 28. Declarations with respect to non-unified legal systems

1. If a State has two or more territorial units in which different systems of law apply in relation to matters dealt with in this Convention, it may at the time of signature, ratification, acceptance, approval or accession declare that the Convention shall extend to all its territorial units or only to one or more of them and may modify this declaration by submitting another declaration at any time.

2. A declaration shall be notified to the depositary and shall state expressly the territorial units to which the Convention applies.

3. If a State makes no declaration under this Article, the Convention shall extend to all territorial units of that State.

4. This Article shall not apply to a Regional Economic Integration Organisation.

Article 29. Regional Economic Integration Organisations

1. A Regional Economic Integration Organisation which is constituted solely by sovereign States and has competence over some or all of the matters governed by this Convention may similarly sign, accept, approve or accede to this Convention. The Regional Economic Integration Organisation shall in that case have the rights and obligations of a Contracting State, to the extent that the Organisation has competence over matters governed by this Convention.

2. The Regional Economic Integration Organisation shall, at the time of signature, acceptance, approval or accession, notify the depositary in writing of the matters governed by this Convention in respect of which competence has been transferred to that Organisation by its Member States. The Organisation shall

promptly notify the depositary in writing of any changes to its competence as specified in the most recent notice given under this paragraph.

3.   For the purposes of the entry into force of this Convention, any instrument deposited by a Regional Economic Integration Organisation shall not be counted unless the Regional Economic Integration Organisation declares in accordance with Article 30 that its Member States will not be Parties to this Convention.

4.   Any reference to a "Contracting State" or "State" in this Convention shall apply equally, where appropriate, to a Regional Economic Integration Organisation that is a Party to it.

Article 30. Accession by a Regional Economic Integration Organisation without its Member States

1.   At the time of signature, acceptance, approval or accession, a Regional Economic Integration Organisation may declare that it exercises competence over all the matters governed by this Convention and that its Member States will not be Parties to this Convention but shall be bound by virtue of the signature, acceptance, approval or accession of the Organisation.

2.   In the event that a declaration is made by a Regional Economic Integration Organisation in accordance with paragraph 1, any reference to a "Contracting State" or "State" in this Convention shall apply equally, where appropriate, to the Member States of the Organisation.

Article 31. Entry into force

1.   This Convention shall enter into force on the first day of the month following the expiration of three months after the deposit of the second instrument of ratification, acceptance, approval or accession referred to in Article 27.

2.   Thereafter this Convention shall enter into force—

(a)   for each State or Regional Economic Integration Organisation subsequently ratifying, accepting, approving or acceding to it, on the first day of the month following the expiration of three months after the deposit of its instrument of ratification, acceptance, approval or accession;

(b)   for a territorial unit to which this Convention has been extended in accordance with Article 28, paragraph 1, on the first day of the month following the expiration of three months after the notification of the declaration referred to in that Article.

Article 32. Declarations

1.   Declarations referred to in Articles 19, 20, 21, 22 and 26 may be made upon signature, ratification, acceptance, approval or accession or at any time thereafter, and may be modified or withdrawn at any time.

2.   Declarations, modifications and withdrawals shall be notified to the depositary.

3.   A declaration made at the time of signature, ratification, acceptance, approval or accession shall take effect simultaneously with the entry into force of this Convention for the State concerned.

4.   A declaration made at a subsequent time, and any modification or withdrawal of a declaration, shall take effect on the first day of the month following the expiration of three months after the date on which the notification is received by the depositary.

5.   A declaration under Articles 19, 20, 21 and 26 shall not apply to exclusive choice of court agreements concluded before it takes effect.

Article 33. Denunciation

1.   This Convention may be denounced by notification in writing to the depositary. The denunciation may be limited to certain territorial units of a non-unified legal system to which this Convention applies.

2.   The denunciation shall take effect on the first day of the month following the expiration of twelve months after the date on which the notification is received by

the depositary. Where a longer period for the denunciation to take effect is specified in the notification, the denunciation shall take effect upon the expiration of such longer period after the date on which the notification is received by the depositary.

HAGUE CONVENTION ON THE INTERNATIONAL RECOVERY OF CHILD SUPPORT AND OTHER FORMS OF FAMILY MAINTENANCE*

(Concluded 23 November 2007)

PREAMBLE

THE STATES SIGNATORY TO THE PRESENT CONVENTION,

Desiring to improve co-operation among States for the international recovery of child support and other forms of family maintenance,

Aware of the need for procedures which produce results and are accessible, prompt, efficient, cost-effective, responsive and fair,

Wishing to build upon the best features of existing Hague Conventions and other international instruments, in particular the United Nations Convention on the Recovery Abroad of Maintenance of 20 June 1956,

Seeking to take advantage of advances in technologies and to create a flexible system which can continue to evolve as needs change and further advances in technology create new opportunities,

Recalling that, in accordance with Articles 3 and 27 of the United Nations Convention on the Rights of the Child of 20 November 1989,

– in all actions concerning children the best interests of the child shall be a primary consideration,

– every child has a right to a standard of living adequate for the child's physical, mental, spiritual, moral and social development,

– the parent(s) or others responsible for the child have the primary responsibility to secure, within their abilities and financial capacities, the conditions of living necessary for the child's development, and

– States Parties should take all appropriate measures, including the conclusion of international agreements, to secure the recovery of maintenance for the child from the parent(s) or other responsible persons, in particular where such persons live in a State different from that of the child,

Have resolved to conclude this Convention and have agreed upon the following provisions:

CHAPTER I – OBJECT, SCOPE AND DEFINITIONS

Article 1. Object
The object of the present Convention is to ensure the effective international recovery of child support and other forms of family maintenance, in particular by—

    (a) establishing a comprehensive system of co-operation between the authorities of the Contracting States;

    (b) making available applications for the establishment of maintenance decisions;

    (c) providing for the recognition and enforcement of maintenance decisions; and

(d)   requiring effective measures for the prompt enforcement of maintenance decisions.

Article 2. Scope

(1)   This Convention shall apply—

(a)   to maintenance obligations arising from a parent-child relationship towards a person under the age of 21 years;

(b)   to recognition and enforcement or enforcement of a decision for spousal support when the application is made with a claim within the scope of sub-paragraph (a); and

(c)   with the exception of Chapters II and III, to spousal support.

(2)   Any Contracting State may reserve, in accordance with Article 62, the right to limit the application of the Convention under sub-paragraph (1)(a), to persons who have not attained the age of 18 years. A Contracting State which makes this reservation shall not be entitled to claim the application of the Convention to persons of the age excluded by its reservation.

(3)   Any Contracting State may declare in accordance with Article 63 that it will extend the application of the whole or any part of the Convention to any maintenance obligation arising from a family relationship, parentage, marriage or affinity, including in particular obligations in respect of vulnerable persons. Any such declaration shall give rise to obligations between two Contracting States only in so far as their declarations cover the same maintenance obligations and parts of the Convention.

(4)   The provisions of this Convention shall apply to children regardless of the marital status of the parents.

Article 3. Definitions

For the purposes of this Convention—

(a)   'creditor' means an individual to whom maintenance is owed or is alleged to be owed;

(b)   'debtor' means an individual who owes or who is alleged to owe maintenance;

(c)   'legal assistance' means the assistance necessary to enable applicants to know and assert their rights and to ensure that applications are fully and effectively dealt with in the requested State. The means of providing such assistance may include as necessary legal advice, assistance in bringing a case before an authority, legal representation and exemption from costs of proceedings;

(d)   'agreement in writing' means an agreement recorded in any medium, the information contained in which is accessible so as to be usable for subsequent reference;

(e)   'maintenance arrangement' means an agreement in writing relating to the payment of maintenance which—

(i)   has been formally drawn up or registered as an authentic instrument by a competent authority; or

(ii)   has been authenticated by, or concluded, registered or filed with a competent authority, and may be the subject of review and modification by a competent authority;

(f)   'vulnerable person' means a person who, by reason of an impairment or insufficiency of his or her personal faculties, is not able to support him or herself.

CHAPTER II – ADMINISTRATIVE CO-OPERATION

Article 4. Designation of Central Authorities

(1)   A Contracting State shall designate a Central Authority to discharge the duties that are imposed by the Convention on such an authority.

(2)   Federal States, States with more than one system of law or States having

autonomous territorial units shall be free to appoint more than one Central Authority and shall specify the territorial or personal extent of their functions. Where a State has appointed more than one Central Authority, it shall designate the Central Authority to which any communication may be addressed for transmission to the appropriate Central Authority within that State.

(3)   The designation of the Central Authority or Central Authorities, their contact details, and where appropriate the extent of their functions as specified in paragraph (2), shall be communicated by a Contracting State to the Permanent Bureau of the Hague Conference on Private International Law at the time when the instrument of ratification or accession is deposited or when a declaration is submitted in accordance with Article 61. Contracting States shall promptly inform the Permanent Bureau of any changes.

Article 5. General functions of Central Authorities
Central Authorities shall—
    (a)   co-operate with each other and promote co-operation amongst the competent authorities in their States to achieve the purposes of the Convention;
    (b)   seek as far as possible solutions to difficulties which arise in the application of the Convention.

Article 6. Specific functions of Central Authorities
(1)   Central Authorities shall provide assistance in relation to applications under Chapter III. In particular they shall—
    (a)   transmit and receive such applications;
    (b)   initiate or facilitate the institution of proceedings in respect of such applications.
(2)   In relation to such applications they shall take all appropriate measures—
    (a)   where the circumstances require, to provide or facilitate the provision of legal assistance;
    (b)   to help locate the debtor or the creditor;
    (c)   to help obtain relevant information concerning the income and, if necessary, other financial circumstances of the debtor or creditor, including the location of assets;
    (d)   to encourage amicable solutions with a view to obtaining voluntary payment of maintenance, where suitable by use of mediation, conciliation or similar processes;
    (e)   to facilitate the ongoing enforcement of maintenance decisions, including any arrears;
    (f)   to facilitate the collection and expeditious transfer of maintenance payments;
    (g)   to facilitate the obtaining of documentary or other evidence;
    (h)   to provide assistance in establishing parentage where necessary for the recovery of maintenance;
    (i)   to initiate or facilitate the institution of proceedings to obtain any necessary provisional measures that are territorial in nature and the purpose of which is to secure the outcome of a pending maintenance application;
    (j)   to facilitate service of documents.
(3)   The functions of the Central Authority under this Article may, to the extent permitted under the law of its State, be performed by public bodies, or other bodies subject to the supervision of the competent authorities of that State. The designation of any such public bodies or other bodies, as well as their contact details and the extent of their functions, shall be communicated by a Contracting State to the Permanent Bureau of the Hague Conference on Private International Law. Contracting States shall promptly inform the Permanent Bureau of any changes.
(4)   Nothing in this Article or Article 7 shall be interpreted as imposing an obli-

gation on a Central Authority to exercise powers that can be exercised only by judicial authorities under the law of the requested State.

Article 7. Requests for specific measures

(1)   A Central Authority may make a request, supported by reasons, to another Central Authority to take appropriate specific measures under Article 6(2)(b), (c), (g), (h), (i) and (j) when no application under Article 10 is pending. The requested Central Authority shall take such measures as are appropriate if satisfied that they are necessary to assist a potential applicant in making an application under Article 10 or in determining whether such an application should be initiated.

(2)   A Central Authority may also take specific measures on the request of another Central Authority in relation to a case having an international element concerning the recovery of maintenance pending in the requesting State.

Article 8. Central Authority costs

(1)   Each Central Authority shall bear its own costs in applying this Convention.

(2)   Central Authorities may not impose any charge on an applicant for the provision of their services under the Convention save for exceptional costs arising from a request for a specific measure under Article 7.

(3)   The requested Central Authority may not recover the costs of the services referred to in paragraph 2 without the prior consent of the applicant to the provision of those services at such cost.

CHAPTER III – APPLICATIONS THROUGH CENTRAL AUTHORITIES

Article 9. Application through Central Authorities

An application under this Chapter shall be made through the Central Authority of the Contracting State in which the applicant resides to the Central Authority of the requested State. For the purpose of this provision, residence excludes mere presence.

Article 10. Available applications

(1)   The following categories of application shall be available to a creditor in a requesting State seeking to recover maintenance under this Convention—

   (a)   recognition or recognition and enforcement of a decision;

   (b)   enforcement of a decision made or recognised in the requested State;

   (c)   establishment of a decision in the requested State where there is no existing decision, including where necessary the establishment of parentage;

   (d)   establishment of a decision in the requested State where recognition and enforcement of a decision is not possible, or is refused, because of the lack of a basis for recognition and enforcement under Article 20, or on the grounds specified in Article 22(b) or (e);

   (e)   modification of a decision made in the requested State;

   (f)   modification of a decision made in a State other than the requested State.

(2)   The following categories of application shall be available to a debtor in a requesting State against whom there is an existing maintenance decision—

   (a)   recognition of a decision, or an equivalent procedure leading to the suspension, or limiting the enforcement, of a previous decision in the requested State;

   (b)   modification of a decision made in the requested State;

   (c)   modification of a decision made in a State other than the requested State.

(3)   Save as otherwise provided in this Convention, the applications in paragraphs (1) and (2) shall be determined under the law of the requested State, and applications in paragraphs (1)(c) to (f) and (2)(b) and (c) shall be subject to the jurisdictional rules applicable in the requested State.

Article 11. Application contents

(1)   All applications under Article 10 shall as a minimum include—

(a)   a statement of the nature of the application or applications;

(b)   the name and contact details, including the address and date of birth of the applicant;

(c)   the name and, if known, address and date of birth of the respondent;

(d)   the name and date of birth of any person for whom maintenance is sought;

(e)   the grounds upon which the application is based;

(f)   in an application by a creditor, information concerning where the maintenance payment should be sent or electronically transmitted;

(g)   save in an application under Article 10(1)(a) and (2)(a), any information or document specified by declaration in accordance with Article 63 by the requested State;

(h)   the name and contact details of the person or unit from the Central Authority of the requesting State responsible for processing the application.

(2)   As appropriate, and to the extent known, the application shall in addition in particular include—

(a)   the financial circumstances of the creditor;

(b)   the financial circumstances of the debtor, including the name and address of the employer of the debtor and the nature and location of the assets of the debtor;

(c)   any other information that may assist with the location of the respondent.

(3)   The application shall be accompanied by any necessary supporting information or documentation including documentation concerning the entitlement of the applicant to free legal assistance. In the case of applications under Article 10(1)(a) and (2)(a), the application shall be accompanied only by the documents listed in Article 25.

(4)   An application under Article 10 may be made in the form recommended and published by the Hague Conference on Private International Law.

Article 12. Transmission, receipt and processing of applications and cases through Central Authorities

(1)   The Central Authority of the requesting State shall assist the applicant in ensuring that the application is accompanied by all the information and documents known by it to be necessary for consideration of the application.

(2)   The Central Authority of the requesting State shall, when satisfied that the application complies with the requirements of the Convention, transmit the application on behalf of and with the consent of the applicant to the Central Authority of the requested State. The application shall be accompanied by the transmittal form set out in Annex 1. The Central Authority of the requesting State shall, when requested by the Central Authority of the requested State, provide a complete copy certified by the competent authority in the State of origin of any document specified under Articles 16(3), 25(1)(a), (b) and (d) and (3)(b) and 30(3).

(3)   The requested Central Authority shall, within six weeks from the date of receipt of the application, acknowledge receipt in the form set out in Annex 2, and inform the Central Authority of the requesting State what initial steps have been or will be taken to deal with the application, and may request any further necessary documents and information. Within the same six-week period, the requested Central Authority shall provide to the requesting Central Authority the name and contact details of the person or unit responsible for responding to inquiries regarding the progress of the application.

(4)   Within three months after the acknowledgement, the requested Central Authority shall inform the requesting Central Authority of the status of the application.

(5) Requesting and requested Central Authorities shall keep each other informed of—
(a)   the person or unit responsible for a particular case;
(b)   the progress of the case,
and shall provide timely responses to enquiries.

(6)   Central Authorities shall process a case as quickly as a proper consideration of the issues will allow.

(7)   Central Authorities shall employ the most rapid and efficient means of communication at their disposal.

(8)   A requested Central Authority may refuse to process an application only if it is manifest that the requirements of the Convention are not fulfilled. In such case, that Central Authority shall promptly inform the requesting Central Authority of its reasons for refusal.

(9)   The requested Central Authority may not reject an application solely on the basis that additional documents or information are needed. However, the requested Central Authority may ask the requesting Central Authority to provide these additional documents or information. If the requesting Central Authority does not do so within three months or a longer period specified by the requested Central Authority, the requested Central Authority may decide that it will no longer process the application. In this case, it shall inform the requesting Central Authority of this decision.

Article 13. Means of communication
Any application made through Central Authorities of the Contracting States in accordance with this Chapter, and any document or information appended thereto or provided by a Central Authority, may not be challenged by the respondent by reason only of the medium or means of communication employed between the Central Authorities concerned.

Article 14. Effective access to procedures
(1)   The requested State shall provide applicants with effective access to procedures, including enforcement and appeal procedures, arising from applications under this Chapter.

(2)   To provide such effective access, the requested State shall provide free legal assistance in accordance with Articles 14 to 17 unless paragraph (3) applies.

(3)   The requested State shall not be obliged to provide such free legal assistance if and to the extent that the procedures of that State enable the applicant to make the case without the need for such assistance, and the Central Authority provides such services as are necessary free of charge.

(4)   Entitlements to free legal assistance shall not be less than those available in equivalent domestic cases.

(5)   No security, bond or deposit, however described, shall be required to guarantee the payment of costs and expenses in proceedings under the Convention.

Article 15. Free legal assistance for child support applications
(1)   The requested State shall provide free legal assistance in respect of all applications by a creditor under this Chapter concerning maintenance obligations arising from a parent-child relationship towards a person under the age of 21 years.

(2)   Notwithstanding paragraph (1), the requested State may, in relation to applications other than those under Article 10(1)(a) and (b) and the cases covered by Article 20(4), refuse free legal assistance if it considers that, on the merits, the application or any appeal is manifestly unfounded.

Article 16. Declaration to permit use of child-centred means test
(1)   Notwithstanding Article 15(1), a State may declare, in accordance with Article 63, that it will provide free legal assistance in respect of applications other

than under Article 10(1)(a) and (b) and the cases covered by Article 20(4), subject to a test based on an assessment of the means of the child.

(2)   A State shall, at the time of making such a declaration, provide information to the Permanent Bureau of the Hague Conference on Private International Law concerning the manner in which the assessment of the child's means will be carried out, including the financial criteria which would need to be met to satisfy the test.

(3)   An application referred to in paragraph (1), addressed to a State which has made the declaration referred to in that paragraph, shall include a formal attestation by the applicant stating that the child's means meet the criteria referred to in paragraph (2). The requested State may only request further evidence of the child's means if it has reasonable grounds to believe that the information provided by the applicant is inaccurate.

(4)   If the most favourable legal assistance provided for by the law of the requested State in respect of applications under this Chapter concerning maintenance obligations arising from a parent-child relationship towards a child is more favourable than that provided for under paragraphs (1) to (3), the most favourable legal assistance shall be provided.

Article 17. Applications not qualifying under Article 15 or Article 16
In the case of all applications under this Convention other than those under Article 15 or Article 16—

(a)   the provision of free legal assistance may be made subject to a means or a merits test;

(b)   an applicant, who in the State of origin has benefited from free legal assistance, shall be entitled, in any proceedings for recognition or enforcement, to benefit, at least to the same extent, from free legal assistance as provided for by the law of the State addressed under the same circumstances.

CHAPTER IV – RESTRICTIONS ON BRINGING PROCEEDINGS

Article 18. Limit on proceedings
(1)   Where a decision is made in a Contracting State where the creditor is habitually resident, proceedings to modify the decision or to make a new decision cannot be brought by the debtor in any other Contracting State as long as the creditor remains habitually resident in the State where the decision was made.

(2)   Paragraph (1) shall not apply—

(a)   where, except in disputes relating to maintenance obligations in respect of children, there is agreement in writing between the parties to the jurisdiction of that other Contracting State;

(b)   where the creditor submits to the jurisdiction of that other Contracting State either expressly or by defending on the merits of the case without objecting to the jurisdiction at the first available opportunity;

(c)   where the competent authority in the State of origin cannot, or refuses to, exercise jurisdiction to modify the decision or make a new decision; or

(d)   where the decision made in the State of origin cannot be recognised or declared enforceable in the Contracting State where proceedings to modify the decision or make a new decision are contemplated.

CHAPTER V – RECOGNITION AND ENFORCEMENT

Article 19. Scope of the Chapter
(1)   This Chapter shall apply to a decision rendered by a judicial or administrative authority in respect of a maintenance obligation. The term 'decision' also includes a settlement or agreement concluded before or approved by such an authority. A decision may include automatic adjustment by indexation and a

requirement to pay arrears, retroactive maintenance or interest and a determination of costs or expenses.

(2)   If a decision does not relate solely to a maintenance obligation, the effect of this Chapter is limited to the parts of the decision which concern maintenance obligations.

(3)   For the purpose of paragraph (1), 'administrative authority' means a public body whose decisions, under the law of the State where it is established—

(a)   may be made the subject of an appeal to or review by a judicial authority; and

(b)   have a similar force and effect to a decision of a judicial authority on the same matter.

(4)   This Chapter also applies to maintenance arrangements in accordance with Article 30.

(5)   The provisions of this Chapter shall apply to a request for recognition and enforcement made directly to a competent authority of the State addressed in accordance with Article 37.

Article 20. Bases for recognition and enforcement

(1)   A decision made in one Contracting State ('the State of origin') shall be recognised and enforced in other Contracting States if—

(a)   the respondent was habitually resident in the State of origin at the time proceedings were instituted;

(b)   the respondent has submitted to the jurisdiction either expressly or by defending on the merits of the case without objecting to the jurisdiction at the first available opportunity;

(c)   the creditor was habitually resident in the State of origin at the time proceedings were instituted;

(d)   the child for whom maintenance was ordered was habitually resident in the State of origin at the time proceedings were instituted, provided that the respondent has lived with the child in that State or has resided in that State and provided support for the child there;

(e)   except in disputes relating to maintenance obligations in respect of children, there has been agreement to the jurisdiction in writing by the parties; or

(f)   the decision was made by an authority exercising jurisdiction on a matter of personal status or parental responsibility, unless that jurisdiction was based solely on the nationality of one of the parties.

(2)   A Contracting State may make a reservation, in accordance with Article 62, in respect of paragraph (1)(c), (e) or (f).

(3)   A Contracting State making a reservation under paragraph (2) shall recognise and enforce a decision if its law would in similar factual circumstances confer or would have conferred jurisdiction on its authorities to make such a decision.

(4)   A Contracting State shall, if recognition of a decision is not possible as a result of a reservation under paragraph (2), and if the debtor is habitually resident in that State, take all appropriate measures to establish a decision for the benefit of the creditor. The preceding sentence shall not apply to direct requests for recognition and enforcement under Article 19(5) or to claims for support referred to in Article 2(1) b).

(5)   A decision in favour of a child under the age of 18 years which cannot be recognised by virtue only of a reservation in respect of paragraph (1)(c), (e) or (f) shall be accepted as establishing the eligibility of that child for maintenance in the State addressed.

(6)   A decision shall be recognised only if it has effect in the State of origin, and shall be enforced only if it is enforceable in the State of origin.

Article 21. Severability and partial recognition and enforcement

(1)   If the State addressed is unable to recognise or enforce the whole of the

decision, it shall recognise or enforce any severable part of the decision which can be so recognised or enforced.

(2) Partial recognition or enforcement of a decision can always be applied for.

Article 22. Grounds for refusing recognition and enforcement
Recognition and enforcement of a decision may be refused if—

(a) recognition and enforcement of the decision is manifestly incompatible with the public policy ('ordre public') of the State addressed;

(b) the decision was obtained by fraud in connection with a matter of procedure;

(c) proceedings between the same parties and having the same purpose are pending before an authority of the State addressed and those proceedings were the first to be instituted;

(d) the decision is incompatible with a decision rendered between the same parties and having the same purpose, either in the State addressed or in another State, provided that this latter decision fulfils the conditions necessary for its recognition and enforcement in the State addressed;

(e) in a case where the respondent has neither appeared nor was represented in proceedings in the State of origin—

(i) when the law of the State of origin provides for notice of proceedings, the respondent did not have proper notice of the proceedings and an opportunity to be heard; or

(ii) when the law of the State of origin does not provide for notice of the proceedings, the respondent did not have proper notice of the decision and an opportunity to challenge or appeal it on fact and law; or

(f) the decision was made in violation of Article 18.

Article 23. Procedure on an application for recognition and enforcement
(1) Subject to the provisions of the Convention, the procedures for recognition and enforcement shall be governed by the law of the State addressed.

(2) Where an application for recognition and enforcement of a decision has been made through Central Authorities in accordance with Chapter III, the requested Central Authority shall promptly either—

(a) refer the application to the competent authority which shall without delay declare the decision enforceable or register the decision for enforcement; or

(b) if it is the competent authority take such steps itself.

(3) Where the request is made directly to a competent authority in the State addressed in accordance with Article 19(5), that authority shall without delay declare the decision enforceable or register the decision for enforcement.

(4) A declaration or registration may be refused only on the ground set out in Article 22(a). At this stage neither the applicant nor the respondent is entitled to make any submissions.

(5) The applicant and the respondent shall be promptly notified of the declaration or registration, made under paragraphs (2) and (3), or the refusal thereof in accordance with paragraph (4), and may bring a challenge or appeal on fact and on a point of law.

(6) A challenge or an appeal is to be lodged within 30 days of notification under paragraph (5). If the contesting party is not resident in the Contracting State in which the declaration or registration was made or refused, the challenge or appeal shall be lodged within 60 days of notification.

(7) A challenge or appeal may be founded only on the following—

(a) the grounds for refusing recognition and enforcement set out in Article 22;

(b) the bases for recognition and enforcement under Article 20;

(c) the authenticity or integrity of any document transmitted in accordance with Article 25(1)(a), (b) or (d) or (3)(b).

(8)   A challenge or an appeal by a respondent may also be founded on the fulfilment of the debt to the extent that the recognition and enforcement relates to payments that fell due in the past.

(9)   The applicant and the respondent shall be promptly notified of the decision following the challenge or the appeal.

(10)   A further appeal, if permitted by the law of the State addressed, shall not have the effect of staying the enforcement of the decision unless there are exceptional circumstances.

(11)   In taking any decision on recognition and enforcement, including any appeal, the competent authority shall act expeditiously.

Article 24. Alternative procedure on an application for recognition and enforcement

(1)   Notwithstanding Article 23(2) to (11), a State may declare, in accordance with Article 63, that it will apply the procedure for recognition and enforcement set out in this Article.

(2)   Where an application for recognition and enforcement of a decision has been made through Central Authorities in accordance with Chapter III, the requested Central Authority shall promptly either—

(a)   refer the application to the competent authority which shall decide on the application for recognition and enforcement; or

(b)   if it is the competent authority, take such a decision itself.

(3)   A decision on recognition and enforcement shall be given by the competent authority after the respondent has been duly and promptly notified of the proceedings and both parties have been given an adequate opportunity to be heard.

(4)   The competent authority may review the grounds for refusing recognition and enforcement set out in Article 22(a), (c) and (d) of its own motion. It may review any grounds listed in Articles 20, 22 and 23(7) (c) if raised by the respondent or if concerns relating to those grounds arise from the face of the documents submitted in accordance with Article 25.

(5)   A refusal of recognition and enforcement may also be founded on the fulfilment of the debt to the extent that the recognition and enforcement relates to payments that fell due in the past.

(6)   Any appeal, if permitted by the law of the State addressed, shall not have the effect of staying the enforcement of the decision unless there are exceptional circumstances.

(7)   In taking any decision on recognition and enforcement, including any appeal, the competent authority shall act expeditiously.

Article 25. Documents

(1)   An application for recognition and enforcement under Article 23 or Article 24 shall be accompanied by the following—

(a)   a complete text of the decision;

(b)   a document stating that the decision is enforceable in the State of origin and, in the case of a decision by an administrative authority, a document stating that the requirements of Article 19(3) are met unless that State has specified in accordance with Article 57 that decisions of its administrative authorities always meet those requirements;

(c)   if the respondent did not appear and was not represented in the proceedings in the State of origin, a document or documents attesting, as appropriate, either that the respondent had proper notice of the proceedings and an opportunity to be heard, or that the respondent had proper notice of the decision and the opportunity to challenge or appeal it on fact and law;

(d)   where necessary, a document showing the amount of any arrears and the date such amount was calculated;

(e)   where necessary, in the case of a decision providing for automatic adjustment by indexation, a document providing the information necessary to make the appropriate calculations;

(f)   where necessary, documentation showing the extent to which the applicant received free legal assistance in the State of origin.

(2)   Upon a challenge or appeal under Article 23(7) (c) or upon request by the competent authority in the State addressed, a complete copy of the document concerned, certified by the competent authority in the State of origin, shall be provided promptly—

(a)   by the Central Authority of the requesting State, where the application has been made in accordance with Chapter III;

(b)   by the applicant, where the request has been made directly to a competent authority of the State addressed.

(3)   A Contracting State may specify in accordance with Article 57—

(a)   that a complete copy of the decision certified by the competent authority in the State of origin must accompany the application;

(b)   circumstances in which it will accept, in lieu of a complete text of the decision, an abstract or extract of the decision drawn up by the competent authority of the State of origin, which may be made in the form recommended and published by the Hague Conference on Private International Law; or

(c)   that it does not require a document stating that the requirements of Article 19(3) are met.

Article 26. Procedure on an application for recognition
This Chapter shall apply mutatis mutandis to an application for recognition of a decision, save that the requirement of enforceability is replaced by the requirement that the decision has effect in the State of origin.

Article 27. Findings of fact
Any competent authority of the State addressed shall be bound by the findings of fact on which the authority of the State of origin based its jurisdiction.

Article 28. No review of the merits
There shall be no review by any competent authority of the State addressed of the merits of a decision.

Article 29. Physical presence of the child or the applicant not required
The physical presence of the child or the applicant shall not be required in any proceedings in the State addressed under this Chapter.

Article 30. Maintenance arrangements
(1)   A maintenance arrangement made in a Contracting State shall be entitled to recognition and enforcement as a decision under this Chapter provided that it is enforceable as a decision in the State of origin.

(2)   For the purpose of Article 10(1)(a) and (b) and (2)(a), the term 'decision' includes a maintenance arrangement.

(3)   An application for recognition and enforcement of a maintenance arrangement shall be accompanied by the following—

(a)   a complete text of the maintenance arrangement; and

(b)   a document stating that the particular maintenance arrangement is enforceable as a decision in the State of origin.

(4)   Recognition and enforcement of a maintenance arrangement may be refused if—

(a)   the recognition and enforcement is manifestly incompatible with the public policy of the State addressed;

(b)   the maintenance arrangement was obtained by fraud or falsification;

(c)   the maintenance arrangement is incompatible with a decision rendered between the same parties and having the same purpose, either in the State addressed or in another State, provided that this latter decision fulfils the conditions necessary for its recognition and enforcement in the State addressed.

(5) The provisions of this Chapter, with the exception of Articles 20, 22, 23(7) and 25(1) and (3), shall apply mutatis mutandis to the recognition and enforcement of a maintenance arrangement save that—

(a) a declaration or registration in accordance with Article 23(2) and (3) may be refused only on the ground set out in paragraph 4 a);

(b) a challenge or appeal as referred to in Article 23(6) may be founded only on the following—

(i) the grounds for refusing recognition and enforcement set out in paragraph (4);

(ii) the authenticity or integrity of any document transmitted in accordance with paragraph (3);

(c) as regards the procedure under Article 24(4), the competent authority may review of its own motion the ground for refusing recognition and enforcement set out in paragraph 4(a) of this Article. It may review all grounds listed in paragraph (4) of this Article and the authenticity or integrity of any document transmitted in accordance with paragraph (3) if raised by the respondent or if concerns relating to those grounds arise from the face of those documents.

(6) Proceedings for recognition and enforcement of a maintenance arrangement shall be suspended if a challenge concerning the arrangement is pending before a competent authority of a Contracting State.

(7) A State may declare, in accordance with Article 63, that applications for recognition and enforcement of a maintenance arrangement shall only be made through Central Authorities.

(8) A Contracting State may, in accordance with Article 62, reserve the right not to recognise and enforce a maintenance arrangement.

Article 31. Decisions produced by the combined effect of provisional and confirmation orders

Where a decision is produced by the combined effect of a provisional order made in one State and an order by an authority in another State ('the confirming State') confirming the provisional order—

(a) each of those States shall be deemed for the purposes of this Chapter to be a State of origin;

(b) the requirements of Article 22(e) shall be met if the respondent had proper notice of the proceedings in the confirming State and an opportunity to oppose the confirmation of the provisional order;

(c) the requirement of Article 20(6) that a decision be enforceable in the State of origin shall be met if the decision is enforceable in the confirming State; and

(d) Article 18 shall not prevent proceedings for the modification of the decision being commenced in either State.

CHAPTER VI – ENFORCEMENT BY THE STATE ADDRESSED

Article 32. Enforcement under internal law

(1) Subject to the provisions of this Chapter, enforcement shall take place in accordance with the law of the State addressed.

(2) Enforcement shall be prompt.

(3) In the case of applications through Central Authorities, where a decision has been declared enforceable or registered for enforcement under Chapter V, enforcement shall proceed without the need for further action by the applicant.

(4) Effect shall be given to any rules applicable in the State of origin of the decision relating to the duration of the maintenance obligation.

(5) Any limitation on the period for which arrears may be enforced shall be determined either by the law of the State of origin of the decision or by the law of the State addressed, whichever provides for the longer limitation period.

Article 33. Non-discrimination
The State addressed shall provide at least the same range of enforcement methods for cases under the Convention as are available in domestic cases.

Article 34. Enforcement measures
(1)   Contracting States shall make available in internal law effective measures to enforce decisions under this Convention.

(2)   Such measures may include—
   (a)   wage withholding;
   (b)   garnishment from bank accounts and other sources;
   (c)   deductions from social security payments;
   (d)   lien on or forced sale of property;
   (e)   tax refund withholding;
   (f)   withholding or attachment of pension benefits;
   (g)   credit bureau reporting;
   (h)   denial, suspension or revocation of various licenses (for example, driving licenses);
   (i)   the use of mediation, conciliation or similar processes to bring about voluntary compliance.

Article 35. Transfer of funds
(1)   Contracting States are encouraged to promote, including by means of international agreements, the use of the most cost-effective and efficient methods available to transfer funds payable as maintenance.

(2)   A Contracting State, under whose law the transfer of funds is restricted, shall accord the highest priority to the transfer of funds payable under this Convention.

CHAPTER VII – PUBLIC BODIES

Article 36. Public bodies as applicants
(1)   For the purposes of applications for recognition and enforcement under Article 10(1)(a) and (b) and cases covered by Article 20(4), 'creditor' includes a public body acting in place of an individual to whom maintenance is owed or one to which reimbursement is owed for benefits provided in place of maintenance.

(2)   The right of a public body to act in place of an individual to whom maintenance is owed or to seek reimbursement of benefits provided to the creditor in place of maintenance shall be governed by the law to which the body is subject.

(3)   A public body may seek recognition or claim enforcement of—
   (a)   a decision rendered against a debtor on the application of a public body which claims payment of benefits provided in place of maintenance;
   (b)   a decision rendered between a creditor and debtor to the extent of the benefits provided to the creditor in place of maintenance.

(4)   The public body seeking recognition or claiming enforcement of a decision shall upon request furnish any document necessary to establish its right under paragraph (2) and that benefits have been provided to the creditor.

CHAPTER VIII – GENERAL PROVISIONS

Article 37. Direct requests to competent authorities
(1)   The Convention shall not exclude the possibility of recourse to such procedures as may be available under the internal law of a Contracting State allowing a person (an applicant) to seise directly a competent authority of that State in a matter governed by the Convention including, subject to Article 18, for the purpose of having a maintenance decision established or modified.

(2)   Articles 14(5) and 17(b) and the provisions of Chapters V, VI, VII and this Chapter, with the exception of Articles 40(2), 42, 43(3), 44(3), 45 and 55, shall apply

in relation to a request for recognition and enforcement made directly to a competent authority in a Contracting State.

(3)   For the purpose of paragraph (2), Article 2(1)(a) shall apply to a decision granting maintenance to a vulnerable person over the age specified in that subparagraph where such decision was rendered before the person reached that age and provided for maintenance beyond that age by reason of the impairment.

Article 38. Protection of personal data
Personal data gathered or transmitted under the Convention shall be used only for the purposes for which they were gathered or transmitted.

Article 39. Confidentiality
Any authority processing information shall ensure its confidentiality in accordance with the law of its State.

Article 40. Non-disclosure of information
(1)   An authority shall not disclose or confirm information gathered or transmitted in application of this Convention if it determines that to do so could jeopardise the health, safety or liberty of a person.

(2)   A determination to this effect made by one Central Authority shall be taken into account by another Central Authority, in particular in cases of family violence.

(3)   Nothing in this Article shall impede the gathering and transmitting of information by and between authorities in so far as necessary to carry out the obligations under the Convention.

Article 41. No legalisation
No legalisation or similar formality may be required in the context of this Convention.

Article 42. Power of attorney
The Central Authority of the requested State may require a power of attorney from the applicant only if it acts on his or her behalf in judicial proceedings or before other authorities, or in order to designate a representative so to act.

Article 43. Recovery of costs
(1)   Recovery of any costs incurred in the application of this Convention shall not take precedence over the recovery of maintenance.

(2)   A State may recover costs from an unsuccessful party.

(3)   For the purposes of an application under Article 10(1)(b) to recover costs from an unsuccessful party in accordance with paragraph (2), the term 'creditor' in Article 10(1) shall include a State.

(4)   This Article shall be without prejudice to Article 8.

Article 44. Language requirements
(1)   Any application and related documents shall be in the original language, and shall be accompanied by a translation into an official language of the requested State or another language which the requested State has indicated, by way of declaration in accordance with Article 63, it will accept, unless the competent authority of that State dispenses with translation.

(2)   A Contracting State which has more than one official language and cannot, for reasons of internal law, accept for the whole of its territory documents in one of those languages shall, by declaration in accordance with Article 63, specify the language in which such documents or translations thereof shall be drawn up for submission in the specified parts of its territory.

(3)   Unless otherwise agreed by the Central Authorities, any other communications between such Authorities shall be in an official language of the requested State or in either English or French. However, a Contracting State may, by making a reservation in accordance with Article 62, object to the use of either English or French.

Article 45. Means and costs of translation

(1)   In the case of applications under Chapter III, the Central Authorities may agree in an individual case or generally that the translation into an official language of the requested State may be made in the requested State from the original language or from any other agreed language. If there is no agreement and it is not possible for the requesting Central Authority to comply with the requirements of Article 44(1) and (2), then the application and related documents may be transmitted with translation into English or French for further translation into an official language of the requested State.

(2)   The cost of translation arising from the application of paragraph (1) shall be borne by the requesting State unless otherwise agreed by Central Authorities of the States concerned.

(3)   Notwithstanding Article 8, the requesting Central Authority may charge an applicant for the costs of translation of an application and related documents, except in so far as those costs may be covered by its system of legal assistance.

Article 46. Non-unified legal systems–interpretation

(1)   In relation to a State in which two or more systems of law or sets of rules of law with regard to any matter dealt with in this Convention apply in different territorial units—

(a)   any reference to the law or procedure of a State shall be construed as referring, where appropriate, to the law or procedure in force in the relevant territorial unit;

(b)   any reference to a decision established, recognised, recognised and enforced, enforced or modified in that State shall be construed as referring, where appropriate, to a decision established, recognised, recognised and enforced, enforced or modified in the relevant territorial unit;

(c)   any reference to a judicial or administrative authority in that State shall be construed as referring, where appropriate, to a judicial or administrative authority in the relevant territorial unit;

(d)   any reference to competent authorities, public bodies, and other bodies of that State, other than Central Authorities, shall be construed as referring, where appropriate, to those authorised to act in the relevant territorial unit;

(e)   any reference to residence or habitual residence in that State shall be construed as referring, where appropriate, to residence or habitual residence in the relevant territorial unit;

(f)   any reference to location of assets in that State shall be construed as referring, where appropriate, to the location of assets in the relevant territorial unit;

(g)   any reference to a reciprocity arrangement in force in a State shall be construed as referring, where appropriate, to a reciprocity arrangement in force in the relevant territorial unit;

(h)   any reference to free legal assistance in that State shall be construed as referring, where appropriate, to free legal assistance in the relevant territorial unit;

(i)   any reference to a maintenance arrangement made in a State shall be construed as referring, where appropriate, to a maintenance arrangement made in the relevant territorial unit;

(j)   any reference to recovery of costs by a State shall be construed as referring, where appropriate, to the recovery of costs by the relevant territorial unit.

(2)   This Article shall not apply to a Regional Economic Integration Organisation.

Article 47. Non-unified legal systems – substantive rules

(1)   A Contracting State with two or more territorial units in which different systems of law apply shall not be bound to apply this Convention to situations which involve solely such different territorial units.

(2)   A competent authority in a territorial unit of a Contracting State with two or more territorial units in which different systems of law apply shall not be bound to recognise or enforce a decision from another Contracting State solely because the decision has been recognised or enforced in another territorial unit of the same Contracting State under this Convention.

(3)   This Article shall not apply to a Regional Economic Integration Organisation.

Article 48. Co-ordination with prior Hague Maintenance Conventions
In relations between the Contracting States, this Convention replaces, subject to Article 56(2), the Hague Convention of 2 October 1973 on the Recognition and Enforcement of Decisions Relating to Maintenance Obligations and the Hague Convention of 15 April 1958 concerning the recognition and enforcement of decisions relating to maintenance obligations towards children in so far as their scope of application as between such States coincides with the scope of application of this Convention.

Article 49. Co-ordination with the 1956 New York Convention
In relations between the Contracting States, this Convention replaces the United Nations Convention on the Recovery Abroad of Maintenance of 20 June 1956, in so far as its scope of application as between such States coincides with the scope of application of this Convention.

Article 50. Relationship with prior Hague Conventions on service of documents and taking of evidence
This Convention does not affect the Hague Convention of 1 March 1954 on civil procedure, the Hague Convention of 15 November 1965 on the Service Abroad of Judicial and Extrajudicial Documents in Civil or Commercial Matters and the Hague Convention of 18 March 1970 on the Taking of Evidence Abroad in Civil or Commercial Matters.

Article 51. Co-ordination of instruments and supplementary agreements
(1)   This Convention does not affect any international instrument concluded before this Convention to which Contracting States are Parties and which contains provisions on matters governed by this Convention.

(2)   Any Contracting State may conclude with one or more Contracting States agreements, which contain provisions on matters governed by the Convention, with a view to improving the application of the Convention between or among themselves, provided that such agreements are consistent with the objects and purpose of the Convention and do not affect, in the relationship of such States with other Contracting States, the application of the provisions of the Convention. The States which have concluded such an agreement shall transmit a copy to the depositary of the Convention.

(3)   Paragraphs (1) and (2) shall also apply to reciprocity arrangements and to uniform laws based on special ties between the States concerned.

(4)   This Convention shall not affect the application of instruments of a Regional Economic Integration Organisation that is a Party to this Convention, adopted after the conclusion of the Convention, on matters governed by the Convention provided that such instruments do not affect, in the relationship of Member States of the Regional Economic Integration Organisation with other Contracting States, the application of the provisions of the Convention. As concerns the recognition or enforcement of decisions as between Member States of the Regional Economic Integration Organisation, the Convention shall not affect the rules of the Regional Economic Integration Organisation, whether adopted before or after the conclusion of the Convention.

Article 52. Most effective rule
(1)   This Convention shall not prevent the application of an agreement, arrange-

ment or international instrument in force between the requesting State and the requested State, or a reciprocity arrangement in force in the requested State that provides for—

(a) broader bases for recognition of maintenance decisions, without prejudice to Article 22(f) of the Convention;

(b) simplified, more expeditious procedures on an application for recognition or recognition and enforcement of maintenance decisions;

(c) more beneficial legal assistance than that provided for under Articles 14 to 17; or

(d) procedures permitting an applicant from a requesting State to make a request directly to the Central Authority of the requested State.

(2) This Convention shall not prevent the application of a law in force in the requested State that provides for more effective rules as referred to in paragraph (1)(a) to (c). However, as regards simplified, more expeditious procedures referred to in paragraph (1)(b), they must be compatible with the protection offered to the parties under Articles 23 and 24, in particular as regards the rights of the parties to be duly notified of the proceedings and be given adequate opportunity to be heard and as regards the effects of any challenge or appeal.

Article 53. Uniform interpretation
In the interpretation of this Convention, regard shall be had to its international character and to the need to promote uniformity in its application.

Article 54. Review of practical operation of the Convention
(1) The Secretary General of the Hague Conference on Private International Law shall at regular intervals convene a Special Commission in order to review the practical operation of the Convention and to encourage the development of good practices under the Convention.

(2) For the purpose of such review, Contracting States shall co-operate with the Permanent Bureau of the Hague Conference on Private International Law in the gathering of information, including statistics and case law, concerning the practical operation of the Convention.

Article 55. Amendment of forms
(1) The forms annexed to this Convention may be amended by a decision of a Special Commission convened by the Secretary General of the Hague Conference on Private International Law to which all Contracting States and all Members shall be invited. Notice of the proposal to amend the forms shall be included in the agenda for the meeting.

(2) Amendments adopted by the Contracting States present at the Special Commission shall come into force for all Contracting States on the first day of the seventh calendar month after the date of their communication by the depositary to all Contracting States.

(3) During the period provided for in paragraph (2) any Contracting State may by notification in writing to the depositary make a reservation, in accordance with Article 62, with respect to the amendment. The State making such reservation shall, until the reservation is withdrawn, be treated as a State not Party to the present Convention with respect to that amendment.

Article 56. Transitional provisions
(1) The Convention shall apply in every case where—

(a) a request pursuant to Article 7 or an application pursuant to Chapter III has been received by the Central Authority of the requested State after the Convention has entered into force between the requesting State and the requested State;

(b) a direct request for recognition and enforcement has been received by the competent authority of the State addressed after the Convention has entered into force between the State of origin and the State addressed.

(2)   With regard to the recognition and enforcement of decisions between Contracting States to this Convention that are also Parties to either of the Hague Maintenance Conventions mentioned in Article 48, if the conditions for the recognition and enforcement under this Convention prevent the recognition and enforcement of a decision given in the State of origin before the entry into force of this Convention for that State, that would otherwise have been recognised and enforced under the terms of the Convention that was in effect at the time the decision was rendered, the conditions of that Convention shall apply.

(3)   The State addressed shall not be bound under this Convention to enforce a decision or a maintenance arrangement, in respect of payments falling due prior to the entry into force of the Convention between the State of origin and the State addressed, except for maintenance obligations arising from a parent-child relationship towards a person under the age of 21 years.

Article 57. Provision of information concerning laws, procedures and services

(1)   A Contracting State, by the time its instrument of ratification or accession is deposited or a declaration is submitted in accordance with Article 61 of the Convention, shall provide the Permanent Bureau of the Hague Conference on Private International Law with—

(a)   a description of its laws and procedures concerning maintenance obligations;

(b)   a description of the measures it will take to meet the obligations under Article 6;

(c)   a description of how it will provide applicants with effective access to procedures, as required under Article 14;

(d)   a description of its enforcement rules and procedures, including any limitations on enforcement, in particular debtor protection rules and limitation periods;

(e)   any specification referred to in Article 25(1)(b) and (3).

(2)   Contracting States may, in fulfilling their obligations under paragraph (1), utilise a country profile form recommended and published by the Hague Conference on Private International Law.

(3)   Information shall be kept up to date by the Contracting States.

CHAPTER IX – FINAL PROVISIONS

Article 58. Signature, ratification and accession

(1)   The Convention shall be open for signature by the States which were Members of the Hague Conference on Private International Law at the time of its Twenty-First Session and by the other States which participated in that Session.

(2)   It shall be ratified, accepted or approved and the instruments of ratification, acceptance or approval shall be deposited with the Ministry of Foreign Affairs of the Kingdom of the Netherlands, depositary of the Convention.

(3)   Any other State or Regional Economic Integration Organisation may accede to the Convention after it has entered into force in accordance with Article 60(1).

(4)   The instrument of accession shall be deposited with the depositary.

(5)   Such accession shall have effect only as regards the relations between the acceding State and those Contracting States which have not raised an objection to its accession in the 12 months after the date of the notification referred to in Article 65. Such an objection may also be raised by States at the time when they ratify, accept or approve the Convention after an accession. Any such objection shall be notified to the depositary.

Article 59. Regional Economic Integration Organisations

(1)   A Regional Economic Integration Organisation which is constituted solely by sovereign States and has competence over some or all of the matters governed by this Convention may similarly sign, accept, approve or accede to this Conven-

tion. The Regional Economic Integration Organisation shall in that case have the rights and obligations of a Contracting State, to the extent that the Organisation has competence over matters governed by the Convention.

(2) The Regional Economic Integration Organisation shall, at the time of signature, acceptance, approval or accession, notify the depositary in writing of the matters governed by this Convention in respect of which competence has been transferred to that Organisation by its Member States. The Organisation shall promptly notify the depositary in writing of any changes to its competence as specified in the most recent notice given under this paragraph.

(3) At the time of signature, acceptance, approval or accession, a Regional Economic Integration Organisation may declare in accordance with Article 63 that it exercises competence over all the matters governed by this Convention and that the Member States which have transferred competence to the Regional Economic Integration Organisation in respect of the matter in question shall be bound by this Convention by virtue of the signature, acceptance, approval or accession of the Organisation.

(4) For the purposes of the entry into force of this Convention, any instrument deposited by a Regional Economic Integration Organisation shall not be counted unless the Regional Economic Integration Organisation makes a declaration in accordance with paragraph 3.

(5) Any reference to a 'Contracting State' or 'State' in this Convention shall apply equally to a Regional Economic Integration Organisation that is a Party to it, where appropriate. In the event that a declaration is made by a Regional Economic Integration Organisation in accordance with paragraph (3), any reference to a 'Contracting State' or 'State' in this Convention shall apply equally to the relevant Member States of the Organisation, where appropriate.

Article 60. Entry into force

(1) The Convention shall enter into force on the first day of the month following the expiration of three months after the deposit of the second instrument of ratification, acceptance or approval referred to in Article 58.

(2) Thereafter the Convention shall enter into force—

(a) for each State or Regional Economic Integration Organisation referred to in Article 59(1) subsequently ratifying, accepting or approving it, on the first day of the month following the expiration of three months after the deposit of its instrument of ratification, acceptance or approval;

(b) for each State or Regional Economic Integration Organisation referred to in Article 58(3) on the day after the end of the period during which objections may be raised in accordance with Article 58(5);

(c) for a territorial unit to which the Convention has been extended in accordance with Article 61, on the first day of the month following the expiration of three months after the notification referred to in that Article.

Article 61. Declarations with respect to non-unified legal systems

(1) If a State has two or more territorial units in which different systems of law are applicable in relation to matters dealt with in the Convention, it may at the time of signature, ratification, acceptance, approval or accession declare in accordance with Article 63 that this Convention shall extend to all its territorial units or only to one or more of them and may modify this declaration by submitting another declaration at any time.

(2) Any such declaration shall be notified to the depositary and shall state expressly the territorial units to which the Convention applies.

(3) If a State makes no declaration under this Article, the Convention shall extend to all territorial units of that State.

(4) This Article shall not apply to a Regional Economic Integration Organisation.

Article 62. Reservations

(1)   Any Contracting State may, not later than the time of ratification, acceptance, approval or accession, or at the time of making a declaration in terms of Article 61, make one or more of the reservations provided for in Articles 2(2), 20(2), 30(8), 44(3) and 55(3). No other reservation shall be permitted.

(2)   Any State may at any time withdraw a reservation it has made. The withdrawal shall be notified to the depositary.

(3)   The reservation shall cease to have effect on the first day of the third calendar month after the notification referred to in paragraph (2).

(4)   Reservations under this Article shall have no reciprocal effect with the exception of the reservation provided for in Article 2(2).

Article 63. Declarations

(1)   Declarations referred to in Articles 2(3), 11(1)(g), 16(1), 24(1), 30(7), 44(1) and (2), 59(3) and 61(1), may be made upon signature, ratification, acceptance, approval or accession or at any time thereafter, and may be modified or withdrawn at any time.

(2)   Declarations, modifications and withdrawals shall be notified to the depositary.

(3)   A declaration made at the time of signature, ratification, acceptance, approval or accession shall take effect simultaneously with the entry into force of this Convention for the State concerned.

(4)   A declaration made at a subsequent time, and any modification or withdrawal of a declaration, shall take effect on the first day of the month following the expiration of three months after the date on which the notification is received by the depositary.

Article 64. Denunciation

(1)   A Contracting State to the Convention may denounce it by a notification in writing addressed to the depositary. The denunciation may be limited to certain territorial units of a multi-unit State to which the Convention applies.

(2)   The denunciation shall take effect on the first day of the month following the expiration of 12 months after the date on which the notification is received by the depositary. Where a longer period for the denunciation to take effect is specified in the notification, the denunciation shall take effect upon the expiration of such longer period after the date on which the notification is received by the depositary.

Article 65. Notification

The depositary shall notify the Members of the Hague Conference on Private International Law, and other States and Regional Economic Integration Organisations which have signed, ratified, accepted, approved or acceded in accordance with Articles 58 and 59 of the following—

(a)   the signatures, ratifications, acceptances and approvals referred to in Articles 58 and 59;

(b)   the accessions and objections raised to accessions referred to in Articles 58(3) and (5) and 59;

(c)   the date on which the Convention enters into force in accordance with Article 60;

(d)   the declarations referred to in Articles 2(3), 11(1)(g), 16(1), 24(1), 30(7), 44(1) and (2), 59(3) and 61(1);

(e)   the agreements referred to in Article 51(2);

(f)   the reservations referred to in Articles 2(2), 20(2), 30(8), 44(3) and 55(3), and the withdrawals referred to in Article 62(2);

(g)   the denunciations referred to in Article 64.

CONVENTION ON JURISDICTION AND THE ENFORCEMENT OF JUDGMENTS IN CIVIL AND COMMERCIAL MATTERS

Done at Lugano on 30 October 2007.

PREAMBLE

THE HIGH CONTRACTING PARTIES TO THIS CONVENTION

DETERMINED to strengthen in their territories the legal protection of persons therein established,

CONSIDERING that it is necessary for this purpose to determine the international jurisdiction of the courts, to facilitate recognition, and to introduce an expeditious procedure for securing the enforcement of judgments, authentic instruments and court settlements,

AWARE OF the links between them, which have been sanctioned in the economic field by the free trade agreements concluded between the European Community and certain States members of the European Free Trade Association,

TAKING INTO ACCOUNT:
– the Brussels Convention of 27 September 1968 on jurisdiction and the enforcement of judgments in civil and commercial matters, as amended by the Accession Conventions under the successive enlargements of the European Union;
– the Lugano Convention of 16 September 1988 on jurisdiction and the enforcement of judgments in civil and commercial matters, which extends the application of the rules of the 1968 Brussels Convention to certain States members of the European Free Trade Association;
– Council Regulation (EC) No 44/2001 of 22 December 2000 on jurisdiction and the recognition and enforcement of judgments in civil and commercial matters, which has replaced the above-mentioned Brussels Convention;
– the Agreement between the European Community and the Kingdom of Denmark on jurisdiction and the recognition and enforcement of judgments in civil and commercial matters, signed at Brussels on 19 October 2005;

PERSUADED that the extension of the principles laid down in Regulation (EC) No 44/2001 to the Contracting Parties to this instrument will strengthen legal and economic cooperation,

DESIRING to ensure as uniform an interpretation as possible of this instrument,

HAVE in this spirit DECIDED to conclude this Convention, and

HAVE AGREED AS FOLLOWS:

TITLE I
SCOPE

Article 1
1. This Convention shall apply in civil and commercial matters whatever the nature of the court or tribunal. It shall not extend, in particular, to revenue, customs or administrative matters.
2. The Convention shall not apply to:
(a) the status or legal capacity of natural persons, rights in property arising out of a matrimonial relationship, wills and succession;
(b) bankruptcy, proceedings relating to the winding-up of insolvent companies or other legal persons, judicial arrangements, compositions and analogous proceedings;

(c)   social security;

(d)   arbitration.

3.   In this Convention, the term 'State bound by this Convention' shall mean any State that is a Contracting Party to this Convention or a Member State of the European Community. It may also mean the European Community.

TITLE II
JURISDICTION

Section 1
General provisions

Article 2

1.   Subject to the provisions of this Convention, persons domiciled in a State bound by this Convention shall, whatever their nationality, be sued in the courts of that State.

2.   Persons who are not nationals of the State bound by this Convention in which they are domiciled shall be governed by the rules of jurisdiction applicable to nationals of that State.

Article 3

1.   Persons domiciled in a State bound by this Convention may be sued in the courts of another State bound by this Convention only by virtue of the rules set out in Sections 2 to 7 of this Title.

2.   In particular the rules of national jurisdiction set out in Annex I shall not be applicable as against them.

Article 4

1.   If the defendant is not domiciled in a State bound by this Convention, the jurisdiction of the courts of each State bound by this Convention shall, subject to the provisions of Articles 22 and 23, be determined by the law of that State.

2.   As against such a defendant, any person domiciled in a State bound by this Convention may, whatever his nationality, avail himself in that State of the rules of jurisdiction there in force, and in particular those specified in Annex I, in the same way as the nationals of that State.

Section 2
Special jurisdiction

Article 5

A person domiciled in a State bound by this Convention may, in another State bound by this Convention, be sued:

1.   (a)   in matters relating to a contract, in the courts for the place of performance of the obligation in question;

(b)   for the purpose of this provision and unless otherwise agreed, the place of performance of the obligation in question shall be:

– in the case of the sale of goods, the place in a State bound by this Convention where, under the contract, the goods were delivered or should have been delivered,

– in the case of the provision of services, the place in a State bound by this Convention where, under the contract, the services were provided or should have been provided;

(c)   if (b) does not apply then subparagraph (a) applies;

2.   in matters relating to maintenance,

(a)   in the courts for the place where the maintenance creditor is domiciled or habitually resident, or

(b)   in the court which, according to its own law, has jurisdiction to entertain proceedings concerning the status of a person if the matter relating to maintenance is ancillary to those proceedings, unless that jurisdiction is based solely on the nationality of one of the parties, or

(c)   in the court which, according to its own law, has jurisdiction to entertain proceedings concerning parental responsibility, if the matter relating to maintenance is ancillary to those proceedings, unless that jurisdiction is based solely on the nationality of one of the parties;

3.   in matters relating to tort, *delict* or *quasi-delict*, in the courts for the place where the harmful event occurred or may occur;

4.   as regards a civil claim for damages or restitution which is based on an act giving rise to criminal proceedings, in the court seised of those proceedings, to the extent that that court has jurisdiction under its own law to entertain civil proceedings;

5.   as regards a dispute arising out of the operations of a branch, agency or other establishment, in the courts for the place in which the branch, agency or other establishment is situated;

6.   as settlor, trustee or beneficiary of a trust created by the operation of a statute, or by a written instrument, or created orally and evidenced in writing, in the courts of the State bound by this Convention in which the trust is domiciled;

7.   as regards a dispute concerning the payment of remuneration claimed in respect of the salvage of a cargo or freight, in the court under the authority of which the cargo or freight in question:

(a)   has been arrested to secure such payment, or

(b)   could have been so arrested, but bail or other security has been given, provided that this provision shall apply only if it is claimed that the defendant has an interest in the cargo or freight or had such an interest at the time of salvage.

Article 6
A person domiciled in a State bound by this Convention may also be sued:

1.   where he is one of a number of defendants, in the courts for the place where any one of them is domiciled, provided the claims are so closely connected that it is expedient to hear and determine them together to avoid the risk of irreconcilable judgments resulting from separate proceedings;

2.   as a third party in an action on a warranty or guarantee or in any other third party proceedings, in the court seised of the original proceedings, unless these were instituted solely with the object of removing him from the jurisdiction of the court which would be competent in his case;

3.   on a counter-claim arising from the same contract or facts on which the original claim was based, in the court in which the original claim is pending;

4.   in matters relating to a contract, if the action may be combined with an action against the same defendant in matters relating to rights *in rem* in immovable property, in the court of the State bound by this Convention in which the property is situated.

Article 7
Where by virtue of this Convention a court of a State bound by this Convention has jurisdiction in actions relating to liability from the use or operation of a ship, that court, or any other court substituted for this purpose by the internal law of that State, shall also have jurisdiction over claims for limitation of such liability.

Section 3
Jurisdiction in matters relating to insurance

Article 8
In matters relating to insurance, jurisdiction shall be determined by this Section, without prejudice to Articles 4 and 5(5).

Article 9
1.   An insurer domiciled in a State bound by this Convention may be sued:

(a)   in the courts of the State where he is domiciled, or

(b)   in another State bound by this Convention, in the case of actions brought by the policyholder, the insured or a beneficiary, in the courts for the place where the plaintiff is domiciled, or

(c)   if he is a co-insurer, in the courts of a State bound by this Convention in which proceedings are brought against the leading insurer.

2.   An insurer who is not domiciled in a State bound by this Convention but has a branch, agency or other establishment in one of the States bound by this Convention shall, in disputes arising out of the operations of the branch, agency or establishment, be deemed to be domiciled in that State.

Article 10

In respect of liability insurance or insurance of immovable property, the insurer may in addition be sued in the courts for the place where the harmful event occurred. The same applies if movable and immovable property are covered by the same insurance policy and both are adversely affected by the same contingency.

Article 11

1.   In respect of liability insurance, the insurer may also, if the law of the court permits it, be joined in proceedings which the injured party has brought against the insured.

2.   Articles 8, 9 and 10 shall apply to actions brought by the injured party directly against the insurer, where such direct actions are permitted.

3.   If the law governing such direct actions provides that the policyholder or the insured may be joined as a party to the action, the same court shall have jurisdiction over them.

Article 12

1.   Without prejudice to Article 11(3), an insurer may bring proceedings only in the courts of the State bound by this Convention in which the defendant is domiciled, irrespective of whether he is the policyholder, the insured or a beneficiary.

2.   The provisions of this Section shall not affect the right to bring a counterclaim in the court in which, in accordance with this Section, the original claim is pending.

Article 13

The provisions of this Section may be departed from only by an agreement:

1.   which is entered into after the dispute has arisen, or

2.   which allows the policyholder, the insured or a beneficiary to bring proceedings in courts other than those indicated in this Section, or

3.   which is concluded between a policyholder and an insurer, both of whom are at the time of conclusion of the contract domiciled or habitually resident in the same State bound by this Convention, and which has the effect of conferring jurisdiction on the courts of that State even if the harmful event were to occur abroad, provided that such an agreement is not contrary to the law of that State, or

4.   which is concluded with a policyholder who is not domiciled in a State bound by this Convention, except in so far as the insurance is compulsory or relates to immovable property in a State bound by this Convention, or

5.   which relates to a contract of insurance in so far as it covers one or more of the risks set out in Article 14.

Article 14

The following are the risks referred to in Article 13(5):

1.   any loss of or damage to:

(a)   seagoing ships, installations situated offshore or on the high seas, or aircraft, arising from perils which relate to their use for commercial purposes;

(b)   goods in transit other than passengers' baggage where the transit consists of or includes carriage by such ships or aircraft;

2.   any liability, other than for bodily injury to passengers or loss of or damage to their baggage:

(a)   arising out of the use or operation of ships, installations or aircraft as referred to in point 1(a) in so far as, in respect of the latter, the law of the State bound by this Convention in which such aircraft are registered does not prohibit agreements on jurisdiction regarding insurance of such risks;

(b)   for loss or damage caused by goods in transit as described in point 1(b);

3.   any financial loss connected with the use or operation of ships, installations or aircraft as referred to in point 1(a), in particular loss of freight or charter-hire;

4.   any risk or interest connected with any of those referred to in points 1 to 3;

5.   notwithstanding points 1 to 4, all large risks.

Section 4
Jurisdiction over consumer contracts

Article 15

1.   In matters relating to a contract concluded by a person, the consumer, for a purpose which can be regarded as being outside his trade or profession, jurisdiction shall be determined by this Section, without prejudice to Articles 4 and 5(5), if:

(a)   it is a contract for the sale of goods on instalment credit terms, or

(b)   it is a contract for a loan repayable by instalments, or for any other form of credit, made to finance the sale of goods, or

(c)   in all other cases, the contract has been concluded with a person who pursues commercial or professional activities in the State bound by this Convention of the consumer's domicile or, by any means, directs such activities to that State or to several States including that State, and the contract falls within the scope of such activities.

2.   Where a consumer enters into a contract with a party who is not domiciled in the State bound by this Convention but has a branch, agency or other establishment in one of the States bound by this Convention, that party shall, in disputes arising out of the operations of the branch, agency or establishment, be deemed to be domiciled in that State.

3.   This section shall not apply to a contract of transport other than a contract which, for an inclusive price, provides for a combination of travel and accommodation.

Article 16

1.   A consumer may bring proceedings against the other party to a contract either in the courts of the State bound by this Convention in which that party is domiciled or in the courts for the place where the consumer is domiciled.

2.   Proceedings may be brought against a consumer by the other party to the contract only in the courts of the State bound by this Convention in which the consumer is domiciled.

3.   This Article shall not affect the right to bring a counter-claim in the court in which, in accordance with this Section, the original claim is pending.

Article 17

The provisions of this Section may be departed from only by an agreement:

1.   which is entered into after the dispute has arisen, or

2.   which allows the consumer to bring proceedings in courts other than those indicated in this Section, or

3.   which is entered into by the consumer and the other party to the contract, both of whom are at the time of conclusion of the contract domiciled or habitually resident in the same State bound by this Convention, and which confers jurisdiction on the courts of that State, provided that such an agreement is not contrary to the law of that State.

Section 5
Jurisdiction over individual contracts of employment

Article 18

1.   In matters relating to individual contracts of employment, jurisdiction shall be determined by this Section, without prejudice to Articles 4 and 5(5).

2.   Where an employee enters into an individual contract of employment with an employer who is not domiciled in a State bound by this Convention but has a branch, agency or other establishment in one of the States bound by this Convention, the employer shall, in disputes arising out of the operations of the branch, agency or establishment, be deemed to be domiciled in that State.

Article 19

An employer domiciled in a State bound by this Convention may be sued:

1.   in the courts of the State where he is domiciled, or

2.   in another State bound by this Convention:

(a)   in the courts for the place where the employee habitually carries out his work or in the courts for the last place where he did so, or

(b)   if the employee does not or did not habitually carry out his work in any one country, in the courts for the place where the business which engaged the employee is or was situated.

Article 20

1.   An employer may bring proceedings only in the courts of the State bound by this Convention in which the employee is domiciled.

2.   The provisions of this Section shall not affect the right to bring a counterclaim in the court in which, in accordance with this Section, the original claim is pending.

Article 21

The provisions of this Section may be departed from only by an agreement on jurisdiction:

1.   which is entered into after the dispute has arisen, or

2.   which allows the employee to bring proceedings in courts other than those indicated in this Section.

Section 6
Exclusive jurisdiction

Article 22

The following courts shall have exclusive jurisdiction, regardless of domicile:

1.   in proceedings which have as their object rights *in rem* in immovable property or tenancies of immovable property, the courts of the State bound by this Convention in which the property is situated.

However, in proceedings which have as their object tenancies of immovable property concluded for temporary private use for a maximum period of six consecutive months, the courts of the State bound by this Convention in which the defendant is domiciled shall also have jurisdiction, provided that the tenant is a natural person and that the landlord and the tenant are domiciled in the same State bound by this Convention;

2.   in proceedings which have as their object the validity of the constitution, the nullity or the dissolution of companies or other legal persons or associations of natural or legal persons, or of the validity of the decisions of their organs, the courts of the State bound by this Convention in which the company, legal person or association has its seat. In order to determine that seat, the court shall apply its rules of private international law;

3.   in proceedings which have as their object the validity of entries in public

registers, the courts of the State bound by this Convention in which the register is kept;

4.   in proceedings concerned with the registration or validity of patents, trade marks, designs, or other similar rights required to be deposited or registered, irrespective of whether the issue is raised by way of an action or as a defence, the courts of the State bound by this Convention in which the deposit or registration has been applied for, has taken place or is, under the terms of a Community instrument or an international convention, deemed to have taken place.

Without prejudice to the jurisdiction of the European Patent Office under the Convention on the grant of European patents, signed at Munich on 5 October 1973, the courts of each State bound by this Convention shall have exclusive jurisdiction, regardless of domicile, in proceedings concerned with the registration or validity of any European patent granted for that State irrespective of whether the issue is raised by way of an action or as a defence;

5.   in proceedings concerned with the enforcement of judgments, the courts of the State bound by this Convention in which the judgment has been or is to be enforced.

Section 7
Prorogation of jurisdiction

Article 23

1.   If the parties, one or more of whom is domiciled in a State bound by this Convention, have agreed that a court or the courts of a State bound by this Convention are to have jurisdiction to settle any disputes which have arisen or which may arise in connection with a particular legal relationship, that court or those courts shall have jurisdiction. Such jurisdiction shall be exclusive unless the parties have agreed otherwise. Such an agreement conferring jurisdiction shall be either:

(a)   in writing or evidenced in writing, or

(b)   in a form which accords with practices which the parties have established between themselves, or

(c)   in international trade or commerce, in a form which accords with a usage of which the parties are or ought to have been aware and which in such trade or commerce is widely known to, and regularly observed by, parties to contracts of the type involved in the particular trade or commerce concerned.

2.   Any communication by electronic means which provides a durable record of the agreement shall be equivalent to 'writing'.

3.   Where such an agreement is concluded by parties, none of whom is domiciled in a State bound by this Convention, the courts of other States bound by this Convention shall have no jurisdiction over their disputes unless the court or courts chosen have declined jurisdiction.

4.   The court or courts of a State bound by this Convention on which a trust instrument has conferred jurisdiction shall have exclusive jurisdiction in any proceedings brought against a settlor, trustee or beneficiary, if relations between these persons or their rights or obligations under the trust are involved.

5.   Agreements or provisions of a trust instrument conferring jurisdiction shall have no legal force if they are contrary to the provisions of Articles 13, 17 or 21, or if the courts whose jurisdiction they purport to exclude have exclusive jurisdiction by virtue of Article 22.

Article 24

Apart from jurisdiction derived from other provisions of this Convention, a court of a State bound by this Convention before which a defendant enters an appearance shall have jurisdiction. This rule shall not apply where appearance was entered to contest the jurisdiction, or where another court has exclusive jurisdiction by virtue of Article 22.

Section 8
Examination as to jurisdiction and admissibility

Article 25
Where a court of a State bound by this Convention is seised of a claim which is principally concerned with a matter over which the courts of another State bound by this Convention have exclusive jurisdiction by virtue of Article 22, it shall declare of its own motion that it has no jurisdiction.

Article 26
1. Where a defendant domiciled in one State bound by this Convention is sued in a court of another State bound by this Convention and does not enter an appearance, the court shall declare of its own motion that it has no jurisdiction unless its jurisdiction is derived from the provisions of this Convention.

2. The court shall stay the proceedings so long as it is not shown that the defendant has been able to receive the document instituting the proceedings or an equivalent document in sufficient time to enable him to arrange for his defence, or that all necessary steps have been taken to this end.

3. Instead of the provisions of paragraph 2, Article 15 of the Hague Convention of 15 November 1965 on the Service Abroad of Judicial and Extrajudicial Documents in Civil and Commercial matters shall apply if the document instituting the proceedings or an equivalent document had to be transmitted pursuant to that Convention.

4. Member States of the European Community bound by Council Regulation (EC) No 1348/2000 of 29 May 2000 or by the Agreement between the European Community and the Kingdom of Denmark on the service of judicial and extrajudicial documents in civil or commercial matters, signed at Brussels on 19 October 2005, shall apply in their mutual relations the provision in Article 19 of that Regulation if the document instituting the proceedings or an equivalent document had to be transmitted pursuant to that Regulation or that Agreement.

Section 9
Lis pendens – related actions

Article 27
1. Where proceedings involving the same cause of action and between the same parties are brought in the courts of different States bound by this Convention, any court other than the court first seised shall of its own motion stay its proceedings until such time as the jurisdiction of the court first seised is established.

2. Where the jurisdiction of the court first seised is established, any court other than the court first seised shall decline jurisdiction in favour of that court.

Article 28
1. Where related actions are pending in the courts of different States bound by this Convention, any court other than the court first seised may stay its proceedings.

2. Where these actions are pending at first instance, any court other than the court first seised may also, on the application of one of the parties, decline jurisdiction if the court first seised has jurisdiction over the actions in question and its law permits the consolidation thereof.

3. For the purposes of this Article, actions are deemed to be related where they are so closely connected that it is expedient to hear and determine them together to avoid the risk of irreconcilable judgments resulting from separate proceedings.

Article 29
Where actions come within the exclusive jurisdiction of several courts, any court other than the court first seised shall decline jurisdiction in favour of that court.

Article 30

For the purposes of this Section, a court shall be deemed to be seised:

1. at the time when the document instituting the proceedings or an equivalent document is lodged with the court, provided that the plaintiff has not subsequently failed to take the steps he was required to take to have service effected on the defendant, or

2. if the document has to be served before being lodged with the court at the time when it is received by the authority responsible for service, provided that the plaintiff has not subsequently failed to take the steps he was required to take to have the document lodged with the court.

Section 10
Provisional, including protective, measures

Article 31

Application may be made to the courts of a State bound by this Convention for such provisional, including protective, measures as may be available under the law of that State, even if, under this Convention, the courts of another State bound by this Convention have jurisdiction as to the substance of the matter.

TITLE III
RECOGNITION AND ENFORCEMENT

Article 32

For the purposes of this Convention, 'judgment' means any judgment given by a court or tribunal of a State bound by this Convention, whatever the judgment may be called, including a decree, order, decision or writ of execution, as well as the determination of costs or expenses by an officer of the court.

Section 1
Recognition

Article 33

1. A judgment given in a State bound by this Convention shall be recognised in the other States bound by this Convention without any special procedure being required.

2. Any interested party who raises the recognition of a judgment as the principal issue in a dispute may, in accordance with the procedures provided for in Sections 2 and 3 of this Title, apply for a decision that the judgment be recognised.

3. If the outcome of proceedings in a court of a State bound by this Convention depends on the determination of an incidental question of recognition that court shall have jurisdiction over that question.

Article 34

A judgment shall not be recognised:

1. if such recognition is manifestly contrary to public policy in the State in which recognition is sought;

2. where it was given in default of appearance, if the defendant was not served with the document which instituted the proceedings or with an equivalent document in sufficient time and in such a way as to enable him to arrange for his defence, unless the defendant failed to commence proceedings to challenge the judgment when it was possible for him to do so;

3. if it is irreconcilable with a judgment given in a dispute between the same parties in the State in which recognition is sought;

4. if it is irreconcilable with an earlier judgment given in another State bound by this Convention or in a third State involving the same cause of action and between the same parties, provided that the earlier judgment fulfils the conditions necessary for its recognition in the State addressed.

Article 35

1. Moreover, a judgment shall not be recognised if it conflicts with Sections 3, 4 or 6 of Title II, or in a case provided for in Article 68. A judgment may furthermore be refused recognition in any case provided for in Article 64(3) or 67(4).

2. In its examination of the grounds of jurisdiction referred to in the foregoing paragraph, the court or authority applied to shall be bound by the findings of fact on which the court of the State of origin based its jurisdiction.

3. Subject to the provisions of paragraph 1, the jurisdiction of the court of the State of origin may not be reviewed. The test of public policy referred to in Article 34(1) may not be applied to the rules relating to jurisdiction.

Article 36

Under no circumstances may a foreign judgment be reviewed as to its substance.

Article 37

1. A court of a State bound by this Convention in which recognition is sought of a judgment given in another State bound by this Convention may stay the proceedings if an ordinary appeal against the judgment has been lodged.

2. A court of a State bound by this Convention in which recognition is sought of a judgment given in Ireland or the United Kingdom may stay the proceedings if enforcement is suspended in the State of origin, by reason of an appeal.

Section 2
Enforcement

Article 38

1. A judgment given in a State bound by this Convention and enforceable in that State shall be enforced in another State bound by this Convention when, on the application of any interested party, it has been declared enforceable there.

2. However, in the United Kingdom, such a judgment shall be enforced in England and Wales, in Scotland, or in Northern Ireland when, on the application of any interested party, it has been registered for enforcement in that part of the United Kingdom.

Article 39

1. The application shall be submitted to the court or competent authority indicated in the list in Annex II.

2. The local jurisdiction shall be determined by reference to the place of domicile of the party against whom enforcement is sought, or to the place of enforcement.

Article 40

1. The procedure for making the application shall be governed by the law of the State in which enforcement is sought.

2. The applicant must give an address for service of process within the area of jurisdiction of the court applied to. However, if the law of the State in which enforcement is sought does not provide for the furnishing of such an address, the applicant shall appoint a representative *ad litem*.

3. The documents referred to in Articles 53 shall be attached to the application.

Article 41

The judgment shall be declared enforceable immediately on completion of the formalities in Article 53 without any review under Articles 34 and 35. The party against whom enforcement is sought shall not at this stage of the proceedings be entitled to make any submissions on the application.

Article 42

1. The decision on the application for a declaration of enforceability shall forth-

with be brought to the notice of the applicant in accordance with the procedure laid down by the law of the State in which enforcement is sought.

2.   The declaration of enforceability shall be served on the party against whom enforcement is sought, accompanied by the judgment, if not already served on that party.

Article 43

1.   The decision on the application for a declaration of enforceability may be appealed against by either party.

2.   The appeal is to be lodged with the court indicated in the list in Annex III.

3.   The appeal shall be dealt with in accordance with the rules governing procedure in contradictory matters.

4.   If the party against whom enforcement is sought fails to appear before the appellate court in proceedings concerning an appeal brought by the applicant, Article 26(2) to (4) shall apply even where the party against whom enforcement is sought is not domiciled in any of the States bound by this Convention.

5.   An appeal against the declaration of enforceability is to be lodged within one month of service thereof. If the party against whom enforcement is sought is domiciled in a State bound by this Convention other than that in which the declaration of enforceability was given, the time for appealing shall be two months and shall run from the date of service, either on him in person or at his residence. No extension of time may be granted on account of distance.

Article 44

The judgment given on the appeal may be contested only by the appeal referred to in Annex IV.

Article 45

1.   The court with which an appeal is lodged under Article 43 or Article 44 shall refuse or revoke a declaration of enforceability only on one of the grounds specified in Articles 34 and 35. It shall give its decision without delay.

2.   Under no circumstances may the foreign judgment be reviewed as to its substance.

Article 46

1.   The court with which an appeal is lodged under Article 43 or Article 44 may, on the application of the party against whom enforcement is sought, stay the proceedings if an ordinary appeal has been lodged against the judgment in the State of origin or if the time for such an appeal has not yet expired; in the latter case, the court may specify the time within which such an appeal is to be lodged.

2.   Where the judgment was given in Ireland or the United Kingdom, any form of appeal available in the State of origin shall be treated as an ordinary appeal for the purposes of paragraph 1.

3.   The court may also make enforcement conditional on the provision of such security as it shall determine.

Article 47

1.   When a judgment must be recognised in accordance with this Convention, nothing shall prevent the applicant from availing himself of provisional, including protective, measures in accordance with the law of the State requested without a declaration of enforceability under Article 41 being required.

2.   The declaration of enforceability shall carry with it the power to proceed to any protective measures.

3.   During the time specified for an appeal pursuant to Article 43(5) against the declaration of enforceability and until any such appeal has been determined, no measures of enforcement may be taken other than protective measures against the property of the party against whom enforcement is sought.

Article 48

1. Where a foreign judgment has been given in respect of several matters and the declaration of enforceability cannot be given for all of them, the court or competent authority shall give it for one or more of them.

2. An applicant may request a declaration of enforceability limited to parts of a judgment.

Article 49

A foreign judgment which orders a periodic payment by way of a penalty shall be enforceable in the State in which enforcement is sought only if the amount of the payment has been finally determined by the courts of the State of origin.

Article 50

1. An applicant who in the State of origin has benefited from complete or partial legal aid or exemption from costs or expenses shall be entitled, in the procedure provided for in this Section, to benefit from the most favourable legal aid or the most extensive exemption from costs or expenses provided for by the law of the State addressed.

2. However, an applicant who requests the enforcement of a decision given by an administrative authority in Denmark, in Iceland or in Norway in respect of maintenance may, in the State addressed, claim the benefits referred to in paragraph 1 if he presents a statement from the Danish, Icelandic, or Norwegian Ministry of Justice to the effect that he fulfils the economic requirements to qualify for the grant of complete or partial legal aid or exemption from costs or expenses.

Article 51

No security, bond or deposit, however described, shall be required of a party who in one State bound by this Convention, applies for enforcement of a judgment given in another State bound by this Convention on the ground that he is a foreign national or that he is not domiciled or resident in the State in which enforcement is sought.

Article 52

In proceedings for the issue of a declaration of enforceability, no charge, duty or fee calculated by reference to the value of the matter at issue may be levied in the State in which enforcement is sought.

Section 3
Common provisions

Article 53

1. A party seeking recognition or applying for a declaration of enforceability shall produce a copy of the judgment which satisfies the conditions necessary to establish its authenticity.

2. A party applying for a declaration of enforceability shall also produce the certificate referred to in Article 54, without prejudice to Article 55.

Article 54

The court or competent authority of a State bound by this Convention where a judgment was given shall issue, at the request of any interested party, a certificate using the standard form in Annex V to this Convention.

Article 55

1. If the certificate referred to in Article 54 is not produced, the court or competent authority may specify a time for its production or accept an equivalent document or, if it considers that it has sufficient information before it, dispense with its production.

2. If the court or competent authority so requires, a translation of the docu-

ments shall be produced. The translation shall be certified by a person qualified to do so in one of the States bound by this Convention.

Article 56
No legalisation or other similar formality shall be required in respect of the documents referred to in Article 53 or Article 55(2), or in respect of a document appointing a representative *ad litem*.

TITLE IV
AUTHENTIC INSTRUMENTS AND COURT SETTLEMENTS

Article 57
1.　A document which has been formally drawn up or registered as an authentic instrument and is enforceable in one State bound by this Convention shall, in another State bound by this Convention, be declared enforceable there, on application made in accordance with the procedures provided for in Article 38, et seq. The court with which an appeal is lodged under Article 43 or Article 44 shall refuse or revoke a declaration of enforceability only if enforcement of the instrument is manifestly contrary to public policy in the State addressed.

2.　Arrangements relating to maintenance obligations concluded with administrative authorities or authenticated by them shall also be regarded as authentic instruments within the meaning of paragraph 1.

3.　The instrument produced must satisfy the conditions necessary to establish its authenticity in the State of origin.

4.　Section 3 of Title III shall apply as appropriate. The competent authority of a State bound by this Convention where an authentic instrument was drawn up or registered shall issue, at the request of any interested party, a certificate using the standard form in Annex VI to this Convention.

Article 58
A settlement which has been approved by a court in the course of proceedings and is enforceable in the State bound by this Convention in which it was concluded shall be enforceable in the State addressed under the same conditions as authentic instruments. The court or competent authority of a State bound by this Convention where a court settlement was approved shall issue, at the request of any interested party, a certificate using the standard form in Annex V to this Convention.

TITLE V
GENERAL PROVISIONS

Article 59
1.　In order to determine whether a party is domiciled in the State bound by this Convention whose courts are seised of a matter, the court shall apply its internal law.

2.　If a party is not domiciled in the State whose courts are seised of the matter, then, in order to determine whether the party is domiciled in another State bound by this Convention, the court shall apply the law of that State.

Article 60
1.　For the purposes of this Convention, a company or other legal person or association of natural or legal persons is domiciled at the place where it has its:
　　(a)　statutory seat, or
　　(b)　central administration, or
　　(c)　principal place of business.

2.　For the purposes of the United Kingdom and Ireland 'statutory seat' means the registered office or, where there is no such office anywhere, the place of incorporation or, where there is no such place anywhere, the place under the law of which the formation took place.

3. In order to determine whether a trust is domiciled in the State bound by this Convention whose courts are seised of the matter, the court shall apply its rules of private international law.

Article 61

Without prejudice to any more favourable provisions of national laws, persons domiciled in a State bound by this Convention who are being prosecuted in the criminal courts of another State bound by this Convention of which they are not nationals for an offence which was not intentionally committed may be defended by persons qualified to do so, even if they do not appear in person. However, the court seised of the matter may order appearance in person; in the case of failure to appear, a judgment given in the civil action without the person concerned having had the opportunity to arrange for his defence need not be recognised or enforced in the other States bound by this Convention.

Article 62

For the purposes of this Convention, the expression 'court' shall include any authorities designated by a State bound by this Convention as having jurisdiction in the matters falling within the scope of this Convention.

TITLE VI
TRANSITIONAL PROVISIONS

Article 63

1. This Convention shall apply only to legal proceedings instituted and to documents formally drawn up or registered as authentic instruments after its entry into force in the State of origin and, where recognition or enforcement of a judgment or authentic instruments is sought, in the State addressed.

2. However, if the proceedings in the State of origin were instituted before the entry into force of this Convention, judgments given after that date shall be recognised and enforced in accordance with Title III:

(a) if the proceedings in the State of origin were instituted after the entry into force of the Lugano Convention of 16 September 1988 both in the State of origin and in the State addressed;

(b) in all other cases, if jurisdiction was founded upon rules which accorded with those provided for either in Title II or in a convention concluded between the State of origin and the State addressed which was in force when the proceedings were instituted.

TITLE VII
RELATIONSHIP TO COUNCIL REGULATION (EC) NO 44/2001 AND OTHER INSTRUMENTS

Article 64

1. This Convention shall not prejudice the application by the Member States of the European Community of the Council Regulation (EC) No 44/2001 on jurisdiction and the recognition and enforcement of judgments in civil and commercial matters, as well as any amendments thereof, of the Convention on Jurisdiction and the Enforcement of Judgments in Civil and Commercial Matters, signed at Brussels on 27 September 1968, and of the Protocol on interpretation of that Convention by the Court of Justice of the European Communities, signed at Luxembourg on 3 June 1971, as amended by the Conventions of Accession to the said Convention and the said Protocol by the States acceding to the European Communities, as well as of the Agreement between the European Community and the Kingdom of Denmark on jurisdiction and the recognition and enforcement of judgments in civil and commercial matters, signed at Brussels on 19 October 2005.

2. However, this Convention shall in any event be applied:

(a) in matters of jurisdiction, where the defendant is domiciled in the territory of a State where this Convention but not an instrument referred to in paragraph 1 of this Article applies, or where Articles 22 or 23 of this Convention confer jurisdiction on the courts of such a State;

(b) in relation to *lis pendens* or to related actions as provided for in Articles 27 and 28, when proceedings are instituted in a State where the Convention but not an instrument referred to in paragraph 1 of this Article applies and in a State where this Convention as well as an instrument referred to in paragraph 1 of this Article apply;

(c) in matters of recognition and enforcement, where either the State of origin or the State addressed is not applying an instrument referred to in paragraph 1 of this Article.

3. In addition to the grounds provided for in Title III, recognition or enforcement may be refused if the ground of jurisdiction on which the judgment has been based differs from that resulting from this Convention and recognition or enforcement is sought against a party who is domiciled in a State where this Convention but not an instrument referred to in paragraph 1 of this Article applies, unless the judgment may otherwise be recognised or enforced under any rule of law in the State addressed.

Article 65
Subject to the provisions of Articles 63(2), 66 and 67, this Convention shall, as between the States bound by this Convention, supersede the conventions concluded between two or more of them that cover the same matters as those to which this Convention applies. In particular, the conventions mentioned in Annex VII shall be superseded.

Article 66
1. The conventions referred to in Article 65 shall continue to have effect in relation to matters to which this Convention does not apply.

2. They shall continue to have effect in respect of judgments given and documents formally drawn up or registered as authentic instruments before the entry into force of this Convention.

Article 67
1. This Convention shall not affect any conventions by which the Contracting Parties and/or the States bound by this Convention are bound and which in relation to particular matters, govern jurisdiction or the recognition or enforcement of judgments. Without prejudice to obligations resulting from other agreements between certain Contracting Parties, this Convention shall not prevent Contracting Parties from entering into such conventions.

2. This Convention shall not prevent a court of a State bound by this Convention and by a convention on a particular matter from assuming jurisdiction in accordance with that convention, even where the defendant is domiciled in another State bound by this Convention which is not a party to that convention. The court hearing the action shall, in any event, apply Article 26 of this Convention.

3. Judgments given in a State bound by this Convention by a court in the exercise of jurisdiction provided for in a convention on a particular matter shall be recognised and enforced in the other States bound by this Convention in accordance with Title III of this Convention.

4. In addition to the grounds provided for in Title III, recognition or enforcement may be refused if the State addressed is not bound by the convention on a particular matter and the person against whom recognition or enforcement is sought is domiciled in that State, or, if the State addressed is a Member State of the European Community and in respect of conventions which would have to be concluded by the European Community, in any of its Member States, unless the judg-

ment may otherwise be recognised or enforced under any rule of law in the State addressed.

5.   Where a convention on a particular matter to which both the State of origin and the State addressed are parties lays down conditions for the recognition or enforcement of judgments, those conditions shall apply. In any event, the provisions of this Convention which concern the procedures for recognition and enforcement of judgments may be applied.

Article 68
1.   This Convention shall not affect agreements by which States bound by this Convention undertook, prior to the entry into force of this Convention, not to recognise judgments given in other States bound by this Convention against defendants domiciled or habitually resident in a third State where, in cases provided for in Article 4, the judgment could only be founded on a ground of jurisdiction as specified in Article 3(2). Without prejudice to obligations resulting from other agreements between certain Contracting Parties, this Convention shall not prevent Contracting Parties from entering into such conventions.

2.   However, a Contracting Party may not assume an obligation towards a third State not to recognise a judgment given in another State bound by this Convention by a court basing its jurisdiction on the presence within that State of property belonging to the defendant, or the seizure by the plaintiff of property situated there:

(a)   if the action is brought to assert or declare proprietary or possessory rights in that property, seeks to obtain authority to dispose of it, or arises from another issue relating to such property, or

(b)   if the property constitutes the security for a debt which is the subject-matter of the action.

TITLE VIII
FINAL PROVISIONS

Article 69
1.   This Convention shall be open for signature by the European Community, Denmark, and States which, at the time of the opening for signature, are Members of the European Free Trade Association.

2.   The Convention shall be subject to ratification by the Signatories. The instruments of ratification shall be deposited with the Swiss Federal Council, which shall act as Depositary of this Convention.

3.   At the time of the ratification, the Contracting Parties may submit declarations in accordance with Articles I, II and III of Protocol 1.

4.   The Convention shall enter into force on the first day of the sixth month following the date on which the European Community and a Member of the European Free Trade Association deposit their instruments of ratification.

5.   The Convention shall enter into force in relation to any other Party on the first day of the third month following the deposit of its instrument of ratification.

6.   Without prejudice to Article 3(3) of Protocol 2, this Convention shall replace the Convention on jurisdiction and the enforcement of judgments in civil and commercial matters done at Lugano on 16 September 1988 as of the date of its entry into force in accordance with paragraphs 4 and 5 above. Any reference to the 1988 Lugano Convention in other instruments shall be understood as a reference to this Convention.

7.   Insofar as the relations between the Member States of the European Community and the non-European territories referred to in Article 70(1)(b) are concerned, the Convention shall replace the Convention on Jurisdiction and the Enforcement of Judgments in Civil and Commercial Matters, signed at Brussels on 27 September 1968, and of the Protocol on interpretation of that Convention by the Court of Justice of the European Communities, signed at Luxembourg on 3 June

1971, as amended by the Conventions of Accession to the said Convention and the said Protocol by the States acceding to the European Communities, as of the date of the entry into force of this Convention with respect to these territories in accordance with Article 73(2).

Article 70

1.   After entering into force this Convention shall be open for accession by:

(a)   the States which, after the opening of this Convention for signature, become Members of the European Free Trade Association, under the conditions laid down in Article 71;

(b)   Member States of the European Community acting on behalf of certain non-European territories that are part of the territory of that Member State or for whose external relations that Member State is responsible, under the conditions laid down in Article 71;

(c)   any other State, under the conditions laid down in Article 72.

2.   States referred to in paragraph 1, which wish to become a Contracting Party to this Convention, shall address their application to the Depositary. The application, including the information referred to in Articles 71 and 72 shall be accompanied by a translation into English and French.

Article 71

1.   Any State referred to in Article 70(1)(a) and (b) wishing to become a Contracting Party to this Convention

(a)   shall communicate the information required for the application of this Convention;

(b)   may submit declarations in accordance with Articles I and III of Protocol 1.

2.   The Depositary shall transmit any information received pursuant to paragraph 1 to the other Contracting Parties prior to the deposit of the instrument of accession by the State concerned.

Article 72

1.   Any State referred to in Article 70(1)(c) wishing to become a Contracting Party to this Convention:

(a)   shall communicate the information required for the application of this Convention;

(b)   may submit declarations in accordance with Articles I and III of Protocol 1; and

(c)   shall provide the Depositary with information on, in particular:

(1)   their judicial system, including information on the appointment and independence of judges;

(2)   their internal law concerning civil procedure and enforcement of judgments; and

(3)   their private international law relating to civil procedure.

2.   The Depositary shall transmit any information received pursuant to paragraph 1 to the other Contracting Parties prior to inviting the State concerned to accede in accordance with paragraph 3 of this Article.

3.   Without prejudice to paragraph 4, the Depositary shall invite the State concerned to accede only if it has obtained the unanimous agreement of the Contracting Parties. The Contracting Parties shall endeavour to give their consent at the latest within one year after the invitation by the Depositary.

4.   The Convention shall enter into force only in relations between the acceding State and the Contracting Parties which have not made any objections to the accession before the first day of the third month following the deposit of the instrument of accession.

Article 73

1.   The instruments of accession shall be deposited with the Depositary.

2. In respect of an acceding State referred to in Article 70, the Convention shall enter into force on the first day of the third month following the deposit of its instrument of accession. As of that moment, the acceding State shall be considered a Contracting Party to the Convention.

3. Any Contracting Party may submit to the Depositary a text of this Convention in the language or languages of the Contracting Party concerned, which shall be authentic if so agreed by the Contracting Parties in accordance with Article 4 of Protocol 2.

Article 74

1. This Convention is concluded for an unlimited period.

2. Any Contracting Party may, at any time, denounce the Convention by sending a notification to the Depositary.

3. The denunciation shall take effect at the end of the calendar year following the expiry of a period of six months from the date of receipt by the Depositary of the notification of denunciation.

Article 75

The following are annexed to this Convention:
- a Protocol 1, on certain questions of jurisdiction, procedure and enforcement;
- a Protocol 2, on the uniform interpretation of this Convention and on the Standing Committee;
- a Protocol 3, on the application of Article 67 of this Convention;
- Annexes I through IV and Annex VII, with information related to the application of this Convention;
- Annexes V and VI, containing the certificates referred to in Articles 54, 58 and 57 of this Convention;
- Annex VIII, containing the authentic languages referred to in Article 79 of this Convention; and
- Annex IX, concerning the application of Article II of Protocol 1.

These Protocols and Annexes shall form an integral part of this Convention.

Article 76

Without prejudice to Article 77, any Contracting Party may request the revision of this Convention. To that end, the Depositary shall convene the Standing Committee as laid down in Article 4 of Protocol 2.

Article 77

1. The Contracting Parties shall communicate to the Depositary the text of any provisions of the laws which amend the lists set out in Annexes I through IV as well as any deletions in or additions to the list set out in Annex VII and the date of their entry into force. Such communication shall be made within reasonable time before the entry into force and be accompanied by a translation into English and French. The Depositary shall adapt the Annexes concerned accordingly, after having consulted the Standing Committee in accordance with Article 4 of Protocol 2. For that purpose, the Contracting Parties shall provide a translation of the adaptations into their languages.

2. Any amendment of the Annexes V through VI and VIII through IX to this Convention shall be adopted by the Standing Committee in accordance with Article 4 of Protocol 2.

Article 78

1. The Depositary shall notify the Contracting Parties of:
   (a) the deposit of each instrument of ratification or accession;
   (b) the dates of entry into force of this Convention in respect of the Contracting Parties;
   (c) any declaration received pursuant to Articles I to IV of Protocol 1;

(d)   any communication made pursuant to Article 74(2), Article 77(1) and paragraph 4 of Protocol 3.

2.   The notifications will be accompanied by translations into English and French.

Article 79

This Convention, drawn up in a single original in the languages listed in Annex VIII, all texts being equally authentic, shall be deposited in the Swiss Federal Archives. The Swiss Federal Council shall transmit a certified copy to each Contracting Party.

...

ANNEX I

The rules of jurisdiction referred to in Article 3(2) and 4(2) of the Convention are the following:

...

– in the United Kingdom: the rules which enable jurisdiction to be founded on:

(a)   the document instituting the proceedings having been served on the defendant during his temporary presence in the United Kingdom, or

(b)   the presence within the United Kingdom of property belonging to the defendant, or

(c)   the seizure by the plaintiff of property situated in the United Kingdom.

ANNEX II

The courts or competent authorities to which the application referred to in Article 39 of the Convention may be submitted are the following:

– in the United Kingdom:

...

(b)   in Scotland, the Court of Session, or in the case of a maintenance judgment to the Sheriff Court on transmission by the Secretary of State.

...

ANNEX III

The courts with which appeals referred to in Article 43(2) of the Convention may be lodged are the following:

– in the United Kingdom:

...

(b)   in Scotland, the Court of Session, or in the case of a maintenance judgment the Sheriff Court.

...

ANNEX IV

The appeals which may be lodged pursuant to Article 44 of the Convention are the following:

...

– in the United Kingdom: a single further appeal on a point of law.

INDEX OF LEGISLATION

Administration of Estates Act 1971, ss 1–6. 19
Administration of Justice Act 1920, ss 9, 12, 14 4
Adoption (Intercountry Aspects) Act 1999, ss 1, 2, 17, 18, Sch 1 126
Adoption (Recognition of Overseas Adoptions) Order 2013 209
Adoption (Recognition of Overseas Adoptions) (Scotland) Regulations   246
   2013. . . . .
Adoption (Scotland) Act 1978, ss 38, 39, 41–44 47
Adoption and Children Act 2002, ss 83–89, 91, 105. 137
Adoption and Children (Scotland) Act 2007, ss 39, 40, 58–70, 119. 159
Adoptions with a Foreign Element (Scotland) Regulations 2009 214
Adoptions with a Foreign Element (Special Restrictions on Adoptions from
   Abroad) (Scotland) Regulations 2008 212
Anti-Social Behaviour, Crime and Policing Act 2014, ss 121, 122 178
Bankruptcy (Scotland) Act 2016, s 15. 184
Brussels I Regulation. 254
Brussels I Regulation (recast) 414
Brussels II *bis* Regulation 278
Child Abduction and Custody Act 1985, ss 1–9, 24A, 25, Sch 1 91
Children (Scotland) Act 1995, s 14 120
Civil Jurisdiction and Judgments Act 1982, ss 1–23, 27, 28, 30–35, 41–45, 49,
   50, Schs 2, 4, 6–8. 52
Civil Jurisdiction and Judgments Order 2001, regs 2–3A, Sch 1 186
Civil Jurisdiction and Judgments Act 1982 (Provisional and Protective
   Measures) (Scotland) Order 1997, arts 2, 3 186
Civil Partnership Act 2004, ss 1, 85, 86, 125, 210–219, 225–227, 233–238. . . . 142
Contracts (Applicable Law) Act 1990, Schs 1, 3 116
Cross–Border Insolvency Regulations 2006. 190
Defamation Act 2013, s 9. 174
Divorce (Religious Bodies) (Scotland) Regulations 2006, regs 1, 2 212
Divorce (Scotland) Act 1976, s 3A. 41
Domicile and Matrimonial Proceedings Act 1973, ss 1, 4, 7, 8, 8A, 10, 11,
   Schs 1B, 3, paras 8, 9. 31
EC/Denmark agreement implementing Regulation (EU) 1215/2012. 442
EC/Denmark agreement on jurisdiction and the recognition and
   enforcement of judgments. 307
European Account Preservation Order Regulation. 442
European Communities (Matrimonial and Parental Responsibility
   Jurisdiction and Judgments) (Scotland) Regulations 2005, regs 1, 6, 7. . . . 212
European Enforcement Order Regulation. 297
Evidence (Proceedings in Other Jurisdictions) Act 1975, s 1 41
Family Law Act 1986, ss 8–15, 17–18, 25–42, 44–52, 54 98
Family Law (Scotland) Act 2006, ss 4, 22, 25–29A, 38–41 153
Forced Marriage etc (Protection and Jurisdiction) (Scotland) Act 2011 168
Foreign Corporations Act 1991, s 1 120
Foreign Judgments (Reciprocal Enforcement) Act 1933 6
Foreign Marriage Act 1892, ss 1, 4(3), 7, 8, 13, 18, 19, 22, 23 1
Hague Convention on Protection of Children (1996) 128
Hague Convention on Choice of Court Agreements (2005). 527
Hague Convention on International Recovery of Child Support and Family
   Maintenance (2007) 456

Hague Convention on the Civil Aspects of International Child Abduction
  (1980).   93
Hague Convention on the Law Applicable to Trusts and on their
  Recognition (1986)   113
Human . . . .
Fertilisation and Embryology Act 2008, s 54.   167
Immigration and Asylum Act 1999, ss 24, 24A.   135
Insolvency Regulation (recast)   471
International Recovery of Maintenance (Hague Convention 2007) (Scotland)
  Regulations 2012   243
Lugano Convention on jurisdiction and the enforcement of judgments
  (2007).   556
Maintenance Orders Act 1950, ss 16–18, 21, 22, 27   11
Maintenance Orders (Reciprocal Enforcement) Act 1972, ss 1, 2, 5–9, 21, 25,
  26, 31   22
Maintenance Regulation.   348
Marriage (Same Sex Couples) Act 2013, ss 1, 9–11, 13, 15, 20.   175
Marriage (Same Sex Couples) (Jurisdiction and Recognition of Judgments)
  (Scotland) Regulations 2014.   248
Marriage (Scotland) Act 1977, ss 1, 3–3B, 5, 7, 20, 20A, 22.   42
Marriage and Civil Partnership (Scotland) Act 2014, ss 4, 9–11, 28(3)   180
Matrimonial and Family Proceedings Act 1984, ss 28, 29, 29A   89
Matrimonial Proceedings (Polygamous Marriages) Act 1972, s 2.   31
Parental Responsibility and Measures for the Protection of Children
  (International Obligations) (Scotland) Regulations 2010.   240
Prescription and Limitation (Scotland) Act 1973, s 23A   40
Private International Law (Miscellaneous Provisions) Act 1995, ss 7, 9–15B .   121
Protocol (No 21) to the TEU and TFEU.   251
Recognition of Trusts Act 1987, s 1, Schedule.   113
Registration of Foreign Adoptions (Scotland) Regulations 2003, regs 1, 2, 7 .   211
Rome Convention on the Law Applicable to Contractual Obligations116
Rome I Regulation   334
Rome II Regulation.   313
Rome III Regulation   374
Scotland Act 1998, ss 29, 30, 57, 126, Sch 5, para 7.   124
Service of Documents Regulation   324
State Immunity Act 1978, ss 1–6, 9, 14   49
Succession Regulation   382
Succession (Scotland) Act 1964, ss 8, 9   16
Succession (Scotland) Act 2016, ss 1, 2, 9.   183
Taking of Evidence Regulation.   270
Treaty of Amsterdam, Arts 61, 65.   251
Treaty on the functioning of the European Union (Consolidated version),
  art 81   250
Unfair Contract Terms Act 1977, s 27   47
Wills Act 1963   15